THE ART OF CERVANTES IN *DON QUIXOTE*
CRITICAL ESSAYS

LEGENDA

LEGENDA is the Modern Humanities Research Association's book imprint for new research in the Humanities. Founded in 1995 by Malcolm Bowie and others within the University of Oxford, Legenda has always been a collaborative publishing enterprise, directly governed by scholars. The Modern Humanities Research Association (MHRA) joined this collaboration in 1998, became half-owner in 2004, in partnership with Maney Publishing and then Routledge, and has since 2016 been sole owner. Titles range from medieval texts to contemporary cinema and form a widely comparative view of the modern humanities, including works on Arabic, Catalan, English, French, German, Greek, Italian, Portuguese, Russian, Spanish, and Yiddish literature. Editorial boards and committees of more than 60 leading academic specialists work in collaboration with bodies such as the Society for French Studies, the British Comparative Literature Association and the Association of Hispanists of Great Britain & Ireland.

The MHRA encourages and promotes advanced study and research in the field of the modern humanities, especially modern European languages and literature, including English, and also cinema. It aims to break down the barriers between scholars working in different disciplines and to maintain the unity of humanistic scholarship. The Association fulfils this purpose through the publication of journals, bibliographies, monographs, critical editions, and the MHRA Style Guide, and by making grants in support of research. Membership is open to all who work in the Humanities, whether independent or in a University post, and the participation of younger colleagues entering the field is especially welcomed.

ALSO PUBLISHED BY THE ASSOCIATION

Critical Texts
Tudor and Stuart Translations • *New Translations* • *European Translations*
MHRA Library of Medieval Welsh Literature

MHRA Bibliographies
Publications of the Modern Humanities Research Association

The Annual Bibliography of English Language & Literature
Austrian Studies
Modern Language Review
Portuguese Studies
The Slavonic and East European Review
Working Papers in the Humanities
The Yearbook of English Studies

www.mhra.org.uk
www.legendabooks.com

STUDIES IN HISPANIC AND LUSOPHONE CULTURES

Studies in Hispanic and Lusophone Cultures are selected and edited by the Association of Hispanists of Great Britain & Ireland. The series seeks to publish the best new research in all areas of the literature, thought, history, culture, film, and languages of Spain, Spanish America, and the Portuguese-speaking world.

The Association of Hispanists of Great Britain & Ireland is a professional association which represents a very diverse discipline, in terms of both geographical coverage and objects of study. Its website showcases new work by members, and publicises jobs, conferences and grants in the field.

Editorial Committee
Chair: Professor Trevor Dadson (Queen Mary University of London)
Professor Catherine Davies (University of Nottingham)
Professor Sally Faulkner (University of Exeter)
Professor Andrew Ginger (University of Bristol)
Professor James Mandrell (Brandeis University, USA)
Professor Hilary Owen (University of Manchester)
Professor Christopher Perriam (University of Manchester)
Professor Philip Swanson (University of Sheffield)

Managing Editor
Dr Graham Nelson
41 Wellington Square, Oxford OX1 2JF, UK

www.legendabooks.com/series/shlc

STUDIES IN HISPANIC AND LUSOPHONE CULTURES

1. *Unamuno's Theory of the Novel*, by C. A. Longhurst
2. *Pessoa's Geometry of the Abyss: Modernity and the* Book of Disquiet, by Paulo de Medeiros
3. *Artifice and Invention in the Spanish Golden Age*, edited by Stephen Boyd and Terence O'Reilly
4. *The Latin American Short Story at its Limits: Fragmentation, Hybridity and Intermediality*, by Lucy Bell
5. *Spanish New York Narratives 1898–1936: Modernisation, Otherness and Nation*, by David Miranda-Barreiro
6. *The Art of Ana Clavel: Ghosts, Urinals, Dolls, Shadows and Outlaw Desires*, by Jane Elizabeth Lavery
7. *Alejo Carpentier and the Musical Text*, by Katia Chornik
8. *Britain, Spain and the Treaty of Utrecht 1713–2013*, edited by Trevor J. Dadson and J. H. Elliott
9. *Books and Periodicals in Brazil 1768–1930: A Transatlantic Perspective*, edited by Ana Cláudia Suriani da Silva and Sandra Guardini Vasconcelos
10. *Lisbon Revisited: Urban Masculinities in Twentieth-Century Portuguese Fiction*, by Rhian Atkin
11. *Urban Space, Identity and Postmodernity in 1980s Spain: Rethinking the Movida*, by Maite Usoz de la Fuente
12. *Santería, Vodou and Resistance in Caribbean Literature: Daughters of the Spirits*, by Paul Humphrey
13. *Reprojecting the City: Urban Space and Dissident Sexualities in Recent Latin American Cinema*, by Benedict Hoff
14. *Rethinking Juan Rulfo's Creative World: Prose, Photography, Film*, edited by Dylan Brennan and Nuala Finnegan
15. *The Last Days of Humanism: A Reappraisal of Quevedo's Thought*, by Alfonso Rey
16. *Catalan Narrative 1875–2015*, edited by Jordi Larios and Montserrat Lunati
17. *Islamic Culture in Spain to 1614: Essays and Studies*, by L. P. Harvey
18. *Film Festivals: Cinema and Cultural Exchange*, by Mar Diestro-Dópido
19. *St Teresa of Ávila: Her Writings and Life*, edited by Terence O'Reilly, Colin Thompson and Lesley Twomey
20. *(Un)veiling Bodies: A Trajectory of Chilean Post-Dictatorship Documentary*, by Elizabeth Ramírez Soto

The Art of Cervantes in *Don Quixote*

Critical Essays

Edited by Stephen Boyd,
Trudi L. Darby and Terence O'Reilly

Studies in Hispanic and Lusophone Cultures 27
Modern Humanities Research Association
2019

*Published by Legenda
an imprint of the Modern Humanities Research Association
Salisbury House, Station Road, Cambridge* CB1 2LA

ISBN 978-1-78188-505-5 (HB)
ISBN 978-1-78188-506-2 (PB)

First published 2019
Paperback edition 2021

All rights reserved. No part of this publication may be reproduced or disseminated or transmitted in any form or by any means, electronic, mechanical, photocopying, recording or otherwise, or stored in any retrieval system, or otherwise used in any manner whatsoever without written permission of the copyright owner, except in accordance with the provisions of the Copyright, Designs and Patents Act 1988, or under the terms of a licence permitting restricted copying issued in the UK by the Copyright Licensing Agency Ltd, Saffron House, 6–10 Kirby Street, London EC1N 8TS, *England, or in the USA by the Copyright Clearance Center, 222 Rosewood Drive, Danvers MA 01923. Application for the written permission of the copyright owner to reproduce any part of this publication must be made by email to legenda@mhra.org.uk.*

Disclaimer: Statements of fact and opinion contained in this book are those of the author and not of the editors or the Modern Humanities Research Association. The publisher makes no representation, express or implied, in respect of the accuracy of the material in this book and cannot accept any legal responsibility or liability for any errors or omissions that may be made.

Trademark notice: Product or corporate names may be trademarks or registered trademarks, and are used only for identification and explanation without intent to infringe.

© *Modern Humanities Research Association 2019*

Copy-Editor: Dr Ellen Jones

CONTENTS

Acknowledgements	viii
Notes on References	ix
Notes on the Contributors	x
Introduction	1
STEPHEN BOYD	

PART I: A BOOK ABOUT BOOKS

1. Books, Readers, Readings, and Writings in *Don Quixote* — 11
   TREVOR DADSON

2. '¿Qué lector será el que no se ría?': Incongruity and Ironic Allusion in *Don Quixote*, II. 60 — 35
   OLIVER NOBLE WOOD

3. An Authorized Version? Siting Authority and Citing *auctores* in *Don Quixote* — 65
   RICHARD RABONE

PART II: A MEETING OF GENRES

4. From Stage to Page: *Don Quixote* as Performance — 93
   B. W. IFE

5. *Don Quixote* and the Picaresque Novel: A Problematic Game of Triangles — 119
   ROBERT OAKLEY

PART III: THE SOCIAL/HISTORICAL CONTEXT

6. Value, Price, and Money: Early Modern Economic Theory in Three Episodes of *Don Quixote* — 133
   BRIAN BREWER

7. Moors, Moriscos, Disbelief: Beyond the Authors of the *Quixote* — 158
   ANTHONY JOHN LAPPIN

8. Reconsidering Literary Criminality in *Don Quixote* — 183
   TED L. L. BERGMAN

PART IV: *BURLAS Y VERAS*

9. Fortune and Providence, *santos y caballeros*, in *Don Quixote* II — 205
   STEPHEN BOYD

10. *Don Quixote*, II. 71–74: The Sense of an Ending — 237
    JEREMY LAWRANCE

Bibliography	263
Index	282

ACKNOWLEDGEMENTS

The editors wish to thank all those who have helped them in their task, most especially Graham Nelson and his team at Legenda. They gratefully acknowledge the award of a grant towards the publication of this volume from the Publications Scheme of the National University of Ireland.

S. B., T. L. D., T. O'R., September, 2019

NOTE ON REFERENCES

All references to the original Spanish text of *Don Quixote* are to Miguel de Cervantes, *Don Quijote de la Mancha: Edición del Instituto Cervantes 1605–2005*, ed. by Francisco Rico and others, 2 vols (Barcelona: Galaxia Gutenberg — Círculo de Lectores, Centro para la Edición de los Clásicos Españoles, 2004).

NOTES ON THE CONTRIBUTORS

❖

Ted L. L. Bergman is Lecturer in Spanish in the School of Modern Languages at the University of St Andrews. His research interests lie in the field of early modern Spanish theatre with a special emphasis on criminality and humour. He is currently preparing a book-length study, provisionally titled: *The Criminal Baroque: Lawbreaking, Peacekeeping, and Theatricality.*

Stephen Boyd is a Lecturer in the Department of Spanish, Portuguese, and Latin American Studies, University College Cork. His research focuses on Spanish Golden Age literature (especially Cervantes) and art. He is co-editor, with Terence O'Reilly, of *Artifice and Invention in the Spanish Golden Age* (London: Legenda, 2014).

Brian Brewer is Assistant Professor in the Department of Hispanic Studies, Trinity College Dublin. His research focuses on the presence of early modern economic theory and political economy in Spanish Golden Age literary fiction (particularly the works of Cervantes). He is currently working on a monograph, provisionally titled: *Quixotic Economics: Early Modern Political Economy in Cervantes.*

Trevor J. Dadson is Emeritus Professor of Hispanic Studies at Queen Mary University of London, and the author of numerous publications on the literature and socio-cultural history of the Spanish Golden Age. His recent publications include: *Tolerancia y convivencia en la España de los Austrias: cristianos y moriscos en el Campo de Calatrava* (Madrid: Cátedra, 2017); *Diego de Silva y Mendoza, conde de Salinas. Obra completa. I: Poesía desconocida* (Madrid: Real Academia Española-Centro para la Edición de los Clásicos Españoles, 2016); and (with Helen H. Reed), *La princesa de Éboli: Cautiva del rey. Vida de Ana de Mendoza y de la Cerda (1540–1592)* (Madrid: Marcial Pons Historia-Centro de Estudios Europa Hispánica, 2015). He is the recipient of many honours, including: the award, in 2015, of the 'encomienda de la Orden de Isabel la Católica' in recognition of his services to Hispanism, and his election, in 2016, as a Corresponding Fellow of both the Real Academia Española and the Real Academia de la Historia.

B. W. Ife is Cervantes Professor Emeritus at King's College London and former Principal of the Guildhall School of Music & Drama, where he is Honorary Senior Research Fellow. He is the author of numerous books, editions, and articles on Spanish and Spanish American literature, history, and music from the fifteenth to the eighteenth centuries. He is currently preparing a book, provisionally titled: *Speaking Prose: The Power of the Voice in Cervantes.* In 2017, he was awarded a Knighthood for services to performing arts education.

Anthony John Lappin is Research Professor at Maynooth University. His research interests lie principally in the fields of medieval religious history and literature, with a particular interest in hagiography, monasticism, and especially Christian–Muslim relations. He is currently completing an edition of the marginal annotations to the earliest Latin translation of the *Qur'an*, the *Alchoran latinus* (from 1143), and editing (with Kurt Villads Jensen and Kim Bergkvist) a two-volume collection of essays on Conflict and Collaboration in Medieval Iberia to be published by Cambridge Scholars.

Jeremy Lawrance is former Professor of Golden Age Studies at the University of Nottingham, and currently Honorary Research Fellow at the University of Oxford. He is a Fellow of the British Academy. He is the author of numerous studies on the cultural history of late medieval and early modern Spain, with special emphasis on the impact of the classical Renaissance upon art and the history of ideas. He is responsible for two editions of Latin texts by Alfonso de Cartagena, and of Ladino translations of the Bible. His more recent publications have focused on the formation of court civilization and the evolution of the Baroque style in the first half of the seventeenth century; on patronage, civil society, new concepts of the role of the artist in the commonwealth, and the interface between all these and the ideologies of absolutism. He maintains an ongoing interest in imperial Spain's colonial and cultural attitudes to foreign cultures, notably its European dominions (Italy, Flanders), Islam, Judaism, Black Africa, and the indigenous civilizations of America. He has articles forthcoming on 'Las utopías en la obra de Cervantes'; Calderon's *La vida es sueño* in the forthcoming Tamesis *Companion to Calderón*; and 'Isidore in the Renaissance (1500–1700): The Role of Golden Age Spain' for a Brill *Companion to Isidore of Seville*.

Oliver Noble Wood is University Lecturer in Golden Age Spanish Literature at the University of Oxford. His research focuses on sixteenth and seventeenth-century Spanish culture, with particular interests in the reception of classical authorities; book history and illustration; satirical and burlesque poetry; and cross-currents between literature and art in Renaissance and Baroque Spain. He is the author of *A Tale Blazed Through Heaven: Imitation and Invention in the Golden Age of Spain* (Oxford: Oxford University Press, 2014), and editor (with J. Andrews and J. Roe) of *On Art and Painting: Vicente Carducho and Baroque Spain* (Cardiff: University of Wales Press, 2016).

Robert Oakley is Honorary Research Fellow in Hispanic Studies at the University of Birmingham. He research interests lie in the fields of Spanish Golden Age prose fiction and drama (especially Tirso de Molina), and in Luso-Brazilian studies. He is the author of *Lima Barreto e o destino da literatura* (São Paulo: Fundação Editora da Universidade Estadual Paulista, 2011).

Richard Rabone is Assistant Professor in Hispanic Studies at the University of Warwick. His research interests are in the literature and culture of Golden Age Spain (with a particular focus on the reception of classical authorities), and also in European emblem books, in literary wit, and in translation. Together with

Peter Such he has published a translation of *The Poem of Fernán González,* Aris and Phillips Hispanic Classics (Oxford: Oxbow, 2015). He is currently working on a book-length study of the reception of the Aristotelian golden mean, provisionally entitled: *A Measure for Measure: Moderation and the Mean in the Literature of Spain's Golden Age.*

INTRODUCTION

Stephen Boyd

The original impulse behind the compilation of this collection of ten essays on *Don Quixote* came from Terence O'Reilly, who pointed out that no book-length study of Cervantes's novel by a British or Irish Hispanist had been published since Anthony Close's *Companion to 'Don Quixote'* (Woodbridge: Tamesis, 2008). He suggested that Golden-Age and Cervantes scholars working in these islands be invited to contribute to a volume of essays that would revisit some of the major aspects of Cervantes's novel and/or open up new avenues of approach. In the interests of giving a coherent shape to the volume as a whole, and of achieving a balance between range and depth, it was decided that contributors would be asked either to explore an individual aspect of the text with reference to selected individual passages or episodes, or to explore an individual passage or episode in a way that would illuminate its significance for understanding a facet of the work as a whole. Although no other direction was given, the essays submitted grouped themselves naturally and more-or-less evenly into four sections corresponding to the following broadly representative thematic areas: writing, reading, and citing texts ('A Book about Books'); generic experimentation ('A Meeting of Genres'); reflections of contemporary reality ('The Social/Historical Context'); and Don Quixote's death as a touchstone for interpretation of the text ('*Burlas y veras*').

A Book about Books

The first section begins with an essay by **Trevor Dadson** which examines the role that books, writing, and reading play in *Don Quixote*, not just in the life of the protagonist, but in those of a whole range of male and female characters, two of whom, the Canon of Toledo and Ginés de Pasamonte, are not only readers but also writers of prose fiction, and many of whom (more than one might suspect) are writers of verse: the shepherd boy Antonio, Grisóstomo, Ambrosio, Cardenio, and Don Luis, among others. Through the figures of Juan Palomeque, his wife and daughter, and Maritornes, we are reminded that even those who could not read had access to books through the practice whereby people gathered together to listen to them being read aloud. The novel's picture of Spain's culture of writing and reading is completed by what we learn of the personal libraries of Don Quixote and Don Diego de Miranda, which accurately reflect the range of books that were read in the period, and, in the case of Don Quixote's collection of romances of chivalry, the precise titles stocked by booksellers in the last decades of the sixteenth century. Professor Dadson takes his discussion of reading and writing to another level through a detailed examination of the linked episodes of the goatherds and of Grisóstomo and Marcela (I. 11–14). These episodes are underpinned by a range of literary genres — principally pastoral romance and courtly love poetry — but they do not so much document what people read as present paradigmatic acts of good and bad reading, and not just of books, but of people and situations and of how these are spoken of and reported. Thus, the goatherds are attentive and judicious readers of their guest, Don Quixote, while he is a bad reader of his hosts, and he and Grisóstomo are, ironically — given that both are well educated and well read — poor readers of Marcela. In this sense, these episodes constitute 'a complete lesson in how to read, in how to interpret the signs of the world-text that surrounds us', all incorporated within an innovative work of fiction, which subsumes and supersedes pre-existing forms, and not only teaches us how to read it but makes the act of reading it its true subject.

In the next essay, which is focused on the incident (in II. 60) of Sancho's resistance to Don Quixote's attempt to force him to complete the penance that will, supposedly, secure the disenchantment of Dulcinea, **Oliver Noble Wood** demonstrates how close reading of the text, and in particular detailed attention to its literary allusions (classical and otherwise), can radically affect its interpretation, and thus constitute 'a necessary correlative to, if not a basic building block for, the construction of overarching grand narratives'. Contesting the widely accepted interpretation of the episode as a peculiarly disturbing act of insubordination, the culmination of a long-drawn-out power struggle, with political implications, in which servant triumphs over master, he argues that it is, in fact, entirely comic in spirit. First, in purely psychological terms, Sancho's reaction to Don Quixote's assault on him while he sleeps represents a perfectly reasonable and restrained act of self-defence — once he has subdued his master, he goes no further than (politely) asking for a guarantee that there will be no repeat performance. Second, throughout the episode (including in the details of its setting — in the open air amidst cork — or evergreen oak? — trees), as in many other places in the novel, Don Quixote is cast as a burlesque version of Alexander the Great: in this case, drawing on accounts by Virgil, Plutarch, Quintus Curtius, and Arrian, Cervantes has him explicitly draw direct inspiration (for the first time) from the great hero of Antiquity as he decides to solve the Gordian-knot-like problem of Sancho's procrastination by cutting the stays that hold up his breeches — only the front part of them, in fact — and, using Rocinante's reins, to administer the lashes himself. Ironically, this latter feature associates him with Arcalaus, the great enemy of his hero and role model, Amadís of Gaul, while other details of phrasing cast him as a crazed Petrarchan lover (with Sancho as the reluctant female object of his attentions), or suggest absurd parallels between this scuffle and the hand-to-hand struggles between King Pedro I (the Cruel) of Castile and his half-brother Enrique of Trastámara on the field of battle at Montiel in 1369, and between Mudarra González and Rodrigo de Lara, as recalled in the ballad, 'A cazar va don Rodrigo'. Based on his re-reading of this particular incident, Noble Wood draws a broader conclusion about the development of Don Quixote and Sancho 'both as individuals and in terms of the dynamic between them' in Part Two, as one characterized by constant flux, and more or less subtle shifts, rather than by the unilinear ascent to power of one (Sancho) and progressive subordination of the other (Don Quixote).

Rather than explore the role of writers and authors within *Don Quixote*, or how Cervantes's allusions to other texts help to illuminate his own, **Richard Rabone** examines the novel's pervasive engagement with the broader issue of *auctoritas*. He begins by observing that a concern with the nature of truth and authority (particularly that of the written word) flows naturally from Cervantes's project of parodying a kind of fiction that posed as history through the invention of a character who believes that it is, and who appeals to its authority to legitimize his behaviour. Distinguishing between general (or abstract) and particular forms of *auctoritas* — the first ascribed to a prestigious writer, the second to concrete citations of his work (with the latter often being deployed to make claim to the former) — Rabone shows that Cervantes most effectively parodies the pseudo historicity of the romances by systematically undermining the authoritativeness of his own text through the fabrication of a 'mutual discrediting society' of discordant narrative voices. Quintilian's observations on the importance of *ēthos* (the perceived character and ability) of a speaker, as well as of decorum (the appropriateness to himself, to the audience, to the time and the place) in determining the persuasiveness of what he says, are adduced to preface an examination of Cervantes's probing of the vulnerabilities of *auctoritas* (in its narrower sense) in non-chivalric contexts at three points in the text. First, in the 1605 prologue, which offers a masterclass in how to manipulate the citation of authoritative sources (even where they are not required). Second, in various places (II. 4, 11, 17, 28) where Aristotle's doctrine of the golden mean (in relation to courage) is misapplied by both Sancho and Quixote, but in ways that point up difficulties inherent in the very flexibility of the doctrine itself. Third, in the episode of the Cave of Montesinos *katabasis*, whose authenticity is doubted by Cide Hamete Benengeli, by Sancho, and by Don Quixote himself. Moreover, it is reported by Cide Hamete that it is said to have been denied by Don Quixote on his deathbed, with 'the *coup de grâce* in the parodic burlesque of *auctoritas*' provided by the humanist cousin's willingness to accept Durandarte's words, as reported by Don Quixote, as an authoritative source for determining the origin of playing cards. The essay concludes by observing that it is characteristic of Cervantes's light-touch engagement with the question of *auctoritas*, that even when (from II. 59 onwards) it really mattered to him to assert the authority of his own or Cide Hamete's text in the face of Avellaneda's rival version, he allows, in the very next chapter, that, in not determining under which precise species of tree Don Quixote settled down for the night, the Arabic author 'did not observe his habitual exactitude'.

A Meeting of Genres

In the first essay in this section, **Barry Ife** begins by pointing to the prominence within Cervantes's prose fiction of musical and theatrical performance, and especially of the singing voice. He then goes on to examine various modalities of performance in *Don Quixote*, and, finally, *Don Quixote as* a performance. He notes how, especially after the introduction of Sancho (who becomes Quixote's permanent audience) in I. 7, diegesis, as the initially predominant narrative mode, increasingly gives way to mimesis as characters present (or perform) themselves. Special attention is paid to a supreme, concentrated example of this, in I. 11–14: improvising his stage and turning his hosts, the goatherds, into an audience, Don Quixote makes his speech on the Golden Age; Antonio is given a theatrical 'build up' before performing on the *rabel*; Grisóstomo's funeral, which is given a masque-like staging, is interrupted by Marcela's speech delivered, like an aria, from an elevated rock, and, as his poem is read out, Grisóstomo's voice reaches us from off stage, beyond death. Also in this episode, and as a foretaste of what is ever more frequently his fate in Part Two, we witness Don Quixote relegated to the role of spectator, but clearly anxious, as he makes his speech about Marcela, to regain his role as 'star' of the show. He is someone constantly performing a part, and doing so unsuccessfully, for it is essential to Cervantes's purpose that the gap between performer and performance should always be visible. In Part Two, as the wider implications of that gap are explored, Professor Ife shows how the novel becomes infused with the sense that life itself is a performance, with the paradoxical result that 'against that ephemeral and insubstantial background Quixote and Sancho gain in stature and moral substance'. He concludes by reflecting on *Don Quixote*, not only as the drama in prose that Cervantes, were it possible, would have wished to write for the stage, but as a performance that invites, anticipates, and consciously depends on its staging in the mind of the audience or reader.

Taking as his starting point J. Hillis Miller's metaphor of the host-parasite relationship as a way of conceptualizing the dynamics of literary influence, **Robert Oakley** examines the impact of *Guzmán de Alfarache* on the shaping of *Don Quixote*. In Mateo Alemán and in the anonymous author of the *Lazarillo*, he argues, Cervantes would have recognized 'artists operating in his field of action', and, in the case of the *Guzmán*, fundamental features in common with his own project: an extended piece of prose fiction, with a non-heroic protagonist, a broad range of settings, ordered in a circular pattern, albeit with the very significant difference that it was a first-person narrative. Cervantes's reservations about what (without being able to label it as the 'picaresque') he would have recognized as a new prose sub-genre are, famously, expressed in Don Quixote's conversation with Ginés de Pasamonte in I. 22, but, Oakley argues, his real difficulty was with the darkly pessimistic vision of life that pervades Alemán's work and, to a lesser extent, the *Lazarillo*. We see him reacting against that dualistic vision of the world and human nature in the way in which he depicts Maese Pedro as a softened but not entirely transformed version of Ginés; in the importance he attaches to friendship in contrast to the solitariness of Guzmán; and in the chapters set in Barcelona, where, while sharing Alemán's interest in urban settings and the sea as a liminal space, he has Don Quixote welcomed aboard a galley rather than being condemned to row in one. Finally, of course, *Don Quixote* ends with the definitive recovery and conversion of its protagonist. If, as Oakley suggests, the *Quixote*, the *Guzmán*, and the *Lazarillo* form a tragic, or iron, triangle, then, the publication in 1605 of Francisco de Úbeda's *La pícara Justina* (whose eponymous heroine ends up marrying Guzmán) generated, together with the *Quixote* and the *Guzmán,* another triangle, a 'golden' one, weighted in the direction of comedy. The essay concludes with the observation that it was Cervantes's comic prose epic that found favour in Spain and beyond, while Alemán's autobiographical prose epic 'was to languish in an international, literary penumbra for another one hundred years' until the publication in 1719 of *Robinson Crusoe*.

The Social/Historical Context

In the opening essay of this section, **Brian Brewer** examines three episodes that exemplify Cervantes's subtle use of 'contemporary theories of value, price, and money as structural elements within the narrative fiction of *Don Quixote*'. First, he shows how, in I. 8, the 'segundo autor' exploits the difference between the 'estimación común' (the subjective, socially agreed commodity value), as paper, of the bundle of papers that he buys from the boy in the Alcaná of Toledo, and his own 'estimación particular' (private estimate) of their nominal value as a manuscript of the history of Don Quixote, to acquire them for half a *real* instead of more than six. While this may reflect a concern on Cervantes's part with the commercialization of literature, Brewer suggests that it is more likely that the willingness of the *morisco aljamiado*, who translates the manuscript, to accept payment in raisins and wheat is designed to contradict the contemporary stereotyping of Moriscos as greedy hoarders of money. Focus falls next on the episode of the Helmet of Mambrino (beginning in I. 21 and concluding in I. 46), which is often invoked in support of 'perspectivist' readings of the text. Having reminded us that the value of the 'helmet' for Don Quixote lies not so much in its supposedly being made of gold as in its having once belonged to Mambrino, Brewer shows that Sancho's intuitive estimate of its utility as a basin and of its value at eight *reales* is objectively borne out when the barber eventually signs a legally citable receipt for precisely that amount. Although in calling the object a *baciyelmo* Sancho appears to go some way to accepting his master's assessment of its nature, he is in reality merely acknowledging the fact that, in protecting the barber's new hat, it is serving temporarily as a helmet. In Don Quixote's reference to part of the object having been cut away to be melted down and sold for its commodity value as gold by those not capable of appreciating its true worth (as Mambrino's helmet), Brewer sees an allusion to the contemporary practice of clipping gold and silver coins and, beyond this, to debates between 'metalists' and 'nominalists' about the nature of money. The former considered that the worth of coins consisted primarily in their commodity value as pieces of metal, while, for the latter, the essence of money *was* its (widely variable) nominal value — the value determined by the state. Thus,

Cervantes suggests an equivalence, with strong political implications, between Don Quixote's fantastical declaration that a brass basin is Mambrino's golden helmet and the contemporary state practice of arbitrarily altering the nominal value of coins by royal fiat. Finally, Brewer examines the intractably ambiguous and politically charged Ricote episode (II. 54). On the one hand, through his accumulation and hoarding of a large sum of money in gold, his attempt to take it out of Spain in contravention of the degree of expulsion, his exploitation of his neighbour Sancho's economic hardship for his own benefit, his association with the foreign 'pilgrims' who exploit the generosity of their Spanish hosts to smuggle gold and silver out of Spain, and his residence in Augsburg (associated with the Fuggers, and with the Declaration of Augsburg), Ricote appears to fulfil many of the negative stereotypes associated with Moriscos as domestic, racially and religiously distinct 'foreigners'. On the other, his love of his homeland, his fluent Castilian, his drinking of wine, his recognition that his wife and daughter (both sincere Catholics) are his most precious treasure, and, above all, the fact that so much of his 'aberrant' behaviour is forced upon him by the decree of expulsion itself, cast him in a very different light. The essay concludes by noting that in *Don Quixote* Cervantes dramatizes all three misuses of money identified by contemporary Spanish economic commenters: its removal (the German false pilgrims); its debasement (the helmet of Mambrino episode); and its hoarding (Ricote's buried treasure). Thus, 'Cervantes incorporates the logic of economic exchange into the essence of the novel' so that '*Don Quixote* represents a true economics of literature, rather than a literature about economics'.

Muslims and Moriscos also feature prominently in the next essay, by **Anthony Lappin**, but in this case as a focus for examining Cervantes's profound engagement with the nature of fiction and the ends that it should serve. It is argued here that his fundamental objection to the romances of chivalry had to with the morally dangerous models of behaviour that they proposed while masquerading as history. The fact that Cervantes's parodic version of a romance narrator/historian, Cide Hamete Benengeli, is a Muslim (in as much as he is imagined living both in the Middle Ages as well as in contemporary Spain) writing in Arabic serves to characterize the *libros de caballerías* as both meretricious and heretical. This is the reason why the episode of the galley slaves (I. 22) which 'takes head-on the conflict between chivalric mores and the requirements of a well-ordered Republic' is prefaced by hyperbolic praise of his skills as an author. The Captive's Tale, on the other hand, is offered by Cervantes as an example of a tale of adventure, prudent heroism and non-miraculous conversion to Christianity rooted in the real world, one that provided readers (in a period that required it) with a picture of the 'enemy' as real people, while dispelling 'the myths of happy captivity'. Pointing out the parallels between them, Lappin goes on to argue that, while the Captive's Tale and those of Ricote and Ana Félix are stories about the possibility of integration — something that 'Cervantes's middle-of-the-road assimilationist position regarding the Moriscos' (and, indeed, his view of literature) suggests that he saw as desirable — it was not his purpose in writing *Don Quixote* to tell readers what to think about the romances of chivalry or any contemporary political or social problem.

Rather, his consistent foregrounding of the fictionality of his novel and the tales within it, allows readers, paradoxically, both to empathize more readily with the characters, and to reflect on their own engagement with them, and so to become more emotionally and intellectually adept readers of the world.

Ted Bergman concludes this section with an essay that seeks to identify and correct the imbalance apparent in critical accounts of Cervantes's depiction of criminals and criminality — as indeed in some works of historiography — that results from over-reliance on picaresque fiction as a frame of reference or as supporting evidence. Recalling that Cervantes had personal experience of prison life (notably in Seville's *Cárcel Real*), he shows, with reference to contemporary first-hand accounts of prison conditions by Cristóbal de Chaves and the Jesuit Pedro de León, how the realities they document are reflected in many details of the galley-slaves episode in *Don Quixote* I. 22 — the bribing of *procuradores* and *escribanos*, for example, and the 'financial give-and-take' integral to the prison system, in Ginés de Pasamonte's pawning of his manuscript autobiography. While allowing that the witty use of *germanía* by Cervantes's criminals may owe a debt to traditional jokes, folkloric *cuentecillos*, and farce in the form of Lope de Rueda's *pasos*, he argues that the *jácara* and the *romances de germanía* are more likely literary generic sources than the picaresque (which tends to skirt serious violence) for the more 'bitterly ironic jokes' about such brutal realities of underworld life as racking or ear-slashing. As an example, he cites the use of the term *gurapas* as a 'specific lexical connection' between the *galeotes* scene in *Don Quixote* and a *jácara* sung in Cervantes's *Entremés del rufián viudo llamado Trampagos*. Noting that Spanish prisons had a relatively high proportion of Portuguese and Italian inmates, and that Italianisms such as *pillar* feature prominently in the *romances de germanía*, he suggests, too, that Maese Pedro's avoidance of them in a context (II. 24–25) in which they are used by three other characters may indicate a desire not to be identified with the criminal world. The essay concludes by referencing the possible influence on Cervantes of another literary genre, the *comedias de valiente*, which, when we remember the criminal violence of which Don Quixote is capable when his chivalric fantasies clash with reality, may allow us to glimpse a possible ambiguity in the references to him as a 'valiente caballero': a 'brave' knight, or a 'brawling' one?

Burlas y veras

Taking initial account of the divergence of critical opinion about the aesthetic coherence and psychological verisimilitude (or otherwise) of the scene of Don Quixote's recovery and death in II. 74, **Stephen Boyd** argues that his recovery, which takes the form of a religious conversion, represents the convergence, culmination and fulfilment of interlocking thematic strands and motifs — in particular of the themes of chivalry versus sanctity, Fortune and Providence, and the related motifs of rising and falling and of omens — that are worked out over the whole course of Part Two. The essay examines three episodes in which Don Quixote confronts (or evades confronting) the relationship between the religious underpinning of chivalry and his own practice of it: the debate with Sancho on the nature of fame (II. 8); his meeting with Don Diego de Miranda (II. 16–18); and his encounter with the images of the 'caballeros santos' (II. 58). In each of these cases, St Paul's metaphor of spiritual warfare appears as an implicit point of reference. In the episode of Don Quixote's contemplation of the image of the apostle's conversion, the themes of chivalry versus sanctity, and the motifs of rising and falling and of omens come together in a way that anticipates the scene of the knight's own conversion, and, Boyd argues, helps to support a reading of it as a work of Providence.

The ending of *Don Quixote* is also the focus of the concluding essay by **Jeremy Lawrance**. In this case, however, the aim is to determine its 'affect' — how Cervantes intended it to be read — , a question which brings the Romantic (soft) versus non-Romantic (hard) reading debate into sharp focus. Essentially, Lawrance sees it as 'teetering on the tightrope between *burlas* and *veras*', as being neither tragic — because of its elements of 'middling low mimetic realism' — , or comic, since its pathos contravenes classical and Renaissance notions of the decorum of comedy. Observing, *en passant*, that there is much to commend Byron's much misunderstood remarks about the novel's sadness being due to its being 'too true [a] tale' and a 'real Epic', the essay goes on to examine some of the clues embedded within the text itself that suggest how we might properly respond to its subtle blend of humour and seriousness. It pays particular attention to a scene set in Don Quixote's bedroom in the ducal palace (II. 44): the narrator remarks that the reader, seeing the knight gazing in deep melancholy at his ravelled green stockings, if not moved to laughter, might well pucker his lips 'con risa de jimia' (in an apish grin). Although 'one of the most important of [the novel's] thousands of self-reflexive remarks', Lawrance notes that Clemencín is the only editor to have proffered a comment on it, and then proceeds to elucidate it by explaining that the ape's negative aspects, as a walking parody of human appearance and conduct, were seen to be heightened when it was imagined as female. Thus, it is not Don Quixote who is cast as a *jimia*, but the reader who laughs at him in a certain way. And not only the reader, but Avellaneda, who created a debased version of him, and who, in II. 71, is tacitly equated with a painter capable of depicting 'Dido with walnut-sized tears or Helen with a whorish grin'. In the light of the foregoing, the essay examines the shifting and subtle dynamics of humour and pathos in the last four chapters, not in order to resolve the 'hard-soft' debate, but to examine 'the ending's artistry and semantic richness, and how it arouses such a variety of responses'. It concludes with a reflection on how the 'kaleidoscopic' nature of Cervantes's style generates an insoluble ambivalence, with the result that 'those that come down on one side tend only to focus on one rotation of the instrument'.

PART I

A Book about Books

CHAPTER 1

Books, Readers, Readings, and Writings in *Don Quixote*

Trevor Dadson

More than twenty-five years ago the North American Hispanist Carroll B. Johnson said of Cervantes's novel that 'It is a book made out of other books and it is a book about books'.[1] This necessarily implies that it is also a book about readers and the ways of reading, that is to say, how to read. This is evident throughout the novel but it is brought into particularly sharp focus in Chapters 1–14 of Part One, chapters that include the well-known episode of Marcela and Grisóstomo.

But before we analyse these rich and complex chapters, let us take a moment to explore the notions of readers and reading that we find at every turn in *Don Quixote*. The novel is based of course on the premise that too much reading, especially of novels of chivalry, can produce madness, and all the action, character development and plot flows from that initial idea. But Alonso Quijano el Bueno (Alonso Quixano the Good, or, Don Quixote) is not alone in his passion for these romances, as we soon discover.[2] Right at the start of the novel we learn that Alonso Quijano had many debates with the village priest ('hombre doctor, graduado en Cigüenza' (I. 1, 41) ('a learned man, a graduate of Sigüenza')[3] regarding 'cuál había sido mejor caballero: Palmerín de Ingalaterra o Amadís de Gaula' (I. 1, 41) ('who had been the greater knight, Palmerín of England or Amadís of Gaul'),[4] debates in which the local barber, Maese Nicolás, also took part: 'decía que ninguno llegaba al Caballero del Febo, y que si alguno se le podía comparar era don Galaor, hermano de Amadís de Gaula' (I. 1, 41) ('[he] said that none was the equal of the Knight of Phoebus, and if any could be compared to him it was Don Galaor, the brother of Amadís of Gaul').[5] When the priest and the barber carry out the scrutiny of Don Quixote's library (I. 6), this prior knowledge comes in very handy as they decide which titles should be burnt and which saved from the (inquisitorial) flames, though even this does not save them from rank prejudice, as we see in the exchange of views over Ariosto's *Orlando furioso*:

> al cual, si aquí le hallo, y que habla en otra lengua que la suya, no le guardaré respeto alguno, pero, si habla en su idioma, le pondré sobre mi cabeza.

> — Pues yo le tengo en italiano, — dijo el barbero — , mas no le entiendo. (I. 6, 87)

> (who, if I find him here, speaking in some language not his own, I will have no respect for him at all; but if he speaks in his own language, I bow down to him.
> 'Well, I have him in Italian,' said the barber, 'but I don't understand it.')[6]

This exchange also reminds us that people could and did own books they could not read or understand.[7]

This passion for romances of chivalry is not limited solely to men, however well or badly educated.[8] In the intercalated tale of Cardenio, Fernando, Luscinda, and Dorotea we find that both female characters are avid readers of these novels. Cardenio is describing his relationship with Luscinda to Don Quixote when he says: 'Acaeció, pues, que habiéndome pedido Luscinda un libro de caballerías en que leer, de quien era ella muy aficionada, que era el de *Amadís de Gaula*' (I. 24, 292) ('It so happened that Luscinda had asked me for a book of chivalry of which she was very fond, which was *Amadís of Gaul*').[9] Needless to say, Don Quixote reacts very positively to this excellent news:

> Con que me dijera vuestra merced al principio de su historia que su merced de la señora Luscinda era aficionada a libros de caballerías, no fuera menester otra exageración para darme a entender la alteza de su entendimiento, porque no le tuviera tan bueno como vos, señor, le habéis pintado, si careciera del gusto de tan sabrosa leyenda [...] que con sólo haber entendido su afición la confirmo por la más hermosa y más discreta mujer del mundo. (I. 24, 293)

> (If your grace had told me at the beginning of your history that her grace the lady Luscinda was fond of books of chivalry, no other embellishment would have been necessary to allow me to grasp the elevation of her understanding, for I would not have considered it as fine as you, Señor, have depicted it, if it had lacked the ability to enjoy such delightful reading [...] by simply knowing of this fondness, I affirm her to be the most beautiful and discrete woman in the world.)[10]

It is a world in which Luscinda is soon to be joined by Dorotea. If Luscinda is presented to us as a bit of a flighty young girl — after all, she reads romances of chivalry, something that priests and moralists railed against from the pulpit and in print on every possible occasion —,[11] Dorotea is initially portrayed as the ideal young woman; indeed, she portrays herself in this way:

> Los ratos que del día me quedaban después de haber dado lo que convenía a los mayorales, a capataces y a otros jornaleros, los entretenía en ejercicios que son a las doncellas tan lícitos como necesarios, como son los que ofrece la aguja y la almohadilla, y la rueca muchas veces; y si alguna, por recrear el ánimo, estos ejercicios dejaba, me acogía al entretenimiento de leer algún libro devoto, o a tocar una harpa [...]. Esta, pues, era la vida que yo tenía en casa de mis padres. (I. 28, 352–53)

> (My times of leisure, after I had attended to overseers, foremen, and other labourers, I spent in activities both proper and necessary for young women, such as those offered by the needle and pincushion and, at times, the distaff;

when I left these activities to refresh my spirit, I would spend the time reading a book of devotions, or playing the harp [...]. This, then, was the life I led in my parents' house.)[12]

In short, Dorotea is the perfect young Spanish lady: she sews and embroiders, she reads devout books and plays the harp. What a paragon of virtue, and what a contrast, the reader is expected to note, between her and Luscinda. But all that glitters is not gold, for only one chapter later, when Dorotea is required to play the part of a chivalresque maiden in distress, she tells us the readers as well as the other characters in the novel that she can play the part much better than the barber 'porque ella había leído muchos libros de caballerías y sabía bien el estilo que tenían las doncellas cuitadas cuando pedían sus dones a los andantes caballeros' (I. 29, 367) ('as she had read many books of chivalry and knew very well the style used by damsels in distress when they begged boons of knights errant').[13] She had kept very quiet about this particular skill when giving us her portrait earlier, which suggests that she was well aware that the reading of these novels was frowned upon by parents as well as the Church, and that it was best done in the privacy of one's own room.

Further female characters who love these novels are Maritornes and the daughter of the innkeeper Juan Palomeque in Part One, Chapter 32. Neither are able to read them but they enjoy hearing them read out aloud, as Maritornes declares:

> a buena fe que yo también gusto mucho de oír aquellas cosas, que son muy lindas, y más cuando cuentan que se está la otra señora debajo de unos naranjos abrazada con su caballero, y que les está una dueña haciéndoles la guarda, muerta de envidia y con mucho sobresalto. Digo que todo esto es cosa de mieles. (I. 32, 405)
>
> (by my faith, I really like to hear those things, too, they're very pretty, especially when they tell about a lady under some orange trees in the arms of her knight, and a duenna's their lookout, and she's dying of envy and scared to death. I think all that's as sweet as honey.)[14]

When asked by the priest what she thinks of these novels, the innkeeper's daughter replies that 'También yo lo escucho, y en verdad que aunque no lo entiendo, que recibo gusto en oíllo' (405) ('I listen, too, and the truth is that even if I don't understand them, I like to hear them').[15]

Throughout the novel Don Quixote is surrounded by people who have read or listened to romances of chivalry, who are able to talk intelligently about them and with passion, and whose lives have been touched by them. And to top it all, we have a canon of Toledo who is writing his own novel of chivalry! As he comments to the priest of Don Quixote's village:

> Yo, a lo menos [...], he tenido cierta tentación de hacer un libro de caballerías, guardando en él todos los puntos que he significado; y si he de confesar la verdad, tengo escritas más de cien hojas, y para hacer la experiencia de si correspondían a mi estimación, las he comunicado con hombres apasionados desta leyenda, dotos y discretos, y con otros ignorantes, que sólo atienden al gusto de oír disparates, y de todos he hallado una agradable aprobación. (I. 48, 603)

(I, at least, have felt a certain temptation to write a book of chivalry in which I followed all the points I have mentioned, and, to tell the truth, I have already written more than a hundred pages. In order to learn if they correspond to my estimation of them, I have given them to intelligent, learned men who are very fond of this kind of reading, and to other men who are ignorant and care only for the pleasure of hearing nonsense, and from all of them I have received a most agreeable approval.)[16]

Men and women, graduates ('hombres [...] dotos y discretos') and illiterates, high and low, ecclesiastics and secular readers, old and young, rich and poor: all have had contact with the books that are supposed to have driven Alonso Quijano mad. In this way Cervantes very cleverly puts doubt into our minds: if so many people read or listened to these tales, and in one case even considered writing one, could they really have been so pernicious? The great irony of course is that the character who spends most time with Don Quixote, his neighbour Sancho Panza, is the one person who has never had any contact with these novels. As a total illiterate he could never have read them,[17] but in addition he seems not to have come into any contact with them via, for example, communal reading aloud. His is certainly a singular case.[18]

The novels of chivalry, however, form only a small part of the rich tapestry of readers, writers and listeners who fill the pages of *Don Quixote*, Part One. The very genesis of the novel brings some of these into play, as for example in the case of the Morisco from Toledo, who translates the Arabic text that the narrator (Cervantes?) has found one day in his wanderings through the 'Alcaná de Toledo' (the old Jewish quarter, around the Plaza del Zocodover) whilst looking for the continuation of *Don Quixote*. What Cervantes has to say here is very instructive. He is talking about the Arabic characters:

> vile con carácteres que conocí ser arábigos. Y puesto que aunque los conocía no los sabía leer, anduve mirando si parecía por allí algún morisco aljamiado que los leyese, y no fue muy dificultoso hallar intérprete semejante, pues aunque le buscara de otra mejor y más antigua lengua le hallara. (I. 9, 118)

> (I saw that it was written in characters I knew to be Arabic. And since I recognised but could not read it, I looked around to see if some Morisco who knew Castilian, and could read it for me, was in the vicinity, and it was not very difficult to find this kind of interpreter, for even if I had sought a speaker of a better and older language, I would have found him.)[19]

That is to say, even if he were looking for a Hebrew translator, he would have had no difficulty in finding one in Toledo, a curious and revealing comment on the multicultural diversity of the City of the Three Religions even at the end of the sixteenth century. Once his Morisco translator makes it clear through his reaction to the 'Arabic' text that he has indeed found the continuation of the novel, Cervantes rapidly buys all the papers from the boy who is selling them in the marketplace and takes the Morisco off to his house, where, in little more than a month and a half, he translates all of them 'en lengua castellana, sin quitarles ni añadirles nada' (I. 9, 119) ('into the Castilian language; without taking away or adding anything').[20] From this point on, readers, writers, and listeners abound in a text supposedly written by an Arab historian, Cide Hamete Benegeli, mediated by a bilingual Morisco, and narrated by a Castilian.[21]

Antonio, a twenty-two-year-old shepherd boy who, we are told 'sabe leer y escribir y es músico de un rabel, que no hay más que desear' (I. 11, 136) ('knows how to read and write and is so good a musician on the rebec that you couldn't ask for anything better')[22], sings a love song about his girlfriend Eulalia which he has written himself. Grisóstomo (to whom we shall shortly return) has written his own 'Canción desesperada' (Song of Despair). His friend Ambrosio, a fellow student, has read the poem and will write the epitaph on his tomb stone. Vivaldo (I. 14) has read the novels of chivalry and reads out Grisóstomo's poem. Ginés de Pasamonte (I. 22), a galley slave, is writing his own autobiography in the style of *Lazarillo de Tormes*. Cardenio has written verses and has a sort of pocket book of his thoughts and jottings; his rival Fernando is well educated and sends notes to his mistresses. Don Luis (of the intercalated tale of Don Luis and Doña Clara) sings his own verses (I. 43). In a world of supposedly high levels of illiteracy, Cervantes gives us the whole gamut of reading, writing, and listening, suggesting that culture was not restricted to just a few but was widely available. The reading out aloud in Palomeque's inn of the *Curioso impertinente* is a case in point. The innkeeper keeps a chest with books and manuscripts in it for when the opportunity arises for a communal reading aloud, especially at harvest time,

> Porque cuando es tiempo de la siega, se recogen aquí las fiestas muchos segadores, y siempre hay algunos que saben leer, el cual coge uno destos libros en las manos, y rodeámonos dél más de treinta y estámosle escuchando con tanto gusto, que nos quita mil canas. (I. 32, 404–05)
>
> (Because during the harvest, many of the harvesters gather here during their time off, and there's always a few who know how to read, and one of them takes down one of those books, and more than thirty of us sit around him and listen to him read with so much pleasure that it saves us a thousand gray hairs.)[23]

We might be surprised by the revelation that there is always a few of the reapers sufficiently educated to be able to read, but the scene that Cervantes describes of thirty or more people sitting around at siesta time listening to a romance of chivalry (which seem to make up the majority of the innkeeper's texts) is not so uncommon and was clearly the way most illiterate people of the age acquired a knowledge of literature and other texts. All that is except Sancho, as we have previously mentioned.

Indeed, throughout the two parts of the novel the number of people who can read (and write) is significantly high,[24] and contrasts quite strongly with the reality of the time, in which the majority of people were illiterate, whichever test of literacy that you use.[25] And the illiterates come from predictable social classes or groups: farm workers, shepherds, lower-class women. Their literate counterparts also come from pretty predictable groups: knights (*hidalgos*), clergy, professionals, students, wealthy or upper-class women.

The effects of reading are clearly something that interested Cervantes, and he explores this not just through the character of Alonso Quijano. If Alonso is the knight of Part One, then Diego de Miranda is very evidently the knight or *hidalgo* of Part Two, a counterweight in many ways to the 'mad' Don Quixote. He is married and has children (unlike the bachelor Quijano) and leads what appears to be an ordered, decorous, and productive life (again, very unlike Alonso). But what sets them apart, and this is a deliberate ploy on the part of Cervantes, are their respective libraries. Don Quixote tells Luscinda in Part One, Chapter 24 that if she were to accompany him to his village 'allí le podré dar más de trecientos libros que son el regalo de mi alma y el entretenimiento de mi vida' (I. 24, 293) ('there I can give you more than three hundred books, which are the joy of my soul and the delight of my life').[26] Earlier we learn that over one hundred of them are bound folio editions of romances of chivalry (I. 6), among the most expensive books on the market. In the course of the text some thirty-seven titles are given to us (i.e. about twelve per cent of the total). In contrast, Diego de Miranda's library has approximately seventy-two volumes, principally of history and devotion, a mixture of works in Spanish and Latin, but no romances of chivalry: 'los de caballerías aún no han entrado por los umbrales de mis puertas' (II. 16, 823) ('books of chivalry have not yet crossed my threshold').[27] Don Diego then makes a very curious observation on his reading habits: 'Hojeo más los que son profanos que los devotos, como sean de honesto entretenimiento, que deleiten con el lenguaje y admiren y suspendan con la invención, puesto que déstos hay muy pocos en España' (823) ('I read more profane books than devout ones, as long as the diversion is honest, and the language delights, and the invention amazes and astounds, though there are very few of these in Spain').[28] It seems that he does not want to appear, from what he has previously said about his books, that he is some sort of prude who does not enjoy contemporary literature; far from it, he prefers works of entertainment to devotional tracts, provided that they are well written and are an honest and morally uplifting form of diversion. In this, as it happens, he is not so far removed from Alonso Quijano. If we examine the titles of the works to be found in this latter's library, we note that, with the exception of the romances of chivalry (the first fourteen of the list), the rest are all relatively contemporary works, dating from the last twenty years or so of the sixteenth century:

15   Jorge de Montemayor, *La Diana*, Valencia, 1558.
16   Alonso Pérez, *Segunda parte de la Diana*, Venice, 1568.
17   Gaspar Gil Polo, *Diana enamorada*, Valencia, 1564.
18   Antonio de lo Frasso, *Libro de la Fortuna de amor*, Barcelona, 1573.
19   Bernardo de la Vega, *El pastor de Iberia*, Sevilla, 1591.
20   Bernardo González de Bobadilla, *Ninfas y pastores de Henares*, Alcalá de Henares, 1587.
21   Bartolomé López de Enciso, *Desengaño de celos*, Madrid, 1586.
22   Luis Gálvez de Montalvo, *El pastor de Fílida*, Madrid, 1582.
23   Pedro de Padilla, *Tesoro de varias poesías*, Madrid, 1580.
24   Gabriel López Maldonado, *Cancionero*, Madrid, 1586.
25   Miguel de Cervantes Saavedra, *La Galatea*, Alcalá de Henares, 1585.
26   Alonso de Ercilla, *La Araucana*, Madrid, 1569.
27   Juan Rufo, *La Austríada*, Madrid, 1584.
28   Cristóbal de Virués, *El Monserrate*, Madrid, 1588.

29 Luis Barahona de Soto, *Las lágrimas de Angélica*, Granada, 1586.
30 Jerónimo de Sempere, *La Carolea*, Valencia, 1560.
31 Pedro de la Vecilla Castellano, *El león de España*, Salamanca, 1586.
32 Luis de Ávila, *Carlo famoso*, Valencia, 1566.
36 *Romances del Marqués de Mantua*, Valencia, 1597; Alcalá de Henares, 1598? (I. 5; I. 10).[29]

If we compare Alonso Quijano's library to the stock held by contemporary booksellers, we can see that he kept very up to date with his purchases. Benito Boyer of Medina del Campo had twenty-three of Alonso's titles for sale in his bookshop (1592), while the Madrid bookseller Cristóbal López had fifteen, in 1606.[30] This library therefore represents the reading tastes of Cervantes's contemporaries towards the end of the sixteenth and beginning of the seventeenth centuries, as far as literature of entertainment is concerned.[31] We should not of course lose sight of the fact that most private libraries of this period contained a far higher proportion of works of law, history, and the classics than they ever did of what we would now call works of literature, though this did not mean that these works were not printed or did not circulate.[32] However, with regard to its size Alonso Quijano's library is larger than the norm; in this respect Diego de Miranda's seventy-two or so books was about average for the time.[33] In these subtle ways Cervantes points out the problems caused by Alonso Quijano's love of books, especially of romances of chivalry. They were large folio volumes, they cost a lot of money, especially if they were bound, and he had a lot of them. No wonder that he forgot about properly administering his estates, gave up hunting, and had to sell 'muchas hanegas de tierra de sembradura para comprar libros de caballerías en que leer' (I. 1, 40) ('acres of arable land in order to buy books of chivalry to read').[34] Whether the reading of them turned him mad or not is not relevant at this stage; what is, is that his counterpoint, Diego de Miranda, is put forward as the ideal *hidalgo*, whose way of life is one of moderation in all things. He is the *hidalgo* Alonso Quijano should have been, Cervantes seems to be saying. But thankfully, he was not, for had he been, there would have been no novel, no hilarious adventures, no clash of reality and fiction. And it is this clash, or rather meeting of reality and fiction in the oft-called 'pastoral interlude' to which I now wish to turn my attention.

After a series of adventures — Part One, Chapters 7–10 — Don Quixote and Sancho Panza go searching for a village where they can stop and spend the night, which is fast approaching. Not finding any inhabited place nearby, they have no choice but to sleep out in the open under the night sky, which fills Sancho with foreboding but Don Quixote with happiness, 'por parecerle que cada vez que esto le sucedía era hacer un acto posesivo que facilitaba la prueba de su caballería' (I. 10, 130) ('for it seemed to him that each time this occurred it was another act of certification that helped to prove his claim to knighthood').[35] Eventually they arrive at a spot where there is a group of goatherds, a place that Sancho has found by following the pleasant smell of the goat stew they are preparing. The goatherds invite the two to share their supper and they spread out on the ground for them some sheep skins so that they will be more comfortable. The most curious thing so far is that at no point do the goatherds show any surprise at the truly bizarre appearance of their supper companions: an elderly man (about fifty years old) dressed as a knight errant in old and broken armour, and wearing on his head a helmet made out of cardboard, accompanied by a short, fat squire riding on a donkey. Where they do show surprise is when Don Quixote and Sancho begin to talk of the rules of knight errantry, and whether Sancho can sit down to eat or whether he has to remain standing to serve his master. As Cervantes says at this point: 'No entendían los cabreros aquella jerigonza de escuderos y de caballeros andantes, y no hacían otra cosa que comer y callar y mirar a sus huéspedes' (I. 11, 132) ('The goatherds did not understand their nonsensical talk about squires and knights errant, and they simply ate and were silent and looked at their guests').[36] A curious and interesting reaction: they do not understand a word of what their two guests are saying, but they do not interfere in the discussion. They simply carry on eating, listening, and watching; in short, they behave impeccably. If we imagine that Don Quixote and Sancho represent a living text, it is evident that the goatherds do not understand the signs (signifier), and if you do not understand the signs you cannot understand the meaning (signified). As a result, they reveal themselves to be potentially very good readers: they listen, watch, and keep silent. They do not want to jump to wrong conclusions or interpretations. They suspend for the time being their judgement of the situation, preferring to see what happens before deciding. A good lesson for any would-be reader: it is important to know how to interpret the signs.

And they do well not to rush into judging the situation, for straightaway comes one of the most memorable moments of the whole novel. In Part One of *El ingenioso hidalgo don Quijote de la Mancha* there are two long and celebrated speeches by the protagonist: that of the 'Golden Age' and that of 'Arms and Letters' (I. 37–38). The two are what we would call today After Dinner Speeches, a talk given at the end of a celebratory meal usually by an invited guest speaker. Everyone has eaten and drunk well, they all feel relaxed, and at this moment the invited speaker stands up and delivers a fifteen- to twenty-minute speech on a topic that usually has something to do with the purpose of the meal or the group who are supping. The key to the speech, and its success, is that it is related to the occasion and to those celebrating, and that it be amenable, agreeable, and, if possible, amusing. This is the context for a successful After Dinner Speech. Don Quixote obviously does not know the rules — and why should he at the beginning of the seventeenth century? — and launches himself into a speech that is the least appropriate for the context in which he finds himself.[37] Cervantes introduces it thus: 'Después que don Quijote hubo bien satisfecho su estómago, tomó un puño de bellotas en la mano y, mirándolas atentamente, soltó la voz a semejantes razones' (132–33) ('After Don Quixote had satisfied his stomach, he picked up a handful of acorns, and, regarding them attentively, he began to speak these words').[38]

As always, Cervantes prepares the scene perfectly: Don Quixote has just had supper with a group of goatherds (real goatherds, let us not forget), he has satisfied the needs of his stomach with the rich meal they have prepared for him, and nearby he sees a handful of acorns (the goatherds' regular food). All of this recalls to him his past readings, though in truth he has no past, and thus no past readings. He is an invention, a creation of Alonso Quijano. Thus, the readings we are going to witness and hear are those of Alonso Quijano, an *hidalgo* gone down in the world thanks to his mania for reading and buying expensive books he can ill afford. This, I believe, is an important point: almost all readers of *Don Quixote* forget about Alonso Quijano after the first chapter where he converts himself into Don Quixote. We think he has disappeared from the text and that he only returns at the end of Part Two when he regains his reason and repents of his supposed madness. But this is not the case. Alonso Quijano never disappears from the text; he is present throughout the whole novel; he is the shadow who accompanies Don Quixote everywhere. It is worth noting that Don Quixote does not read anything during the course of the novel (unlike almost all the other characters), but he continually quotes texts that his alter ego, his creator Alonso Quijano, certainly has read: texts learnt when a child, such as the ballads of the Marquis of Mantua (a basic primary school text for initiating young children into the art of reading),[39] or the works of sixteenth-century poets such as Garcilaso de la Vega and Jorge de Montemayor and classical texts by Virgil and Horace. The North-American critic Daniel Eisenberg has carried out a study of all the texts cited in *Don Quixote* in order to try to reconstruct Cervantes's imaginary 'library', and he noted more than three hundred of them.[40]

All these readings carried out by Alonso Quijano are going to shape Don Quixote's great speech on the Golden Age of Man, which begins thus:

> Dichosa edad y siglos dichosos aquellos a quien los antiguos pusieron nombre de dorados, y no porque en ellos el oro, que en esta nuestra edad de hierro tanto se estima, se alcanzase en aquella venturosa sin fatiga alguna, sino porque entonces los que en ella vivían ignoraban estas dos palabras de *tuyo* y *mío*. Eran en aquella santa edad todas las cosas comunes: a nadie le era necesario para alcanzar su ordinario sustento tomar otro trabajo que alzar la mano y alcanzarle de las robustas encinas, que liberalmente les estaban convidando con su dulce y sazonado fruto. Las claras fuentes y corrientes ríos, en magnífica abundancia, sabrosas y transparentes aguas les ofrecían. (I. 11, 133)

> (Fortunate the age and fortunate the times called golden by the ancients, and not because gold, which in this our age of iron is so highly esteemed, could be found then with no effort, but because those who lived in that time did not know the two words *thine* and *mine*. In that blessed age all things were owned in common; no one, for his daily sustenance, needed to do more than lift his hand and pluck it from the sturdy oaks that so liberally invited him to share their sweet and flavoursome fruit. The clear fountains and rushing rivers offered delicious, transparent waters in magnificent abundance.)[41]

And so it goes on, praising the goodness of nature which gave man all he needed without his having to toil or sweat, a world where 'todo era paz entonces, todo amistad, todo concordia' (133) ('all was peace, friendship and harmony')[42], where 'andaban las simples y hermosas zagalejas de valle en valle y de otero en otero, en trenza y en cabello' (134) ('simple and beautiful shepherdesses could wander from valley to valley and hill to hill, their hair hanging loose or in braids').[43] In short, a perfect world of justice, decorum, and good customs, and all in contrast with 'estos nuestros detestables siglos' (135) ('these our detestable times')[44] where 'no está segura ninguna' (135) ('no maiden is safe').⁴⁵ Now that we have arrived at this point, we realize that the speech so far has just been preparation for what is to come: praise of knight errantry, for as he says: 'Para cuya seguridad, andando más los tiempos y creciendo más la malicia, se instituyó la orden de los caballeros andantes, para defender las doncellas, amparar las viudas y socorrer a los huérfanos y a los menesterosos' (135) ('It was for their protection, as time passed and wickedness spread, that the order of knights errant was instituted: to defend maidens, protect widows, and come to the aid of orphans and those in need').⁴⁶

The sequence of ideas is perfect: the goatherds and then the acorns which our knight finds on the ground take him to the theme of the Golden Age, where nature was abundant and good; from there he moves on to the young damsels who were safe in this perfect age and honourable in their morals; the security and defence of damsels is the prime motive for the existence of knights errant, hence his speech ends with praise of its institution. And just in case we have not caught on to this chain of ideas, Cervantes spells it out for us: 'Toda esta larga arenga [...] dijo nuestro caballero, porque las bellotas que le dieron le trujeron a la memoria la edad dorada, y antojósele hacer aquel inútil razonamiento a los cabreros' (135) ('This long harangue [...] was declaimed by our knight because the acorns served to him brought to mind the Golden Age, and with it the desire to make that foolish speech to the goatherds').⁴⁷ With his characteristic irony, Cervantes calls this speech a 'larga arenga (que se pudiera muy bien escusar)' ('long harangue, which could very easily have been omitted')⁴⁸ and 'aquel inútil razonamiento' ('that foolish speech').⁴⁹ If it were redundant and so foolish, he surely would not have written it. If it is there, then it is for a reason, and as always in Cervantes that reason is to teach the reader something, in this case, I believe, something about the mechanisms and nature of fiction.

As just noted above, this speech is completely inappropriate for the context in which it is given. The public listening to it is made up of goatherds and Sancho, all of them one hundred per cent illiterate, who will not recognize a single text hidden in the discourse of our knight and who are, in addition, very tired after a long day of hard work looking after their goats. More appropriate for such an audience would have been perhaps some inconsequential chitchat, a short conversation on what everyone had been doing during the day, where they had been, what they had seen, and so forth. Anything really but an erudite speech made up from various classical texts, such as the *Idylls* of Theocritus, the *Eclogues* of Virgil, the *Odes* of Horace, Seneca's *Hipolitus*, various works by Ovid, and more modern authors such as Jacobo Sanazzaro and his *Arcadia*, Garcilaso, Fray Luis de León, and so on. The Golden Age is a literary fiction that deals with an era that never existed, but which all societies have recreated as a moment in the past in which everything functioned perfectly, when man did not have to sweat and toil and when nature gave abundantly of its fruits. We are looking at Paradise, which, according to the Bible, was lost with Adam and Eve, a paradise to which all cultures have wished to return. To offer this speech (and vision) to an illiterate public, worn out from hard work and made up of real goatherds and not the literary shepherds who people, for example, the eclogues of Garcilaso or Cervantes's own pastoral novel *La Galatea*, is hugely amusing and a further example of how out of place and time Don Quixote is. In any case, as we have noted above, the only person who could have given this speech was Alonso Quijano and not Don Quixote.

And what about the poor goatherds during all of this? This is what Cervantes has to say: 'sin respondelle palabra, embobados y suspensos, le estuvieron escuchando' (135) ('stupefied and perplexed, [they] listened without saying a word').[50] 'Embobados y suspensos': these are key words, absolutely fundamental words, because with them Cervantes gets to the heart of fiction, and he does so centuries before the celebrated term 'suspension of disbelief' was coined to describe the effects of fiction on the reader.[51] We, as readers, when we pick up a novel, have to suspend our disbelief in order to be able to read and enjoy what we are reading. That is to say, we know that what we are reading is a book full of fictional characters created by the author, who do not exist and have never existed. But for fiction to function, the reader has to believe in this fiction, in these fictional characters, and amazingly this is what happens. When we read we suspend our disbelief and believe that the characters are real. We identify with them, we feel what they feel, we may even fall in love with some of them. What fiction, the novel to be more exact, has, and this is why it has surpassed all forms of literature in popularity over the ages, is its capacity to make us believe in it, to believe that its characters are real. We get absorbed in the novel, all notion of time is suspended when we are reading a good novel, and when we get to the end, we feel something like a loss or bereavement, as if someone had died and left a void behind them. And while their readers have passed from this life, the characters of great novels live on. Everyone has heard of Don Quixote and Sancho Panza; they are immortal characters who still live on four centuries after their creation, but their millions of readers since 1605, those who did live in reality, are completely unknown to us. And all of this is conveyed to us in that wonderful phrase 'embobados y suspensos'. Chapters 11–14 of Part One of *Don Quixote* are like a seminar on the art of narration and the art of reading, and we are only just a few pages into Chapter 11 at this point! We should also note that this is not the only time Cervantes employs the concept. Just after Juan Palomeque has been waxing lyrical about the effects on him of listening to the romances of chivalry, 'que querría estar oyéndolos noches y días' (I. 32, 405) ('and I'd be happy to keep hearing about them for days and nights on end'),[52] his wife interjects with the following pointed observation: 'Y yo ni más ni menos [...], porque nunca tengo buen rato en mi casa sino aquel que vos estáis escuchando leer, que estáis tan *embobado*, que no os acordáis de reñir por entonces' (405; my emphasis) ('The same goes for me, because I never have any peace in my house except when you're listening to somebody read; you get so caught up that you forget about arguing with me').[53] Again, the idea of a suspension of or from reality.[54]

From the episode of the goatherds and the after-dinner speech on the Golden Age, we move on to another famous and probably better-known episode, that of Marcela and Gristóstomo. In order to make the link between the two, Cervantes employs first of all the references in the Golden Age speech to 'las simples y hermosas zagalejas [que andaban] de valle en valle y de otero en otero, en trenza y en cabello' (I. 11, 134) ('the simple and beautiful shepherdesses [who] could wander from valley to valley and hill to hill, their hair hanging loose or in braids'),[55] and then introduces the goatherd Antonio, who sings a poem of frustrated love about his lover Olalla (Eulalia). Apart from reminding us that in this age of mass illiteracy the principal form of communication was oral, the poem serves to introduce the history of Marcela and Grisóstomo, another story of unrequited love. As soon as Antonio finishes his poem, Pedro, a young lad from the nearby village, turns up with sad news:

> murió esta mañana aquel famoso pastor estudiante llamado Grisóstomo, y se murmura que ha muerto de amores de aquella endiablada moza de Marcela, la hija de Guillermo el rico, aquella que se anda en hábito de pastora por esos andurriales'. (I. 12, 140)
>
> (This morning the famous student shepherd named Grisótomo died, and they say he died of love for that accursed girl Marcela, the daughter of Guillermo the rich man, the same girl who dresses up like a shepherdess and wanders around the wild, empty places.')[56]

Straightaway we discover that a group of young students, from well-off backgrounds, have been playing at being shepherds, but not real shepherds (like our real goatherds), rather fictional ones. If the speech of Don Quixote on the Golden Age was a contrast with his audience of real goatherds, then the story of Marcela and Gristóstomo affords an even greater contrast, for here two pastoral worlds collide: the real and the fictional. As always, the goatherds act as an audience (or, in our terms, readers) of what takes place before their eyes.

The story is as follows: it seems that Grisóstomo, a student for a number of years at Salamanca university who has returned to his village 'con opinión de muy sabio y muy leído' (141) ('with a reputation for being very learned and well-read'),[57] has fallen in love with a girl from the same village called Marcela, the daughter of a father even richer than Grisóstomo's. As her father has died, she has been brought up by an uncle, a priest and an incumbent, who keeps her 'con mucho recato y con mucho encerramiento' (144) ('carefully and modestly secluded'),[58] for she has become a very beautiful young girl and word of her beauty has spread. Rich and beautiful, she is a good marriage prospect, but her uncle, although he wants to marry her off, does not wish to do so without her consent, an attitude that merits very positive comments in the village. Every so often her uncle would propose to her possible candidates for her hand in marriage, but she always rejected them saying that 'por entonces no quería casarse y que, por ser tan muchacha, no se sentía hábil para poder llevar la carga del matrimonio' (145) ('she didn't want to marry just then, and since she was so young she didn't feel able to bear the burdens of matrimony').[59] And then, suddenly, without consulting with her uncle, Marcela decides to dress up as a shepherdess and 'dio en irse al campo con las demás zagalas del lugar, y dio en guardar su mesmo ganado' (145) ('started to go out to the countryside with the other shepherdesses and to watch over her own flock').[60] Naturally, by doing this, she makes herself visible for the first time to the young men of the village; they had probably heard about her fabled beauty, but they had not actually seen her in person. The result is inevitable: they all fall in love with her. As Cervantes says with great humour:

> No está muy lejos de aquí un sitio donde hay casi dos docenas de altas hayas, y no hay ninguna que en su lisa corteza no tenga grabado y escrito el nombre de Marcela, y encima de alguna una corona grabada en el mesmo árbol, como si más claramente dijera su amante que Marcela la lleva y la merece de toda la hermosura humana. Aquí sospira un pastor, allí se queja otro; acullá se oyen amorosas canciones, acá desesperadas endechas. (146)

> (Not very far from here is a place where there are almost two dozen tall beech trees, and there's not one that doesn't have the name of Marcela carved and written on its smooth bark, and at the top of some there's a crown carved into the tree, as if the lover were saying even more clearly that Marcela wears and deserves the crown more than any other human beauty. Here a shepherd sighs, there another moans, over yonder amorous songs are heard, and farther on desperate lamentations.)[61]

They are all so much in love with Marcela that the one who brings the news talks of 'los amantes de Marcela (147) ('the lovers of Marcela')[62] as if they were a collective. And, even worse, they have left the poor trees in a disastrous state with so many names and crowns inscribed on them, rather like young people do nowadays when they write on the tree bark 'John loves Mary' and put a heart with an arrow through it.

Among this group of environmental hooligans we find of course Gristóstomo. In order to get close to Marcela, for he too is madly in love with her, Grisóstomo along with his student friend Ambrosio decides to dress up as a shepherd also 'con su cayado y pellico' (142) ('with a staff and a sheepskin jacket')[63] and recreate the world of the eclogues and pastoral novels, which is what Marcela seems to have done. In other words, we the readers find ourselves in another fictional world, this time the pastoral novel, a genre which Cervantes had practised in his first published work *La Galatea* (1585) and which was very popular for most of the sixteenth century. It is worth recalling that among the books possessed by Alonso Quijano we find the following: Jorge de Montemayor, *La Diana*, 1558; Alonso Pérez, *Segunda parte de la Diana*, 1568; Gaspar Gil Polo, *Diana enamorada*, 1564; Luis Gálvez de Montalvo, *El pastor de Fílida*, 1582; Bernardo de la Vega, *El pastor de Iberia*, 1591; Bernardo González de Bobadilla, *Ninfas y pastores de Henares*, 1587; and, of course, *La Galatea* by Cervantes himself. Alonso Quijano had almost all the principal novels of the genre in his library.

The pastoral novel is essentially made up of amorous and philosophical dialogues between shepherds and shepherdesses, all of them courtiers who have received a good education and have escaped from the court into a pastoral world, which acts as a backcloth against which to explore and discuss their emotions. These shepherds would not know one end of a sheep from the other, even though sheep do appear in this fiction, mainly however as a decoration or prop. If there are shepherds, then there must be sheep, but these are incredibly well-educated sheep which do not wander off everywhere, like real sheep, but stay still listening to the songs of their shepherds and waiting patiently for their laments to come to an end. It is a completely artificial world, but with rivers, riverbanks, meadows, and trees to make it look real, indeed, whose only function is to give the appearance or veneer of reality. This is Arcadia, as in the famous classical phrase 'Et in Arcadia ego'. All is artificial: the scene, the protagonists, the props, but not the speeches.

In Chapters 12–14 of Part One of *Don Quixote* Cervantes recreates this fiction in the tale of Marcela and Grisóstomo, two rich young people who play at being shepherds, like those who appear in the pastoral novels, which they have obviously read and read well. The problem for Marcela and Grisóstomo is that fiction is one thing and the real world another, and in the end neither is able to distinguish very well between the two, although, as we shall see, Marcela does a better job of it than Grisóstomo. Naturally, in this they remind us of Alonso Quijano who was also unable to distinguish between what he read — the world of fiction — and what surrounded him — the world of reality —, and to overcome the dilemma (or, at least, to escape from it) he turned himself into the knight errant Don Quixote. From the evidence before us, neither Marcela nor Grisóstomo are happy in the real world and wish to flee from it to the fictional world of the pastoral novel. In this scene, which is so rich in nuances and suggestions, Cervantes places before us two fictional worlds or, rather, two literary forms: the pastoral novel and the romance of chivalry. Both were without doubt the most popular forms of fiction in the sixteenth century among all social classes. The romances of chivalry were immensely popular from the beginning of the century, with sales peaking in the years 1520–30, 1550, and 1570–80, which is when the majority of them were published and when many enjoyed numerous editions throughout the century.[64] The pastoral novel was popular more or less at the same time, although by 1585, when Cervantes published *La Galatea*, its readership had fallen off somewhat. To his great annoyance, he published his first novel at the very moment when the genre had entered into decline. But in *Don Quixote* Cervantes is able to recreate this artificial world in the episode of Marcela and Grisóstomo and again in Chapter 67 of Part Two when Don Quixote and Sancho Panza play with the idea of becoming shepherds and calling themselves 'Shepherd Quixotiz' and 'Shepherd Pancino', and, according to Don Quixote's speech, roaming 'los montes, por las selvas y por los prados, cantando aquí, endechando allí, bebiendo de los líquidos cristales de las fuentes, o ya de los limpios arroyuelos o de los caudalosos ríos' (II. 67, 1284) ('the mountains, the woods and the meadows, singing here, lamenting there, drinking the liquid crystal of the fountains, or the limpid streams, or the rushing rivers').[65] Once again the memory of the Golden Age comes back to him:

> Daranos con abundantísima mano de su dulcísimo fruto las encinas, asiento los troncos de los durísimos alcornoques, sombra los sauces, olor las rosas, alfombras de mil colores matizadas los estendidos prados, aliento el aire claro y puro, luz la luna y las estrellas, a pesar de la escuridad de la noche, gusto el canto, alegría el lloro, Apolo versos, el amor conceptos, con que podremos hacernos eternos y famosos, no sólo en los presentes, sino en los venideros siglos. (II. 67, 1284)
>
> (With a copious hand the oaks will give us their sweetest fruit; the hard cork trees, their trunks as seats, the willows, their shade; the roses, their fragrance; the broad meadows, carpets of a thousand shades and colours; the clear, pure air,

our breath; the moon and stars, our light in spite of night's darkness; pleasure will give us our songs; joy, our weeping; Apollo, our verses; love, our conceits; and with these we shall make ourselves eternal and famous, not only in the present but in times to come.)[66]

We will return to this episode at the end of the chapter because it contains something important, I believe, for understanding the novel, but to return to where we were, in Chapters 13 and 14 of Part One, Cervantes brings face to face two fictional worlds, both very popular at the time: the pastoral novel represented by Marcela and Grisóstomo, and the romance of chivalry represented by Don Quixote. In both cases we are confronted by characters who for one reason or another are ill at ease in the society of their time. Alonso Quijano flees a boring, conventional life without a future as a bachelor *hidalgo* come down in the world; Marcela flees a society which imposes marriage upon her as the only solution for a young female orphan, even though wealthy; Grisóstomo, however, does not seem to be fleeing anything, rather he throws himself into the pastoral world in order to be with Marcela, a decision which will literally cost him his life.

For, in spite of his love for Marcela, she does not respond; she has no interest in marrying anyone and least of all, it would appear, a student who leaves off the gown and hood of a graduate to dress up as a false shepherd. The result of her scorn is that Grisóstomo dies and Don Quixote and the rest arrive in time to witness his burial. What is not totally clear in the text is the manner of his death, although it would appear to have been suicide, for which reason Ambrosio and the rest of his friends bury him in the open countryside and not in a consecrated place (which was not possible). Alongside the corpse are placed various pieces of paper, among them the story of Grisóstomo's love for Marcela, papers which he had asked Ambrosio to consign to the flames, thus following in the footsteps of so many other writers who asked for the destruction of their literary work, and anticipating by a few years, for example, what Lupercio Leonardo de Argensola asked his brother Bartolomé to do with his poems when he died in Naples in 1613.[67]

One of the gentlemen who has joined the group, Vivaldo, tries to save the papers from the fire and manages to get hold of one which has as its title 'Canción desesperada' ('Desperate Verses') which, according to Ambrosio, was the last thing his friend wrote. Chapter 14, thus, begins with the reading out aloud of Grisóstomo's 'Canción desesperada'. It is the typical Petrarchan poem of the sixteenth century on the theme of unrequited love, in which the lover is rejected and in despair, and the beloved is 'la belle dame sans merci' of tradition, just as Ambrosio had described it all previously:

> Quiso bien, fue aborrecido; adoró, fue desdeñado; rogó a una fiera, importunó a un mármol, corrió tras el viento, dio voces a la soledad, sirvió a la ingratitud, de quien alcanzó por premio ser despojos de la muerte en la mitad de la carrera de su vida. (I. 13, 158)

> (He loved deeply and was rejected; he adored and was scorned; he pleaded with a wild beast, importuned a piece of marble, pursued the wind, shouted in the desert, served ingratitude, and his reward was to fall victim to death in the middle of his life.)[68]

When Ambrosio finishes reading the poem, Vivaldo is on the point of reading another paper from those he saved from the flames when he is disturbed by a marvellous vision (in Cervantes's words)

> que improvisamente se les ofreció a los ojos; y fue que por cima de la peña donde se cavaba la sepultura pareció la pastora Marcela, tan hermosa, que pasaba a su fama su hermosura. Los que hasta entonces no la habían visto la miraban con admiración y silencio, y los que ya estaban acostumbrados a verla no quedaron menos suspensos que los que nunca la habían visto. (I. 14, 166)
>
> (that suddenly appeared before his eyes; at the top of the crag where the grave was being dug, there came into view the shepherdess Marcela, whose beauty far surpassed her fame for beauty. Those who had not seen her before looked at her in amazement and silence, and those who were already accustomed to seeing her were no less thunderstruck than those who had not seen her until then.)[69]

Let us note the words which Cervantes, with extreme care, chooses for his description of Marcela: those who see her for the first time — that is to say, another public or audience — look at her with amazement and silence; and those who know her already are no less astonished or thunderstruck ('suspensos'). Inevitably, we are reminded of the reaction of the goatherds after hearing Don Quixote's speech: 'sin respondelle palabra' = 'silencio'/silence; they listened to him 'embobados y suspensos'. 'Embobados' (amazement), 'suspensos (astonishment) and 'silencio' (silence). Cervantes presents Marcela as another text to be deciphered, another text whose meaning is not at a first reading obvious, and difficult to understand if we do not recognize the signs.

To begin with, it is evident that even before Marcela appears on the scene we all have an idea of her, just as the 'readers' of our text have been forming an idea, assuredly quite negative, of this young lady. Up to this moment our only information about Marcela has come from Grisóstomo's friends (Ambrosio and the goatherd Pedro, who is the first to inform us of the death of the student cum shepherd) and the 'Canción desesperada' written by Grisóstomo shortly before taking his own life. In other words, the idea that we have been forming in our minds about this rich and very beautiful young girl — and also disdainful, angry and haughty — comes from a single source and not exactly the most objective. It is almost certainly the case that we, just like the character-readers in the text, have arrived at wrong conclusions about her because we have received only a partial description of the truth. We have seen the signs, but we have not known how to interpret them correctly because we lack the full information. With Marcela herself on the scene we have the opportunity, the possibility of seeing more of the portrait, although who knows if it will be a complete or, indeed, truthful or accurate portrayal.

No sooner does he see her than Ambrosio attacks her verbally as the cause of the death of his friend: she is a fierce basilisk, another merciless Nero who watches on while Rome burns, another Tullia who drives in her chariot over the body of Tarquin.[70] Just as Don Quixote drew from his memory the echoes of classical quotations about the Golden Age, so too does Ambrosio make use of other commonplaces of classical literature to characterize Marcela.

Ambrosio's attack gives rise to one of the most powerful, brilliant, magnificent speeches ever put in the mouth of a woman. No convinced feminist of the twenty-first century could overshadow Marcela in her speech. It is one of the great moments of the novel, a moment when Cervantes creates one of his best female characters. Basically, what she says is that just because she is beautiful she does not have to let herself be loved by anybody or everybody:

> Yo conozco, con el natural entendimiento que Dios me ha dado, que todo lo hermoso es amable; mas no alcanzo que, por razón de ser amado, esté obligado lo que es amado por hermoso a amar a quien le ama. (I. 14, 167)
>
> (I know, with the natural understanding that God has given me, that everything beautiful is lovable, but I cannot grasp why, simply because it is loved, the thing loved for its beauty is obliged to love the one who loves it.)[71]

For Marcela the most important thing of all is the will, free will, the capacity of every human being to choose:

> Yo nací libre, y para poder vivir libre escogí la soledad de los campos [...]. Yo, como sabéis, tengo riquezas propias, y no codicio las ajenas; tengo libre condición, y no gusto de sujetarme; ni quiero ni aborrezco a nadie; no engaño a éste ni solicito aquel; ni burlo con uno ni me entretengo con el otro. (I. 14, 168–70)
>
> (I was born free, and in order to live free I chose the solitude of the countryside [...]. As you know, I have wealth of my own and do not desire anyone else's; I am free and do not care to submit to another; I do not love or despise anyone. I do not deceive this one or solicit that one; I do not mock one or amuse myself with another.)[72]

She cannot be held responsible for the death of one who has fallen in love with her when she has not given him any reason or motive to do so: 'antes le mató su porfía que mi crueldad' (168) ('his obstinacy, not my cruelty, is what killed him'),[73] she says. And with this 'volvió las espaldas y se entró por lo más cerrado de un monte que allí cerca estaba, dejando admirados tanto de su discreción como de su hermosura a todos los que allí estaban' (170) ('she turned her back and entered the densest part of a nearby forest, leaving all those present filled with admiration as much for her intelligence as for her beauty').[74] We note once again the use of the term 'dejando *admirados* [...] a todos los que allí estaban' ('leaving all those present filled with *admiration*'; my emphasis). As I have just said, Marcela is another text we have to decipher. Now, with her own words ringing in our ears, we are in a better position to decipher it than previously when we just had the point of view of her enemies, but that we are totally prepared for the task is something that Cervantes quickly disabuses us of: 'Y algunos dieron muestras [...] de quererla seguir, sin aprovecharse del manifiesto desengaño que habían oído' (170) ('And some [...] gave indications of wishing to follow her, disregarding the patent discouragement they had heard').[75] In spite of her forceful speech in favour of female freedom, and her right to choose and decide, some of those present still have not understood her. Don Quixote appears to have done so when he shouts out at those about to follow her:

> Ninguna persona, de cualquier estado y condición que sea, se atreva a seguir a la hermosa Marcela, so pena de caer en la furiosa indignación mía. Ella ha mostrado con claras y suficientes razones la poca o ninguna culpa que ha tenido en la muerte de Grisóstomo y cuán ajena vive de condescender con los deseos de ninguno de sus amantes; a cuya causa es justo que, en lugar de ser seguida y perseguida, sea honrada y estimada de todos los buenos del mundo, pues muestra que en él ella es sola la que con tan honesta intención vive. (I. 14, 170)
>
> (Let no person, whatever his circumstances or condition, dare to follow the beautiful Marcela lest he fall victim to my fury and outrage. She has shown with clear and sufficient reasons that she bears little or no blame in the death of Grisóstomo, and she has also shown how far she is from acquiescing to the desires of any who love her, and therefore it is just that rather than being followed and persecuted, she should be honoured and esteemed by all good people in the world, for she has shown herself to be the only woman in it who lives with so virtuous a desire.)[76]

No one does follow her, but we do not know if this is because of the threats of Don Quixote or because Ambrosio tells them that he has to get on with the task in hand, which is to bury his friend Grisóstomo. With the grave dug and his papers thrown into the fire, they lay his body to rest, placing over it a tombstone which carries the following epitaph in verse:

Yace aquí de un amador	(Here lies the sad cold
el mísero cuerpo helado,	body of a lover,
que fue pastor de ganado,	a shepherd destroyed
perdido por desamor.	by an icy heart.
Murió a manos del rigor	The pitiless hand
de una esquiva hermosa ingrata,	of cruel beauty killed him,
con quien su imperio dilata	extending the power
la tiranía de amor. (171)[77]	of love's tyranny.)[78]

Yet another text.

With the burial over, each one takes a separate path and abandons the scene, talking as they go about 'la historia de Marcela y Grisóstomo como de las locuras de don Quijote' (171) ('from the history of Marcela and Grisóstomo to the madness of Don Quixote').[79] And Don Quixote, what does he do?: 'determinó de ir a buscar a la pastora Marcela y ofrecerle todo lo que él podía en su servicio' (171) ('Our knight resolved to seek out the shepherdess Marcela and offer to serve her in any way he could').[80] Incredible, although perhaps not, because a little before Cervantes had said, when Marcela finished her speech, that it seemed to Don Quixote that this was an appropriate time to 'usar de su caballería, socorriendo a las doncellas menesterosas' (170) ('put his chivalry into practice by coming to the aid of a maiden in distress').[81] In other words, and in spite of what Marcela has just said to the rest, that they leave her in peace, that they do not follow or persecute her, he has decided to offer her his services as a knight errant because she is a damsel in distress and in need. If ever there was a damsel less in distress and in need of anyone's assistance (and this includes grown up men playing at being knights errant), that person is Marcela.

As a result, Don Quixote reveals that once again he too is a bad reader: he has heard what she has said, but he has not interpreted the signs correctly. And as we know, this is a failing of his throughout the novel: windmills become giants, inns castles, prostitutes damsels, sheep and goats armies, the shaving basin of a barber Mambrino's helmet. Cervantes knew that the real world is a text full of signs that we have to learn how to decipher in order to be able to live and lead a normal life, and to be able to navigate our way through its choppy waters. The problem is that signs are rarely of a single meaning: they are ambiguous and polyvalent. Seen from a distance and with the sun shining on it, a barber's basin can easily appear to be a helmet, especially if it is being worn on the head and we are reading the signs as if everything was from a romance of chivalry. The same can be said of the dust raised by hundreds of sheep and goats: that too could be the dust raised by a troop of soldiers. Our eyes and our brain are constantly deciphering ambiguous and polyvalent signs to try to give meaning to what we see and to the world in which we live.

Don Quixote, as I have just said, is a bad reader; so too is Grisóstomo, who did not know how to interpret Marcela's behaviour and actions. He wanted to see in her flight to the countryside dressed as a shepherdess a recreation of the pastoral novel, and, thus, he became a shepherd to accompany her and make her fall in love with him, as traditionally happens in such novels. But she has not wished to recreate that fictitious world. As she very clearly states:

> La conversación honesta de las zagalas destas aldeas y el cuidado de mis cabras me entretiene. Tienen mis deseos por término estas montañas, y si de aquí salen es a contemplar la hermosura del cielo, pasos con que camina el alma a su morada primera. (I. 14, 170)
>
> (The honest conversation of the shepherdesses from these hamlets, and tending to my goats, are my entertainment. The limits of my desires are these mountains, and if they go beyond here, it is to contemplate the beauty of heaven and the steps whereby the soul travels to its first home.)[82]

From the pastoral novel we have passed, almost imperceptibly, to the mystical poetry of a Saint John of the Cross or a Fray Luis de León — with the reference to the soul's 'morada primera' (first home) — , and thus to another world full of even more ambiguous signs. Marcela has read a lot, that is clear, but her reading does not seem to have influenced her behaviour as it did Alonso Quijano's or, indeed, Grisóstomo's. The tragedy of Grisóstomo — his death — is that he turned his life into a courtly love poem, something akin to his own 'Canción desesperada'. In fact, he has mixed together two fictitious worlds: that of the pastoral novel and that of courtly love poetry. In both the shepherd lover suffers the disdain of the beloved, he weeps bitterly, he complains about her conduct, about her ingratitude, and so on. And, this is the key point, he threatens to end his life. He is always talking of death, of his death. As Garcilaso de la Vega wrote in one of his most famous sonnets: 'por vos nací, por vos tengo la vida, | por vos he de morir, y por vos muero' (I was born for you, I owe my life to you, | I must die for you, and so I die for you) (Sonnet v). But here is the most curious thing of all: nobody dies of love in the real world, only in poetry; or, rather, nobody does but Grisóstomo who, unable to distinguish between reality and fiction, commits suicide. If Don Quixote turns the fictional world of romances of chivalry into reality, then Grisóstomo does the same with courtly love poetry, but with disastrous results. The poets and their beloveds (real or fictitious) knew very well that poetry is one thing and the real world another altogether. In 1604, in some Motes de Palacio, Diego de Silva y Mendoza, Count of Salinas (lord of Villarrubia de los Ojos, where local legend locates 'La Peña de Marcela'), wrote the following verses: 'Sintiera vivir acaso | más que morir de propósito' ('I would perhaps regret living | more than dying on purpose'). His young beloved and poetic muse, Leonor Pimentel, wrote by the side, in the margin: 'Lo que se siente es morir, | pero ya no muere nadie' ('What you regret is dying, | but nobody any longer dies').[83] Her reply (and she is referring of course to dying of love) could not be more direct or more cynical. It is a pity that Grisóstomo did not take the same sceptical attitude towards Marcela's disdain.

What we have then in these marvellous Chapters 11–14 of Part One of *Don Quixote* is a complete lesson in how to read, in how to interpret the signs of the world-text that surrounds us, and, at the same time, a seminar on the different forms of fiction available in those years: the romances of chivalry, the pastoral novel, courtly poetry, and, of course, hovering above them all, and outdoing them, the new modern novel that Cervantes is creating. The world of the knight errant comes face to face with the real world of the goatherds, who listen 'embobados y suspensos' to a literary discourse on the Golden Age about as far away from their own reality as it is possible to get. Then, this world of real goatherds is carried off into another fictitious world, this time pastoral, inhabited by real people like them — Marcela and Grisóstomo — but disguised as fictional characters. The death of Grisóstomo from having believed too much in the fictional world he has created — courtly love poetry — reveals the dangers of reading badly. Marcela, on the other hand, seems to know how to interpret the signs better, and she does not confuse the real world with literature. As a result, she lives on. What Cervantes does is to put us in a labyrinth and let us find our own way out by interpreting the signs we find on the way. All the different elements that I have discussed and analysed here are like Chinese boxes or Russian dolls, one inside another and another and another. If we do not wish to lose ourselves forever in this labyrinth, we have to learn how to read, how to interpret our world, but at the same time we can behave like the goatherds who listened in silence 'embobados y suspensos', that is, we can enjoy this marvellous thing called fiction and which nobody handled better than Miguel de Cervantes, for, as he said in Chapter 67 of Part Two, it is thanks to fiction that 'podremos hacernos eternos y famosos, no sólo en los presentes, sino en los venideros siglos' (II. 67, 1284) ('we shall make ourselves eternal and famous, not only in the present but in times to come').[84] Four hundred years on those words have lost none of their relevance — or poignancy.

Notes to Chapter 1

1. Carroll B. Johnson, *Don Quixote: The Quest for Modern Fiction* (Boston: Twayne, 1990), p. 71.
2. For ease of reference I refer to Don Quixote's original persona as Alonso Quijano, fully aware that he only receives this name in the final chapter of Part Two: 'Yo fui loco y ya soy cuerdo; fui don Quijote de la Mancha y soy agora, como he dicho, Alonso Quijano el Bueno' (II. 74, 1333) ('I was mad and now I am sane; I was Don Quixote of La Mancha, and now I am, as I have said, Alonso Quixano the Good'; *Don Quixote*, trans. by Edith Grossman (London: Vintage, 2005), p. 937). Only then does Cervantes sort out the deliberate confusion created in Part One Chapter 1 over his possible names: 'Quieren decir que tenía el sobrenombre de "Quijada", o "Quesada", que en esto hay alguna diferencia en los autores que de este caso escriben, aunque por conjeturas verisímiles se deja entender que se llamaba "Quijana"' (I. 1, 39) ('Some claim that his family name was Quixada, or Quexada, for there is a certain amount of disagreement among the authors who write of this matter, although reliable conjecture seems to indicate that his name was Quexana'; pp. 19–20). Quijana, we are told in II. 74, is the surname of his niece, Antonia. In this Cervantes shows his knowledge of a custom of the Mancha which frequently feminized surnames, thus Ricote's wife, we recall, is known as La Ricota. It would be quite normal, therefore, for the niece of the knight Alonso Quijano to be known as Antonia Quijana. All page references for translations into English of the novel are to Grossman's edition. Translations from other original works into English are mine.
3. p. 20.
4. p. 20.
5. p. 20.
6. p. 48. The reference is almost certainly to the translation into Castilian of *Orlando furioso* by Jerónimo Jiménez de Urrea (1549).
7. There is an excellent and subtle analysis of the scrutiny of Don Quixote's library in Ryan Prendergast, *Reading, Writing, and Errant Subjects in Inquisitorial Spain* (Farnham: Ashgate, 2011), Chapter 1.
8. The reference to the priest's having studied at Sigüenza university, from which he emerged as a learned graduate, is of course highly ironic, as Sigüenza was rated at the time as one of the weakest universities in the kingdom; it was where many mediocre graduates went to finish their studies and get a degree. The University of Osuna was another similar institution.
9. p. 187.
10. p. 188.
11. As the Franciscan Juan de la Cerda wrote: 'Qué tienen que ver las armas con las donzellas, ni los cuentos de deshonestos amores con las que han de ser honestíssimas? [...] Ay algunas doncellas que por entretener el tiempo, leen en estos libros, y hallan en ellos vn dulce veneno que les incita a malos pensamientos, y les haze perder el seso que tenían. Y por esso es error muy grande de las madres que paladean a sus hijas desde niñas con este azeyte de escorpiones, y con este apetito de las diabólicas lecturas de amor' (*Libro intitulado vida política de todos los estados de mugeres* (Alcalá de Henares: Juan Gracián, 1599), fol. 41ᵛ), cited in Edward Glaser, 'Nuevos datos sobre la crítica de los libros de caballerías en los siglos XVI y XVII', *Anuario de Estudios Medievales*, 3 (1996), 393–410 (p. 406)) (What have arms to do with damsels, or unchaste love stories with those who should be most chaste? [...] There are some damsels who, in order to pass the time, read these books, finding in them a sweet poison that incites them to evil thoughts and makes them lose their minds. And because of this, it is a mother's grave error to mollify their daughters from childhood with such scorpion oil, and to awaken their appetite for diabolical love stories). For the library of a mother who probably encouraged her daughter to read these works, see Trevor Dadson, 'The Education, Books and Reading Habits of Ana de Mendoza y de la Cerda, Princess of Éboli (1540–1592)', in *Women's Literacy in Early Modern Spain and the New World*, ed. by Anne J. Cruz and Rosilie Hernández-Pecoraro (Aldershot: Ashgate, 2011), pp. 79–102.
12. p. 231.
13. pp. 241–42.
14. p 268.

15. p. 268.
16. p. 414.
17. He makes this very clear in 1.10: 'La verdad sea [...] que yo no he leído ninguna historia jamás, porque ni sé leer ni escrebir'(125) ('The truth is that I never read any history because I don't know how to read and write'; p. 71).
18. For some of the ramifications of this, see José María Arbizu, *Sancho, primer intérprete de don Quijote* (Salamanca: Publicaciones Universidad Pontificia de Salamanca, 2001), and Trevor Dadson, 'Los libros de caballerías, *Don Quijote* y sus lectores en el siglo XVII', in *Antes y después del 'Quijote' en el cincuentenario de la Asociación de Hispanistas de Gran Bretaña e Irlanda*, ed. by Robert Archer (Valencia: Biblioteca Valenciana, 2005), pp. 59–78 (pp. 73–74).
19. p. 67.
20. pp. 67–68.
21. For a more nuanced reading of this passage, and the likelihood that what the Morisco boy is actually translating is not Arabic as such but the Arabic characters of an Aljamiado text, in which case he is in fact transliterating, see Trevor Dadson, 'The Multicultural World of *Don Quijote*', *In Other Words*, 2016 (47), 86–94. If this is the case, then the translation of 'morisco aljamiado' as 'some Morisco who knew Castilian' is clearly wrong. All Moriscos living in Toledo at the start of the seventeenth century knew Castilian; what our author needs is a Morisco who knows enough Arabic to be able to transliterate the Arabic characters on the page into the Castilian that lies beneath. That is why, after all, he is called a 'morisco aljamiado'.
22. p. 78.
23. p. 267.
24. Although most of my examples are taken from Part One, this is simply for reasons of space; one could find an equal number of readers, writers, and listeners from Part Two, if not more, given the extended scenes that take place in the ducal palace.
25. For a discussion of literacy and the tests used to measure it, see my 'Literacy and Education in Early Modern Rural Spain: The Case of Villarrubia de los Ojos', in *The Iberian Book and its Readers: Essays for Ian Michael*, ed. by Nigel Griffin, Clive Griffin, and Eric Southworth, *Bulletin of Spanish Studies*, 81 (2004), 1011–37.
26. p. 188.
27. p. 554.
28. p. 554.
29. Numbers 33–35 and 37 in my list are more romances of chivalry: 33 Feliciano de Silva, *Don Florisel de Niquea*, Valladolid, 1532 (1, 1); 34 Diego Ortúñez de Calahorra, *Caballero del Febo*, Zaragoza, 1555 (1, 1); 35 *Don Reinaldos de Montalbán*, Alcalá de Henares, 1564 (1, 1; 1, 7); 37 Feliciano de Silva, *Don Rogel de Grecia*, Medina del Campo, 1535 (1, 24).
30. For the bookshop of Benito Boyer, see Vicente Bécares and Alejandro Luis Iglesias, *La librería de Benito Boyer (Medina del Campo 1592)* (Salamanca: Junta de Castilla y León, 1992); for that of Cristóbal López, see Trevor Dadson, 'La librería de Cristóbal López (1606): estudio y análisis de una librería madrileña de principios del siglo XVII', in *El libro antiguo español IV: Coleccionismo y Bibliotecas (Siglos XVI–XVIII)*, ed. by Pedro M. Cátedra and María Luisa López-Vidriero (Salamanca: Universidad de Salamanca, Sociedad Española de Historia del Libro, 1998), pp. 167–234.
31. For an excellent analysis of Don Quixote's library, see Edward Baker, *La biblioteca de don Quijote* (Madrid: Marcial Pons, 1997).
32. On this, see Trevor Dadson, 'The Dissemination of Poetry in Sixteenth-Century Spain', *Journal of the Institute of Romance Studies*, 8 (2000 [2003]), 47–56; 'La difusión de la poesía española impresa en el siglo XVII', *Bulletin Hispanique*, 113.1 (2011), 13–42; and 'La publicación y diseminación de obras de entretenimiento en la España del siglo XVII', in *Del autor al lector: el comercio y distribución del libro medieval y moderno*, ed. by Manuel José Pedraza Gracia, Yolanda Clemente San Román, and Nicolás Bas Martín (Zaragoza: Prensas de la Universidad de Zaragoza), pp. 69–95.
33. See Trevor Dadson, *Libros, lectores y lecturas: estudios sobre bibliotecas particulares españolas del Siglo de Oro* (Madrid: Arco/Libros, 1998), Chapter 1, for a discussion of the size of different libraries in this period.

34. p. 20.
35. p. 75.
36. p. 76.
37. Although not discussed here, it should be noted that the 'Arms and Letters' speech in Part One, Chapters 37–38 is also totally inappropriate given its audience of soldiers and men who have seen real fighting, in contrast to Don Quixote whose thoughts on the matter are drawn entirely from what he has read.
38. p. 76.
39. Crucially, Don Quixote has recourse to these ballads in moments of great stress as, for example, when he has just been beaten up by the merchants at the end of Part One, Chapter 4: 'Viendo, pues, que, en efeto, no podía menearse, acordó de acogerse a su ordinario remedio, que era pensar en algún paso de sus libros, y trújole su locura a la memoria aquel de Valdovinos y del marqués de Mantua, cuando Carloto le dejó herido en la montiña, historia sabida de los niños, no ignorada de los mozos, celebrada y aun creída de los viejos' (I. 5, 76–77) ('Seeing, then, that in fact he could not move, he took refuge in his usual remedy, which was to think about some situation from his books, and his madness made him recall that of Valdovinos and the Marquis of Mantua, when Carloto left him wounded in the highlands, a history known to children, acknowledged by youths, celebrated and even believed by the old'; p. 41). The newly created Don Quixote cannot ignore his childhood education when he was plain Alonso Quijano.
40. For Cervantes's possible library, see Daniel Eisenberg, 'Did Cervantes Have a Library?', in *Hispanic Studies in Honor of Alan D. Deyermond: A North American Tribute* (Madison: Hispanic Seminary of Medieval Studies, 1986), pp. 93–106, and 'La biblioteca de Cervantes', in *Studia in honorem prof. M. de Riquer*, 3 vols (Barcelona: Quaderns Crema, 1986–88), II, 271–328.
41. p. 76.
42. p. 76.
43. p. 77.
44. p. 77.
45. p. 77.
46. p. 77.
47. pp. 77–78.
48. p. 77.
49. p. 78.
50. p. 78.
51. The credit for coming up with this term goes to Samuel Taylor Coleridge who, in 1817, suggested that if a writer could infuse a 'human interest and a semblance of truth' into a fantastic tale, the reader would suspend judgement concerning the implausibility of the narrative (Samuel Taylor Coleridge, *Biographia Literaria: Or, Biographical Sketches of My Literary Life and Opinions* (London: R. Fenner, 1817), chapter XIV) <http://www.english.upenn.edu/~mgamer/Etexts/biographia.html> [accessed 23 April 2019].
52. p. 267.
53. p. 267.
54. We should note that this is precisely what Diego de Miranda, already mentioned, appreciated in his reading: works 'que deleiten con el lenguaje y admiren y suspendan con la invención' (II. 16, 823) ('the language delights, and the invention amazes and astounds'; p. 554).
55. p. 77.
56. p. 81.
57. p. 82.
58. p. 84.
59. p. 84.
60. p. 84.
61. p. 85.
62. p. 86.
63. p. 82.
64. See Dadson, 'Los libros de caballerías, *Don Quijote* y sus lectores en el siglo XVII', and Daniel

Eisenberg and María Carmen Marín Piña, *Bibliografía de los libros de caballerías castellanos* (Zaragoza: Prensas Universitarias de Zaragoza, 2000).
65. p. 899. Amusingly, on the same page, Don Quixote also tells Sancho that he will buy some sheep and 'todas las demás cosas que al pastoral ejercicio son necesarias' ('all the other things needed for the pastoral exercise').
66. pp. 899–900.
67. On this and similar episodes, see Trevor Dadson, *Historia de la impresión de las 'Rimas' de Lupercio y Bartolomé Leonardo de Argensola* (Zaragoza: Institución 'Fernando el Católico', 2010), pp. 18–20.
68. p. 93.
69. p. 98.
70. Legend has it that Tullia passed in her chariot over the dead body of her father Servius Tullius, King of Rome, killed by her husband Tarquin, but the Spanish ballad tradition makes her the daughter of Tarquin (as recounted here by Cervantes).
71. p. 99.
72. pp. 99–100.
73. p. 99.
74. pp. 100–01.
75. p. 101.
76. p. 101.
77. I have set out the poem in this fashion, since it consists of two 'redondillas' in the form of a 'copla castellana'.
78. p. 101.
79. p. 102.
80. p. 102.
81. p. 101.
82. p. 100.
83. For the poem in question, see Trevor Dadson (ed.), *El conde de Salinas. Obra completa: la poesía desconocida* (Madrid: Anejos de la Real Academia Española, 2016), p. 164. On the amorous and literary relationship between Salinas and Leonor Pimentel, see Dadson, 'El conde de Salinas y Leonor Pimentel: cuando se juntan el amor y la poesía', in *Spanish Golden Age Poetry in Motion: The Dynamics of Creation and Conversation*, ed. by Jean Andrews and Isabel Torres (Woodbridge: Tamesis, 2014), pp. 185–212.
84. p. 900. These words recall, no doubt deliberately, the opening remarks of Don Quixote when he sets out on his first journey: '¿Quién duda sino que en los venideros tiempos, cuando salga a luz la verdadera historia de mis famosos hechos [...]' (I. 2, 49) ('Who can doubt that in times to come, when the true history of my famous deeds comes to light...'; p. 25). Just as, a few sentences further on, his words recall his later speech on the Golden Age: 'Dichosa edad y siglo dichoso aquel adonde saldrán a luz las famosas hazañas mías [...]' (50) ('Fortunate the time and blessed the age when my famous deeds will come to light [...]'; p. 25).

CHAPTER 2

'¿Qué lector será el que no se ría?': Incongruity and Ironic Allusion in *Don Quixote*, II. 60

Oliver Noble Wood

> The Second Worthy, was Great Alexander,
> That Valiant Captain, and renown'd Commander.
> He in his youth did the known World subdue
> And wept because he found no more to do.[1]

When posed by Diego Clemencín in the late 1830s, to round off a note found towards the beginning of II. 60, the question '¿Qué lector será el que no se ría? (What reader wouldn't laugh?)'[2] was clearly intended as rhetorical. Of the scene under discussion, which sees Don Quixote unsuccessfully attempt to strip Sancho Panza in order to administer some of the 3,300 strokes purportedly required for Dulcinea's disenchantment, Clemencín went on to say that 'el presente pasaje es tan gracioso como verosímil en vista del descuido de Sancho, y de los desvelos y deseos vehementes de Don Quijote' (The present passage is as funny as it is realistic in view of Sancho's negligence and Don Quixote's impassioned efforts and desires).[3] Over the next century or so, however, the very same passage — which culminates in Sancho tripping his master, pinning him to the floor, and proclaiming his own autonomy — came to be read in a rather different light. Miguel de Unamuno held it to be 'el más triste suceso de tantos tan tristísimos como la historia de nuestro Don Quijote encierra' (the saddest of such extremely sad events as the story of our Don Quixote contains), viewing Sancho's rebellion as a form of 'suprema tortura' (supreme torture) for his master.[4] For Vladimir Nabokov, this, Don Quixote's 'Nineteenth Defeat' — making it '20–19 (5–6 in the fourth set)' — was 'the most grotesque, ignoble, and atrocious [of all]'.[5] And Salvador de Madariaga went as far as to dismiss 'aquella desagradable escena en que el escudero pone mano sobre su amo' (that disagreeable scene in which the squire lays his hands on his master) as 'la página más deplorable' (the most deplorable page), one that 'todo lector noble desearía no escrita' (every right-minded reader would wish not to have been written).[6] Later commentators could have been forgiven, therefore, for reformulating Clemencín's question with one small but significant deletion: '¿Qué lector será el que ~~no~~ se ría?'

Whilst, under the influence of Peter Russell, Anthony Close, and others, the last half century has seen the balance between hard and soft readings of Cervantes's novel in part redressed, the opening of II. 60 — up until the moment when Quixote and Sancho are captured by the Catalan bandit Roque Guinart — has continued to draw little detailed critical comment.[7] The most influential assessment of it from the last decade is that of Edwin Williamson, for whom the scene constitutes a moment of 'crisis' in the 'power-struggle' between master and squire, the last of four 'turning-points which change irreversibly the relations between Quixote and Sancho' (the other three occurring at the fulling mills in I. 20 and then with Dulcinea's enchantment in II. 10 and Merlin's prophecy for her disenchantment in II. 35).[8] For Williamson, Sancho's behaviour here — 'insubordination', 'brazen self-assertion', 'the climax of [his] steady rise to power in Part Two' — sees him 'withdrawing his consent to be governed by the authority of Don Quixote', with the result that 'the pact between lord and vassal which was confirmed at the Fulling Mills [is] broken'.[9] It is through this avowedly political account of the development of the pair's relationship that the passage is now often viewed. In a recent section-by-section close reading of the novel, from the year of the quatercentenary of the publication of Part Two, Roberto González Echevarría, for example, mentions the tussle between master and squire only in passing, as part of a brief summary of Williamson's reading of this facet of the work.[10] The aim of this chapter is to offer more sustained engagement with what is, therefore, a controversial but often neglected episode, one of profound significance in terms of both the dynamics between Quixote and Sancho and, more broadly, the balance between comedy and tragedy in the novel. Following González Echevarría's own mantra of 'details, details, details', I hope to show in the following pages how close reading — in particular, here, examination of often incongruous intra- and intertextual references — is a necessary correlative to, if not a basic building block for, the construction of overarching grand narratives.[11]

When, in II. 59, Quixote and Sancho first learn of Avellaneda's spurious sequel whilst dining at an inn en route to Zaragoza, each is scandalized by their portrayal therein, the former as 'ya desenamorado de Dulcinea del Toboso' ('no longer in love with Dulcinea del Toboso'), the latter as 'comedor y simple y nonada gracioso' (I. 59, 1213, 1215) ('a glutton, and simple-minded, and not at all funny').[12] Chapter 60 begins with Don Quixote setting out the very next morning intent upon giving the lie to 'aquel nuevo historiador' ('that novice historian') by changing course and heading for Barcelona 'sin tocar en Zaragoza' (1218) ('without going through Saragossa').[13] Nothing worthy of note happens for almost a week, quite long enough for the pair to put significant distance between themselves and Zaragoza:

> Sucedió, pues, que en más de seis días no le sucedió cosa digna de ponerse en escritura, al cabo de los cuales, yendo fuera de camino, le tomó la noche entre unas espesas encinas o alcornoques, que en esto no guarda la puntualidad Cide Hamete que en otras cosas suele. (II. 60, 1218–19)

(What happened next was that for more than six days nothing happened, nothing at least worth writing about; and at the end of that time, while he was riding off the road, night overtook him in a dense copse of evergreen oaks or cork-oaks — on this point Cide Hamete isn't as meticulous as usual.)[14]

Here, the very deliberate and drawn-out repetition and then negation of the verb *suceder* ('sucedió [...] que [...] no le sucedió'), the conversational 'pues', the acknowledged uncertainty over seemingly insignificant detail, the switch from the preterite to the present (as the *segundo autor* moves from narrative to commentary), and the attribution of the blame for the aforementioned uncertainty to an uncharacteristic lack of precision from Cide Hamete Benengeli, elsewhere praised, ironically, as 'puntualísimo escudriñador de los átomos desta verdadera historia' (II. 50, 1130) ('that painstaking investigator of the most minute details of this true history'),[15] together serve to set the stage for what follows in a playful and highly self-aware fashion. Of particular note is the equivocation over the trees in question and the accompanying metanarrative, a variant of which recurs in II. 68: 'Don Quijote, arrimado a un tronco de una haya, o de un alcornoque (que Cide Hamete Benengeli no distingue el árbol que era), al son de sus mesmos suspiros cantó de esta suerte [...]' (1291) ('Don Quixote, leaning against the trunk of a beech or a cork-oak (Cide Hamete Benengeli doesn't specify which it was), sang as follows, to the accompaniment of his own sighs [...]').[16] Clemencín's notes address the question of arboreal codominance in parts of Catalonia, but the issue here is not one of faithful reflection of the real world but rather of knowing refraction of the literary one. In each instance, we find humorous reworking of the pastoral topos of 'arbore sub quadam' ('under a certain tree') inspired by Virgil, *Eclogue* I. 1 ('Tityre, tu patulae recubans sub tegmine fagi' ('You, Tityrus, lie under the canopy of a spreading beech')[17], allusion to contemporary polemic over the correct translation of *fagus* ('¿Haya, encina o alcornoque?'), and parody of pedants — writers and theorists — who 'equate "truth" with the accumulation of trivial detail'.[18] In II. 60, the equivocation is specifically between *encinas* and *alcornoques*. Dedicated to Jupiter, the former are associated with both physical strength and the sublime style.[19] Symbolic, by contrast, of the low style, the latter are associated with both hard-heartedness and nakedness/stripping: 'Es nombre arábigo, *aldorque*, y vale tanto como el desnudado o mal vestido, aludiendo a lo que tenemos dicho de la corteza, que le desnudan della para hacer calzado a las mujeres pequeñas' ('It is an Arabic noun, *aldorque*, and its meaning approximates to the one that is stripped or poorly dressed, in reference to what has already been said about its bark, of which it is stripped in order to make footwear for small women').[20] In a parallel scene in II. 12, Sancho was linked with the *alcornoque*, Quixote with the *encina*: 'Sancho se quedó dormido al pie de un alcornoque, y don Quijote, dormitando al de una robusta encina' (787) ('Sancho finally fell asleep at the foot of a cork-oak, and Don Quixote dozed at the foot of a stout evergreen oak').[21] As will become evident, such links, and the trees' various associations, establish an eminently appropriate backdrop for the scene about to unfold.

The stage now set, both master and squire dismount and then settle down against tree-trunks, the subordinate clause 'acomodándose a los troncos de los árboles' ('settled down against a tree-trunk')[22] neatly completing the 'arbore sub quadam' motif.[23] As on many previous occasions in the novel, contrast between the pair is then re-established through focus on food and sleep:

> Sancho, que había merendado aquel día, se dejó entrar de rondón por las puertas del sueño; pero don Quijote, a quien desvelaban sus imaginaciones mucho más que la hambre, no podía pegar sus ojos, antes iba y venía con el pensamiento por mil géneros de lugares. (II. 60, 1219)
>
> (Sancho, who that day had enjoyed an afternoon meal, slipped without knocking through the doors of sleep; but Don Quixote, kept awake by his imagination much more than by his hunger, couldn't manage to drop off, and he wandered in his thoughts through thousands of different places.)[24]

Having eaten that afternoon, Sancho drops off, slipping 'de rondón' — that is, 'de golpe y sin reparar' (suddenly and without realizing) (Cov. s.v. *rendón*) — through 'las puertas del sueño'. Here, though no distinction is drawn between the gates of horn and ivory, the knowing circumlocution for *dormirse* gives rise to incongruous echoes of Aeneas's exit from the Underworld in *Aeneid*, VI. 893–98 (which begins, in Gregorio Hernández de Velasco's translation, 'Dos puertas tiene el sueño [...]' ('Two gates of Sleep there are [...]')[25]) and, by extension, Virgil's own model, found in the discussion of dreams between Penelope and her disguised husband in *Odyssey*, XIX. 562–67.[26] Quixote, meanwhile, cannot sleep a wink. Whereas sleepless nights spent reading chivalric romances were the initial cause of the humoral imbalance that led to his madness in I. 1 ('del poco dormir y del mucho leer, se le secó el celebro de manera que vino a perder el juicio' (42) ('until the lack of sleep and the excess of reading withered his brain, and he went mad')[27]), ever since sleepless nights spent thinking of Dulcinea have been a cornerstone of his subsequent imitation of chivalric models:

> Toda aquella noche no durmió don Quijote, pensando en su señora Dulcinea, por acomodarse a lo que había leído en sus libros, cuando los caballeros pasaban sin dormir muchas noches en las florestas y despoblados, entretenidos con las memorias de sus señoras. (I. 8, 106–07)[28]
>
> ([Don Quixote] didn't sleep in all the night, thinking about his lady Dulcinea, to conform with what he'd read in his books, where knights errant spent many sleepless nights in glades and deserts, engrossed in the recollection of their ladies.)[29]

The latest iteration of this motif sees Quixote kept up by a raging imagination, his thoughts racing to and fro, not through 'mil [...] lugares' but through the even more hyperbolic 'mil *géneros* de lugares' (my emphasis). A sense of the frantic, exasperated movements of his mind is captured as memories of earlier episodes featuring the enchanted Dulcinea flood back:

> Ya le parecía hallarse en la cueva de Montesinos; ya ver brincar y subir sobre su pollina a la convertida en labradora Dulcinea, ya que le sonaban en los oídos las palabras del sabio Merlín que le referían las condiciones y diligencias que se habían de hacer y tener en el desencanto de Dulcinea. (II. 60, 1219)

(Now he was in the Cave of Montesinos; now he was watching Dulcinea, transformed into a peasant girl, vaulting on to her donkey; now he could hear the sage Merlin's words ringing in his ears, telling him of the conditions to be met and the actions to be taken to disenchant Dulcinea.)[30]

The ascending tricolon underscored by the anaphora of 'ya' sees a progression from Quixote's descent into the Cave of Montesinos (II. 23) and the emblematic moment of his first encounter with the enchanted Dulcinea (II. 10) to the terms and conditions of Merlin's prophecy-cum-prescription for her disenchantment (II. 35). Set within the elegant frame of this sentence are further elements of humour and incongruity: first, another reminder of the *villana*'s unladylike, animalistic 'brinco sobre la pollina' (II. 33, 992) ('leapt on to the donkey')[31] etched, as Close notes, 'indelibly on the hero's imagination'; then, unusually, *lack* of uncertainty over the gender of Dulcinea's mount (in light of the earlier 'sobre tres pollinos, o pollinas, que el autor no lo declara'; II. 10, 767 ('on three jackasses, or she-asses, because the author isn't explicit on this point')[32]); followed by the substitution of the customized but awkward epithet 'la convertida en labradora' for the clichéd but idealizing 'la sin par' used on so many previous occasions; and, finally, the ironic epithet 'sabio', befitting the Merlin of legend but not the 'figura de la muerte, descarnada y fea' ('Death itself, fleshless and hideous')[33] played by the *mayordomo* in the farcical parade orchestrated by the Duke and Duchess (II. 35, 1006).[34]

The words ringing in Quixote's ears are the following hendecasyllables delivered earlier by Merlin 'con voz algo dormida y con lengua no muy despierta' ('in a sleepy voice and with a tongue only half awake'):[35]

> A ti digo, ¡oh varón como se debe
> por jamás alabado!, a ti, valiente
> juntamente y discreto don Quijote,
> de la Mancha esplendor, de España estrella,
> que para recobrar su estado primo
> la sin par Dulcinea del Toboso
> es menester que Sancho tu escudero
> se dé tres mil azotes y trescientos
> en ambas sus valientes posaderas,
> al aire descubiertas, y de modo,
> que le escuezan, le amarguen y le enfaden.
> Y en esto se resuelven todos cuantos
> de su desgracia han sido los autores,
> y a esto es mi venida, mis señores. (II. 35, 1008)

> (To you I say, O hero never praised
> Enough, to you, Don Quixote sir, O man
> Of courage and of wisdom intertwined,
> You splendour of La Mancha, star of Spain:
> In order to recover and restore
> Your peerless mistress to her pristine state,
> Your squire, your Sancho, has to lash himself
> Three thousand times and then three hundred more
> On both his buttocks, big and bold and bare

> Unto the air exposed, in such a way
> That they will smart and sting and vex him sore.
> For this has been decided by all those
> Who worked the spells that cost the maid so dear;
> And this, my noble lords, is why I'm here.)[36]

Each element of the prescription is patently absurd: the central role given to Sancho, not Quixote; the inflated number of lashings set (three thousand, with three hundred more added for good measure); the requirement for them to be self-administered, in a form of mock-penitence or mortification of the flesh; the stipulation that they be to Sancho's backside, not his back, and that it be bare; and the emphasis given to the need for the strokes to actually hurt ('que le escuezan, le amarguen y le enfaden'). Sancho's initial response is incredulity ('¡Yo no sé qué tienen que ver mis posas con los encantos!' (1008) ('I don't see what my bum has got to do with magic spells!')[37]) and a refusal to cooperate ('¿azotarme yo...? ¡Abernuncio!' (1009) ('as for me taking the lashes, I announce them and all their works')[38]), but, in the face of protestations — and the odd threat — from Merlin, 'Dulcinea' herself, and the Duke and Duchess, he eventually gives his assent.

The conditions he sets in doing so give him complete control over all questions of timing, and thus an easy rebuff to subsequent pleas from his master for him to begin the task in hand. In II. 41, for example, as the pair prepares to mount Clavileño, Quixote takes Sancho to one side and, grasping him by the hands, implores him to withdraw to his room and make a start before they set off on their latest adventure:

> — Ya vees, Sancho hermano, el largo viaje que nos espera y que sabe Dios cuándo volveremos de él, ni la comodidad y espacio que nos darán los negocios; y, así, querría que ahora te retirases en tu aposento, como que vas a buscar alguna cosa necesaria para el camino, y en un daca las pajas te dieses, a buena cuenta de los tres mil y trecientos azotes a que estás obligado, siquiera quinientos, que dados te los tendrás, que el comenzar las cosas es tenerlas medio acabadas. (II. 41, 1046–47)
>
> ('You can see, brother Sancho, what a long journey lies ahead of us, and you must realize that God alone knows when we shall come back or how much leisure or time off this business is going to allow us; so I would like you now to retire to your room, as if you were going to look for something that you need for the journey, and in the twinkling of an eye, in part payment of the three thousand three hundred lashes to which you're committed, give yourself five hundred of them at least, and that will be five hundred less to suffer later on; because well begun is half done.')[39]

Sancho responds by pointing out that this is not the appropriate moment to scourge himself — '¿Ahora que tengo de ir sentado en una tabla rasa quiere vuestra merced que me lastime las posas?' (1047) ('Now that I've got to ride along sitting on a bare board you expect me to do an injury to my bum?')[40] — and then promises speedy completion of his obligation at a later date. In II. 59, as master and squire recover from their recent trampling by bulls, Quixote accepts Sancho's advice to get some sleep but again calls on him to begin:

— Si tú, ¡oh Sancho!, quisieses hacer por mí lo que yo ahora te diré, serían mis alivios más ciertos y mis pesadumbres no tan grandes: y es que mientras yo duermo, obedeciendo tus consejos, tú te desviases un poco lejos de aquí y con las riendas de Rocinante, echando al aire tus carnes, te dieses trecientos o cuatrocientos azotes a buena cuenta de los tres mil y tantos que te has de dar por el desencanto de Dulcinea, que es lástima no pequeña que aquella pobre señora esté encantada por tu descuido y negligencia. (II. 59, 1210)

('If, Sancho, you would like to do for me what I am about to explain, my improvement would be more assured and my dejection less oppressive, and it is this: while, obeying your advice, I sleep, I should like you to go some way from here and, exposing your flesh to the air, give yourself with Rocinante's reins three or four hundred lashes in part payment of the three thousand odd that you must give yourself to disenchant Dulcinea; because it is a great shame that the poor lady is still enchanted just because of your gross negligence.')[41]

On this occasion, Sancho neatly sidesteps the request, but reassures his master by reaffirming 'el deseo de cumplir con lo que h[a] prometido' (1211) ('I still intend to do what I promised to do').[42] Quixote is oddly grateful: he thanks his squire, eats, and then proceeds to sleep.

In II. 60, by contrast, when Dulcinea's disenchantment once more resurfaces as Quixote's overriding concern, his thoughts on Sancho are decidedly less positive: 'Desesperábase de ver la flojedad y caridad poca de Sancho su escudero, pues, a lo que creía, solos cinco azotes se había dado, número desigual y pequeño para los infinitos que le faltaban' (1219) ('It made him despair to consider Sancho's lassitude and lack of charitable feeling, because it was his belief that his squire had only given himself five lashes to far, a ridiculously small number in comparison with all those that still remained').[43] His diagnosis of 'flojedad y caridad poca' — a duplet in which the second element is foregrounded through addition and emphatic placement of the adjective — and the reasoning behind it once more give rise to the ironic conjunction of Sancho's parodic penance and (considerations of) the religious virtue of charity (or lack thereof), recalling both Merlin's earlier claim that 'esta disciplina [...] os será de mucho provecho, así para el alma como para el cuerpo: para el alma, por la caridad con que la haréis; para el cuerpo, porque [...] no os podrá hacer daño sacaros un poco de sangre' (II. 35, 1013) ('this penance [...] will be of the greatest benefit to you, both body and soul: good for your soul because of the charity with which you will perform it, and for the body because [...] it will do you no harm to lose a little blood')[44] and — in one of the novel's most controversial sentences — the Duchess's warning to Sancho that 'las obras de caridad que se hacen tibia y flojamente no tienen mérito ni valen nada' (II. 36, 1016)[45] ('works of charity performed in a lukewarm and half-hearted way have no merit or value whatsoever').[46] The disparity between the number of *azotes* that Quixote thinks Sancho has self-administered and the number prescribed by Merlin — five versus 3,300 — is made even more humorous by another duplet, the adjectival pair 'desigual y pequeño', and the sense that, to Quixote at least, Sancho's target is so far off that a finite number may just as well now be infinite. Of course, there is the additional irony that Sancho's true running tally may well not even have reached the heady heights of five, for, as the narrator's addition of the clause 'a lo que creía' hints, his earlier claim to have begun 'la tarea de la disciplina' by slapping himself five times ('Dijo que [...] aquella noche se había dado cinco azotes [...] con la mano' (1015) ('He replied that [...] during the night he'd given himself five lashes [...] with his hand')[47] may have been pure fabrication.

Fuelled by 'tanta pesadumbre y enojo' ('[being] so furious')[48] — distress at Dulcinea's current state, anger at Sancho's indolence — , Quixote launches into a *discurso* in which, drawing inspiration from Alexander the Great's conquest of Asia, he signals his intention to take matters into his own hands:

> — Si nudo gordiano cortó el Magno Alejandro, diciendo: 'Tanto monta cortar como desatar', y no por eso dejó de ser universal señor de toda la Asia, ni más ni menos podría suceder ahora en el desencanto de Dulcinea, si yo azotase a Sancho a pesar suyo; que si la condición deste remedio está en que Sancho reciba los tres mil y tantos azotes, ¿qué se me da a mí que se los dé él, o que se los dé otro, pues la sustancia está en que él los reciba, lleguen por do llegaren? (II. 60, 1219)
>
> ('If Alexander the Great cut the Gordian knot saying, "To cut is as good as to untie," and if that didn't prevent him from becoming the lord and masterof all Asia, the same could apply to the disenchantment of Dulcinea if I lash Sancho whether he likes it or not; because if the conditions is that he must receive three thousand odd lashes, what do I care whether he applies them himself of someone else does so for him, since what matters is that he must receive them, wherever they come from?')[49]

Quixote's models are not just knights from chivalric romance and Carolingian epic but also figures from the classical world. Memorable earlier examples of this include his imitation or emulation of Mars, in the episode of Mambrino's helmet (I. 21, 247); Cato, in relation to advice given to Sancho on governorship (II. 42, 1059); and even Dido, to Doña Rodríguez's Aeneas, in the context of a furtive encounter with a member of the opposite sex (II. 48, 1111). This is the latest in a number of references in the novel to Alexander the Great, stretching as far back as the *prólogo* ('si de capitanes valerosos [...] Plutarco os dará mil Alejandros' (17) ('if it's valiant captains [...] Plutarch will give you a thousand Alexanders')[50]) and the first of the satirical paratextual poems in Part One ('en el cual floreció un du- | que es nuevo Alejandro Ma-' (22)[51] ('on which dukes were procrea — ; | And one's a modern Alexa — ,')[52]). In I. 1, Quixote's *rocín*, at that point unnamed, was compared favourably — despite being no more than skin and bones — to Alexander's steed Bucephalus: 'Fue luego a ver su rocín, y aunque tenía más cuartos que un real y más tachas que el caballo de Gonela, que "tantum pellis et ossa fuit", le pareció que ni el Bucéfalo de Alejandro ni Babieca el del Cid con él se igualaban' (45) ('Then he went to visit his nag, and although it had more corns than a barleyfield and more wrong with it than Gonella's horse, which *tantum pellis et ossa fuit*, it seemed to him that neither Alexander's Bucephalus nor the Cid's Babieca was its equal.').[53] In II. 59, criticism of Avellaneda's sequel sees the inn-goer Don Juan state that 'si fuera posible, se había de mandar que ninguno fuera osado a tratar de las cosas del gran don Quijote, si no fuese Cide Hamete, su primer autor, bien así como mandó Alejandro que ninguno fuese osado a retratarle sino Apeles' (1216–17) ('if it were possible a law ought to be passed that nobody should presume to write about the doings of the great Don Quixote, except the first author Cide Hamete, just as Alexander ordered that nobody should presume to represent him on canvas except Apelles').[54] On these occasions, and others in between — most notably, I. 6, where a link is established between Don Quixote's copy of *Palmerín de Inglaterra* and Alexander's copy of the *Iliad* (89), and I. 52, when Sancho praises his master as 'liberal sobre todos los Alejandros' (643) ('more open-handed than all the Alexanders')[55] — , Don Quixote is associated by extension with Alexander. As De Armas observes in relation to the mentions of Alexander in Part One, 'a medida que la hipérbole quijotesca aumenta la comparación con Alejandro traerá consigo un movimiento deflacionario' (as quixotic hyperbole amplifies the comparison with Alexander there is an accompanying movement towards deflation).[56]

The effects of this deflation are felt even more strongly on the occasions when Quixote himself invites direct comparison with the Macedonian king. In I. 5, whilst being escorted home following his disastrous first sally, a bruised and battered Don Quixote alludes to Alexander in claiming that his future exploits will surpass those of not only the Twelve Peers of France but also the Nine Worthies: 'a todas las hazañas que ellos todos juntos y cada uno por sí hicieron se aventajarán las mías' (79) ('because all the deeds performed by them both singly and together will be exceeded by mine').[57] The culmination of mentions of Alexander in the novel, the reference in II. 60 is the first instance of Quixote naming him outright and thus drawing direct inspiration from him.[58] The allusion is, of course, to a particular event in the life of Alexander, namely his solving of the problem of the Gordian knot and his subsequent conquest of Asia. The episode is recorded, in the context of Alexander's conquest of the Phrygian city of Gordium, in most major classical accounts of his life, including Plutarch, *Life of Alexander* (XVIII.1–5), Quintus Curtius, *History of Alexander* (III. 1. 14–18), and Arrian, *Anabasis of Alexander* (II. 3). Plutarch, for example, recounts how:

> Alli ovo de mirar el carro en que estava la ligadura dela delgada corteza del alcornoque. Del qual carro entre los Barbaros se avia esparzido aquesta opinion en sus fablas por ellos creydas que qualquier que aquella ligadura desatasse a aquel otorgavan los fados el señorío dela redondez dela tierra. [...] las cabeças delos nudos eran ciegas y rebueltas entre sy girando unas sobre otras y que non los podia desatar: ovo alexandre de sacar la espada: y de cortar todos los nudos, y recortados los dençima dizen que se descubrieron otras muchas cabeças de nudos los quales segun dize Aristobolo que alexandre supo ligeramente desatar.[59]

> (There he saw the wagon that was tied up with the fine bark of the cork oak. On the subject of that wagon, through the tales held by them to be true, there had spread amongst the Barbarians the belief that whoever undid that tie would be granted dominion over the whole world by the Fates. [...] the knot ends were invisible and tangled, all intertwined with one another, and impossible to undo. Alexander drew his sword — and from cutting all the knots, once those on top had been cut away, it's said there were revealed many other knot ends which Aristobulus says Alexander was able to undo easily.)

Cervantes may well have been familiar with the accounts of one or more of Plutarch, Quintus Curtius, and Arrian — the existence of a number of late fifteenth- and sixteenth-century editions of their works, either in the original or in Latin or vernacular translation, suggesting that such accounts circulated freely — , but there were innumerable other possible sources of knowledge of the episode in question. Entries in Sebastián de Covarrubias's *Tesoro de la lengua castellana* (1611) and Gonzalo Correas's *Vocabulario de refranes* (1627) attest to the fact that the tale and sayings derived from it were popular and widely known in the early seventeenth century. The former, for example, notes how: 'Viniendo allí Alejandro, y no pudiéndole desatar, le cortó con la espada, dando a entender que montaba tanto cortar como desatar' (Coming there, and not being able to untie it, Alexander cut through it with his sword, leading to the conclusion that cutting and untying amounted to the same thing) (s.v. *desañudar*). Both the former (s.v. *montar*) and the latter record the very *refrán* cited by Quixote, 'Tanto monta cortar, como desatar', Correas noting in passing that 'Es lo del "nodus gordianus"' (It's the 'Gordian knot' episode).[60] Both knot and saying were also associated with the Catholic Monarchs, having inspired the personal emblem of Ferdinand of Aragon:

> Así el católico rey Don Fernando, viendo que no podía por maña y destreza destejer la liga de los príncipes, sus émulos, determinó de contrastarla por las armas, y romper la guerra, valiéndose de aquellas palabras de Alejandro, cuando cortó el nudo gordiano: 'Tanto monta cortar como desatar', y después lo acomodó en ingeniosa empresa el famoso Antonio de Nebrija, a quien tanto debieron las letras humanas de España.[61]

> (Thus the Catholic king Don Ferdinand, seeing that he could not dissolve the league of princes, his rivals, through skill and ingenuity, decided to come against it with arms, and declare war, appealing to those words of Alexander, when he cut the Gordian knot: 'Cutting and untying amount to the same thing.' Afterwards the saying was incorporated into an ingenious device by the famous Antonio de Nebrija, to whom the humanities in Spain owed so much.)

For a contemporary audience, then, the explicit reference to Alexander, the Gordian knot, and the words 'Tanto monta [...]' would have carried with it an implicit allusion to a ruler, or rulers, closer to home: 'el nudo gordiano, blasón de los Reyes Católicos' (the Gordian knot, emblem of the Catholic Monarchs).[62]

Quixote's reference to the knot is his second in the novel, having earlier drawn on the metaphor of the 'nudo gordiano' in passing to describe the indissoluble tie of marriage, undone only by the 'guadaña de la muerte' (II. 19, 856) ('scythe of death').[63] In II. 60, the reference is more significant. As on previous occasions, the juxtaposition of Quixote, an aged *hidalgo* striving to revive the art of knight-errantry, and a classical figure, here, one of the most revered, and feared, rulers of Antiquity, is absurd. Alexander the Great was associated with a wide range of qualities, for the most part positive (e.g. liberality, magnanimity, vigilance) but also at times negative (e.g. hubris, profligacy, alcoholism).[64] Prominent amongst the former were attributes associated with combat and conquest: strength, valour, and invincibility. 'Con razon alcanço nombre de Magno Alexandre, pues fue tal su esfuerço y valentia, que no se hallo en batalla de que no fuesse vencedor, ni puso cerco sobre ciudad que no la tomasse, ni movio guerra contra alguna nacion que no la subjetasse' (It was right that Alexander came to be known as 'the Great', because his strength and bravery were such that there was no battle in which he engaged that he did not win, no city that he besieged that he did not take, no nation on which he declared war that he did not conquer).[65] Alexander's solution of the Gordian knot was held up as the classical example *par excellence* of how thinking out of the box can help solve a seemingly insuperable problem. If Alexander could bend the rules associated with one prophecy, why, Quixote muses, can he not do the same in relation to another? His train of thought is easy to follow — 'Si nudo gordiano cortó el Magno Alejandro, [...], y no por eso dejó de ser [...], ni más ni menos podría suceder ahora [...], si yo azotase [...]' (II. 60, 1219) — but the contrast between Alexander slicing through the indissoluble knot and thus securing the conquest of Asia, on the one hand, and Quixote preparing to whip his sleeping squire to secure his lady's disenchantment, on the other, is farcical. Don Quixote's *discurso* culminates in a striking rhetorical question which begins with an implausibly long series of monosyllables: '¿qué se me da a mí que se los dé él, o que se los dé otro, pues [...]?' (II. 60, 1219). Echoing Sancho's earlier retort '¿Qué se me da a mí que mis vasallos sean negros?' (I. 29, 372) ('Who cares if my vassals are negroes?')[66] and the anaphora that runs through the parodic *romance* '¿Qué se me da a mi que el mundo [...]?' (What do I care if the world [...]?), this string of words cuts through Quixote's customary lofty rhetoric, laying the ground for the moment when he finally tries to take matters into his own hands.[67]

Voiced outside, and in the middle of the night, Quixote's soliloquy is delivered to an audience whose only member is, for the time being at least, fast asleep. With the example of Alexander in mind, and the conviction that the essence ('sustancia') of the problem lies in Sancho receiving the 'tres mil y tantos azotes [...] lleguen por do llegaren', Quixote proceeds to try to strip his squire of his trousers in order to beat him with Rocinante's reins:

> Con esta imaginación se llegó a Sancho, habiendo primero tomado las riendas de Rocinante, y, acomodándolas en modo que pudiese azotarle con ellas, comenzole a quitar las cintas (que es opinión que no tenía más que la delantera) en que se sustentaban los greguescos; pero apenas hubo llegado, cuando Sancho despertó en todo su acuerdo y dijo:
> — ¿Qué es esto? ¿Quién me toca y desencinta? (II. 60, 1219–20)
>
> (With these thoughts in mind he went over to Sancho, having first taken Rocinante's reins and fashioned them into a whip, and began to loosen the laces that held Sancho's breeches up, although it is believed that there was only one lace, the front one; but scarcely had he begun when Sancho was wide awake and crying:
> 'What's this? Who's touching me, who's unlacing me?')[68]

Ironically, with reins in hand, Quixote can be seen to adopt the role of Amadís de Gaula's 'mortal enemigo Arcalaús el encantador' ('mortal enemy the enchanter Arcalaus') who, Quixote mistakenly claims, administered to Quixote's hero 'más de docientos azotes con las riendas de su caballo' (I. 15, 178) ('more than two hundred lashes with the reins of his horse').[69] Even more disconcerting, however, is the fact that Quixote's actions place his squire in two or more incongruous roles. The attempt to debag him, in accordance with the stipulation that the lashes be administered to his bare backside, sets Sancho up as a child being punished for minor misdemeanours: '*Bajarle las calzas* al muchacho, azotarle' (To take the lad's breeches down, to whip him) (Cov. s.v. *calzas*). But even the young Andrés was not subjected to the ignominy of being beaten by his master below the waist: 'vio atada una yegua a una encina, y atado en otra a un muchacho, desnudo *de medio cuerpo arriba*, hasta de edad de quince años' (I. 4, 68; my emphasis) ('saw a mare tied by the reins to an evergreen oak, and tied to another a lad of about fifteen, naked from the waist up').[70] Only Doña Rodríguez had the misfortune to be beaten 'de medio cuerpo abajo' when slippered on her rump in the farcical culmination of her night time appeal to Quixote: 'sintió la pobre dueña que la asían de la garganta [...] y que otra persona [...] le alzaba las faldas, y con una al parecer chinela le comenzó a dar tantos azotes, que era una compasión' (II. 48, 1116) ('the poor duenna felt two hands seizing her by the throat [...] while someone else [...] hoisted her skirts and with what seemed to be a slipper gave her so many slaps that anyone would have felt sorry for her').[71] Yet more incongruous is the air of bedroom farce, with Sancho as an unsuspecting woman subjected to the indecent advances of a male figure operating under the cloak of night.[72] That Sancho's *greguescos* are held up with *cintas*, articles more commonly associated with women's attire, supports this suggestion. Covarrubias notes not only that 'La cinta es propia de la mujer' (Girdles are appropriate for women), but also that: 'La cinta es símbolo de la castidad; y cerca de los gentiles se usaba una ceremonia, que el marido antes de ayuntarse con la mujer le desataba él mesmo esta cinta, dicha *caesto*, que vale correa' (The girdle is a symbol of chastity; amongst the pagans there was a ceremony whereby, before sleeping with her, the husband himself would untie his wife's girdle, or *caesto*, which means strap) (Cov. s.v. *cinta y cinto*).[73] The most ridiculous image conjured up here is, then, of a groom undressing a chaste bride, complete with girdle, in preparation for the consummation of their marriage.

Added to this is the narrator's parenthetical remark that 'es opinión que no tenía más que la [cinta] delantera', the latest in a long line of playful interruptions to the narrative and yet another hint at the existence of other parallel accounts of Quixote's adventures ('dicen que [...]', 'quieren decir que [...]', 'hay alguna diferencia [...]', and so on). Most significant here, however, is the suggestion that Sancho's breeches are only half tied up. The lack of support at the back — i.e. of any 'cinta *trasera*' — means that his trousers must already be on the way to falling down. These are no *ñudos ciegos*; the gulf between Quixote's undertaking and that of his classical model grows ever greater. Quintus Curtius's description of the problem that faced Alexander underlines the disparity between the flimsy and effeminate *cintas* that only half maintain Sancho's modesty and the indissoluble nature of the Gordian knot:

> Y lo que en el carro avia mas de notar era el yugo que a el estava atado: porque las ataduras o ligaduras con que estava ligado eran hechas de tal manera y tenian tantos ñudos y tan inesplicables e intricados que por ninguna manera se podia ver ni hallar el principio ni cabo de ellos.[74]

(The most noteworthy feature of the wagon was the yoke that was tied to it, because the ties or bonds with which it was bound were made in such a way and had so many knots that were so resistant and intricate that by no means could one see or find where they began or ended.)

Everything points to Quixote scoring a quick win, or at least having a good chance of being successful in stripping his squire. However, Sancho immediately wakes up, regaining instant control of all of his faculties: 'despertó en todo su acuerdo.' This is in stark opposition to earlier scenes in which emphasis is placed on the difficulty he has shaking off the effects of sleep. In I. 16, amidst the farcical scrap that ensued from Quixote's night time encounter with Maritornes, Sancho had come round fully only when punched by her repeatedly: 'dio el retorno a Sancho con tantas, que, a su despecho, le quitó el sueño' (191) ('gave him so many punches in return that he was soon wide awake, much against his will').[75] The contrast between II. 60 and the scene in II. 20 when Quixote wakes Sancho with the tip of his lance after delivering another soliloquy over his sleeping squire is particularly acute:

[Don Quijote] se puso en pie y llamó a su escudero Sancho, que aún todavía roncaba; lo cual visto por don Quijote, antes que le despertase, le dijo:
— ¡Oh tú, bienaventurado sobre cuantos viven sobre la haz de la tierra, pues sin tener invidia ni ser invidiado duermes con sosegado espíritu, ni te persiguen encantadores ni sobresaltan encantamentos! [...] Duerme el criado, y está velando el señor, pensando cómo le ha de sustentar, mejorar y hacer mercedes. La congoja de ver que el cielo se hace de bronce sin acudir a la tierra con el conveniente rocío no aflige al criado, sino al señor, que ha de sustentar en la esterilidad y hambre al que le sirvió en la fertilidad y abundancia.
A todo esto no respondió Sancho, porque dormía, ni despertara tan presto si don Quijote con el cuento de la lanza no le hiciere volver en sí. Despertó, en fin, soñoliento y perezoso, y volviendo el rostro a todas partes [...]. (II, 20, 862–63)

(Don Quixote [...] rose to his feet and called to his squire Sancho who was still snoring; seeing which, Don Quixote addressed him thus before waking him:
'O happy you above all who dwell upon the face of the earth for, neither envying nor envied, you sleep with a tranquil spirit and without enchanters to pursue you or enchantments to alarm you! [...] The servant sleeps and the master lies awake, worrying about how to maintain him, better him and favour him. The anguish of seeing the heavens turning to brass and refusing to succour the earth with their necessary moisture does not afflict the servant but only the master, who in times of barrenness and hunger must provide for one who ministered to him in times of fertility and abundance.'
Sancho didn't reply to all this, because he was fast asleep, and he wouldn't have awoken as soon as he did if Don Quixote hadn't revived him by prodding him with the butt of his lance. In the end he did wake up, stretching and yawning, and he said as he peered all around [...].)[76]

Recalling this earlier scene throws some of the multiple ironies of the opening of II. 60 into sharper relief. It also underlines, through contrast, the humorous nature of Sancho's instantaneous response to Quixote's attempt to undress him. His immediate riposte — '¿Qué es esto? ¿Quién me toca y desencinta?' — may contain an echo of Jesus's words in the miracle of the healing of the bleeding woman in Luke 8. 43–48: 'Who touched me?' If so, the question '¿Quién me toca?' would suffice to add this further layer of incongruity; the addition of '[...] y desencinta?' is perhaps, therefore, more significant, serving not only to cement the absurdity of any possible biblical parallel but also to reinforce the impression of Sancho as a potentially vulnerable female seeking to ward off unsolicited male advances.

Quixote's calm, measured response to Sancho's short, sharp questions confirms the rude nature of this particular awakening:

> — Yo soy — respondió don Quijote — , que vengo a suplir tus faltas y a remediar mis trabajos: véngote a azotar, Sancho, y a descargar en parte la deuda a que te obligaste. Dulcinea perece, tú vives en descuido, yo muero deseando; y, así, desatácate por tu voluntad, que la mía es de darte en esta soledad por lo menos dos mil azotes. (II. 60, 1220)

> ('It is I', Don Quixote replied, 'come to make up for your deficiencies and to remedy my woes: I have come to lash you, Sancho, and to discharge in part the debt into which you have entered. Dulcinea is languishing, you are living on regardless, I am dying of desire — so now undo your breeches yourself, because what I am going to do now that we are alone is to give you two thousand lashes at least.')[77]

Here, *faltas* has both a general sense, of 'failings', 'failures', or 'defects', and a more specific one, given its immediate context (i.e. the disparity between five and 3,300), relating to 'insufficiency' or 'shortage(s)'. A third meaning may also be in play in a grotesque extension of the parodic gender dynamics outlined above: '*Faltas*, en la mujer preñada, los meses que ha tenido faltos de su regla' (*Faltas*, in a pregnant woman, the months elapsed since her last period) (Cov. s.v. *falta*). The balanced parallelism of Quixote's declaration — 'vengo a suplir tus faltas y a remediar mis trabajos' — sets up the hammerblow delivered in the clear and concise explanation that follows: 'véngote a azotar, Sancho'. The ironic disparity between the knight's intended actions, on the one hand, and how he perceives them and presents them to his squire, on the other, is developed further in Quixote's suggestion that whipping Sancho is equivalent to relieving him of part of a particular burden ('[...] a descargar [...]'), debt ('la deuda [...]'), or obligation ('a que te obligaste'). The implication, it seems, is that the squire who was only moments before sound asleep should actually be grateful to his master for waking him up and promising to beat him.

Quixote's next rhetorical flourish brings an elegant tricolon summing up what he sees as the current state of affairs: 'Dulcinea perece, tú vives en descuido, yo muero deseando.' The order of the three elements — Dulcinea (death), Sancho (life), Quixote (death) — both underlines the contrast between Dulcinea and Quixote, on the one hand, and Sancho, on the other, and makes Sancho's alleged culpability for both Dulcinea's demise and Quixote's own figurative death clear. Quixote thus picks up on and develops his earlier assertion to Sancho 'que es lástima no pequeña que aquella pobre señora esté encantada por tu descuido y negligencia' (II. 59, 1210). Quixote's latest self-presentation as the archetypal courtly lover whose burning desire causes him to experience a form of living death is immediately juxtaposed with, and undercut by, the simple imperative 'desatácate'. Having failed in his first attempt to strip Sancho, he now commands him to untie his breeches voluntarily. As if the original revelation that Quixote intends to beat Sancho were not enough, the point is reiterated, only this time with the added detail that Sancho is facing the prospect of at least two thousand lashes. Once more, a reminder of the total prescribed by Merlin highlights the ridiculous nature of the mission. Even two thousand far exceeds the maximum number of strokes dispensed as punishment either for wrongdoing in the Bible — 'Forty stripes he may give him, and not exceed: lest, if he should exceed, and beat him above these with many stripes, then thy brother should seem vile unto thee' (Deuteronomy 25.3; see also, for example, II Corinthians 11.24) — or for crimes in contemporary society, where public whippings were administered in hundreds, four or more *centenarios* being effectively akin to the death sentence, as Pablos's uncle so tactfully outlines to his nephew in *Buscón*, I. 7: 'vuestra madre [...] está presa en la Inquisición de Toledo [...]. Dicen que representará en un auto el día de la Trinidad, con cuatrocientos de muerte' (your mother [...] has been arrested by the Inquisition in Toledo [...]. It's said she'll take part in an *auto* on Trinity Sunday, accompanied by a lethal four hundred).[78]

A final point to note in relation to Quixote's declaration is the attention drawn once again to the setting for this episode, and in particular, here, to the notion of *soledad*: '[mi voluntad] es de darte en esta soledad por lo menos dos mil azotes.' If, earlier, the narrator's description of master and squire 'acomodándose a los troncos de [las espesas encinas o alcornoques]' pointed to playful reworking of one pastoral topos, now Quixote's words offer humorous recontextualization of another. On one level, in line with its meaning as a 'wilderness' or 'deserted place', *soledad* simply underscores that Quixote intends to take advantage of the fact that nobody else is around in order to make significant inroads into the target of 3,300 lashings; on another, however, in line with a well-established tradition stretching back through Góngora (e.g. *Soledades*), Fray Luis de León (e.g. '¡Qué descansada vida [...]!' ([What a peaceful life [...]!), 'Huid, contentos [...]' (Flee, pleasures [...])), Garcilaso (e.g. *Eclogue* II. 38–76), and others, to Horace, *Epode* II ('Beatus ille [...]'), it carries positive moral connotations associated with retreat, repose, self-sufficiency, and a network of other broadly Neo-Stoic virtues.[79] The setting is, therefore, more appropriate as a context for, or a stimulus to, reflective solitude, as it will later prove to be again in the frame to Lope de Vega's famous *romance* 'A mis soledades voy' (To my solitudes I go), than as a backdrop for the prospective administering of thousands of blood-raising lashes.

Sancho's response, in which he counters Quixote's plan by reminding him of the need for any strokes to be voluntary, draws a curt and notably less rhetorical rejoinder from his master, the exchange between the pair continuing as follows:

> — Eso no — dijo Sancho — , vuesa merced se esté quedo; si no, por Dios verdadero que nos han de oír los sordos. Los azotes a que yo me obligué han de ser voluntarios, y no por fuerza, y ahora no tengo gana de azotarme; basta que doy a vuesa merced mi palabra de vapularme y mosquearme cuando en voluntad me viniere.

— No hay que dejarlo a tu cortesía, Sancho — dijo don Quijote — , porque eres duro de corazón, y, aunque villano, blando de carnes. (II. 60, 1220)

('Oh no you're not,' said Sancho, 'you just stay where you are, because if you don't I swear to the one true God that even the deaf are going to hear us. The lashes I said I'd give myself have got to be voluntary ones, not forced on me, and right now I don't feel like lashing myself. It's enough if I promise to give myself a good hiding or at least a good swatting just as soon as I get the urge.'

'No, it can't be left to your goodwill, Sancho,' said Don Quixote, 'because your heart is hard and, although you're a peasant, your flesh is soft.')[80]

The opening 'Eso no' rebuffs Quixote's proposition in the most direct and immediate terms. This is followed by the striking juxtaposition of a polite form of address and an abrupt command, 'vuesa merced se esté quedo', as Sancho parries Quixote's earlier imperative 'desatácate'. A peak is then reached in the third and final element of Sancho's rejection, the oath-cum-warning 'si no, por Dios verdadero nos han de oír los sordos'. The hyperbole — a variation of another *refrán* recorded by Correas ('*Oírnos los sordos*: "Tener rencilla y voces"' (*To be heard by the deaf*: 'To quarrel loudly')) — is especially humorous in the light of the mock pastoral associations of *soledad*, the impending ruckus threatening to introduce a discordant note into a setting more usually accustomed to the harmonious sounds of gently running streams, untutored birdsong, and the drowsy humming of bees (e.g. Garcilaso, *Eclogue* II. 64–76). Having rejected Quixote's proposal, ordered him to desist from his intended course of action, and reminded him of a key condition for Dulcinea's disenchantment — echoing Merlin's earlier admonition to Quixote that 'los azotes que ha de recebir el buen Sancho han de ser por su voluntad, y no por fuerza, y en el tiempo que él quisiere' (II. 35, 1009) ('the worthy Sancho must take his lashing of his own free will, not by force, and at a time of his own choosing, for no deadline has been established')[81] — , Sancho reiterates his promise to whip himself at some future point in time. Another playful duplet throws his chosen terms into sharp relief: whereas the infinitive *vapularme*, the first of two synonyms for *azotarme*, points to a flogging in line with Merlin's proscription that the lashes 'le escuezan, le amarguen y le enfaden', *mosquearme*, the second, suggests something rather more light touch — 'Es defenderse de los que pretenden picar a uno, como hace el buey o el caballo de las moscas, moviendo la cola' (It means to defend oneself from potential sources of irritation, just as oxen and horses do from flies, by swishing their tails) (Cov. s.v. *mosquearse*) — , recalling another of the stipulations originally set by Sancho: 'Ha de ser también condición que no he de estar obligado a sacarme sangre con la diciplina, y que si algunos fueren de mosqueo, se me han de tomar en cuenta' (II. 35, 1013–14) ('And there's another condition too — I'm not to have to make myself bleed, and if some of the lashes turn out to be more like swatting flies they're still valid').[82]

On this occasion, of course, Quixote is not mollified by Sancho's promise of deferral: as a humble *villano*, and thus someone ill-equipped to embody true *cortesía* ('yo soy un pobre escudero, y no puedo llevar a cuestas tantas cortesías'; II. 41, 1046) ('I'm just a poor squire and I can't take all that courtesy'),[83] Sancho cannot be expected to keep his word. The complaint that he is 'duro de corazón' sets him up as a hard-hearted, disdainful Petrarchan beloved refusing to cede to the wishes of a frustrated suitor. The parallelism 'duro de corazón, y [...] blando de carnes' underlines the contrast between Sancho's hardness of heart, on the one hand, and his softness (or weakness) of flesh, on the other. Here, the suggestion that Sancho is 'aunque villano, blando de carnes' contains a thinly veiled accusation of indolence, for, as a peasant, the implication is that he must *not* have spent much time labouring outdoors. It contains an ironic echo of Quixote's earlier admission to the Duchess that he himself is made of similar substance: 'muchas veces la experiencia me ha mostrado que soy de carnes blandas y nonada impenetrables' (II. 32, 982) ('experience has often shown me that I am made of soft and not at all impenetrable flesh').[84] And, finally, it also further develops the humorous gender play, for, as Huarte de San Juan outlines, *blandura de carne* is a quality associated primarily with women (and children): 'las carnes de las mugeres, y de los niños [...] exceden en blandura a la de los hombres' (the flesh of women and children [...] is softer than that of men).[85] In sum, in the words of Molho, 'corazón duro y carne blanda, más que de hombre y villano, son de mujer desdeñosa y huidiza, indiferente a toda amorosa solicitación' (a hard heart and soft flesh are characteristic less of a rustic man, more of a disdainful and evasive woman, indifferent to all amorous advances).[86]

The climactic moment of this episode arrives when Quixote follows through with his threat and tries once more to strip Sancho, only this time by force:

> Y, así, procuraba y pugnaba por desenlazarle; viendo lo cual Sancho Panza, se puso en pie y, arremetiendo a su amo, se abrazó con él a brazo partido y, echándole una zancadilla, dio con él en el suelo boca arriba, púsole la rodilla derecha sobre el pecho y con las manos le tenía las manos de modo que ni le dejaba rodear ni alentar. Don Quijote le decía:
> — ¿Cómo, traidor? ¿Contra tu amo y señor natural te desmandas? ¿Con quién te da su pan te atreves? (II. 60, 1220)
>
> (And as he spoke he was struggling to untie him, to which Sancho responded by jumping to his feet, hurling himself at his master, grappling with him and then sticking a leg in, to leave him lying face upwards on the ground; and then Sancho clamped his right knee to his master's chest and held his wrists to the ground so that he couldn't move and could hardly even breathe. Don Quixote was gasping:
> 'What, you traitor? You defy your own natural lord? You raise your hand against the man who feeds you?')[87]

Quixote's determination is underscored by the humorous double 'procuraba y pugnaba', in which the initial plosive alliteration highlights the contrast between one verb that is cerebral and another that is decidedly more physical. When Sancho responds to his master's aggression, the pair finally engages in a form of hand-to-hand combat. The verbs *arremeter* and *abrazarse* and the adverbial phrase 'a brazo partido', which introduces a striking pleonasm and polyptoton following 'se abrazó con él', capture first Sancho's own recourse to force and then, momentarily, a sense of the pair being equally matched: '*Luchar a brazo partido*, es proceder igualmente, sin ventaja de uno a otro' (*Luchar a brazo partido*, to proceed on an equal footing, without either party having the advantage) (Cov. s.v. *brazo*). It is ironic that, on previous occasions, Sancho had actually saved his master from the ignominy of unarmed combat with a social inferior, arguing, in the aftermath of a fight with Cardenio, that it was inappropriate for Quixote to engage 'mano a mano' with the *cabrero*, a 'villano [que] no está armado caballero' (I. 24, 295) ('just a peasant [...] and he's never been knighted');[88] (see also Sancho's encounters with the owner of the *baciyelmo* and later with the *cabrero*, in I. 44 and I. 52 respectively). That master and squire should end up wrestling is certainly striking, and it is easy to see how the latter could be accused of wilful insubordination, but, given the circumstances, it is hard to see any other course of action available to Sancho. Significantly, the level of violence that ensues here is considerably lower than in Sancho's earlier altercations, as, for example, in his defeat by the deranged Cardenio: 'Sancho Panza [...] arremetió al loco con el puño cerrado, y el Roto le recibió de tal suerte, que con una puñada dio con él a sus pies y luego se subió sobre él y le brumó las costillas muy a su sabor' ('Sancho Panza [...] took his fist to the madman, and the Ragged Knight received him with a punch that left him spread-eagled at his feet, and then jumped on to him and trampled his ribs to his heart's content') and, just moments later, 'Replicó Sancho Panza y tornó a replicar el cabrero, y fue el fin de las réplicas asirse de las barbas y darse tales puñadas, que si don Quijote no los pusiera en paz se hicieran pedazos' (I. 24, 295) ('Sancho made his reply to this, and the goatherd replied to Sancho, and all this replying ended up with them grabbing each other by the beard and exchanging such punches that if Don Quixote hadn't pacified them they'd have thumped each other to pieces').[89]

The nature and outcome of the encounter render Quixote's proposed imitation of Alexander even more absurd. Strong and athletic, Alexander was an expert warrior, revered for his skills in fighting unarmed at close quarters and widely held to be invincible: 'Invencible eres, o hijo, no ay quien te vença' (You are invincible, O son, there is no one who can defeat you).[90] Here, any sense of parity, of the pair fighting 'a brazo partido', is only fleeting, for Quixote is soon conquered. Instead of resorting to his fists, Sancho instead trips his master up, pins him to the ground by placing a knee on his chest, and restrains his hands so that he cannot move or recover his breath. Sancho's recourse to the *zancadilla* is notable: 'Lo asombroso de esta escena estriba en la asociación de expresiones que remiten al universo caballeresco: *arremeter, abrazarse, la rodilla sobre el pecho*, con palabras que le son totalmente ajenas como *zancadilla*' (What is striking about this scene stems from the conjunction of expressions drawn from the world of chivalry, such as *arremeter, abrazarse, la rodilla sobre el pecho*, and words that are totally alien to it, like *zancadilla*).[91] Whilst, on one level, the phrase 'echar la zancadilla' simply means 'hacer caer, derribar' (topple, knock down) (Cov. *Suplemento*, s.v. Iacob), on another, it carries associations of deliberate deceit, of 'ardid y engaño' [ruse and deception] (Cov. s.v. *zanca, traspié, estropezar*), and of the work of the Devil: '¿y sé yo por ventura si en esos gobiernos me tiene aparejada el diablo alguna zancadilla [...]' (II. 4, 720) ('And how am I to know that the devil hasn't been fixing up tripwires on those islands [...]').[92] Sancho's tactic could be read, therefore, as an instance of underhand behaviour, as a 'gesto poco heroico', but, first and foremost, it serves to underscore the ease with which his master is defeated. Moments later, the motif of Sancho's knee on Don Quixote's chest presents an ironic reworking of similar victory scenes in earlier chivalric romances: 'Grumedán tenía al uno de los romanos de espaldas en el suelo, y él las rodillas sobre sus pechos, y dávale en el rostro grandes golpes de la mançana de la espada' (Grumedan had one of the Romans on his back on the ground, with his knees on his chest, and was hitting him in the face with lusty blows from the pommel of his sword) (*Amadís de Gaula*, II. 3. 80).[93] Such brutality is, however, absent here: the *zancadilla* brings a sudden and relatively non-violent end to the encounter, and it is significant that when atop his master Sancho does not follow up with a torrent of blows, but chooses instead to subdue him and thus bring an immediate conclusion to their struggle.

Quixote's response to being overcome takes the form of yet another tricolon, his incredulity conveyed through three short questions all beginning with the same initial sound: '¿Cómo [...]? ¿Contra [...]? ¿Con quién [...]?' Through use of the slur *traidor*, the first echoes a number of earlier instances of Quixote upbraiding Sancho for his failure to act and/or speak in accordance with his master's worldview, as seen in the context of the pair's disagreement over the nature of the barber's basin in I. 21 ('¿Cómo me puedo engañar en lo que digo, traidor escrupuloso?' (244) ('How can I be wrong, you doubting Thomas?')[94]), discussion of Dulcinea in the light of Sancho's (non-)delivery of the letter in I. 30 ('¿Cómo que no la has visto, traidor blasfemo?' (387) ('How can you say that you have never seen her, you blasphemous traitor?')[95]), and the fallout from Sancho's decision to store his recently acquired curds in Quixote's helmet in II. 17 ('Por vida de mi señora Dulcinea del Toboso, que son requesones los que aquí me has puesto, traidor, bergante y malmirado escudero' (830) ('By the life of my lady Dulcinea del Toboso, these are curds you've put in here, you treacherous, villainous, ill-mannered squire!')[96]). In his relations with Sancho, Quixote's recourse to this and a range of other insults — *hereje*, *ladrón*, *mentecato*, *pecador*, *villano*, and others — is frequent, contrasting neatly with other more positive forms of address that run through the novel — notably, those based on *amigo*, *hermano*, or *hijo*.[97] An example of Quixote at his vituperative best is seen in the hyperbolic enumeration of terms of insult that forms the backbone of his response to Sancho's initial refusal to accept the conditions of Merlin's prophecy in II. 35:

> — ¡Oh malaventurado escudero, alma de cántaro, corazón de alcornoque, de entrañas guijeñas y apedernaladas! Si te mandaran, ladrón, desuellacaras, que [...]; si te pidieran, enemigo del género humano, que [...]. Pon, ¡oh miserable y endurecido animal!, pon, digo, esos tus ojos [...]. Muévate, socarrón y malintencionado monstro [...]. Date, date en esas carnazas, bestión indómito, y saca de harón ese brío, que [...]. (II. 35, 1009–10)

('O wretched squire, soul of lead, heart of cork, bowels of flint and granite! If you were being commanded, you thieving cutthroat, to [...]; if you were being asked, you enemy of human kind, to [...] Rest, O miserable callous animal, rest, I say, those eyes [...] Relent, you sly and spiteful monster [...] Come on, lash that fat carcass of yours, you untamed beast, and arouse that slothful spirit, that [...]')[98]

In II. 60, Quixote's use of the term *traidor* is, therefore, both unexceptional and comparatively understated. The wording of Quixote's second question also recalls an earlier exchange, in which, in the wake of the fulling mills episode, Sancho promised not to mock his master: 'puede estar seguro que de aquí adelante no despliegue mis labios para hacer donaire de las cosas de vuestra merced, si no fuere para honrarle, como a mi amo y señor natural' (I. 20, 242) ('you can take it from me that from this moment on I won't open my mouth to make fun of your doings, but only to honour you as my master and natural lord').[99] Rather than establishing a formal feudal pact between lord and vassal, Quixote's response at the time, ending with the assertion that 'después de a los padres, a los amos se ha de respetar como si lo fuesen' (243) (next to our parents, our masters should be respected as if they were our parents'),[100] brought an ironic close to a chapter in which Sancho had first deceived his master and then openly ridiculed him. In II. 60, the emphasis on the hierarchical nature of their relationship in Quixote's second and third questions underlines the absurdity of his defeat at the hands of his own squire, the one person who would normally, by default, be unfailingly respectful towards him. The contrast with Alexander grows even greater in the light of the fear and respect he is reputed to have inspired in those who served him, a fact reflected in the following brief anecdote recorded by Fray Luis de Granada:

> De un paje de Alejandro Magno se lee que como se le fuese acabando una candela que tenía en la mano, con que estaba alumbrando a su señor, y se le comenzasen ya a quemar los dedos, no la osó soltar, ni hacer desdén con el cuerpo, por el temor y reverencia de Alejandro.[101]

> (Of one of Alexander the Great's servants one reads that as a candle that he was holding to give his master light was coming to an end, despite his fingers having already started to burn, he did not dare let go of it, or show any physical signs of displeasure, on account of his fear and reverence of Alexander.)

That Quixote is vanquished in such an unbecoming manner and then subdued instantly by his own squire, one whose own childlike and effeminate nature has recently been drawn out, only adds to the incongruity of the imitation of Alexander.

The episode draws to a memorable conclusion as Sancho's assertive response to Quixote's succession of questions leaves his master no other option than to back down:

> — Ni quito rey ni pongo rey — respondió Sancho — , sino ayúdome a mí, que soy mi señor. Vuesa merced me prometa que se estará quedo y no tratará de azotarme por agora, que yo le dejaré libre y desembarazado; donde no,
>   aquí morirás, traidor,
>   enemigo de doña Sancha.
> Prometiósele don Quijote y juró por vida de sus pensamientos no tocarle en el pelo de la ropa y que dejaría en toda su voluntad y albedrío el azotarse cuando quisiese. (II. 60, 1220–21)

> ('I don't make the king or break the king,' Sancho replied, 'I only help my master — in other words me. You promise to leave me alone, and not try to lash me yet, and I'll let you go, but if not,

You'll die here and now, you traitor,
Doña Sancha's enemy.'
Don Quixote made his promise, and swore by his life not to lay a finger on him, and to leave it to him to choose with absolute freedom when to lash himself.)[102]

The first part of Sancho's retort reworks another *refrán* recorded by Correas, 'Ni quito rey ni pongo rey, mas ayudo a mi señor'. As reflected in Correas's accompanying explanation, Sancho's words, and the saying on which they are based, contain an allusion to the defeat of Pedro I of Castile at the hands of his half-brother Enrique of Trastámara following the battle of Montiel in 1369 and, in particular, to the role played therein by a third party held to have tipped a fight to the death between them in favour of Enrique before uttering the above words. Correas attributes the saying to 'un caballero Andrada' (a knight called Andrada), that is, to the Galician knight Fernán Pérez de Andrade, but notes that 'otros lo atribuyeron a otro' (others attributed it to someone else).[103] Clemencín credits the role to the French knight Bertrand du Guesclin, or, in the castilianized version of his name, Beltrán (de) Claquín, before proceeding to cite lines from the ballad 'Los fieros cuerpos revueltos', in which the crucial part is played by an unnamed servant to Enrique.[104] The closing quatrains of the ballad read:

> Viendo el page a su señor
> en tan peligroso paso,
> por detras al Rey allega
> reziamente del tirando.
> Diziendo: No quito Rey,
> ni pongo Rey de mi mano:
> pero hago lo que debo
> al oficio de criado.
> Y dio con el Rey de espaldas,
> y Enrique vino a lo alto,
> hiriendo con un puñal
> en el pecho del Rey falso.
> Donde abueltas de la sangre
> el vital hilo cortando,
> salió el alma mas cruel,
> que vivió en pecho Cristiano.[105]

(Seeing his master in such a dangerous position, the page moves up behind the king pulling on him hard, and saying 'I neither depose nor make the king, but do my duty in my role as servant'. And he forced the king onto his back, and Henry, climbing on top, thrust a dagger into the false king's chest. Upon which, on cutting the thread of life, along with the blood there came out the cruelest soul that ever resided in a Christian chest.)

Sancho's words thus give rise to one of the passage's most extreme incongruities. The parallel drawn between the fleeting scuffle that takes place between him and Quixote over the *azotes* required for Dulcinea's disenchantment, on the one hand, and the ferocious hand-to-hand combat between Pedro and Enrique resulting in the fratricide that represents the climax of their protracted struggle for control of the kingdom of Castile, on the other, is preposterous. If Quixote plays the part of Pedro, then Sancho plays those of both his bastard half-brother and the loyal partisan of Enrique whose intervention proves decisive. Whilst Sancho's words could be seen as a proclamation of his autonomy, first and foremost they constitute a witty reworking of the well-known *refrán* — the second half modified from 'pero ayudo a mi señor', and variations on the theme of loyal service (e.g. the above 'pero hago lo que debo | al oficio de criado'), to 'sino ayúdome a mí, que soy mi señor' — necessitated by the absence of any third party.

The ultimatum offered by Sancho is delivered through a second humorous piece of recontextualisation, this time of the closing lines of the *romance* 'A cazar va don Rodrigo', which begins and ends as follows:

> A cazar va don Rodrigo,
> y aun don Rodrigo de Lara,
> con la grande siesta que hace
> arrimádose ha a una haya,
> maldiciendo a Mudarrillo,
> hijo de la renegada,
> que si a las manos le hubiese
> que le sacaría el alma.
> [...]
> — Espéresme, don Gonzalo,
> iré a tomar las mis armas.
> — El espera que tú diste
> a los infantes de Lara.
> Aquí morirás, traidor,
> enemigo de doña Sancha. (1–8, 39–44)[106]

(A-hunting goes Don Rodrigo, Don Rodrigo de Lara no less, and with the great early afternoon heat he's leant up against a beech tree, cursing Mudarrillo, son of the renegade woman, because if he had him in his hands he would tear out his soul. [...] 'Wait for me, Don Gonzalo, I will go to fetch my arms.' 'I'll lie in wait just as you did for the princes of Lara. You'll die here and now, you traitor, enemy of Doña Sancha.')

The ballad's closing lines point, through characteristic *saber callar a tiempo*, to the revenge taken by Mudarra González, the above 'Mudarrillo', for Rodrigo de Lara's betrayal of his own nephews, the Siete Infantes de Lara. It ends with the prospect of one-on-one combat between the *caballero* Rodrigo ('Dios te salve, caballero, | debajo de la verde haya' (God save you, knight, underneath the green beech), lines 11–12) and the *escudero* Mudarrillo ('Así haga a ti, escudero, | buena sea tu llegada' (You too, good squire, | may your arrival be blest), 13–14), and the violent demise of the former at the hands of the latter. Once again, the link drawn between an infamous fight to the death and the brief fallout from Quixote's attempt to strip Sancho by force is jarring. Here, however, there is no need for any modification to the lines cited. As on previous occasions (most notably, his injudicious recycling of the opening lines of the 'Romance de Lanzarote y el orgulloso' to Doña Rodríguez in II. 31 (963)), Sancho's recitation of verses from a well-known ballad is inherently humorous, containing a striking switch into the *tú* form, witty reversal of Quixote's own accusation of treachery, and the incongruous introduction of the figure of Doña Sancha, who is displaced from the context of the cycle of the Siete Infantes and reimagined as a participant in the present fight.[107] Sancho's verbatim quotation of lines voiced by Mudarrillo sets him up as a 'nuevo Mudarra', to Quixote's Rodrigo, but the content of the lines, and the play on his own name, equates him not with Mudarra González but with the female figure of Doña Sancha.[108] As such, it represents the culmination of a series of allusions to, and plays on, Sancho's 'condición [...] mujeril' and of his resistance to the advances of Quixote, the 'seductor frustrado'.[109]

Sancho's ultimatum has the desired effect, eliciting a promise from Quixote that he will not lay a hand on him and that 'dejaría en toda su voluntad y albedrío el azotarse cuando quisiese'. In the very next lines, Sancho's discovery of bodies hanging in nearby trees leads straight into the Roque Guinart episode, with the result that the narrative of Dulcinea's disenchantment is put on hold. The subject of the *azotes* resurfaces in II. 62, in one of Quixote's questions to the enchanted head, and again in II. 63, on board the galley in Barcelona, before peaking again in II. 68, when Quixote once more wakes Sancho at night to address the issue. Recalling his earlier defeat, he implores Sancho to whip himself, now recognizing the futility of force: 'no quiero venir contigo a los brazos como la otra vez, porque sé que los tienes pesados' (1288–89) ('I don't want to fight you like the last time, for I know that you have a heavy hand').[110] The promise of compensatory amoebean song and of the inception of their pastoral careers fails to convince Sancho, who defers once again. The question arises for the final time when, following the feigned resurrection of Altisidora in II. 69–70, Quixote's offer of payment in II. 71 brings a sudden and dramatic change of heart from his squire. At a *cuarto* per *azote*, Sancho cannot wait to scourge himself; that very night, having stripped off 'de medio cuerpo arriba' ('to the waist') (1312), he begins, only to pause after 'hasta seis o ocho' (1313) ('six or eight'),[111] double his financial rate, and then resume, only this time flaying not his own back but the trunks of nearby trees. The dramatic irony of the scene that ensues comes to a head when, following so many attempts to persuade Sancho to begin, Quixote now beseeches him to stop, fearing for his squire's very survival. The *entremés*-style farce ends with an incongruous allusion to Samson pulling down the pillars of the temple, Quixote's repeated insistence that Sancho break from the task, and Sancho donning Quixote's cape to cover his back before sleeping until daybreak. It resumes the following night, after the encounter with Don Álvaro Tarfe, with Sancho reaching, by his master's reckoning, 3,029 lashes. The task is finally completed the night after that, only for Quixote's joy to be shattered by the *malum signum* that greets him when he reaches his home village at the start of II. 73.

Returning to the scene in hand, Madariaga's famous dismissal of the start of II. 60 is on the grounds of both content and style: 'Lugar ya duro y desalmado de por sí y que apena más todavía por el descuido con el que está escrito y por la indiferencia con la que el autor pasa a la aventura siguiente sin pararse a meditar, comentar o sentir tan significativo momento en la vida de su héroe' (A passage that is already cruel and heartless in itself and which generates even greater sadness on account of the carelessness with which it is written and the indifference with which the author moves on to the next adventure without stopping to think about, comment on, or lament such an important moment in the life of his hero).[112] The page in question is, however, far from carelessly written. Rather than an all-too-brief account of an apparently momentous event, it is in fact a laconic treatment of one that is much less serious. As such, it contains a series of unmistakably humorous touches ranging from subtle irony to patent absurdity. The cornerstone of the passage in this regard is Quixote's proposed imitation of Alexander the Great, and the gap that opens up between the Macedonian's public cutting of the Gordian knot and the Manchegan's private attempt to undo his squire's breeches. As is often the case, explicit reference to an archetype to be emulated results not in ennoblement but in bathetic deflation. Following on from many previous night time scenes in the novel, including those set in the inn (e.g. I. 16, I. 35) and those orchestrated by the Duke and Duchess (II. 35–36, II. 48), here there is an overriding impression of farce, one that is further developed through the inclusion of allusions to Sancho's womanly attributes and attire. Knowing reworking of pastoral topoi, playful narratorial intrusion, and humorous recontextualization of famous lines from historical legend and the ballad tradition all introduce further elements of incongruity. Through a series of parallels and analogies, some direct, others more nuanced, Quixote appears as shepherd, frustrated suitor, Alexander the Great, Pedro I of Castile, and Rodrigo de Lara, with Sancho under the guises of disobedient child, hard-hearted Petrarchan lady, Enrique II, Mudarra González, and Doña Sancha. Humour thus arises from the conflation of details drawn from multiple, often incompatible, traditions, and from the speed of transition from one frame of reference to the next.

Such humour should be taken into account in assessments of this passage. In his critique of Madariaga's influential chiastic model of the relationship between master (*sanchificación*) and squire (*quijotización*), and his insistence instead on an openly political account of the development of the pair's relationship, Williamson downplays the comic aspects of his four chosen moments of 'crisis'. In the case of this particular exchange, this tendency is seen both in relation to the details of the episode itself and the question of how it fits into the work more broadly. Much of the humour of this passage, and of many others, depends on contrast and dissonance, visible on both a local level and across the novel as a whole. On the back of II. 59, Quixote's actions here undermine any suggestion that he is 'ya desenamorado de Dulcinea del Toboso', thus serving further to discredit Avellaneda's spurious sequel. Sancho's actions, meanwhile, are framed by praise of Quixote as 'mi amo, valiente, discreto y enamorado' (1216) ('my master, brave and wise and in love'),[113] on the one hand, and instinctive and immediate reversion to asking him for protection when he discovers the bodies in the trees ('Dio voces llamando a don Quijote que le favoreciese' (1221) ('He screamed to Don Quixote for help')[114]), on the other. Beyond this immediate context, the passage is one of a series of parallel scenes centred on Quixote's reactions to Sancho sleeping, ironically undercutting that in II. 20, at the same time as setting up a later contrast with Sancho's eulogy of sleep in II. 68 (1289). Looking across both parts, this is also one of many episodes stemming from Merlin's prophecy that together rewrite and invert Quixote's imitation of Amadís's penance at Peña Pobre in the Sierra Morena. Here, Sancho's extreme reluctance to bare his 'valientes posaderas' and to take on the role of the *disciplinante* is in stark opposition to Quixote, or 'don Azote' (as he is addressed by Dorotea, disguised as Micomicona, in I. 30 (382)), 'desnudándose con toda priesa los calzones' ('pulling down his breeches as fast as ever he could')[115] at the end of I. 25 (317), setting up the humorous reversal that comes with the offer of payment in II. 71.

Readings of the relationship between Quixote and Sancho based on the model and language of feudalism, according to which events at the start of II. 60 constitute 'a shocking infraction of the hierarchical relationship, an open physical rebellion against the authority of the master', see Sancho emerge with little credit.[116] When taken to extreme lengths, they characterize him as anything from a biblical Lucifer, in his refusal to serve a higher authority, to the dogs of the classical figure of Actaeon, who tore their master apart when he was transformed into a stag.[117] Reading the scrap between master and squire as a supreme act of treachery, which paves the way for the 'merciless exploitation' of Quixote by a 'cynical, greedy and thoroughly deceitful' Sancho, is, however, possible only if one ignores the presence of much of the episode's humour.[118] Williamson's character assassination of Sancho flows from the conclusion that 'Madariaga's theory [...] will scarcely do to describe the dynamics between knight and squire over the course of the entire narrative', but the same criticism could be levelled at his own model based on the theory of a power-struggle between master and squire culminating in the latter's overthrowing of the former. The construction of a narrative arc of Sancho's steady rise to power, based on the plotting of four discrete but interconnected points in the novel, offers too schematic a view of the development of a relationship that is in a constant state of flux, at times shifting markedly, at others varying more subtly. The development of Quixote and Sancho, both as individuals and in terms of the dynamic between them, does not follow a clear-cut path. Attempts at neat demarcation, along the lines of Madariaga or Williamson, are ultimately frustrated by the all-pervasive ironies and incongruities that are found not only in the most overtly parodic episodes of the novel but also in its more serious-seeming passages, including that often viewed as 'la más grave de las disputas sobre los azotes [...] para desencantar a Dulcinea'.[119]

Notes to Chapter 2

1. R. B. [pseudonym for Nathaniel Crouch], *The History of the Nine Worthies of the World* (London: Nath[aniel] Crouch, 1687), p. 30.
2. All translations are mine, unless otherwise indicated.
3. See notes to Miguel de Cervantes Saavedra, *El ingenioso Don Quijote de la Mancha, compuesto por Miguel de Cervantes Saavedra, y comentado por Don Diego Clemencín*, 6 vols (Madrid: D. E. Aguado, 1833–39), VI, 223.
4. Miguel de Unamuno, *Vida de Don Quijote y Sancho*, ed. by Alberto Navarro, Letras Hispánicas, 279 (Madrid: [n. pub.], 1905, repr. Cátedra, 1992), pp. 454–55.
5. Vladimir Nabokov, *Lectures on 'Don Quixote'*, ed. by Fredson Bowers (San Diego: Harcourt Brace Jovanovich, 1983), p. 109.
6. Salvador de Madariaga, *Guía del lector del 'Quijote': ensayo psicológico sobre el 'Quijote'*, 2nd edn (Buenos Aires: Editorial Sudamericana, 1943), pp. 146, 19.

7. For a basic outline of some of the most influential 'hard' and 'soft' (and 'perspectivist') readings, see Howard Mancing, *Cervantes' 'Don Quixote': A Reference Guide*, Greenwood Guides to Multicultural Literature (Westport, CT: Greenwood Press, 2006), pp. 193–96.
8. Edwin Williamson, 'The Power-Struggle between Don Quixote and Sancho: Four Crises in the Development of the Narrative', *Bulletin of Spanish Studies*, 84 (2007), 837–58 (p. 839), developing ideas nascent in his *The Half-Way House of Fiction: 'Don Quixote' and Arthurian Romance* (Oxford: Clarendon Press, 1984), pp. 193–94, 197–98. For a Spanish version of the article, with minor changes, see 'La autoridad de Don Quijote y el poder de Sancho: el conflicto político en el fondo del *Quijote*', in *Autoridad y poder en el Siglo de Oro*, ed. by Ignacio Arellano, Christoph Strosetzki, and Edwin Williamson (Madrid: Iberoamericana, 2009), pp. 241–66.
9. Williamson, 'Power-Struggle', pp. 853–55.
10. Roberto González Echevarría, *Cervantes' 'Don Quixote'*, Open Yale Courses (New Haven: Yale University Press, 2015), pp. 294–95.
11. González Echevarría, *Cervantes' 'Don Quixote'*, p. 283.
12. Miguel de Cervantes Saavedra, *Cervantes: Don Quixote*, trans. by John Rutherford (London: Penguin, 2000), pp. 887, 888. All translations from *Don Quixote* are from this edition. My discussion builds on several of the footnotes in I, 1218–21, and on the accompanying notes in the 'Volumen complementario', in addition to Clemencín.
13. p. 891.
14. p. 891.
15. p. 822.
16. p. 946.
17. The translation is from Virgil, *Eclogues, Georgics, Aeneid: Books 1–6*, trans. by H. R. Fairclough, rev. by George P. Goold, Loeb Classical Library, 63 (Cambridge, MA: Harvard University Press, 1999), p. 25.
18. Stephen Boyd, 'Cervantes's Exemplary Prologue', in *A Companion to Cervantes's 'Novelas Ejemplares'*, ed. by Stephen Boyd, Serie A: Monografías, 218 (Woodbridge: Tamesis, 2005), pp. 63–64, n. 18. Compare the following scene from *La gitanilla*: 'Sucedió, pues, que [...] una noche, por entretenerse, sentados los dos, Andrés al pie de un alcornoque, Clemente al de una encina, cada uno con una guitarra, convidados del silencio de la noche, [...] cantaron estos versos [...]' (It happened, then, that [...] one night, to amuse themselves, with both of them sat down, Andrés at the foot of a cork oak, Clemente at that of an evergreen, each with a guitar, moved by the silence of the night, [...] they sang these verses [...]) (*Novelas ejemplares*, ed. by Harry Sieber, 22nd edn, Letras Hispánicas, 105–06, 2 vols (Madrid: Cátedra, 1997), I, 119). For more on debates on the meaning of *fagus*, see José Antonio Izquierdo Izquierdo, '¿Haya, encina o alcornoque? Ecos de una polémica virgiliana en el *Quijote*', *Minerva: Revista de filología clásica*, 5 (1991), 293–304; and Manuel Mañas Núñez, 'Sanctius Brocensis, "El Brocense"', *Alcántara: Revista del Seminario de Estudios Cacereños*, 61–62 (2005), 11–26 (p. 12).
19. See, for example, the commentary on Alciato's emblem 'Quercus' in Diego López, *Declaración magistral sobre las Emblemas de Andres Alciato* (Nájera: Juan de Mongastón, 1615), fols 401^v–02^v.
20. Sebastián de Covarrubias Horozco, *Tesoro de la lengua castellana o española* [1611], ed. by Ignacio Arellano and Rafael Zafra (Madrid: Iberoamericana, 2006), s.v. *alcornoque*. All subsequent references to this work will be incorporated into the main text (using the abbreviation Cov.). Georgina Dopico Black, 'Canons Afire: Libraries, Books, and Bodies in *Don Quixote*'s Spain', in *Cervantes' 'Don Quixote': A Casebook*, ed. by Roberto González Echevarría (Oxford: Oxford University Press, 2005), pp. 95–123 (p. 117): 'The word [i.e. *alcornoque*] means nakedness, on account of that covering — bark — the tree is repeatedly made to give up.'
21. p. 560.
22. p. 891.
23. On this pastoral topos, see, for example, Ernst Robert Curtius, *European Literature and the Latin Middle Ages* [1953], trans. by Willard R. Trask, intro. by Colin Burrow, Bollingen Series, 36 (Princeton: Princeton University Press, 2013), pp. 190–93.
24. p. 891.
25. Loeb Classical Library 63, p. 597.

26. Evidence that these specific sources were widely known is found in the commentaries of both El Brocense and Fernando de Herrera on Garcilaso, *Eclogue* II.117 ('con prestas alas por la ebúrnea puerta'). Herrera, for example, begins his comment on *ebúrnea* as follows: 'Omero, en el 19 de la *Odissea*, pone dos puertas del sueño; i Virgilio, en el 6, a su imitación, dize assí: "Sunt geminae Somni portae [...]"' (Homer, in *Odyssey* XIX, gives two gates of Sleep; and Virgil, in *Aeneid* VI, in imitation, says as follows: 'Two gates of Sleep there are [...]') (see Fernando de Herrera, *Anotaciones a la poesía de Garcilaso*, ed. by Inoria Pepe and José María Reyes, Letras Hispánicas, 516 (Madrid: Cátedra, 2001), pp. 812–14 (p. 812)). For Hernández de Velasco's translation, see *Los doze libros de la Eneida de Vergilio, Principe de los Poetas Latinos* (Toledo: Juan de Ayala, 1555), fol. 58^v.
27. pp. 26–27.
28. On the effects of Quixote's insomnia, see, for example, the epilogue to Robert Folger, *Images in Mind: Lovesickness, Spanish Sentimental Fiction and 'Don Quijote'*, North Carolina Studies in the Romance Languages and Literatures (Chapel Hill: The University of North Carolina, 2002), pp. 234–48: 'Sleep deprivation and intense mental activity, which involves the consumption of pneuma, lead to the corruption of bodily humors or adust melancholy' (p. 237).
29. p. 66.
30. p. 891.
31. p. 716.
32. p. 546.
33. p. 727.
34. Anthony J. Close, *Miguel de Cervantes: 'Don Quixote'*, Landmarks of World Literature (Cambridge: Cambridge University Press, 1990), p. 98.
35. p. 727.
36. pp. 728–29.
37. p. 729.
38. p. 729.
39. p. 757.
40. p. 758.
41. pp. 884–85.
42. p. 885.
43. pp. 891–92.
44. p. 732.
45. *Novus index librorum prohibitorum et expurgatorum* [...] *D. Antonii Zapata* (Seville: Francisco de Lyra, 1632), p. 980: 'Miguel Cervantes Saavedra. Segunda parte de don Quixote cap. 36. al medio, borrese, *las obras de caridad que se hazen tibia, y floxamente, no tienen merito, ni valen nada*' (Miguel Cervantes Saavedra. Second part of *Don Quixote*, chapter 36, in the middle, delete 'las obras de caridad que se hazen tibia, y floxamente, no tienen merito, ni valen nada'). On the much-discussed suppression of the Duchess's warning from the 1616 Valencia edition, and this related entry in the 1632 *Index*, see, for example, Américo Castro, 'Cervantes y la Inquisición', *Modern Philology*, 27 (1930), 427–33; José López Navío, 'Sobre la frase de la duquesa: "las obras de caridad hechas floja y tibiamente" (*Don Quijote*, 2, 36)', *Anales Cervantinos*, 9 (1961), 97–112; and José Antonio Escudero, 'El *Quijote* y la Inquisición', in his *Estudios sobre La Inquisición* (Madrid: Marcial Pons, 2005), pp. 333–47.
46. p. 734.
47. p. 734.
48. p. 892.
49. p. 892.
50. p. 15.
51. On references to Alexander in Part One, see Frederick A. de Armas, 'Don Quijote y Alejandro Magno: vidas paralelas', in *Cervantes, la lectura interminable*, ed. by Roberto González Echevarría (= *Cuadernos hispanoamericanos*, 790 (April 2016)), 32–47. See also Antonio Barnés Vázquez, *'Yo he leído en Virgilio': la tradición clásica en el 'Quijote'*, Biblioteca Cátedra Miguel de Cervantes: Publicaciones Académicas, 12 (Vigo: Editorial Academia del Hispanismo, 2009), pp. 144–51.

52. p. 18.
53. p. 28. 'The Latin means "was all skin and bone" (Plautus, *Aulularia*, III. 6, 28)' (p. 986, n. 9).
54. pp. 889–90.
55. p. 471.
56. De Armas, 'Don Quijote y Alejandro Magno', p. 34.
57. p. 50.
58. Avellaneda's Quixote also compares himself to Alexander: 'Osariate apostar (y esto es sin duda) que si me abriessen por medio, y sacasen el corazón, que le hallarían como aquel de Alejandro Magno, de quien se dice que le tenía lleno de vello, señal evidentísima de su gran virtud y fortaleza' (I would dare bet you (and this is certain) that if I were cut open in the middle, and my heart were removed, it would be found to be like that of Alexander the Great, who was said to have one that was covered in hair, a very clear mark of his considerable virtue and strength); see Alonso Fernández de Avellaneda, *El Quijote apócrifo*, ed. by Alfredo Rodríguez López-Vázquez, Letras Hispánicas, 685 (Madrid: Cátedra, 2011), p. 150. The hairy heart was, though, an attribute not of Alexander but of Aristomenes of Messene (Cov. s.v. Aristómenes).
59. Plutarch, *La primera y segunda parte de Plutharcho*, trans. by Alfonso de Palencia, 2 vols (Seville: Paulo de Colonia, 1491), II, 100^{r-v}.
60. Gonzalo Correas, *Vocabulario de refranes y frases proverbiales* [1627], ed. by Louis Combet (Bordeaux: Institut d'études ibériques et ibéro-américaines de l'Université de Bordeaux, 1967), p. 495a.
61. Baltasar Gracián, *Agudeza y arte de ingenio*, ed. by Evaristo Correa Calderón, Clásicos Castalia, 14–15, 2 vols (Madrid: Castalia, 1987), II, 62.
62. Tirso de Molina, *Cigarrales de Toledo*, ed. by Luis Vázquez Fernández, Clásicos Castalia, 216 (Madrid: Castalia, 1996), p. 164.
63. p. 611.
64. For the latter, see, for example, Francisco de Quevedo's burlesque retelling of Alexander's visit to the Cynic philosopher Diogenes in the ballad 'En el retrete del mosto' (*Poesía original completa*, ed. by José Manuel Blecua (Barcelona: Planeta, 2004), pp. 889–93 (no. 745)).
65. Alonso de Villegas, *Flos sanctorum: segunda parte y historia general en que se escrive la vida de la Virgen* (Barcelona: Damian Bages, 1586), fols 245^r–46^v (at 246^v).
66. p. 266.
67. *Romancero general, en que se contienen todos los Romances que andan impressos aora nuevamente añadido, y emendado por Pedro Flores* (Madrid: Juan de la Cuesta, 1614), fols 387^r–88^r.
68. p. 892.
69. p. 119.
70. p. 42.
71. p. 811.
72. The comments that follow build on Maurice Molho's discussion of Sancho's 'condición [...] mujeril', in his 'Doña Sancha (*Quijote*, II, 60)', in *Homenaje a José Manuel Blecua ofrecido por sus discípulos, colegas y amigos*, ed. by Dámaso Alonso (Madrid: Gredos, 1983), pp. 443–48 (p. 446). Molho takes as his starting point the fact that Sancho rides side-saddle, that is 'sentado a la mujeriega' (I.23, 274) or 'a mujeriegas' (II.41, 1048).
73. Cf. John Minsheu, *A Dictionarie in Spanish and English* (London: Ed[mund] Bollifant, 1599) p. 67: '*Cinta, f. a girdle of silke, cruell, or riband for a woman.*'
74. Quintus Curtius Rufus, *De los hechos del magno Alexandre rey de macedonia* (Seville: Juan Cromberger, 1534), fols 27^{r-v}.
75. p. 127.
76. pp. 615–16.
77. p. 892.
78. Francisco de Quevedo, *El Buscón*, ed. by Domingo Ynduráin, Letras Hispánicas, 124 (Madrid: Cátedra, 2001), p. 164.
79. See, for example, Jeremy Lawrance, '"Mal haya el que en señores idolatra" (1609): Poetry of Gardens and Solitude', in *A Poet for All Seasons: Eight Commentaries on Góngora*, ed. by Oliver Noble Wood and Nigel Griffin (New York: Hispanic Seminary of Medieval Studies, 2013), pp.

25–46; and Karl Vossler, *La soledad en la poesía española*, trans. by José Miguel Sacristán, 2nd edn, Biblioteca Filológica Hispana, 49 (Madrid: Visor, 2000).
80. p. 892.
81. p. 729.
82. p. 733.
83. p. 757.
84. p. 709.
85. Juan Huarte de San Juan, *Examen de ingenios para las sciencias* (Baeza: Juan Baptista de Montoya, 1594), fol. 144^r, further noting that 'los humores que hazen las carnes blandas [...] hazen los hombres simples y bobos' (the humours that make the flesh weak [...] make men simple and stupid).
86. Molho, 'Doña Sancha', p. 446.
87. pp. 892–93.
88. p. 203.
89. p. 203.
90. Quintus Curtius, *De los hechos del magno Alexandre*, fol. 37^v.
91. Bénédicte Torres, *Cuerpo y gesto en 'El Quijote' de Cervantes* (Alcalá de Henares: Centro de Estudios Cervantinos, 2002), p. 79.
92. p. 512.
93. Torres, *Cuerpo y gesto*, p. 79.
94. p. 166.
95. p. 277.
96. p. 591.
97. On forms of address used between the pair, see Helen Phipps Houck, 'Substantive Address Used between Don Quijote and Sancho Panza', *Hispanic Review*, 5 (1937), 60–72.
98. p. 730.
99. p. 165.
100. p. 165.
101. Fray Luis de Granada, *Adiciones al Memorial de la vida Cristiana* (Salamanca: Mathias Gast, 1574), p. 318.
102. p. 893.
103. *Vocabulario*, p. 234a: 'Sabido es que lo dijo un *caballero* Andrada, volviendo de abajo a don Enrique el Bueno contra su hermano el Rey don Pedro; *otros lo atribuyeron a otro*' (It is known that it was said by a knight called Andrada, as he turned Don Henry the Good from underneath against his brother, the king, Don Peter; others attributed it to someone else). Both the saying and its attribution to Fernán Pérez de Andrade are recorded in Juan de Molina, *Descripcion del Reyno de Galizia* (Mondoñedo: Agustín de Paz, 1551), fol. 49^v, and, also, with a slight variation ('[...] sino libro a mi Señor'), in Gonzalo Argote de Molina, *Nobleza del Andaluzia* (Seville: Fernando Díaz, 1588), fol. 110^v. By contrast, for example, Jerónimo Zurita does not record the saying, and identifies the third party as the Viscount of Roquebertin, in *Los cinco libros postreros de la primera parte de los Anales de la Corona de Aragón* (Zaragoza: Juan de Lanaja y Quartanet, 1610), fol. 354^v. In his account, Pedro López de Ayala makes no mention of any decisive third party intervention, and thus records no saying either, in *La cronica del rey do[n] pedro* (Toledo: Remon de Petras, 1526), fols 132^v–34^r.
104. See note to Cervantes, *El ingenioso Don Quijote de la Mancha* (1833–39), VI, 225.
105. *Romancero general*, fols 249^v–50^r.
106. The ballad was included in innumerable editions of sixteenth- and seventeenth-century anthologies; see, for example, *Cancionero de romances (Anvers, 1550): Edición, estudio, bibliografía e índices*, ed. by Antonio Rodríguez-Moñino (Madrid: Castalia, 1967), pp. 83 and 232; and Lorenzo de Sepúlveda, *Cancionero de romances (Sevilla, 1584): Edición, estudio, bibliografía e índices*, ed. by Antonio Rodríguez-Moñino (Madrid: Castalia, 1967), p. 119.
107. Roger Wright sees the 'poetic justice' of the ballad's final lines as a source of 'delighted laughter', in 'Humour in the Oral *Romancero*: How Would We Know?', *Bulletin of Hispanic Studies*, 86 (2009), 26–36 (p. 29). On Cervantes's use of elements of the ballad tradition more generally,

see, for example, Daniel Eisenberg, *Estudios cervantinos* (Barcelona: Sirmio, 1991), pp. 57–82 ('El romance visto por Cervantes'); and Julio Alonso Asenjo, 'Quijote y romances: usos y funciones', in *Historia, reescritura y pervivencia del Romancero: estudios en memoria de Amelia García-Valdecasas*, ed. by Rafael Beltrán (Valencia: Universitat de València, 2000), pp. 25–65.
108. Alonso Asenjo, 'Quijote y romances', p. 52.
109. Molho, 'Doña Sancha', pp. 445–46.
110. p. 944.
111. p. 963.
112. Madariaga, *Guía del lector*, p. 19.
113. p. 889.
114. p. 893.
115. p. 220.
116. Carroll B. Johnson, *Cervantes and the Material World* (Urbana: University of Illinois Press, 2000), p. 32.
117. See, for the former, Unamuno, *Vida de Don Quijote y Sancho*, p. 455, and, for the latter, Bienvenido Morros Mestres, 'Cervantes y la revolución cultural del Renacimiento: Acteón y don Quijote', *Anales Cervantinos*, 37 (2005), 167–77 (pp. 173–75).
118. Williamson, 'Power-Struggle', p. 857.
119. Martín de Riquer, *Para leer a Cervantes* (Barcelona: Acantilado, 2003), p. 331.

CHAPTER 3

❖

An Authorized Version? Siting Authority and Citing *auctores* in Don Quixote

Richard Rabone

The elusive nature of truth and certainty in *Don Quixote*, as real and fictional worlds leech into one another within the pages of the novel, is well chronicled. Indeed, some form of engagement with such problems follows logically from the novel's conception, as Don Quixote's apparently wholehearted belief in the truth of his chivalry books suggests the relevance of more general notions of the authority of the written or printed word as a guarantee of the truth value of the contents. Moreover, when seen in this light, such convictions are not particular to the protagonist, but are shared in some form by characters as different as the innkeeper of I. 32, for whom no lie could bear the royal imprimatur, and Basilio's humanist cousin, whose proof for his discovery of original *inventores* consists simply in the testimony of other *autores*. Yet the authority of the written word is more than a matter of its truth value, as the legitimizing sanction of textual authority may be invoked as justification either for belief or for action. Indeed, such a distinction is suggested by the innkeeper himself, for whom the anachronistic irrelevance of chivalric matters is no impediment to believing them true, but does imply that their value as a model for action which authorizes a particular mode of conduct is now nil.[1] This is of course precisely the use Don Quixote makes of his reading, routinely claiming legitimacy for his actions by the old rhetorical technique of citing prestigious *auctores*; but his use of that technique inevitably backfires, and his repeated appeals to textual precedent only serve to draw our attention to the ludicrous illegitimacy of his actions, grounded as they are in texts whose relevance and truth value are routinely undermined. However, while it is thus suggested by the novel's declared purpose of chivalric parody, the rhetorical strategy of imparting *auctoritas* by adducing *auctores* is not limited to Don Quixote's reliance on chivalric romance; instead, that strategy underpins a significant aspect of Cervantes's parodic art, as the text repeatedly gestures towards various potential sources of authority while in the same breath obliquely questioning their validity. That playful dynamic of Cervantes's treatment of *auctoritas* is my focus in this chapter, which begins by outlining the heritage of the concept and its easy relevance to the novel's declared purpose, before examining three areas of the novel where some claim to authority might ordinarily be expected: the preliminaries to the text in which the innkeeper placed his trust, focusing especially on the prologue; speeches or exchanges where the speaker is intending to persuade; and the margins of the page, which the prologue suggested might be filled with the names of *auctores* cited in the text, but which harbour instead the doubting words of those who transmit Don Quixote's tale.[2]

The above outline relies implicitly on distinguishing two kinds of authority, following A. J. Minnis's discussion of the medieval notion of *auctoritas*, a term which referred either to an abstract sense of the veracity or sagacity of an author's writings, or to concrete references and quotations from a particular *auctor*.[3] Similar logic underpins rhetoricians' discussion of the concept, which refers both to the weight of legitimacy which a prestigious figure can lend, and to the citation of particular precedents and examples.[4] Yet these species of *auctoritas* are closely related, since the purpose of invoking particular *auctores* will often be to claim in a new context precisely that abstract sense of veracity which the original was seen to possess; it is Cervantes's interest in disrupting this dynamic which this chapter seeks to explore. However, the concept's classical and rhetorical heritage should not imply that Cervantes's interest in it is an abstruse or particularly technical one; instead, it may be seen to grow naturally from the mechanics of the novel's chivalric parody, while attention to the treatment of chivalric authorities will also provide important guidance for the novel's wider engagement with *auctoritas*.

The relevance of authority to the romances of chivalry is clearly indicated by their obsession with provenance, as the fiction of historicity which they so frequently peddle may be seen as a device designed to claim Minnis's more abstract sense of authority, exploiting the trappings of historical presentation in order to authenticate implausible and miraculous content.[5] Cervantes's parody then relies on Don Quixote assuming that those legitimizing strategies are successful, and that chivalry books thus constitute a true record of the feats of illustrious knights errant. Since he does see these texts as authoritative, Don Quixote is free to take them as the basis for his worldview, and as a result he will regularly assess the validity of what he sees around him by reference to chivalric precedent; in other words, the authority (in the abstract sense) of textual authorities is required for the evidence of his senses to be validated, and may trump it where the two kinds of evidence conflict. It is thus his inability to cite chivalric authorities for the manner of his 'enchanted' journey in a purpose-built cage which leads him to doubt the validity of his experience, while the guiding principle of the scheming *duques* is of course to ensure that their actions conform to his revered textual precedents.[6] These appeals to chivalric authority may take various forms, from Don Quixote's imitation of exemplary figures to his references to *autores* he has read, but all are essentially designed to transfer that abstract guarantee of validity which is the currency of reputable authors, and which Don Quixote finds in the historical pose of chivalric fiction. Both kinds of *auctoritas* outlined by Minnis are thus implicitly suggested by Cervantes's parody and Don Quixote's madness, and it comes as little surprise that these species of authority, and the relationship between them, should occupy a substantial portion of the author's attention over the course of the work.[7]

However, neither kind of authority is allowed to function straightforwardly in Cervantes's pages. If Montalvo and his ilk suggested a raft of authentication strategies which gesture towards validating impossible feats as a matter of historical record, Cervantes exploits those same techniques to undermine the authority of his narrative. The clearest example of this is once again the text's supposed provenance, as the image of a venerable manuscript requiring translation, familiar (for example) from the prologue to *Amadís de Gaula*, gives way instead to a text written in Arabic script by a Moorish historian mistrusted by his own hero, translated on the hoof for an excitable *segundo autor*, and ultimately edited by a shadowy figure whom we are permitted only to glimpse. The various layers of Cervantes's narratorial construct thus echo the authentication strategies of chivalric romance, yet here those narrative voices instead form a 'mutual discrediting society' whose various criticisms and inadequacies serve only to raise doubts about the validity of the tale they transmit. In effect, then, Don Quixote's tale has no author of renown to impart authority, but a collection of unreliable narrative voices who query rather than reinforce the text's authenticity.[8] Moreover, this unstable provenance is never far from the reader's mind, thanks to the various interventions of the different narrative voices in the text, and the omnipresent tag 'cuenta la historia que' ('the history says that'): this phrase and its variants are regularly used as a way of getting the narrative underway in a new chapter, but Willis has shown that they also represent an implicit claim to the text's underlying historical authenticity, as equivalent phrases do in chivalric romance, and very possibly also in Arabic historiography.[9] The consistent use of an authority formula such as this to cite a history whose own authority is undermined at every turn thus forms a constant, ironic reminder of its dubious validity.

If the abstract *auctoritas* of *Don Quixote* is thus fatally undermined, our second kind of authority fares no better, as appeals to chivalric *autores* are not always as secure as might be hoped, and often fall foul of at least one of two recurring problems: inaccuracies in the reference, and implausible misapplication. Don Quixote thus finds himself blithely untroubled by details such as an author's name, content to refer instead to 'un autor secreto, y de no poco crédito' (I. 15, 178) ('an anonymous author of no small credit'),[10] openly invoking the authoritative reputation of an author he cannot even identify, in relation to a tale which is not readily corroborated. If citing authorities is designed to persuade others of the validity of your case, this kind of mangled reference has the opposite effect, and speaks perhaps of a rattled Don Quixote in the aftermath of his drubbing by muleteers, groping for some precedent for his painful and dishonourable suffering. A similar disregard for precision in these matters is nicely displayed after his encounter with the Basque, as Don Quixote flies into a rage on seeing the damage to his helmet, and swears to live sparely until winning vengeance, in the manner of the Marquis of Mantua:

> Yo hago juramento [...] de hacer la vida que hizo el grande marqués de Mantua cuando juró de vengar la muerte de su sobrino Valdovinos, que fue de no comer pan a manteles, ni con su mujer folgar, y otras cosas que, aunque dellas no me

acuerdo, las doy aquí por expresadas, hasta tomar entera venganza del que tal desaguisado me fizo. (I. 10, 126–27)

(I swear [...] that I will lead the life led by the great Marquis of Mantua when he swore to avenge his nephew Baldwin's death, and until then 'ne'er at table to eat bread nor with his wife to lie', and other such things that, although I cannot remember them now, can be taken as spoken, until I have exacted full vengeance on the perpetrator of this outrage.)[11]

Here it is the content of the oath which escapes Don Quixote, but no matter: we can be sure that it must be the right type of thing to do, because of the man who did it, and doubtless our protagonist is confident he will remember the missing actions in time to perform them in due course. The unconcerned inaccuracy in this reference may perhaps be read as a smiling comment on the novel's protagonist, delicately drawing our attention to the extent of his uncritical zeal in these matters of heroism: imitating the actions of the Marquis in a loosely similar situation is a good course of action regardless of what that involves in detail, simply because his authoritative precedent makes it an appropriately heroic thing to do. However, as Sancho immediately points out, the situation is not really similar enough for the reference to be appropriate at all, since Don Quixote has already given his word that he will do his foe no further harm, provided the Basque presents himself to Dulcinea, as promised; he has already forsworn further vengeance. These examples thus alert us to two important ways in which such recourse to corroborating textual authorities may be undermined: by inaccurate citation or attribution of the material, and by employing it in a new situation where its relevance is questionable. However, neither of these issues is particular to chivalric material, since both are also discussed in rhetorical treatments of *auctoritas*, while the example of the Marquis of Mantua has already brought us away from strictly chivalric figures and onto ballad lore. Accordingly, I now turn away from the material of chivalric romance, to examine in more detail how this concept of *auctoritas*, so closely bound up in the logic of Cervantes's parody, is treated in other contexts, briefly outlining its position in rhetoric before analysing its deployment in the 1605 prologue, in speeches of persuasion, and in the margins of the Cave of Montesinos.

The essentials of the concept are concisely summarized by Lausberg, and confirm what has already been deduced from Cervantes's text: the reference cited as an *auctoritas* must be external material not directly arising from the case at hand, which lends a persuasive sense of impartiality and universal appeal; the speaker must then work to establish its relevance, precisely in order to forestall the kind of applicability objection which Sancho raised to Don Quixote's material on the Marquis of Mantua.[12] Properly speaking, the *auctor* cited should also be an expert in the relevant discipline, as Petrus Hispanus makes clear in his *Summulae Logicales*: 'Auctoritas, ut hic sumitur, est iudicium sapientis in scientia sua' (v. 36) ('As used here, "authority" is the judgment of an expert about his field').[13] However, while this reinforces the importance of the applicability criterion in another sense, since authors by implication should only be cited as authorities in their own specialist areas ('in scientia sua'), we may begin to see here the relevance of another facet of *auctoritas*: prestige. These experts are not found persuasive simply because of their clear articulation of a truth; rather, their judgement carries weight because of their perceived expertise, as the prestige of their expert reputation bolsters the case they are called in to support. An extreme form of such persuasion by prestige is recorded by Petrarch, in a letter which recalls an altercation sparked by his own partially critical view of Cicero: his interlocutor's reverence for Cicero's reputation simply brooked no criticism, leading Petrarch to claim that in his case, 'authority usurped the place of reasoning.'[14] Importantly, such phrasing is not uncommon, and recalls Quintilian's prominent statement of *auctoritas* as one criterion for good Latinity, where the prestige of the model is again decisive, and answers any rational quibble over linguistic correctness:

> Auctoritas ab oratoribus vel historicis peti solet [...] cum summorum in eloquentia virorum iudicium pro ratione, et vel error honestus sit magnos duces sequentibus. (*Institutio Oratoria* I. 6, 2)
>
> (Authority is generally sought from orators and historians. [...] This is because the judgement of the supreme orators replaces Reason, and even error is honourable if it comes from following such great guides.)[15]

Though Quintilian is here discussing correct speech rather than argumentative technique, the appeal to *auctoritas* functions similarly in both cases, being external evidence whose persuasive appeal can bypass reason and convince by the prestige of its source. Yet despite its persuasive power, such a technique is clearly open to exploitation and parody, in exactly the ways advertised for us in Don Quixote's garbled references, above: by creating doubt about the value of the supposedly prestigious source, or about its relevance to the case at hand. Cervantes's playful undermining of Don Quixote's chivalric authorities thus strikes at the heart of their persuasive power as defined by the rhetorical logic of *auctoritas*, and we should expect these twin targets of the source and applicability of a reference to repay scrutiny in non-chivalric contexts too.

However, the inaccuracy or otherwise of such references does not only affect their own persuasive force in buttressing a specific argument; rather, just as Don Quixote's inaccuracies prompted reflections on his character and mood, above, a tendency to handle these references confidently or haphazardly will similarly affect our perception of the speaker. In rhetorical terms, this is *ēthos*: a broad impression of the speaker's character and ability which, if favourable, will render that speaker's arguments more convincing; a sure-footedness in selecting and presenting the kind of authorities that will convince a particular audience is one way in which this positive impression of competence may be built.[16] Nor are formal citations from acknowledged authors the only technique which follows this logic, as Quintilian's discussion of *auctoritas* allows for proverbs to be cited as authorities in a comparable way, defining the *auctoritas* as:

> si quid ita visum gentibus, populis, sapientibus viris, claris civibus, inlustribus poetis referri potest. Ne haec quidem vulgo dicta et recepta persuasione populari sine usu fuerint. (*Institutio Oratoria* V. 11, 36–37)

(opinions which can be attributed to nations, peoples, wise men, distinguished citizens, or famous poets. Even common sayings and popular beliefs may be useful.)

This is clearly reflected in *Don Quixote*, where the authority of proverbs as *sentencias* is acknowledged at least four times.[17] Moreover, the important applicability criterion remains in play here, as Sancho is repeatedly admonished for *refranes* which do not quite fit the situation at hand:

> y si no me acuerdo mal, otra vez te he dicho que los refranes son sentencias breves, sacadas de la experiencia y especulación de nuestros antiguos sabios, y el refrán que no viene a propósito antes es disparate que sentencia. (II. 67, 1287)
>
> (and if I remember correctly I've told you on other occasions that proverbs are brief maxims, derived from the experience and speculation of the wise men of former times, but the proverb that isn't relevant isn't a maxim but an absurdity.)[18]

When cited as supporting evidence, proverbs and attributed references should thus be seen as two sides of the same coin, as both are capable of bringing that persuasive, abstract kind of *auctoritas*, but both also remain vulnerable to inaccurate or inappropriate citation. In part this is of course a matter of decorum: proverbial wisdom is the everyday equivalent of the revered *auctores* whom Don Quixote might have read but Sancho will not know, and for a speech to be persuasive it must be appropriate to the speaker, as well as to its audience and its time and place.[19] Yet it also, I suggest, hinges on a question of familiarity: as a proverb is repeatedly spoken and endorsed as true, it acquires a kind of familiarity which predisposes a listener to agree, just as the prestigious name of an Aristotle or a Cicero does with references attributed to them. Familiarity may thus do duty for prestige, which suggests an important caveat in the case of unattributed references to *auctores*: the lack of attribution may undermine the appeal, as was the case with Don Quixote's 'autor secreto'; but where the doctrine alluded to has effectively acquired the currency of a proverb, then that familiarity may ensure that it retains its persuasive appeal even if the source goes unmentioned, as we will see below. This, then, is the guidance offered by rhetoric and by Don Quixote's chivalric authorities: we expect references which are cited as supporting evidence to be drawn from outside the immediate situation, and their persuasive force will often reside in the prestige of the source or the familiarity of the reference itself. Proverbs and reputable authors alike may be invoked in these terms, but the speaker must take special care when establishing their relevance to the situation, and when attributing a reference to its source, since missteps in those two areas are liable to undermine both the speaker's own authority and the immediate success of any attempt to persuade.

The 1605 prologue is a masterpiece in undermining and displacing *auctoritas*. Any expectation that the censors' declarations and royal privilege would allow the preliminaries even to masquerade as a site of authority guaranteeing the truth of the novel's content is radically undermined by the prologue, and the rhetorical logic of *auctoritas* is serially exploited to that end.[20] The clearest anti-authority strategy is of course the fiction of the friend, as the author affects an inability to compose, denying us the definitive reflection on the completed text which prologues often supply, and passing responsibility for it to a third party. Yet this is in itself an ideal introduction to the authority problems caused by the multiple and untrustworthy narrators, outlined above: as Salvador J. Fajardo has shown in a valuable study, the prologue's structure of a short, framed narrative laced with critical commentary on the task of writing prefigures the novel as a whole, with its untrustworthy narrative layers which interrupt the narrative to pass comment on the text.[21] Moreover, the friend is effectively quoted as an external authority, but there is no prestige whatsoever in this unknown and anonymous figure; instead, the prologue's author purports to accept his words because of their convincing logic:

> Con silencio grande estuve escuchando lo que mi amigo me decía, y de tal manera se imprimieron en mí sus razones, que, sin ponerlas en disputa, las aprobé por buenas y de ellas mismas quise hacer este prólogo. (I. Prólogo, 19)
>
> (I listened in profound silence to what my friend said, and his words so stamped themselves on my mind that I accepted them without any argument and decided to use them for this prologue.)[22]

Yet the friend's advice is clearly fraudulent, and is revealed as such by its flouting of the logic of *auctoritas*, as we will see, while Fajardo has argued that this slippery approval of the friend's words as 'buenas', which looks like an endorsement of the truth of his account, really only commits to endorsing their value as material for this prologue.[23] This sophistic approval of patently dubious and apparently external advice thus serves to introduce the playful undermining of authority that so pervades the novel, as Cervantes hints at where we might expect to find such authority while simultaneously undermining its claim, giving with one hand but taking away with the other.

Nor is the friend the only figure to whom authority is teasingly or fraudulently passed in this way. The prologue also claims to empower the reader, granting a king-like authority to make an independent judgement of the text, yet even that regal authority is undermined in the same breath:

> y estás en tu casa, donde eres señor della, como el rey de sus alcabalas, y sabes lo que comúnmente se dice, que 'debajo de mi manto, al rey mato', todo lo cual te esenta y hace libre de todo respeto y obligación, y, así, puedes decir de la historia todo aquello que te pareciere, sin temor que te calunien por el mal ni te premien por el bien que dijeres della. (I. Prólogo, 10)
>
> (and you are sitting in your own home, where you are the lord and master just as much as the king is of his taxes, and you know that common saying, 'Under my cloak a fig for the king'. All of which exempts you and frees you from every respect and obligation, and so you can say whatever you like about this history, without any fear of being attacked for a hostile judgement or rewarded for a favourable one.)[24]

While the proverb quoted would ordinarily reinforce this gift of authority, implying that everyone is free to make whatever judgements they see fit, the context of that regal authority of judgement hints that the reader's role may be closer to the king than the insurgent; the fate of the proverb's king then becomes an oblique note of caution which implicitly limits the authority of the reader, whose judgement may not quite be exercised with impunity after all.[25] It is this suggestive but evasive balancing act that the prologue really alerts us to, purporting to present the reader and the friend as figures of authority able to pass judgement on the text, the latter even being cited as a source of authoritative comment on it; yet neither's authority is secure, as further voices in Cervantes's slippery text instantly give the lie to that portrayal.

However, we may go still further. We noted above that such authority as is claimed for the friend rests not on his prestige or prior reputation, but on the apparent endorsement of his words in 'las aprobé por buenas'. Any assessment of his authority must therefore assess the content of his advice, at the heart of which is cynical counsel to exploit the logic of *auctoritas*. Indeed, the original speaker himself frames the friend's intervention in these terms, by claiming that the lamented lack of marginal notes, endnotes, and indexed authors, which bear witness to erudition in other works, all remain absent in *Don Quixote* precisely because of an inability to cite *autores*, and much of the friend's reply is focused on what is here identified as an underlying common cause:

> De todo esto [quotations and annotations of various kinds] ha de carecer mi libro, porque ni tengo qué acotar en el margen, ni qué anotar en el fin, *ni menos sé qué autores sigo en él*, para ponerlos al principio, como hacen todos. (I. Prólogo, 12; my emphasis)
>
> (There won't be any of this in my book, because I haven't anything to put in the margins or any notes for the end, still less do I know what authors I have followed in my text so as to list them at the beginning, as others do.)[26]
>
> yo me hallo incapaz de remediarlas, por mi insuficiencia y pocas letras, y porque naturalmente soy poltrón y perezoso de andarme buscando autores que digan lo que yo me sé decir sin ellos. (I. Prólogo, 13)
>
> (I'm not up to it, because of my inadequacy and my scanty learning, and because I'm naturally lazy and disinclined to go hunting for authors to say for me what I know how to say without them.)[27]

This is of course typically read as Cervantes taking a stand against the indiscriminate citation that often adorns other prologues in a parade of pointless (and frequently second-hand) erudition, while the friend's unashamedly cynical techniques for countering this lack of *autores* may be seen as a continuation of such criticism, implying that those who do follow that path are engaged in a manipulative sham. Those techniques, however, merit scrutiny, since they respond directly to the root cause of the speaker's problems: all these vaunted trappings of erudition rely on having citations of *autores* to refer to. Moreover, while clearly meretricious, the friend's strategies are not easily dismissed out of hand, but rather represent in some respects a cynical *tour de force*, revealing a genuine vulnerability in the logic of *auctoritas* even as we are moved to reject his advice.

It is clear enough that the friend is thinking in these terms himself, as he explains the benefit of listing cited authors using a textbook definition of the relationship between abstract and specific *auctoritas*: 'y cuando no sirva de otra cosa, por lo menos servirá aquel largo catálogo de autores a dar de improviso autoridad al libro' (I. Prólogo, 18) ('Even if it serves no other purpose, your long list will at least lend your book an instant air of authority').[28] However, throughout his speech he shows a flagrant disregard for the two potential dangers identified earlier as a risk to persuasive power: inaccurate attributions and references that do not really fit the situation at hand. His promised endnotes thus rely on only the most tangential kind of relevance to the content of the narrative, as the appearance of any giant is reason enough for the text to be emended to Goliath, allowing the notes to be filled with banalities which, since they are specific to Goliath, cannot logically bear much relevance to a context where his appearance was so arbitrarily engineered. That particular note then concludes with a deliciously incomplete Bible reference, as the friend will not stoop to looking up the authors that he cites: '"según se cuenta en el libro de los Reyes", en el capítulo que vos halláredes que se escribe' (I. Prólogo, 16) ('"according to what is narrated in the Book of Kings," in the chapter where you'll find it written').[29] Indeed, it is in attributing his references that the friend most frequently flouts the principles of *auctoritas*, as he is made to refer surprisingly to Virgil's Circe and not Homer's, after Virgil had all but written her out of the *Aeneid*, and incongruously to attribute an (admittedly harmless) Ovidian couplet to Cato, an author who could scarcely be more different in spirit.[30] Once again, these cited authors thus represent sites of authority that are gestured towards but simultaneously undermined. However, the cardinal example of this burlesque of *auctoritas* is the treatment of the Latin tag 'Non bene pro toto libertas venditur auro' ('Freedom should not be sold for all the gold in the world'),[31] which any kind of discussion of freedom and captivity is sufficient justification to include, and which is deceitfully attributed as follows: 'Y luego, en el margen, citar a Horacio, o a quien lo dijo' (I. Prólogo, 15) ('And then, in the margin, you mention Horace or whoever it was that said it').[32] In using the margin to record (and so draw attention to) his source's prestigious name, the friend's advice fits the normal logic of *auctoritas*, but his sublimely unconcerned 'o a quien lo dijo' only serves to highlight the inaccuracy of his reference to Horace, with a final twist to come in the following sentence, where Horace is indeed quoted — but, ironically, not named. As we expect, these obviously haphazard references and the friend's utter lack of any scruples affect his *ēthos*, helping forge an image of an untrustworthy huckster whose tactics we fancy we can see through. Yet what is really interesting here is that while that picture of the friend is a true one, he does nonetheless have something of a point. The above analysis of rhetorical background suggested that when notable *auctores* are cited to bolster a case, it is really the prestige of the name that does the heavy lifting of persuasion. The friend's position is a *reductio ad absurdum* of that legitimate position, revealing for us a vulnerability in its logic: the role played by the source's reputation is an important insight into how these references actually manage to persuade, but it also suggests how the technique might be abused, to persuade people of nonsense by a false or specious reference attributed to an authoritative 'source'. We may well see through the friend's specific suggestions in the examples he offers; indeed, we are surely supposed to, given how the Horatian misattribution is dwelt on, and it is important that we are not taken in by his deceit if we are to form a clear view of his cynical character. Yet that is a matter of the specific references in question and does not imply that a similar strategy could not be pursued more subtly and with greater success; the onus is after all entirely on the audience or the reader to catch any such misattributed or misapplied references. For all that we judge him negatively, then, and his lazy attributions undermine him, the friend's advice nonetheless reveals an important potential risk in rhetoric's focus on an *auctor*'s prestige, as Cervantes counsels caution in scrutinizing authorities.

This more nuanced position also fits well with the earlier suggestion that the friend's advice is designed to recall other authors' proemial strategies: such displays of erudition are potentially a powerful tool for bolstering the writer's authority, as the popular strategy is built on sound rhetorical logic; yet the only thing preventing easier, counterfeit erudition from garnering similar authority for a writer is the reader's ability to assess such references, scorning mishandled erudition as vacuous, in the way which Cervantes's presentation of the friend suggests here. If the friend's disingenuous appropriation of legitimate rhetorical principles may thus be read as a tart comment on the practice of other authors, that may also suggest why this lengthy exploration of *auctoritas* is present in the prologue at all, since the friend himself will go on to declare that this kind of reference has no place in chivalric romance or its parody, deftly undermining his own lengthy solutions for the problem of dealing with *auctores* and rendering them, on his own terms, something of an empty sideshow. However, as well as registering Cervantes's implicit objection to other *prologuistas*, this playful deconstruction of authority also sets up one of the novel's major themes, both in its broad undermining of chivalric authority tropes, and in its specific manipulation of cited authors to similar purpose. The prologue thus marks the beginning of a wry commentary on this rhetorical trope that will be developed over the course of the novel, while also introducing an important feature of how that concept will be treated: Cervantes does not deny authority outright, but gestures towards it in places where we might expect to find it, even as he knowingly undermines that claim. This distinctive gesture of simultaneously suggesting and undermining authority is key to Cervantes's art of parody, and it is his exploitation of the logic of *auctoritas* which makes it possible, as we have seen, as the reader works to keep up with these hints over the validity of particular authority claims. In the second half of this chapter, I turn to analysis of this aspect of Cervantes's parody in two other contexts where we might also expect claims to *auctoritas*: when speaking to persuade, and in the framing of the episode of the Cave of Montesinos, which features both the translator's record of Cide Hamete's marginalia, and the humanist cousin's collation of different *auctores*.[33]

Although substantial speeches which seek to persuade by deploying the tools of forensic rhetoric are not extremely common in *Don Quixote*, isolated examples of the appeal to *auctores* are not far to seek. An ideal example of how the technique should work is provided by Lotario in his attempt to dissuade Anselmo from testing Camila's virtue: among his arguments is the claim that concern over secrecy and public disgrace is something of a false trail, because Anselmo will himself know what he has done and that private knowledge alone will be his undoing;

he then cites 'el famoso poeta Luis Tansilo' ('the famous poet Luis Tansillo') on a similar case of internal emotional torture, explicitly as supporting evidence 'para confirmación desta verdad' (I. 33, 20) ('as a confirmation of this truth').[34] Particular sources may also be of interest, as when the truth value of chivalric romance is challenged on the grounds of including giants, in response to which Don Quixote is made to cite the Bible, the ultimate textual authority, alongside evidence of bones dug up in Sicily (II. 1, 693–94); Don Quixote's sources thus branch out into new and more empirical kinds of knowledge here, an interesting development from his default position noted above, whereby chivalric texts were the ultimate arbiters of reality, and needed no further corroboration themselves. We might think too of Marcela, who directly invokes the authority of an external source when justifying her conduct, referring to familiar commonplaces on love that may be recognizably Platonic in form but might also be found persuasive by dint of simple familiarity, as we recognize an argument that will have been seen and accepted without question elsewhere: 'Y, según yo he oído decir, el verdadero amor no se divide, y ha de ser voluntario, y no forzoso' (I. 14, 167) ('And, according to what I've heard, true love can't be divided, and must be voluntary, not forced on you').[35] Moreover, her appeal to what she has 'oído decir' is a deceptively important one, since that phrase is repeated very frequently in the novel, and often serves to advertise exactly this kind of reference to corroborating external authorities. One particularly neat example is that of the Aristotelian golden mean, cited by Sancho with exactly this phrase (II. 4, 719–20), similarly without mention of Aristotle's name but with the assumption that the reference will be familiar and authoritative, just as Marcela presumes here. However, this reference to Aristotle is much more than an isolated case, and begins a more lengthy engagement with the topic in the first third of Part Two, which features a succession of arguments about courage and the concept of prudent retreat. Indeed, this succession of references demands more detailed analysis, as the flexible deployment of the mean in these chapters invites reflection both on Aristotle's doctrine itself, and on the practice of citing *auctores* in this way.

The mean is primarily relevant here in its application to the virtue of courage: for Aristotle, proper courage consists in assessing the situation at hand and responding appropriately to the dangers it presents, feeling neither more nor less than a proportionate amount of fear; excessively confident and unduly timorous reactions are both considered vices, the latter being cowardice, and the former recklessness, or temerity. It is this reckless excess which concerns us here, where insufficient fear is felt in situations which ought really to provoke it, a vice typically branded as *temeridad* or, perhaps less consistently, *atrevimiento*.[36] The mean in this sense thus begins with an assessment of the danger of a situation; however, it therefore fits easily into one of the novel's recurring narrative patterns, as adventures often begin with Don Quixote and Sancho articulating wildly different assessments of a new apparent danger, with the squire imploring his master to retreat. Their dispute about whether to take on the adventure promised by the fearful sound of the fulling-mills may stand as an example of a disagreement which is restaged many times, as Sancho denies any cowardice and tries to bring Don Quixote to the popular and biblical view he attributes to the village priest, that 'quien busca el peligro perece en él' (I. 20, 229) ('danger loved is death won').[37] Don Quixote is inevitably impervious to such attempts, precisely because his attitude to danger is radically different: though he acknowledges that the noise would terrify even Mars, it seems to cause him no fear at all, merely whetting his appetite for what he sees as a heaven-sent opportunity to prove his worth (I. 20, 227–28). The potential danger of the situation is thus tacitly acknowledged but essentially ignored, a move which clearly leaves Don Quixote susceptible to accusations of temerity, and when Sancho introduces the framework of the mean in II. 4, it should therefore be read as a straightforward development of this familiar tactic whereby aspects of the two protagonists' characters are revealed by contrasting their attitudes to danger.

What is less straightforward is that this ultimately Aristotelian framework should occur to the unlettered Sancho, a point made in a different context by the translator, who considers the very next chapter inauthentic as Sancho displays just this kind of implausibly high-level speech (II. 5, 723). Recalling the logic of *auctoritas*, the initial risk here is apparently of breaking decorum, by trying to cite an authority which others will not believe you really know, and thereby losing persuasive power as you paradoxically draw attention to your own lack of expertise. Yet Sancho seems to attempt to mitigate this by giving a more plausible attribution for this reference:

> Y más, que yo he oído decir, y creo que a mi señor mismo, si mal no me acuerdo, que entre los estremos de cobarde y de temerario está el medio de la valentía: y si esto es así, no quiero que huya sin tener para qué, ni que acometa cuando la demasía pide otra cosa. (II. 4, 719–20)
>
> (What's more, I've heard it said, by my master himself if I remember rightly, that being brave is halfway between the extremes of being a coward and being foolhardy, and if that's right I don't want him to go running away when there isn't any reason to, or attacking when the odds are hopeless.)[38]

As we expect of an *auctoritas*, the mean is not the focus of Sancho's entire speech, but one of several pieces of supporting evidence brought in to support his case for a more circumspect approach to danger, eagerly agreeing with Sansón's sly argument that Don Quixote should try to keep out of harm's way to preserve himself for aiding those who are in need. However, Sancho at no point mentions Aristotle, whose name would certainly provide the kind of prestige cynically exploited by the friend in the prologue, but whose work Sancho could hardly claim credibly to know. Instead, he uses the citation phrase we observed in Marcela's speech not in allusion to the grand original *auctor*, but to identify where he himself has learnt the idea, thus mitigating any offence to decorum and offering a plausible explanation for his apparently disconcerting spark of erudition. Yet in line with what Howard Mancing has suggested for another such appeal to what Sancho has 'oído decir', he may often fairly assume that whoever he learnt the idea from also endorsed it, and that kind of endorsement from someone Sancho considers learned must for him be analogous to the prestigious expertise of a traditional *auctor*.[39] This important citation phrase thus performs two functions here, purporting to assuage any concerns about decorum while also seeking to imply the endorsement of a figure who ought to be considered authoritative, at least as far as the speaker is concerned.

Sancho's brief reference thus engages with several aspects of the important logic of *auctoritas*. However, the picture as outlined so far is too straight-laced to tell the full story. The dual purpose of Sancho's citation phrase is important, but the reader might just suspect that Sancho is misidentifying his source here: Don Quixote's own words would be an excellent persuasive weapon to use against him, but Sancho is clearly unsure about the attribution, and Antonio Barnés Vázquez has argued that Don Quixote has said no such thing before now, and that Sancho must be recalling the Canon's discussion of excessive *temeridad* and moderate *valentía* instead.[40] It may also of course remain possible that Sancho has indeed learnt this from Don Quixote in a conversation to which we were not privy, but in any case this citation phrase, which is ordinarily used to signpost authoritative external references, is playfully manipulated here to sow seeds of doubt instead. It thus comes as no surprise that this speech fails to persuade Don Quixote to circumspection, though in truth Sancho does not press that case here: the argument for Don Quixote's prudent retreat seems to suggest to Sancho the possibility that he himself might have to fight in his master's stead, and that particular self-interest then takes over with a lengthy account of the terms of his squireship, which preclude any fighting and favour loyalty over valour; by the time he finishes, the notion of prudent courage is long forgotten. Yet this example serves to outline exactly the terms in which Cervantes treats the mean in these chapters: it is a potentially serious supporting *auctoritas* in arguments about the proper response to danger, but its persuasive force is undermined as it here gives way to burlesque comment on Sancho's knowledge and the issue of decorum; moreover, we might also suspect that this venerable ethic is being made subordinate to a more self-interested approach, which is clearest in the following discussion of rewards for Sancho's service, but surely also lies behind the zeal of his advocacy of circumspection at the beginning of the speech, for Sancho is no impassioned abstract moralist, but real danger and violence are anathema to him. All this will be playfully developed in the subsequent appearances of the mean.

The doctrine next surfaces in II. 11, as Don Quixote makes to attack the band of costumed actors in retaliation for one of their number making off with Sancho's ass, the beast now delightfully invested with the dignity of a chivalric squire's mount as Don Quixote sees in it a pretext for his attack. Sancho, however, more concerned with the danger represented by a group of men poised for a stoning, thinks retreat the wiser choice, and again has recourse to the mean in an attempt to dissuade Don Quixote from attacking:

> y también se ha de considerar que es más temeridad que valentía acometer un hombre solo a un ejército donde está la Muerte y pelean en persona emperadores, y a quien ayudan los buenos y los malos ángeles. (II. 11, 782)

> (and another thing you must bear in mind is that it's more foolhardy than brave for one man alone to attack an army that's got death on its side, as well as emperors fighting in person, and good and bad angels helping out.)[41]

Once again, the logic of the mean is playfully employed: the danger itself is quite real, but it is hardly the costumes that provide it, for all that Don Quixote might scorn the threat of sharp-edged stones. Again, too, the mean does not take centre stage here: it is exactly the kind of supplementary argument we expect for an *auctoritas*, with the familiar lexis implying at least for the reader the doctrine's weighty heritage; but Sancho advances more than one argument in his cause, and it is another which successfully convinces Don Quixote to withdraw, as he ultimately accepts that these opponents are not fitting foes for a knight errant but does not acknowledge the charge of temerity. Even in a successful speech of persuasion, then, the deployment of the mean as authority subtly questions its efficacy: we have no reason to believe that the Aristotelian logic deployed played any major role in the persuasion of Don Quixote, while a perfectly legitimate use of the argument given the danger of the situation at hand is slyly problematized by the suggestion that this danger comes from fighting with costumed angels, as the further voices in Cervantes's text gently disrupt the logic of the reference to foster an incongruity at which the reader can only smile.

A similar argument is put to Don Quixote again when he insists on challenging the lions. This time, however, its effect is not easily passed over, but lingers much longer after the initial Aristotelian reference, and Don Quixote is eventually moved to respond in kind, with unsettling implications for the doctrine itself and for the logic of *auctoritas*. Don Diego is the first to apply the concept here, in its familiar position as external evidence cited in support of a case to dissuade Don Quixote from his foolhardy challenge:

> Señor caballero, los caballeros andantes han de acometer las aventuras que prometen esperanza de salir bien dellas, y no aquellas que de todo en todo la quitan; porque la valentía que se entra en la juridición de la temeridad, más tiene de locura que de fortaleza. (II. 17, 832)
>
> (Sir knight: knights errant should undertake adventures that offer some chance of success, and not those that are utterly hopeless; because courage that crosses the border into foolhardiness has more of insanity than fortitude about it.)[42]

The reference once again goes unattributed, but the familiar lexis serves to identify the Aristotelian concept. At this stage, the argument carries no weight for Don Quixote, who rejects Don Diego's call to retreat, but without mention in his reply of the Aristotelian portion of the latter's argument. However, the idea is not simply forgotten this time, as a series of lexical echoes serve to keep the Aristotelian framework in the reader's mind throughout the episode: Cide Hamete praises Don Quixote as an 'espejo donde se pueden mirar todos los valientes del mundo' (II. 17, 835) ('mirror for all brave men in the world'),[43] a suspicious claim that might rather put us in mind of the *temeridad* to which *valentía* was contrasted in Sancho's earlier example, especially if the partisan, emotional interjection in which the historian's praise is couched already inclines the reader to distrust it; a higher narrator then labels Don Quixote an 'indignado y atrevido caballero' (II. 17, 835) ('bold and angry knight'),[44] in which we might hear notes of boldness and recklessness alike; and most significantly, the sight of the lion poking its head out of its cage is described as a 'vista y ademán para poner espanto a la misma temeridad' (II. 17, 836) ('the sight of which would have struck terror into temerity itself'),[45] perhaps leaving Don Quixote, who shows no sign of such fear, more impossibly extreme in his temerity than temerity itself. The Aristotelian logic introduced as an unsuccessful *auctoritas* thus remains relevant throughout the chapter, culminating in Don Diego and Don Quixote's different interpretations of the scene, which both apply the familiar lexis with its implicit Aristotelian framework, but come to opposite conclusions, as Don Quixote thinks he has displayed 'la verdadera valentía' (II. 17, 838) ('true valour'),[46] while Don Diego thinks his effort 'disparatado, temerario y tonto' ('absurd, foolhardy and stupid'),[47] and the height of 'temeridad' (II. 17, 838). Clearly we remain on Don Diego's side, yet there is perhaps something of a sense of the mean as a flexible concept here, whose logic can be applied in quite different ways. Indeed, Don Quixote's view does make a certain kind of sense, given that how dangerous a situation is for a given individual will partly depend on that individual's own strength and ability to respond, while Don Quixote's mad faith in the strength of his arm is unshakeable: it remains unconvincing, but there would be a logic to his position, if the impossible premise of his mad overestimation of his strength could be granted.[48] Yet even he seems aware on some level that he is misapplying Aristotle's framework here, as he is moved to offer a mitigating justification of his actions in precisely these Aristotelian terms, recognizing his temerity but pitching it as the better extreme:

> y, así, el acometer los leones que ahora acometí derechamente me tocaba, puesto que conocí ser temeridad esorbitante, porque bien sé lo que es valentía, que es una virtud que está puesta entre dos estremos viciosos, como son la cobardía y la temeridad: pero menos mal será que el que es valiente toque y suba al punto de temerario que no que baje y toque en el punto de cobarde, que así como es más fácil venir el pródigo a ser liberal que el avaro, así es más fácil dar el temerario en verdadero valiente que no el cobarde subir a la verdadera valentía. (II. 17, 840)

> (and attacking those lions a moment ago was therefore something that I had to do, even though I was well aware that it was foolhardy beyond measure, for I know what courage is, a virtue situated between two extremes, the vices of cowardice and foolhardiness; but it is less reprehensible for the man who is courageous to rise up as far as the extreme of foolhardiness than to sink down to the extreme of cowardice; for just as it is easier for the spendthrift than for the miser to be generous, so it is easier for the foolhardy man than for the coward to become a truly courageous man.)[49]

Don Quixote's words offer a classic account of this Aristotelian triad of a mean between two vices, and indeed, this suggestion that courage is closer to recklessness than to cowardice does have legitimate Aristotelian precedent; Don Quixote is thus in effect appealing to his own Aristotelian *auctoritas* in an attempt to counter the temerity charge that has dogged him throughout this encounter.[50] Yet while that heritage might certainly lend prestige, Don Quixote's use of it still surely strikes us as specious (though not malicious) special pleading, a last-ditch attempt to justify his actions that misappropriates a potentially valid concept which does not quite suit his situation: it is not at all clear, for example, what would constitute the contemptible cowardice to which the temerity of his challenging the lions would be preferable, in a situation where the obvious choice is between evidently prudent non-engagement and reckless confrontation. If attribution and applicability were the two warning areas of misguided *auctoritas*, both have now been explored in these references to Aristotle's mean, as Sancho's hesitant attribution to Don Quixote is now complemented by this misapplied haggling over the value of the knight's unthinking boldness. Yet while that haggling is partly down to the flexibility of Aristotle's individually calibrated concept, the fact that his logic can be invoked with some degree of plausibility on both sides of the argument here is perhaps a new reminder of the potential for more deceitful or unreliable invocations of authority, as the weight of prestige or familiarity which accompanies the reference is no real indication of its truth, and it is up to the audience to fend for themselves in establishing the validity of the reference.

The burlesqued golden mean then returns for its swansong in II. 28, a chapter which opens with a grand endorsement of the vital concept of prudent flight, here embodied by Don Quixote turning tail from the angry townsfolk and their firearms after Sancho's ill-advised braying. When justifying his actions, Don Quixote again has recourse to the familiar logic of the mean:

> No huye el que se retira — respondió don Quijote — , porque has de saber, Sancho, que la valentía que no se funda sobre la basa de la prudencia se llama temeridad, y las hazañas del temerario más se atribuyen a la buena fortuna que a su ánimo. (II. 28, 943)
>
> ('He who withdraws does not flee,' Don Quixote replied, 'because I would have you know, Sancho, that courage which is not based on prudence is called foolhardiness, and the achievements of the foolhardy man are more to be credited to good fortune than to his courage.')[51]

As so often, however, the details of this claim to authority only serve obliquely to undermine it. That sublime 'has de saber' is an essential marker of relative expertise, frequently used throughout the novel to lend a tone of superiority in explanations where one party knows vastly more than the other. Yet if read literally it is nonsense in this case, since we know full well that Sancho is already quite familiar with this topic, and indeed it was Sancho himself who first applied the mean to the concept of prudent flight. Don Quixote, however, rejected or ignored earlier arguments that were put to him in these terms, yet he airily advances the same logic now that it suits him, as if his position were unimpeachable. Such splendid confidence in an authority we have seen him repeatedly ignore develops still further that suspicious flexibility with which *auctores* can be cited, as II. 17 and the 1605 prologue each in their own way suggest. That flexibility offers Cervantes innumerable possibilities for parody, as the examples we have explored so frequently display that characteristic gesture of appearing to cite good and authoritative models while simultaneously causing the details and applicability of the reference subtly to undermine its claim. Moreover, it also re-emphasizes that implicit warning about *auctoritas*: if this device persuades by associated prestige, the reader must work hard to establish the validity of the reference in the ways we have seen; prestige is certainly convincing, but it is ultimately no guarantee of truth or relevance.

Cervantes's arch probing of the concept of *auctoritas* reaches its climax in the *katabasis* of the Cave of Montesinos. Critical responses to this episode have been legion, but my analysis here will focus on the relationship of the descent to its frame narrative involving the humanist cousin, and how that advances the novel's wider parody of authority.[52] However, this is not quite the same approach as we have seen so far, where external authorities are cited in supporting evidence; here, instead, the cave episode is designed to be the 'external' authority cited as evidence by others within the novel. This is most immediately true for Don Quixote himself, for whom the episode should provide trustworthy testimony on the issue which he finds most pressing, corroborating Sancho's account of Dulcinea's enchantment with the word of Montesinos himself, 'a more reputable romance authority than Sancho'.[53]

However, if this tale is supposed to offer authoritative confirmation, what is most striking about it is how utterly devoid it is of verifiably true content, as several features explored on different narrative levels provoke doubts over the episode's veracity. Within the main narrative, the various burlesque and incongruous details of Don Quixote's account all conspire to make its content seem implausible, from Montesinos's oversized rosary with its ludicrously precise bead measurements, each one the size of a specifically average ostrich egg (II. 23, 893), to the various temporal incongruities, including Don Quixote's belief that his hour-long sojourn lasted three sleepless days (II. 23, 900), and Belerma's ridiculous schedule for mourning, working a four-day week into eternity (II. 23, 898).[54] Observers of various kinds also voice their uncertainty, as Basilio's cousin and Sancho are both immediately struck by the impossibly long time Don Quixote claimed to have been away, while the Dulcinea story, so desirable for Don Quixote as authoritative proof of her enchantment, has quite the opposite effect on Sancho, confirming to him the falsity of the episode, as it corroborates an account which he knows he invented (II. 23, 901–02). The narrators of the novel are similarly preoccupied with the episode's authenticity, as the first and last words of the chapter dwell on its dubious veracity, from the chapter heading's promise of an event 'cuya imposibilidad y grandeza hace que se tenga esta aventura por apócrifa' (II. 23, 892) ('the magnitude and impossibility of which cause this adventure to be considered apocryphal'),[55] to Don Quixote's promise that Sancho will be convinced of its truth once he has only heard more details (II. 23, 904). Most deliciously of all, the translator claims to record Cide Hamete's own marginalia to the story; yet if margins are potentially a place for recording sources and thereby bolstering authority, these instead contain a (remarkably long) account of Cide Hamete's scepticism over the truth of the episode just related, as the historian insouciantly washes his hands of any responsibility for judging the truth of what he has recorded (II. 24, 904–05). The Cave of Montesinos is thus a tale conceived as a source of authority and unusually adorned with paratextual comment, yet at every turn that authority is undermined, as all those who encounter the story immediately struggle to believe it as true.

The most prominent doubters, however, are Don Quixote and Sancho themselves, and the fact that this doubt continues to gnaw at them means that we return to the issue of the cave's dubious veracity at several points during Part Two. Don Quixote's impressive speech to the page heading for war moves Sancho to draw a private contrast with the 'disparates imposibles' (II. 24, 912) ('crazy nonsense')[56] of the cave episode, while his doubts are made public when he voices them to Don Quixote and they together seek clarification from Maese Pedro's monkey (II. 25, 922). Don Quixote continues to dwell on the issue, and Sancho to disbelieve the tale, before the adventure of the enchanted boat (II. 29, 948), and it still preys on the knight's mind while he and Sancho are staying with the Duke and Duchess (II. 34, 1003), by which time the Duchess has craftily persuaded Sancho to believe his own lie about Dulcinea, leading him instantly to reassess the truth of the cave episode too (II. 33, 993). The sense that belief in the tale is difficult to justify and has to be negotiated is reconfirmed by the pact offered by Don Quixote after the 'flight' astride Clavileño (II. 41, 1055), while doubts continue to worry him at least long enough for him to seek further inconclusive corroboration from a second false oracle in the talking head that belongs to Don Antonio Moreno (II. 62, 1245). The question of the cave's authenticity is thus raised frequently and clearly bothers the protagonists, yet it is never resolved, and even the phrasing of Don Quixote's supposed retraction of the story on his deathbed is so indirect and oblique that it is hard to think it any more credible than empty hearsay, especially since it forms part of Cide Hamete's abdication of responsibility over the truth of the cave episode, a tacit suggestion perhaps that Cide Hamete may have little faith in this retraction himself.[57] An encounter that was supposed to provide Don Quixote with authoritative answers is thus consistently thrown into doubt over the course of Part Two, as the cave could scarcely be a site of weaker authority.

Don Quixote is not the only figure to rely on this impossibly weakened testimony, as the cave episode is cited as a legitimate authority by the humanist cousin who serves as their guide; its use as an *auctoritas* thus represents one way in which the descent itself is yoked to the wider narrative. However, by including it in his book, the cousin implicitly endorses the truth of the episode against all the above evidence, and this uncritical willingness to seek out and endorse such unreliable and useless knowledge inevitably reflects negatively on his character; as a result, his presence is often read as a means for Cervantes to attack the vogue for fruitless erudition and simple credence in classical mythology, or an extension of the criticism of pedantic learning first voiced in the 1605 prologue.[58] However, the use of the Montesinos episode as a source for the cousin's scholarship also provides the *coup de grâce* in the parodic burlesque of *auctoritas*, with which I bring this exploration of authority to a close.

Details from Don Quixote's descent find their way into two of the cousin's projects: his *Ovidio español*, and his supplement to Polydore Vergil's *De Inventoribus Rerum*. The former is effectively concerned with aetiology, providing a ludicrously overblown mythological back-story for 'notable, and notably mundane, Spanish landmarks', here via the invented lore of the lamenting Guadiana, and Ruidera with her daughters and nieces, whose tears saw them metamorphosed by Merlin into the bodies of water still visible nearby.[59] It is in the *Suplemento*, however, that Cervantes's parodic purpose really comes into its own. This reference to the work of a humanist compiler is usually seen as a way of satirizing that kind of humanist project, poking fun at the ultimately futile learning on display in the work of Polydore Vergil, Pedro Mexía, and others of their ilk, by having the cousin take the same approach but with patently fatuous material.[60] Yet the potential legitimacy of the project is perhaps subtler than this, while I suggest that the relevance of Polydore Vergil's work lies less in it being a compilation *per se*, and more in what that implies about the nature of the evidence it cites. The cousin's own account of his project sees it designed to complement its forebear, by adding in the material 'de gran sustancia' ('matters of substance')[61] which Polydore Vergil had omitted, as follows:

> Olvidósele a Virgilio de declararnos quién fue el primero que tuvo catarro en el mundo, y el primero que tomó las unciones para curarse del morbo gálico, y yo lo declaro al pie de la letra, y lo autorizo con más de veinte y cinco autores, porque vea vuesa merced si he trabajado bien y si ha de ser útil el tal libro a todo el mundo. (II. 22, 887)
>
> (Polydore Virgil forgot to tell us who was the first person in the world to catch a cold, and the first person to use ointment to treat the pox, and I give precise details about all this, and substantiate them with references to more than twenty-five authorities; so you can see how hard I've worked, and how useful the book will be to everyone.)[62]

These examples hardly seem to be the matters of substance we were promised, offering instead a ridiculously trivial version of a potentially legitimate project, though we are perhaps also prompted to reflect on what the genuine criteria for inclusion in such compilations might be: the first 'catarro' sounds impossibly trivial, yet there is plenty of triviality in Polydore Vergil's original; similarly, while ointments for venereal disease seem unlikely material on which to seek notable *auctores*, we might recall that syphilis was a theme on which Fracastoro wrote three books of hexameter verse, with a section on remedies that does at least touch on a role for ointments.[63] The key here, however, is what these lines tell us about the nature of this compilation's criterion of proof: like Polydore Vergil's own work, it is essentially a catalogue of citations, as the testimony of earlier authors is the sole strategy for authentication. The cousin's own presentation of his work might thus suggest that its method is at least as relevant as its content, as the format of a collection of legitimizing *auctores* provides the perfect context for this parodic undermining of *auctoritas*.

Challenges to this mode of authorization come quickly and from various corners. Sancho's immediate questions about the first man to scratch his head, and the identity of the first acrobat, are so ridiculously pedestrian that they have not yet crossed the cousin's path, yet while he promises to seek the answer to the second query once he is reunited with his revered books, the testimony of those *auctores* is instantly rendered otiose as Sancho answers both questions on the strength of his own powers of logic. The *Suplemento*'s authority-based methodology is thus implicitly undermined at once, as the cousin proceeds to endorse Sancho's answers, obviating the need for his *auctores* (II. 22, 887–88). Sancho's quick replies also catch Don Quixote's attention, and lead him to a withering assessment of the hours of wasted effort which other methods of proof often require, even in the validation of inconsequential trivia:

> Más has dicho, Sancho, de lo que sabes — dijo don Quijote — , que hay algunos que se cansan en saber y averiguar cosas que después de sabidas y averiguadas no importan un ardite al entendimiento ni a la memoria. (II. 22, 888)

> ('You have spoken a greater truth, Sancho, than you realize,' Don Quixote said, 'for there are some people who weary themselves discovering facts that, once discovered, are of no use whatsoever either to the understanding or to the memory.')[64]

In context, and especially as a response to Sancho's statement that he is well capable of dealing with such trivial matters himself without seeking others' opinions (II. 22, 888), we are naturally put in mind of the cousin's method once again, with the hours of trawling through sources it entails, in pursuit of exactly the kind of useless information which Don Quixote and Sancho have in mind here. Yet if we are therefore suspicious of the cousin's employment of *auctoritas* from the outset, it is his reaction to Don Quixote's account which most spectacularly undermines him, drawing our attention to the credulous process of his book's composition.

The feature of Don Quixote's tale which the cousin picks out for the *Suplemento* is Durandarte's response to Merlin's prophecy:

> — Y cuando así no sea [sc. should Don Quixote not fulfil the prophecy] — respondió el lastimado Durandarte con voz desmayada y baja — , cuando así no sea, ¡oh primo!, digo, paciencia y barajar. (II. 23, 898)

> ('And if not,' replied the afflicted Durandarte, in a faint and feeble voice, 'if not, cousin: shuffle the pack and deal again, you never know your luck.')[65]

In itself, this is another of the tonal incongruities present throughout the account, as the noble Durandarte employs a phrase more suited to a tavern gambler to express his doubt that Merlin's prophecy about Don Quixote will come to fruition; moreover, the phrase which the cousin will cite as his *auctoritas* is thus originally used not to build authority but to undermine it, questioning the prophecy of the supposedly infallible Merlin.[66] The cousin, however, is more taken with the phrase's semantic field, assuming it to be evidence that such card games were current in Durandarte's time and announcing that it therefore fills an important gap in Polydore Vergil's compilation. Once again, there is a certain sense to this: Polydore Vergil does indeed have a lengthy section on gambling and games of chance, among which he includes 'chartae lusoriae' (playing cards) as an example (II. 13, 14), but without giving details of the first to play cards specifically; the cousin's apparent discovery would not necessarily be an irrelevant one, then, on Polydore Vergil's own terms. Yet the cousin ludicrously overplays his findings, which he sees as important not only because of their omission from Polydore Vergil, but also because of the prestige of his source — to which any purveyor of authorities should be alert:

> creo que en el suyo no se acordó de poner la de los naipes, como la pondré yo ahora, que será de mucha importancia, y más alegando autor tan grave y tan verdadero como es el señor Durandarte. (II. 24, 906)

(I do believe that he didn't remember to include the beginnings of playing cards in his book, so I shall include the subject in mine, and it will be a matter of great importance, and even more so adducing an authority as weighty and reliable as Sir Durandarte.)[67]

Moreover, if this claim that a model hero could serve as a guarantor of truth were not risible enough in a novel founded on the folly of taking the accounts of such heroes literally, the issue of dubious *auctores* is carried still further as the cousin comes piquantly close to establishing Don Quixote himself as the source, acknowledging that the entry to his supplement rests not simply on the authority of Durandarte, but on 'las palabras que vuesa merced dice que dijo Durandarte' (II. 24, 906) ('the words that you say Durandarte said').[68] The cousin's project on *inventio*, cataloguing inventors on the authority of printed *auctores*, is thus made to rely on the unlikely testimony of a fictional *auctor* as reported by Don Quixote himself, the novel's most extreme example of the dangers of believing the wrong authors, in a scene whose authenticity is repeatedly undermined, being at worst not *inventio* but baseless invention. Problems of context and attribution combine here as the cousin's utterly uncritical approach to *auctores* marks the climax of Cervantes's parodic engagement with this rhetorical concept, as he is only too happy to include in his compilation an *auctoritas* that is rigorously and ostentatiously stripped of all authority.

Throughout this study, what has stood out above all else is the playful nature of Cervantes's engagement with these issues. Prompted by certain features of its starting point of chivalric parody, the novel probes some potentially serious epistemological questions, from the value of the written or printed word as a guarantee of truth, to the nature of persuasive appeals to external authorities, and the ways in which such appeals can be misused; yet these questions are treated with a delicate touch and an evident delight in the self-undermining complexity of these references, as particular appeals to an external *auctoritas* do not bring the abstract, legitimizing sense of authority we expect. However, all of this takes on more personal and immediate importance with the appearance of Avellaneda's rival chronicle, a new potential source of textual authority which poses a challenge both for Don Quixote and for his author. In response comes a new, positive intent to reinforce authority, establishing Cide Hamete as the chronicler of the true Don Quixote and exposing the rival character as a fraud. That brings a new set of authentication strategies, from Don Quixote's attempt to produce empirical proof of the falsity of Avellaneda's version by his resolve never to enter Zaragoza, *contra* the rival chronicler's claim that he had (II. 59, 1217–18), to textual authority of a different kind in the legal testimony affirming Don Quixote's identity signed by a character pulled from Avellaneda's pages (II. 72, 1320–21). Yet even here, where Cervantes has a more obvious vested interest in establishing the authenticity of his own creation and denying the legitimacy of imposters, we nonetheless find that subversive further voices within the text continue to cause problems, as the Zaragoza ruse designed to prove the exclusive truth of Cide Hamete's version is immediately followed by one of his characteristic lapses of detail, to which our attention is pointedly drawn: 'le tomó la noche entre unas espesas encinas o alcornoques, que en esto no guarda la puntualidad Cide Hamete que en otras cosas suele' (II. 60, 1219) ('night overtook him in a dense copse of evergreen oaks or cork-oaks — on this point Cide Hamete isn't as meticulous as usual').[69] There is no question of such doubts being taken too seriously, but it is at the last one final, supreme irony that despite the premium placed in these chapters on the authenticity of Cide Hamete's authorship, that irrepressible vein of parody that so defines the novel's engagement with *auctoritas* is not entirely suppressed, but briefly surfaces even alongside the contention that this is the only authorized version.[70]

Notes to Chapter 3

1. See the innkeeper's reasoning for why his belief in the truth of these tales will not tempt him to imitate them, for knights errant have no place in the modern world: 'que bien veo que ahora no se usa lo que se usaba en aquel tiempo, cuando se dice que andaban por el mundo estos famosos caballeros' (I. 32, 409) ('it's clear enough to me that things are different now from what they were then, when all those famous knights are supposed to have roamed about all over the world'; p. 294). Translations of *Don Quixote* are reproduced from Miguel de Cervantes Saavedra, *Cervantes: Don Quixote*, trans. by John Rutherford (Harmondsworth: Penguin, 2000).
2. The project of undermining authority in the novel of course extends far beyond the particular technique I focus on here; for more general discussion, see especially James A. Parr, *'Don Quixote': A Touchstone for Literary Criticism* (Kassel: Reichenberger, 2005), pp. 33–50; cf. Ralph Flores, *The Rhetoric of Doubtful Authority: Deconstructive Readings of Self-Questioning Narratives, St. Augustine to Faulkner* (Ithaca: Cornell University Press, 1984), pp. 88–115. For a more general account of Cervantes's treatment of authority, experience, and reason as sources of knowledge, see Juan Bautista Avalle Arce, 'Conocimiento y vida en Cervantes', in *Nuevos deslindes cervantinos* (Barcelona: Ariel, 1975), pp. 17–72. A related argument, suggesting that *Don Quixote* 'has to do with methods of defining the world around us and with the role of books in the process', is made by Edward H. Friedman, 'Reading Redressed; or, the Media Circuits of *Don Quijote*', *Confluencia*, 9.2 (1994), 38–51 (p. 42). For a recent analysis of the concept of *auctoritas* in 'El curioso impertinente', arguing that the *novela* directly opposes authority-based and experiential knowledge, see David Arbesú Fernández, '*Auctoritas* y experiencia en "El curioso impertinente"', *Cervantes: Bulletin of the Cervantes Society of America*, 25.1 (2005), 23–43.
3. See Alastair J. Minnis, *Medieval Theory of Authorship: Scholastic Literary Attitudes in the Later Middle Ages*, 2nd ed. (Aldershot: Scolar Press, 1988), p. 10.
4. See *Oxford Latin Dictionary*, s.v. 'auctoritas', entries 2, 8, 9, 10. For rhetorical discussion of the concept, see especially Quintilian, *The Orator's Education [Institutio Oratoria]*, v. 11, 36–44, and relevant sections in Heinrich Lausberg, *Handbook of Literary Rhetoric: A Foundation for Literary Study*, trans. by Matthew T. Bliss, Annemiek Jansen, and David E. Orton, ed. by David E. Orton and R. Dean Anderson (Leiden: Brill, 1998).
5. For this view of chivalric fiction, and the suggestion that these techniques are already straining at the seams to accommodate narrative implausibility in Montalvo, see Edwin Williamson, *The Half-way House of Fiction: 'Don Quixote' and Arthurian Romance* (Oxford: Clarendon Press, 1984), especially pp. 54–69. The chivalric background would thus suggest not only the relevance of this abstract kind of *auctoritas*, but also its susceptibility to being undermined.
6. Don Quixote's lengthy list of the elements of his enchanted journey which fail to convince him is founded on a double appeal to the authority of chivalric tales: 'Muchas y muy graves historias he yo leído de caballeros andantes, pero jamás he leído ni visto ni oído que a los caballeros encantados los lleven desta manera' (I. 47, 590) ('Many weighty histories of knights errant have I read, but never have I read, or seen, or heard of enchanted knights being carried off in this way'; p. 433). The importance of *auctoritas* for Don Quixote's submission to the machinations of the Duke and Duchess is clearly advertised from the beginning of their association, and hinges on his response to seeing a world which finally conforms to his litmus test of textual authority: 'y

aquél fue el primer día que de todo en todo conoció y creyó ser caballero andante verdadero, y no fantástico, viéndose tratar del mesmo modo que él había leído se trataban los tales caballeros en los pasados siglos' (II. 31, 962) ('and that was the first day when he was fully convinced that he was a real knight errant, not a fantasy one, seeing himself treated in the same way as he'd read that such knights used to be treated in centuries past'; p. 693). Howard Mancing, *The Chivalric World of 'Don Quijote': Style, Structure, and Narrative Technique* (Columbia: University of Missouri Press, 1982), p. 199, argues that Cide Hamete misrepresents Don Quixote's psychology here, but the basic point that the *duques* aim to convince by creating experiences that tally with Don Quixote's *auctores* will nonetheless stand.

7. For reasons of space, I focus in the text on the specific rhetorical technique of citing *auctores* and familiar or proverbial *sententiae* to impart *auctoritas*, but the practice of imitating exemplary models would of course follow similar logic, and is one of Don Quixote's most prominent methods of invoking chivalric authority. For studies of how such chivalric *exempla* are parodically exploited in the novel, see especially Timothy Hampton, *Writing from History: The Rhetoric of Exemplarity in Renaissance Literature* (Ithaca: Cornell University Press, 1990), pp. 237–96; Edward C. Riley, 'Don Quixote and the Imitation of Models', *Bulletin of Hispanic Studies*, 31 (1954), 3–16. On similarities between *exemplum* and *auctoritas*, see for example Lausberg, *Handbook*, pp. 196, 202–03.

8. See especially Parr, *Touchstone*, pp. 33–50, from where the description of a 'mutual discrediting society' is borrowed (p. 39). As was the case with the notion of *auctoritas* in general, the problematic narrator may be read partly in an epistemological key, conveying a degree of scepticism towards the written word as a guarantee of truth, or an idea of the difficulty of perceiving and representing phenomenological reality: see, for example, Parr, *Touchstone*, pp. 43, 48–50; E. Michael Gerli, *Refiguring Authority: Reading, Writing, and Rewriting in Cervantes*, Studies in Romance Languages, 39 (Lexington: University Press of Kentucky, 1995), p. 77; Friedman, 'Reading Redressed', p. 44. Nonetheless, these possibilities are brought about by what is primarily a matter of chivalric parody, toying with the implications of the historian-narrator and in so doing opening the way for an exploration of questions of the written word as epistemological guarantor, along with the present topic of *auctoritas*.

9. On this phrase and its possible origins, see Raymond S. Willis, Jr., *The Phantom Chapters of the 'Quijote'* (New York: Hispanic Institute in the United States, 1953), pp. 99–103; cf. Mancing, *Chivalric World*, pp. 195–96; Parr, *Touchstone*, pp. 35–36, 41.

10. p. 119.

11. p. 80.

12. See Lausberg, *Handbook*, pp. 202–03.

13. Text and translation are quoted from Peter of Spain, *Summaries of Logic: Text, Translation, Introduction, and Notes*, ed. and trans. by Brian P. Copenhaver, with Calvin Normore and Terence Parsons (Oxford: Oxford University Press, 2014).

14. 'Itaque nichil aliud vel michi vel aliis quod responderet habebat, nisi ut adversus omne quod diceretur, splendorem nominis obiectaret, et rationis locum teneret autoritas' (*Epistolae familiares* XXIV. 2, 8) ('So he had no other answer to me or the others, but simply opposed every statement by putting forward the glory of Cicero's reputation, and authority usurped the place of reasoning'). Text and translation follow Francesco Petrarca, *Selected Letters*, vol. II, trans. by Elaine Fantham, The I Tatti Renaissance Library, 77 (Cambridge, MA: Harvard University Press, 2017).

15. Text and translation are quoted from Quintilian, *The Orator's Education*, ed. and trans. by Donald A. Russell, Loeb Classical Library 124–27 and 494, 5 vols (Cambridge, MA: Harvard University Press, 2002).

16. On the importance of the presentation of the speaker's character in general terms, see Kevin Dunn, *Pretexts of Authority: The Rhetoric of Authorship in the Renaissance Preface* (Stanford: Stanford University Press, 1994), p. 4. On *ēthos* and *Don Quixote*, see the analysis of Marcela's speech in Thomas R. Hart and Steven Rendall, 'Rhetoric and Persuasion in Marcela's Address to the Shepherds', *Hispanic Review*, 46.3 (1978), 287–98 (pp. 288–89, 292–93); cf. Mary Mackey, 'Rhetoric and Characterization in *Don Quijote*', *Hispanic Review*, 42.1 (1974), 51–66 (p. 54).

The relevance of a sure touch in citing authorities for building this favourable presentation of the speaker is suggested by the entries for 'ethos' and 'anamnesis' in Gideon O. Burton's 'Silva Rhetoricae' <http://rhetoric.byu.edu/> [accessed 26 September 2017].

17. See I. 21, 243; I. 39, 494; II. 43, 1064; II. 67, 1287.
18. p. 943.
19. For these aspects of decorum, see Lausberg, *Handbook*, p. 461.
20. On this misguided expectation of authority, suggested by Juan Palomeque's words quoted in n. 1, see further Hampton, *Writing from History*, p. 246; Bruce W. Wardropper, 'Cervantes' Theory of the Drama', *Modern Philology*, 52.4 (1955), 217–21 (p. 220).
21. See Salvador J. Fajardo, 'Instructions for Use: The Prologue to *Don Quixote I*', *Journal of Interdisciplinary Literary Studies*, 6.1 (1994), 1–17 (p. 6).
22. p. 16.
23. Fajardo, 'Instructions for Use', p. 11.
24. pp. 11–12.
25. On the implications of this phrase for the limits of the reader's authority and as a warning against overconfidence in interpretation, see especially Carolyn A. Nadeau, *Women of the Prologue: Imitation, Myth, and Magic in 'Don Quixote I'* (London: Associated University Presses, 2002), pp. 39, 44; Williamson, *Half-way House*, pp. 82–83.
26. p. 12.
27. p. 13.
28. p. 15.
29. p. 15.
30. On the implications of the reference to Virgil's Circe as a classical reference which itself suggests the reworking and rejecting of such references, given Virgil's treatment of his Homeric figure, see especially Nadeau, *Women of the Prologue*, pp. 38, 49–50, 114–17.
31. p. 983 n. 4.
32. p. 14.
33. I focus here on its implications for Cervantes's art of parody, but the void of authority which the prologue produces and the novel develops has also been mined for epistemological implications, as a way of contesting the authority of the written word, or a means of leading the reader to adopt a default position of sceptical doubt: for more on these approaches, see, for example, Nadeau, *Women of the Prologue*, p. 38; Maureen Ihrie, 'Classical Skepticism and Narrative Authority in *Don Quijote de la Mancha*', in *Studies on 'Don Quijote' and Other Cervantine Works*, ed. by Donald W. Bleznick (York: Spanish Literature Publications Company, 1984), pp. 31–37). However, as Nadeau also notes (p. 52), this should not obscure the playful way in which these questions are suggested, as the simultaneous suggesting and undermining of authority outlined in the text may be read as part of what she calls Cervantes's game of 'hide-and-seek with his readers', as the prologue's teasing hints of authority begin a game which is played for fun on both sides.
34. p. 302.
35. p. 109. On possible Platonic background, see the extended note *ad loc.* in the second volume of the Rico et al. edition, and the references there cited.
36. See especially Aristotle, *Nicomachean Ethics*, 1115b17–20, 1115b28–1116a9. On *temeridad* in particular as a marker of this vice, along with its Latin cognate *temeritas*, see Richard Rabone, 'Fallen Idols? Vice and Virtue in the Iconography of Icarus and Phaethon', in *The Routledge Companion to Iberian Studies*, ed. by Javier Muñoz-Basols, Laura Lonsdale, and Manuel Delgado (London: Routledge, 2017), pp. 249–63 (p. 252). For more general discussion of the golden mean in *Don Quixote*, see Francisco Rico, 'Don Quijote, Cervantes, el justo medio', *Estudios Públicos*, 100 (2005), 63–70.
37. p. 155.
38. p. 512.
39. See Mancing, *Chivalric World*, p. 75 on Sancho's reference to the priest in the dispute about danger in I. 20; cf. pp. 171–76 for further discussion of Sancho citing his sources, including the translator's sceptical reaction and the above reference to the mean.

40. See Antonio Barnés Vázquez, *'Yo he leído en Virgilio': la tradición clásica en el 'Quijote'*, Biblioteca Cátedra Miguel de Cervantes: Publicaciones Académicas, 12 (Vigo: Editorial Academia del Hispanismo, 2009), p. 184. For the Canon's brief reference to being 'valiente sin temeridad, osado sin cobardía' ('brave but not rash'; p. 453), reproducing exactly the familiar lexis of the mean, see I. 49, 617.
41. p. 556.
42. p. 593.
43. p. 595.
44. p. 595.
45. p. 595.
46. p. 596.
47. p. 598.
48. The necessity of incorporating an individual's capabilities and particular needs into the situational data to be considered when assessing a situation is of course not limited to the virtue of courage; for the Aristotelian heritage of the idea in other contexts, see, for example, Lesley Brown, 'What Is the "Mean Relative to Us" in Aristotle's Ethics?', *Phronesis*, 42.1 (1997), 77–93 (p. 86).
49. p. 599.
50. For Aristotelian expression of this thought, see the claim that one extreme can be 'more opposed' to the mean than the other at *Nicomachean Ethics* 1108b35–1109a5.
51. p. 677.
52. A useful summary of the wide range of critical approaches brought to bear on this episode is provided by Henry W. Sullivan, *Grotesque Purgatory: A Study of Cervantes's 'Don Quixote', Part II* (University Park, Pennsylvania: Pennsylvania State University Press, 1996), pp. 30–48.
53. Williamson, *Half-way House*, p. 116.
54. For more on these and other incongruities within the tale, see Peter N. Dunn, 'Two Classical Myths in *Don Quijote*', *Renaissance and Reformation*, 9.1 (1972), 2–10 (pp. 6–8).
55. p. 638.
56. p. 653.
57. 'puesto que *se tiene por cierto* que al tiempo de su fin y muerte *dicen que* se retrató della y dijo que él la había inventado, por parecerle que convenía y cuadraba bien con las aventuras que había leído en sus historias' (II. 24, 905; my emphasis, indicating Cide Hamete's oblique phrasing as he withholds his own judgement) ('even though it is believed to be the case that when he was dying he is said to have retracted it all and stated that he had made it up because he thought it tallied well with the adventures that he had read about in his histories'; p. 648).
58. See Aurora Egido, 'La cueva de Montesinos y la tradición erasmista de ultratumba', in *Cervantes y las puertas del sueño: estudios sobre 'La Galatea', 'El Quijote', y 'El Persiles'*, Estudios universitarios (Barcelona: PPU, 1994), pp. 137–78 (p. 173) (first publ. as 'Cervantes y las puertas del sueño: sobre la tradición erasmista del ultramundo en el episodio de la cueva de Montesinos', in *Studia in honorem prof. M. de Riquer*, ed. by Carlos Alvar and others, 4 vols (Barcelona: Quaderns Crema, 1988), III. 305–41); Barnés Vázquez, *La tradición clásica*, p. 82.
59. The phrase is borrowed from Anthony Close, *A Companion to 'Don Quixote'*, Colección Támesis Serie A: Monografías, 262 (Woodbridge: Tamesis, 2008), p. 197.
60. See, for example, E. C. Riley, 'Metamorphosis, Myth, and Dream in the Cave of Montesinos', in *Essays on Narrative Fiction in the Iberian Peninsula in Honour of Frank Pierce*, ed. by R. B. Tate (London: Dolphin, 1982), pp. 105–19 (p. 118); Sullivan, *Grotesque Purgatory*, p. 23.
61. p. 633.
62. pp. 633–34.
63. See 'Syphilis, sive de morbo gallico'; ointment is used as part of the treatment of sores at II. 245–47. The poem is available in Girolamo Fracastoro, *Latin Poetry*, trans. by James Gardner, The I Tatti Renaissance Library, 57 (Cambridge, MA: Harvard University Press, 2013), pp. 1–85. I am not suggesting that Cervantes had Fracastoro in mind here, nor that the cousin's project in fact constitutes a topic of real substance, but merely that the legitimate criteria for inclusion in such compilations are not quite so strictly highbrow as the cousin's initial words might lead us

to suspect, with his burlesque examples here entertainingly close to being material on which it would be possible to find weighty humanist authority.

64. p. 634.
65. p. 642.
66. See especially Dunn, 'Two Classical Myths', pp. 6–7; Peter N. Dunn, 'La cueva de Montesinos por fuera y por dentro: estructura épica, fisonomía', *MLN*, 88.2 (1973), 190–202 (p. 193).
67. p. 649.
68. p. 649.
69. p. 891.
70. I am grateful to Roy Norton for his comments on an earlier version of this chapter.

PART II

A Meeting of Genres

CHAPTER 4

From Stage to Page: *Don Quixote* as Performance

B. W. Ife

I

In January 1760, in an early review of *Tristram Shandy*, the English novelist Tobias Smollett described Toby, Trim, and Slop as 'excellent imitations of certain characters in a modern, truly Cervantic performance'.[1] Smollett's use of the word 'performance' to describe a novel is, on the face of it, odd. A novel has few, if any, of the obvious features of a performance: the embodiment in real time by a performer or performers of a script or score in the presence of an audience, and in a place designed for that purpose.[2] But Smollett had published his own translation of *Don Quixote* five years earlier, in 1755, and in characterizing *Tristram Shandy* as a 'Cervantic performance' he was clearly responding to some obvious features that both novels have in common: they are both vividly and dramatically written and their protagonists are opinionated, larger than life characters, determined to make their voices heard with quasi-theatrical relish.

Smollett was not the first writer to pick up on the dramatic qualities of Cervantes's fiction in prose. Alonso Fernández de Avellaneda had commented on the theatrical dimension of Cervantes's novels when, in the prologue to his spurious second part of *Don Quixote* (1614), he described the first part as 'much like a play'.[3] And if Lope de Vega did have a hand in this prologue, as many suppose, we could say that 'it takes one to recognize one'.[4]

Cervantes was an ambitious if ultimately frustrated dramatist, as he is the first to admit in the prologue to his *Ocho comedias y ocho entremeses nuevos, nunca representados* published in 1615, the year of the second part of *Don Quixote*.[5] His view of what the theatre could and should achieve far outstripped the capacity of the contemporary playhouse, the taste of its audience and the willingness of producers to take a risk. It could be argued that he sublimated this frustration in prose. His novels often incorporate *coups de théâtre* that would have been technically impossible to achieve on the early-modern stage: the shaft of moonlight that illuminates the crucifix that Leocadia will use, years later, to identify the man who abducted and dishonoured her (*La fuerza de la sangre*); or the opening of the shutters in *Las dos doncellas* to reveal that the man with whom Teodosia had shared the room that night was her brother. And Peralta's silent reading of the script of the conversation between two dogs was a smart way of avoiding what would have been a rather surreal afternoon in the *corral de comedias*.[6]

The purpose of this essay is to discuss and illustrate Cervantes's fascination with performers and performance, both actors and musicians; to examine some of the many instances where he represents and recreates performance in his writing; and ultimately to suggest that, in prose fiction, he found a way of bypassing and overcoming the limitations of theatrical performance and the personal frustrations he experienced as a dramatist. In short, he found a way of giving the novel many, if not all, of the qualities of live performance. The current reappraisal of Cervantes as a dramatist lies in the background to this discussion, but in the foreground are a number of influential studies of what has been called the 'performative turn' in theory and some recent important work on the impact of playbooks and silent reading on the development and dissemination of dramatic literature in early seventeenth-century England and Spain.

The concept and language of performance has become a common feature of contemporary society and social thought. In an extremely influential study, ominously called *Perform or Else*, Jon McKenzie identifies three paradigms of performance that function both normatively and transgressively in modern society: organizational, cultural, and technological.[7] Technological performance, he argues, was born out of the American cold-war apparatus and the military-industrial complex of the 1960s. Its midwives were the engineers and computer scientists who responded successfully to Kennedy's challenge in May 1961, to land a man on the moon and return him safely to earth, before the decade was out. The Challenger disaster of 1986 demonstrated graphically and tragically the limits of technological effectiveness; but it has left us with a vocabulary of performance that we apply indiscriminately to everything from fast cars and computers to bag-less vacuum cleaners.

Organizational performance has similarly given us the language of 'key performance indicators', 'performance management', rewards for good performance and penalties for under-performance, in every walk of life from business and academia to professional sport. This has nothing to do with acting but everything to do with acting effectively. The challenge of organizational performance is one of efficiency, of minimizing inputs and maximizing outputs; the aim is to control, and the consequence is to promote regression to a norm. In this respect, cultural and organizational performance overlap. Anthropologists, sociologists, and cultural theorists all use performance as a way of analysing ritual, social interaction, race, gender, and sexual politics, and the concept of performance as the embodied enactment of cultural forces has become one of the dominant concepts of contemporary theory.[8] As McKenzie himself concludes: 'performance will be to the twentieth and twenty-first centuries what discipline was to the eighteenth and nineteenth, that is, an onto-historical formation of power and knowledge'.[9]

Nevertheless, what performance embodies, performance can also resist. Some of the most interesting recent discussions of the subversive power of performance have centred on the anti-war demonstrations and performance art movement of the 1970s and 1980s, culminating in the so-called 'culture wars' of the 1990s.[10] When conservative politicians in the USA were calling for funding to be withdrawn from the National Endowment for the Arts, performance was on the front line.[11] If the threat from organizational management is always 'perform — or be fired', the cry from the arts is 'perform — or be socially normalized'. It is this ability of performance both to embody values and subvert them that will be central to the argument of this essay.

The discussion falls broadly into three sections, starting with music and ending with drama. In the middle comes a pivotal episode from *Don Quixote* — the story of Grisóstomo and Marcela that illustrates the process by which Cervantes starts to think of his novel less as a story to be told and more as a script to be enacted, embodied, and performed. Common to all three parts of the essay is the role of the voice. In Cervantes's mind the essence of self lies in the voice. The voice is the key to character and the mark of a character's integrity. The challenge that Cervantes faces in his prose fiction is to make the voices of his characters heard as loudly and clearly as if we were hearing them, live, in the theatre.

II

We do not know if Cervantes himself was a musician, whether he played an instrument, sang well or badly, or composed music for the many verses that feature in his published work. But his literary world is full of musical allusions and there are hundreds of references to playing and singing. This is hardly surprising, given Cervantes's firm grip on the facts of life in early seventeenth-century Spain.[12] This was a world in which, if one wanted to hear music, someone had to play or sing.

Cervantes was certainly no musical theorist and left no lasting description of music akin to Leonardo's 'figurazione delle cose invisibili' ('the expression of invisible things') or Shakespeare's 'food of love'. For Cervantes, music is simply 'suave', 'agradable', 'concertada', or 'triste'. For Sancho, music brings jollification: 'indicio de regocijos y de fiestas' (II. 34, 1005) ('a sign of happiness and fiestas').[13] For Dorotea, 'la música compone los ánimos descompuestos y alivia los trabajos que nacen del espíritu' (I. 28, 353) ('music settles the distressed mind and eases the troubles that are born of the spirit').[14]

Don Quixote, however, certainly was a musician. In II. 46, he asks for a lute to be placed in his room so that later that evening he can console the lady Altisidora:

> — Haga vuesa merced, señora, que se me ponga un laúd esta noche en mi aposento, que yo consolaré lo mejor que pudiere a esta lastimada doncella. (II. 46, 1091–92)

> ('Please have a lute placed in my room tonight, and I shall console this afflicted maid as best I can.')[15]

On awakening from her swoon, Altisidora urges her companion to comply, no doubt expecting some further amusement at his expense:

> — Menester será que se le ponga el laúd, que sin duda don Quijote quiere darnos música, y no será mala, siendo suya. (II. 46, 1092)

('We'd better let him have his lute — it looks as if Don Quixote wants to give us some music, and coming from him it can't be bad!')[16]

They go to see the Duchess to bring her up to date and pass on Don Quixote's request:

> Fueron luego a dar cuenta a la duquesa de lo que pasaba y del laúd que pedía don Quijote. (II. 46, 1092)
>
> (So they went straight off to tell the Duchess what had happened and how Don Quixote had asked for a lute.)[17]

But when he gets to his room at eleven o'clock, things are not quite what he anticipated:

> [...] llegadas las once horas de la noche, halló don Quijote una vihuela en su aposento. (II. 46, 1092)
>
> ([...] it was soon eleven o'clock at night, and Don Quixote found a guitar in his room.)[18]

Three times a lute is requested but what turns up is a vihuela. It is, of course, possible that the Duke and the Duchess did not have a lute to hand; or that Cervantes did not know the difference between a lute and a vihuela; or maybe none of them thought it made much difference.

More likely, it is a joke at Don Quixote's expense, and quite a subtle one. Cervantes uses the word 'laúd' only seven times in his work: four times in *Don Quixote* (three of them in this episode) and three in *La Galatea*. In his mind, at least, the lute is an aristocratic instrument, whereas the vihuela is more popular. So we have a joke based on literary decorum, the intersection of genres and musical types that, once again, gently debunks Don Quixote's literary and social aspirations.

This episode may also play into the hands of the relativists: 'el laúd' but 'la vihuela'; two near-synonyms distinguished by a difference in grammatical gender. Could Cervantes be channelling Mambrino's helmet: 'eso que a ti te parece vihuela a mí me parece laúd y a otro le parecerá guitarra'.[19]

So Don Quixote picks up the 'vihuelaúd' and starts to play:

> Templola, abrió la reja y sintió que andaba gente en el jardín; y habiendo recorrido los trastes de la vihuela y afinádola lo mejor que supo, escupió y remondose el pecho, y luego, con una voz ronquilla aunque entonada, cantó [...]. (II. 46, 1092)
>
> (he ran his fingers over the strings, opened the window and heard people moving about in the garden and, after adjusting the frets and tuning the instrument as best he could, he cleared his tubes, spat, and, in a voice that was somewhat hoarse but well-pitched, he sang [...].)[20]

'Cantó.' Pausing the quotation at this point prompts a key question: when Don Quixote starts to sing, what are we supposed to hear? The works of Cervantes teem with singers and players, and he mentions virtually every instrument known to early seventeenth-century Spain: wind, strings, keyboards, and percussion.[21] Yet if we put the *Obras completas* to our ear, we cannot hear a thing — total silence. How does a writer stimulate the auditory imagination of a reader in the same way that he fires the other dimensions of the imagination through description, narrative, and dialogue? If we have ever heard someone play the lute or the vihuela, our real-world knowledge will enable us to imagine the tuning and the warming up. And we can imagine the hawking and the spitting, which is so prevalent in Cervantes as to constitute a minor topos of its own. There is an instance in II. 12; la Gananciosa does it in *Rinconete y Cortadillo*; and Lope does it twice in *La ilustre fregona* while he is thinking about what he is going to sing.[22] But we cannot hear the music.

That music features so prominently in Cervantes is one more indication of the innate theatricality of his approach to prose fiction. Like many playwrights, Cervantes specifies music several times in his plays. But he is remarkably unspecific about what he wants. Grand entrances and exits demand shawms — *chirimías* — and sad scenes demand flutes. 'Suene música de flautas tristes' ('sad flutes play') is about as specific as he gets (in *La casa de los celos*); and one of the directions in *Los baños de Argel* even reads: 'Canten lo que quisieren' ('let them sing whatever they like').[23] Cervantes may simply have left this to his director or even to the musicians themselves, since they were more likely to have improvised than to have played specially composed incidental music.[24]

But this degree of imprecision will not do in prose fiction. Cervantes enjoyed a challenge and, in his novels, he seems consciously to have sought solutions to the difficulty of conveying the sound of music through the written word. This is why songs come to be so prominent in his work. Song is the one musical form in which the two dimensions of music and text intersect through the medium of the voice. Through song, abstract relationships between real-world sounds are grounded in language; song has the capacity to stimulate the auditory imagination; and song enables the characters to express their authenticity and to 'find their voice'.

So let us rejoin Don Quixote as he attempts to console the lady Altisidora:

> [...] cantó el siguiente romance, que él mismo aquel día había compuesto:
>
>> — Suelen las fuerzas de amor
>> sacar de quicio a las almas,
>> tomando por instrumento
>> la ociosidad descuidada. (II. 46, 1092–93)
>
> ([...] he sang the following ballad, which he'd composed himself that day:
>
>> The soul, by Love's most mighty power,
>> Can often be upset
>> If Love can count on careless sloth
>> To aid and to abet.)[25]

and there follow a further thirty-two lines of a song text that someone (Don Quixote or Cervantes) had composed earlier that day.

When Cervantes writes 'había compuesto' does he mean composed as a poet or composed as a composer? We have no way of knowing, but this type of ambiguity is commonplace throughout his work. There are literally hundreds of verses that appear on the page as poems but are framed in the text as songs. None of them has survived as a musical composition attributed to Cervantes himself and few of them have survived in settings by other composers. Most of them could be sung to a pre-existing tune but there are no clues to indicate that Cervantes had a particular tune in mind. The nearest he comes to suggesting a tune comes when he quotes snatches of ballads that he must have assumed would sound in the reader's inner ear.

There is an extended riff on this theme in *El celoso extremeño* when Loaysa is offering singing lessons to Luis, the black eunuch who guards Carrizales's house:

> — No canto mal, respondió el negro, — pero ¿qué aprovecha, pues no sé tonada alguna, si no es la de *La estrella de Venus* y la de *Por un verde prado* y aquella que ahora se usa que dice:
>
> >A los hierros de una reja
> >la turbada mano asida?
>
> — Todas ésas son aire, dijo Loaysa, — para las que yo os podría enseñar, porque sé todas las del moro Abindarráez, con las de su dama Jarifa, y todas las que se cantan de la historia del gran Sofí Tomunibeyo, con las de la zarabanda a lo divino, que son tales, que hacen pasmar a los mismos portugueses. (338–39)
>
> ('I'm not a bad singer,' replied the Negro, 'but what use is that when I don't know any songs apart from "The Star of Venus" and "Through Pastures Green" and that one that everyone is singing these days, which goes:
>
> >*The bars of a window*
> >*I clasped with a trembling hand...?'*
>
> 'All of those are nothing,' said Loaysa, 'compared to what I could teach you, because I know all the ballads about the Moor Abindarráez and about his lady Jarifa and those sung about the times of the great Sufi, Tuman Bey together with the sacred sarabands that drive the Portuguese themselves to distraction.')[26]

In setting out his stall as a singing teacher, Loaysa makes several references to ballads and popular songs that Cervantes could reasonably have expected his readers to know. Among them, 'Madre, la mi madre, / guardas me ponéis' (p. 357) ('Mother, o mother of mine, / you keep me ever in view'),[27] encapsulates one of the primary lessons of the *novela*, that physical constraints are powerless against the freedom of the will. These and many other examples show how alert was Cervantes to the sounds of popular culture, and that he understood the power of words and music to achieve an emotional response that words alone could not. Loaysa's skill at singing is the means by which he gains access to the impenetrable fortress of Carrizales's jealousy, but as he implies in this passage, a song well sung can move the hardest of hearts.

It would be wrong to assume that Cervantes uses song as a mere pretext, a way of smuggling his poetry into his prose. Of course, there are in the background the conventions of the pastoral novel and Cervantes has many singing shepherds in *La Galatea*. But *Don Quixote*, the *Novelas ejemplares* and the *Persiles* are not primarily pastoral fiction and yet they draw on the conventions of singing and song texts in a number of unconventional ways. From the doomed Portuguese lover of the *Persiles* to the nun with the beautiful voice in *La española inglesa*, the ethereal sound of the singing voice is never very far away.[28]

The significance of the singing voice is underlined in a central episode of Cervantes's last novel *Persiles y Sigismunda* — the episode of Feliciana de la Voz.[29] In this episode, Cervantes creates a character with such a beautiful singing voice that she and her voice become one, to the extent that her very name encapsulates her most striking characteristic. She is an extreme example of a character who does more than find her voice in music: she *is* her voice in music.

But Cervantes treats her terribly in the novel. He subjects her to such a gruelling succession of vicissitudes — this is, after all, a Byzantine romance — that she is continually prevented from expressing herself/her self through her voice. For most of the episode she is on the run from an arranged marriage, having had a child out of wedlock by a man of her own choosing. She is so exhausted that she can barely speak, let alone sing, and when she does eventually sing — a hymn to the Virgin in the church of Guadalupe — her voice is strangely disembodied, as if it were emanating from a source outside herself:

> puesta de hinojos, y las manos puestas y junto al pecho, la hermosa Feliciana de la Voz, lloviendo tiernas lágrimas, con sosegado semblante, sin mover los labios ni hacer otra demostración ni movimiento que diese señal de ser viva criatura, soltó la voz a los vientos y levantó el corazón al cielo, y cantó unos versos que ella sabía de memoria (los cuales dio después por escrito), con que suspendió los sentidos de cuantos la escuchaban, y acreditó las alabanzas que ella misma de su voz había dicho, y satisfizo de todo en todo los deseos que sus peregrinos tenían de escucharla. (III. 5, 473)
>
> (kneeling with the other, her eyes full of tears, her hands on her stomach, her lips closed, and the rest of her body without motion or token that she was a living creature, [she] gave passage to her voice and began to sing verses which she had perfectly by heart, whereby she suspended the minds of all that gave ear unto her, satisfied the desire which they had to hear her, and made the praises which she had given herself to be believed.)[30]

If speech is the embodiment of self and song is a heightened form of speech, then song is a more intense expression of self. By suppressing Feliciana's singing voice Cervantes conveys with even greater emphasis the suppression of self that Feliciana suffers by virtue of her position in contemporary society. And when she does get her voice back, she seems to owe it to divine intervention. As her father comments on entering the church: 'O aquella voz es de algún ángel de los confirmados en gracia o es de mi hija Feliciana de la Voz' (p. 474) ('Either this is the voice of an angel confirmed in grace, or of my daughter Feliciana').[31]

It is extraordinary that Cervantes, who evidently knew a great deal about the practice and theory of music, and so often recreates the act of singing through the printed song text, should have described her singing in such an improbable manner. As the narrator says and she confirms, she is in no state to sing at all. There is an odd disjunction between her singing, interrupted after four stanzas, and the full printed text of twelve stanzas (ninety-six lines), which is only given later in the chapter once all the reconciliations have taken place. And the character who asks to see the text is Auristela, a pilgrim from Scandinavia who has been in Spain less than a week and has had no chance to learn Spanish in that time.

Cervantes seems to be doing everything possible to break down the alignment between the singer, the act of singing, the sung text and the reader's reading of it, an alignment that, as we have seen, would normally allow him to convey the sound of the singing voice on the printed page. But in this case, the disruption is deliberate: it makes Feliciana's singing extraordinary in the proper sense of the word. Hers is not a human voice, but a divinely-inspired voice, and what starts as a hymn with a text becomes, in the latter stages, a song without words. Her singing is in fact a minor miracle, a Marian intervention just like those celebrated by Alfonso el Sabio, showing that, as Dorotea says in I. 28, 'la música compone los ánimos descompuestos y alivia los trabajos que nacen del espíritu' (I. 28, 353).[32]

Preciosa, *La gitanilla*, is another character who is most clearly distinguished by her singing voice:

> De entre el son del tamborín y castañetas y fuga del baile salió un rumor que encarecía la belleza y donaire de la gitanilla, y corrían los muchachos a verla, y los hombres a mirarla. Pero cuando la oyeron cantar, por ser la danza cantada, ¡allí fue ello! (pp. 30–31)

> (Above the sound of the tambourine and the castanets and the movement of the dance came a murmur of praise for the beauty and grace of the little gypsy girl; boys came running up to see her, and men stopped to look at her. But when they heard her sing, because it was a dance accompanied by a song, that was the climax!)[33]

The songs that Cervantes and the *paje poeta* give Preciosa to sing in the first half of the *novela* convey that special mix of integrity and *desenvoltura* ('spontaneity') that makes her such an exceptional character. But, as we all know, because Cervantes tells us as much in his opening paragraph, Preciosa is not a gypsy and, like Feliciana — though not in so brutal a manner — she too loses her voice as she is absorbed back into conventional society once her true origins are revealed.

Perhaps the finest example of song as a heightened form of speech comes at the end of the Captive's Tale (I. 42), when Don Quixote is keeping watch outside the inn and dawn is about to break.

> Sucedió, pues, que faltando poco por venir el alba, llegó a los oídos de las damas una voz tan entonada y tan buena, que les obligó a que todas le prestasen atento oído. Nadie podía imaginar quién era la persona que tan bien cantaba, y era una voz sola, sin que la acompañase instrumento alguno [...] estando en esta confusión muy atentas, llegó a la puerta del aposento Cardenio, y dijo:
> — Quien no duerme, escuche, que oirán una voz de un mozo de mulas que de tal manera canta, que encanta. (I. 42, 547)

> (A little before dawn the ladies heard a voice which was so fine and tuneful, that they all had to listen [...]. None of them could imagine who it was singing so well, and unaccompanied. [...] As they lay there listening in bewilderment Cardenio came to their door and said: 'If any of you are awake, do listen and you'll hear a young footman singing. It's the most gorgeous sound: enchanting chanting, one might say'.)[34]

And these are the words that they heard:

> Marinero soy de amor
> Y en su piélago profundo
> Navego sin esperanza
> De llegar a puerto alguno. (I. 42, 548)

> (A mariner of love am I
> Who, far from any strand,
> Sails on, although without a hope
> Of ever reaching land.)[35]

...and a further sixteen lines.

Two things are interesting here. One is the fact that this is a *romance nuevo*, newly composed and not traditional, so there is nothing to guide the reader's inner ear. The other is the way Cervantes in effect interrupts the song before it is finished. Instead, when the singer gets to this point Dorotea wakes Clara from her sleep so that she can listen:

> Llegando el que cantaba a este punto [the song clearly continues, but no further text is given], le pareció a Dorotea que no sería bien que dejase Clara de oír una tan buena voz, y, así, moviéndola a una y a otra parte, la despertó, diciéndole:
> — Perdóname, niña, que te despierto, pues lo hago porque gustes de oír la mejor voz que quizá habrás oído en toda tu vida. (I. 42, 549)

> (When the singer reached this point in his song, Dorotea thought it would be a pity if Clara missed hearing such a good voice, so she shook her awake and said: 'Forgive me for waking you up, my child, but I did it so that you can enjoy the finest voice perhaps you've ever heard'.)[36]

It is curiously appropriate that, once again, at this moment of extreme beauty, the muleteer's song parts company from the text. As with Feliciana, Cervantes peels the text from the song, sets the song free, letting it become pure voice, recorded wholly in terms of its effect on those listening, the audience. The muleteer's song, unaccompanied, disembodied, almost otherworldly, creates a moment of ecstasy in which Cervantes celebrates the power of music to convey heightened emotion, express the deepest self and elevate the written word to a higher level. This is perhaps the closest Cervantes ever came to recreating music in words.

III

The very first note of music to sound in *Don Quixote* (leaving aside the whistling of the 'castrador de puercos' at the inn that Don Quixote takes for a castle in I. 2), comes in I. 11 when Quixote is with the goatherds. Taking up a handful of acorns, he delivers himself of his first great discourse on the Golden Age ('Dichosa edad y siglos dichosos aquellos a quien los antiguos pusieron nombre de dorados', 133) ('Happy the age and happy the centuries were those on which the ancients bestowed the name of golden').[37] After the speech comes the dinner, and after the dinner comes the after-dinner entertainment:

> queremos darle solaz y contento con hacer que cante un compañero nuestro que no tardará mucho en estar aquí; el cual es un zagal muy entendido y muy

> enamorado, y que, sobre todo, sabe leer y escribir y es músico de un rabel, que no hay más que desear. (I. II, 136)
>
> (we want to offer you some pleasant entertainment by getting a companion of ours, who'll soon be here, to sing to us — he's a bright lad, fond of the ladies, and, what's more, he can read and write and he plays the fiddle as prettily as can be.)[38]

The end of Don Quixote's speech to the goatherds and the introduction to the episode of Grisóstomo and Marcela is one of the most subtle transition passages in the whole novel and it merits a moment or two of careful attention. The challenge for Cervantes is to bring variety into the work and he does this by changing the generic focus from chivalry to pastoral.[39] A change of genre means a change of scene from the flat plain to the rocky uplands; of tone, from gentle comedy to heightened emotion; and of role for Don Quixote and Sancho, from protagonists to spectators. These shifts of emphasis undoubtedly contribute to our perception of the novel as a performance.

At that very moment, as if on cue, the sound of the rebec is heard:

> Apenas había el cabrero acabado de decir esto, cuando llegó a sus oídos el son del rabel, y de allí a poco llegó el que le tañía, que era un mozo de hasta veinte y dos años, de muy buena gracia. (I. II, 136)
>
> (The goatherd had hardly finished speaking when the sound of the fiddle reached their ears, and soon after that the fiddler himself appeared, a well-graced lad of maybe twenty-two.)[40]

Every detail of this meeting is staged. Antonio, the young musician, will arrive very shortly; he will make an appearance. He is given a bit of a build-up: he is clever, educated, skilled at the rebec, and in love. As with the muleteer and the Portuguese lover, we hear the music before we see the musician. Cervantes is using music as a structural device to move us from one world to another while reminding us that what we are about to see and hear is just another kind of performance on another kind of stage.

The goatherd asks Antonio if he has eaten and then asks him to sing, so that their guest can see that even these rustic folk have among them someone who understands music.

> Preguntáronle sus compañeros si había cenado, y, respondiendo que sí, el que había hecho los ofrecimientos le dijo:
> — De esa manera, Antonio, bien podrás hacernos placer de cantar un poco, porque vea este señor huésped que tenemos que también por los montes y selvas hay quien sepa de música. (I, II, 136)
>
> (His companions asked him if he'd had his supper, and when he replied that he had, the goatherd who'd offered Don Quixote the song said to the lad: 'In that case, Antonio, you could give us the pleasure of hearing you sing, just to show our guest here that there's someone among us who can, and that in these woods and forests there are people who know music'.) [41]

This is one example among many of the *topos* of 'menosprecio de corte y alabanza de aldea', the idea that the village is just as civilized as the city, if not more so, and it is important that their metropolitan guest should understand that music is an art that is practised as much in the countryside as in the town.

> Hémosle dicho tus buenas habilidades y deseamos que las muestres y nos saques verdaderos; y, así, te ruego por tu vida que te sientes y cantes el romance de tus amores, que te compuso el beneficiado tu tío, que en el pueblo ha parecido muy bien.
> — Que me place, respondió el mozo.
> Y sin hacerse más de rogar, se sentó en el tronco de una desmochada encina [a very stagey detail], y, templando su rabel, de allí a poco, con muy buena gracia, comenzó a cantar, diciendo desta manera:
> > Yo sé, Olalla, que me adoras,
> > puesto que no me lo has dicho [...]. (I. 11, 136–37)

('We've told him about your abilities, and now we want you to air them and show that we're right; so go on, sit yourself down and sing us that ballad about your sweetheart that your uncle the priest made up for you — everyone in the village thought it was very good.
'All right,' the lad replied.
And, not needing to be asked again, he sat down on the stump of an evergreen oak and, after tuning his fiddle, soon began, with great charm, to sing this song:
> *Although, Olalla, you love me,*
> *you never say you do [...].*)[42]

And there follow sixty-eight lines of song text.

The theme of Antonio's ballad ('I know that you adore me even though you haven't said so') anticipates the central theme of the shepherd Grisóstomo's self-deluded and self-destructive love for the shepherdess Marcela. Intrigued by what he hears of Grisóstomo's suicide, Don Quixote decides to join the goatherds at the funeral, where Marcela appears on a rocky outcrop overlooking the grave (another stagey detail) and delivers herself of a long and extremely eloquent defence against the charge of hard-heartedness: she doesn't love Grisóstomo and has told him so several times; she doesn't want to get married; and 'si a Grisóstomo mató su impaciencia y arrojado deseo, ¿por qué se ha de culpar mi honesto proceder y recato?' (p. 169) ('If Grisóstomo was killed by his own impatience and uncontrolled passion, why should anyone blame my modest and circumspect behaviour for that?').[43]

If it were not for the fact that opera had not yet been invented, one might be tempted to describe this episode as operatic. It is certainly pure theatre, from the characters to the set, to the roles they play and the lines they speak. Neither Grisóstomo nor Marcela is a shepherd. He is the son of a rich farmer and has studied at Salamanca; she is the niece of an even richer farmer. Grisóstomo became a shepherd in the same way that Don Quixote became a knight errant and Marcela has fled the town simply to escape from a forced marriage. Grisóstomo's burial (at his own insistence) in unhallowed ground gives Cervantes a first-rate setting, both for the entry of the funeral procession along a defile in the rocks, and a prominent position from which Marcela can deliver her concluding aria. And the roles that the two protagonists act out — the doomed lover and the supposedly hard-hearted object of his love — both resonate down the centuries.

What is most interesting about this episode, however, is the almost complete absence of a narrator. Cervantes gets us where we need to be and makes sure we know who is speaking to whom, but absolutely everything we know about Grisóstomo and Marcela and their doomed relationship we learn from them and from the other characters involved. Cervantes gives us a kaleidoscopic reconstruction of the circumstances of Grisóstomo's death, pieced together from several partial accounts from those who knew him and those who heard about him at second hand. Even Gristóstomo gets to speak from the grave through the medium of his long *canción desesperada*, the last poem he wrote, read aloud by his friend Vivaldo, before Marcela bursts on the scene with her display of muscular rationality that completely rearranges our conception of the whole episode.

The overwhelming predominance of first-person over third-person narrative in the episode of Grisóstomo and Marcela shows how far we have come from the narrative stance of the opening chapters of the novel. With the invention of Sancho, Cervantes inevitably started to shift the balance from third to first and second persons, and the dynamic from narrative to dialogue. From that point on Cervantes began a process of delegating the narrative task to his characters, so that even in the most apparently conventional third-person narrative, the narrative voice quickly dissipates and becomes difficult to locate. This shift from diegesis to mimesis makes sense of some of the showier tricks that Cervantes pulls in the intervening chapters: the way he runs out of material at the end of I. 8; the subdivision of narrators; the creation of a 'segundo autor' and so on. This all seems part of a strategy to withdraw the narrator as much as possible from the text and to give it a much more performative, provisional feel.

All of which allows Cervantes to unlock the power of the voice. In II. 44, Cide Hamete Benengeli is said to have regretted embarking on the history of Don Quixote because it is so dry and one-dimensional ('tan seca y tan limitada' (II. 44, 1069)) and because it did not give him scope to include weightier and more entertaining episodes ('digresiones y episodios más graves y más entretenidos' (1070)). These 'digressions' (which he included nevertheless) relieved him of the insufferable task ('trabajo incomportable') of having to write about a single subject and to speak through the mouths of very few characters ('escribir de un solo sujeto y hablar por las bocas de pocas personas'). Grisóstomo and Marcela is Cervantes's first systematic excursion in *Don Quixote* into a world of many characters, each of whom is given the chance to tell the story from their own point of view.

Cervantine criticism talks a lot about the voices of the implied author and the narrator, and the tone of irony that characterizes so much of his writing; and it talks about the importance of dialogue and his preference for doubleton characters as against the singleton *pícaro*, for example. But perhaps more attention should be given to the primacy of the individual voice in driving action and conveying character. Irony may be Cervantes's preferred tone of voice, but he is an extremely deferential narrator, content to absent himself almost entirely from the narrative for long periods of time, much as Don Quixote and Sancho sit out long periods of their novel while other characters and other issues take centre stage.

I have suggested elsewhere that there may be a subtle political purpose behind Cervantes's approach to narrative.[44] The move, in such a few chapters, from a single self-conscious yet controlling voice ('En un lugar de La Mancha, de cuyo nombre no quiero acordarme' (I. 1, 37)) ('In a village in La Mancha, whose name I don't wish to remember')[45] to a plurality of voices is not accidental. We do not have to take an aggressively relativistic approach to the novel to appreciate the skill with which Cervantes presents a richly textured account in which many people, great and small, have their voices heard. And all of this takes place within a controlling political context, under Philip III and Lerma, which was concerned to limit the number of voices in play. This kind of tension, between official and literary discourse, needs to be fully recognized when we come to consider the significance of *Don Quixote* within the political context of early seventeenth-century Spain. 'Giving voice' is an important feature of Cervantes's approach to narrative and he manages to do it, ironically enough, through the silent reading of a printed text.

But there is one important voice that has remained virtually silent throughout this episode, and that is Don Quixote's own. Cervantes may be content to step back and give others their chance, but in this episode Quixote and Sancho are reduced to little more than onlookers, minimally involved in the action and only present to the extent that they shift their position and vantage point as the action unfolds across this rather barren pastoral setting. They have given up their place in the drama and retired to seats at the edge of the stage, still on the stage but as spectators rather than actors. And with this change of position comes loss of control. That is one reason why, at the end of the episode, Don Quixote tries to reassert his authority. As judge and critic, he steps in to pronounce upon the clarity and persuasiveness with which Marcela has demonstrated that she is not responsible for Grisóstomo's death.[46] And he resumes his chivalric role by forbidding anyone to pursue Marcela, on pain of incurring his 'furious indignation'. But let's be clear about his real motive: Quixote cannot let this episode pass without reminding us that he, and he alone, is the star of the show.

IV

In Chapter 11 of Part Two, Don Quixote meets a group of travelling players. As usual, he challenges them to say who they are and what they are doing. Their leader, who is dressed as the devil, explains that they belong to the company of Angulo el Malo. They have just performed an *auto sacramental* in the previous village, are about to play it again in the next and are travelling in costume to save having to change again later. Don Quixote lets them pass, but not before offering to help them out, with a thinly-veiled hint: 'desde mochacho fui aficionado a la carátula, y en mi mocedad se me iban los ojos tras la farándula.' (II .11, 779) ('as a boy I loved Talia, and as a young man I could not tear my eyes away from Melpomene').[47]

We might have known it. Not content with neglecting his household, selling off his estate and sitting up all night reading books of chivalry, Don Quixote has misspent his youth messing about in the theatre. Almost from the outset of the novel it has been clear that Alonso Quijano has not just been playing a role but acting a part. He has spent years learning the script from the novels of chivalry; he has the costume ready in the shape of the suit of armour; he makes, tests, and then re-makes one of his key props, the cardboard visor on his helmet; he mounts his pantomime horse and sets off on his travels:

> una mañana, antes del día, que era uno de los calurosos del mes de julio, se armó de todas sus armas, subió sobre Rocinante, puesta su mal compuesta celada, embrazó su adarga, tomó su lanza y por la puerta falsa de un corral salió al campo. (I. 2, 48–49)
>
> (one morning, before dawn because it was going to be one of those sweltering July days, he donned his armour, mounted Rocinante, with his ill-devised visor in place, took up his leather shield, seized his lance and rode out into the fields through a side door in a yard wall.)[48]

There are several layers of meaning here that are inevitably lost in translation. The 'puerta falsa' is both a back door and, jocularly, the back passage, so there is nothing grand about this departure. And the word order that Cervantes chooses is particularly significant because it brings the words 'corral' and 'salió' into close juxtaposition. At one level, a *corral* is a farmyard and *salió* means that he went out. But both words have secondary, theatrical meanings that are highlighted by their proximity: a *corral* is also an inn yard or outdoor theatre — a *corral de comedias* — and, in that context, *salir* is what actors do when they make their entrance. As he leaves the yard, Don Quixote comes on stage.[49]

The first two chapters of *Don Quixote* are as clear an instance as we might wish to find of what Stephen Greenblatt came to call 'renaissance self-fashioning', a characteristic he first discerned in the behaviour of Sir Walter Ralegh and later developed into a book-length account of the forces at work in sixteenth-century England that 'caused individuals to conceive of themselves as malleable roles in life as well as in writing'.[50]

Greenblatt started from a reading of Ralegh's poem 'Ocean's Love to Cynthia' and 'its tormented sense of a world and a self in pieces' that put him in mind of Eliot's *Waste Land*, and asked 'why would a tough-minded Elizabethan courtier, monopolist, and adventurer [like Sir Walter Ralegh] have written poetry at all, let alone poetry that had the ring of a modernist experiment?'. He found the answer in Ralegh's role-playing, his sense of himself as a character in a fiction. Fallen from Elizabeth's favour, he cast himself as Orlando Furioso, driven mad by disappointed love, writing anguished verses intended to display his state of distraction. Ralegh's desperation may not have been entirely feigned, as he was, after all, imprisoned in the Tower. But, as Greenblatt observes, 'he turned that desperation into a literary performance that was in turn part of a lifelong practice of staging himself'. Greenblatt does not reference Erving Goffman's classic account of the presentation of self in everyday life, but he arrives at much the same conclusion: individuals design their actions according to the impression of themselves they want to project onto others.[51]

Alonso Quijano is not in the same league as Sir Walter Ralegh, and it would be unfair perhaps to characterize his role-play as no more than a pose, but there is a strong parallel between the ways in which both he and Ralegh assume the role of a character in fiction as a way of embodying a state of mind and a political or ideological standpoint.[52] The extent to which they do adopt a pose comes precisely in the way they both leave a discernible gap between the role and their playing of it, between the actor and the mask. No one can accuse Alonso Quijano of being a convincing actor. No one is taken in by his performance — his 'mal compuesta celada' — and Cervantes needs that gap because that is where he locates the humour and the satire.

Perhaps the strongest parallel with Ralegh's self-fashioning comes in the episode in the Sierra Morena (I. 25), when Alonso Quijano, now firmly established as an actor who is playing the part of Don Quixote, also plays the part of Amadís de Gaula, who is playing the role of Beltenebros, who is playing the role of Orlando, a lover sent mad by love, 'haciendo del desesperado, del sandío y del furioso'. There is, however, a limit to Don Quixote's readiness to play the part in full. Orlando lays waste to the land in his fury, but Quixote stops short at Amadís's more considerate behaviour: 'que sin hacer locuras de daño, sino de lloros y sentimientos, alcanzó tanta fama como el que más' (I. 25, 302) ('his madness did not involve doing any damage, but just weeping and being heartbroken, and he achieved as much fame as the best of them').[53] In sparing the trees, the shepherds, the sheep and the cottages — all destroyed in Orlando's original fit of fury — Don Quixote is underlining the fact that it is not real emotion he is expressing: 'el toque está en desatinar sin ocasión' (302) ('[t]he thing is to become mad without a cause').[54]

The whole point is to act mad without reason, to show what he might be capable of if he had good cause.

Ann Davies has also highlighted the significance of the gap between the actor and the character in her fascinating study of Penélope Cruz.[55] Unsurprisingly, in a book about a prominent screen actor, the notions of 'perform' and 'performance' figure extensively in Ann Davies's analysis, but even on a first reading, it is clear that they mean very different things according to context and theoretical viewpoint. The four sections of the book are headed 'Performing Youth', 'Performing Nation', 'Performing Otherness', and 'Performing Performance'. These are clearly not phrases drawn from common parlance but Davies uses them to show how Penélope Cruz's emerging public persona — a young, attractive, Spanish, female actor working successfully in an international industry largely dominated by Anglo-American expectations and values — intersects and resonates with the roles she plays in films like *Jamón Jamón*, *Vicky Christina Barcelona*, *Abre los ojos* (remade as *Vanilla Sky*), *Volver*, and *Los abrazos rotos*.

A key passage in Davies's book comes when she analyses the scene in *La niña de tus ojos* when Macarena, played by Penélope Cruz, is playing the part of an actress, usually assumed to be Imperio Argentina, who is weeping over the body of Antonio in the film within the film, usually assumed to be *Carmen, la de Triana*. 'In the first take,' Davies writes,

> Macarena gives a false and exaggerated performance of grief. Before the second

> take Fontiveros tells Macarena that her father has died in prison. Macarena then gives a moving and tearful performance in the second take that appears genuine, and emotional enough to move the other actors who all comment on her performance.[56]

The scene itself, and Ann Davies's reading of it, both highlight the central paradox about artistry and authenticity in performance: the more skilful the pretence, the more convincing the result. In this instance, Penélope Cruz demonstrates her skill as an actor in portraying an actress who can only produce a convincing performance when she is herself bereaved.

The collocations with 'performance' that Davies uses most frequently in her book are 'active', 'deliberate', 'explicit', 'exaggeration', 'hyperbole', and 'fakery'. These are not qualities that one normally associates with successful performance. But, as Ann Davies demonstrates, there are times when acting is an art that both conceals and reveals its own artistry. Sometimes the gap between the actor and the role can be more eloquent than a perfect congruence between them.

Alonso Quijano is, to use Ann Davies's formulation, 'performing chivalry', but in such a way that his performance is, again in her words, 'active, deliberate, explicit, exaggerated, hyperbolic — fake'. Sometimes the actor needs to be convincing, sometimes not.

V

As Richard Schechner has written, and most practitioners and theorists agree, there is no performance without an audience: 'even where audiences do not exist as such [...] the function of the audience persists.'[57] In the early chapters of Part One, Don Quixote has very little exposure to an audience. During the early stages of the first sally he has no one to talk to but himself: he is reduced to dictating to himself the chronicle that he imagines will be written about his exploits on that first morning on the campo de Montiel. But he does have a prospective readership in mind, so 'the function of the audience persists'.

When he reaches the inn in I. 2, the two prostitutes, the innkeeper, and the other occupants provide him with a more tangible though less appreciative audience. The priest and the barber who sweep him up and bundle him into his bed complete the sum total of those who can bear witness to his achievements. The introduction of Sancho moves the performance onto a different plane. In one sense, Sancho joins the cast of Don Quixote's play, marking a distinctive shift in the texture of the novel from narrative to dialogue; but he also provides Quixote with an audience.[58]

In practice, Don Quixote, like all good actors, turns out to be a very skilful manager of his audience. He has to be: there are no theatres in La Mancha, only strolling players and puppet shows. Nowadays, performances normally take place in spaces designed for the purpose — arenas, stadia, theatres — places that are 'uniquely organized so that a large group can watch a small group — and become aware of itself at the same time'.[59] Both aspects of this definition are important: the audience has to be able to see and be seen. It has to have a common point of focus and a strong sense of its own group dynamic, because performances are not just about entertainment, they exist to foster celebratory and ceremonial feelings and encourage social solidarity. Nick Starr, former Executive Director of the National Theatre, has called this the 'congregational' quality of theatre and its importance has been underlined by recent research on audience responses to live opera relays in the cinema. Almost without exception, respondents to questionnaires value the solidarity they feel with their fellow audience members above any other consideration — the singing, the sound quality, the subtitles, the price of the ice cream, anything. They just like watching the show together.[60]

Other recent empirical research has focused on the way street performers create for themselves a performance space, build an audience, and elicit payment. Researchers have filmed street performers — jugglers and escapologists — in the west plaza of Covent Garden in London using cameras fixed on the roof of the central market buildings as well as at street level. The performers have a very short time to transform a public space (a physical environment) into a performance place (a social construct) that passers-by acknowledge as such; and in the same short period of time they have to turn a group of passers-by into an audience. In order to achieve this, the performers design their words and actions so as to help audience members identify themselves as part of a performance, and to understand the role that they must play in it, not least, of course, by showing their appreciation at the end, when the hat is passed around.[61]

All of this happens extremely rapidly, and there is a repertoire of phrases, gestures, repartee, loud noises, bangs, and objects (bins, boxes, ropes, and chainsaws) that they use to do it. Speeded up films of this process show with breath-taking vividness crowds of up to two hundred people apparently spontaneously organizing themselves into an attentive and well-behaved audience.[62] It is instructive to see how mechanistically we all behave in these situations, underlining very graphically the point that there is no performance without an audience; the audience embodies the performance just as much as the performer does.

There is a text-book illustration of this process at work in Book III Chapter 10 of *Persiles y Sigismunda* which features two false redeemed captives who play the large and attentive audience ('mucha gente junta, todos atentos mirando y escuchando') in much the same way as our Covent Garden performers do. They have with them some objects, a painted canvas which they use as a visual aid and two heavy chains to signify their recent release from captivity. And one of them speaks 'con voz clara y en todo estremo esperta lengua' ('in a clear and expert voice') while cracking a whip to retain their attention throughout his patter, variously described as a 'larga plática' ('long discourse') and an 'arenga' ('harangue').[63]

Don Quixote is also very good at doing exactly what these street performers do: organizing random bystanders into an audience by stopping people in their tracks, catching their attention, making them listen and engage with what he is saying; making them think of themselves as a group and deliver some sort of verdict at the end. An early example comes in I. 11 with the goatherds, where just a handful of acorns and a 'larga arenga' has them 'embobados y suspensos' ('bemused and bewildered').[64] He will repeat the trick countless times throughout the novel, with the galley slaves (something of a captive audience, admittedly), in taverns, at dinner tables, at the Cave of Montesinos, in the ducal palace, using attention-grabbing language, gestures, and objects to focus the attention of the people around him and organize them into an audience.

Of course, the reception he and others get for their performances is not always rapturous — it is frequently ironic, often hostile, sometimes bored, and in the case of the two false captives they find their story challenged to destruction by the two *alcaldes*. Periandro's narration in Book II of the *Persiles* is met with deeply divided, gender-specific, critical response from an audience that, nevertheless, turns up night after night to hear him tell his tale. But it is characteristic of Cervantes's fiction that his audiences express their critical appreciation or amazement as a way of bringing down a metaphorical curtain on a quasi-theatrical event.

The foregoing discussion heavily underlines the significance of Don Quixote's intervention at the end of the episode of Grisóstomo and Marcela. This performance, or masque, brings to a close what was originally the second of four parts to the original novel (what we now think of as Part One) and it shows how far Don Quixote has come in fourteen chapters: from a singleton, self-fashioning protagonist with only himself to talk to, to a fully-staged drama of unrequited love and self-inflicted destruction in which everyone is playing a part. Cervantes has also come a long way in terms of his role as narrator, from omniscience and total control ('de cuyo nombre no quiero acordarme' — 'I *don't wish to* remember') to the exact opposite, where everything we know we learn from the characters themselves. With Grisóstomo and Marcela, Cervantes has broken the mould of third-person narrative and has moved via dialogue to a world of multiple first persons all telling their own story in their own words. But these actors are also spectators within the site-specific playing spaces that Cervantes finds both outdoors in the mountains and indoors at the inn. Faced with this rising tide of multiple voices, Don Quixote often finds himself sharing the stage, and sometimes vacating it altogether. His defiant intervention on Marcela's behalf is his own cry for attention.

VI

The sequence just outlined is masterly and it foreshadows in many ways the profound shift of emphasis in Part Two that causes Don Quixote such discomfort — the onset of celebrity.

The principal distinctive features of Part Two of *Don Quixote*, and those which contribute most to the success of the sequel, all arise from Cervantes's own critical reading of Part One, and the opening chapters in particular. Virtually all the material that appeared in 1615 can be traced back to the opening six chapters of 1605; even the very status of the novel itself undergoes a critique which has its origins in the scrutiny of the books (I. 6). On the face of it, there is no equivalent passage in Part Two to the sustained exercise of practical criticism carried out by the priest and the barber as they go through Don Quixote's library, sorting the worthwhile from the rubbish and throwing the latter on the fire. Nor could there be, since Don Quixote's original library no longer exists.

But there is a scrutiny of a book at the beginning of Part Two and that is the discussion in Chapter 2 that follows the news, broken excitedly first by Sansón Carrasco and then by Sancho, that a book has been published about Quixote and Sancho's exploits. Sequels always include, to some extent, at least a reference to a previous episode or episodes, but Cervantes goes further and incorporates Part One into Part Two both physically and intellectually. Whereas Part One began with a list of the thirty or so books that the contemporary reader really ought to have read to get the best out of *Don Quixote*, at the beginning of Part Two there is only one book in town. Everyone has read it; everyone is talking about it; Don Quixote and Sancho are famous.

This elbowing aside of a literary tradition by a work of Cervantes's own is not just a piece of vanity publishing. The stroke of genius arises from Cervantes's decision to promote his protagonist from obscurity to celebrity. In Part One Don Quixote is a socially obscure and economically dysfunctional *hidalgo*; Part Two answers the question 'what if we make him famous?'. Everything that follows stems from this fundamental change in the dynamic between Don Quixote and the world: Quixote's loss of control over the chivalric vision; Sancho's growing confidence in his manipulation of his master; and the knight's tragic confusion at not being able to see what others profess to see; his pathetic recourse to inventing what he claims to have seen in the Cave of Montesinos; and his cynical bargain with Sancho that he will believe what Sancho claims to have seen from the back of Clavileño if Sancho will believe what he claims to have seen in the Cave of Montesinos.

In Part Two, Don Quixote and Sancho in effect become members of a much larger troupe of actors. Everyone they meet has read the book, knows the plot and plays along. As Part Two unfolds, Quixote no longer knows what role he is supposed to play. He is used to playing to a hostile audience and now everyone is queuing up to play along with him. Hence the power shift away from him to Sancho. Increasingly, Don Quixote finds himself an onlooker in his own show.

The visit to El Toboso and the enchantment of Dulcinea (II. 8–10) is a key turning point, a stroke of genius arising from a letter undelivered ten years earlier. Desperate to see the lady Dulcinea, Quixote allows Sancho to persuade him that she and her two ladies in waiting have been transformed into three peasant girls by the wicked enchanters. But, as in Part One, Quixote knows what things look like — he knows that the giants look like windmills; he knows that the helmet looks like a basin; and he knows that the three peasant girls look (and smell) like peasants. In Part Two he has simply lost the ability to pretend, to play along. Quixote's closing words of Chapter 10 are perpetually moving: '¡Y que no viese yo todo eso, Sancho! [...] Ahora torno a decir y diré mil veces que soy el más desdichado de los hombres' (II. 10, 774) ('And to think that I could not see any of that, Sancho! [...] I say it again, and I shall say it a thousand times: I am the most unfortunate of men').[65] Like Quixote himself, Part Two is a sadder and a wiser book.

Sancho gains control of the privileged vision and Quixote is left disconcerted and deeply saddened, but it is the long episode at the ducal palace (II. 30–54) that sets the seal on Quixote's change of role from protagonist to audience. These twenty-four chapters are in some ways structurally equivalent to the sequence in I. 27–36 that deal with Cardenio's story. The power of this sequence depends crucially on Cervantes's decision to capitalize on the new-found celebrity of the knight and the squire. The result is to reduce the world of Part Two to a series of masques in which all the men and women are merely players. The shift in dynamic is brilliant and it moves the novel onto a different plane. Never in control, constantly bewildered and frequently humiliated, Don Quixote (and Sancho) both lurch through a series of chivalric episodes staged by the estate workers at the behest of the Duke and the Duchess for their amusement. For once, Cervantes seems to take an uncharacteristically clear position on these representatives of the new rich nobility living out their superficial lives by playing trivial games at the expense of their celebrity guests. Everything on the estate is a performance until the performers lose interest. And when they do, it is Sancho who saves the day with an outstanding display of dignity in defeat that puts everyone else to shame.

This is one reason why Part Two is such a different work from Part One: in the ten-year interval between the two parts, Cervantes has ushered in a different kind of fiction, one in which dialogue with the literary past is supplanted by dialogue with the contemporary world. The scope of Part Two is much greater; its satire is much sharper; its sensitivity to the limits of political achievement goes much deeper; and its awareness of the boundless ability of mankind to inflict pain and humiliation on its fellow human beings is much more eloquent.

Part Two is just as episodic as Part One, but the episodes have their justification and their unity in their origin as drama. Changes of scene are what happens in theatre. What holds the episodes together is a view of the world as representation, as appearance. And against that ephemeral and insubstantial background, Quixote and Sancho gain in stature and moral substance.

VII

Cervantes's interest in performance, whether musical or dramatic, his foregrounding of multiple individual voices and his readiness to allow his characters to carry much of the narrative load, undoubtedly colours his prose fiction (not just in *Don Quixote*, but also in the *Novelas ejemplares* and *Persiles y Sigismunda*) and gives it its unmistakable vividness and truth to life. But are we saying anything more than that all the world's a stage, and is the representation of performance *in* the work the same as the representation of the work *as* performance? What does it mean to say that a work of prose fiction, read silently in private, without actors to embody the words or fellow spectators to share in the moment, is a performance?[66]

Part of the answer lies in Richard Schechner's comment that 'even where audiences do not exist as such [...] the function of the audience persists'. In this essay I have, in effect, argued that Cervantes conceived of *Don Quixote*, at least in part, as a drama in prose, realized as a performance in the mind of the reader; the audience does not exist as such but the reader fulfils that function, without which there is no performance, no drama. The critic J. L. Styan goes further, insisting that, even in the theatre, 'the play is not on the stage but in the mind.'[67] Cervantes would undoubtedly have subscribed to this view. If he worked out his ideas in prose rather than in drama it is because he wanted to go further than was possible, even conceivable, on the contemporary stage. Jean Canavaggio has characterized Cervantes's approach to drama as *un théâtre à naître* ('a theatre yet to be born') and it seems clear that his drama occupies a middle ground between the *corral* and the printed copy.[68]

None of *Don Quixote* takes place in a theatre. The nearest Don Quixote gets to a theatre is Maese Pedro's puppet show. In that sense the whole of the novel is site-specific; it all takes place in what we would call today 'found' spaces. That is why Don Quixote has to work so hard to create places for performance and capture and manage his audiences. But once Cervantes pulls back and shows the full extent of the stage on which he is operating, and once the full extent of the performance becomes apparent, the reader's role as audience starts to take on a new significance. The reader's role is fore-grounded on a number of occasions in the novel but perhaps most clearly during the reading of *El curioso impertinente* (I. 33–35), when for three chapters there is an absolute alignment of time and place between the fictional world of the reading and the real world of the reader.

We may not always notice it, but that alignment is there throughout our reading of the novel even when it is not foregrounded. These players who are playing out their performance in front of us, who have our full attention and who hold us 'embobados y suspensos', can only do so, unlike real actors in a real theatre, because they are as much immersed in our minds as we are in theirs. When we are reading, we are a fully immersed audience of one, co-creating the performance with the performers. And as the texture becomes more and more fluid and porous, especially in Part Two, and the characters repeatedly switch their roles between actors and onlookers, the reader's spectatorship becomes an important unifying factor.

As we have seen, when Don Quixote rides out, he does so 'por la puerta falsa de un corral'. He leaves the confines of the *corral*. Cervantes's dramatic sense stretched well beyond the boundaries of the contemporary playhouse and that, as much as his resentment of Lope de Vega, accounts for at least some of his ambivalence towards the contemporary theatrical scene. When he wrote *Don Quixote* — or at least once he had started writing *Don Quixote* — he was determined to take performance to a place he knew no-one, not even Lope, could follow him. And prose was the only medium in which the drama in his imagination could be performed.

Notes to Chapter 4

1. Quoted in Robert Folkenflik, '*Tristram Shandy* and Eighteenth-Century Narrative', in *The Cambridge Companion to Laurence Sterne*, ed. by Thomas Keymer (Cambridge: Cambridge University Press, 2009), p. 49. Writing in the *Monthly Review* for December 1759, the same month in which the first two volumes were published in York, William Kenrick also invokes the word 'performance' when commenting on the extended title of Sterne's novel — *The Life and Opinions of Tristram Shandy, Gentleman*. Kenrick speculates that the public have had enough of lives and *adventures*, 'a consideration that probably induced the droll Mr Tristram Shandy to entitle the performance before us, his Life and *Opinions*' (Folkenflik, p. 49).

2. Richard Schechner, *Performance Theory* (London: Routledge, 2003): 'a performance is an activity done by an individual or group in the presence of and for another individual or group. I had thought it best to centre my definition of performance on certain acknowledged qualities of live theatre, the most stable being the audience-performer interaction. Even where audiences do not exist as such [...] the function of the audience persists' (p. 22, n. 10). Many aspects of a performance can be virtual (an improvisation as opposed to a composition), asynchronous (a broadcast to a distributed audience), or makeshift (a found space); but 'the presence of an audience is central to the definition of theatre' (Helen Freshwater, *Theatre and Audience* (London: Palgrave Macmillan, 2009), p. 1). Peter Brook famously stated that 'a man walks across this empty space whilst someone else is watching him, and this is all that is needed for an act of theatre to be engaged' (*The Empty Space* (London: Penguin, 1968), p. 11, cited by Freshwater, *Theatre and Audience*, p. 1).
3. 'Como casi es comedia toda la historia de don Quijote de la Mancha, no puede ni debe ir sin prólogo'; Alonso Fernández de Avellaneda, *El ingenioso hidalgo don Quijote de la Mancha*, ed. by F. García Salinero (Madrid: Castalia, 1971), p. 51.
4. Lope de Vega had long been included in the list of potential suspects behind the publication of the false *Quixote* and although he has been fairly comprehensively ruled out as the author on linguistic and stylistic grounds, Nicolás Marín has argued that he may have written the prologue: 'La piedra y la mano en el prólogo del *Quijote* apócrifo', in *Homenaje a Guillermo Guastavino: miscelánea de estudios en el año de su jubilación como Director de la Biblioteca Nacional* (Madrid: Asociación Nacional de Bibliotecarios, Archiveros y Arqueólogos, 1974), pp. 253–88. See also Daniel Eisenberg, 'Cervantes, Lope y Avellaneda' in *Estudios cervantinos* (Barcelona: Sirmio, 1991), pp. 119–41. Although there is a strong consensus among critics that the author was Gerónimo de Pasamonte, the most recent editor of the false *Quixote* argues that Lope may have taken a proactive role in the preparation of the manuscript (Alonso Fernández de Avellaneda, *El ingenioso hidalgo Don Quijote de la Mancha*, ed. by Luis Gómez Canseco (Madrid: Biblioteca Nueva, 2000), p. 59).
5. After a brief history of Spanish theatre, culminating in the triumph of Lope de Vega, that 'monstruo de la naturaleza' who carried all before him, Cervantes says that when he himself later resumed his interest in the theatre, he could not find anyone to produce his plays. A publisher had shown some interest until he was advised by a licensed producer ('autor de título') that although his prose was very promising, his verse was not ('que de mi prosa se podía esperar mucho, pero que del verso, nada'): Miguel de Cervantes, *Teatro completo*, ed. by Florencio Sevilla Arroyo (Barcelona: Penguin Random House, 2016), p. 271.
6. On the theatricality of the *Novelas ejemplares* see Eduardo Olid Guerrero, *Del teatro a la novela: el ritual del disfraz en las 'Novelas ejemplares' de Cervantes*, Biblioteca de Estudios Cervantinos, 34 (Alcalá de Henares: Universidad de Alcalá Servicio de Publicaciones, 2015). I had sight of this important study too late to make greater reference to it in this essay.
7. Jon McKenzie, *Perform or Else: From Discipline to Performance* (New York: Routledge, 2001).
8. McKenzie, p. 8.
9. McKenzie, p. 18.
10. Marvin Carlson, *Performance: A Critical Introduction*, 2nd edn, (New York: Routledge, 2004).
11. The threat has not gone away. While this essay was in the final stages of preparation, President Trump, in his first federal budget plan, proposed eliminating both the National Endowment for the Arts and the National Endowment for the Humanities.
12. Emilio Moreno, liner notes to Orphénica Lyra, *Música en el 'Quijote'*, dir. by José Miguel Moreno, (San Lorenzo de El Escorial: Glossa Music, GCD 920207, 2005): 'la gran mayoría de las obras cervantinas acogen entre sus líneas a músicos y músicas, a cantantes e instrumentistas populares y cultos, danzas y canciones y hasta referencias, en algún caso de cierta erudición, a hechos musicales que ofrecen una interesante visión de relativa amplitud de la vida musical de finales del siglo XVI y principios del XVII, que el escritor, como buen hijo de su época, conocía y valoraba' (p. 7) ('a vast majority of Cervantes' works accommodate music and musicians in their lines: popular and cultured singers and players, dances and songs and even occasionally erudite references to musical events that offer an interesting and relatively broad view of musical life at

the end of the 16th and the beginning of the 17th centuries, which the writer knew and valued, being as he was, a faithful son of his times'; p. 12).
13. p. 726. Page references to the English translations are to *Cervantes: Don Quixote*, trans. by John Rutherford (Harmondsworth: Penguin, 2000).
14. p. 251.
15. p. 792.
16. p. 793.
17. p. 793.
18. p. 793. Note that, *pace* Rutherford, a guitar is not a vihuela.
19. Cf I. 25, 303–04: 'eso que a ti te parece bacía de barbero me parece a mí el yelmo de Mambrino y a otro le parecerá otra cosa' ('what looks to you like a barber's basin looks to me like Mambrino's helmet and will look like something else to another person'; p. 209).
20. p. 793.
21. Emilio Moreno lists, in addition to the lute and vihuela already mentioned, 'la guitarra morisca y la cristiana [...] tocadas normal y a lo rasgado, y arpas, salterios, órganos, *clavicímbanos*, gaitas zamoranas y zampoñas, flautas, *pífaros*, chirimías, dulzainas, trompetas, cornetas y clarines, sacabuches [...] tambores, atabales y tamborinos, *albogues*, castañuelas, sonajas, panderos, cascabeles, los malhadados cencerros, matracas [...]. Y de arco, solamente el rabel, siempre en pastoriles manos, y nunca el violín' (*Música en el 'Quijote'*, p. 8) ('the Moorish and the 'Christian' guitars [...] played normally or strummed on, as well as harps, psalteries, organs, *clavicímbanos* [predecessors of the harpsichord], Zamora bagpipes, hurdy-gurdies, pastoral flutes, pipes, oboes, cornets, bugles, sackbuts [...] [drums], timpani, [tabors, cymbals, castanets, rattles], tambourines, brass plates, timbrels, hawk bells, the ill-fated cow bells ['ill-fated' because they are used to interrupt Don Quixote's singing in II. 46, 1094], rattles [...]. And among the bow[ed] instruments, only the fiddle, always in pastoral hands, and never the violin'; p. 13). (My additions and amendments.)
22. 'Pero escucha, que a lo que parece [un andante caballero] templando está un laúd o vigüela, y, según escupe y se desembaraza el pecho, debe de preparase para cantar algo' (p. 788) ('But listen: it seems he [a wandering knight] is tuning a lute or a viol and, to judge from his way of spitting and clearing his throat, he must be making himself ready to sing'; p. 560). Note that, *pace* Rutherford, a vihuela is not a viol, either. For the Gananciosa and Lope examples see Miguel de Cervantes, *Novelas ejemplares*, ed. by Jorge García López (Madrid: Real Academia Española, 2013), pp. 205, 402. All other references are to this edition.
23. *Teatro completo*, pp. 400, 555. Note that, in the third act of *Los baños de Argel*, Cervantes describes the entrance of Halima 'con música y hachas encendidas, guitarras y voces y grande regocijo, cantando los cantares que yo daré' (p. 571) ('with music and lit torches, guitars and singing and great revelry, singing the songs that I will provide'; my translation). This stage direction, and a similar one, in *La casa de los celos* (p. 428) show that Cervantes intended to have a hand in the direction of these plays, even though they were 'nunca representadas' ('never performed') and may even have provided music for them.
24. Contrast this with stage directions like this one, from Noël Coward's *Hay Fever*: 'Clara proceeds to clear away the dirty breakfast things, which she takes out singing 'Tea for Two' in a very shrill voice.' Or Peter Shaffer's stage direction in *Amadeus*: 'The Adagio from the Serenade for Thirteen Wind Instruments (K361) begins to sound.' That K361 leaves no doubt about what we are supposed to hear, and the director only has to decide whether to go with the Academy of St Martin in the Fields (who recorded the original soundtrack) or the Berlin Philharmonic Wind Ensemble, as recommended in the *Gramophone Classical Music Guide*.
25. p. 793.
26. Cervantes, *The Complete Exemplary Novels*, ed. by Barry Ife and Jonathan Thacker (Oxford: Oxbow Books, 2013), p. 355. All subsequent references are to this edition and translation. *The Jealous Old Man from Extremadura* was translated by Michael Thacker and Jonathan Thacker.
27. p. 375.
28. Manuel de Sosa Coutiño (*Persiles y Sigismunda*, I. 9–10) makes his, initially disembodied, appearance in the novel by singing, first in Portuguese and then in Castilian, thus enabling Cervantes to set down the words of his song in the language of his intended readership. Having

explained to the other refugees from the Barbaric Isle how he came to be there, the Portuguese lover promptly dies. See B. W. Ife, 'Cervantes's Portuguese Lover', in *'A primavera toda para ti.'. Homenagem a Helder Macedo*, ed. by Margarida Calafate Ribeiro (Lisbon: Presença, 2004), pp. 117–21. The nun with the beautiful voice is used as a locator in *La española inglesa*, as part of Isabel's instructions to Ricaredo to allow him to find her: 'Los padres de Isabela alquilaron una casa principal, frontero de Santa Paula, por ocasión que estaba monja en aquel santo monasterio una sobrina suya, única y estremada en la voz; y así, por tenerla cerca, como por haber dicho Isabela a Ricaredo que, si viniese a buscarla la hallaría en Sevilla y le diría su casa su prima la monja de Santa Paula, y que para conocella no había menester más de preguntar por la monja que tenía la mejor voz en el monasterio, porque estas señas no se le podían olvidar (p. 252)' ('Isabella's parents rented a fine house opposite the convent of Santa Paula, to be near a niece of theirs who happened to be a nun there, a young woman with a beautiful voice, and also because Isabella had told Ricaredo that if he came to look for her, he would find her in Seville, and that her cousin, the nun of Santa Paula, would tell him wherever her house was, and in order to find her he need only ask for the nun who had the most beautiful voice in the convent, something which would be easy to remember'; p. 257; translated by R. M. Price). In the event, Ricaredo does not need that extra indicator, the singing nun does not sing and does not even make an appearance in the novel, another example of imaginative excess in the mind of a great writer.

29. See B. W. Ife, 'Feliciana's Little Voice', *Bulletin of Hispanic Studies*, 86.1 (December 2009), 867–76.
30. References to *Persiles y Sigismunda* are to the edition by Carlos Romero Muñoz (Madrid: Cátedra, 2004). Anonymous English translation (London: Matthew Lownes, 1619), p. 244, ed. by B. W. Ife and T. L. Darby, available at <http://ems.kcl.ac.uk> [accessed 4 April 2017].
31. p. 244.
32. See note 14.
33. p. 5; translated by R. M. Price.
34. p. 401.
35. p. 401.
36. p. 402.
37. p. 84.
38. p. 86. A 'rabel', *pace* Rutherford, is not what most people would think of as a fiddle (played under the chin) but is best translated as a viol (played on the knee).
39. There is a strongly held and convincingly argued view among textual critics, that the episode of Grisóstomo and Marcela was originally intended to come between Chapters 23 and 25 but that Cervantes brought it forward in the interests of spreading the interpolated episodes more evenly throughout the novel. See Ellen M. Anderson and Gonzalo Pontón, 'La composición del *Quijote*', in Rico (ed.), pp. cxcii–ccxx, especially section 2 (pp. cxcvi–ccvii) which was revised by Geoffrey Stagg, the leading authority on this aspect of the textual history of *Don Quixote*. See Geoffrey Stagg, 'Revision in *Don Quixote* Part I', in *Studies in Honour of I. González Llubera*, ed. by Frank Pierce (Oxford: Dolphin, 1959), pp. 347–66, and 'Sobre el plan primitivo del *Quijote*', in *Actas del I Congreso Internacional de Hispanistas*, ed. by Frank Pierce and Cyril A. Jones (Oxford: Dolphin, 1964), pp. 463–71. If the episode had been moved forward in this way, it would explain the strong contrast, discussed below, between the narrative approaches adopted in this episode and the main narrative thread.
40. p. 86.
41. p. 86.
42. p. 86. It is interesting to note that if Antonio's uncle, the priest who wrote the song ('el beneficiado tu tío'), is the same priest ('sacerdote y beneficiado') (p. 144) who is Marcela's uncle, then Antonio and Marcela are cousins in this very small world.
43. p. 110.
44. Barry Ife, 'Drama as Novel/Novel as Drama' in *Cervantes–Shakespeare 1616–2016*, ed. by José Manuel González, José María Ferri, and María del Carmen Irles (Kassel: Reichenberger, 2017), pp. 350–68.
45. My translation. Rutherford's 'cannot quite recall' does not convey the wilfulness of 'no quiero acordarme'.

46. 'Ninguna persona, de cualquier estado y condición que sea, se atreva a seguir a la hermosa Marcela, so pena de caer en la furiosa indignación mía. Ella ha mostrado con claras y suficientes razones la poca o ninguna culpa que ha tenido en la muerte de Grisóstomo' (170) ('Let no man, of whatever estate or condition, dare to follow the beautiful Marcela, under pain of incurring my furious indignation. She has shown with clear and sufficient reasons that she bears little or no blame for Grisóstomo's death'; p. 111).
47. p. 554.
48. p. 30.
49. On Don Quixote as an actor see Mark Van Doren, *Don Quixote's Profession* (New York: Columbia University Press, 1958): 'he was first and last an actor, a skilful and conscious actor, who wrote his own play as he proceeded and of course kept the center of its stage' (pp. 8–9). See also Dale Wasserman, '*Don Quixote* as Theatre', *Cervantes: Bulletin of the Cervantes Society of America*, 19.1 (1999), 125–30. Simon Leys, 'The Imitation of Our Lord Don Quixote', *New York Review of Books*, 11 June 1998 reads Van Doren's lectures rather differently: 'The occupation which Don Quixote chooses for himself is that of knight errant. He is not under the delusion that he is a knight errant [...]; he is not pretending to be someone else, like an impostor, or impersonating a character, like an actor on stage'. While there can be little doubt that Don Quixote is acting a part, his being an actor is not sufficient to make the novel a performance. When he is acting, Quixote's audience is represented within the fiction. For the novel to be a performance, the audience has to be located outside its frame of reference. As Robert Sawyer argues ('Tilting at Convention: Orson Welles's *Don Quixote* and *Chimes at Midnight*' in González, Ferri, and Irles, *Cervantes–Shakespeare 1616–2016*, pp. 369–85), Cervantes, like Shakespeare, challenges simplistic binary boundaries: 'In using metatheatrical ploys such as plays-within-plays, role-playing and direct addresses to the audience, both early modern writers call attention to the imaginary world of novelistic writing as well as to the illusory capacity of theatrical performance' (p. 372).
50. Stephen Greenblatt, *Renaissance Self-Fashioning: From More to Shakespeare* (Chicago: University of Chicago Press, 2005). All quotations are from the Preface: 'Fashioning *Renaissance Self-Fashioning*', p. xii.
51. Erving Goffman, *The Presentation of Self in Everyday Life* (Garden City: Doubleday Anchor, 1959).
52. Ralegh and Quixote are in fact both modelling themselves on the same character — Orlando Furioso —, although Quixote is simultaneously channelling him through Amadís de Gaula: 'quiero imitar a Amadís, haciendo aquí del desesperado, del sandío y del furioso, por imitar juntamente al valiente don Roldán (I. 25, 301) ('I intend to imitate Amadís, and to act the desperate, foolish, furious lover so as also to imitate the valiant Orlando'; p. 208).
53. p. 208.
54. p. 208
55. Ann Davies, *Penélope Cruz*, BFI Film Stars (London: Palgrave MacMillan, 2014). I am very grateful to Professor Davies for providing me with an electronic copy of her text so that I could readily identify and study all 197 instances of 'performance' in her book.
56. Davies, *Penélope Cruz*, pp. 49–50.
57. Schechner. See note 2.
58. It could be argued that the shift from predominantly third-person narrative to dialogue marks the point at which the argumentative gap opens up in Don Quixote's performance and it starts to attain the richness of texture that will become a hallmark of the novel. As Tom Stoppard has commented: 'I write plays because writing dialogue is the only respectable way of contradicting yourself. I put a position, rebut it, refute the rebuttal, and rebut the refutation.' In Mel Gussow, *Conversations with Stoppard* (London: Nick Hern Books, 1995), p. 3.
59. Schechner, p. 14.
60. Sinéad O'Neill, Joshua Edelman and John Sloboda, *Opera Audiences and Cultural Value: A Study of Audience Experience*, Working Paper, 2 (London: Creativeworks London, 2014) <http://www.creativeworkslondon.org.uk/publications/working-paper-2> [accessed 3 April 2017]. Karen Wise, *English Touring Opera*, 'Opera in Cinemas', Working Paper, 3 (London: Creativeworks London, 2014). <http://www.creativeworkslondon.org.uk/publications/working-paper-3> [accessed 3 April 2017].

61. The research has been carried out by Colombine Gardair, Patrick Healy, and Martin Welton in the Interaction, Media and Communication Research Group in the School of Electronic Engineering and Computer Science at Queen Mary University of London. Dr Gardair has reported her analysis of street performers in Covent Garden in 'Performing Places', in *C&C'11: Proceedings of the 8th ACM Conference on Creativity and Cognition* (New York: Association for Computing Machinery, 2011), pp. 51–60.
62. Body torque is an extremely important indicator of this process. 'A torque occurs when the upper body orientation, usually led by the eyes, followed by the head, and eventually the shoulders, deviates from the lower body orientation, starting from the feet up to the hips' (Gardair, p. 52). Because the lower body is usually orientated towards the main activity and the upper body towards lower priority activities, a realignment eventually takes place, and when the passer-by aligns their lower body with their upper body the performer has their attention and her audience.
63. Cervantes, *Persiles*, pp. 527–28. My translation.
64. p. 86.
65. p. 551.
66. For a full discussion of the importance of silent, private reading of printed playbooks in England and Spain, see Ife, 'Drama as Novel/Novel as Drama'.
67. J. L. Styan, *The Elements of Drama* (Cambridge: Cambridge University Press, 1960), p. 288, cited in David Edgar, *How Plays Work* (London: Nick Hern Books, 2009), p. 7.
68. In Florencio Sevilla Arroyo, introduction to Miguel de Cervantes, *Teatro completo* (Barcelona: Planeta, 1987), p. 30.

CHAPTER 5

Don Quixote and the Picaresque Novel: A Problematic Game of Triangles

Robert Oakley

Don Quixote, wanting to resuscitate knight errantry, leaves home one July morning in search of adventures that might match up to those he has read in his books. He also dreams that a gifted chronicler will relate his chivalric deeds so powerfully that Don Quixote, man of action, and his deeds, will be immortalized by the chronicler's pen. In Chapter 22 of Part One of the subsequent chronicle of those deeds, Don Quixote comes face to face with a gaggle of convicts — all of them condemned to row in His Majesty's galleys for the crimes they have committed. Among these is another man of action who has written his own account of his deeds — in short, the story of his life. He introduces himself as Ginés de Pasamonte and through him Don Quixote and his creator encounter the picaresque.

Jerónimo de Pasamonte, Aragonese soldier who, like Cervantes, fought at Lepanto and then suffered captivity in Africa, had in fact written his memoirs (although the text remained in manuscript until early in the twentieth century) which cover the eighteen years he spent in the Middle East. It is now believed by many that Cervantes's Pasamonte was designed to lampoon the literary efforts of a man who shared his fate in the Magreb. Be that as it may, the meeting of Don Quixote with Ginés de Pasamonte is the meeting of two missions — one of them, the chivalric quest of Don Quixote related in the first part of *Don Quixote de la Mancha*, published in 1605. The second mission had already been related by Mateo Alemán in the first part of his *Guzmán de Alfarache* published six years earlier in 1599 — ostensibly a campaign against the professional beggary that plagued Spain.

The facts are well known, have been much commented on, and demonstrate arguably the most important case of intertextuality in the whole of European literature at the turn of the seventeenth century. *Guzmán de Alfarache*, Part One, went on sale in March 1599. Nine weeks later another book-seller published *Lazarillo de Tormes*. This was the first time in twenty-six years that the *Lazarillo* had been published in Madrid, albeit in an expurgated version. Two editions of the *Guzmán* came out in Barcelona and one in Zaragoza — all these in the year in which the princeps was published. It is of interest to note that one of the Barcelona editions as well as the Aragonese edition included the *Lazarillo* in the same volume.

Booksellers, reading Part One of *Guzmán de Alfarache* in 1599, had clearly perceived the fundamental links between Mateo Alemán's book and *Lazarillo*. Cervantes too. That is to say, these men, writers, readers, and book-sellers had between them taken part in 'el descubrimiento espontáneo de una clase por parte de un lector-escritor que pertenece al más amplio de los públicos' (the spontaneous discovery of a new literary form and yet these people are simply members of the general public.)[1] It was in fact the birth of a new sub-genre in the world of prose fiction, although it is only twenty-first-century hindsight that allows us to speak here in terms of genre and sub-genre. As for Cervantes himself, he had not created a genre, but he had provided his reader in 1605 with the first constructive commentary on a sub-genre that he recognized without being able to give it a name. Don Quixote asks anxiously if Ginés's *Life* is any good:

— Es tan bueno, respondió Ginés — , que mal año para *Lazarillo de Tormes* y para todos cuantos de aquel género se han escrito o escribieren. (I. 22, 265–66)

('It's so good,' replied Ginés, 'that I wouldn't give a fig for *Lazarillo de Tormes* and all the others of that kind that have been or ever will be written.')[2]

While Ginés's use of 'género' may well simply refer to the autobiographical narrative structure of a *Lazarillo* or a *Guzmán*, Cervantes had undoubtedly seen more than this: a peripatetic trajectory — from master to master, from profession to profession, from place to place; and in *Guzmán de Alfarache*, Part One, despite its immense size (more than ten times that of *Lazarillo de Tormes*), a text of epic dimensions, but the protagonist of which makes no secret of his total lack of heroism. The phenomenal success of *Guzmán de Alfarache*, Part One, was confirmed by the appearance three years later of a spurious second part authored by one Juan Martí under the pseudonym Mateo Luján de Sayavedra — a fate which Cervantes himself was to suffer in due course at the hands of the mysterious Avellaneda. Let it be noted *de pasada* that *Lazarillo de Tormes*, not *Guzmán de Alfarache*, is the named proto-picaresque narrative in Chapter 22 of *Don Quixote*, Part One, while Ginés de Pasamonte appears to be merely its fool. I am far from being the first to see Cervantes's portrayal of Mateo Alemán's protagonist as a way to resolve what Harold Bloom has called the anxiety of influence.[3]

Bloomian anxiety is, of course, the poet's desperate fear that he may prove to be not as strong as his admired precursor who, in addition to his manifest genius, enjoys an apparently unassailable literary immortality. Yet there is no choice: the successor must respond to the challenge. His response is to carry out a strong re-reading, or better, misreading, as Bloom would have it, avoiding above all a mere repetition of his precursor's work in order to achieve emancipation and be strong himself.[4] Mere repetition signals defeat. Indisputably, Cervantes and Alemán were strong readers although at that literary moment, the dying days of the sixteenth century, the genre we now call the Novel remained to be created. As Gonzalo Sobejano demonstrated in his pioneer essay, Alemán had read the *Lazarillo* with attention and perpetrated what Bloom would call a misreading of the little masterpiece.[5] Let us recall at this point the classic definition of a picaresque novel formulated by Fernando Lázaro Carreter in his essay 'Para una revisión del concepto "Novela Picaresca"'. For

Lázaro Carreter, a picaresque novel is

> la autobiografía de un desventurado sin escrúpulos, narrada como una sucesión de peripecias [...]; la articulación de la autobiografía mediante el servicio del protagonista a varios amos, como pretexto para la crítica; y el relato como explicación de un estado final de deshonor.[6]
>
> (the autobiography of an unscrupulous wretch consisting of his career in the service of diverse masters, affording the opportunity for satire. The narrative takes the form of an explanation for his fall and ultimate state of dishonour.)

Alemán adopts the first of these three wholesale but abandons the second (the formula 'mozo de muchos amos' (lad with many masters) disappears entirely at the close of Part One of the *Guzmán*). And the 'relato'? The story as epistle to one 'Vuestra Merced' is replaced in *Guzmán de Alfarache*, Part One, by the confessions of an inveterate sinner/criminal who, we are given to understand by Mateo Alemán in his prefatory 'Declaración para el entendimiento deste libro' (Address for the understanding of this book), tells the story of his life 'desde las galeras, donde queda forzado al remo, por delitos que cometió, habiendo sido ladrón famosísimo, como largamente lo verás en la segunda parte' (from his position in the galley to which he has been condemned, having been a notorious thief as, in detail, you will learn in Part Two).[7]

How much about *Guzmán de Alfarache*, Part Two, could Cervantes have known in the middle of 1604? Given the manner in which manuscripts habitually circulated in those times, he may even have had a sight of the entire work. It is surely to be supposed that Chapter 22 of the first part of *Don Quixote* was already written long before, while thanks to that prefatory 'Declaración', he had had plenty of time to meditate on the fate of Alemán's protagonist in the galleys at the close of Part Two of the *Guzmán*. Finally, it is now well established that he had taken note of the spurious *Guzmán* composed by Juan Martí in 1602. Harold Bloom can be entertaining, but he may prove less inspirational when the time comes to analyse the clash of two writers whose master-works happen to arrive on the literary scene almost simultaneously. The *Lazarillo de Tormes* was certainly a Bloomian precursor for Mateo Alemán. Bloomian precursors are sometimes remote in time if not in space, and more often than not, dead. Cervantes and the booksellers in the year 1599 saw Alemán as a follower or emulator of the anonymous author of the *Lazarillo*. Alemán's proto-realist programme in support of the war currently being waged against false beggary is unlikely to have seemed a threat in any way whatever, but the first part of *Guzmán* had nevertheless found an extraordinary favour with the general public. Cervantes must have been aware of the threat, and of its sheer immediacy, as he completed his own Part One. He was approaching what I can only describe as a moment, less of influence than of confluence that makes it worthwhile for us, four hundred years later, to seek a different metaphor. Instead of father and son, we borrow from another critic, J. Hillis Miller, a different relationship: that of host and parasite.[8]

The struggle between poets of flesh and blood is appealing; but less appealing is its Freudian inspiration, given that the precursor is a father who must be vanquished in order that his successor, his son, can be liberated and supersede him. Moreover, for Bloom, given that no one can choose his own father, likewise no poet, no matter how strong, can choose his precursor.⁹ But Mateo Alemán, strong poet and strong reader, evidently chose his precursor, the anonymous author of the *Lazarillo*. Harold Bloom's metaphor implies a struggle between two creative artists, the former, the predecessor, being more powerful than the successor. Both metaphors can be useful in that they force us to concentrate on the act of reading without which there can be no struggle of any kind. But while Miller's retains the sense of struggle that grounds Bloom's theory, instead of the two contestants being viewed as father and son, they are now seen as parasite and host. For anyone who has not read Miller's essay, the use of the words 'host' and 'parasite' may seem strange in the context of literary theory and its application to intertextuality. The eternal debates concerning influence and its supposed role in the tracing of the creation of genres make Miller a more attractive option because his metaphor would appear to possess an antithetical, as well as ambiguous quality capable of circumnavigating the customary explanations that envelop the picaresque and the part it may have played in the creation of the Novel. Miller has in mind the meaning of the word 'host' in antiquity. Nowadays, the host is s/he who offers hospitality while s/he can also be the guest who receives it. Readers of *Don Quixote*, however, know better than anyone that 'host' and 'guest' must have the same etymological root given that when a Cervantine innkeeper is not being called 'ventero', he is the 'huésped'. Certainly, in Old French, Old Norse and Slavic, the double antithetical relation obtains so that, more brutally, the host both eats and is eaten. Thus, Miller is referring to 'guest in the bifold sense of friendly presence and alien invader'.¹⁰ 'Parasite' is equally antithetical, coming as it does from the Greek 'parasitos'. 'Para' is 'beside' or 'near'. 'Sitos' is 'grain', or 'food'. Thus, host and parasite are fellow guests 'beside' the food. They share it, but the host is guest as well. S/he eats and is eaten when the fellow guest turns alien invader. The literary work, like the food at the table, is an 'ambiguous gift, food, host in the sense of victim, sacrifice. It is broken, divided, passed around, consumed by the critics [...] who are in that odd relation to one another of host and parasite.'¹¹ In the case of a host-parasite relationship between the *Lazarillo* and the *Guzmán*, Miller's metaphor names the former a text that is, by definition, the established, published work that has been admired by a logical successor. It is therefore automatically the host that awaits a visit from its parasite.

Lazarillo de Tormes attracted Mateo Alemán *qua* reader and he entered the little tale as a parasite enters its host. The predecessor, the already published and often much celebrated text, awaits its assailant, but once the two are united by the act of reading, the passage of the would-be successor sets off a reverse attack whereby the predecessor ineluctably leaves its mark on the parasite (in this case Mateo Alemán qua writer) that came and went and will come again. In perfect reciprocity, the two works can be seen to invade and colonize, sacking the thematics and structure of one another: the son does not choose his father, but the parasite does choose its host. In his turn, Cervantes *qua* reader must have recognized the anonymous author of the *Lazarillo* and Mateo Alemán as artists operating in his field of action. Now, as we have seen, the host-parasite relationship is initiated when the potential parasite, through an act of reading, is attracted to a host through admiration of its structure. Thus it was that, in his turn, Cervantes chose to read the *Guzmán de Alfarache*, Part One somewhere between 1599 and 1604. The extraordinary confluence of the *Guzmán*, Part Two and *Don Quixote*, Part One in 1604 sets in motion a host-parasite relationship. *Guzmán de Alfarache*, Part One constitutes a threat that creates fear — fear deriving from admiration. This admiration transforms *Don Quixote*, Part One into a parasite of a logical host: the already published and astonishingly well received *Guzmán*, Part One.

We shall never know to what extent the reading of the *Guzmán* Parts One and Two affected or altered Cervantes's own personal view of the structure and content of the first and second parts of *Don Quixote*, any more than we can know if he experienced fear or admiration when faced with the vast and majestic bulk of Alemán's text. And yet anyone who has read both works with any degree of care cannot fail to have noted the fact that the structure of Cervantes's tale and that of the *Guzmán* are remarkably similar. Some consideration of the role of Ginés de Pasamonte in Cervantes's novel helps one to appreciate the nature of the confluence of these two texts as well as their similarities. It could be conjectured, for example, that Cervantes, faced with the sheer size and ambition of Alemán's work, driven to compete, chose to abandon the much discussed conception of *Don Quixote* as novella. The novella was an already well established sub-genre in late sixteenth-century Spain. Miller's theory is helpful at this point. Cervantes qua reader, elaborating the meeting with the galley slaves, has invaded the *Guzmán*, returning home thereafter, qua writer, to his own work-in-progress. At this point it is important to bear in mind that Miller's host and parasite are not to be seen in polar opposition with one another but rather that 'the relation is a triangle, not a polar opposition [...]. There is always a third to whom the two are related, something before them or between them, which they divide, consume, or exchange, across which they meet' while the

> relation in question is always in fact a chain [...] without beginning or end [...] a chain in which no commanding element [...] can be identified [...] while the poem is neither the host nor the parasite but the food they both need, host in another sense, the third element in this particular triangle.[12]

Cervantes, in a manner of speaking, steals his rival's protagonist as well as the structure of his rival's work. To put it another way, he returns home with an apparent mocking effigy of Alemán's protagonist under another name. But is that all he is?

If Cervantes had simply wanted to put a rival in his place, he would have been more than contented with the gladiatorial combat in Chapter 22 of his own Part One. However, Edward Riley has remarked on the extent to which Ginés de Pasamonte goes on to haunt the rest of *Don Quixote*.[13] A little while later, Sancho's ass goes missing and in Chapter 4 of Part Two Sancho reveals to Sansón Carrasco that the thief was Ginés de Pasamonte — and finally in Chapters 25 and 26 of Part

Two Ginés reappears transformed into Maese Pedro, puppeteer and divine. The fact that Maese Pedro is a *pícaro* and charlatan could make him appear the villain of the piece, but Riley calls attention to his curious and unexpected behaviour. First, he insists on offering Don Quixote a free show; and secondly, when Don Quixote destroys a number of figures taking part in the puppet drama, he will accept only a proportion of the costs by way of reparation. It is at this point that we return to the literary conversation between Don Quixote and Ginés. Martín de Riquer is pre-eminent among those critics who think that Ginés is a device invented by Cervantes to avenge himself on his fellow-slave, Jerónimo de Pasamonte, who may have authored the spurious continuation of *Don Quixote*.[14] Certainly, everyone seems to agree that in inventing Ginés, Cervantes is commenting ironically upon the supposed structural defect or drawback that first-person narrative implies. But to reduce this clash to mere satire seems superficial and perfunctory. Cervantes was surely neither of these things. He knew perfectly well that the able story-teller will always fashion a satisfactory ending so as to give a convincing structure to his story. The awesome *desenlace* (dénouement) of *Guzmán de Alfarache*, Part Two, on which I believe Cervantes meditated long and hard, illustrates this beautifully. Lazarillo had tasted *buena fortuna* (good fortune) according to the close of his account and boasts in the famous prologue of having reached his *buen puerto* (safe haven). Guzmán may end up the *hombre perfecto* his creator promised at the opening of his Part One. Having read Part One of the *Guzmán*, Cervantes knows all this, but only after the publication of Part Two does he know of Guzmán's epiphany in the galleys. At this stage he may well have planned Don Quixote's conversion and return to sanity. Equally, he may even have been at a loss to know what to do with the figure he had created — one as anti-heroic as Guzmán de Alfarache. How to end his story without plagiarizing or copying in one way or another, the closure of the *Guzmán* Part Two? Surely not by simply and lamely reminding his reader of the famous conversion of the great *pícaro* at the close of *Guzmán de Alfarache* Part Two. And yet, right the way through to 1615, it seems to me legitimate to regard Cervantes as preoccupied by the fate of Alemán's anti-hero. The reappearance of Ginés de Pasamonte in Part Two of *Don Quixote* is the spectacular confirmation of this. Commenting on the sympathetic portrayal accorded by Cervantes to his own *pícaro*, Riley concludes that 'en este episodio, observamos un inequívoco movimiento en la dirección, contrario a sus orígenes picarescos. Vestido de maese Pedro, Ginés empieza a solidificarse como ser humano' (in this episode we can see an unmistakable movement in the direction contrary to his picaresque origins. Clothed as master Peter, he begins to solidify as a human being).[15] We glimpse here that familiar, humanizing tendency in Cervantine characterization. Recreating Guzmán in his own story was a challenge for the successor who is struggling, and possibly failing, to overcome his rival and precursor by effecting this deft transformation of Mateo Alemán's anti-hero, Guzmán de Alfarache:

> Sigue siendo una figura transitoria en todos los sentidos: está a punto de desaparecer de nuevo, y quien sabe lo que le va a pasar. Lo que sí es cierto es que ya demuestra un potencial para cambiar.[16]

(He remains never more than a transitory figure in any sense: at this stage he is on the point of vanishing yet again and who knows what may become of him. The only certainty is that already he is showing signs of possessing the potential for change.)

Change is also supposed to be at the heart of the unfolding narrative of the *Guzmán*, Part Two. Alemán informs his reader at the opening of his second part that his story of conversion and redemption can only be closed out after Guzmán has suffered 'trabajos y miserias, después de haber bajado a la más ínfima de todas, puesto en galera por curullero della' (trials and tribulations after having descended to the most base and miserable position of all — charge of the storage).[17] Such is the second and final section of his life, the homeward half, indeed, the wicked half of a story that I summarize thus: Seville, the wide world, and Seville again where Fernando Lázaro's *estado final de deshonor* (final state of dishonour) awaits him. Whatever Cervantes thought of the ending of Part Two of his rival's tale, zealous of his own protagonist's destiny in this world and the next, he brings his own circular narrative to an almost identical conclusion: Don Quixote reverts to being harmless Alonso Quijano — and dies the good Christian death. Of course, he dies in part so as to close the door in the face of any future Avellanedas or Pasamontes. But clearly, the renunciation of the chivalric fairyland means the acceptance of the world as it is. Many critics have across the years celebrated the way Cervantes turns his back on what Carlos Blanco Aguinaga called the *Guzmán*'s dialectic of truth and falsehood, claiming that there existed in the Golden Age two fictional worlds, one true, the other false. The false one is that of the baroque dogmatist who knows best as he contemplates 'el mundo en guerra que siempre se resuelve' (a world constantly at war except when it chooses otherwise).[18] But no; for Blanco this reality is false. Strip it aside and then you find the truth. Such is the process of *desengaño* (disillusionment). Blanco argues in his influential essay that the Cervantine invention of *parejas* (pairs) — Don Quixote and Sancho, Cipión and Berganza, Rincón and Cortado, and so on — reveals a world that is all uncertainty, ambiguity, openness, in which ultimately the creator loses or relinquishes control of the creation. Such for Blanco is the true realism, the realism which is free. But the distinguished French *alemanista*, Edmond Cros, declares that the power of the *Guzmán* lies precisely in its dogged portrayal of 'un universo radicalmente fementido' (a universe that is radically flawed).[19] Is this world one from which Cervantes would want to distance himself? Apparently so, but his choice does not make a nonsense of Alemán's realism, baroque or otherwise. Given the initial push that gave momentum to his mighty narrative, the portrayal by Américo Castro of Alemán as the bitter outsider is wholly logical — most obviously and obsessively in Castro's late collection of essays, *Cervantes y los casticismos españoles*, where, like so many who came after him, he finds his own way of accounting for 'la melancolía desesperada del *Guzmán de Alfarache*, sobre su insinuación de haberse equivocado Dios irremediablemente al crear al hombre' (the desperate melancholy in *Guzmán de Alfarache* and for the feeling that God had made a dreadful mistake when he made mankind).[20] Castro found painful this 'mundo grandiosamente atroz del *Guzmán* (falsía, injusticia, iniquidad universales), era la sombra que proyectaba sobre cuanto existe' (overwhelmingly appalling existence (universal duplicity, injustice, iniquity) and such was the shadow with which it enveloped the entire world).[21] However, Castro and many others have not understood until recent times that Alemán is offering his reader what we would nowadays call programmatic realism. The logical opposite to the *Guzmán* must be *Amadís de Gaula*, reasons Castro. He saw *Amadís* as the choice model for a Cervantes appalled by what today is beginning to be seen as the sheer modernity of Guzmán and his world. Meanwhile, choice in *Guzmán de Alfarache* has a distinctly existential ring.[22]

In the world of the galley-slave, Guzmán's overseers make cruel sport of him in what passes for an application of justice. Readers of the second part of *Don Quixote* who have also read *Guzmán de Alfarache* should be reminded of the great *pícaro*'s agony when they come to Chapter 63 of Part Two in which Don Quixote and Sancho are received as honoured guests by officers of one of His Majesty's galleys. In this episode, rarely visited by the critics, Sancho is playfully made fun of by the *galeotes* so that *Don Quixote*, Part Two, can demonstrate for the umpteenth time its credentials as a *libro de entretenimiento* (amusing book) while Don Quixote is vouchsafed yet again an opportunity to be reminded of his state of dishonour as well as his degree of dishonour. Thus did Cervantes show his awareness in Part One, Chapter 22, of the obvious triangle that can be formed using Miller's metaphor: the *Lazarillo*, the *Guzmán*, and *Don Quixote*, Part One. I choose to call this a tragic triangle as well as an iron triangle if only because iron, Hesiod's Fifth Age, speaks to us of the material world and therefore we tend to discount its ambivalent value. Within this triangle *Guzmán de Alfarache*, Part Two, must certainly have been awaited by a public demanding more of the same, while the first part of *Don Quixote* was the unknown quantity, although rumour already had it that the book would please. But there was another triangle taking shape in 1603–04. This was a comic triangle, and because the *vulgo* loved comedy above all else, its constituent parts were guaranteed commercial success. It was in other words a golden triangle: the *Guzmán*, Part Two, *Don Quixote*, Part One, and Francisco de Úbeda's *La pícara Justina*. This last author hoists his colours in the very title of his book: *Libro de entretenimiento, de la pícara Justina* — a tale in which the anti-heroine will end up marrying Guzmán de Alfarache. By 1603 *Don Quixote* was already circulating in manuscript and was eagerly awaited — for its comedy. So when we speak here of this trio of texts as golden, it is no longer gold's superior spiritual quality we have in mind but rather its material value. Thoughtful *cervantistas* have had cause in recent times to remind us of the sometimes inconvenient fact that *Don Quixote* is a funny book. On the other hand, long before Mateo Alemán journeyed to Lisbon in order to see his Part Two through the press in 1604, Part One of his magnum opus had become in the popular mind quite simply *El Pícaro*. The word 'pícaro' features heavily in Part One because the author's programme demanded it.[23]

From our point of view four hundred years later, membership of which of these two triangles best suits *Don Quixote*? Which triangle enables Cervantes to transcend and, indeed, supersede the *Guzmán*? Or had the established work, *Guzmán de Alfarache*, Parts One and Two, turned the tables? How important at this stage of our deliberations is the structure of the *Guzmán*? Does it still attract Cervantes as late as 1614 by which time he must have penned the episode in which Don Quixote visits the galleys, striving all the while to leave Avellaneda in his wake? Is Cervantes, reader and writer, host and parasite, still sacking his host as his own narrative reaches its closure? Or has the host turned parasite? Bloom has warned all would-be successors against repetition, and yet, readers discover that both sequels concern urban space and the sea. Andrés Murillo observes:

> Thus, as Don Quixote and Sancho move towards Barcelona in the company of Roque, they move towards the historical moment of 1614 that will complete the mock hero's destination amidst the life of the city and the sea.[24]

Margaret Doody has defined this particular space as the 'Trope of the Shore or Margin'.[25] She suggests that the novel and the epic share this interest, but the novel

> makes much more of its beach front property. It is more openly and insistently fascinated by the implication of the point at which water and land mingle. The ambiguous area [...] becomes a special kind of space or setting for the Novel.[26]

Doody has called this the 'Threshhold Trope'[27] whose function is often to signal profound change in a story's trajectory. It goes without saying that Cervantes has no need of that space between water and land, but piratical circumstances beyond his control, tickling his inventive genius, guide the destination of Quixote and Sancho. Cervantes's anti-hero will return to rural Castile where he belongs. But let it not be forgotten that the same applies to Guzmán de Alfarache. He, too, is going home. Guzmán leaves home, travels around Europe and then returns home to endure some of the most extreme pain and humiliation that can be experienced in this world. Home for him is therefore the seemingly unavoidable maritime Seville, the new Babylon circa 1600. The sea claims him as its ultimate picaresque prize. We are then asked to believe that he transcends the threatening *desenlace* to find redemption and know *desengaño*. Don Quixote has never known *desengaño* so that when, after leaving home and doing his share of travelling, he finally encounters the Caballero de la Blanca Luna, the humiliation and *desengaño* are as profound as Guzmán's. Indeed, they proceed to dismantle his fairyland slowly — in that Cervantine comic mode. After all, as late as Chapter 67 of Part Two, a year's sojourn in a pastoral paradise still beckons and tempts. This story of rise and fall terminating in the second part of *Don Quixote* completes the textual triangle that can be formed by the *Lazarillo*, the *Guzmán*, and the *Quixote* — three texts and the critical awareness they demand. Lazarillo tells us that he was as good as born in water — that of the Tormes. These beginnings will serve him ill. Alemán describes at considerable as well as grisly length his anti-hero's brutal sojourn on water in the galleys of His Majesty. Did Don Quixote, country *hidalgo* who was born, lived and died in the heart of rural Spain, really have to follow Guzmán into the galleys? Briefly, it is true, but also, absurdly. J. Hillis Miller tells us that

> the previous text is both the ground of the new one and something the new one must annihilate by incorporating it, turning it into ghostly insubstantiality,

so that the new poem may perform its possible-impossible task of becoming its own ground.[28]

The fact that Don Quixote and Sancho can share their humiliation in the galleys would appear to grant a somewhat dubious victory for Cervantes over Mateo Alemán, if indeed the *Guzmán* was still on Cervantes's mind at this stage in the elaboration of his narrative. For Guzmán, of course, there can be no death, but the meaning of Guzmán's saga must manifest itself in some way. Clearly, its *desenlace* cannot be comic. For Cervantes, of course there is always the comic escape from any adventure. So he can easily be a member of either of my triangles in 1604. Cervantes can follow Alemán by having his two anti-heroes accept an invitation to enter the galley. For Alemán, this is not so. The only named comrade to follow Guzmán into the galley is Soto, the last of a series of individuals who have betrayed him along the way. Luis Gómez Canseco notes that amongst the multitude of journeys and adventures

> hay algo que permanece inalterable a lo largo de todo el libro: la soledad del héroe. A pesar de la multitud que le rodea, Guzmán está siempre solo [...] De acuerdo con la doctrina de la carta sobre la verdadera Amistad que Alemán compuso en octubre de 1597, no hay amistad alguna en el *Guzmán* y menos verdadera.[29]

> (one thing remains constant throughout the entire book: the solitude of the hero. Despite the multitudes that surround him, Guzmán is always alone. When set alongside the doctrinal drift of the letter Alemán composed in October of 1597, the absence of friendship was total.)

Neither Cervantes nor Alemán could possibly have known that the latter had written what in the literary parlance of today can legitimately be called the first true novel of betrayal. Soto will betray Guzmán; but equally, Guzmán will betray Soto with terrifying consequences. A story this brutal demands a tone that should have been quite enough to dampen considerably by 1604 the enthusiasm of Alemán's public of 1599. And such is the tone of the second part of the *Guzmán*. Here, the *pícaro* no longer belongs. Yet hardly anyone has noticed. The preeminent feature of the literary era ushered in by Mateo Alemán

> iba a ser el hallazgo de una ambigua expresividad capacitada para comunicar en distintos niveles de significación con los múltiples estratos y contracorrientes de aquel fenómeno que por primera vez cabe llamar un verdadero 'público' de característicos modernos.[30]

> (was going to be the discovery of an ambiguous mode of expression with the capacity to communicate at different levels of meaning so as to connect with the multitude of levels and crosscurrents to be found in that phenomenon that for the first time could be called a genuine public.)

But not even the intellectual public in 1604 was ready to embrace the modernity of either of these two writers. Peter Dunn has pointed out forcefully Cervantes's awareness of the significance of *La pícara Justina* in 1604.[31] He draws attention to Cervantes's treatment of its author in his *Viaje del Parnaso*. López de Úbeda's presence in our golden triangle becomes a shocking and shameful necessity.

Pace Cervantes's invention of a wonderful comic polyphony, is it still possible to draw him back into the tragic triangle? Indeed, is it necessary? Mateo Alemán saw the tragedy of the Spain of Philip II and Phillip III. He also had the temerity to write about it in a work of prose fiction. So did Cervantes, and like Alemán, he found a fresh way of doing so. Of course, at this point, we should be remembering that although *Don Quixote de la Mancha* and *Guzmán de Alfarache* have much in common, our game of triangles always presupposes that they are also adversaries in what is also a game of genres and subgenres. Cervantes had also performed the enormous critical feat of recognizing that the solution to his critical dilemma was not to try to replace either the *Guzmán* or the *Lazarillo*. He had seen in these two works when they sat alongside the *Quixote* in the same triangle of texts, that they were not there to be suppressed but to be ignored. Out in the wide world, the *Quixote* and the *Guzmán* were to have other battles to fight. The Aristotelian, hierarchical division or separation of styles still obtained for many in seventeenth-century Spain, as it did elsewhere. This meant that *Don Quixote* could at least find a noble place within the Middle or Low Styles. But it also meant that it was barred from reaching out in the direction of the Sublime. The High Style as understood in the seventeenth century was beyond it. Comedy could never be sublime, but neither could the *Guzmán* be deemed sublime since it was neither a tragic play nor a secondary epic in verse. In brief, *Guzmán de Alfarache*, despite its literary ambition, had no place in the Spain in which it was composed. *Don Quixote* almost suffered a similar fate with the advent of Romanticism. One would have thought that the virtual evaporation of such separation by style, at the latest, by the close of the eighteenth century, would have guaranteed full canonization to *Don Quixote,* but for the Romantics, comedy was the wrong generic code and the wrong canon in which to insert the literary flagship of a seriously declining Spain. In short, it was decided that *Don Quixote* needed to be re-invented.

As things turned out, Cervantine genius shone brightly and steadily enough in those early days (1599 to 1605 and beyond) for a successful launch of the comic prose epic narrated in the third person. The reverse fate befell the *Guzmán* — a work that nobody knew what to do with. The result was that Alemán's generic achievement, the autobiographical prose epic, was to languish in an international, literary penumbra for another one hundred years. This was bad enough, but worse was to follow because when *Guzmán de Alfarache* re-emerged in the year 1719, its title had been changed to *Robinson Crusoe*.

Notes to Chapter 5

1. Claudio Guillén, 'Luis Sánchez, Ginés de Pasamonte y los inventores del género picaresco', in *Homenaje a Rodríguez-Moñino: estudios de erudición que le ofrecen sus amigos o discípulos hispanistas norteamericanos*, 2 vols (Madrid: Castalia, 1966), I, 221–31 (p. 228) (repr. as 'Luis Sánchez, Ginés de Pasamonte y el descubrimiento del género picaresco' in Claudio Guillén, *El primer siglo de oro: estudios sobre géneros y modelos* (Barcelona: Editorial Crítica, 1988), pp. 197–211). See also Claudio Guillén, 'Genre and Counter genre: The Discovery of the *Picaresque*', in his *Literature as System* (Princeton: University Press, 1971), pp. 135–58. This last is a translation and development of the previous essay. All translations in the present chapter are mine unless otherwise stated.

2. Miguel de Cervantes Saavedra, *Cervantes: Don Quixote*, trans. by John Rutherford (London: Penguin, 2000), p. 182.
3. Harold Bloom, *The Anxiety of Influence: A Theory of Poetry* (New York: Oxford University Press, 1997)
4. Bloom, *The Anxiety of Influence*, p. 83.
5. Gonzalo Sobejano, 'De la intención y valor del *Guzmán de Alfarache*', *Romanische Forschungen*, 71 (1959), 267–311.
6. This essay is the final part of Lázaro Carreter's book-length study, '*Lazarillo de Tormes*' *en la picaresca* (Barcelona: Ariel, 1972), pp. 195–229 (pp. 206–07).
7. Mateo Alemán, *Guzmán de Alfarache*, ed. by José María Micó, 2 vols (Madrid: Cátedra, 1987), II, 113.
8. J. Hillis Miller, 'The Critic as Host', in Harold Bloom and others, *Deconstruction and Criticism* (London: Routledge & Kegan Paul, 1979), pp. 217–53.
9. Harold Bloom, *A Map of Misreading* (Oxford: Oxford University Press, 1980), p. 12.
10. Miller, 'Critic as Host', p. 220.
11. Miller, 'Critic as Host', p. 225.
12. Miller, 'Critic as Host', pp. 224–25.
13. Edward C. Riley, 'Sepa que yo soy Ginés de Pasamonte', in his *La rara invención: estudios sobre Cervantes y su posteridad literaria* (Barcelona: Editorial Crítica, 2001), pp. 51–71.
14. Martín de Riquer, *Para leer a Cervantes*, El Acantilado, 74 (Barcelona: Acantilado, 2003), pp. 393–550.
15. Riley, 'Sepa que yo soy Ginés de Pasamonte', p. 69.
16. Daniel Eisenberg has commented on Ginés de Pasamonte's presence in *Don Quixote*, Part Two, accepting Riquer's thesis concerning Avellaneda as Pasamonte but finding the change in character not one of Cervantes's more felicitous touches. See Eisenberg, *Estudios cervantinos* (Barcelona: Sirmio, 1991), pp. 128–41.
17. Alemán, II, 22.
18. Carlos Blanco Aguinaga, 'Cervantes y la picaresca: notas sobre dos tipos de realismo', *Nueva Revista de Filología Hispánica*, 11 (1957), 314–42 (p. 324).
19. Edmond Cros, *Mateo Alemán: introducción a su vida y a su obra* (Salamanca: Anaya, 1971), p. 104.
20. Américo Castro, *Cervantes y los casticismos españoles* (Madrid: Alfaguara,1966), p. 32.
21. Castro, *Cervante y los casticimos españoles*, p. 165.
22. Benito Brancaforte, '*Guzmán de Alfarache*': ¿*Conversión o proceso de degradación?* (Madison: Hispanic Seminary of Medieval Studies, 1980). This study represents well the robust view of Mateo Alemán's proto-realism.
23. Alemán, II, 115. For the most authoritative explanation of the nature and context of his programme, see the following: Edmond Cros, *Le protée et le gueux: recherches sur les origins et la nature du récit picaresque dans 'Guzmán de Alfarache'* (Paris: Didier, 1967); Michel Cavillac, *Pícaros y mercaderes en el 'Guzmán de Alfarache'* (Granada: Universidad de Granada, 1994); Michel Cavillac, *'Guzmán de Alfarache' y la novela moderna* (Madrid: Casa de Velázquez, 2010).
24. Louis A. Murillo, *The Golden Dial: Temporal Configuration in 'Don Quijote'* (Oxford: Dolphin, 1975), p. 154.
25. Margaret Anne Doody, *The True Story of the Novel* (New Brunswick, NJ: Rutgers University Press, 1999), p. 319.
26. Doody, *True Story*, p. 320.
27. Doody, *True Story*, p. 321
28. Miller, 'Critic as Host', p. 225.
29. Mateo Alemán, *Guzmán de Alfarache*, ed. by Luis Gómez Canseco, Biblioteca Clásica de la RAE, 42 (Madrid: Real Academia Española, 2012), p. 799.
30. Francisco Márquez Villanueva, 'La interacción Alemán-Cervantes', in *Actas del Coloquio Internacional de la Asociación de Cervantistas* (Barcelona: Anthropos, 1991), pp. 149–81 (p. 156).
31. Peter N. Dunn, *Spanish Picaresque Fiction: A New Literary History* (Ithaca: Cornell University Press, 1993), pp. 205–08.

PART III

The Social/Historical Context

CHAPTER 6

Value, Price, and Money: Early Modern Economic Theory in Three Episodes of *Don Quixote*

Brian Brewer

Introduction: Economics and *Don Quixote*.

Miguel de Cervantes's *Don Quixote* is, as critic Carroll Johnson has observed, 'a book about books' that 'simultaneously incorporates into itself and carries on a dialogue with all the forms of imaginative literature current in late sixteenth-century Spain'.[1] *Don Quixote*, however, also engages with a plethora of other, non-literary discourses prevalent in early modern Iberia. Among these, one that has come into increasingly prominent critical focus is the discourse of economics. Although the term 'economics' was not common at the time, issues such as utility value, price, and monetary theory were widely discussed within a conceptual framework derived from medieval scholasticism and applied to a new context of incipient globalization. In the essay that follows, I propose to demonstrate that Cervantes was both well apprised of the state of economic thinking at the turn of the seventeenth century and that he incorporated contemporary theories of value, price, and money as structural elements within the narrative fiction of *Don Quixote*. My analysis will focus on three episodes from both parts of the novel: the discovery of the *Quixote* manuscript in Toledo (Part One, Chapter 9); the adventure of the helmet of Mambrino (Part One, Chapter 21); and the encounter between Sancho Panza and the exiled Morisco Ricote (Part Two, Chapter 54).

Don Quixote: Story, History, or Wrapping Paper?

Don Quixote, Part One, Chapter 9 consolidates many of the outstanding tropes of the preceding chapters (literary referentiality, parody, problematic narrative truth, uncertainty of authorship, etc.), while deepening the text's complexity and ambiguity via the introduction of an ostensibly historical text written in Arabic by the Moorish historian Cide Hamete Benengeli. The discovery of this manuscript in the market of Toledo by the so-called second author of *Don Quixote* does not introduce, but does significantly enrich, the novel's economic discourse, by means of the brief but suggestive description of the book as both physical object and intellectual artefact subject to various uses and therefore susceptible of varying criteria of value. The process of discovery begins when the second author casually interrupts an act of commercial exchange:

> Estando yo un día en el Alcaná de Toledo, llegó un muchacho a vender unos cartapacios y papeles viejos a un sedero; y como yo soy aficionado a leer aunque sean los papeles rotos de las calles, llevado desta mi natural inclinación tomé un cartapacio de los que el muchacho vendía y vile con carácteres que conocí ser arábigos. (I. 9, 118)

> (One day when I was in the main shopping street in Toledo, a lad appeared, on his way to sell some old notebooks and loose sheets of paper to a silk merchant; and since I'll read anything, even scraps of paper lying in the gutter, this leaning of mine led me to pick up one of the notebooks that the lad had for sale, and I saw it was in written in characters that I recognized as Arabic.)[2]

He quickly finds a 'morisco aljamiado', a man of Muslim origin who is proficient in both Spanish and Arabic, to translate these sheaves, which turn out to be a fragment of *Don Quixote* itself:

> Mucha discreción fue menester para disimular el contento que recebí cuando llegó a mis oídos el título del libro, y, salteándoselo al sedero, compré al muchacho todos los papeles y cartapacios por medio real; que si él tuviera discreción y supiera lo que yo los deseaba, bien se pudiera prometer y llevar más de seis reales de la compra. (I. 9, 118–19)

> (I had to draw on all the discretion I possess not to reveal how happy I felt when I heard the title of the book; and, getting in ahead of the silk merchant, I bought all the papers and notebooks from the lad for half a real and if the lad himself had had any discretion and had noticed how much I wanted them, he could well have expected and indeed exacted more than six reals.)[3]

This description of the discovery and purchase of *Don Quixote* not only recounts an economic transaction, it dramatizes the exchange precisely, albeit humorously, in the terms of contemporary price theory. The dominant intellectual force in this regard was a resurgent late scholasticism, whose theoretical and practical economic precepts were predicated upon moral postulates drawn from Aristotle and Thomas Aquinas. For the neo-scholastics, the foundational principle that governed the legitimacy of any purchase agreement was commutative justice, i.e. equality of value between the items exchanged in the deal. Thus, if a book, for example, had a value of six *reales*, then six *reales* was the just price of the item and sellers were morally obligated to charge, and buyers to pay, that price for the book. This was a matter of immutable justice; violating the principle was a mortal sin that could only be assuaged by establishing equality through monetary restitution.[4]

With regard to value, despite potentially confusing overlap in the use of the terms *valor* and *precio* in the source texts, in the context of market exchanges these words were completely interchangeable synonyms that referred exclusively to price. Value was not, in this sense, an ontological category but a description of monetary price, which was, in turn, a function of the general use value that buyers ascribed to a given item within a specific market. Other factors, such as scarcity and cost of production, could influence the price of a good, but ultimately economic value was primarily seen to be the result of the subjective social evaluation of an object's general utility.[5] It is important to recognize that this subjective judgement was social, not individual, and that, in most cases, a good's utility value had to be measured in general, not particular, terms. Hence the emphasis on the so-called common estimate (*estimación común*) of the price of an item, as well as the recognition that this price legitimately fluctuates according to market conditions. Given the volatility of the market, the natural price of a good, which was the monetary expression of the *estimación común*, was subject to frequent alteration (it was as changeable as a chameleon, averred Tomás de Mercado).[6] For this reason there was latitude in the just price, which could be high (*riguroso*), medium (*mediano*), or low (*piadoso*). The king (or his agents) had the legitimate authority to fix the legal price of a good, but in order to be just this price had to take into account the pre-existing *estimación común*.[7]

Let us return now to *Don Quixote* in order to observe how Cervantes situates the episode of the discovery of the manuscript within the parameters of this general theory of prices. Firstly, one should note that there are two competing buyers involved in the process of evaluating and pricing the manuscript (there is also a seller, about whom more anon). For the silk merchant, the object is merely a collection of loose sheaves, presumably useful as wrapping paper for his wares. Johnson supposes that the *sedero* intends to use the paper as food for his silk worms, a possibility that heightens the story's comedy but does not fundamentally alter the basic economic point: for the merchant, *Don Quixote* is, not a text, but a bundle of papers with a use value far removed from its original purpose as an historical document.[8] For him, it is quite literally worth only the paper it is written on. For the second author, however, the manuscript is valuable precisely because of its content; that it should be written on paper is immaterial to his evaluation of the text's worth.

This representation of variable use values dramatizes exactly the kind of illustrative anecdotes commonly found in sixteenth-century guides to commercial ethics for merchants. One of the best of these is the *Tratado utilísimo y muy general de todos los contratos*, written by the Dominican friar Francisco García and published in Valencia in 1583. As befits a practical guide to ethical commerce, García's *Tratado* is replete with real-world examples of the legitimate variability of market prices according to buyers' particular estimates of a good's utility. One of his recurrent examples is that of a book, the price of which may depend upon whether a buyer values it as a book or as a bundle of paper:

> Así vemos que los libros se consideran de una manera, en cuanto son papel solamente, bueno para aforrar bonetes o gorras, y para jabón, y para enlomar otros libros, y para otros servicios semejantes. De otra manera se consideran en cuanto libros, y por esta parte tienen dos usos: el uno es principal, cual es el leer en ellos y el estudiar la materia que tratan, el otro es menos principal y segundario, cual es el mercadear con ellos, como lo hacen los libreros granjeando con libros, comprándolos y vendiéndolos, y alquilándolos. Lo mismo se puede ver en todas las otras cosas artificiales, como los zapatos se pueden considerar en cuanto son un pedazo de cuero, o en cuanto zapatos.[9]

(So we see that books can be considered in one way as only paper, good for lining bonnets and caps, and for soap, and for binding other books, and for similar purposes. In another way they can be considered as books, and in this way they have two uses: the principal use is to read them and study their content; the secondary use is to trade in them, like merchants do, buying, selling, and lending them. The same is true of all manufactured goods, such as shoes, which can be considered either as pieces of leather or as shoes.)[10]

Even if a buyer values the book qua book, however, the same object will have a different value according to its relative utility for different users:

> se ha de notar que el valor de las cosas, así como la utilidad de aquéllas, es en dos maneras: uno, es general y común, el cual tienen ellas para quien quiera que las compre y en poder de quien quiera que esté; otra, es particular, el cual de tal suerte les conviene estando en poder de uno, que no les conviene estando en poder de otro. Así vemos que un libro de astrología tiene un valor común, cual es el que comúnmente vale y se estima en poder de libreros y mercaderes, y de otro cualquiera que no fuere astrólogo; y tiene otro particular, cual sería el que en poder de un astrólogo le conviniese, para el cual podría ser de muy grande provecho. Estos dos valores se pueden hallar el uno sin el otro, pues el general se halla sin el particular, aunque no el particular sin el general, como vemos en el dicho libro que, estando en poder del librero, tiene su valor general y no el particular; y estando en poder de un astrólogo, tiene el uno y el otro.[11]

(note that the value of things, like their utility, is double: the general and common value is the one that they have for anyone who might buy or possess them; the other value is particular, which they have according to whoever uses them. Thus we see that a book of astrology has a common value and price for booksellers and merchants, or anyone else who is not an astrologer. It has a particular value for an astrologer, for whom it could be very useful. These two values can exist separately, the general one without the particular one, although not the other way around, as we see with the aforementioned book, which has a general but not particular value for a bookseller, and both values for an astrologer.)

García's lucid exposition explains the price theory that underpins the interaction between the silk merchant and the second author in *Don Quixote*. We might say that the former appraises the manuscript according to its commodity value, while the latter does so for its nominal value. Both estimates are utilitarian and equally legitimate within the moral postulates of the period, but they lead to divergent evaluations and, ultimately, different prices for each buyer for the same good.

Because the second author values *Don Quixote* more highly than the silk merchant, the boy who is selling the manuscript accepts his offer for the item. The description of the transaction is especially intriguing, however, because it refers directly to contemporary theories of ethical pricing in commercial exchanges: 'salteándosele al sedero, compré al muchacho todos los papeles y cartapacios por medio real; que si él tuviera discreción y supiera lo que yo los deseaba, bien se pudiera prometer y llevar más de seis reales de la compra' (I. 9, 119). In part this is an inside joke, since *Don Quixote* Part One carried an official *tasa* of 290.5 *maravedís*, or just over 8.5 *reales* (I, Tasa, p. 3). In other words, the second author values *Don Quixote* at two-and-a-half *reales* less than the novel itself actually cost in 1605. This might be an example of slyly self-deprecating humour on the part of Cervantes, or a subtle indication that the second author intends to sell copies of the *Quixote* at their (expected) official market price and thus earn a profit.

In any case, for our purposes the more important part of the cited passage is the suggestion that the seller could have capitalized on the second author's desire to buy the manuscript in order to charge him a higher price than he in fact paid. This is precisely the kind of ethical problem that contemporary moralists addressed in their commercial guides. As before, García provides an especially clear exposition of the relevant moral principles:

> una misma cosa puede ser del vendedor estimada y apreciada de una manera, y a un precio, y del comprador puede ser estimada y apreciada de otra, y a otro mayor precio, por otro respecto. Pues para que la venta no se diga fraudulenta y engañosa por parte del comprador, no es menester que él informe al vendedor de lo que vale la cosa comprada, conforme a como él mismo la estima, pues no cae debajo de venta conforme a la estimación del que compra, sino conforme a la estimación del que vende. Ni pretende el vendedor vender sus cosas conforme a cómo el comprador las puede estimar, sino conforme a cómo él las estima, y como él las suele vender. Y porque cuanto a la voluntad y propósito del que vende no entreviene ignorancia alguna, pues sabe muy bien cuánto precio pueden valer las cosas que vende, estimadas y vendidas de la manera que él las estima y vende, y de la manera que caen debajo de vendición; por eso no tiene el comprador necesidad alguna de declararle lo que a sí mismo ha de valer la cosa comprada, conforme a su propia estimación y necesidad.[12]

> (the same thing can be valued at one price by the seller and, for some other reason, at a higher price by the buyer. In order for the sale not to be deceitful and fraudulent on the buyer's part, it is unnecessary for him to inform the seller of its worth to him, since the sale proceeds according to the seller's estimation of its worth, not the buyer's. Neither does the seller expect to sell his goods according to their value for the buyer but, rather, at the price at which he usually sells them. As to the seller's willingness to sell, since he knows very well how much his goods usually sell for, the buyer has no obligation at all to reveal how much the purchased good is worth to him.)

Applying this doctrine to the second author's acquisition of *Don Quixote* in the Toledo market, we see that it would have been morally illegitimate, although certainly not uncommon, for the boy (the seller) to price the manuscript according to its utility and value for the buyer, since the latter's estimation of the object's worth has no bearing on its use value, and hence its legitimate price, for the former. The seller's ignorance of the content of the document that he is selling is irrelevant, since he accurately prices the sheaves of paper according to their value as such within this particular market. The second author's casual, humorous reference to the possible immorality latent in the transaction remains enigmatic. Is it meant as an ethical statement on the potential illegitimacy of all commercial exchanges? Does it disguise an implicit authorial lament for the commercialization of literature, which in some cases is so undervalued as to be appreciated merely for the paper it is written on? Or is it simply an accurate portrayal of real-world market processes, whatever the moralists of the period might have intoned?

There is a further economic transaction to consider in this episode, which may help to guide our reading of the purchase of the *Don Quixote* manuscript. Once in possession of the document, the second author hires the *morisco aljamiado* to translate it into Castilian, 'ofreciéndole la paga que él quisiese' (I. 9, 119) ('I offered to pay him whatever he desired').[13] The offer of any payment that the translator requests marks a contrast with the second author's rather parsimonious evaluation of the manuscript as being worth up to six *reales*, but there is no ethical issue here in regard to the just price because buyers and sellers could legitimately offer or accept any price for a good (or service, in this case), so long as they did so willingly. In the event, the Morisco accepts, not money, but a quantity of raisins and wheat in payment for the translation. Cervantes is here trading on an ethnic stereotype based upon the dietary habits of Spanish Muslims (just as he does with the reference to the aubergine, *berenjena*, in the name of the fictional Moorish historian, Cide Hamete Benengeli), but this detail also cuts against the widespread accusation that the Moriscos were greedy hoarders of wealth. Cervantes himself reproduces this aspect of the standard bigotry of the age via the dog Berganza in the exemplary novel *El coloquio de los perros*:

> todo su intento es acuñar y guardar dinero acuñado, y para conseguirle trabajan y no comen; en entrando el real en su poder, como no sea sencillo, le condenan a cárcel perpetua y a escuridad eterna; de modo que ganando siempre y gastando nunca, llegan y amontonan la mayor cantidad de dinero que hay en España. Ellos son su hucha, su polilla, sus picazas y sus comadrejas; todo lo llegan, todo lo esconden y todo lo tragan.[14]
>
> (all their efforts are to mint and hoard coined money, and to get it they work and do not eat. When they get their hands on anything more than a single *real*, they condemn it to a life sentence and eternal darkness. By always working and never spending, they heap up the biggest pile of money in Spain. They are its moneybox, its moth, its magpies and its weasels. They hoard everything, hide it and swallow it.)

In contrast, the Morisco translator of *Don Quixote* works, not for money, but for food that he will very literally consume, unlike the metaphorical consumption ('todo lo tragan') that Berganza, echoing the popular sentiment of the day, attributes to the Moriscos in financial matters. This character thus challenges the contemporary stereotype of greed and hoarding by choosing payment in foodstuffs, when the second author has explicitly offered to allow him to name his price for translating the *Don Quixote* manuscript.

Just as significantly, the second author and the Morisco translator go into the cathedral to agree the terms of the contract. Toledo was the seat of the Church in Spain, and so the choice to locate a business deal between a Christian and a Morisco, whom contemporary readers would simply assume to be a covertly practising Muslim, in this space is an ideologically loaded one. The biblical story of Christ's expulsion of the moneychangers from the Temple would have been familiar to all contemporary readers, and there was literary precedent for this detail, as well. In *Lazarillo de Tormes*, Lázaro agrees to work as a water seller for a chaplain of this very cathedral. As Maurice Molho has shown, the chaplain is a crypto-Jew, running a business out of the nerve centre of Spanish Catholicism.[15] If the business transacted between the second author and the Morisco in *Don Quixote* does not represent so obvious a criticism of the contemporary Church, it is nevertheless suggestive of Christian hypocrisy towards both material gain generally and the specific condemnation of the Morisco population for their ostensible greed. These issues resurface in the encounter between Sancho Panza and the Morisco Ricote in *Don Quixote*, Part Two, which we will consider presently.

The 'Baciyelmo', Price Theory, and the Nature of Money: Economic Perspectivism

Cervantes again turns to the economic concepts of use value and divergent estimation of utility and price in the narration of Don Quixote's acquisition of what he believes to be the magical, golden helmet of Mambrino. Given that the object in question is, in fact, a humble barber's basin made of brass, and especially in light of Sancho Panza's attempt to reconcile these two divergent perspectives with the neologism *baciyelmo*, the episode has occasioned a great deal of scholarly debate about Cervantes's apparent 'perspectivism', that is, his relativistic presentation of life as containing not one, but multiple, equally real although differently perceived, realities.[16] Here I would like to approach this episode from the perspective of economic value and contemporary price theory, which straightforwardly emphasizes the social, not particular, nature of evaluating, and valuing, reality.

After Don Quixote has divested the barber of his basin, which he was wearing on his head to protect his (presumably) new hat from the rain, Sancho retrieves the object and immediately assigns it a monetary value: 'Por Dios que la bacía es buena y que vale un real de a ocho como un maravedí' (I. 21, 246)[17] ('By God this is a good basin — it's worth a piece of eight if it's worth a maravedí).[18] The mad knight, in contrast, evaluates the same object very differently:

> ¿Sabes qué imagino, Sancho? Que esta famosa pieza deste encantado yelmo por algún estraño acidente debió de venir a manos de quien no supo conocer ni estimar su valor y, sin saber lo que hacía, viéndola de oro purísimo, debió de fundir la mitad para aprovecharse del precio, y de la otra mitad hizo esta que parece bacía de barbero, como tú dices. (I. 21, 246–47)

> (Do you know what I think, Sancho? I think that this famous piece of this enchanted helmet must, by some strange accident, have fallen into the hands of a person who did not understand or appreciate its value, and, not knowing what he was doing, he must, on seeing that it is made of the purest gold, have melted down the other half to sell it, and with the remaining half made this, which seems as you say, like a barber's basin.)[19]

Both knight and squire apply the language and logic of contemporary price theory to their respective evaluations of the object, the former explicitly and obviously with some knowledge of the relevant terms and concepts, the latter only intuitively. Their estimations of both the basin's utility and its value diverge radically, but ultimately Sancho is proven to be absolutely correct in his assessment, which does indeed represent the *estimación común* of the basin's nature and worth.

How do we know? Because the matter is eventually settled economically. Near the end of Part One, when Quixote and Sancho find themselves, along with many other principal characters, in Juan Palomeque's inn, the despoiled barber suddenly enters, recognizes the man who attacked him on the road, and demands the return of his property. After much broad comedy at the expense of both the madman and his increasingly exasperated victim, including a farcical trial in which the other characters satirically confirm the former's insane assessment of the basin's nature as mythical helmet, the matter is concluded in purely financial and legal terms:

> Y en lo que tocaba a lo del yelmo de Mambrino, el cura, a socapa y sin que don Quijote lo entendiese, le dio por la bacía ocho reales, y el barbero le hizo una cédula del recibo y de no llamarse a engaño por entonces, ni por siempre jamás, amén. (I. 46, 580–81)
>
> (And as regards Mambrino's helmet, the priest, surreptitiously and behind Don Quixote's back, let the barber have eight reals for the basin, and the barber made out a receipt and a written promise not to claim that he's been unfairly treated, now and for ever and ever, amen.)[20]

This payment and the issuing of a receipt confirm both Sancho's initial assessment of the helmet's value and that the price accurately reflects the *estimación común* of the object. The proof is not just in the fact that Sancho and the barber each assign to the basin a value of eight *reales*, but also because, by issuing a receipt of sale and forgoing any right to sue for fraud ('llamarse a engaño'), the barber recognizes, legally, that he has received the just price for the item. As we have noted, sixteenth-century scholastic moral philosophers allowed some latitude in determining the just price of an object in a market transaction, because the process was fluid and the price subject to frequent oscillations. Civil law extended this leeway to *la mitad del justo precio*, i.e. fifty per cent above or below the just price.[21] So, the barber's receipt is explicit acknowledgement that the price paid for the basin falls within these parameters.

This outcome puts paid to the question of the basin's nature and value, as sanctioned by the common evaluation of its utility through the *estimación común* and expressed in the just price. But what of Sancho's famous description of the object as a *baciyelmo* (I. 44, 570)? Sancho coins the neologism at the end of an argument between Don Quixote and the barber as to the nature of the basin, as well as to whether the packsaddle from the barber's mule, which Sancho kept for himself, is the bridle of a war horse. The context is important for understanding Sancho's attempt to describe the object as both basin and helmet. Don Quixote's explanation for the difference in perspectives is his standard one: 'que como ésas transformaciones se ven en los sucesos de la caballería; para confirmación de lo cual, corre, Sancho hijo, y saca aquí el yelmo que este buen hombre dice ser bacía' (I. 44, 569) ('that these transformations do occur in the affairs of chivalry; for confirmation of which, Sancho my son, hurry and fetch the helmet that this fellow says is a basin).[22] Sancho's response decisively indicates that he does not believe the basin actually to be a helmet: ' — ¡Pardiez, señor — dijo Sancho — , si no tenemos otra prueba de nuestra intención que la que vuestra merced dice, tan bacía es el yelmo de Malino como el jaez deste buen hombre albarda!' (I. 44, 569) ('"By God, sir," said

Sancho, "if we haven't got any better proof to support us than that, Malino's helmet is as much a barber's basin as this character's comparisons are a pack-saddle!' ").[23]

Nevertheless, Sancho does, in fact, describe the basin as a *baciyelmo*. The reason, however, is unrelated to either the unstable nature of the object or the legitimate variance in perception of its essence. Rather, it is a description of the uses to which the basin has actually been put, both in its primary function as a barber's implement and, secondarily, as a helmet. Don Quixote, in fact, put the basin to such a use when freeing the galley slaves, who subsequently pelted him with stones, as Sancho relates:

> desde que mi señor le ganó hasta agora no ha hecho con él más de una batalla, cuando libró a los sin ventura encadenados; y si no fuera por este baciyelmo, no lo pasara entonces muy bien, porque hubo asaz de pedradas en aquel trance. (I. 44, 570)

> (because from the time my master won it up to now he's only fought one battle wearing it, when he freed those poor wretches in chains, and it hadn't been for this here basinelmet he'd have had a bad time of it, because there was lots of stonethrowing on that occasion.)[24]

This use of the basin recalls that of the barber to whom it belonged, who was wearing it on his head, like a helmet, to keep his new hat dry. Furthermore, Don Quixote himself previews the utility of the basin as a helmet to protect against rocks: 'bien será bastante para defenderme de alguna pedrada' (I. 21, 247) ('it will certainly be adequate to protect me against stonings').[25] Thus, the same object has two uses, as basin and improvised helmet, and it can be evaluated and priced according to both of them, just as the manuscript of *Don Quixote* itself could be valued either as a bundle of paper or as the historical account of a knight from La Mancha, and then priced appropriately by competing buyers in an open market.

In the case of both the manuscript and the basin, value is ultimately the product of the objects' general utility within particular markets. We see this principle more clearly because of the contrast in how the 'true' nature of each item is valued. The second author is able to purchase the *Don Quixote* manuscript at such a bargain price because the seller (the young boy) and the other potential buyer (the silk merchant) do not recognize the object for what it is, i.e. an historical document with a value as such that exceeds the material worth of the paper. Their ignorance is no impediment to a just transaction, however, because each party to the contract accurately evaluates the document's value for himself, according to its intended use. In this market, the *estimación común* may be lower than it might otherwise be if more information were available, but such ignorance does not invalidate the legitimacy of the transaction because it does not fundamentally affect the nature of the manuscript as a collection of paper sheaves. García terms this kind of inconsequential ignorance *ignorancia negativa* and distinguishes it from the more serious *ignorancia privativa*, which does pertain to the essential nature of an object in an exchange.[26]

The same issues play out, in reverse, in the case of the barber's basin, despite its more outlandish parody. Don Quixote deplores the woeful ignorance 'de quien no supo conocer ni estimar su valor' (I. 21, 246). If he were correct about the essence of the object, this would count as an example of *ignorancia privativa*, but his estimation of the basin's nature and value ultimately proves irrelevant to the appropriate, communal assessment of those qualities, as well as to the adequate pricing of the basin according to its generally accepted social utility, as detailed above. Thus, we see that, when determining the price of any good within a market, the core principle is the *estimación común*, which, when genuinely common, is the basis for the establishment of commutative justice and therefore moral legitimacy.

There is a further aspect to Quixote's fabulous evaluation of the basin's essence and worth, one with more immediately political overtones. According to the madman, the ignoramus who did not recognize the helmet's true nature deformed it, which explains the object's strange appearance: 'viéndola de oro purísimo, debió de fundir la mitad para aprovecharse del precio, y de la otra mitad hizo esta que parece bacía de barbero' (I. 21, 247). What Don Quixote describes here is, by analogy, the widespread practice of clipping gold and silver coins in order to take advantage of their metal content. The description of the mythical helmet as having two, separable, values, one the magical ability to ward off spells and the other as a mere commodity, reproduces analogically a long-running debate about the dual nature of money, which was both an immaterial sign and a quantity of precious metal with a potentially different material value. In this way, the episode responds to a theoretical problem about the essence of money that had acquired urgency as a matter of political economy following a series of currency manipulations by the crown in the first years of the seventeenth century.

Sixteenth-century moral philosophers recognized the double aspect of money. According to Domingo de Soto, money can be considered either as a coin or as a piece of metal. In this view, a coin's face value is like a weight or measure, and it reflects the pre-existing commodity value of the metal from which it is minted. Even if it were not coined, the metal would have the same exchange value as the money, 'mas el Estado con la acuñación atestigua el valor del metal' (but the State by coining it certifies the value of the metal).[27] Martín de Azpilcueta held a similar view: 'la bondad intrinseca del dinero, no es el precio que la republica le pone, sino la qualidad y bondad de la material, de que el es' (the intrinsic worth of money is not the price that the republic puts on it, but the quality and worth of the material of which it is made).[28] Soto and Azpilcueta thus tended towards a metalist perspective, because they maintained that the intrinsic value of money was derived from the commodity value of its metal content.

Not all sixteenth-century scholastics shared this opinion, however. Mercado, in a burst of pure nominalism, averred that gold and silver have no value beyond that which the crown assigns to them. Money can therefore be made of any material, and a coin can be stamped with any value, which then becomes immutable: 'Así, no mudándola el rey, de quien depende, no se puede lícitamente variar, ni dar más ni menos por ella' (Thus, if the king, upon whom its value depends, does not alter it, it may not legitimately vary in value, nor may more nor less be given in exchange for it).[29] Nevertheless, experience showed that money did indeed vary considerably in value from place to place and in time, a phenomenon that Mercado both described and legitimized by ingeniously adapting standard contemporary price theory to monetary theory. In most goods, he explains, the price is an extrinsic or accidental value, determined not by ontology but by the common estimate of utility. Money, however, is unique in that its price, or nominal value, *is* its essence or intrinsic value. And, as with other goods, that price will change following the common estimate of value, according to local conditions in particular markets.[30]

Other theorists of the period reasoned similarly. Responding to Azpilcueta's above-cited claim that the intrinsic value of money derives from its commodity value, García declares that the famous 'Doctor Navarro' was deceived ('se engañó'), because it is merely accidental that a piece of any metal (such as gold, silver, or copper) should have a given numeric value. Once coined into money, however, that value becomes intrinsic

> bien así como la vara, si se considera por parte de su material, en cuanto es un pedazo de palo, o de hierro, accidental y extrínseca cosa le es tener cuatro palmos; pero considerándola en cuanto es vara de medir, cosa intrínseca y esencial le es tener cuatro palmos
>
> (just as, if one considers a rod as a piece of the material it is made of, such as wood or iron, its length is accidental and extrinsic; but considering it as a measuring rod, its length is intrinsic and essential to it).[31]

We see these concepts reflected in the language with which Don Quixote describes the unfortunately misshapen helmet of Mambrino and, more generally, in the resolution of the episode according to the common estimate of the basin's nature and value as expressed through the price system and formalized with a mutually agreeable, legally binding monetary transaction. Quixote, we recall, attributes the deformation of the helmet to the 'estraño acidente' by which the object came into the hands of one who clearly valued only its accidental, i.e. non-intrinsic, commodity value as a piece of gold. This is the explicit meaning of his presumption that this person 'no supo conocer ni estimar su valor y, sin saber lo que hacía, viéndola de oro purísimo, debió de fundir la mitad para aprovecharse del precio' (I. 21, 246–47). As we have seen, the madman's very peculiar evaluation of the basin's essence and worth is completely superseded by the common estimate of its utility and price, which completely disregards the magical, intangible, properties that Quixote deems to be the source of its intrinsic value.

This collision of values reproduces very precisely an urgent debate then playing out in the field of monetary theory and Castilian political economy. Strapped for cash, the crown, for the first time since the successful currency reforms implemented by the Catholic Monarchs in the Medina del Campo pragmatic of 1497, began to manipulate the coinage as a means of generating revenue. Gold and silver coins were not directly affected, however. Instead, Philip III chose to alter the *monedas de vellón*, fractional currency made of copper alloyed with a small amount of silver. In 1602 this silver plug was removed, on the claim that the coins' value was purely nominal. In 1603, these copper *monedas de vellón* were collected at royal mints and re-stamped at double their face value. The owners received one-half the number of coins submitted, which constituted the whole of their original face value, while the crown kept the difference, i.e., one hundred per cent, minus costs (in practice, roughly ninety-two per cent).[32] In response, there were howls of popular protest and a spate of critical writings by influential individuals, who adopted the familiar language of monetary theory from the sixteenth-century moral philosophers while emphasizing that the commodity value of coinage constituted its intrinsic value, while its nominal value was reduced to an 'accidental' quality.[33]

In truth, the Spanish scholastics of the sixteenth century could hardly be inflexibly categorized as either nominalist or metalist. They tended to vary their opinions depending on whether they considered money qua money, or coins as discs of precious metal with a commodity value of their own.[34] Even a rigid nominalist such as Bartolomé de Albornoz recognized that gold and silver coins would be priced as pieces of precious metal outside the political boundaries of Castile.[35] Nevertheless, what is striking about the theoretical debate regarding the *moneda de vellón* at the beginning of the seventeenth century is how previous theories about the nature of money and the source of its intrinsic value were narrowly interpreted and precisely applied in direct response to new political realities. The humanist and royal chronicler Pedro de Valencia, for example, wrote in a treatise of 1605: 'La moneda legítima en común derecho y estimación universal de las gentes es la que tiene [...] el valor por la materia y peso, sin consideración de la forma' (Coins that are legitimate according to common law and the universal esteem of the people are those whose value derives from their material and weight, irrespective of its form).[36] That same year Pedro de Oña, bishop of Gaeta, wrote a memorial to Philip III in which he affirmed that coinage is not stamped with an official seal in order to give it value, 'sino totalm[en]te para verificar y hazer testimonio del valor y pesso que ella en si tiene como en las pessas y marcos publicos' (but exclusively to verify and attest to the value and weight that it has, as with public weights and measures).[37]

Also in 1605, the Jesuit Juan de Mariana published a second edition of his work *La dignidad real y la educación del Rey*, which contained only one significant addition with respect to the original version of 1599, a discussion of money that prefigured Mariana's later, and much better known, treatise, *Tratado y discurso sobre la moneda de vellón* (1609). Like Valencia and Oña, Mariana insists that the intrinsic value of money derives from the price of the metal from which it is minted:

> El valor de la moneda es de dos clases. Tiene un valor natural, tomado de la calidad del metal y de su peso, que se llama intrínseco, y otro legal, o extrínseco, que le da el príncipe mediante la ley [...] Sería un necio el que separe estos dos valores de tal forma que el legal no corresponda al natural, como sería un malvado el que mandase vender a diez una cosa que la gente solo aprecia en cinco, y para que así no se haga se despliega el mayor cuidado y severidad.[38]
>
> (Coins have two kinds of value. They have a natural value, derived from the quality and weight of the metal, which is called intrinsic, and another legal or extrinsic one, which the prince applies through the law [...] Only a fool would separate these two values so that the legal one did not correspond to the natural one, just as only a wicked man would order that a good be sold for double the price that the people value it, and the greatest care is taken and the severest penalties are imposed to ensure that it does not happen.)

Valencia, Oña, and Mariana take the same terms and concepts used by Soto, Azpilcueta, Mercado, García, and many others, but in light of the crown's manipulations of the *moneda de vellón* they insist not upon the royal prerogative to coin money, but on the royal obligation to mint coinage that reflects the popular *estimación común* of the commodity value of the currency's metal. Because early modern monetary theory was largely predicated upon contemporary price theory, it was a relatively straightforward matter for Cervantes to reference the controversy surrounding currency manipulation in an episode that is built upon, and finds resolution in, then-current ideologies of values and prices in market exchanges. By associating commodity value with the commonly perceived, and legally certified, nature and price of the barber's basin, the episode of the helmet of Mambrino suggests that the crown's contention that the value of money was determined by royal fiat is the monetary equivalent of Don Quixote's fantastical evaluation of a brass basin as an enchanted piece of armour. What counts, as Valencia, Oña, and Mariana affirmed, is the communal perception of utility and value, not the aberrant claim of a single individual.

The Morisco Ricote and the Foreign Hoard

Issues of money, wealth, and contemporary political economy are central to the episode of Sancho Panza's encounter with his former neighbour, the Morisco Ricote, in *Don Quixote* Part Two. In this instance, however, the economic material is foregrounded and much more openly political than in the helmet of Mambrino adventure. Having left Spain in search of a new homeland shortly before the crown ordered the expulsion of the Castilian Moriscos in 1609, Ricote now returns to Spain in the company of five German pilgrims in order to reclaim a treasure that he left buried in his village and begin the work of reuniting with his wife and daughter, who are living in exile in Algeria. Cervantes's portrait of this conflicted individual, who longs to return to the home from which he has been banished, is deeply humane and strikes modern readers as profoundly sympathetic. Indeed it is, but, in keeping with the tensions that transect the episode, Ricote's characterization is also highly ambiguous, for Cervantes has included in it several of the most widespread stereotypes then used to vilify the Morisco minority. The master anti-Morisco trope was their innate otherness, their refusal to assimilate either culturally or religiously to the Old Christian majority, and Cervantes will play repeatedly and ambivalently upon this theme in his representation of Ricote.[39]

The character himself refers to his fellow Moriscos as 'mi nación' (II. 54, 1168), a term with which the Old Christian population labelled this minority group precisely in order to highlight its presence as a foreign element within the Spanish body politic.[40] Ricote also references the notorious resistance of the Moriscos to intermarriage with Old Christians when confiding in Sancho his lack of concern that his daughter would entertain the romantic advances of a rich man's son and heir: 'las moriscas pocas o ninguna vez se mezclaron por amores con cristianos viejos' (II. 54, 1175) ('Morisco girls have seldom if ever become involved in love affairs with men from Old Christian families).⁴¹ Even so, Ricote himself straddles both Christian and Muslim cultures. While his wife and daughter are sincere Catholics, he is conflicted in his faith: 'aunque yo no lo soy [=católico] tanto, todavía tengo más de cristiano que de moro' (II. 54, 1172) ('although I'm not much of [a Catholic] myself I'm still more of a Christian than a Moor').⁴² Ricote reveals a similar duality in his speech, as he speaks to Sancho 'sin tropezar nada en su lengua morisca, en la pura castellana' (II. 54, 1170) ('in pure Castilian, without once lapsing into his Morisco language').⁴³ Above all, Ricote is a member of a distinct, largely unassimilated ethnic and religious minority who nonetheless strongly self-identifies as Spanish: 'agora conozco y experimento lo que suele decirse, que es dulce el amor de la patria' (II. 54, 1171) ('now I know and I feel in my bones the truth of the saying that the love of one's country is sweet').⁴⁴

Cervantes further underscores Ricote's ambiguous foreignness by explicitly assimilating him to the Germans with whom he travels. Upon recognizing his exiled neighbour, Sancho exclaims, 'Dime quién te ha hecho franchote' (II. 54, 1167) (But tell me now — who's turned you into a bloody foreigner'),⁴⁵ *franchote* being a pejorative term that could equally mean 'Frenchman' or, more generically, 'foreigner'. When the other pilgrims begin taking out their wineskins, Ricote joins them, 'transformado de morisco en alemán o en tudesco' (II. 54, 1169) ('who'd turned himself from a Morisco into a German').⁴⁶ The presence of this wine, as well as the hambones that form part of the pilgrims' repast, further highlights the ambivalence of Ricote's characterization. As Américo Castro points out, these items could act as markers of Old Christian identity, and thus serve as safeguards against detection for Muslims.⁴⁷ In contrast, Monique Joly describes a countervailing tradition in which both wine and hambones were also associated in the Spanish popular imagination of the time with foreigners, the latter specifically with proverbially greedy Frenchmen.⁴⁸

The episode's economic content reinforces this ambiguous characterization through its association of Ricote's wealth, and more precisely the manner in which it was accumulated, with the actions of his German companions. These foreigners are, in fact, false pilgrims, who have come to Spain to take financial advantage of its famously charitable people (a trait embodied, in this episode at least, by Sancho, who is here described as 'caritativo además' (II. 54, 1166) ('a most charitable man')⁴⁹). As Ricote explains to Sancho:

> tienen por costumbre de venir a España muchos dellos cada año a visitar los santuarios della, que los tienen por sus Indias, y por certísima granjería y conocida ganancia: ándanla casi toda, y no hay pueblo ninguno de donde no salgan comidos y bebidos, como suele decirse, y con un real, por lo menos, en dineros, y al cabo de su viaje salen con más de cien escudos de sobra, que, trocados en oro, o ya en el hueco de los bordones o entre los remiendos de las esclavinas o con la industria que ellos pueden, los sacan del reino y los pasan a sus tierras, a pesar de las guardas de los puestos y puertos donde se registran. (II. 54, 1172)
>
> ([They] come to Spain each year to visit shrines here, because for them they are what the Americas are for us, rich pickings and certain profits. They wander

over almost the whole country, and there isn't a village they leave without having been wined and dined, as the expression is, and without a real at least in small change; and at the end of their travels they leave with more than a hundred escudos that they've saved, and that, converted into gold, they smuggle out of this country and into their own, hidden in hollows in their staffs or sewn into the patches on their cloaks or in whatever way they can devise, despite all the precautions that are taken in the custom-houses where money has to be declared.)[50]

What Ricote describes is a dramatization of one of the greatest economic concerns in early modern Spain, namely, the drain of precious metals to foreign rivals.[51] One important cause of this capital flight was the system of *asientos*, short-term, high-interest loans signed with foreign creditors, such as the German Fuggers and Weslers during the reign of Charles V and, subsequently, Genoese bankers under Philip II and Philip III. Following the royal manipulation of the *moneda de vellón* in 1602 and 1603, however, the so-called *arbitristas*, the political economists of the period, identified the influx of counterfeit copper coins as a contributing factor to the outward flow of gold and silver. As Pedro de Valencia wrote in 1605:

> si el cobre en calderas no vale más que antes y en moneda vale dos, tanto de plata y oro, cierto es que todo el cobre [...] se labrará en moneda semejantísima a la que ahora corre en España, y vendrá acá a venderse a peso de plata y oro; y, si corre diez años este género de moneda de vellón en este Reino, tendremos todo el cobre del mundo, porque lo pagamos muy bien.[52]

> (if copper in pots is worth no more than before, but in coins it is worth double in relation to both silver and gold, it is certain that all the copper will be made into coins practically indistinguishable from those that now circulate in Spain, and it will be brought here to be sold for silver and gold. If this kind of fractional coin (*moneda de vellón*) circulates for ten years in this kingdom, we will have all the copper in the world, because we pay very well for it.)

The Catalan *arbitrista* Gaspar de Pons, who in 1602 was appointed to the *Consejo de Hacienda*, addressed the problem of capital flight in a memorial published in 1600:

> Para que la moneda de cada prouincia no se saque della, ni la deshagan, ni la encierren por la dicha causa, el vnico medio es, que sea de tal calidad, que no sea de prouecho, o por lo menos de poco, para sacarla de las prouincias, y para deshazerla, y de poco gusto, y de poca cudicia para encerrarla.[53]

> (So that each province's coinage will not be drained from it, nor melted down, nor hoarded for the same reason, the only solution is for it to be of such quality that it is of no value, or at least of very little, to remove it from the provinces and to melt it down, and not attractive, and not worth hoarding.)

Pons's solution, radical for the time, was to issue coins of no commodity value whatsoever, while gold and silver money 'de verdadero valor intrinseco' (of true intrinsic value) would be held in reserve in order to 'trocarlo por la moneda corriente' (exchange it for money in circulation) with official consent.[54]

In *Don Quixote* Cervantes dramatizes all three misuses of coinage that Pons identifies in the cited passage: 'sacarla' (the German false pilgrims); 'deshazerla' (by analogy, the helmet of Mambrino, as discussed above); 'encerrarla' (Ricote's buried treasure). Clipping gold and silver coins or exporting them out of Spain were simply illegal. Hoarding was a more complicated matter, however, and central to the complex and contradictory characterization of Ricote. Johnson analyses the Morisco shopkeeper's amassed wealth as a potential source of capital for investment, while Benjamín Liu, reading the episode in light of Mariana's 1609 *Tratado*, views Ricote's hoarding as symmetrical to the Germans' export of precious metals, both of which are examples of what came to be called Gresham's Law ('bad money drives out good') and, thus, rational acts undertaken in response to inflation caused by the crown's manipulation of *monedas de vellón*. Both critics see the character as a positive, though ultimately frustrated, alternative to the Old Christian privileging of frivolous expenditure in pursuit of the symbolic social capital of honour over the pragmatic bourgeois activities of saving and investment.[55] These are plausible, well-reasoned interpretations of the episode. However, they adopt the perspective of the historical fact of subsequent economic development and the displacement of the feudal aristocracy by the bourgeoisie, a process that they implicitly accept as inevitable and that they tacitly assume Cervantes to have viewed favourably. Consequently, both readings downplay the negative conceptual parameters, based upon ethno-religious prejudice and anti-foreigner bias, within which the episode develops. I find compelling Michel Moner's counter argument that then-current literary and ideological considerations distort the documentary quality of Ricote's story. Moner contends that both the character's name (*rico* + *ote*) and his considerable fortune make reference to 'uno de los temas antimoriscos más remachados y popularizados: su afición al dinero y su propensión a acumular riquezas' (one of the most insistent and popular anti-Morisco themes: their desire for money and their tendency to accumulate wealth). Thus, despite his positive aspects, Ricote 'viene a coincidir [...] con el estereotipo del morisco acumulador de riquezas que es precisamente el que denunciaban los apologistas en sus requisitorios' (coincides [...] with precisely the stereotype of the wealth-accruing Morisco that the apologists [for expulsion] denounced in their treatises).[56]

Indeed, despite the fact that royal policy itself (enormous amounts of debt to international creditors largely financed through the issuing of domestic debt and currency devaluation, with pernicious knock-on effects in the productive sectors of the economy) manifestly spurred capital flight in the sixteenth- and seventeenth- centuries, contemporary observers frequently blamed foreigners for Spain's economic troubles. Mercado engages in such scapegoating: 'España, reino fecundísimo, está falto, porque no vienen tantos millones de nuestras Indias cuantos extranjeros pasan a sus ciudades' (Spain, a most fertile kingdom, is lacking, because more foreigners pass through our cities than the millions in wealth that come from our Indies).[57] In one of the earliest mercantilist memorials (1558), the *contador* (royal accountant) from Burgos Luis Ortiz says of those foreigners who buy Spanish exports of raw materials and sell in return manufactured goods:

> nos tratan muy peor que a indios porque a los indios para sacarles el oro o plata llevámosles algunas cosas de mucho o de poco provecho, mas a nosotros, con las nuestras propias, no solo se enriquecen y aprovechan de lo que les falta en

sus naturalezas, mas llevanos el dinero del Reino con su industria sin trabajar de sacarlo de las minas como nosotros hacemos.[58]

(they treat us much worse than Indians, because to get their gold or silver we took them some more or less useful goods, but [foreigners], with our own goods, not only get rich and take advantage of the things that they are lacking by nature, but they also take away the money from the kingdom with their craftiness, without even working to dig it out of the mines like we do.)

Six decades later, Lope de Deza echoed the same complaint in his condemnation of the 'mercaderías supérfluas' (luxury goods) sold in Spain by foreign merchants:

todas las que vienen de este género se permutan a oro y plata, con que las demás naciones se enriquecen y empobrece la nuestra, burlándose ya de nosotros como nosotros hicimos de los indios y Negros, que por cascabeles y toda quinquillería rescatan o dan su oro, su plata, su marfil, y otras cosas preciosas; no se ya que diferencia haya de ellos a nosotros, llevándoles de ventaja la religión y la policía.[59]

(all such things are changed into gold and silver, with which other nations get rich while impoverishing ours, swindling us the way we did to the Indians and Negroes, who for little bells and all manner of trifles gather up and hand over their gold, their silver, their ivory, and other precious things. I don't know what difference there is between them and us anymore, except that we have religion and civilization.)

There is no hint of irony in these laments that others treat Spaniards in precisely the same manner (in reality, much better) than they treat Native Americans and Africans. So much for the Golden Rule. Consider, also, Pons's explanation for the drain of precious metals from Spain. He does not attribute this phenomenon principally to flawed policy but, rather, to personal greed:

la [causa] efectiva y principal de sacarse la moneda destos Reynos, y deshazerse, y de auer agabelladores, y regatones della, es la ganancia, y de encerrarse por algunos, y en otros sola prudencia particular, sin mirar por el beneficio publico, y en otros sola auaricia y gusto de tenerla.[60]

(the real cause of capital flight from these kingdoms, and melting it down, and the presence of hoarders and resellers, is profit, and some people's monopolizing it, and only self-interest in others, with no consideration of the public good, and in others only greed and desire to hold it.)

Cervantes makes direct reference to this context in Ricote's statement that his German companions make their annual pilgrimage to Spain's shrines because 'los tienen por sus Indias, y por certísima granjería y conocida ganancia' (II. 54, 1172). Few readers would have viewed such foreign interlopers with any sympathy, but the Morisco's Old Christian contemporaries would likely have tarred him with the same brush. Mercado cites with approval a contemporary law that reveals the explicitness of the economic connection between foreigners and Moriscos: 'Mandamos que ningún extranjero pueda tratar en Indias, ni ningún extranjero ni morisco ni arriero pueda mercar oro ni plata en barra ni en pasta, so pena de perderlo y destierro perpetuo' (We decree that no foreigner can do business in the

Indies, nor that any foreigner nor Morisco nor mule driver may trade in unminted gold nor silver, on pain of its confiscation and permanent banishment).[61] Joly asserts that in his portrayal of Ricote, Cervantes blends both popular anti-foreigner and anti-Morisco prejudices with the *arbitristas*' political and economic reform proposals in a critical depiction of 'esos "elementos foráneos" (gitanos, moriscos y gabachos) que destruyen, según él, la economía española' (those 'foreign elements' (gypsies, Moriscos and Frenchmen) that, according to him, are destroying the Spanish economy).[62] I do not believe that the characterization of Ricote is so categorically negative, but it certainly exploits widespread hostility to social outgroups that were perceived to be equally pernicious to the republic.

Given that Ricote is a humble shopkeeper in a rural village in La Mancha, how has he has managed to amass so much wealth that it qualifies as a 'tesoro' (II. 54, 1172)? Based upon the general perception that Moriscos were greedy hoarders, as illustrated by the dog Berganza's representative tirade cited above, many contemporaries would surely have assumed that he has done so illegitimately, through monopoly practices. The moralists of the period condemned any hoarding used to corner the market and raise prices, particularly of primary goods such as 'trigo, cebada, paja, centeno, avena, carnes, vacas, carneros, ovejas, aceites, vino, lienzos, sedas, paños' (wheat, barley, hay, rye, oats, meat, cows, rams, sheep, olives, wine, linen, silk, cloths).[63] These are, of course, precisely the products in which a *tendero* would trade. Mercado calls hoarding of such goods 'un trato odioso y escrupuloso' (a hateful and immoral business), but he also recognizes that the practice was widespread: 'es grande la multitud que en estos tratos y ganancias se ocupan, negocian y pecan' (a great multitude engage, trade and sin in these dealings and earnings).[64] García likewise condemns hoarders, whom he, like Pons, terms 'agabelladores', because they commit an act of implicit violence by forcing their customers to pay higher prices: 'otro modo de hacer violencia tácita es agabellando las mercaderías o mantenimientos para que, habiendo de esta suerte pocos vendedores, ellos las vendan al precio que quisieren' (another way to do tacit violence is by hoarding goods and foodstuffs, so that there will be few sellers and they can sell them at any price they want).[65]

The connection that García makes between hoarding and violence is important. The philosophical background is the scholastic doctrine, first elaborated in the Middle Ages, that one who exploits the need of another for personal gain commits violence against the other.[66] Financial need ('necesidad') is therefore a coercive force that can compel desperate individuals to undertake involuntary actions, such as agreeing to repay a loan with interest.[67] The Ricote episode contains a detail that harks back to these concepts, when the Morisco attempts to persuade Sancho to help him recover his treasure through an appeal to the latter's precarious financial situation: 'si tú, Sancho, quieres venir conmigo y ayudarme a sacarlo y a encubrirlo, yo te daré docientos escudos, con que podrás remediar tus necesidades, que ya sabes que sé yo que las tienes muchas' (II. 54, 1173) ('Sancho, if you'd like to come and help me dig it up and hide it on me, I'll give you two hundred escudos, which will solve a lot of your money problems, and you know I know you've got a lot of those').⁶⁸ Ricote's request is not just that his former neighbour help a friend in need, but that he commit an act of high treason, as Sancho recognizes: 'haría traición a mi rey en dar favor a sus enemigos' (II. 54, 1173) ('I'd be betraying my king by helping his enemies').⁶⁹ The fact that Ricote appeals openly to Sancho's material need in an effort to compel him to undertake an illegal and dangerous action is direct textual evidence that links Ricote to the kind of illicit commercial and financial practices that the moral philosophers condemned. This connection would likely explain for contemporary readers, already accustomed to viewing Moriscos as avaricious hoarders, a modest shopkeeper's seemingly incongruous ability to amass a considerable fortune in a poor village.

Much of the scholastics' commentary concerning need and coercion related to usury.⁷⁰ One strand of contemporary anti-Morisco discourse accused the thrifty members of this community of using their accumulated wealth in order to lend money at interest to their Old Christian neighbours. When the act of expulsion was first ratified in 1582, Juan de Ribera, archbishop of Valencia, declared that 'la hazienda en ellos no sirve para otra cosa, que empobreçer con logros y reventas a los cristianos viejos' (they only use their wealth to impoverish Old Christians with usury and reselling).⁷¹ In fact, there is evidence that this kind of activity did occur. L. P. Harvey reports that 'there is abundant confirmation of Morisco participation in money-lending, speculation, and in small-scale banking'.⁷² At the time that the first wave of the expulsion was implemented (1608), in the Kingdom of Valencia Morisco moneylenders had outstanding credit to Christians in the considerable amount of £197,679.⁷³ Beyond usurious lending, Ribera's reference to 'reselling' ('reventas'), i.e. buying and selling goods without altering them (in other words, normal commercial activity), was strongly associated with hoarding and immoral business practice generally, and specifically with Moriscos, in the period.⁷⁴ Cervantes himself included this accusation in Berganza's anti-Morisco screed in *El coloquio de los perros*: 'róbannos a pie quedo, y con los frutos de nuestras heredades, que nos revenden, se hacen ricos' (they steal from us on the sly, and with the fruits of our own inherited lands, which they resell to us, they become rich).⁷⁵ Note, too, how Ribera's language reflects the anti-foreigner tirades of Ortiz and Deza cited above, and how this shared semantic field tends to further conflate rapacious foreigners with the Moriscos, a greedy foreign 'sect' or 'nation' within Old Christian Spain. Within this context, it is very plausible that Cervantes's readers would have perceived in Ricote's characterization the kind of highly negative traits of avarice, hoarding, and usurious lending traditionally ascribed to the Moriscos.

The various economic threads that we have been unravelling separately in the Ricote episode, currency manipulation, capital flight, hoarding, predatory pricing, and illicit credit practices, were all potentially knotted together in the perception of some observers in the period. In his 1605 memorial, Pedro de Oña relates the following lucrative scheme based on the import of counterfeit *monedas de vellón*:

> me an referido que los estrangeros meten grandissima cantidad de esta moneda baxa contrahecha por todos los puertos de Castilla y Vizcaya que traen por lastre de sus baxeles y se conciertan con los naturales por no dezir con las mismas

guardas y les dan dos barriles digamos de quartos porque de ay a un año y dos les bueluan la mitad en plata o en oro, en que ganan una infinidad, y los que las reciben otro tanto y mayor porque hazen empleos gruesissimos y luego por justicia les hazen recebir la paga en la moneda baxa y falsa del estrangero y atrauiessan con din[er]o ageno, y tan inorme daño no solo mercadurias sino bienes raizes sobre que despues fundan censos que los recibe[n] en reales, con que pagan enteram[en]te al estrangero la mitad y ellos quedan riquissimos sin un real suyo y el R[ei]no destruido.[76]

(I have been told that foreigners smuggle a great quantity of these worthless, counterfeit coins, which they carry as ballast in their ships, through all the ports in Castile and Biscay, and they conspire with the locals, not to say with the customs officials, to whom they give, for example, two barrels of *cuartos* so that within a year or two they return half of that amount to them in silver or gold. In this way they earn an astonishing amount, and those who accept the *cuartos* as much again and more, because they negotiate very lucrative deals and then use the law to force the other party to accept payment in the foreign counterfeit coins, and they hoard the others' money. They do enormous damage not only in commerce but also in real estate, because then they purchase *censos* [annuities secured with the seller's mortgaged land] and take their payments in *reales* [silver coins]. Half the money goes straight to the foreigners and they end up very rich without having had a *real* of their own, and the kingdom is destroyed.)

Note that this is mere hearsay ('me an referido'), but it is evidence that such rumours circulated in the period. I suggest that many readers in 1615 would have perceived in the Ricote episode a similar matrix of greed, counterfeiting, collusion with rapacious foreigners, hoarding ('atrauiessan'), and predatory credit (some *arbitristas* asserted that *censos* were more damaging than usury).[77] From this majoritarian perspective, Ricote, as a Morisco and therefore a member of a foreign, heretical 'nation' to begin with, is explicitly assimilated to the figure of the greedy foreigner ('franchote', 'alemán o tudesco') who impoverishes Christian Spain by smuggling away its hard-earned American treasure. The fact that a humble village shopkeeper was able to accrue a considerable fortune, which he then buried in contravention of the edict of expulsion so as not to surrender it to the crown, both plays upon popular anti-Morisco stereotypes (avarice, hoarding) and reinforces the connection with the kind of financial malfeasance blamed for despoiling the kingdom that the German false pilgrims represent. Ricote's choice of Augsburg as his new home is particularly important in this regard because, as Johnson notes, that Bavarian city was both the seat of the Fugger banking dynasty and the place of declaration of the Augsburg Confession:

> Of all the cities in Europe and around the Mediterranean basin where Cervantes might have sent his fictional Ricote into exile, Augsburg is the only one that brings together the religious and economic themes bound up in the expulsion of the moriscos.[78]

Moreover, as Chad Leahy has shown, Ricote's hoarded coins, with their stamped crosses and coats of arms, are an even more concentrated distillation of those same tensions. However, because they materialize in themselves the contradictions and limits of enforced religious, political, and ethnic uniformity, Ricote's gold *escudos* explicitly confound straightforward exegesis by virtue of their inherent polyvalence:

> On the one hand, they materially signal the collective tragedy at the heart of the expulsion, exposing the cracks and porous borders undermining official narratives of control, homogeneity, and purity. On the other hand, they simultaneously reproduce through numismatics the very exclusionary ideology deployed to legitimate the expulsion in the first place.[79]

Much like Ricote himself, therefore, these coins are susceptible of competing interpretations in accordance with each reader's ideological orientation.

More than illustrating that, with regard to the so-called Morisco problem, 'Cervantes milita de lleno en el campo de la opinión moderada' (Cervantes is a fully-fledged moderate), as Márquez Villanueva asserts, the Ricote episode appears to simply present the issue in all its contradictory complexity and then allow individual readers to make their own judgments.[80] The highly negative economic stereotypes that we have identified in the Morisco's tale, particularly Ricote's open assimilation to a band of rapacious foreigners, are counterbalanced by his integration into Spanish society; his love of his homeland; his fluent Castilian; his consumption of wine (not just a disguise to pass unnoticed, to judge by his exclamation upon seeing Sancho that 'ni duermo ni estoy ahora borracho' (II. 54, 1167) ('I'm not asleep and as yet I'm not drunk!')[81]); the fact that his wife and daughter are sincere Catholics; and his recognition that the latter, not his material wealth, constitutes 'el tesoro que más [le] enriquece' (II. 63, 1262) ('the treasure that's most precious of them all').[82] Ricote's characterization is undeniably humane and empathetic, and Cervantes surely intended it as a purposeful rejoinder to the villainous caricature of the Moriscos as uniformly inveterate enemies of Christian Spain. Furthermore, even if we accept that Ricote is rich through ill-gotten gain, Cervantes certainly does not associate such practices exclusively with greedy Moriscos and Protestant heretics. Sancho encounters his former neighbour immediately after abandoning his governorship of the Ínsula Barataria: 'un oficio dejé yo esta mañana de las manos donde pudiera hacer las paredes de mi casa de oro y comer antes de seis meses en platos de plata' (II. 54, 1173) ('[I] walked out of a job this morning where I could have built the walls of my house in solid gold and where before six months were out I could have been eating off silver platters').[83] The fact that Sancho has not lined his own pockets at his subjects' expense is a pointed, albeit non-specific, indictment of those Spanish rulers who do fleece the populace in pursuit of their own interests. Finally, if Ricote, in his efforts to smuggle his treasure out of the country, acts like the false pilgrims who represent the avaricious foreign merchants and bankers in the Spanish popular imagination, it is only because Christian Spain has *made* him a foreigner, as well, much against his wishes. Rather than a treatise for or against the expulsion of the Moriscos, therefore, the Ricote episode demonstrates Cervantes's mastery at interlacing multiple discursive elements, both literary and non-literary, into a cohesive narrative that illuminates his characters in all their human ambiguity.

Coda: *Don Quixote* as Cultural Appropriation.

Similar ambivalence is evident in the nature of *Don Quixote* itself. Just like the helmet of Mambrino, the Arabic manuscript that the second author discovers in Toledo can be understood as the analogue of a coin, similarly endowed with two values: a face value, represented here by the words on the page, and a commodity value, in this case the sheaves of paper of which it is made. From this perspective, the document functions in precisely the same way as a coin, whose face value is inconsequential beyond the political boundaries in which it is legal tender. Likewise, the manuscript is only valuable for its base material outside the linguistic community in which it circulates. Because the second author recognizes the document's unique nature, he is able to purchase it at a very low commodity price within the relatively small market in Toledo, where its value is merely a function of its material worth. He then essentially exports the manuscript by having it translated and selling it in a much larger Castilian-language market, where it commands a much higher price. This is precisely the same process by which Ricote's German companions amass copper coins in Spain, which they exchange for gold and silver ones based on the fractional coins' artificially inflated nominal value within this local market. They then smuggle the precious metal out of Spain, where it attains a higher value in the globalized currency exchange market. In this comparison between the book and the coins, the valuable half of the dyad (face value / commodity value) changes, but the principle remains the same. Logically, then, the very same complaints that Spaniards made against foreign merchants and bankers for despoiling the kingdom of its rightful hoard of gold and silver could be applied to the second author, who has, by this reasoning, robbed the Morisco community of a cultural artefact for personal profit by exporting it to a foreign constituency. Whether this symmetry, or the irony to which it gives rise, would have been perceptible to Cervantes or his contemporaries remains highly speculative. Be that as it may, by explicitly describing his own literary creation in terms of the interplay of competing, and potentially radically divergent, uses, values, and prices, Cervantes incorporates the logic of economic exchange into the essence of the novel. In this way, *Don Quixote* represents a true economics of literature, rather than a literature about economics.

Notes to Chapter 6

1. Carroll B. Johnson, *Don Quixote: The Quest for Modern Fiction* (Boston: Twayne, 1990), p. 71.
2. Miguel de Cervantes Saavedra, *The Ingenious Hidalgo Don Quixote de la Mancha*, trans. by John Rutherford (London: Penguin, 2000), p. 74. All translations from *Don Quixote* are from this edition.
3. p. 75.
4. Tomás de Mercado, *Suma de tratos y contratos*, ed. by Nicolás Sánchez Albornoz, 2 vols (Madrid: Instituto de Estudios Fiscales, Ministerio de Hacienda, 1977), I, 49–50; Francisco García, *Tratado utilísimo y muy general de todos los contratos*, ed. by Idoya Zorroza and Horacio Rodríguez Penelas (Pamplona: EUNSA, 2003), pp. 138–42.
5. Mercado, I, 118–19; Luis de Molina, *La teoría del justo precio*, ed. by Francisco G. Camacho (Madrid: Editora Nacional, 1981), pp. 159–74.
6. Mercado, I, 173.

7. Domingo de Soto, *De la justicia y del derecho*, trans. by Marcelino González Ordóñez, 5 vols (Madrid: Instituto de Estudios Políticos, 1967), III, 546–49; Molina, *La teoría*, p. 162.
8. Carroll B. Johnson, *Cervantes and the Material World* (Urbana: University of Illinois Press, 2000), p. 6.
9. García, pp. 387–88.
10. My translation. With the exception of passages translated from *Don Quixote*, all translations are my own.
11. García, p. 140.
12. García, p. 222; Molina, *La teoría*, p. 171.
13. p. 75.
14. Miguel de Cervantes, *El coloquio de los perros*, in *Novelas ejemplares*, ed. by Harry Sieber, 22nd edn, Letras Hispánicas, 105–06, 2 vols (Madrid: Cátedra, 2003), II, 299–359 (pp. 349–50).
15. Maurice Molho, 'El pícaro de nuevo', *Modern Language Notes*, 100.2 (1985), 199–222 (p. 208).
16. Américo Castro, 'La palabra escrita y el *Quijote*', in *Hacia Cervantes* (Madrid: Taurus, 1967), repr. in Américo Castro, *Obra reunida*, ed. by José Miranda, 3 vols (Madrid: Trotta, 2002 (1967)), I, 341–702 (pp. 614–15) (originally published in 1947); Joaquín Casalduero, *Sentido y forma del 'Quijote', (1606–1615)*, Colección Biblioteca Cervantina, X (Madrid: Visor Libros, 2006), p. 28; Manuel Durán, *La ambigüedad en el 'Quijote'*, Biblioteca de la Facultad de Filosofía y Letras (Xalapa: Universidad Veracruzana, 1960), p 173; Helena Percas de Ponseti, *Cervantes y su concepto del arte*, 2 vols, Biblioteca Románica Hispánica, II: Estudios y Ensayos, 217 (Madrid: Gredos, 1975), I, 138–39; Augustin Redondo, *Otra manera de leer el 'Quijote': historia, tradiciones culturales y literatura*, Nueva Biblioteca de Erudición y Crítica (Madrid: Castalia, 1997), p. 483; Leo Spitzer, 'Linguistic Perspectivism in the *Don Quijote*', in his *Linguistics and Literary History: Essays in Stylistics* (Princeton: Princeton University Press, 1948), pp. 41–85. For rejoinders to Castro and Spitzer see, respectively, Alexander A. Parker, 'El concepto de la verdad en el *Quijote*', *Revista de Filología Española*, 32 (1948), 287–305 <http://cvc.cervantes.es/literatura/quijote_antologia/parker.htm> [accessed 23 April 2019]; and Thomas R. Hart, '¿Cervantes perspectivista?', *Nueva Revista de Filología Hispánica*, 40.1 (1992), 293–303.
17. The *real* was a silver coin worth 34 *maravedís*, and the *real de a ocho* was worth eight *reales*, or 272 *maravedís*.
18. p. 167.
19. p. 168.
20. p. 426.
21. *Recopilación de las leyes de estos reynos*, 3 vols (Madrid: Catalina de Barrio y Angulo y Diego Diaz de la Carrera, 1640; repr. Valladolid: Lex Nova, 1982), II, 27^r.
22. p. 417.
23. p. 418.
24. p. 418.
25. p. 168.
26. García, pp. 222–24.
27. Soto, III, 585.
28. Martín de Azpilcueta, *Comentario resolutorio de cambios*, ed. by Alberto Ullastres, José M. Pérez Prendes, and Luciano Pereña (Madrid: Consejo Superior de Investigaciones Científicas, 1965), p. 71.
29. Mercado, I, 218.
30. Mercado, II, 394.
31. García, p. 128.
32. José I. García del Paso, 'El problema del vellón en *El chitón de las tarabillas*', *La Perinola*, 6 (2002), 323–62 (pp. 331–32).
33. Elena María García Guerra, *Las alteraciones monetarias en Europa durante la Edad Moderna*, Cuadernos de Historia, 78 (Madrid: Arco Libros, 2000) and *Moneda y arbitrios: consideraciones del siglo XVII* (Madrid: Consejo Superior de Investigaciones Científicas, 2003).
34. Abelardo del Vigo, *Cambistas, mercaderes y banqueros en el Siglo de Oro español* (Madrid: Biblioteca de Autores Cristianos, 1997), p. 253.

35. Bartolomé de Albornoz, *Arte de los contractos* (Valencia: Pedro de Huete, 1573), fol. 131^v.
36. Pedro de Valencia, 'Discurso de Pedro de Valencia acerca de la moneda de vellón. Zafra, 1605', in *Obras completes IV/I: Escritos sociales I; Escritos económicos*, ed. by Rafael González Cañal (León: Universidad de León, 1994), pp. 111–23 (p. 113).
37. Pedro de Oña, 'Tratado y memorial de los inconuenientes y daños que a causado en los Reynos la moneda de Vellon que estos años se labro y doblo en Castilla y del Remedio y reparo de todos ellos', Madrid, Biblioteca Nacional de España, MS 6279, fol. 4^v.
38. Juan de Mariana, *La dignidad real y la educación del Rey (De rege et regis institutione)*, ed. by Luis Sánchez Agesta (Madrid: Centro de Estudios Constitucionales, 1981), pp. 342–43.
39. Chad Leahy, '"Dineros en Cruzados": The *Morisco* Expulsion, Numismatic Propaganda, and the Materiality of Ricote's Coins', *Hispanic Review*, 84.3 (2016), 273–98 (pp. 281–83).
40. Francisco Márquez Villanueva, *Personajes y temas del 'Quijote'* (Madrid: Taurus, 1975), p. 251; Julio Vélez-Sainz, '¿Amputación o ungimiento?: Soluciones a la contaminación religiosa en el *Buscón* y el Quijote (1615)', *Modern Language Notes*, 122.2 (2007), 233–50 (pp. 244–45).
41. p. 857.
42. p. 855.
43. p. 853.
44. p. 854.
45. p. 852.
46. p. 853.
47. Américo Castro, *Cervantes y los casticismos españoles* (Barcelona: Alfaguara, 1966), pp. 13–23. See also Carolyn A. Nadeau, '*Moscatel morisco*: The Role of Wine in the Formation of Morisco Identity', *Bulletin of Hispanic Studies*, 90.2 (2013), 153–65.
48. Monique Joly, 'Afición de los extranjeros al vino y al jamón: nota sobre el sentido de una síntesis cervantina', *Nueva Revista de Filología Hispánica*, 22.2 (1973), 321–28.
49. p. 851.
50. p. 855.
51. José Larraz, *La época del mercantilismo en Castilla (1500–1700)*, 3rd edn (Madrid: Aguilar, 1963), p. 105. As Luis Perdices de Blas points out, this critique was fundamentally predicated upon the recognition that a lack of domestic productivity allowed 'industriosos extranjeros' to drain Castilian capital (*La economía política de la decadencia de Castilla en el siglo XVII: investigaciones de los arbitristas sobre la naturaleza y causas de la riqueza de las naciones* (Madrid: Editorial Síntesis, 1996), p. 42).
52. Valencia, p. 115.
53. Gaspar de Pons, *Untitled Memorial* (Madrid: [n. pub.], 1600), fol. 37^r. This long and compendious memorial is unsigned, but it is unquestionably the work of Pons, since it contains elements taken from at least two memorials of certain attribution, *Diez puntos* (Madrid, Biblioteca Nacional de España, VE/28/26) and *Expos[ici]on de 10 puntos q[ue] se tocaron en Villete q[ue] se embio al Rey N[ue]s[tr]o s[eñ]or D. Ph[elip]e 3º año 1599* (Madrid, Biblioteca Nacional de España, MS 2346, 63^r–159^r). It was probably printed at the *Imprenta Real*. For this latter information I am grateful to Professor D. W. Cruickshank, who generously agreed to share his time and expertise by examining my copy of the manuscript.
54. Pons, fols 37^{r-v}.
55. Johnson, 'Ricote the *Morisco* and Capital Formation', in *Cervantes and the Material World*, pp. 51–68; Benjamín Liu, 'Ricote, Mariana y el patrón oro', in *Cervantes y la economía*, ed. by Miguel-Ángel Galindo Martín (Cuenca: Ediciones de la Universidad de Castilla-La Mancha, 2007), pp. 53–66.
56. Michel Moner, 'El problema morisco en los textos cervantinos', in *Las dos grandes minorías étnico-religiosas en la literatura española del Siglo de Oro: los judeoconversos y los moriscos. Actas del 'Grand Séminaire' de Neuchâtel: Neuchâtel 26 a 27 de mayo de 1994*, ed. by Irene Andres-Suárez (Paris: Les Belles Lettres, 1995), pp. 85–100 (p. 94).
57. Mercado, II, 495.
58. Luis Ortiz, *Memorial del contado Luis Ortiz a Felipe II*, ed. by José Larraz (Madrid: Instituto de España, 1970), pp. 30–31.

59. Lope de Deza, *Gobierno político de agricultura*, ed. by Ángel García Sanz (Madrid: Instituto de Cooperación Iberoamericana, 1991), pp. 170–71.
60. Pons, fol. 37^r.
61. Mercado, I, 93.
62. Joly, p. 325.
63. Mercado, I, 226.
64. Mercado, I, 227, 229.
65. García, p. 193.
66. Odd Langholm, *The Legacy of Scholasticism in Economic Thought: Antecedents of Choice and Power* (Cambridge: Cambridge University Press, 1998), pp. 34–42, 59–66.
67. Mercado, I, 187; II, 578.
68. p. 855.
69. p. 856.
70. Soto, III, 510.
71. Quoted in Márquez Villanueva, p. 263.
72. L. P. Harvey, *Muslims in Spain, 1500 to 1614* (Chicago: University of Chicago Press, 2005), p. 253.
73. Antonio Domínguez Ortiz and Bernard Vincent, *Historia de los moriscos: vida y tragedia de una minoría*, Biblioteca de la Revista de Occidente, 36 (Madrid: Revista de Occidente, 1978), p. 126.
74. Mercado, I, 229; Domínguez Ortiz and Vincent, pp. 110, 120, 124.
75. Cervantes, 'El coloquio de los perros', p. 350.
76. Oña, fols 14^v–15^r.
77. Deza, p. 57.
78. Johnson, *Material World*, p. 63.
79. Leahy, p. 293.
80. Márquez Villanueva, p. 324.
81. p. 852.
82. p. 924.
83. p. 856.

CHAPTER 7

Moors, Moriscos, Disbelief: Beyond the Authors of the *Quixote*

Anthony John Lappin

In memoriam amicorum nunc absentium

Prohemium

Let me, for the sake of argument, assert somewhat wholeheartedly that, when we read fiction, we 'entertain the proposition that *p* unasserted'.[1] And if we imagine ourselves reading fiction, we may be drawn into thinking that we engage in a game of make-believe with the products of our fancy, a game which takes its inspiration from the text before our eyes, crediting these fancies with enough existence for the duration of our game to make the game itself worth the candle.[2] Such a description can soon fold in upon itself, as imaginings upon imaginings project themselves into an infinity of reflexions in one's mirror neurons.[3] Yet, although the neuroscientific jury is still out on how we imagine, or how we relate with those imaginings, it is clear that, when we read, if the spell of fiction is successfully cast over us, we accept (perhaps implicitly) that what we are reading is at once 'real within itself' as well as being 'not wholly or necessarily real with regard to everything else'.

As readers, we give ourselves permission to imagine and also to discount, to let ourselves enjoy the story whilst at the same time not commit ourselves to that story's congruence to actual, bald and hard facts either in our present or about the past. We possess a category of *fiction* by which we categorize certain types of written, oral and staged stories; and we gain pleasure from them, through distraction from present concerns via the variations of a narrative (often termed 'suspension' or 'transportation'), attention paid to details ('focus'), combined with suspense, the tension created by an unknown outcome. Another level of enjoyment is produced by the appreciation of the artifice (the structure of the plot, the evocation of fictionality), which depends upon the work being accepted as fiction in the first place — that the story is not constrained in its course by the requirement that it retells something that actually happened in the 'real world'. The propositions contained within the envelope of the fiction may be entertained, accepted, without their having to be justified beyond themselves. Within this category of 'fiction', it has been noted how works adopt what is accepted as reality as their default, departing from it only when they make this explicit; and so, in Umberto Eco's characterization, they are 'parasitic' on the real world.⁴

The means, however, by which we award ourselves this important permission, of reading a work as fictional, is a complex process, depending upon numerous cues and clues which we interpret in line with our social formation, following rules and conventions we pick up as we go along. Those conventions are socially formed, co-operative, and mutually recognized, so that the narrative may be accepted as fiction without leading to mistaken beliefs or conclusions which lead to unsuitable responses.⁵ One of the most important elements in this type of negotiation with a text, as it takes place on an individual level and within a wider social context, is the claim to (on the text's side), and the attribution of (on the readers'), genre. To make these choices clearer (and to relate the issue directly to *Don Quixote*), we may wish some similar types of writing into two categories. The first, *history writing*, concerned with the establishment of facts based upon documentary evidence marshalled into a narrative, combined with interpretation based upon those facts (and philosophical and psychological beliefs about the nature of human beings — in other words, informed cultural assumptions). The second, *fiction writing*, concerned with the establishment of an enjoyable story which takes place within a conceivable world filled out by philosophical and psychological beliefs about the nature of human beings within that world — in other words, informed critical assumptions. Even within such a Manichean division of texts written either to inform or to delight, the negotiations of fictionality are ever-present: decisions about whether a piece of information is a golden nugget of real world fact or the fools' gold of fictional invention are constant: the parasite, as it happens, shares a good deal of DNA with its host, and the limits of one organism and the other are not necessarily perfectly clear, but will vary with the sophistication and knowledge of each reader. But this is a cavill to the broader point, which seeks to underline the importance of our classification, or taxonomy, of narrations: genre is established by conformity to familiar styles and through recognition of the familiar formatting of, for example, the print, the illustrations, the paratexts to the narrative proper.⁶ This method of navigation or parsing the type of story we are presented with is extremely helpful, saving time, confusion, and no little embarrassment on the way.

One should not take what is fictional as being simply historical, for example. And one certainly would not take what is fictional as being simply historical, as long as one has a clear-cut definition of the one and the other, a clear generic separation. The DNA of one is quite distinct — and is manifested in different behaviours — from the DNA of the other. But narrative can exist quite happily without almost any generic conceits, as was the case through much of the Middle Ages; styles and themes seeped across diverse subject-matters without any undue concerns.⁷ And, we should remember, that it was in the Middle Ages when the novels of chivalry were born. Their absence from classical canons caused a certain discomfiture to the renascimental preceptists concerned with establishing their genre, and their rules.⁸ Yet we — modern, sophisticated readers, like your good self, my gentle friend — are familiar with the chivalresque genre: the fantastic accounts of imaginary yet noble heroes, motivated by absurdly punctilious honour and by ridiculous devotion to a beautiful lady, containing incredible marvels of enchantment and outlandishly monstrous wonders. It can be clearly placed in the compartment marked *fiction (do not open)*, and left alone for the fustian-infused tosh it is.

Nevertheless, whatever *sanbenito* we insist they wear, the chivalresque books themselves do not take our designation lying down. No: they ride out to the lists asserting their truthfulness, proud to define themselves as a 'true history' in an unabashed and unsophisticated direct apostrophe to the Reader, loud in presenting the words of an authentic and credible witness to the events they narrate, faithfully translated by the author of the vernacular work who selflessly handed it over to the printer.[9] Continuations of the stories by various hands also maintained the affirmations of veracity, expanding the reach in time and space. This would be all good fun, in a rocambolesque way, a happy joke between author and reader, if there were no individuals who took the affirmations seriously, and so credited the magico-martial morass not as agreeable fantasy but straight-down historical narrative.

I

Cervantes was quite clear, both in the prologue to Part One and in the final paragraph of Part Two, that his principal aim in writing was to bring low the novels of chivalry. I think I am not exceeding the natural caution of the historian in asserting that the Spain of Cervantes's day was hardly overwhelmed by an epidemic of stark, staring madness brought on by overexposure to the novels of chivalry. But the attitude of the illiterate innkeeper, unable to distinguish between the derring-do of Fortinbras and the notable deeds of the Gran Capitán — a confusion, above all, of genre — gives us more of a glimpse of the target. Set in a distant past, with some claim to mentioning historical figures or places, the fine tissue of the chivalresque could be granted a (distant) reality. But that reality entailed, from any contemporary intellectual's view, ridiculous beliefs about magic, and witchcraft, and martial prowess that could no longer be held at the beginning of the seventeenth century: blades might once have been enchanted, but bullets certainly could not be. In Cervantes's day, the intelligentsia of Catholic Europe had almost completely abandoned any faith it had in witches' powers or the efficacy of magic spells: any slither of success for either came from poisons and natural potions, or (very rarely) from actual demons — although, fortunately for all, because of this potential for demonic involvement, witchcraft fell under the Inquisition's jurisdiction as a possible heresy, rather than civil crime.[10] At that time, there was as concrete a need felt to combat such superstitions, as there is felt in the present to champion evolution and vanquish the vanishingly small number of people that believe that the world was created in seven days according to the time-and-motion analysis provided by the first chapter of Genesis. Part of Cervantes's campaign against the novels of chivalry is through the strong association he makes between them and heresy: the interrogation and burning of Don Quixote's books as if they were heretics, although ironic and comic, has a serious point. Yet the debate and the concern was not so much simply a question of what stories might be deemed historical facts — any more than the debate over creationism is a matter of getting mutual agreement over the date for the world's birthday — ; but, rather, the issue lay in the attitude one should take to the information presented. Although fiction could be enjoyable, history offered models of exemplarity, precedents to follow, actions to copy, attitudes to adopt: the presentation of the romances and novels of chivalry as history was flooded with the danger that they could overflow their proper course of puerile distractions and inundate society with their faulty models of behaviour. Cervantes's struggle was not at all about abstract facts, and all about practical virtues.

Chivalric authors were quite clear that their readers should be taking their works as improving literature by which to be inspired in their deeds and which they should copy in their lives. Jerónimo Fernández, creator of the most magnanimous knight, Don Belianís, outlined the importance of historical exemplars for the Romans, in both war and science; and, down to his present, the same importance was ascribed to the valour of Spanish nobility, especially his clerical patron's family. In this context, Fernández raises his 'translation from the Greek' to rub shoulders with other Greek forebears, such as Homer and Aristotle:

> Quien hiziera a los valerosos romanos tan pujantes de coraçon, tan atreuidos en esfuerços, tan valerosos en personas, tan esclarescidos en la moral philosophia, si no tuuieran ante los ojos los troyanos, de quien en las armas y linaje se tenían por successores, con aquellas lumbreras de caualleria, Ector, Troylus, Paris, y Deyfebo, con los otros sus valedores y en la ciencia ha aquellos tan profundos griegos con sus esclarescidos maestros Socrates, Platon, Aristotiles, Solon, con los demas de que en los libros estan poblados, donde se siguieron en Roma aquellos tan excelentes romanos, Romulos en lo humano y Numa Pompilio en lo diuino, con tantos y tan esclarescidos consulados que por cosa notoria se pueden dexar de contar, donde finalmente, ylustre señor, procediera tanto valor en nuestras Españas como el que al presente tienen. [...] Por lo qual, determinado de hazer a vuestra illustre persona vn pequeño seruicio, me determiné, siguiendo la memoria de estos tan insignes varones, ha restituyr en nuestro español, la Hystoria del valeroso principe don Belianis de Grecia, la qual el sabio Friston, en lengua griega, dexò escripta, certificando que aunque al parescer se represente ser cosa para occupar ociosos, tiene sentencias admirables que no dexaran de dar algun contentamiento.[11]

> (How would the brave Romans have had such strength in their hearts, such daring in their efforts, such valour in their persons, such excellence in ethics, if they did not hold the Trojans before their eyes, of whom they thought themselves the successors in arms and descent, with those luminaries of chivalry, Hector, Troylus, Paris, and Deiphebus, with their followers; and in the fields of knowledge, those deep-thinking Greeks with their illustrious teachers, Socrates, Plato, Aristotle, Solon, with the others who fill up their books, whence there followed in Rome those most excellent Romans, Romulus in human matters and Numa Pompilio in divine, with so many and so illustrious consuls who are so famous they do not need to be mentioned, whence finally, illustrious lord, their came to be such bravery in our Spains as there is now [...]

> Therefore, intending to do your illustrious person a small service, I made up my mind, following the recollection of which signal men, to restore in our Spanish the History of the brave prince don Belianis of Greece, which the magus Friston, in the Greek tongue, wrote down, assuring that although it seems to be something to occupy those who have nothing to do, it contains wonderful *sententiae* which will not fail to give some pleasure.)

The author of the *Platir* (part of the Primaleón cycle) goes one better, and invokes the deeds of representatives of major noble houses of Spain (the Osorio, the Pimentel, and the Velasco), together with the universally-acclaimed 'Cir Rudyes [*sic*]' and the Gran Capitán, and, furthermore, contemporary Spanish soldiers by sea and by land; invokes all of this as a means of asserting the humdrum credibility of his frankly incredible tale. But if the story was credible, then it should be modelic:

> me dava muchas alas tener la obra gran semejança de virtud, porque, viendo los buenos cavalleros presentes que en aquellos tiempos se obravan tan excelentes hazañas, perseverassen en sus bondades y los perezosos tomassen exemplo para mejorar sus obras.[12]
>
> (I was much enthused that the work should have the a great appearance of virtue, since, when good knights of the present-day should see that in those times such excellent deeds were accomplished, they might persevere in goodness, and the stay-a-beds might take an example to improve their own actions.)

And so, the disasters that follow from Don Quixote's acting out of chivalresque *mores* are not simply motors for laughter; they make a point about the morally unacceptable role that chivalric literature was claiming for itself. This is already signalled early in the book, where Don Quixote's favourite knight's behaviour is exposed as ludicrously fictitious, highly misleading and simply unacceptable:

> Pero, sobre todos, estaba bien con Reinaldos de Montalbán, y más cuando le veía salir de su castillo y robar cuantos topaba, y cuando en allende robó aquel ídolo de Mahoma, que era todo de oro, según dice su historia. (I. 1, 43)
>
> (But, above all, he enjoyed Reinaldos de Montalbán, and more when he saw him come out of his castle, and rob all those he came across, and when, in foreign lands, he robbed that idol of Muhammad, which was pure gold, according to what it says in his History.)

In a period in which understanding of Muslims was crucial within Spain's own geopolitical space, and a measured appreciation of Islam was a political necessity, idiocies such as a golden mammet could not be allowed to pass unnoticed. One of Spain's greatest intellectuals of the period, the Valencian Jesuit, Benedictus Pererius, would append a refutation, at the end of his commentary on the Apocalypse, of the idea that had taken form in the late fifteenth century that Muhammad (or Islam or the Turks) was the Antichrist himself. This was published a year after Part One of the *Quixote*, and written at exactly the same time.[13]

The key means of relegating these pestilential books of chivalry to the category of *fiction (do not open)* is the ruthless parody of what become the generic markers of fictionality: the apparatus by which the tales were purportedly recorded, retold, translated (that is, their claims to truthfulness). Cervantes, in the prologue and first chapters of Part One, placed himself under the spotlight. In the prologue, we see him toiling over the words we read, until 'a friend' (unnamed, obviously) provides him with his subject matter: a condemnation of the pseudo-learned apparatus that by force adorned improving literature; and a third-person affirmation that the book was written against chivalric literature, at once avoiding too sententious a declaration from Cervantes himself, and making doubly sure that no illiterate innkeeper would get the wrong end of the stick (although this seems not to have dissuaded a generation or two of Romantic Germans from grasping it with both hands and swinging it with all the force of their own will).[14]

Unless we are willing to affirm that the prologue is pure biography, and Cervantes was for once lost for words and needed a friend to tell him what to do; unless we are sure that an author of fiction is obliged to write the truth about himself; and unless we wish to slide into the rest of the book with a vision of Miguel de Cervantes Saavedra (as the author is named on the frontispiece) trawling the highways and byways of La Mancha and assembling his biography of a modern-day knight errant from various authorities;[15] then we must conclude that Cervantes is presenting a fictionalized version of himself: not the historical author (born, enslaved, imprisoned, recipient of payment from the publisher: the author-function outside the text); but, rather, an author-function within the text, a creation of the text itself which explains its own origin as part of an encapsulating fiction.[16] The fiction's author-function is a compiler, fortunate in his *trouvailles*; and that author-function is as much a vehicle for Cervantes's (the historical author's) irony as any other character.[17] One should note the indications that the historical Cervantes had also passed through his own story without being associated with the author-function ('compiler', 'second author'): the amicable yet adverse criticism of his *La Galatea* by the village priest (I. 6, 94); the unnamed traveller who abandons the box containing his own works at the inn, together with some of the dregs of the chivalresque genre (I. 32, 410); the Saavedra mentioned as the luckiest of captives in Algiers (I. 40, 507). The author-function within *Don Quixote* apes the role of the 'faithful translator' presented as the means of transmission of chivalresque novels from distant lands and foreign tongues, when he discovers the Arabic manuscript(s) containing the continuation of Don Quixote's story, by one Cide Hamete Benegeli. One should note the verisimilitude of the circumstances of the discovery (useless Arabic manuscripts destined for pulping), his ignorance of Arabic, the use of an intermediary (I. 9, 118–19); and yet one should also note the incredible notion that an author should write a romance of chivalry in Arabic adorned with a frontispiece which would not be out of place at the beginning of a contemporary printed book (I. 9, 119–20).

The choice of identifying the original text as Arabic was well within the confines of previous chivalresque accounts: although Greek was a particular favourite due to the fascination with long-fallen Constantinople, at least one work claimed to have been translated from the Arabic: the resolutely un-miraculous and crusade-oriented *Lepolemo* (otherwise known as the *Caballero de la Cruz*), written in Valencia in the early sixteenth century and much concerned with Egypt; and, appearing in eleven editions, amongst the top sellers of the range.[18] The tale is narrated by Xarton, a

Muslim sorcerer and *vates*, who himself recognizes the innate qualities of the noble captive, Lepolemo, and prophesies his future greatness; he writes at the command of the Sultan of Cairo, whom Lepolemo served faithfully for many years, fighting against the Turks.

Benengeli, then, might simply be a stand-in for all the magician-storytellers that provide the authorship of a slew of chivalric tales; indeed, the first line of the third part of the first book, 'Cuenta el sabio Cide Hamete Benengeli' (I. 15, 173; As the *sabio* Cide Hamete Benengeli tells the tale), is a calque on the first words of another of the genre's blockbusters: 'Cuenta el sabio Friston', the dastardly antagonist and wizardly narrator of the noble deeds of the invincible Don Belianís de Grecia, son of the magnificent and magnanimous emperor, Don Belanio de Grecia, who *etc*.[19]

Yet the choice of an author writing in Arabic was another easy means of indicating fictionality, or, at least, that the story, whatever it might claim to be, was not to be taken as 'true history'. Histories and documents composed in Arabic had been received with a brief period of enthusiasm during the late sixteenth century, but quickly attracted censure and were dismissed as impostures.[20] Indeed, the Cervantes-author-function within the text is rather sniffy about the historical reliability of his source:

> Si a ésta se le puede poner alguna objeción cerca de su verdad, no podrá ser otra sino haber sido su autor arábigo, siendo muy propio de los de aquella nación ser mentirosos; aunque, por ser tan nuestros enemigos, antes se puede entender haber quedado falto en ella que demasiado. Y ansí me parece a mí, pues cuando pudiera y debiera estender la pluma en las alabanzas de tan buen caballero, parece que de industria las pasa en silencio. (I. 9, 120)

> (If any objection might be made over the truth of this [history], it would not be other than that its author wrote in Arabic, since it is natural for those of that ethnicity to be liars; although, since they are such enemies of ours, he is rather more scarce than excessive in it. And thus it seems to me, since when he could and should have drawn out his quill in the praises of such a good knight, it seems that in craftiness he passes over them in silence.)

The anti-Islamic sentiment is quite palpable; but, in fact, all the author-function is doing here is echoing the pseudo-author of the *Lepolemo*: Xarton is granted his own prologue, and observes,

> Bien se yo que no podre escapar de murmaradores en mi escriptura mas que todos los que escriuen: pero soy cierto que no me juzgaran que escriuo mas delo que el hizo: sino menos: por que todo no pudo uenir ami noticia.[21]

> (I well know that I will not be able to fly from critics of my writing any more than all of those who write; but I am certain that they will not judge me that I write more than he did, rather I write less than he did, since I could not become aware of everything.)

The compiler's complaint against his source material in *Don Quixote* is furthermore undercut by his immediate insistence that the historian required a dispassionate and equitable approach.[22] Both the author-function/compiler and his Arabic source are involved in presenting fiction as fact; both are undercut by Cervantes's irony.

The choice of Xarton as narrator makes sense in *Lepolemo*, since it is a tale of triumphant Christianity in league with opponents of the Turk, and takes place on Xarton's home ground, Egypt. Cide Hamete Benengeli, it transpires, is also writing on home ground, and provides an uncomfortable reminder that much of Spain's medieval history had been written by Muslims, originally set down in Arabic, and composed on what was very much their home ground. Although the origin and the veracity of such Muslim-inspired tales were hotly debated,[23] the burgeoning number of national histories were forced to quarry and elaborate from them — or were themselves half-cocked re-imaginings dependent upon an invented witness after the supposed discovery of an authentic and antique manuscript.[24] Indeed, the affirmation that the Arabic author was also rooted in the landscape he wrote about comes with the emphasis that he was, without any doubt, a Muslim, with a clarification that *Hamete* was not a form of *Hamid* or *Ahmed*, but of the Prophet (and, from a Christian point of view, let us remember, the arch-heretic) himself:

> porque era uno de los ricos arrieros de Arévalo, según lo dice el autor desta historia, que deste arriero hace particular mención porque le conocía muy bien, y aun quieren decir que era algo pariente suyo. Fuera de que Cide Mahamate Benengeli fue historiador muy curioso y muy puntual en todas las cosas. (I. 16, 186)
>
> (since it was one of the rich muleteers from Arevalo, as was said by the author of this history (who makes special mention of this muleteer because he knew him well, and even suggests that he was something of a relation). Although Cide Mahamate Benegeli was a very gifted and exact historian in all things.)

Cervantes's intention here, I think, is to jumble the chronology of the work: the form of our Arabic historian's name looks back to the Middle Ages, with the archaic *Çide* (lord, 'Don') combined with a name which would not have been much used after the conversion of the Moriscos. This is but part of the parody of the chivalresque style, which Cervantes follows in its unblushing blend of historical figures and periods, its discontinuities, and even its tendency to get chapter headings wrong, or simply omit them.[25] At least, I think that is Cervantes's purpose; yet, given the details in the Captive's Tale which place that narration squarely in the late 1580s or early 1590s, an Old Christian reader might be forgiven (if that were ever possible) for assuming that the Arabic narrator was a contemporary *manchego*, writing in forbidden Arabic, and evidently one of the crypto-Muslims that had been causing such a degree of agitation in various high-placed clerics that they had been demanding, for over a decade, the exile of all Moriscos and not just the execution of the recalcitrant few. Admittedly, when the first part of *Don Quixote* appeared, it did seem that these extremists arguing for the economic self-harm of expulsion were a tiny number, and the voices of reason and sanity in Spain — backed up by the pope — were firmly in the ascendant. But the extreme can quickly move to occupy the centre, particularly as fear of the Turk and the pressure exerted by Barbary piracy turned a question of religious conscience best left to local clerics and the Holy Office into a full-blown threat to national security that demanded drastic action.[26] A crypto-Muslim writing harmless chivalresque reportage in La Mancha might seem perfectly innocent; but the archbishop of Valencia was arguing the point that even fully Christian Moriscos would be little harmed by their deportation to Algiers, since they already dwelt amongst practising Muslims, who (in a twist bound to tip the scales) were unafraid to show their sympathies for Spain's Turkish foe.[27]

Such an unfortunate political nexus aside, the suspicion which enveloped Benengeli as a narrator, however, fitted well with Cervantes's main and broader aim, which, in the early chapters of Part One, was to depict the novels of chivalry as heretical tomes, fit only for the fire. Belief in the books was equated with heresy; and Muslim heresy at that. Thus the *Amadís* is accused (although finally reprieved) of being the 'dogmatizador de una secta tan mala' (I. 6, 84) (the instructor into the dogma of such a vicious sect) — recalling Muhammad himself — , and *Lepolemo* is condemned for its Muslim narrator:

> Abriose otro libro y vieron que tenía por título *El Caballero de la Cruz*.
> — Por nombre tan santo como este libro tiene, se podía perdonar su ignorancia; mas también se suele decir 'tras la cruz está el diablo'. Vaya al fuego. (I. 6, 86)
>
> (He opened another book, and they saw its title was *The Knight of the Cross*. 'For a holy name such as belongs to this book, one might be willing to pardon its ignorance; but, besides, you do say, "Behind the Cross the Devil abides". To the flames'.)

At another point, Don Quixote calls to mind a well-known scene from his reading for use in a crisis; its celebrity is treated with hyperbolic praise, only to be equated with a whole genre of damnable Islamic superstition:

> Viendo, pues, que, en efeto, no podía menearse, acordó de acogerse a su ordinario remedio, que era pensar en algún paso de sus libros, y trújole su locura a la memoria aquel de Valdovinos y del marqués de Mantua, cuando Carloto le dejó herido en la montiña, historia sabida de los niños, no ignorada de los mozos, celebrada y aun creída de los viejos, y, con todo esto, no más verdadera que los milagros de Mahoma. (I. 5, 76–77)
>
> (So, seeing that, essentially, he could not shift, he remembered to latch onto his habitual remedy, which was to think of some incident from his books, and his madness brought forth into his memory the story of Valdovinos and the Marquis of Mantua, when Carloto left him wounded on the mountain-side, a story familiar to children, not unknown to young lads, famed and even believed by old men, and, with all this, was no more true than Muhammad's miracles.)

Cervantes, however, was not a writer who would leave a rich vein of irony unexplored, and Cide Hamete Benengeli becomes a means by which he can offer a seemingly objective comment on the development of his own story (rather like the 'friend' of the prologue). Chapter 22 takes head-on the conflict between chivalric *mores* and the requirements of a well-ordered Republic, when Don Quixote frees the gang of convicts who had been condemned to the galleys (used, let us not forget, to hold at bay the opportunism of the corsairs, the rapine of the pirates, and the fearsome might of the Turks). The chapter-title presents the events in a straightforward chivalric key ('De la libertad que dio don Quijote a muchos desdichados que mal de su grado los llevaban donde no quisieran ir') (I. 22, 257) (Regarding the freedom which don Quixote gave to many unfortunates who were being led where they did not want to go), and the beginning of the chapter itself offers us two characterizations: one of Cide Hamete, the other of the story itself; 'Cuenta Cide Hamete Benengeli, autor arábigo y manchego, en esta gravísima, altisonante, mínima, dulce e imaginada historia, que después que [...]' (257) (So narrates Cide Hamete Benengeli, an author in Arabic and of La Mancha, in this most serious, high-sounding, descriptive, sweet, and illustrated history, that, after [...]).

Exoticism (*arábigo*) meets parochialism (*manchego*), although *arábigo* always meant, when applied to a person, 'Arabic-speaking', rather than Arabian or Arab;[28] the designation 'autor arábigo' was particularly associated with scientific learning.[29] The author's style is summed up in five adjectives:

gravíssima, with serious mein, and with well-chosen words, and with thoughtful and grave bearing;[30]
altisonante, having a high and polished style, harmonious and divine;[31]
mínima, finely-grained, detailed;[32]
dulce, easy on the ear and pleasing to literary taste;[33]
imaginada, provided with suitable and ingenious decoration, thought-through, planned.[34]

Alternatively, one might read all this in an ironic key, condemning the chivalresque style for its self-important sententiousness, its bombast, its utter inconsequentiality, its saccharine overload, and its evident falsity. A reader attuned to the chivalric ethos, however, would be more inclined to accept the first. By the end of the episode, they may have changed their minds.

The second description of Cide Hamete's work, however, admits of no ironic readings, and prepares the reader for the interlocking nature of the intercalated stories built around the arrivals at the inn, with a pun on the production of the 'thread' of the narrative which, in fact, goes nowhere:

> [G]ozamos ahora en esta nuestra edad, necesitada de alegres entretenimientos, no sólo de la dulzura de su verdadera historia, sino de los cuentos y episodios della, que en parte no son menos agradables y artificiosos y verdaderos que la misma historia; la cual prosiguiendo su rastrillado, torcido y aspado hilo, cuenta que así como el cura comenzó a prevenirse para consolar a Cardenio [...]. (I. 28, 347)

> (Let us now enjoy in our own time, lacking in happy pastimes, not only the sweetness of his true history, but even of its tales and its episodes, which in part are no less agreeable and well-made and truthful as that same history; which, proceeding with its combed, twisted, and wound thread, relates that just as the priest began to gather himself to console Cardenio [...])

Rastrillado, torcido, aspado: combed, twisted, wound; purified, criss-crossing, chiastic.[35]

The key intercalated story in this part of the book is the Captive's Tale, following on from — and illustrating in a modern (i.e., non-chivalric) key — Don Quixote's own praise for the valour of the soldier over the industry of the scholar.[36] And, in the figure of the beautiful Mooress, Zoraida, we find a contrary figure to the potential of Cide Hamete: a Muslim who desires to become a true Christian, not a false Christian who remains Muslim. The story draws on Cervantes's own experience of captivity (and mentions him in passing, modestly reducing his considerable bravery to an example of good fortune).[37] Indeed, we might be led to present the story as an evident retelling of a captive's fantasy of escape, through the passionate love of a beautiful and rich woman. But this is not quite that type of fantasy; even less is it a narrative born of trauma.[38]

The Captive's Tale is a skilfully woven story of a conversion to Christianity, kept consistently within the confines of the natural, the believable, the coherent, whilst maintaining suspense through its numerous twists and turns, underpinned with serious symbolic import. It could be a miracle story, but refrains from outlandish supernatural involvement, of any type. Zoraida's introduction to Christianity is from a female slave brought from Spain; her confirmation in the faith is brought about by dreams, not visions; and her faith is devotional, not theological. Her desire is to become Christian, and she places her trust in the Virgin Mary — whose name she insists she will take; but there is no miraculous intervention; Zoraida seeks a direct and rational means of fulfilling her desires. Given her situation, all she can opt for is to escape with a captive; and rather than being overcome with desire for a man, she makes a rational choice from amongst the captives she can see from her house, and works to have him freed. The choice of husband is secondary to the choice of Christianity. This is an important narrative refutation to her father's betrayed and reproachful accusations that she seeks merely sexual licence amongst the Christians, since women had more liberty amongst them. That this occurs when they are forced to take shelter at the headland where La Cava was supposed to have been buried adds an added element to the tale: 'el [cabo] de la "Cava Rumia", que en nuestra lengua quiere decir "la mala mujer cristiana"' (I. 41, 530) (Cava Rumia's headland; in our language, that means 'the bad Christian woman'). According to Arabic histories, La Cava's seduction by King Roderick led to the loss of Spain to the Muslims; Zoraida's chastity brings a return to Christian Spain for the captive and his associates in prison. There is even a half-miraculous preservation of Zoraida's virginity, which is explained (or explained away, or joked away) by observing that the French corsairs were interested only in money (534). The corsairs' desire for money, though, strips the escapees of any wealth they had preserved; the renegade sensibly dropped the chest containing Zoraida's gold into the sea (534), lest the corsairs realize who had fallen into their hands, and sell them, for a suitably high price, back to certain death in Algiers. So the captive gains his freedom, but without the wealth that would have eased his return.

Yet what of Gil Pérez de Biedma, the captive himself? He distinguishes himself as a soldier by his religious faith and through his devotion to the cause of the Holy League against the Ottomans, and in the bravery which leads to his capture; and through his forbearance in refusing to plead with his family for his redemption price (I. 39, 500). His wanderings around the Mediterranean as a slave allow him an inside-view of historical events, on which he maintains a providentialist attitude, which, however, is still rooted in simple economics.[39] Realism — both in description, and in evaluation of experience — holds sway; prudence and fortitude are to the fore in his dealings with others. His depiction of the Muslim Other is, in the text, a series of evaluations of people, based on categorizations of bravery, humanity, cruelty: the renegade Uchalí Fartax is described with some admiration, even in his conversion to Islam (I. 40, 505–06); Azán Agá — Uchalí's protégé and successor — is recognized as being uniquely evil, even by the Turks themselves, whose own fame throughout Europe was of immoral butchers (I. 40, 506). Gradations, distinctions, assessments. The depiction of capitivity is harrowing, with the constant fear and the horror evoked by senseless and brutal executions taking place on a daily basis (I. 40, 507). As such, the account falls in well with early modern literary taste which had a vivid interest in captives' narratives providing ethnographic and historical descriptions of an alien and hostile civilization as well as an individual's physical and psychological experience of captivity.[40]

Against the background of the novels of chivalry, however, the anguish of the *baños* should be understood as a reproof to the myths of 'happy captivity' which they used as yet another narrative chess-piece.[41] Furthermore, from the earliest descriptions of Turkish captivity in the sixteenth century — particularly Bartholomeus Georgievitz's much-published and oft-translated account of his own experience of slavery — [42] to Haedo's account of the depravity of Algiers,[43] magic was an important instrument of control. These superstitious credences find no place in Cervantes's account. The Muslim Other is resolutely this-worldly, another reproof to the easy invocation of Moorish magicalness conjured up in Don Quixote's madness.

> — Por donde conjeturo que el tesoro de la fermosura desta doncella le debe de guardar algún encanto moro, y no debe de ser para mí.
> — Ni para mí tampoco, — respondió Sancho — , porque más de cuatrocientos moros me han aporreado a mí, de manera que el molimiento de las estacas fue tortas y pan pintado. (I. 17, 194)

> ('Thence I conjecture that the treasure of this lady's beauty must be kept by some enchanted Moor or other, and must not be destined for me.'
> Nor me, neither,' replied Sancho, 'because more than four hundred Moors have given me a beating, to the point that the thrashing with the stakes was a walk in the park.')

Yet Cervantes's concern is not simply to mock the simple, nor just to educate them. Part of his literary programme was to create a common literary culture, shared between the educated, the *discretos* and *prudentes* (those possessed with good, practical wisdom), and the common people. As Aristotelian precepts (and worse) took hold amongst the educated, this shared culture was collapsing; the gap was being widened thanks to malformed novels of chivalry which looked irredeemably heretical and superstitious, and to drama which pandered exclusively to the groundlings even when a solid commercial case could also be made for suitably august productions of properly conceived and executed plays.[44] *Don Quixote* itself was designed to bridge the widening gap, to reset the dial with regard to acceptable means of representation in fiction, establish the level to which — if we return to

Umberto Eco for a moment — it should be parasitic upon the real world. And — extremely important for Cervantes — to refocus attention on what ends fiction should serve. The experience of brutal warfare from which he lost the use of his left hand, the further anguish and horror of captivity, and subsequently the hardships of Spanish prisons when he had regained his freedom; these had left him with an over-riding sense of the importance of fortitude and of the need for virtue. But not in a bland, blanket sense of doing the impossible before bedtime and working miracles and wonders after breakfast, the misplaced piety that assumes that virtue is both easy to attain and the choices one faces are simple.[45]

II

The second part of *Don Quixote* was published in a world which had changed, and changed radically. The Moriscos, a seemingly safe minority in Spain, who troubled only the overworked judges of the Inquisition, had been expelled: in an ostensibly Christian polity, Christians — good, bad, and false — had been driven by armed guards onto ships and dumped in Barbary. And the literary market place, so empty of *Don Quixote*s before the first book had been published that Cervantes would have been willingly paid the worth of up to three chickens for Benengeli's single surviving manuscript (I. 9, 119), was now adorned not only by the first volume but also by a spurious tome in continuation claimed to be authored by a pseudonymous Alonso Fernández de Avellaneda, and done, it would seem, as much to spite Cervantes as to profit from, in an absolutely *castizo* authorial tradition within the chivalresque, a continuation not by the original author.[46]

The question of legitimacy becomes paramount, and the second part is published with the important qualification: *Segunda parte del ingenioso cauallero don Quixote de la Mancha. Por Miguel de Ceruantes Saauedra, autor de su primera parte* (661) (Second Part of the Witty Knight don Quixote of La Mancha. By Miguel de Cervantes Saavedra, Author of its First Part). The three divisions of the first part are forgotten (since Avellaneda's title indicated that it contained the 'fifth part'),[47] and, rather, the books as complementary units are brought to the fore; the first words of Chapter One are: 'Cuenta Cide Hamete Benengeli en la segunda parte desta historia y tercera salida de don Quijote' (II. 1, 681) (Cide Hamete Benengeli narrates in the second part of this history and third journey of Don Quixote). The learned Moor then becomes a useful cipher for Cervantes, as the authenticity of the story can be drawn from the former's writing; it provides a humorous and jocular manner of insisting on Cervantes's own primacy as creator of the characters and director of the story-line. Nevertheless, the Arabic-speaking author is increasingly characterized as an uncomprehending voice from the world of chivalry. Don Quixote and Sancho are informed by Sansón Carrasco of their literary celebrity as if it were truly taken from true novels of chivalry (II. 3, 705–06), and Benengeli becomes invested with much more of the aura of an unreliable narrator — thus leaving more space to Cervantes to be seen through the gaps.[48] No doubt due to the demands of celebrity (on which Part Two is itself a long essay), and to the usurping of his role by a mal-intentioned adversary, the author-function within the text can no longer be left playfully distant from the author-function outside the text, and so they are both brought together, to point to the author whose works were an international success and whose name was celebrated by the cream of French aristocracy.[49] Benengeli thus becomes much more fully associated with the chivalric world which was to be done away with, as José de Valdivielso notes in his *Aprobación* (given on 17 March 1615) to Part Two, identifying Cervantes's purpose (with no little contemporary reference) as 'la expulsión de los libros de caballerías, pues con su buena diligencia mañosamente ha limpiado de su contagiosa dolencia a estos reinos' (666–67) (the explusion of chivalric literature, since with finesse he has diligently cleansed these kingdoms of their contagious infection).

Yet concrete reference to the expulsion of the Moriscos in Part Two must await the latter chapters of the book. They had been exiled, region by region, beginning in 1609; but, with a certain amount of royal tolerance, had begun to drift back during the following years: we might say that the general attitude had been a steadfast support for the idea of expelling all Moriscos, combined with a widespread determination that the expulsion should not penalize those Moriscos whom people knew and liked as neighbours.[50]

Ricote first appears as an affectionate friend to Sancho: indeed, he trusts Sancho not to discover him to the authorities (II. 54, 1167–68). The motif of his return for buried treasure was perfectly comprehensible at the time, and the motif of the Morisco's Buried Treasure may have already become part of oral tradition.[51] Ricote's daughter and wife are faithful Catholics, whereas he is honest enough to be unsure of himself, even to an old Christian such as Sancho:

> Que, en resolución, Sancho, yo sé cierto que la Ricota mi hija y Francisca Ricota mi mujer son católicas cristianas, y aunque yo no lo soy tanto, todavía tengo más de cristiano que de moro, y ruego siempre a Dios me abra los ojos del entendimiento y me dé a conocer cómo le tengo de servir. (II. 54, 1172).
>
> (So, to sum up, Sancho, I know for certain that my daughter, Ricota, and my Francisca Ricota my wife are Catholic Christians, and although I am not so much, I still have more Christian than Moor to me, and I always ask God to open the eyes of my understanding and let me know how I am to serve him.)

If anything, in Ricote's being mostly Christian, Cervantes aligns himself here with the old view that it required time and effort to convert the Moors, despite Ricote's praise for the royal edict of expulsion. But Ricote's preference for Augsberg and the 'libertad de conciencia' found in Germany reflects the widespread view that Protestantism was far too close — doctrinally and politically — to Islam, and too willing to ally with the Ottomans, for Spanish and Catholic comfort.[52] Ricote again reaffirms his theme of the justness of the Morisco expulsion when he refuses Don Antonio Moreno's offer of intercession at the Court for both himself and his daughter. On the one hand, it shows how much more upright he is than the courtiers who can be turned by gifts; but also, in his repeated loyalty to the Crown and its officers, he shows how fit he is, in fact, to remain. In any case, Ricote's now out-of-date insistence that the eradication of the Moriscos was necessary for the health of the kingdom is simply ignored by Don Antonio: 'Una por una, yo haré, puesto allá, las diligencias posibles' (Step by step, I will, when I am there, carry out what can be done), and, echoing Ricote's previous words to Sancho, 'y haga el cielo lo que más fuere servido' (II. 65, 1274) (and may Heaven do what it will be best served by). Ricote, after all, was speaking for himself, his own more-than-half-Christian-less-than-half-Moorish self; but his daughter, Ana Félix, remained a Catholic Christian throughout her travails: she, too, deserved some consideration, and a judicious revision of her standing, now supported not only by Don Antonio, but the Viceroy himself. Decrees were one thing; desserts another. Marriage to Don Gregorio, the pretty boy she almost consigned to a fate worse than death, was obviously desired by all.

Ana Félix's story is marked by comic cross-dressing which Cervantes invokes for humour and suspense in his narration. Ana Félix is first presented as the unnamed 'mozo, que es el arráez del bergantín' (II. 63, 1257) (young man, who is the captain of the brig), apprehended after a high-speed naval chase; bound, ready for execution, and revealing through her speech that, of the three possibilities for a pirate on the high seas, 'Ni soy turco de nación, ni moro, ni renegado' (1258) (I am not a Turk, nor a Moor, nor an apostate). The primary definition she chooses, however, after these negations, is not a *nación* (i.e., *natio*, 'ethnicity'), but 'Mujer cristiana' (1258) (Christian woman).[53] Yet *her* cross-dressing is only part of the story.

Her admirer, Don Gregorio, son of the local *señor*, had followed her to Algiers, and was about to be summoned to the king's presence on account of his beauty, as Ana Félix had also been. Such examinations were not without carnal purposes. Able to extract herself from unwanted sexual relations through the promise of buried treasure, she attempted to provide Don Gregorio a means of escaping similar sexual intimacy: 'el peligro que don Gregorio corría, porque entre aquellos bárbaros turcos en más se tiene y estima un mochacho o mancebo hermoso que una mujer, por bellísima que sea' (1259) (the danger which Don Gregorio ran, since amongst those barbarian Turks a beautiful boy or young man is more highly esteemed than a woman, however beautiful she is). This was not simply a wish to avoid Don Gregorio becoming an object of homosexual desire.[54] From Gregorievitz's accounts on, it was common knowledge that castration was what awaited pretty young men, particularly if they were destined for the satisfaction of their owners' lust.[55] She dresses him as a women to avoid him *becoming* like a woman in a very literal sense; yet also thereby preserves her own sexual interest in him. Cervantes's telling of the tale keeps a certain propriety, but that should not be confused with naivety. Cross-dressing was beloved by contemporary theatre for its dramatic effects,[56] but seems to have attracted little of the shock and horror that moderns seem to think it should. It was canonized in Christian hagiography, in such figures as Saint Marina, who dressed as a monk, entered a monastery, and was ejected because she caused all of the cenobites to be overwhelmed with (so the monks themselves thought) homosexual desires.[57] She was by no means alone; there were many others who donned male garb for impeccable spiritual purposes to join their male confrères in monasteries.[58] But such transvestite saints did not only dwell in sandy coenobia of Late Antique deserts that were inscribed within inaccessible Latin *vitae*. They would even slip into something more masculine in the public theatres, to popular acclaim.[59] And so, in referring to Ana's own choice of gendered clothing, Don Antonio can make a pointed quip, suggesting she stay either 'con mi mujer en mi casa, o en un monasterio' (II. 64, 1274) (with my wife in my house, or in a monastery), and not, as would be expected for a young, unmarried woman, a convent.

Don Gregorio, dressed in women's clothes, and destined for the Ottoman sultan's harem, has to maintain a pretence before the noble women set to keep watch over him/her. He is rescued in a high-risk operation (which only takes place after Ricote guarantees the ransoms of any of the oarsmen captured) and is spared humiliation by being able to change into male garb — that of a captive — on the boat. No explanation for the presence of the captive is provided. Don Gregorio goes into very few details in his explanation of his adventures, 'donde mostró que su discreción se adelantaba a sus años' (1272) (whence he showed that his discretion was greater than his years). Given the drama of the escape, one may complain, as the author-function of Part One did against Cide Hamete Benengeli, that rather too much has remained in the inkwell. Cervantes was perhaps rather constrained at this point, assailed by poverty and old age, needing to get the book to the publisher, who also would have had a limit on how long even such a commercially successful work could be.[60]

Obviously, there are echoes in the Ricote–Ana Félix story of the Captive's Tale.[61] Earthly treasure, buried or sunk contrasted with true treasure (for Zoraida, her virginity; for Ricote, his daughter) (II. 63, 1262); both Zoraida and Ana Félix escape deflowerment because of the desire for money being stronger than the desire to rape;[62] men rescued from captivity at considerable risk; and, importantly, the crucial role of the *renegados*, the turncoats, the Christians who for whatever reason had decided to throw in their lot with their former enemies and current captors, and put themselves at great risk in order to return to Christendom. In these stories of conversion (Zoraida) or perdurance in the faith (Ana Félix), there are also the accounts of re-integration of the renegades to the Church and to Spanish society. Cervantes chooses to express this in unwonted theological language, without any traces of irony, referring to the renegade: 'Reincorporose y redújose el renegado con la Iglesia, y de miembro podrido volvió limpio y sano con la penitencia y el arrepentimiento' (II. 65, 1272–73) (the turncoat humbled himself and joined himself to the Church, and from a rotted limb became clean and sound through penitence and repentance).[63] Both of these are, in effect, tales about integration, offering a vision in which a making whole of the shattered Catholic unity of Spain was still possible, even regarding those often deemed beyond the pale. A similar position to his view of literature. Cervantes's middle-of-the-road assimilationist position regarding the Moriscos, 'la fusión biológica de sangres' (the biological fusion of bloodlines) in Márquez Villanueva's words,[64] was part of a much wider, accommodating and forgiving view. Indeed, the number of times that women are agents and instigators of solutions and salvation should lead us to consider carefully Cervantes's own attachment to the contemporary devotion towards the Mother of God as a gently salvific force.

Both accounts of captivity reveal one important way in which fiction involves us: by the presentation of dangers and sufferings, peripecies and disappointments, our sympathetic faculties are engaged, a response to characters that has been termed by primatologists and literary critics as 'empathy'.[65] One must be cautious, however, in assuming that 'empathy' is a one-size-fits-all for individuals and cultures, and that there might not be significant differences in levels and types of empathetic responses in readers and listeners of other ages and places.[66] A keen awareness of the fictionality of the tale, however, allows us to engage our empathetic understanding *more*, rather than less; unconstrained by quite rational concerns over empathizing too much with a living human being, a fictional character — and the more 'real', the better — can be the unknowing and unaffected recipient of our empathetic concerns.[67] In sympathizing with the plight of the protagonists of the Captive's Tale, we are not under any obligation to send our servant out to inquire if Zoraida–María is indeed happily married and wants not for the necessities of life. We can afford to be transported by the narrative, and make an emotional investment in the characters.[68] Real life usually places limits on our self-association with others; fiction removes those barriers.

And so in *Don Quixote*, we may say that Cervantes explores this fundamental danger of empathetic engagement with fiction, that the process of emotional investment does not find a way to *dis*engage itself, particularly with the open-ended and immersive story-worlds of the chivalric genre.[69] Reality may be (incorrectly) seen through a fictional frame,[70] rather than the recognition of the fictional frame allowing a dynamic but well-defined engagement with the fiction.[71]

The elaborate architecture of the references to Cide Hamete Benengeli's Arabic work, that author's own interjections and marginal annotations — interruptions to the 'flow' of the work and the narrative illusion of a completed story-world — offer a means of standing back from our immersion in the fiction, an opportunity to admire the artifice; that is, to engage other faculties beyond simple empathy, run other mental processes beyond imagination, gain other intellectual appraisals of the action that is presented to us. So, whilst we cradle the fiction warmly in our mind, we are also led to use other parts of our brain, making judgements, comparing, contrasting, being aware of both the fiction and our own responses to it. One of the aims — perhaps the fundamental aim — of *Don Quixote* is not to espouse the correct view on the novels of chivalry, nor to inculcate Aristotelian literary fashion, nor to take the correct line on what to do about the Morisco problem or the crusade against the Turk; rather, it is to produce an engaged reading of the text; engaged, however, not simply on an emotional level, but also an intellectual one. *Don Quixote* survives beyond the demise of the chivalric tomes it brought about, because it offers not simply a parody of them, but a highly sophisticated view of fiction, and offers a means for the reader to take part at a number of levels in the particular fiction which is presented by the work itself. It is no simple thing to affirm that fiction does not have to be true, nor that what presents itself as true should be, in fact, read as fiction.

Notes to Chapter 7

1. Roger Scruton, *Art and Imagination: A Study in the Philosophy of Mind* (London: Methuen, 1974), p. 88.
2. Here I paraphrase Kendall L. Walton, *Mimesis as Make-Believe: On the Foundations of the Representational Arts* (Cambridge, MA: Harvard University Press, 1990).
3. For the (by no means wholly accepted) argument that mirror neurons play a crucial role: Zanna Clay and Marco Iacobini, 'Mirroring Fictional Others', in *The Aesthetic Mind: Philosophy and Psychology*, ed. by E. Schellekens and P. Goldie (New York: Oxford University Press, 2011), pp. 313–29.
4. Umberto Eco, *Sei passeggiate nei boschi narrativi: Harvard University Norton Lectures 1992–93* (Milano: Bompiani, 1994), p. 101; see, further, Peter Bondanella, *Umberto Eco and the Open Text: Semiotics, Fiction, Popular Culture* (Cambridge: Cambridge University Press, 1997), pp. 165–66.
5. Peter Lamarque and Stein Haugom Olsen, *Truth, Fiction and Literature: A Philosophical Perspective* (Oxford: Oxford University Press, 1994), p. 37.
6. Gérard Genette, *Seuils* (Paris: Éditions du Seuil, 1987).
7. Kevin Sean Whetter points out that even if key themes are habitually grouped together in certain types of stories, neither were they discussed as such from a literary critical point of view nor were the themes limited to just those types of stories (*Understanding Genre and Medieval Romance* (Avalon: Ashgate, 2008), p. 155). Ingrid Nelson and Shannon Gayk also argue for medieval genre's implicit yet expansive nature: 'Introduction: Genre as *form-of-life*', *Exemplaria*, 27 (2015), 3–7.
8. Benedetto Croce, *Estetica come scienza dell'espressione e linguística generale: teoria e storia*, 4th edn (Bari: Laterza, 1912), p. 517: 'I critici italiani del Rinascimento, mentre lavoravono sul modello aristotelico alle loro Poetiche, si trovavono di fronte alla poesia cavalleresca, e dovettero intendersi alla meglio con lei, e l'assegnarono ai generi di poemi non previsti degli antichi [... o a] un eroico mal composto' (The Italian critics from the Renaissance, whilst they worked on the Aristotelian model for their Poetics, found themselves before chivalresque poems, and had to understand it as best they could, and assigned it to poetic genres unforeseen by the ancients [or to] an ill-formed heroic poetry). All translations in the article are my own.
9. See Daniel Eisenberg, 'The Pseudo-Historicity of the Romances of Chivalry', *Quaderni Ibero-Americani*, 45–46 (1975), 253–59.
10. See my introduction to the edition of Lope de Vega's *El Caballero de Olmedo* (Manchester: Manchester University Press, 2007), pp. 13–14.
11. I have taken the text from *Libro Primero, del valeroso e inuencible principe don Belianis de Grecia; hijo del Emperador don Belanio de Grecia. En el qual se cuentan las estrañas y peligrosas auenturas que le succedieron con los amores que tuuo con la princesa Florisbella: hija del Soldan de Babylonia. Y como fue hallada la princesa Policena: hija del Rey Priamo de Troya. Sacado de lengua Griega: en la qual se escriuio el Sabio Friston. Dirigio al illustre y muy Magnifico y Reuerendo señor don Pero Xuarez de Figueroa y de Velasco: Dean de Burgos, y Abad de Hermedes, y Arcediano de Valpuesta: señor de la villa de Cozcurrita* (Medina del Campo: Diego Despinosa, 1564), fol. 1^{r-v}. The title itself is a good example of the incoherent mixture of the classical with the modish and the flagrantly unhistorical: see Lilia E. F. de Orduna, 'Héroes troyanos y griegos en la *Hystoria del magnánimo, valiente e inuencible cauallero don belianís de grecia* (Burgos, 1547)', in *Actas del IX Congreso de la Asociación internacional de hispanistas*, 2 vols (Frankfurt: Vervuert, 1986), I, 559–68; a translation of the work's title might be as follows: *The First Book, regarding the Brave and Invincible Prince, Don Belianis of Greece, Son of the Emperor, don Belanio of Greece. In which are recounted the extraordinary and dangerous adventures which befell him through his love for the Princess Florisbella, the Sultan of Babylon's daughter. And how Princess Polycena, King Priam of Troy's daughter, was discovered. Done out of the Greek tongue, in which the Magus Friston wrote it. Dedicated to the high-born and most magnificent and reverend sir, don Pero Xuarez de Figeroa y de Velasco, dean of Burgos, and abbot of Hermedes, and archdeacon of Valpuesta, lord of the town of Cozcurrita.* The work was first published as *Comiença la Hystoria del magnanimo y valiente, y inuencible cauallero don Belianis de Grecia:* [...] *Traduzida de lengua Griega, en vulgar Castellano* (Burgos, 1547) — *So Begins the History of the magnanimous and brave, and invincible knight, don Belanis of Greece* [...] *Translated from the Greek language into common Castilian.*

12. *Platir: Valldolid, Nicolás Tierri, 1533*, ed. by María Carmen Marín Pina (Alcalá de Henares: Centro de Estudios Cervantinos, 1997), p. 4; the original title was *Cronica del muy valiente y esforçado cauallero Platir: hijo del inuencible emperador Primaleón* (Valladolid: Nicolas Tierri, 1533) — Chronicle of the very brave and strong knight, Platir, son of the invincible Emperor Primaleón.
13. Benedictus Pererius, *Centum octoginta tres disputationes selectissimae super libro Apocalypsis beati Ioannis apostoli: quibus adiectae sunt [...] viginti tres disputationes, aduersus eos qui putarunt, Maometem Saracenorum legislatorem fuisse verum illum antchristum* (Venice: Antonius Leonardus, 1607).
14. See Anthony Close, *The Romantic Approach to 'Don Quixote': A Critical History of the Romantic Tradition in 'Quixote' Criticism* (Cambridge: Cambridge University Press, 1978).
15. 'Quieren decir que tenía el sobrenombre de "Quijada", o "Quesada", que en esto hay alguna diferencia en los autores que deste caso escriben' (I. 1, 39) (they mean that his surname was Quijada or Quesada, since in this the authors who write about this subject differ); 'Autores hay que dicen que la primera aventura que le avino fue la del Puerto Lápice; otros dicen que la de los molinos de viento; pero lo que yo he podido averiguar en este caso, y lo que he hallado escrito en los anales de la Mancha es que [...]' (I .2, 51–52 (there are authors who say that the first adventure to come his way was that of the Lapice Pass, others say that it was that of the windmills; but what I have been able to verify in this case, and what I have found written in the annals of La Mancha is that [...]).
16. Michel Foucault, 'Qu'est-ce qu'un auteur?', *Bulletin de la Société française de philosophie*, 63:3 (1969), 73–104. For a fine attempt at unstringing the Gordian knot of knowing narratorial presences in the first book, see Shannon L. Polchow, 'Manipulation of Narrative Discourse: From *Amadís de Gaula* to *Don Quixote*', *Hispania*, 88 (2005), 72–81.
17. *Pace* Howard Mancing, 'Cide Hamete Benengeli vs. Miguel de Cervantes: The Metafictional Dialectic of *Don Quijote*', *Cervantes*, 1 (1981), 63–81 (pp. 63–64). The author-function defines himself as the book's 'padrastro' in the prologue (I. 10), and, later, as its 'segundo autor' (I. 8, 113).
18. Anna Bognolo, 'El "Lepolemo", "Caballero de la Cruz" y el "Leandro el Bel"', *Edad de Oro*, 21 (2002), 271–88.
19. *Don Belianis*, fol. A iii^r.
20. Richard Hitchcock, 'Cervantes, Ricote and the Expulsion of the Moriscos', *Bulletin of Spanish Studies*, 81 (2004), 175–85 (p. 176).
21. *El libro del inuencible cauallero Lepolemo hijo del emperador de Alemaña y de los hechos que hizo llamandose el Cauallero de la Cruz* (Toledo: Iuan Ferrer, 1552) — The Book of the Invincible Knight, Leoplemo, son of the Emperor of Germany and of the Deeds he Accomplished whilst Calling Himself the Knight of the Cross. The work was first printed in Seville around 1521.
22. 'cosa mal hecha y peor pensada, habiendo y debiendo ser los historiadores puntuales, verdaderos y nonada apasionados, y que ni el interés ni el miedo, el rancor ni la afición, no les hagan torcer del camino de la verdad, cuya madre es la historia, émula del tiempo, depósito de las acciones, testigo de lo pasado, ejemplo y aviso de lo presente, advertencia de lo por venir' (I. 9, 120–21) (an ill-wrought and worse-intended deed, since historians have the obligation to be exact, truthful and not at all biased, whom neither gain nor fear, hatred nor suffering will turn from the way of truth (whose mother is History, the copy of Time, Treasure-House of actions, witness to what has passed, example and warning for the present, counsel for what is to come)).
23. The *Crónica del moro Rasis*, for example, was at the centre of a long dispute over its authenticity; nevertheless, it was constantly cited and developed: Francisco José Aranda Pérez, 'Cide Hamete Benengeli, inventor inventado del *Quijote*, y otros historiadores arábigos más o menos invencioneros', *eHumanista/Conversos*, 3 (2015), 9–44, <http://www.ehumanista.ucsb.edu/conversos/volumes/3> [accessed 22 February 2018]. Benengeli's expression of agnosticism regarding the events in the Cave of Montesinos is itself a calque on Juan de Mariana's own definitive doubts about the story of Roderick, last king of the Goths, La Cava (see below, n. 29), and the fall of Spain: Mary Malcolm Gaylord, 'Pulling Strings with Master Peter's Puppets', *Cervantes: Bulletin of the Cervantes Society of America*, 18 (1998), 117–47 (pp. 139–40).
24. Pedro del Corral's fourteenth-century *Crónica sarracina*, partially based upon the account by one Eleastras, who claimed to be courtier and historian to Roderick, the last of the Visigothic kings:

Frédéric Alchalabi, 'L'écriture de l'histoire dans la *Crónica sarracina* de Pedro de Corral: le roi et son conseiller sous le regard d'Eleastras, l'historien', *e-Spania* [Online], 12 (2011), <http://dx.doi.org/10.4000/e-spania.20595>.

25. See the incisive essay by Thomas A. Lathrop, 'The Mysterious Missing Title of Chapter 43, of *Don Quixote*, Part I ', in *Cervantes y su mundo*, ed. by A. Robert Lauer and Kurt Reichenberger, 3 vols, (Kassel: Reichenberger, 2005), III. 275–82; I am not, however, as confident as he is that the 'missing title' in the list of contents is due to a nervous typesetter, and not just another jest by Cervantes himself. Further chronological uncertainty is found right at the end of Part One, where poems in Castilian are found allegedly underneath an old rural chapel, written 'con letras góticas' (I. 52, 647) (in Visigothic letters). Visigothic script had, together with Arabic, become a byword for illegibility: for example, *Relaciones histórico-geográficas-estadísticas de los pueblos de España. Reino de Toledo*, ed. by Carmelo Viñas and Ramón Paz, 3 vols (Madrid: CSIC, 1951–63), I, 486–87: 'Hay junto de la iglesia un arco grueso de ladrillo tosco y ruinado, y en una piedra del pico de la torre una inscripcion de letra antigua, goticas o arabigas, que no se dexan bien leer.' (There is, next to the church, a thick arch, made of coarse and ruined bricks, and on a stone at the top of the tower there is an inscription in an old script, either Visigothic or Arabic, which cannot be easily deciphered.) The maintenance of Visigothic script by the Toledan Mozarabs into the late fifteenth century may be here combined with the novel's faux-Arabic origin. For the long period in which Visigothic continued to be written flawlessly as an imitative script, see A. M. Mundó, 'La datación de los códices litúrgicos visigóticos toledanos', *Hispania sacra*, 18 (1965), 1–25.

26. Benjamin Ehlers, *Between Christians and Moriscos: Juan de Ribera and Religious Reform in Valencia, 1568–1614* (Baltimore: Johns Hopkins University Press, 2006), pp. 142–43. Much of the debate reads as a re-run of the victory of extremist intolerance with regard to the *conversos* during the fifteenth century, on which see Rosa Vidal Doval, '"Nos soli sumus christiani": *Conversos* in the Texts of the Toledo Rebellion of 1449', in *Medieval Hispanic Studies in Memory of Alan Deyermond*, ed. by A. M. Beresford, L. M. Haywood, and J. Weiss (Woodbridge: Tamesis, 2013), pp. 215–36.

27. Ehlers, p. 104.

28. The clearest example is from Luis de Mármol Carvajal, *Rebelión y castigo de los moros*, ed. by Cayetano Rosell (Madrid: Ribadeneira, 1852), p. 279: 'tres soldados grandes arábigos' (three highly-skilled Arabic-speaking soldiers) who were sent out from a besieged city to slip through the enemy lines; the only examples where the word means 'Arabian' up to the publication of the *Quixote* is in poetic bombast, from Góngora himself — 'arábigos olores' (scents of Arabia): Luis de Góngora y Argote, *Romances*, ed. by Antonio Carreira, (Barcelona: Quaderns Crema, 1998), p. 42 — and from Pedro de Espinosa, in an early example of a *Silva* from 1605, fol. 126^r: 'Ya un tiempo mi presencia | Grangeaste con votos, | Y en los templos de Cipria | Quemaste con devota reverencia | Bálsamo de Iudea, encienso arábigo, | Porque ni yo adorasse otra belleza | Ni tardase á tus braços.' (*Flores de poetas ilustres*, in *Poetas líricos de los siglos XVI y XVII*, ed. by Adolfo de Castro, 2 vols (Madrid: Rivadeneyra, 1857), II. 1–43 (pp. 27–28) (Once, long ago, you won my presence with vows, and in the temples of Cyprus you burnt with devout reverence Judean balsam, Arabian incense, so that I would not adore any other beauty, nor tarry returning to your arms). Both occurrences are related to gum arabic (*goma arábiga*), mentioned by Francisco Núñez, *Libro intitulado del parto humano. Madrid, Universidad Complutense, Facultad de Medicina, ms. 618.4*, transcr. by María Teresa Herrera and María Estela González de Fauve (Madison: Hispanic Seminary of Medieval Studies, 1997), fol. 154^v; Jerónimo Soriano, *Libro de experimentos médicos, fáciles y verdaderos*, transcr. by María Teresa Herrera and María Estela González de Fauve (Madison: Hispanic Seminary of Medieval Studies, 1997), fols 24rb, 72rb.

29. Juan de Jurava, *Historia de yerbas y plantas con los nombres griegos, latinos y españoles*, ed. by María Jesús Mancho (Salamanca: CILUS, 1999), s.v. *Hissopum montanum cilicum*: 'Mesué, autor arábigo, dezía que el isopo lleva la flor colorada, de la qual se avía de usar en medicina, mas, no aviéndola, usamos del otro, porque, como dize Dioscórides, ay dos maneras de Isopo, doméstico y agreste' (Masawaih, an Arabic author, said that hyssop has a red flower, with which one should create medicines, but, if it is not available, we may use another, because, as Dioscorides says, there are

two types of hyssop, garden and wild.) The initial reference is probably not to *Hyssopus officinalis* or related sub-species but to *Capparis spinosa*.

30. *Diccionario de autoridades*, 6 vols (Madrid: Real Academia Española, 1726–39), IV, s.v. *grave*[(6) — (7)], 'Se dice tambien del estilo, del discurso, de las palabras sérias y circunspectas: como Escribió en estilo grave, &c. Latín. *Gravis. Serius.* PINC[iano]. Philos. Epist. 6. Fragm. 7. No tenía para qué usar de conceptos agúdos, sino graves, severos, urbanos y cortesanos. VALDIV. S. Joseph, Cant. 1. Oct. 7. *Suene mi voz en dulce y grave estilo, | Del patrio Tajo al inundante Nilo.* (It is also used regarding style, discourse, serious, and well-considered words, such as 'He wrote in a grave manner [...]'. Latin: *gravis. serius* [grave, slow]. Pinciano, Philosophical Letters 6, fragment 7, 'There was no need to use witty conceits, but rather grave, severe, polished and courtly.' Valdivio, Saint Joseph, Canto 1, Octava 7: 'Let my voice sound in a sweet and grave style, from our homeland's Tagus to the flooding Nile'.) Moreover, the word also 'significa muchas veces importante, y de mucha entidad y gravedad: como Negocio grave, cáusa grave, &c. Latín. *Gravis. Ponderosus*' (often means important, of much weight and seriousness, such as 'grave buisiness', 'grave reason', and so on. Latin: *gravis, ponderous* [grave, weighty]).

31. *Diccionario de autoridades*, I, s.v. *altisonante*: 'Altamente sonoro, u de alto sonido. Voz jocósa compuesta de alto, y de sonante. Lat. *Altisonans,* que es de donde viene. CERV. Quix. tom. 1. cap. 22. En esta gravíssima *altisonante*, mínima, dulce, è imaginable história.' (altisonante: highly sonorous, or with a high pitch. A comic word, composed of *alto* [high] and *sonante* [sounding]. Latin: *altisonans*, which is whence it comes. Cervantes, Quixote, Vol. 1, Chapter 22: In this most grave, high-sounding, minimal, sweet and believable history.) One notes the citation of the passage under consideration, although with an illuminating misreading of the ultimate adjective. In renaissance Latin, however, *altisonans* evoked the music of the spheres ('sounding on high', perhaps a calque (or misreading even) of *altitonans* (thundering on high)): cp. Franciscus Georgii, *De harmonia mundi totus cantica tria* (Venice: Bernardinus de Vitalibus, 1525), fol. CLXVI[r]: 'percipiemus ipsam [psalmodiam] altisonantem omnia intersonare facientem' (we will perceive this heavenly hymnody making all things sound together); Marco Cipriani, 'Il *De orthographia* di L. Caecilius Minutianus Apuleius: introduzione, edizione, traduzione e commento' (unpublished doctoral thesis, Università degli Studi Roma Tre, 2009), p. 27. This would seem to be the first use of the word in Castilian, however.

32. *Diccionario de autoridades* IV, s.v. *minimo*: 'Lo que tiene el grado último de diminución, comparado con otra cosa de su especie. Es del Latino *Minimus, a, um.* MARM. Rebel. lib. 1. cap. 11. Y quando la voluntad de Dios ocurre, las más mínima ocasión nos mata. CERV. Galat. lib. 3. f. 150. *Si de mi mal insano | La más mínima parte conocieras, | Cessaran tus porfias*' (that which possesses the ultimate point of reduction, compared with another thing of the same type. It is from the Latin *minimus* [smallest, least]. Luis del Mármol Carvajal, *Historia de la rebelión y castigo de los moros de Granada*, Book 1, Chapter 11: 'And when the will of God comes about, the slightest adversity kills us'. Cervantes, *La Galatea*, Book 3, folio 150: 'If you should know the smallest part of the pain that drives me mad, you would insist on rejecting me'.)

33. *Diccionario de autoridades*, III, *dulce*[(4)–(5)]: 'Se usa translaticiamente en lo espiritual, moral y político, por grato, gustoso y apacible. Latín. *Suavis. Jucundus*'. (It is used in an expanded sense in spiritual, ethical and political writing for pleasing, enjoyable, and pleasurable. Latin: *suavis* [sweet], *jucundus* [congenial]). And, further, 'En la Pintúra es lo que está pintado con blandúra y suavidad. Latín. *Lenioris vel mollioris penicilli ductus*.' (In Painting, it is what is painted with softness and charm. Latin [softer and more beguiling brush-strokes].)

34. *Diccionario de autoridades*, IV, s.v. *imaginar*[(3)]: 'Significa tambien disponer con imágenes, o adornar con ellas alguna pieza de architectúra. En este sentido es verbo activo. Latín. *Imaginare. Imaginibus ornare.* CLAVIJ. Embax. f. 9. Es todo imaginado de imágines y figuras mui fermosas, de obra musáica.' (It means also to arrange with images, or adorn an architectural structure with them. In this sense, it is an active verb. Clavijo, *Embajada a Tamerlán*, fol. 9, 'It is completely decorated with very fine images and figures, made of mosaic'.) The word was also used for a concept (or figure) held in the mind, or something which is planned before being put into practice. Geometry: 'las demas lineas, las quales tambien considera el Matematico no tener latitud, o anchura, que solo se imagina su longitud, que es linea visual imaginada derecha al

sujeto' (Cristoual de Rojas, *Teorica y practica de fortificacion, conforme las medidas y defensas destos tiempos, repartida en tres partes* (Madrid: Luis Sanchez, 1589), fol. 4^v) (the other lines, which the mathematician will also consider to have no latitude, or width, since the only thought is their length, which is a straight, imagined, visual line); planning: 'Llegada la noche después de ymaginada la vengança ordenó los medios' (Sebastián de Horozco, *Libro de los proverbios glosados*, ed. by Jack Weiner (Kassel: Reichenberger, 1994), p. 496) (Night having come, after imagining what the vengeance would be, he arranged the means to achieve it).

35. *Diccionario de autoridades*, V, *s.v. rastrillar*: 'Limpiar el lino o cáñamo de la arista y estopa. Latín. *Linum pectere*' (to clean the flax or stalk of its woody stalk and tow fibres. Latin [to comb flax]); I, *s.v. aspado*: 'del verbo Aspar en todas sus acepciónes. Lat. *Decussatus, a, um. In decussatam crucem actus, a, um.*' (from the verb, *aspar*, in all of its meanings. Latin [arranged cross-wise, placed on a saltire]); and *aspa*: 'Instrumento de dos palos atravesados con sus cabézas para recoger lo hilado, y hacerlo madéjas. [...] Covarr. dedúce esta voz del verbo Griego *Aspazo*, que vale abrazar, por estar abrazado un palo con otro. Tamarid y otros dicen que es voz Arábiga. Lat. *Machinula decussata ad fila evolvenda ex fuso.*' (An instrument of two crossed stick with raised pegs [heads] to gather the spun thread and make it into skeins [...] Covarrubias gets this word from the Greek *aspazo* which means to embrace, since one stick is in an embrace with the other. Tamarid and others say that it is Arabic. Latin [a small tool in the shape of a cross to draw the thread from the spindle]).

36. I. 38, 489–91; I. 53–54. Scholarship gets its subsequent turn in the intercalated limelight through the pursuit of Doña Clara by Don Luis.

37. For which, see Diego de Haedo, *Topographia e historia general de Argel, repartida en cinco tratados, do se veran casos estraños, muertes espantosas, y tormentos exquisitos; que conuiene se entiendan en la Christiandad: con mucha doctrina, y elegancia curiosa* (Valladolid: Diego Fernandez de Cordova y Oviedo for Antonio Coello, 1612), fols 184^v–185^r.

38. As argued by María Antonia Garcés, *Cervantes in Algiers: A Captive's Tale* (Nashville: Vanderbilt University Press, 2002).

39. For example, the loss of Goleta being, in the end, a 'particular gracia y merced que el cielo hizo a España' (I. 39, 501) (an especial grace and mercy which Heaven granted Spain).

40. Joe Snader, *Caught between Worlds: British Captivity Narratives in Fact and Fiction* (Lexington: University Press of Kentucky, 2000), p. 18.

41. On the theme of the happy captivity where, whilst maintaining an irreproachable Christian faith, the noble knight rises to the great offices of state in Muslim lands, see Albert Mas, *Les Turcs dans la littérature espagnole du Siècle d'Or: recherches sur l'evolution d'un thème littéraire*, 2 vols (Paris: Follope, 1967), II, 367. In Cervantes's description, only renegades are even vaguely trusted by their masters.

42. First published: Bartholomeus Georgievitz, *De afflictione tam captivorum quam etiam sub turcae tributo viventium* (Antwerp: Copenius, 1514) — *On the affliction of both captives and also those living under tribute to the Turks*. The work was published nearly fifty times by 1600 in a range of languages (Norman Housley, *Religious Warfare in Europe 1400–1536* (Oxford: Oxford University Press, 2002), p. 137). I cite from Bartolomeus Georgievitz, *De afflictione* [...] (Worms, 1544), fol. A8^v: 'Habent quoddam genus incantationis, quo inuitos retrahunt. Nomen serui in schedula scriptum suspenditur in tabernaculo uel domicilio serui, deinde diris uerbis et deuotionibus illius caput impetunt, deinde fit ui daemoniaca, ut fugiens putet sibi in itinere uel leones uel dracones incurrere, uel mare uel flumina contra se exundare, uel omnia tenebris nigrescere, iisque terriculis repulsis ad herum redit.' (They have a certain type of incantation, by which they bring them back against their will. The slave's name, written on a scrap of paper, is hung up in the slave's tent or room, then by dire words and devotions they attack his mind [*lit.* 'head'], next it comes about by the devil's power that the escapee thinks that before him either lions or dragons are running at him, or the sea or rivers are gushing out towards him, or that everything grows dark as night, and thwarted by these terrors he returns to his owner.)

43. Haedo, *Topographia*, fol. 121vb, where Georgevitz's account is used with perhaps some local embellishments.

44. The thrust of the canon's long disquisition on literary tastes (I. 47–48). This matches Cervantes's

practice: the announcement of the half-completed novel of chivalry by the canon, according to the preceptive rules of Art (I. 48, 603); the composition of the *Novelas ejemplares* and the *Entremeses*.

45. Here the debt is to casuistry, explored by Roberto González Echevarría, *Love and the Law in Cervantes* (New Haven: Yale University Press, 2005), pp. 22–34.
46. José Antonio Millán, 'El Quijote apócrifo de "Alonso Fernández de Avellaneda"', *Revista digital universitaria*, 6.5 (2005), 1–8.
47. Alonso Fernández de Avellaneda, *Segundo tomo del ingenioso hidalgo don Quixote de la Mancha, que contiene su tercera salida: y es la quinta parte de sus auenturas. Compuesto por el Licenciado Alonso Fernandez de Auellaneda, natural de la Villa de Tordesillas. Al Alcalde, Regidores, y hidalgos, de la noble villa de Argamesilla, patria feliz del hidalgo Cauallero Don Quixote de la Mancha* (Tarragona: Felipe Roberto, 1614) — Second volume of the witty noble Don Quixote de la Mancha, which contains his third foray: and represents the fifth part of his adventures. Composed by the licenciate Alonso Fernández de Avellaneda, citizen of the town of Tordesillas. To the Mayor, Councillors and nobles of the noble town of Argamesilla, lucky birthplace of the noble knight, Don Quixote of La Mancha. 'Argamasilla' picks up the final lines of Part One, where the verses are attributed to 'Los académicos de la Argamasilla, lugar de la Mancha, en vida y muerte del valeroso don Quijote de la Mancha, "hoc scripserunt."' (The academicians of Argamasilla, a town of La Mancha, "hoc scripserunt" [Latin: wrote this] on the life and death of the valorous Don Quixote of La Mancha) (I. 52, 648)).
48. John J. Allen, 'The Narrators, the Reader, and Don Quijote', *MLN*, 91 (1976), 201–12; Mancing, pp. 74–80.
49. As reported, with a few *bons mots*, by Licenciado Márquez Torres in his *Aprobación*, given on 27 February 1615 (669–70).
50. See, for example, Trevor J. Dadson, *Los moriscos de Villarubia de los Ojos (siglos XV–XVIII). Historia de una minoría asimilada, expulsada y reintegrada* (Madrid; Frankfurt: Iberoamericana; Vervuert, 2007).
51. *Relaciones histórico-geográficas-estadísticas de los pueblos de España*, I, 484: 'no hay edificio señalado sino es la iglesia, que tiene una capilla de cal y canto bien labrada y recia, y no hay otro rastro de edificios antiguos salvo un arco viejo medio caido muy ancho, questa pegado con la dicha iglesia, de argamasa y ladrillo tosco, y muy grueso, y que el pie de la torre de la dicha iglesia parece de algun fuerte antiguo, y, que en una piedra de la dicha torre o pie della se señalan ciertas letras, que parecen goticas o arabigas, y no se pueden leer, y que habra como diez años poco mas o menos que vinieron a la dicha villa ciertos hombres, que dicen algunos que eran moriscos, y diz que traian una memoria que decia que en Hocar a la parte del cierço en un huerto a la mano derecha del camino habia un tesoro, y buscaron, y se tornaron vacios.' (There is no particularly interesting building there except the church, which is a well-built chapel of lime-washed stone, and there is no other trace of any old building bar a very wide old arch which is half-fallen-down and fixed to the aforesaid church, thick-set, of crude bricks and mortar, and which, at the foot of the tower of the aforesaid church, seems to be from some ancient castle, and that in a stone of the aforesaid tower or foot of the same a few letters are pointed out, which seem Visigothic or Arabic, and which cannot be deciphered, and, perhaps more-or-less ten years ago there came to the aforesaid town a number of men, that some say were *moriscos*, and the story goes that they brought a note with them that said that in Hocar, to the north, in an orchard on the right of the road there was a treasure, and they dug, and they went back empty-handed.)
52. See Jonathan Burton, *Traffic and Turning: Islam and English Drama, 1579–1624* (Newark: University of Delaware Press, 2005), pp. 62–63, for rapprochement between the Sultan, Murad III, and Spanish and Dutch Protestants in the last quarter of the sixteenth century; for Catholic polemics linking Protestantism with Islam, see S. J. Barnett, *Idol Temples and Crafty Priests: The Origins of Enlightenment Anticlericalism* (New York: St Martin's Press, 1999), p. 88.
53. She later defines her ethnicity as *morisca*: 'De aquella nación más desdichada que prudente sobre quien ha llovido estos días un mar de desgracias, nací yo, de moriscos padres engendrada' (II. 63, 1258) (I came into the world out of that race — more unfortunate than prudent — on whom has rained a sea of misfortunes, born from Morisco parents). Like her father, she criticizes the Moriscos in general, here for their lack of prudence, and stresses her purity from Morisco

customs both in her behaviour and — rather interestingly — in her language, whence the rather convoluted manner in which she describes her origins.
54. As assumed by Leyla Rouhi, 'A Handsome Boy Among Those Barbarous Turks: Cervantes's Muslims and the Art and Science of Desire', in *Islamicate Sexualities: Translations across Temporal Geographies of Desire*, ed. by Kathryn Babayan and Afsaneh Najmabadi (Cambridge, MA: Harvard University Press, 2008), pp. 41–71.
55. Georgievitz, *De afflictione*, fol. A4^r: 'Reliqui proh nefas, in quibus maior gratia formae, ita abscinduntur ut nihil uirile in toto corpore appareat, grauissimo cum discrimine uitae: quod si euadant, non in aliud sunt incolumes quam in obsequium sceleratissimae libidinis, mox senescente pulchritudine, ad officia eunuchorum, ut matronas seruent deputantur, aut custodientis equis et mulis, aut culinae ministeriis addicuntur.' (Those who remain [i.e., not destined for military service] in whom there is more physical beauty, are castrated so that there should appear nothing male in any part of their body, at great danger to their lives, which (if they survive) are in no way protected other than to serve the most heinous desire; then, as their beauty decays, they are set to serve the women, or keep the horses and mules, or put to the service of the kitchen.) For the later sixteenth and seventeenth centuries, see Alison Games, *The Web of Empire: English Cosmopolitans in an Age of Empire* (Oxford: Oxford University Press, 2008), pp. 59–60.
56. Marcela Beatriz Sosa, '(Más)caras de la sexualidad en el Siglo de Oro español: travestismo y metateatro en géneros breves', *Texturas: estudios interdisciplinares sobre el discurso*, 4 (2004), 105–15; Amy L. Tigner, 'The Spanish Actress's Art: Improvisations, Transvestism, and Disruption in Tirso's *El vergonzoso en palacio*', *Early Theatre*, 15 (2012), 169–92.
57. Agnes Smith Lewis, 'The Story of the Blessed Mary Who Was Called Marina', *Vox Benedictina*, 2 (1985), 305–17.
58. See, for example, John Anson, 'The Female Transvestite in Early Monasticism: The Origins and Development of a Motif", *Viator*, 5 (1974), 1–32; Evelyne Patlagean, 'L'histoire de la femme deguisée en moine et l'évolution de la sainteté feminine en Byzance', *Studi medievali*, 3rd series, 17 (1976), 597–623.
59. Natalia Fernández Rodríguez, ' "Suele el disfraz varonil agradar mucho": las santas travestidas de la hagiografía en la comedia nueva', in *Cuatrocientos años del 'Arte nuevo' de hacer comedias' de Lope de Vega: actas selectas del XIV Congreso de la Asociación Internacional de Teatro Español y Novohispano de los Siglos de Oro*, ed. by G. Vega García-Luengos and H. Urzáiz Tortajada (Valladolid; Olmedo: Universidad de Valladolid; Ayuntamiento de Olmedo, 2010), pp. 455–66; Fernando Baños Vallejo, 'El transformismo de santa Eugenia: del cuerpo medieval al ingenio barroco', *Bulletin of Hispanic Studies*, 93 (2016), 1–28.
60. Márquez Torres describes Cervantes to his French admirers: 'Halléme obligado a decir que era viejo, soldado, hidalgo y pobre' (Aprobación, 669–70) (I found myself obliged to say he was old, a [former] soldier, noble and poor).
61. But, it must be said, the tales are not designed to be read as exact parallels, and the tone of each story offers one of many contrasts: austere sobriety in the first, much racier innuendo in the second; further, the fathers' role.
62. 'Tuvo noticia el rey de mi hermosura, y la fama se la dio de mis riquezas [...]. Todo esto le dije, temerosa de que no le cegase mi hermosura, sino su codicia' (II. 63, 1259); (the king had been informed of my beauty, just like the repute of my wealth [...] All of this I told him, fearful that he should not be blinded by my beauty, but his avarice).
63. There is no *espejismo* at this point, as if the supposedly Muslim narrator were expressing himself as a Christian.
64. Francisco Márquez Villanueva, *Personajes y temas del Quijote* (Madrid: Taurus, 1975), p. 313.
65. Suzanne Keen, 'A Narrative Theory of Empathy', *Narrative*, 14 (2006), 207–36; Frans de Waal, *The Age of Empathy: Nature's Lessons for a Kinder Society, With Drawings by the Author* (New York: Harmony, 2009).
66. Douglas W. Hollan and C. Jason Throop, 'The Anthropology of Empathy: *Introduction*', in *The Anthropology of Empathy: Experiencing the Lives of Others in Pacific Societies*, ed. by D. W. Hollan and C. J. Throop (New York: Berghahn Books, 2001), pp. 1–24 (pp. 6–8). It is worth

bearing in mind that Cervantes's drawing a discreet veil over Don Gregorio's experience *inter mulieribus* in Algiers may be as much to save his readers' blushes and preserve the nobility of his characterization of the young lad as a wish to get on and finish the damn book.

67. David Comer Kidd and Emanuele Castano, 'Reading Literary Fiction Improves Theory of Mind', *Science*, 342 (2013), 377–80 <http://dx.doi: 10.1126/science.1239918>.

68. Raymond A. Mar, Keith Oatley and Jordan B. Peterson, 'Exploring the Link between Reading Fiction and Empathy: Ruling Out Individual Differences and Examining Outcomes', *Communications*, 34 (2009), 407–28; for 'transportation' as a key ingredient in our experience of fiction, see Victor Nell, *Lost in a Book: The Psychology of Reading for Pleasure* (New Haven, CT: Yale University Press, 1988).

69. For 'story-worlds', see Frank Zippel, 'Fiction across Media: Towards a Transmedial Concept of Fictionality', in *Storyworlds Across Media: Towards a Media-Conscious Narratology*, ed. by Marie-Laure Ryan and Jan-Noël Thon (Lincoln: University of Nebraska Press, 2014), pp. 103–25.

70. For example, the neo-crusading zeal of Don Quixote in supposing that a group of knight-errants could defeat the Turk quite happily reproduces the fantastic ethos of the *Amadís* family, but also reflects on still recent events, such as the catastrophic defeat of the Portuguese at Alcácer Quibir in 1578.

71. Werner Wolf, 'Framings of Narrative in Literature and the Pictorial Arts', in *Intermediality and Storytelling*, ed. by Marina Grishakova and Marie-Laure Ryan (Berlin: de Gruyter, 2010), pp. 126–47 (p. 126), 'narrative is a major cognitive frame whose application is elicited by certain clues, "keys", or "framings", typically and preferably at the outset of the reception process.'

CHAPTER 8

Reconsidering Literary Criminality in *Don Quixote*

Ted L. L. Bergman

While the picaresque has been studied extensively in *Don Quixote*, the use of a single literary genre to study a particular aspect of an author's production, namely criminality, can have its limitations. References to criminality are simply deemed 'picaresque', and the picaresque nature is confirmed by citing a picaresque work featuring a similar reference, and again we are led around in a somewhat circular investigation. This circularity can persist, even when sidestepping questions of genre by focusing on biographical information in an effort to obtain a different perspective on criminals and their behaviour in Cervantes's novel. References to criminals or prison life can be linked to the author's own experience, but these are in turn confirmed by adducing yet more of his own literary references, leading us critics around in the same vicious circle. These references are often framed within the picaresque, a tendency reinforced by the fact that Cervantes has written straightforward picaresque fiction elsewhere. This framing is guided by the notion that as many as three of his *Novelas ejemplares* 'should be considered as full participants in the genre',[1] and driven by the reasonable assumption that Cervantes's strictly picaresque writing must overlap considerably with different sections of his larger novel. While it is sensible and productive to use well-known biographical details and the picaresque genre as a lens through which to study criminal characters, actions, and themes in *Don Quixote*, there is also much to be gained by widening the scope of Cervantes's experience and by including criminality-themed genres other than the picaresque. A different approach is helpful since the topic of lawbreaking and law enforcement is difficult to avoid in the novel and is broached as early as the prologue to Part One:

> ¿qué podía engendrar el estéril y mal cultivado ingenio mío, sino la historia de un hijo seco, avellanado, antojadizo y lleno de pensamientos varios y nunca imaginados de otro alguno, bien como quien se engendró en una cárcel, donde toda incomodidad tiene su asiento y donde todo triste ruido hace su habitación? (I. Prólogo, 9).

> (And so what could my barren and poorly cultivated wits beget but the history of a child who is dry, withered, capricious, and filled with inconstant thoughts never imagined by anyone else, which is just what one would expect of a person

begotten in a prison, where every discomfort has its place and every mournful sound makes its home?)²

The author's imprisonment in the *Cárcel Real de Sevilla* must have informed his thoughts on crime and punishment, but it is important to resist the temptation solely to fall back on literary examples when seeking to explore the topic further. An example of this limiting point of view is found in a passage from José Miguel Cabañas Agrela's *Breve historia de Cervantes* in which he seeks to paint a vivid picture of the criminal element that surrounded the author inside and outside of jail:

> [Sevilla] era la meca de la picaresca por antonomasia, como lo demuestran las novelas de este género de la época. Existía en España una ruta de la picaresca que recorría el reino de norte a sur, desde Burgos hasta Sevilla, pasando por Madrid, Toledo y Córdoba, por donde, como peregrinos de la delincuencia, se dirigían todos los desheredados y maleantes a Sevilla, su santuario ideal. Y es que aquí, como en el crimen organizado, incluso se reunían en cofradías de rufianes, con una estricta organización jerárquica y un respeto escrupuloso a sus leyes, por parte de quienes, paradójicamente, no respetaba las oficiales. Nadie ha descrito mejor este submundo sevillano y estas organizaciones del delito como Cervantes en su famosa novela *Rinconete y Cortadillo* cuando nos muestra el patio de Monipodio y su mundo, que él mismo controla y mantiene alrededor suyo como un padre que se ocupa de su numerosa familia para que no les falte un mendrugo de pan que llevarse a la boca, pero también bajo unas estrictas reglas que cumplir. Pícaros, ladrones y rufianes de toda laya convivían, por tanto, asociados, con una organización, una jerarquía y uno o varios jefes — como el Monipodio cervantino, personaje real y al que con toda seguridad Cervantes conoció.³

> (Seville was the picaresque mecca *par excellence*, as shown by the novels of the era belonging to this genre. In Spain there was a picaresque route that wound its way through the kingdom from north to south, from Burgos to Seville, passing through Madrid, Toledo and Cordoba. Along this road, like a group of pilgrim delinquents, all those who were villainous and disenfranchised made their way to Seville, their ideal sanctuary. And it is here, as in organized crime, that we find brotherhoods of thugs, with a strict hierarchical organization and a careful respect for its laws on the part of those who paradoxically did not respect official law. Nobody has described this Sevillian underworld and these criminal organizations better than Cervantes in his famous *Rinconete and Cortadillo* when he shows us Monipodio's courtyard and his world. The character controls and maintains order in his surroundings like a father looking after a large family to ensure that they have a crust of bread to eat, but it is also a world with strict rules that must be followed. Rogues, thieves, and pimps of every stripe lived together, and in this way are associated with an organization, a hierarchy and one or several bosses — like Cervantes's Monipodio, a real person and whom Cervantes surely met.)⁴

The words 'picaresca' or 'pícaro' are used three times above, and in the paragraph previous to the one in the quotation, Cabañas Agrela cites the picaresque novels *La vida del escudero Marcos de Obregón* and *Guzmán de Alfarache* as sources on Seville's underworld, while conceding that Mateo Alemán may have used poetic licence when describing the abundant wealth of the city. The historian Cabañas Agrela's reliance on fictional accounts is not unusual, although he seems overly dependent when he writes: 'Nadie ha descrito mejor este submundo sevillano y estas organizaciones del delito como Cervantes en su famosa novela *Rinconete y Cortadillo*' (Nobody has described this underworld of Seville better than Cervantes in his famous *novela Rinconete and Cortadillo*). Mary Elizabeth Perry, who literally wrote the book on *Crime and Society in Early Modern Seville*, is more circumspect:

> Monipodio's organization is fictional, and Cervantes' motives in writing this story must be examined. Undoubtedly he wanted to delight his public as well as to describe in loving irony a society that he had known on the streets and in the Royal Prison of Seville. The many details he included and the evidence of criminal organization he amassed suggests that he was consciously trying to make a point about it. His story satirized a society in which each person had his role and his territory secure so long as he did not question the people above him who took a share of his earnings.[5]

In order to see what the city was really like, it is useful to read first-hand accounts when dealing with very specific locations such as the *Cárcel Real de Sevilla*. The historian and criminality-in-Seville scholar Herrera Puga would agree:

> al considerar el ambiente de la Cárcel en todas sus dimensiones picarescas, se llega al convencimiento de ser éste uno de sus aspectos más importantes y, al mismo tiempo, el foco principal de donde irradia gran parte de la fuerza secreta de nuestra literatura.[6]
>
> (when considering the atmosphere of the Jail in all its picaresque dimensions, one arrives at the conclusion that this is one of its most important aspects, and at the same time, the main focal point from which a great deal of the secret power of our literature emanates.)

This *ambiente* must not be not accessed through Cervantes himself, nor other writers of the picaresque, but can be read through modern historians and their primary sources. Returning to Cervantes's prologue, a single word can take on new significance if we momentarily turn away from picturesque satire as the reference point for our criticism. Simultaneously, it is important to remain focused on the criminal *ambiente*, a context wider than the immediate biographical circumstances of the author. In their notes about Cervantes's prologue cited above, Ellen M. Anderson and Gonzalo Pontón Gijón write:

> La frase no aclara de suyo si tiene un sentido literal o metafórico, pero el cervantismo ha optado mayoritariamente por creer que la expresión debe tomarse al pie de la letra: el *Quijote* se ideó, e incluso empezó a escribirse, mientras Cervantes permanecía recluido en una prisión.[7]
>
> (This phrase in itself does not make clear if it is meant literally or metaphorically, but the majority of Cervantes scholars have opted for the view that the expression should be taken at face value: *Don Quixote* was conceived, and also began to be written, while Cervantes was locked up in a prison.)

The two critics then briefly examine a debate about how much of the novel was actually written in prison. They conclude that it is best to 'suponer únicamente que el primer aliento de la historia, la percepción de su contenido, le sobrevino a Cervantes mientras permanecía en prisión' (suppose only that the inspiration for the story, the idea for its content, came to Cervantes while he was in prison).[8] The focus here moves to the novel's date of composition, and attendant debate about reality-versus-metaphor has ignored the concrete sense of such words as *incomodidad* (discomfort) whose mundane appearance masks a deeper understanding of the *ambiente* in question. Historical accounts reveal that the *Cárcel de Sevilla* was more than a place of misery. It was also a business operation in which *incomodidad* was a driver of profit. Not only the wardens, but the prisoners themselves preyed financially on the incarcerated population through any number of scams and small entrepreneurial ventures. Drawing on Cristóbal de Chaves's *Relación de las cosas de la cárcel de Sevilla y su trato* as a source, Perry writes: 'The assistant warden had up to 400 special cells that he could rent for fourteen or fifteen *reales* a month', and,

> some enterprising prisoners stood guard at an entrance to the prison latrine and charged prisoners a small amount to use the stepping stones they had placed there to pass through the filth. Others charged a fee for providing a support that helped make more bearable the punishment of suspension by wrist shackles high above the ground.[9]

Within this quotation we can find inspiration for Cervantes's thoughts on crime, punishment, and corruption. *Don Quixote* features a complex web of interconnected points of reference, seeds of ideas that later bear fruit; and the author's stay in the *Cárcel Real de Sevilla* can be used to illuminate other areas of the novel in which criminality is manifest. The *galeotes* (galley slaves) episode (I. 22) is a good example of this. The common course for investigation is to follow up allusions to *Guzmán de Alfarache* and explicit references to *Lazarillo de Tormes*, meaning to start and likely end with the picaresque as a point of reference. In his notes to a chapter on Ginés de Pasamonte, Gerald R. Gingras points out that not every critic follows this path unreflectively.[10] He cites Peter N. Dunn, who insists that Cervantes was not inserting fragments of a coherent and consensus-driven picaresque genre into his novel. Dunn's approach contrasts with that of E. C. Riley, who seven years later would reinforce the more common interpretation that 'Cervantes has contrived powerfully to suggest a confrontation between two kinds of prose fiction: the picaresque and [...] the new novel of Cervantes'.[11] Among modern critics, the picaresque as a foundation for analysing criminality in *Don Quixote* is difficult to avoid. For example, Juergen Hahn's study mixes in the topics of giants and savagery but has the picaresque at its core. He writes:

> [Don Quixote] does after all live out his imagination beyond the pale of normal society, the more or less orderly, acceptable bourgeois existence, just like the picaro. And even though his value system is miles apart, his disruptive effect on 'normal' societal values is often similar. For while the picaro indulges his frequently petty, and sometimes grandiose criminality, Don Quijote, in spite of his lofty intentions, too manages to place himself in a criminal position vis-a-vis normal society. This is especially evident in his encounter with the galeotes.[12]

There are many different ways to shift the focus from the picaresque when looking at criminality in *Don Quixote*, but the pull of the genre remains strong. When explaining the significance of an omniscient narrator in *El licenciado Vidriera*, Michael Gerli contrasts it with the 'the first-person narrations of picaresque novels in the Galeotes episode of *Don Quijote* (I. 22)'.[13] At the same time, studying another narrator, neither omniscient, nor first-person, can lead us to another point of view that breaks us free from the picaresque paradigm. While Ginés de Pasamonte is a captivating figure and can influence our own judgements as critics, we should also heed the words of his guardian, the *comisario*, who tells us that 'él [Ginés] mesmo ha escrito su historia, que no hay más que desear, y deja empeñado el libro en la cárcel en docientos reales' (I. 22, 265) ('He wrote his own history himself, as fine as you please, and he pawned the book for two hundred *reales* and left it in prison').[14] When studying criminality in this context, the natural next step would be to head mentally towards the *galeotes*'s destination, the *galeras* (galleys), leading to inevitable comparisons with *Guzmán de Alfarache*. But why not take a different route, or indeed reverse direction entirely? Why not focus more on the *comisario*'s words and look backwards to the *cárcel* itself, quite possibly the same *Cárcel Real de Sevilla* where Cervantes himself stayed? That Ginés has pawned his book at the prison may seem purely picturesque and picaresque, but only if we disregard Cristóbal de Chaves's account of the financial give-and-take that was an integral part of the prison system and no doubt integral to Cervantes's day-to-day *incomodidad*. Likewise for other prisoners, the evidence of the justice system's corrupt nature does not need support from picaresque fiction and such a focus may even obscure real-world connections between the fictional and factual prisoners. One *galeote* explains that 'si a su tiempo tuviera yo esos veinte ducados que vuestra merced ahora me ofrece, hubiera untado con ellos la péndola del escribano y avivado el ingenio del procurador' (I. 22, 261) ('if I'd had those twenty *ducados* your grace is offering me now at the right time, I'd have greased the quill of the clerk and sharpened the wits of my attorney').[15] In Don Diego Clemencín's notes to the 1833 edition for this passage, he explains that 'nuestros libros de entonces hablan de la corrupción y venalidad de los escribanos como de cosa ordinaria' (our books from back then speak of the corruption and venality of the scribes as something ordinary).[16] Clemencín calls one of the *galeotes*'s reference to 'perder los tragaderos' ('having one's gullet in a noose')[17] a 'metáfora picaresca' that must also be treated as a 'testimonio' among many.[18] According to the nineteenth-century critic, similar 'testimonios' by 'infinitos escritores coetáneos' (countless contemporary writers) can be found in such works as the *Corbacho*, *Celestina*, *Propalladia*, *Lazarillo de Tormes*, *Guzmán de Alfarache*, *La pícara Justina*, *El coloquio de los perros*, *Rinconete y Cortadillo*, 'el *Tacaño* de Quevedo, y el *Teatro* de Lope y de Calderón': in short, all fictional sources.[19] Such a judgement from nearly two hundred years ago may seem antiquated, but still today it is difficult to shake off the influence of literary tradition and take account of the real-world context that informs a genre. This is particularly true if one takes genre itself as a starting point. In his *Crítica de los géneros literarios en el 'Quijote'*, Jesús G. Maestro writes first that 'el encuentro con los galeotes cita a don Quijote directamente con el mundo de la picaresca' (the encounter with the galley slaves places Don Quixote directly in the world of the picaresque).[20] The foundation of this 'mundo' is *Lazarillo de Tormes*, and built upon it are '*Guzmán de Alfarache, Vida del escudero Marcos de Obregón, Vida del Buscón, La pícara Justina, La hija de Celestina, Vida y hechos de Estebanillo González* [...]'.[21] Returning to the passage from the *galeotes* episode about bribing the *escribano* and *procurador*, a new perspective requires a source that stands apart from the picturesque satire of the picaresque. Padre de León, a sort of early-modern 'prison worker', wrote about the lack of money among prisoners at the *Cárcel Real* in graphic and sincere terms, with sympathy instead of the acerbic wit that is integral to the picaresque:

> Habiendo, pues, considerado con mucha atención el grande número de presos indefensos y olvidados por no haber quien diese un paso por ellos sin interés, sino a poder de dineros, haciéndoles increyentes los escribanos y procuradores que con tantos reales que les diesen (como tengo dicho), y aunque yo y otros veinte de la Compañía de Jesús anduviéramos en la solicitud de estos presos olvidados, no hiciéramos la centésima parte de lo que era menester.[22]

> (I thus considered with great attention the large number of defenceless and forgotten prisoners for whom nobody would intervene unless for some gain, through the power of money, and how scribes and prosecutors had ruined the faith of the prisoners by all the *reales* that they demanded of them, as I have mentioned. Even if I and twenty more from the Company of Jesus were to advocate for these forgotten prisoners, we would not manage to do one hundredth of what was necessary.)

This example casts the fictional *galeote*'s words in a much less cheeky, less picaresque light, and directly connects the fictional character's circumstances with Cervantes's own *incomodidad* mentioned in the prologue. The destitute *galeote*, and the officials who wanted money and were of no help to the prisoner, do not have to be treated as objects lifted from an assembly line of picaresque novels and made into the butt of a simple joke. Instead, these characters can be considered reflections of unfiltered real-life experience suffered by Cervantes's fellow inmates. It is difficult to argue against the heavy influence that *Lazarillo* and *Guzmán de Alfarache*, or even their successors, must have had on the *galeotes* episode. Nevertheless, one cannot deny the usefulness of casting a wider net for catching sources that have always been available but neglected due to a one-sided generic approach. Historical sources are only one resource, while another is found in criminality-themed genres that are distinct from the picaresque prose of *Lazarillo*, *Guzmán*, and company.

The specificity of language in the *galeotes* episode opens a pathway to a more varied exploration of genre influences. Both fictional *galeotes* and Cervantes survived incarceration with their wit(s) intact, and a sense of humour is useful in dealing with the *incomodidad* of going to jail. The jokes told by the prisoners in Chapter 22 take the form of what Clemencín called 'metáfora picaresca', but more accurately should be described as a playful use of *germanía*, witty and stylized underworld jargon. Once again, the tendency to use the picaresque as a lens through which to view the episode is difficult to avoid. Over a century after Clemencín's comments, when listing the puns used by the *galeotes*, Joaquín Casalduero wrote:

Cervantes se sitúa en este juego verbal: 'por enamorado', 'por cantor', 'por faltarme diez ducados', 'por haber sido corredor de oreja', 'porque me burlé', y este juego verbal es la sordina irónica que se pone a la visión picaresca de la vida.[23]

(Cervantes positions himself amidst this wordplay: 'for being a lover', 'for being a singer', 'for not having ten gold *ducados*', 'for trading in ears', 'because I made too merry' and this wordplay is the ironic damper placed upon the picaresque view of life.)[24]

Sixty years after that, Anthony Close also refers to the picaresque, but only after listing a number of other influences: 'The Quixotic adventures of Part I, including [the *galeotes* episode], are saturated with echoes of robustly comic species of previous literature and folklore: farcical interludes and other motifs of theatre, fabliaux and novellas, popular jests, the picaresque novel.'[25] For Close, farce plays a big role in the form of Lope de Rueda's *pasos*, and the critic cites a very good example from the fourth *paso* of the *Registro de representantes*. The sketch features a conversation of 'comic casuistry' that ends with the punch line, 'Pues ¿qué afrenta recibo yo que me azoten, si es contra mi voluntad y por fuerza?' (And another thing: one can't call it an affront if what a man suffers is inflicted on him by force, not freely consented to).[26] Close also cites jokes based on 'euphemistic allusions to shameful punishments to be inflicted on his nearest and dearest, like being pilloried, whipped, tortured', and implies that such jokes mostly stem from a folklore tradition.[27] As he writes elsewhere, 'The relation of *DQ* to folklore and popular traditions has been the speciality of traditional Spanish philology and French Hispanism' and includes 'important considerations on C[ervantes]'s portrayal of character and its roots in popular jests in Maxime Chevalier' and 'Monique Joly's innovative *La bourle et son interprétation* analyses the terminology and practices of popular jokes, taunts, hoaxes and their assimilation in picaresque literature'.[28] Studying both Lope de Rueda and Cervantes within the *cuentecillo* (short story) tradition is a productive enterprise, but following the lead of Chevalier or Joly when examining bitterly ironic jokes about crime and punishment is only one path among many that we can take in deepening our understanding. While it makes sense to start with folklore and move towards the picturesque as an endpoint, such a direction draws our attention away from another genre that can shed light on the *galeotes* episode. That genre is the *jácara*, of which a key characteristic is *germanía*-based wordplay that communicates the harshest violence in an understated comical tone. The criminal jargon so common to the *jácara* is part of a popular tradition, but not one born in the countryside or marketplace. Instead, *germanía* reflects the folklore of urban prisons like the *Cárcel Real de Sevilla*, a context quite different from that found in a typical *cuentecillo*:

> los germanos utilizaban permanentemente la lengua popular, en alguna de sus variedades más bajas, y las estructuras generales del registro coloquial. Y en él insertaban sus peculiaridades léxicas e introducían algunas rupturas propias; es decir, que no utilizaban germanía de manera permanente al comunicarse, si bien procuraban insertar sus variedades con la mayor frecuencia posible. Por otra parte, estas creaciones no se programaban: eran fruto de la agudeza de ingenio de algún germano, que por la oportunidad de la creación, por el

prestigio de su creador entre la germanesca o por convenio de un pequeño grupo, se difundía, generalizaba y estabilizaba.²⁹

(underworld figures always used popular language, in some of its basest varieties, along with the general structures of a colloquial register. Into this they injected lexical peculiarities and introduced their own breaks from the norm. In other words, they did not use underworld jargon as a fixed mode of communication, since they attempted to add variations as frequently as possible. What is more, these creations were not programmatic: they were the fruits of the sharp wit of some criminal, that through the opportunity for creation, through the prestige of their creator in the underworld, or by the agreement of a small group, were disseminated, generalized, and stylized.)

Because 'agudeza de ingenio' was integral to *germanía*, its appeal was immediate to Francisco de Quevedo, who wrote *jácaras* that, according to José Manuel Blecua, were greatly admired by Cervantes.³⁰ Blecua cites a *romance* from *La ilustre fregona* as an example of this admiration and imitation, while the example cited by most critics is the *Entremés del rufián viudo llamado Trampagos*. The sketch ends with an appearance by the *jaque* (thug) Escarramán whose signature dance is accompanied by musicians who play his theme song, one lifted from one of Quevedo's own *jácaras*.³¹ Aside from the broader theme of criminality, there is a specific lexical connection between *Don Quixote*'s *galeotes* scene, Cervantes's *entremés*, and the *jácara* genre as a whole. The connection is through the word 'gurapas'. In the *entremés*, the musicians sing:

> Ya salió de las gurapas
> El valiente Escarramán
> Para asombro de la gura,
> Y para bien de su mal.³²

> (That tough guy Escarramán,
> Once in the galleys, just got out.
> It's quite a shocker for the cops,
> But good for curing what ails him.)

'Gurapas' is a term that separates Don Quixote's understanding of the world from that of the *galeotes* whom he feels compelled to liberate: ' — ¿Qué son *gurapas*? — preguntó don Quijote. — *Gurapas* son galeras — respondió el galeote' (1. 22, 259) ('What are gurapas?' asked Don Quixote 'Gurapas are galleys,' responded the galley slave).³³

The word also signals a lack of generic awareness in the hero because it is tightly bound to the 'euphemistic allusions to shameful punishments' (to repeat Anthony Close's observation) so often used in the *jácara* genre. It is this lack of awareness that presents the main obstacle to communication between Don Quixote and the prisoners. The following lines from different *jácaras* in Juan Hidalgo's 1609 collection *Romances de germanía* demonstrate the irony, violence, and humour surrounding 'gurapas' in a literary context:

> Al fin el Guro ha mandado,
> que en pago de lo servido,
> le corten entrambas Mirlas [orejas]

> por el lugar mas crecido.
> Y esté recluso diez años
> en las Gurapas metido,
> en orden de Tercero [galeote de tercer banco],
> escribano sin partido [...].
>
> [...]
>
> El reside en las Gurapas
> Cumpliendo lo prometido:
> Un argolla y su palabra
> son fiadores del partido [...].³⁴
>
> (In the end the cops demand
> Payment for his services:
> Both ears must be cut off
> From that magnificent head.
> And he's secluded for ten years,
> Cloistered in the galleys,
> A scribe without a district to attend [...]
>
> [...]
>
> He resides in the galleys,
> Completing his end of the deal:
> A shackle and his word
> Will vouch for his agreement.)

In another *jácara*, we hear the equally cynical voice of a *jaque*'s *marca* (moll):

> Solo a ti por quien he hecho
> en la Trena y en la Altana,
> y en las Gurapas metido
> sin mancar de tu demanda.
> Y en los destierros y clamos
> de ti sin faltar hallada,
> agora es tiempo alma mía,
> que sea remunerada.³⁵
>
> (Only for you, for whom
> I've done so much while
> You were stuck in either
> Prison, Sanctuary, or Galleys.
> Through banishments and bounties,
> ever at your service,
> Now it is time my love,
> That I get what is my due.)

The *jaque* Maladros suffers a similar punishment as the figure in the first *jácara* cited above:

> Vino desde allí a Sevilla
> do le fue otro cotón dado:
> y cortadas ambas mirlas
> y a las ansias entregado.
> Donde sirvió de Proel

> a la Corulla amarrado,
> cumplida su penitencia
> y pasados ya seis años
> [...]
> Y dejando las Gurapas
> a Sevilla volvió el calco,
> y por sustentar el Rozo
> altanóse en allegando.[36]

> (He came from there to Seville,
> Where he was given more lashes:
> And had both ears cut off,
> And was stretched on the rack.
> He served as a sailor at the prow,
> Tied to the bridle of the oars,
> And did his penance,
> After six years gone by.
> [...]
> And leaving the galleys,
> He headed for Seville,
> And to earn his bread
> He made himself a pimp.)

When Maladros from the *jácara* above is tortured on the rack, he 'sings' in a manner that is full of wordplay but generically far removed from the bulk of 'the first-person narrations of picaresque novels',[37] whose scenes of torture or mutilation are exceedingly rare compared to the constant presence of these in the *jácara* genre.

> Llegué aquí a Babilonia,
> y en su confusión mezclado
> usé de todas las chanzas,
> cual me acumuló el Padrastro,
> pues me puso en las Gurapas
> mi vida y obras pagando.
> El Guro que lo está oyendo
> ansioso de oír su Charlo,
> entrevado su cantar,
> mandole cesar el garlo [...].[38]

> (I came here to Babylon [Seville],
> And mixed up in its confusion
> I used every trick I could,
> Which led me to the prosecutor
> Who put me in the galleys
> To pay for my life and deeds.
> The guards who are listening,
> Dying to hear him talk,
> Having understood his singing,
> Demand that he shut his mouth.)

'Cantar' is the common *jácara* reference to torture spoken by the *galeote* who says to Don Quixote, 'no hay peor cosa que cantar en el ansia' (I. 22, 260) ('there's nothing worse than singing when you're in difficulty').[39] To call a joke such as this a 'metáfora picaresca', as Clemencín does, for 'perder los tragaderos', is to undercut the painfulness of a situation that no amount of irony can mask. Having one's body twisted on the rack or, as in the *jácaras* above, having one's ears sliced off, is far more cruel than the beatings suffered by Lazarillo, Guzmán, Pablos, Estebanillo, and their ilk. To this torture we must add the hundred lashes, mentioned by one of those guarding the *galeotes*. This takes us quite far from the standard playful tone of the picaresque, barring extreme exceptions. If *Guzmán de Alfarache* did inspire Cervantes, then what are we to make of the following observation: 'Closing [Guzmán's] novel with the description of his own torture for a crime he did not commit changes the entire tenor of the novel'?[40] The non-picaresque level of harshness of punishment can be debated by way of discussions about Cervantes's ambivalence towards the picaresque or handling of the genre;[41] but the analysis can be taken in another direction by ignoring specific references to the picaresque altogether and instead focusing on the *jácara*. For Emma Nishida, the use of *germanía* and indebtedness to a *jácara* tradition lead her to Quevedo's Escarramán in a search for 'mensajes pícaros de Cervantes hacia Alonso Fernández de Avellaneda' (cheeky-picaresque messages sent by Cervantes to Alonso Fernández de Avellaneda).[42] Such is the draw of the picaresque, but why not continue to move in another direction and thus grant a larger role to the *jácara* in the novel? To borrow Felipe Pedraza Jiménez's term, why not describe the *galeotes* episode as a 'jácara en prosa de Cervantes'? Pedraza Jiménez uses the idea to study an example from *Los trabajos de Persiles y Sigismunda* and not so much Chapter 22 of *Don Quixote*. Despite this shift away from criminality-themed genres, the critic helpfully reminds us that Francisco Rodríguez Marín drew attention to the *jácara* as a literary inspiration for Cervantes back in 1947.[43] Since the days of Rodríguez Marín, few critics have taken a look at the role of *romances de germanía* in Cervantes's supremely inter-generic novel, and those who do rarely look beyond Quevedo. This is likely due to an overall neglect of the *jácara* genre in comparison to the attention lavished upon the picaresque. An imbalance of scholarly interest is justified, as the picaresque undoubtedly had more impact than the *jácara* on prose authors, but the current degree of critical attention deficit requires some amount of remedy.

Returning to the relationship between language, literature, and prison life in *Don Quixote*, there remain some autobiographical connections that, like the generic ones examined above, deserve more attention. Cervantes's understanding of different cultures is attributed to his travels, especially when he is forced into close contact with them, as in the case of his imprisonment in Algiers. On the other hand, since many of Cervantes's brethren in the *baños* were not strictly imprisoned for breaking the law *per se*, the relationship between explicit criminality and diverse cultural perspectives is better studied in the context of Cervantes's other incarceration, namely in the *Cárcel Real de Sevilla*. Mary Elizabeth Perry writes that the prison was 'a cultural meeting place', explaining further that,

> as a meeting place for prisoners and outside groups, the prison emphasized the subordination of prisoners to the larger society and their dependence on outside

support, but it also provided a meeting place for the variety of people who came together as prisoners. They were from Portugal, Italy, and most parts of Spain. They were between fourteen and eighty years of age. Many were penniless, a few were wealthy — although the wealthy prisoners often kept to their own better quarters. Some, such as Lope Ponce, came from well-known noble families. In no other place in Spain could so many varieties of people meet together to enrich and reinforce an underworld culture.[44]

This context may help us better understand the concentration of *italianismos* (Italianisms) in the second part of *Don Quixote* within the span of Chapters 24–25. These are comprised mostly of the 'aventura del rebuzno' (II. 25, 912) ('braying adventure')[45] and Maese Pedro episodes, the second of which features the disguised master criminal facing the novel's hero. Carlos Romero Muñoz lists *italianismos* uttered by three characters: the man with the lances on his way to the inn ('*hacer placer*', '*no que*', '*contraseño*') (II. 25, 913, 914, 915) ('to have one appreciate', 'let alone', 'signal'),[46] the innkeeper ('es *hombre galante*, como dicen en Italia, *y bon compaño*') (II. 25, 918), ('gallant man and a good companion, as they say in Italy')[47] and Don Quixote himself ('*espilorchería*', '*¿qué peje pillamo?*') (II. 24, 910 and II. 25, 918) ('miserliness or stinginess', 'what are we up to?).[48] Maese Pedro stands apart from the other three because he does not employ such phrases.[49] Why does he refuse? Perhaps he resists contributing Italian affectations to the conversation because he is wary of being identified, even tangentially, with the criminal underworld. The *italianismos* are affectations because they are functionally unnecessary, unlike the use of Italian as a *lingua franca* when a German pilgrim takes Sancho's hand in Part Two, Chapter 54, and says, '*Español y tudesqui, tuto uno: bon compaño*' ('Spaniard and German, together: good friends'), to which Sancho responds: '*¡Bon compaño, jura Di!*' (II. 54, 1169) ('Good friends, by God!').[50] Romero Muñoz suggests that while it is possible that the innkeeper thinks that Maese Pedro is Italian, it is more likely that 'la venta es lugar donde el italiano más o menos genuino de los veteranos suena con frecuencia' (the inn is a place where one frequently hears the more-or-less genuine Italian of veterans).[51] Given Ginés de Pasamonte's skill in disguising himself, it is telling that as a traveller he does not directly respond to *italianismos*, further suggesting that his fear of being detected as a criminal outweighs any possible benefit of rejoining Don Quixote's unusual '*¿qué peje pillamo?*' (II. 25, 918) as Maese Pedro attempts to blend in. The puppeteer-rogue's aversion to using Italian is even more noticeable when one considers many *cervantistas*' explanation of the character's connection to Italy. These critics have reasonably suggested that the puppet-theatre portion of the episode in question is inspired by Cervantes's experiences with Sicilian *puppi*, and still others have invoked another Italian figure, that of the 'charlatan'. Despite the *italianismos* that surround him, Ginés de Pasamonte tellingly does not take the title 'Maestro', like 'Maestro Paolo da Arezzo', cited by Tomasso Garzoni in the sixteenth century as leading a troupe of mountebanks, including a certain 'Zan della Vigna with his performing monkey', who perfectly anticipates Maese Pedro's non-puppet-show act.[52] The criminal-turned-mountebank is surrounded by inadvertent intimations of criminal behaviour through the use of *italianismos*. Instead of looking towards Italy as a source of these phrases, can they not be derived from Cervantes's incarceration in the 'cultural meeting place' that was the *Cárcel Real de Sevilla*? Critics have stretched farther than this in making claims about the origin of Italian-inspired loan-words in relation to criminality: 'En cuanto al mote de "Ginesillo de Parapilla", según recuerda Augustin Redondo, el apelativo Ginés se aplicaba a los villanos y el pillar es un italianismo que significa robar [...] (Recordemos que [Gerónimo de Pasamonte] vivió en Italia.)' (Regarding the moniker 'Ginesillo de Parapilla', as Augustin Redondo reminds us, the soubriquet Ginés was applied to country folk and 'pillar' is Italian in origin, meaning 'to steal' [...] (Let us recall that [Gerónimo de Pasamonte] lived in Italy)).[53] If we leave aside the question of whether the fictional Ginés de Pasamonte was created in a convoluted attempt to ridicule the real-life Gerónimo de Pasamonte, what remains is the association of 'robar' with 'pillar' by way of criminal behaviour. Such an association could have been observed by Cervantes while imprisoned in Seville, at least with the same likelihood that he learned of it while a free man in Italy. When looking further into the word 'pillar' from a different perspective, the question of genre overlaps with that of biography. In Juan Hidalgo's 1609 *Romances de germanía*, the word 'pillar' and variations thereof appear eleven times, while in both parts of *Don Quixote*, it appears only once in obvious fashion, in the significant example of '*¿Qué peje pillamo?*' cited above. If we interpret the use of *italianismos* as a reflection of incarceration in Seville, then the use of such expressions can be read as evidence of the overlap between the 'cultural meeting place' of the *Cárcel Real de Sevilla* and a Spanish *venta* that is a much more cheerful, if only slightly less comfortable, 'meeting place for travellers in the journey of life'.[54]

Romero Muñoz's observation that 'la venta es lugar donde el italiano más o menos genuino de los veteranos suena con frecuencia',[55] reminds us of Cervantes's travels in Italy, and also of the peripatetic soldier's life in general. *Cervantistas* rightly look to works such as *El licenciado Vidriera* to find further insight into this life and connections between that novel's characters, settings and situations and those in *Don Quixote*. In the case of *El licenciado Vidriera*, the search for insight in a literary vein can lead one to the genres of travel literature, folktales and the picaresque.[56] Independent of the work in question, the picaresque is a genre that seems to have captured most critics' imagination when studying how an author encapsulates the soldier's life in prose. Even the sub-genre of soldiers' autobiographies are described in terms of the picaresque. For example, the autobiography of Gerónimo de Pasamonte has been described as 'a lively picaresque narration of his troubles as a child, journey to Italy, participation in the battle of Lepanto (1571) and the battle of Tunis (1573)'.[57] It has been observed of another soldier's autobiography, Catalina de Erauso's *Vida y sucesos de la monja alférez*, that 'while [...] not a picaresque novel, some scholars have found sequences ['cross-dressing and boundary-crossing adventures'] that recall picaresque adventures'.[58] When studying any soldier's autobiography, we should be wary of ascribing too many picaresque elements, especially where criminal behaviour is concerned. Gerónimo de Pasamonte's *Vida* may feature 'a lively picaresque narration of his troubles as a child', but this is not some sort of generic pattern followed in other works. In *Vida, nacimiento, padres y crianza del capitán Alonso de Contreras*, the real-life hero of the story has a childhood featuring violent criminal behaviour that pushes the narrative outside of the realm of the picaresque. At one point in Contreras's narration he recounts how he exacted vengeance for a classmate's treachery by bringing him to the ground, stabbing him in the back, and then turning around the traitor to subsequently stab him in the stomach for good measure.[59] A modern historian cites the same 'Alonso de Contreras, [and his] picaresque account of his cruises with the knights [of Malta]' after introducing him as 'the Knight of Malta who bragged of torturing the Greeks he encountered', revealing that the 'picaresque' label can be somewhat misleading.[60] Another genre category can be helpful in order to move in another direction and escape the dominance of picaresque fiction in the analysis of criminality in Spanish Golden Age literature. On the many occasions when the term pícaro does not apply to wandering soldiers and their violent adventures, we may instead refer to a *valiente*: the character type that has more in common with a *jaque* like the 'valiente Escarramán' from Cervantes's *jácara*, and less to do with the stereotypical cheeky and non-threatening pícaro. After the publication of *Don Quixote*, the term *valiente* was commonly used to describe a brawling character who gains literary prominence through *comedias* defined by such a protagonist. Consequently, *comedias de valiente* (or *valentón*) are full of action scenes, although many of these may be re-enacted in stirring *romance*-style poems, if not performed in spectacular swordfights on stage. A great many *comedias de capa y espada* (cloak and dagger plays) have their share of swordfights, but these are used to punctuate complicated love plots, adding moments of tension or confusion. In the separate generic category of the *comedia de valiente*, the action mostly exists for action's sake. While fighting on stage adds excitement in its own right, the main purpose is simply to demonstrate the *valiente*'s unerring *valentía* which is indistinguishable from a pure love of brawling. The early twentieth-century critic Emilio Cotarelo y Mori is still an excellent guide for studying lesser-known genres, and his list of *valiente* plays includes the following:

> *El valiente sevillano*, de Enciso, *El valiente Diego de Camas*, de Enríquez Gómez; *El valiente toledano*, de Luis Vélez; *El afanador el de Utrera*, de Belmonte; *Añasco el de Talavera*, de Cubillo; *El más valiente andaluz, Antón Bravo*, de Monroy; *Pero Vázquez de Escamilla*, de Quevedo; *El valiente Barrionuevo*, de Cantón Salazar; *El valiente Campuzano*, de Zárate, hasta llegar a la famosa del *Guapo Francisco Estevan*, al *Valiente Pedro Ponce*, al *Valor nunca vencido, hazañas de Juan de Arévalo* y otras aún más disparatadas del siglo XVIII.[61]

> (*El valiente sevillano*, by Enciso, *El valiente Diego de Camas*, by Enríquez Gómez; *El valiente toledano*, by Luis Vélez; *El afanador el de Utrera*, by Belmonte; *Añasco el de Talavera*, by Cubillo; *El más valiente andaluz, Antón Bravo*, by Monroy; *Pero Vázquez de Escamilla*, by Quevedo; *El valiente Barrionuevo*, by Cantón Salazar; *El valiente Campuzano*, by Zárate, until we arrive at the famous *Guapo Francisco Estevan*, or *Valiente Pedro Ponce*, or *Valor nunca vencido, hazañas de Juan de Arévalo* and others from the eighteenth century that are even more ridiculous.)

Despite the prevalence of the word *valiente* in *comedia* titles, no generic distinction is perfect, and one must be sensitive to shades of meaning in Cervantes's use of the word, given the author's playful attitude towards genre conventions of all sorts.

However he uses the word, it seems reasonable that there is always the potential that it refers to 'brawler' and not simply 'brave'. The expression *valiente caballero* is an operating cliché that serves Cervantes's chivalric parody well, but one cannot neglect his pervasive irony and love of double meaning for describing contradictory situations. Although Don Quixote claims chivalric knights as his model, the hero repeatedly and senselessly breaks the law in order to fulfil his fantasies. When he is accused of a crime or misconduct, Don Quixote answers in a manner foreshadowing his fellow *valientes* who will later populate the seventeenth-century stage. Despite the trail of bodies that those brawling and bullying characters leave behind them, the *comedia* protagonists must point out that, while they may be lawbreakers, they are honourable men, and certainly not thieves. Likewise, nobody can accuse Don Quixote of stealing or acting dishonourably, but by his own admission he remains a lawbreaker. More than that, he is a self-professed threat to law enforcement: '¿qué caballero andante ha habido, hay ni habrá en el mundo que no tenga bríos para dar él solo cuatrocientos palos a cuatrocientos cuadrilleros que se le pongan delante?' (I. 45, 580) ('what knight errant ever was, is, or will be in the world who does not have the courage to single-handedly deliver four hundred blows to four hundred Brotherhoods if they presume to oppose him?').[62] Compare this statement with that of the title character of *El valiente Juan de Heredia*:

> Volvíme a Guadalcanal,
> de donde fue salir fuerza
> dentro de muy breve tiempo,
> huyendo de las molestias
> que la justicia me hacía
> por desgarros y pendencias,
> muertes y heridas, efetos
> de mi condición traviesa,
> si bien alabarme puedo
> que jamás, sin que tuviera
> ocasión, saqué la espada,
> que hay hombres que sin tenerla
> en sacarla cada instante
> para hacer mal se deleitan,
> bárbaramente imprudentes.[63]

> (I came back to Guadalcanal,
> From where I was forced to leave,
> After very little time,
> Fleeing from the annoyances,
> That the police caused me,
> Because of the brawls and scraps,
> Murders and assaults, the results
> Of my mischievous nature,
> Though I can boast
> Of never drawing my sword
> Without good reason.
> There are men who always draw theirs
> Without justification,

And enjoy doing harm,
Like senseless beasts.)

The *valiente* insists that he never drew his sword without cause, but the phrase 'las molestias que la justicia me hacía' reveals that (as with Don Quixote) when his cause is just, he may attack at will and ignore the repercussions of the law. Don Quixote's justification is that 'son esentos de todo judicial fuero los caballeros andantes, y que su ley es su espada, sus fueros, sus bríos, sus premáticas, su voluntad' (I. 45, 579) ('knights errant are exempt from all jurisdictional authority, [...] their law is their sword, their edicts their courage, their statutes their will'),[64] but this does little to distinguish him from later *valientes de comedia*. Because Don Quixote is obsessed with books of chivalry, he easily conflates very real *cuadrilleros* with the typical hordes hewn down by fictitious superhero knights. This genre-based conflation does not distance him much from any saner, but equally violent, *valiente* literary type. However, there is one important distinction. In *El valiente Juan de Heredia*, the father figure and peacemaker the Conde de Palma intercedes on the hero's behalf in payment for Juan de Heredia's assistance in fighting off thieves. This intercession erases any potential for the *valiente*'s criminal past to prevent his marriage to the Count's daughter. In *Don Quixote*, despite the protagonist's insistence that he is fighting for a noble cause while being pursued by the authorities, there is no powerful arbiter that can save him. He presents all the behaviour of a *valiente de comedia* without the means of escaping prosecution that the theatrical genre provides. The generic clash is also a clear reminder of what happens when the violent wish-fulfilment fantasies of Don Quixote's favourite books are brought into the plane of reality. If we reflect upon the different appealing aspects of the books of chivalry, as outlined by the innkeeper, his wife, his daughter, and Maritornes in the first part of the novel, we will recall how the innkeeper exclaims, 'cuando oyo decir aquellos furibundos y terribles golpes que los que los caballeros pegan, que me toma gana de hacer otro tanto' (I. 32, 405) ('when I hear about those furious, terrible blows struck by the knights, it makes me want to do the same').[65] His wife the *ventera* is glad that the stories are so engrossing that the men sit still and do not fulfil their violent fantasies. Citing tension between pacification and incitement only underlines the fact that Don Quixote has no break on his behaviour, is not content to simply sit and listen, and has instead become an uncontrollable brawler. Of course, as a multi-dimensional character, he is more than that. He is also a lover who takes his cues in romance from the same books, but if forced to decide between being a lover or a fighter, Don Quixote would squarely fall into the second camp. At the end of Chapter 45, he swore in his rhetorical questions to be among those who will deal 'cuatrocientos palos a cuatrocientos cuadrilleros que se le pongan delante' (580). At the very beginning of Chapter 46, titled 'De la notable aventura de los cuadrilleros y la gran ferocidad de nuestro buen caballero don Quijote' ('Regarding the notable adventure of the officers of the Holy Brotherhood, and the great ferocity of our good knight Don Quixote'),[66] the law-enforcement officials effectively drop their charges against Don Quixote by reason of his insanity and the hero's status reverts from threatening *valiente* to bumbling madman. After the tension drops and the tone shifts, the narrator leaves us with a lingering ironical commentary. If we keep in mind the ambiguity of the word *valiente*, the sub-text rises to the surface as we read about the lovers and fighters who occupy the inn:

> Sosegadas, pues, estas dos pendencias, que eran las más principales y de más tomo, restaba que los criados de don Luis se contentasen de volver los tres, y que el uno quedase para acompañarle donde don Fernando le quería llevar; y como ya la buena suerte y mejor fortuna había comenzado a romper lanzas y a facilitar dificultades en favor de los amantes de la venta y de los valientes della, quiso llevarlo al cabo y dar a todo felice suceso. (I. 46, 581)
>
> (Having settled these two disputes, which were the most important and most pressing, it remained only for Don Luis's servants to agree that three would return home while one stayed behind to accompany him wherever Don Fernando wished to take him; since good luck had begun to intervene in favor of the lovers and the valiant people at the inn, overcoming all difficulties, a better fortune wished to bring everything to a happy conclusion.)[67]

The '*amantes*' refer to the embedded love story of Doña Clara and Don Luis, and '*valientes*' can only be ascribed to the narrowly-avoided confrontation between the novel's hero and *la justicia*, a scene that would have been reminiscent of many from the *comedias de valiente*.

Those familiar with the *comedias de valiente* can argue that most of these plays were written well after the first part of *Don Quixote*, and many may indeed wonder if the connections made above are tenuous. I believe that the comparisons are fair and fruitful, especially if one considers the extremely common use of the word 'picaresque' in studies on *Don Quixote*. Before publication of the first part of the novel, only two widely recognized picaresque works circulated in printed form, namely *Guzmán de Alfarache* and, half a century before, the work that started them all, *La vida de Lazarillo de Tormes, y de sus fortunas y adversidades*. The bulk of picaresque fiction, in the loosest use of the term, was published after the first part of *Don Quixote*, yet the designation is used as though Cervantes had read all of these works years or even decades before they were printed. If the term 'picaresque' is licit for analysing the representation of criminality in Cervantes, then so is the word *valiente* in reference to the theatrical genre based upon the character-type. Since we know that Cervantes had an eye fixed on Lope de Vega's works, and Lope did write *El valiente Céspedes* between 1612 and 1615,[68] we can be sure that the novelist was aware of the word's current usage before he died and most likely when he began to write *Don Quixote*. Also, Lope wrote another play about a figure associated with the underworld, *El rufián Castrucho*, likely in 1598.[69] Although that play's protagonist has been called a combination of *fanfarrón* (braggart) and *pícaro*,[70] when Castrucho the protagonist declares, 'verás lo que se llama valentía | [...] arrímate a la esquina, que es en vano | estorbar la venganza y el cuchillo [...],'[71] ('I'll show you who's tougher | [...] go head for the corner, it's useless | trying to stop vengeance and a knife') it is evident that Lope has fashioned this figure in the *valiente* mould and was aware of the reckless love for brawling often implied in the word *valentía*.

If we add together prison narratives, *jácaras*, *comedias de valiente*, all genres that specifically deal with lawbreakers and peacekeepers, we begin to see that the expression 'picaresque' is inadequate for a holistic study of cultural and literary influences on the portrayal of criminality in *Don Quixote*. In addition to an expanded generic approach, we have the option of returning to the historical moment, as recorded by those working within and around the early modern prison system of Seville. It is my hope that with the examples given above we might take a respite from using the picaresque as a point of reference and in this way explore more deeply and more widely crime and punishment in the novel.

Notes to Chapter 8

1. Howard Mancing, '*Guzmán de Alfarache* and After: The Spanish Picaresque Novel in the Seventeenth Century', in *The Picaresque Novel in Western Literature: From the Sixteenth Century to the Neopicaresque,* ed. by J. A Garrido Ardila (Cambridge: Cambridge University Press, 2015), pp 40–59 (p. 50).
2. Miguel de Cervantes Saavedra, *Don Quixote*, trans. by Edith Grossman (London: Secker & Warburg, 2004), p. 3. All translations from *Don Quixote* are taken from this edition except where otherwise stated.
3. José Miguel Cabañas Agrela, *Breve historia de Cervantes* (Madrid: Nowtilus, 2016), pp. 222–23.
4. All translations from texts other than *Don Quixote* are my own.
5. Mary Elizabeth Perry, *Crime and Society in Early Modern Seville* (Hanover, NH: University Press of New England, 1980), p. 28.
6. Pedro Herrera Puga, *Sociedad y delincuencia en el Siglo de Oro: aspectos de la vidasevillana en los siglos XVI y XVII* (Granada: Universidad de Granada, Secretariado de Publicaciones, 1971), p. 117.
7. Ellen M. Anderson and Gonzalo Pontón Gijón, 'La composición del *Quijote*', in DQ, pp. cxcii–ccxx (p. cxcii).
8. Anderson and Pontón, p. cxciii.
9. Mary Elizabeth Perry, *Crime and Society in Early Modern Seville*, pp. 77, 79.
10. Gerald L. Gingras, 'Relación de cómo Ginés de Pasamonte se desprendió de su cárcel literaria', in *Cervantes y su mundo*, ed. by Kurt Reichenberger and Darío Fernández-Morera, 3 vols (Kassel: Reichenberger, 2004), II, 193–226.
11. As quoted in Gingras, p. 215, n.1.
12. Juergen Hahn, '*Rinconete y Cortadillo* in *Don Quijote*: A Cervantine Reconstruction', *Modern Language Notes*, 116.2 (2001), 211–34 (p. 219).
13. E. Michael Gerli, *Refiguring Authority: Reading, Writing, and Rewriting in Cervantes*, Studies in Romance Languages, 39 (Lexington Kentucky: The University Press of Kentucky, 1996), p. 20.
14. p. 168.
15. p. 165.
16. Miguel de Cervantes, *El ingenioso hidalgo Don Quijote de la Mancha*, ed. by Diego Clemencín, 6 vols (Madrid: Aguado, 1833–39; repr. Madrid: Castilia, 1967), II, single footnote on p. 198.
17. Adapted from Grossman's translation, p. 167.
18. Cervantes, *El ingenioso hidalgo*, ed. Clemencín, II, single footnote on p. 204; translation based on Grossman, p. 167.
19. Cervantes, *El ingenioso hidalgo*, ed. Clemencín, II, single footnote on p. 205.
20. Jesús G. Maestro, *Crítica de los géneros literarios en el 'Quijote': idea y concepto de género en la investigación literaria* (Vigo: Academia del Hispanismo, 2009), p. 248.
21. Maestro, p. 248.
22. As cited in Pedro Herrera Puga and Pedro de León, *Grandeza y miseria en Andalucía: testimonio de una encrucijada histórica, 1578–1616* (Granada: Facultad de Teología, 1981), p. 221.
23. Joaquín Casalduero, *Sentido y forma del 'Quijote', (1605–1615)*, 3rd edn (Madrid: Ínsula, 1970), p. 119.
24. My translation of the phrases in commas is based on Grossman, p. 167.

25. Anthony Close, 'The Liberation of the Galley Slaves and the ethos of *Don Quijote* Part I', *Cervantes: Bulletin of the Cervantes Society of America*, 27.1 (Spring 2007 [2008]), 7–30 (p. 15).
26. Close, 'The Liberation', p. 16; translation from same page.
27. Close, 'The Liberation', p. 17.
28. Anthony Close, *A Companion to 'Don Quixote'*, Colección Támesis Serie A: Monografías (Woodbridge: Tamesis, 2010), p. 262.
29. César Hernández Alonso and Beatriz Sanz Alonso, *Germanía y sociedad en los siglos de oro: la cárcel de Sevilla* (Valladolid: Secretariado de Publicaciones e Intercambio Editorial, Universidad de Valladolid, 1999), p. 175.
30. José M. Blecua, *Sobre poesía de la Edad de Oro: ensayos y notas eruditas* (Madrid: Gredos, 1970), p. 189.
31. See Luis Astrana Marín, *La vida turbulenta de Quevedo* (Madrid: Gran Capitán, 1945), p. 181; Elena Di Pinto, *La tradición escarramanesca en el teatro del Siglo de Oro* (Madrid: Iberoamericana, 2005), p. 29; Vicente Pérez de León, *Tablas destempladas: los entremeses de Cervantes a examen* (Alcalá de Henares, Madrid: Centro de Estudios Cervantinos, 2005), p. 169.
32. As cited in Emma Nishida, 'Los romances y el lenguaje de germanía en el entremés del *Rufián viudo*: ¿mensajes pícaros de Cervantes hacia Alonso Fernández de Avellaneda?', in *Tus obras los rincones de la tierra descubren. Actas del VI Congreso Internacional de la Asociación de Cervantistas. Alcalá de Henares, 13 al 16 de diciembre de 2006*, ed. by A. Dotras Bravo and others (Alcalá de Henares: Centro de estudios cervantinos, 2008), pp. 591–600 (p. 596).
33. p. 134.
34. As cited in John M. M. Hill, *Poesías germanescas* (Bloomington: Indiana University Press, 1945), pp. 65, 66.
35. As cited in Hill, *Poesías*, p. 70.
36. As cited in Hill, *Poesías*, p. 84.
37. Gerli, *Refiguring Authority*, p. 20.
38. As cited in Hill, *Poesías*, p. 89.
39. p. 165.
40. Ryan Prendergast, *Reading, Writing, and Errant Subjects in Inquisitorial Spain* (Farnham: Ashgate, 2011), p. 84.
41. See, for example, Chad M. Gasta, 'Cervantes and the Picaresque: A Question of Compatibility', in *The Picaresque Novel in Western Literature: From the Sixteenth Century to the Neopicaresque*, ed. by J. A Garrido Ardila (Cambridge: Cambridge University Press, 2015), pp. 96–112 (p. 99).
42. Nishida, 'Los romances y el lenguaje de germanía', p. 596.
43. Felipe B. Pedraza Jiménez, 'De Quevedo a Cervantes: la génesis de la jácara', in *Edad de Oro Cantabrigense: Actas del VII Congreso de la Asociación Internacional Siglo De Oro (AISO): (Robinson College, Cambridge, 18–22 Julio, 2005)* (Madrid: Iberoamericana, 2006), pp. 77–88 (p. 81).
44. Perry, *Crime and Society*, p. 83.
45. p. 620.
46. pp. 621, 621 again, 622, respectively.
47. p. 624, emended. Grossman's translation puts '*uomo galante*' for the Spanish 'hombre galante' and '*bon compagno*' for '*bon compaño*'.
48. p. 618 fn. 3, 'The word means "miserliness" or "stinginess"'; p. 624, fn. 1, 'literally, "what fish are we catching?" or "what are we up to, what are we doing?"'.
49. Carlos Romero Muñoz, 'Nueva lectura de *El retablo de Maese Pedro*', in *Actas del I Coloquio Internacional de la Asociación de Cervantistas* (Madrid: Anthropos, 1990), pp. 95–130 (pp. 108–09).
50. My translation; Grossman's translation leaves this interchange untranslated (p. 812).
51. Romero Muñoz, p. 109.
52. Winifred Smith, *The Commedia dell'Arte: A Study in Italian Popular Comedy* (New York: Columbia University Press, 1912), p. 34.
53. Helena Percas de Ponseti, 'Un misterio dilucidado: Pasamonte fue Avellaneda', *Cervantes: Bulletin of the Cervantes Society of America*, 22.1 (2002), 127–54 (pp. 131–32).
54. Frederick A. de Armas, 'The Artful Gamblers: Wagering Danaë in Cervantes' *Don Quixote* I. 33–35', in *Objects of Culture in the Literature of Imperial Spain*, ed. by Mary E. Barnard and Frederick A. de Armas (Toronto: University of Toronto Press, 2013), pp. 54–79 (p. 55).

55. Romero Muñoz, p. 109.
56. Stephen Rupp, 'Soldiers and Satire in *El Licenciado Vidriera*', in *A Companion to Cervantes's 'Novelas Ejemplares'*, ed. by Stephen Boyd (Woodbridge: Tamesis, 2005), pp. 134–47 (pp. 134–35).
57. Germán Bleiberg, Maureen Ihrie, and Janet Pérez, *Dictionary of the Literature of the Iberian Peninsula*, 2 vols (Westport, CT: Greenwood, 1993), II, 1234.
58. Sonia Pérez-Villanueva, *The Life of Catalina de Erauso, the Lieutenant Nun: An Early-Modern Autobiography* (Madison: Fairleigh Dickinson University Press, 2014), p. 101.
59. Alonso de Contreras, *Vida, nacimiento, padres y crianza del capitán Alonso de Contreras*, ed. by Fernando Reigosa (Madrid: Alianza Editorial, 1967), p. 52.
60. Molly Greene, *Catholic Pirates and Greek Merchants: A Maritime History of the Mediterranean* (Princeton: Princeton University Press, 2010), pp. 121, 11.
61. *Obras de Lope de Vega*, ed. by Emilio Cotarelo y Mori, 13 vols. (Madrid: Revista de Archivos, Bibliotecas y Museos, 1916–1930), II, p. xv.
62. p. 397.
63. [Attributed in] *Obras de Lope de Vega*, II, p. 649.
64. p. 397.
65. p. 267.
66. p. 398.
67. pp. 398–99.
68. Edwin S. Morby, 'Some Observations on *tragedia* and *tragicomedia* in Lope', *Hispanic Review*, 11.3 (1943), 185–209 (p. 189).
69. Lope de Vega, *El rufián Castrucho* (Madrid: RESAD, 2000), p. 20
70. Juan Oleza, 'La propuesta teatral del primer Lope de Vega', in *Teatro y prácticas escénicas: II*, ed. by Ana Giordano Gromegna (London: Tamesis, 1986), pp. 251–308 (p. 305).
71. Lope de Vega, *El rufián Castrucho*, p. 150.

PART IV

Burlas y Veras

CHAPTER 9

Fortune and Providence, *santos y caballeros*, in *Don Quixote* II

Stephen Boyd

Writing, in 1956, about the scene of Don Quixote's death in the final chapter of the second part of Cervantes's novel, Jorge Luis Borges contended, primarily on aesthetic grounds, that 'el libro entero ha sido escrito para esta escena' (the whole book was written for this scene).[1] Just four years earlier, the poet, Jorge Guillén, placing rather more emphasis on what he saw as its psychological verisimilitude, had argued, similarly, that the knight's death was well prepared for: 'Así, de aventura en aventura, de fracaso en fracaso, descendemos a la aventura del fracaso final: desenlace nada brusco' (Thus, from adventure to adventure, from disaster to disaster, we descend to the adventure of the final disaster: a far from abrupt ending).[2] Of course, there are Cervantes scholars who see things quite differently. For Steven Hutchinson, for example, the notion that Don Quixote's increasingly acute melancholy requires his death, or that 'el argumento desde el inicio de la primera parte, o incluso desde el comienzo de la segunda parte, requiere este cierre como fin de ciclo' (the plot, from the beginning of the first part, or even from the start of the second, requires this ending as the completion of a cycle) is a debatable one because 'semejante intención autorial no se trasluce ni vemos ninguna prolepsis al respecto' (there is no sign of any such authorial intention nor do we see any prolepsis in this respect). Although allowing that Cervantes capitalizes on the sheer abruptness and banality (as he sees it) of Don Quixote's death to achieve 'una luminosa poética de la disolución, del anticlímax' (a luminous poetics of dissolution, of anticlimax), for him, it functions primarily as 'el medio para proteger la novela' (the means to protect the novel) from other would-be Avellanedas.[3] In his survey of critical commentary on the final chapter of *Don Quixote* II, Jaime Fernández notes, however, that the view of Don Quixote's death as a 'blunder' or as 'something unnecessary or forced' is a minority one.[4] Similar questions, and more, arise with respect to Don Quixote's, or Alonso Quijano's, return to sanity, and here critical opinion is rather more divided. For Borges, a champion of the aesthetic inevitability of the knight's return to sanity, as of his death, although a lesser author 'hubiera cedido a la tentación de que don Quijote muriera en su ley, combatiendo con gigantes o paladines alucinatorios' (would have yielded to the temptation to have Don Quixote die as he lived, fighting giants or hallucinatory paladins), 'la forma de la novela exige que don Quijote vuelva a la cordura' (the form of the novel requires that Don Quixote regains his sanity), ultimately because 'el sueño de Alonso Quijano cesa con la cordura y también el sueño general del libro, del que pronto despertaremos' (the dream of Alonso Quijano comes to end with his sanity and also the overall dream of the book from which we shall shortly awaken).[5] On the other hand, Edwin Williamson's view that 'Don Quixote's release from the grip of madness is as sudden and unaccountable as its onset' is a widely shared one.[6] While allowing that 'the sheer abruptness of [Don Quixote's] transition from madness to sanity, with the consequent renunciation of chivalry, suggests the author's arbitrary resolve to bring things to a conclusion', and arguing that, in this instance, 'function prevails to a considerable extent over psychological verisimilitude', Anthony Close, in his summary of debate on the question, concludes that, at least from an aesthetic point of view, the functionality of Don Quixote's recovery is positive since it allows Cervantes to end the novel with some 'satisfying symmetries' — between the recovery and the onset of his madness, for example — , and, thus, in keeping with neo-Aristotelian literary theory, to achieve the kind of 'poetic truth [that] is more universal than the historical kind'.[7] Although there can be no doubt that Don Quixote does die, a number of critics have questioned the extent, or indeed, the very fact, of his return to sanity; for them, the absolute nature and sheer vehemence of his renunciation of chivalry indicate that, although manifesting itself in a different — now religious — mode, his madness continues unabated.[8] How one answers these questions about the aesthetic and psychological fittingness of Don Quixote's recovery and death will depend upon and influence how one interprets the work as a whole.[9] In this essay, I would like to consider some of the textual evidence that would reinforce the notion that the way for Don Quixote's recovery (as I take it to be) and death, and for the redirection of his imagination specifically to the sphere of religion, is prepared throughout Part Two, and that what happens in the final chapter represents the culmination of processes which are, paradoxically, both slow and sudden, and which, although they may appear accidental — a matter of the caprice of Fortune or of authorial convenience — , are intimated to be a work of Providence. This evidence relates to two inter-connected and often overlapping thematic strands that surface and resurface at intervals throughout the text: first, that centred on the tension between the pursuit of sanctity on the one hand and of chivalry on the other, a tension that Don Quixote is initially reluctant to acknowledge, but which he is progressively led to confront; second, that of the ups and downs of Fortune, manifested, above all, in the series of literal and metaphorical ascents and descents that marks his progress throughout Part Two. Beginning with the theme of the rival claims of sanctity and chivalry, I propose to examine the working out of these strands by looking (in sequential order) at selected points in the text where they come into prominence, concluding with the final chapter, where (it will be argued) that working out reaches its culmination. It is convenient, however, to begin at the end with a reminder of how Don Quixote's physical decline, mental recovery, and death are presented in Chapter 74.

We can begin by saying that, subjectively, Don Quixote's death does indeed seem to come out of no-where: there has been no mention of physical illness, and no indication that he himself has felt that he was close to death — quite the opposite, in fact, since we are told that 'llegó su fin y acabamiento cuando él menos lo pensaba' (II. 74, 1328) ('[he] reached [his] end when he was least expecting it').[10] On the other hand, it may be observed, first, that readers are given at least immediate forewarning (in the most literal and banal sense) of his imminent demise in the epigraph to the final chapter, 'De cómo don Quijote cayó malo y del testamento que hizo y su muerte' ('Concerning how Don Quixote fell ill, the will that he made, and his death')[11] and in a rather more gentle and gradated way, in its gracefully cadenced, elegiac opening words about death as the universal lot of humankind:[12]

> Como las cosas humanas no sean eternas, yendo siempre en declinación de sus principios hasta llegar a su último fin, especialmente las vidas de los hombres, y como la de don Quijote no tuviese privilegio del cielo para detener el curso de la suya, llegó su fin y acabamiento cuando él menos lo pensaba. (1328)
>
> (Since what is human is not eternal, but is in continuous decline from its beginnings to its conclusion, this being particularly true of men's lives, and since Don Quixote's life had not been granted any special privilege by heaven to halt the course of its decline, it reached its end when he was least expecting it to.)[13]

Second, two different, but clearly complementary rather than mutually exclusive, reasons are suggested for the fever which is the immediate cause of his death: 'la melancolía que le causaba el verse vencido o [...] la disposición del cielo, que así lo ordenaba' (1328) ('the depression brought on by his defeat or [...] divine ordination').[14] The narrator's speculation about the psychosomatic cause ('melancolía') of Don Quixote's decline coincides with the diagnosis of his doctor: 'Fue el parecer del médico que melancolías y desabrimientos le acababan' (1329) ('The doctor's opinion was that depression and despondency were killing him)'.[15] Thus, readers are provided with a plausible explanation for his illness and death, and reminded (if they need to be) of the ever-deepening mood of dejection that has afflicted him throughout Part Two, even before his defeat on the beach of Barcelona. It might be added that it is not altogether strange that a man of Don Quixote's advanced age (as it would have been considered to be in the period), especially one who has undergone as much self-imposed physical hardship as he has, should fall ill and die. If his death still comes as something of a shock, which it does, this may represent a transference and intensification of the sadness that readers tend to feel when a fictional character, especially one whom they have come to know and like over the course of many pages and a long period of reading, 'disappears' as the work of fiction ends.[16] Or, might there be an additional and more subtle reason?: in the case of Don Quixote, the surprise and sadness, along with a sense of strangeness, may also be connected with the fact that, although he acquires greater psychological depth in Part Two,[17] Don Quixote is, to a considerable degree, a fantastical, larger-than-life invention of Alonso Quijano's, a strange and largely impenetrable cypher, and, for that reason, difficult to imagine being subject to death.[18]

Don Quixote's, or Alonso Quijano's, recovery of sanity, on the other hand, really does appear to come as a bolt from the blue, a turn of events for which it seems that

Cervantes has in no way prepared the reader. It is surprising, strange, and may well appear implausible, for several reasons: its suddenness and apparent completeness — it happens in the space of just six hours; its manner — it happens while Don Quixote is asleep; its cause — according to him, it is an act of divine mercy; and its form — it is presented not just as a recovery of sanity but as a religious conversion, and even, perhaps, a miracle.[19] Don Quixote had announced a need to be left alone to sleep after hearing the doctor intimate that he might be near to death ('dijo que, por sí o por no, atendiese a la salud de su alma, porque la del cuerpo corría peligro' (1329) ('[he] said to be on the safe side he should look to the well-being of his soul, because the well-being of his body was in some danger')[20]), news that he receives 'con ánimo sosegado' ('with great composure'), unlike his housekeeper, his niece, and Sancho. The sleep is clearly a deep one: 'durmió de un tirón, como dicen, más de seis horas: tanto, que pensaron el ama y la sobrina que se había de quedar en el sueño' (1329) ('he slept for more than six hours at a stretch, as the saying goes: indeed he slept for so long that the housekeeper and the niece thought that he was going to die in his sleep').[21] It ends with a double awakening, both literal and spiritual, as, after giving a loud, triumphant shout ('una gran voz'), Don Quixote declares: 'Yo tengo juicio ya libre y claro [...] ya yo no soy don Quijote de la Mancha, sino Alonso Quijano' (1330) ('My mind has been restored to me, and it is now clear and free [...] I am no longer Don Quixote de la Mancha but Alonso Quixano').[22] This is a recovery which he identifies, in effect, as a conversion: God has shown mercy to him, restoring him to his rightful mind, in spite of his sins, and delivering him from 'las sombras caliginosas de la ignorancia' ('those gloomy shadows of ignorance') into which he was plunged by his 'amarga y continua leyenda de los detestables libros de las caballerías' (1330) ('wretched, obsessive reading of those detestable books of chivalry').[23] He would have been better advised, he now realizes, to have devoted himself to 'leyendo otros que sean luz del alma' (1330) ('reading other books that might be a light for my soul').[24] Something remarkable and mysterious has happened to him in his sleep. He believes that God has shed his light on him, but readers can never know exactly what has caused this dramatic change of heart and mind. In contrast to this impression of abruptness, we might recall that, in the first chapter of Part Two, we are told that Don Quixote's niece and housekeeper report intermittent signs of what appears to be a very great improvement in his mental health: 'echaban de ver que su señor por momentos iba dando muestras de estar en su entero juicio' (I. 1, 681) ('they could see that their master was showing every sign of recovering his sanity').[25] Even when it emerges, in the course of the experiment conducted by his friends, the priest and the barber, that his chivalric delusions remain as strong as ever, in his superbly indignant response to the barber's story of the madman from Seville, he reveals an entirely new awareness of being perceived as mad: ' — Pues ¿este es el cuento, señor barbero — dijo don Quijote — , que por venir aquí como de molde no podía dejar de contarle? ¡Ah, señor rapista, señor rapista, y cuán ciego es aquel que no vee por tela de cedazo!' (689) ('"And this is the tale, mister barber", said Don Quixote, "that fitted the bill so perfectly that you could not refrain from telling it? Oh mister shaver, mister shaver, how blind is the man who can see no further than the end of his nose!' ").[26] If a madman is conscious that others see him as mad, it suggests that he may well have begun to emerge from his madness. Later on, he shows a similar awareness in the course of his encounter with Don Diego de Miranda (II. 16), which we shall consider in due course. And there is, of course, that other much commented upon sign of improvement that differentiates the Don Quixote of Part Two from that of Part One: the fact that, with a very few exceptions, he no longer spontaneously mistakes ordinary people and things for the fantastical people and things of the romances of chivalry. In the final chapter itself, Cervantes does go a little way towards accounting for the suddenness of his recovery — its most striking aspect for his family and friends (as for readers) — by alluding to the contemporary belief that mad people could recover their sanity when on the point of death: 'una de las señales por donde conjeturaron se moría fue el haber vuelto con tanta facilidad de loco a cuerdo' (II. 74, 1331) ('one of the signs that led them to conclude that he really was dying was the ease with which he had turned from a madman into a sane man').[27] In addition, and as we have observed, just as the melancholy to which the doctor attributes his final illness has gradually been building up throughout the whole course of his third sally, Don Quixote's final descent into sleep and awakening to sanity, and his renunciation of the romances of chivalry in favour of devotional literature, may be seen as the thematically coherent culmination of his encounters, in different modes, with the ideal of the holy life, and of the pattern of rising and falling, of descents in one sense that are ascents in another (and vice versa), which is present throughout Part Two. In what follows, these patterns, and the way in which they prepare the way for the knight's recovery and conversion in the final chapter, will be explored in greater depth.

Knights and Saints

There are three points in the course of Don Quixote's third sally at which he is forced to consider the merits of the holy life as opposed to those of the life of knight errantry: in the conversation with Sancho about the nature of fame in Chapter 8; in his meeting with Don Diego de Miranda in Chapters 16 to 18; and in his encounter with the images of four soldier saints in Chapter 58. In the first, he engages with the idea of sanctity; in the second, he meets someone who, at least by his own account, leads a saintly life, and whom Sancho considers to be a saint; and, in the third, he views images of *caballeros* who were also saints. We shall now consider each of these episodes in turn.

In Chapter 8, when they have just set out on their third expedition, Don Quixote and Sancho engage in a sustained discussion about the nature of fame and the human thirst to achieve it, even if only, like Herostratus, in the form of infamy.[28] Don Quixote draws a distinction between the vanity and evanescence of the worldly fame that 'en este presente y acabable siglo se alcanza' ('can be achieved in this present transient life') and the everlasting fame, the 'gloria de los siglos venideros, que es eterna en las regiones etéreas y celestes' ('the glory of the life to come, to be enjoyed throughout eternity in the ethereal and celestial regions')[29] to which 'los cristianos, católicos y andantes caballeros más habemos de atender' (754) (we Christian and Catholic knights errant must most attend), the kind of fame which is achieved, he says, not through spectacular displays of valour such as those of Horatius on the bridge, Marcus Curtius in his self-sacrifice in the Forum, Mucius Scaevola burning his hand, Julius Caesar crossing the Rubicon, or Hernán Cortés scuttling his ships at Veracruz, but by dedication to inner, spiritual warfare against the 'giants' of pride, envy, wrath, greed, sloth, and lust.[30] Just a little before this (in Chapter 7), Sancho had registered his annoyance at having his linguistic slips constantly corrected by his socially and intellectually superior and better educated master ('Una o dos veces — respondió Sancho — , si mal no me acuerdo, he suplicado a vuestra merced que no me emiende los vocablos, si es que entiende lo que quiero decir en ellos' (741) ('"If I remember rightly," Sancho replied, "I've already asked you once or twice not to correct my words, if you understand what I mean by them"')[31]), and had tried to make his participation in the third expedition conditional on being paid a salary. At the beginning of Chapter 8, he had interpreted his ass's making louder sounds (from both ends of its body) than Rocinante as an omen signifying that 'su ventura había de sobrepujar y ponerse encima de la de su señor' (748) ('his good fortune was going to surpass his master's').[32] Now, he scents an opportunity — at last — to get the upper hand of Don Quixote and defeat him in the sphere of the intellect where his superiority has always been unquestioned. Having got him to admit that, unlike the shrines of the saints, the monuments erected to commemorate famous pagans have either been forgotten or converted to other uses, and slyly echoing back, in their literal sense — the one in which he more usually understands them — Don Quixote's words about giants (while simultaneously misappropriating those of Christ), he asks his master, '¿cuál es más, resucitar a un muerto o matar a un gigante?' (756) ('what's better, bringing a corpse back to life, or killing a giant?').[33] Having received what he knows is the only possible correct answer, he crows triumphantly, 'Cogido le tengo' ('And now I've got you'), and then — one can almost sense him surfing a rolling wave of inexorable logic and inspired eloquence — moves in for the kill:

> Luego la fama del que resucita muertos, da vista a los ciegos, endereza los cojos y da salud a los enfermos [...], mejor fama será, para este y para el otro siglo, que la que dejaron y dejaren cuantos emperadores gentiles y caballeros andantes ha habido en el mundo. (756)

> (From that it follows that the fame of the man who brings the dead back to life, gives sight to the blind, gets the lame walking and makes the sick healthy [...] must be a better sort of fame, for this world and for the next, than all the fame of all the pagan emperors and knight errants that ever were and ever will be on the face of the earth.)[34]

When, as he must, Don Quixote, admits that this is true, Sancho reminds him that the tombs of the saints, adorned with ex-votos and votive lamps, are thronged with pilgrims, and that kings regard it as a singular privilege to carry their relics in procession or kiss tiny fragments of their bones. Finally, in response to his master's mystified enquiry, '¿Qué quieres que infiera, Sancho, de todo lo que has dicho?' (756) ('What do you want me to infer, Sancho, from all this you have just said?')[35], he peremptorily unleashes the wonderfully improbable proposal that he must have been keeping up his sleeve all along: 'que nos demos a ser santos' (756) ('let's go in for being saints').[36] The 'buena fama', the kind won through heroic virtue, which Don Quixote had just declared preferable to any other, he tells his master, is much more likely to be attained, and attained more readily, by imitating the holy life of two recently canonized or beatified 'little discalced friars' than by continuing to pursue the path of chivalry:

> Así que, señor mío, más vale ser humilde frailecito, de cualquier orden que sea, que valiente y andante caballero; más alcanzan con Dios dos docenas de diciplinas que dos mil lanzadas, ora las den a gigantes, ora a vestiglos o a endriagos. (756–57)[37]
>
> (So you see, sir, it's better to be a humble little friar of any order than a brave knight errant, and as far as God's concerned a couple of dozen strokes of the lash are worth more than a couple of thousand thrusts of the lance, whether given to giants, monsters or dragons.)[38]

The logic, as Sancho well knows, is incontestable: who could reasonably prefer to pursue a professed aim by means other than the most efficient and effective? Don Quixote can only try to wriggle out of the corner into which he has been so astutely backed by resort to pseudo-logical hair-splitting: God leads people to heaven by many paths; one of them is chivalry; there are many saintly knights in heaven; if the number of religious there is greater, that is merely the accidental logical corollary of the fact that there are more religious than knights in the first place. Sancho is aware, as is the reader, that Don Quixote has no real interest in engaging in the kind of spiritual battles or in pursuing the kind of otherworldly fame that he professes to believe are of the essence of chivalry.[39] The reader knows, equally well, that the venal Sancho does not have the remotest intention of becoming a friar and leading a life of ascetic self-denial.[40] The argument between the two men is not, of course, about what kind of vocation they should be pursuing, but a means by which Cervantes allows tensions between them, which will play out over the whole course of the second part, to manifest themselves in a significant way for the first time.[41] It is also important on a deeper, thematic, level, and in a way that goes to the heart of Don Quixote's madness and its meaning. He imagines, as he later tells Don Diego de Miranda, that he has already 'cumplido gran parte de mi deseo, socorriendo viudas, amparando doncellas y favoreciendo casadas, huérfanos y pupilos' (II. 16, 821) ('been fulfilling my desires, succouring widows, rescuing maidens, protecting wives, orphans and wards')[42], all of which, as he notes, are acts of Christian charity particularly and naturally enjoined upon knights errant ('propio y natural oficio de caballeros andantes' (821)). In fact, of course, he has done none of these things; the only attempt he has made to right what may have been a real injustice — the cruel punishment meted out by his employer to the shepherd boy, Andrés — ended up by making the victim's suffering much worse.[43] The terms in which Don Quixote's initial motivation for wanting to be a knight are set out, and most of his subsequent actions make it clear that, for him, it is not the desire to help others, but the thirst for a fantastical form of worldly fame, that is primary:

> y fue que le pareció convenible y necesario, así para el aumento de su honra como para el servicio de su república, hacerse caballero andante y irse por todo el mundo con sus armas y caballo a buscar las aventuras y a ejercitarse en todo aquello que él había leído que los caballeros andantes se ejercitaban, deshaciendo todo género de agravio y poniéndose en ocasiones y peligros donde, acabándolos, cobrase eterno nombre y fama. Imaginábase el pobre ya coronado por el valor de su brazo, por lo menos del imperio de Trapisonda. (I. 1, 43–44)

> (considering it desirable and necessary, both for the increase of his honour and for the common good, to become a knight errant, and to travel around the world with his armour and his arms and his horse in search of adventures, and to practise all those activities that he knew from his books were practised by knights errant, redressing all kinds of grievances, and exposing himself to perils and dangers that he would overcome and thus gain eternal fame and renown. The poor man could already see himself being crowned Emperor of Trebizond, at the very least, through the might of his arm.)[44]

Not only has he shown no interest in engaging in the kind of inner spiritual warfare that he describes to Sancho — the only 'giants' he has fought against are windmills rather than any or all of the deadly sins — but he has preferred precisely to seek to imitate the deeds of fictional knights that, typically, do exceed the 'límite que nos tiene puesto la religión cristiana que profesamos' (II. 16, 754) ('limits imposed by the Christian religion that we profess')[45] rather than those of real soldiers.[46] In short, pride is the motor of his 'knightly' activity rather than a prime enemy to be defeated by means of it.[47] If Don Quixote were to accept Sancho's arguments — precisely calculated to open up and exploit the gap between his words and his actions, his lofty theory and preposterous practice — along with the proposal that he change vocation, he would have to renounce the glamour of literary chivalry, which is so fundamentally important to him; it would signify putting the end before the means, and before the manner of the means. Not surprisingly, he is reluctant to do so. Thus, Don Quixote's eloquent excursus (II. 8) on the true, or deep, meaning of chivalry, serves not only to remind the reader of the magnitude of the gap between theory and practice, but, as is well recognized, of St Paul's words about spiritual warfare in his Letter to the Ephesians 6, 11–17:[48]

> induite vos armaturam Dei, ut possitis stare adversus insidias diaboli: quoniam non est nobis colluctatio adversus carnem et sanguinem, sed adversus principes, et potestates, adversus mundi rectores tenebrarum harum, contra spiritualia nequitiæ, in cælestibus. Propterea accipite armaturam Dei, ut possitis resistere in die malo, et in omnibus perfeci stare. State ergo succincti lumbos vestros in veritate, et induti loricam justitiæ, et calceati pedes in præparatione Evangelii pacis, in omnibus sumentes scutum fidei, in quo possitis omnia tela nequissimi ignea extinguere: et galeam salutis assumite, et gladium spiritus (quod est verbum Dei).

> (Put on the whole armour of God, that ye may be able to stand against the wiles of the devil. For we wrestle not against flesh and blood, but against principalities,

against powers, against the rulers of the darkness of this world, against spiritual wickedness in high places. Wherefore take unto you the whole armour of God, that ye may be able to withstand in the evil day, and having done all, to stand. Stand therefore, having your loins girt about with truth, and having on the breastplate of righteousness; And your feet shod with the preparation of the gospel of peace; Above all, taking the shield of faith, wherewith ye shall be able to quench all the fiery darts of the wicked. And take the helmet of salvation, and the sword of the Spirit, which is the word of God.)

In his *Liber ad milites Templi: De laude novae militae* (*Book for the Knights of the Temple: In Praise of the New Knighthood*) (written between 1128 and 1131), and making a clear theoretical distinction between 'militia saeculi' and the 'milites Christi', St Bernard of Clairvaux, like so many other medieval theologians, spiritual writers and preachers,[49] drew on this text to remind Christian knights of their duty to behave in a way that accorded with the spirit of the religion in defence of which they professed to fight.[50] As is well known, these attempts to civilize and Christianize the practice of warfare were, hardly surprisingly, not very effective in practice, and knights by and large continued to engage in it for the sake of worldly power, honour, and glory. As Antonio Regalado puts it:

> Y es que cuanto más elevado es el ideal, mayor es la disparidad con la realidad. Ya en los últimos dos siglos de la Edad Media, la brecha que se abre entre el ideal caballeresco y la práctica es objeto de burlas, parodias y escarnios.[51]
>
> (And so it is that the more exalted the ideal, the greater the disparity with the reality. In the last two centuries of the Middle Ages, the gulf that opens up between the ideal of chivalry and its practice is the object of mockery, parody and ridicule.)

Let us turn now to consider Don Quixote's encounter (Chapters 16 to 18) with a man who, if not a saint, possesses (at least ostensibly) many saintly qualities: Don Diego de Miranda.[52] Unlike the 'little discalced friars' mentioned by Sancho in Chapter 8, with their 'cadenas de hierro con que ceñían y atormentaban sus cuerpos' (756) ('the iron chains they girded and tormented their bodies with'),[53] he is not a member of a religious order, but a married man, of some social standing and substance, living in the world; unlike the friars, and unlike the 'santos caballeros' (warrior saints) whose images Don Quixote contemplates in Chapter 58, his life is one marked by quiet moderation rather than spectacularly harsh penance or heroically virtuous action.[54] Don Quixote's reactions to and interactions with Don Diego are remarkable for several reasons: first, he has never before shown such a degree of attention to, or appreciation of, another person in his or her own right:[55] 'si mucho miraba el de lo verde a don Quijote, mucho más miraba don Quijote al de lo verde, pareciéndole hombre de chapa' (820) ('if the man in green gazed at Don Quixote, Don Quixote gazed even more at the man in green, thinking that he must be a fine upright citizen').[56] It seems that Cervantes's emphasis in this passage on the act of looking, conveyed through the repeated use of the verbs 'mirar' and 'admirar', together with the etymological significance of Don Diego's surname, 'Miranda', is intended to suggest that the meeting has for each man a specular quality, and that, at least in part, Don Quixote is initially drawn to Don Diego because of an unconscious recognition of physical similarity ('La edad mostraba ser de cincuenta años; las canas, pocas, y el rostro, aguileño' (820) ('He seemed to be about fifty, with not many hairs turned grey, [and] the face of an eagle')[57]). However, the narrator seems to make it clear that what principally attracts him is a sense of the other man's goodness: he strikes him at once as being an 'hombre de chapa'. This impression tallies with the narrator's comment that 'en el traje y apostura daba a entender ser hombre de buenas prendas' (820) ('his clothes and his demeanour made him seem like a man of admirable qualities').[58] A second remarkable feature of Don Quixote's initial response to meeting Don Diego is the unusual level of self-consciousness that it seems to provoke in him: he is acutely aware of being looked at — 'Notó bien don Quijote la atención con que el caminante le miraba' (820) ('Don Quixote noted the care with which the traveller was examining him')[59] — , and of how strange he is likely to appear in the eyes of the other man:

> Esta figura que vuesa merced en mí ha visto, por ser tan nueva y tan fuera de las que comúnmente se usan, no me maravillaría yo de que le hubiese maravillado [...] así que [...] ni la amarillez de mi rostro, ni mi atenuada flaqueza, os podrá admirar de aquí adelante, habiendo ya sabido quién soy y la profesión que hago. (820, 821)

> (The appearance that I present to you is so strange and out of the ordinary that it would not surprise me to learn that it has filled you with wonder [...] and thus [...] [neither] the pallor of my face, nor my extreme thinness should surprise you from henceforth, now that you know who I am and the profession I follow.)[60]

Likewise, a little later, after his abortive attempt to do battle with the caged lions, he shows that he is conscious of how reckless and unhinged his behaviour must have seemed to his host: '¿Quién duda, señor don Diego de Miranda, que vuestra merced no me tenga en su opinión por un hombre disparatado y loco? Y no sería mucho que así fuese, porque mis obras no pueden dar testimonio de otra cosa' (839) ('Who can doubt, Don Diego de Miranda sir, that your opinion of me is that I am a man who is both foolish and mad? And it would be no wonder, if you did, because it is the only conclusion to be drawn from my deeds').[61] As mentioned earlier, this awareness of being perceived as mad recalls his reaction to the barber's tale of 'el loco de Sevilla' in II. 1, but with some notable differences: in this case, there is no mention of Don Diego (unlike the barber) having given any indication, overt or subtle, that he does think Don Quixote mad, and although the knight goes on vehemently to defend his sanity, he acknowledges that it is perfectly reasonable and understandable for Don Diego to think that he is so. Quite unlike Don Quixote, Don Diego, by his own account, leads a life marked by attention to his family and friends ('paso la vida con mi mujer y con mis hijos y con mis amigos' (822–23) ('I spend my time with my wife, my children and my friends')[62]), prudent moderation, balance, and moral probity ('ni gusto de murmurar ni consiento que delante de mí se murmure; no escudriño las vidas ajenas ni soy lince de los hechos de los otros') ('I neither like to gossip, nor do I allow others to gossip in my presence; I make no scrutiny of others' lives, nor do I spy on their deeds')), religious faith and devotion ('oigo misa cada día'; 'soy devoto de Nuestra Señora y confío siempre en la misericordia infinita de

Dios Nuestro Señor') ('I hear mass every day'; 'I am a devotee of Our Lady, and I trust forever in the infinite mercy of Our Lord God')), and to the good of the wider community ('reparto de mis bienes con los pobres'; 'procuro poner en paz los que sé que están desavenidos' (823) ('I distribute my wealth aming the poor'; 'I strive to make peace among those who have quarreled')[63]). We may note, too, that he is conscious (as, in theory, is Don Quixote — we recall his words in Chapter 8: 'Hemos de matar en los gigantes a la soberbia [...]') of the need to exercise constant vigilance 'por no dar entrada en mi corazón a la hipocresía y vanagloria, enemigos que blandamente se apoderan del corazón más recatado' (823)[64] ('so as not to allow hypocrisy and vainglory into my heart, for they are enemies that steal into the wariest breast').[65] He may not be a saint as Sancho, naively and amusingly, thinks him to be ('me parece vuesa merced el primer santo a la jineta que he visto en todos los días de mi vida' (823) ('to my mind you're the first saint riding Arab-style I've ever come across in all the days of my born life')[66] but the evidence of his uniquely kind behaviour towards Don Quixote — his careful and balanced assessment of his character ('un cuerdo loco y un loco que tiraba a cuerdo' (II. 17, 838) ('a sane man with madness in him, and as a madman with sane tendencies')[67]), the patience he shows him, and his hospitality — suggests that he is indeed an 'hombre de chapa', the kind of person, in fact, that Don Quixote could and should have been.[68] In Don Diego's presence — perhaps stimulated by it? — , Don Quixote seems, at moments, to come closer than ever to sanity. Paradoxically, however, his attempt to do battle with the lions is one of the most extravagant manifestations of his madness in Part Two. As the epigraph to the Chapter 17 ironically puts it, it is an episode about 'el último punto y estremo adonde llegó y pudo llegar [su] inaudito ánimo' (829) ('about events that revealed the very highest peak ever reached by Don Quixote's unprecedented courage').[69] In like manner, Don Quixote's overall reaction to Don Diego is contradictory: he finds him to be an attractive person and enjoys his four-day stay in his house, but shows no inclination to consider taking him as a model, or to abandon his pursuit of knightly adventure and glory in favour of a life of quiet moderation. In fact, when Don Diego tries to dissuade him, through rational argument, from confronting the lions, Don Quixote's rudely dismissive response — 'Váyase vuesa merced, señor hidalgo [...], a entender con su perdigón manso y con su hurón atrevido, y deje a cada uno hacer su oficio' (832) ('Sir hidalgo [...], pray go away and play with your tame decoy partridge and your intrepid ferret, and let others proceed with their own business')[70] — reveals an underlying contempt for what he obviously regards as Don Diego's insufficiently heroic virtue.

Bearing this in mind, it scarcely seems accidental that when, in Chapter 58, Don Quixote is brought, for a second time, explicitly to confront the relationship between sanctity and chivalry, one of the four images of 'santos caballeros' (warrior saints) that he inspects is that of St Paul. This image acquires special prominence, and is differentiated from the others, in several ways: it is the last one presented for Don Quixote's inspection; unlike St George, St Martin of Tours, and St James (the Great), St Paul was not, and is not represented as, a soldier, and only as a 'caballero' in the most literal sense. Instead of being shown seated confidently on his horse and engaged in heroic military or even charitable action, he is portrayed falling from it in the humiliating yet sublime moment of his conversion.[71] Not surprisingly, Don Quixote is particularly enthusiastic in his appraisal of the obviously heroic images of St George and St James: the former, for him, is 'uno de los mejores andantes que tuvo la milicia divina' ('one of the finest errants in the heavenly army') and, as a 'defendedor de doncellas' (II. 58, 1197) ('defender of maidens'),[72] an exemplar of chivalry; the latter, 'uno de los más valientes santos y caballeros que tuvo el mundo y tiene agora el cielo' (1197) ('one of the bravest saints and knights who once lived in this world and now live in heaven').[73] On the other hand, and again not surprisingly, given Don Quixote's proclivities, his reaction to the image of St Martin, shown dressed as a soldier, but giving part of his cloak to a beggar rather than engaged in combat, is rather more lukewarm: 'Este caballero también fue de los aventureros cristianos, y creo que fue más liberal que valiente' (1197)[74] ('This knight was another of the Christian adventurers, and in my opinion he was more generous than courageous').[75] It is notable, then, that he should, perhaps unexpectedly, reserve his highest, most extended and elaborate praise for St Paul, the saint who was not a soldier but who invented the metaphor of the Christian as soldier and, clearly aware of the purely figurative sense of 'caballero andante por la vida' (1198) ('a knight errant in life'),[76] eulogize him as a defender of the Church. It is remarkable, too, that he should evoke him in terms that recall St Paul's own words: 'doctor de las gentes'[77] ('the teacher of the Gentiles')[78]; 'a quien sirvieron de escuelas los cielos y de catedrático y maestro que le enseñase el mismo Jesucristo' (1198)[79] ('with heaven as his school and Jesus Christ himself as his Master').[80] Before considering the implications of Don Quixote's encounter with the image of St Paul, and of the fact that it is the last of the images that he views, we need to remind ourselves of some of the key features of the episode in general. For both Don Quixote and Sancho, it has been an unusually pleasant one: Don Quixote hails it, first, as a 'buen agüero' (1198) ('good omen'),[81] and then, more cautiously, but equally appreciatively, as a 'felicísimo acontecimiento' (1200) ('a most happy coincidence').[82] Sancho declares the encounter to be 'de las más suaves y dulces que en todo el discurso de nuestra peregrinación nos ha sucedido' (1199) ('one of the gentlest and mildest ones we've ever had in the whole course of our wanderings').[83] Both speak of it as an usually privileged act of seeing: 'Por buen agüero he tenido, hermanos, haber visto lo que he visto' (1198) (Don Quixote)[84] ('I consider it a good omen, my friends, to have seen what I have just seen');[85] 'Bendito sea Dios, que tal me ha dejado ver con mis propios ojos' (1199) (Sancho) ('God be blessed for letting me see such a marvel with my own two eyes').[86] Other circumstantial factors are likely to have heightened both men's strong sense of the pleasantness of the event. First, it comes directly after they have left the palace of the Duke and Duchess; they find themselves in the open countryside ('en la campaña rasa' (1195)), and Don Quixote is starting to enjoy a sense of freedom regained: 'libre y desembarazado de los requiebros de Altisidora, le pareció que estaba en su centro y que los espíritus se le renovaban para proseguir de nuevo el asumpto de sus caballerías' (1195) ('free at last from Altisodora's amorous advances, he felt that he was in his own element again, and that his spirits were reviving for the fresh pursuit of his chivalresque goals').[87] Second, the setting for the encounter is a pleasant green meadow ('un pradillo verde' (1196)), and the atmosphere is the relaxed one of a picnic: 'encima de la yerba [...], encima de sus capas, estaban comiendo hasta una docena de hombres vestidos de labradores' (1196) ('about a dozen men in farmers' clothes [were] sitting on their cloaks on the grass [...] eating').[88] The inspection of the images provokes a rare moment of apparent humility in Don Quixote, as he admits that his achievements pale into insignificance in comparison with those of the four saints:

> la diferencia que hay entre mí y ellos es que ellos fueron santos y pelearon a lo divino y yo soy pecador y peleo a lo humano. Ellos conquistaron el cielo a fuerza de brazos, porque el cielo padece fuerza, y yo hasta agora no sé lo que conquisto a fuerza de mis trabajos. (1198)
>
> (the difference between them and me is that they were saints, and fought in the manner of angels, and I am a sinner, and fight in the manner of men. They conquered heaven by force of arms, for heaven suffers violence, and so far I do not know what I conquer by force of toils.)[89]

This amounts to an acknowledgement that he has not engaged in the kind of spiritual warfare that he eulogized in Chapter 8, but rather pursued what he called 'la vanidad de la fama que en este presente y acabable siglo se alcanza' (754) ('the vanity of the fame that can be achieved in this present transient life').[90] It seems for a moment that he has come to a real turning point, but his very next words show that this is not the case: 'pero si mi Dulcinea del Toboso saliese de los [trabajos] que padece, mejorándose mi ventura y adobándoseme el juicio, podría ser que encaminase mis pasos por mejor camino del que llevo' (1198) ('but if my Dulcinea del Toboso were to be delivered from her own toils, it could well be that my luck would change, and my understanding would improve, and I should direct my steps along a better road than I am following at present').[91] Clearly, Don Quixote's belief in his mission and in Dulcinea and her enchanted state remains as strong as ever. However, he also speaks about his judgement being set right and the possibility of his following a better path in future. These are ambiguous remarks. Read in the context of his observations about the saints, it looks as though they might add up to an admission, however fleeting, of his folly, and of a need to reorder his life in a completely different direction; yet, in the immediate context of his words about Dulcinea, it seems that they refer rather to a need to be more judicious — perhaps more like the saints — in his practice of knight errantry itself.[92] Whichever way one interprets them, it is clear that viewing the images of the saints has inspired in Don Quixote a moment of unprecedentedly humble self-reflection and awareness of limitation. Why did Cervantes create this encounter and order it in this way? It seems obvious that it harks back to the debate between Don Quixote and Sancho in Chapter 8 which underscores the tension between chivalry and sanctity, implying, in turn, that this is a thematically significant question. On this occasion, a humbler Don Quixote, disillusioned by the enchantment of Dulcinea and the experience of the Cave of Montesinos, and wearied by his stay with the Duke and Duchess, comes a little closer to acknowledging that there may be a better way of life, or at least a better way of carrying out his mission.[93]

The significance of the episode comes into yet sharper focus when we take account of two motifs and an associated thematic strand, recurrent throughout Part Two, which resurface here: the motifs of omens, of rising and falling, and the theme of Fortune. Having at first hailed the encounter with the images of the saints as a 'good omen', Don Quixote almost immediately afterwards dismisses as superstitious the belief in omens, which, when they seem favourable, should, he says, rather be called 'buenos acontecimientos' (1199) ('mere happy coincidences'),[94] leading him to conclude that what he has just experienced is a 'felicísimo acontecimiento'. As his anecdote about the man who retreats into his house on catching sight of a Franciscan friar (superstitiously considered unlucky) (II. 58, 1199) indicates, his quarrel is not with the notion that an apparently fortuitous encounter may have a special significance — even a transcendent one — but with the belief that it is a predictor of particular future events; it is not that heaven does not ordain certain conjunctions of circumstances, but that one should be very careful about ascribing particular meanings to them: 'El discreto y cristiano no ha de andar en puntillos con lo que quiere hacer el cielo' (1199) ('The wise Christian shouldn't pry into what heaven intends to do').[95] In proof of this, he cites the famous story of Scipio Africanus's fall on reaching the shores of Africa, an accident interpreted by his men as a bad omen, but by him as a positive one — his close contact with the land as he covered it with his body signifying his future dominion over it. Of course, the last of the images that Don Quixote has just inspected, and the sight of which he called a 'good omen', depicted St Paul falling from his horse. Although Don Quixote himself does not make any connection between them, readers surely must? This is particularly the case because falls and descents form such a significant part of Don Quixote's trajectory in Part Two: he is brought to the ground in the episode of 'Las Cortes de la Muerte' (Chapter 11), descends into the Cave of Montesinos (Chapter 22), falls into the river Ebro (Chapter 29), falls from his horse on his first meeting with the Duke and Duchess (Chapter 30), is thrown off Clavileño (Chapter 41), knocked down and trampled by bulls shortly after his encounter with the images of the saints (Chapter 58), thrown off his horse as he enters Barcelona (Chapter 61), left sprawling on his back on the beach of Barcelona by Sansón Carrasco (Chapter 64), and, finally, is run over by pigs in the same spot where he had previously been trampled by bulls (Chapter 68).[96] Although Don Quixote does not mean it quite literally, clearly, there is more literal truth than he might care to acknowledge in his words to Don Diego de Miranda about the manner of his career (as there is a lack of it with regard to the substance): 'ha muchos días que tropezando aquí, cayendo allí, despeñándome acá y levantándome acullá, he cumplido gran parte de mi deseo, socorriendo viudas [...]' (821) ('for some time now, stumbling here, falling there, I have in large measure been fulfilling my desires, succouring widows [...]').[97] The falls Don Quixote experiences towards the end of Part Two are increasingly humiliating and his reaction to them shifts from indignation towards ever greater resignation, sometimes verging on despair. If we look at the episodes of his trampling by bulls, his defeat on the beach of Barcelona, and his trampling by pigs, this pattern can be seen to emerge clearly.

Rising and Falling

The trampling by the bulls, which follows on Don Quixote's meeting with the 'shepherds and shepherdesses' enacting their version of Arcadia, would not have happened if he had not insisted on carrying out his 'arrogante y nunca visto ofrecimento' (II. 58, 1207) ('arrogant and unprecedented gesture')[98] to stand for two days in the middle of the road and, against all comers, uphold his claim that the 'señoras zagalas contrahechas que aquí están son las más hermosas doncellas y más corteses que hay en el mundo, excetando solo a la sin par Dulcinea del Toboso' (1206)[99] ('these [...] damsels disguised as shepherdesses are the most beautiful and courteous maidens in the world, only excepting the peerless Dulcinea del Toboso').[100] When a group of men (some armed with lances) at the head of a herd of bulls and oxen bears down on him at great speed,[101] he refuses to heed the warning to get of their way, abuses them as 'wretches' and 'knaves', haughtily dismisses the danger posed by the animals as insignificant ('para mí no hay toros que valgan, aunque sean de los más bravos que cría Jarama en sus riberas' (1208) ('I care nothing for bulls [...], even if they are the fiercest bulls ever bred on the banks of the Jarama')[102]), and insists that they admit the truth of his claim about Dulcinea or take the consequences ('Confesad, malandrines, así, a carga cerrada [an all too well-chosen expression] que es verdad lo que yo aquí he publicado; si no, conmigo sois en batalla' (1208) (Confess, in one fell swoop, you scoundrels, that what I've proclaimed here is true; or, if not, into battle with you!). Even though his anger and embarrassment — he is described as 'encendido el rostro y colérico' ('his face flushed with fury') — at Sancho's earlier, well-meant but clumsily prefaced, praise of him ('¿Es posible que haya en el mundo personas que se atrevan a decir y a jurar que este mi señor es loco?' (1206) ('Can there really be people in this world who dare to say and to swear that master of mine's a madman?')[103] goes some way to explain his behaviour, it is exceptionally foolhardy, and, thus, seems to mark another reversion to the kind of violently deranged behaviour that we associate with him in Part One.[104] Yet, in a sense, this is worse: when he attacks the flocks of sheep in I. 18 he thinks that they are the armies of Alifanfarón and Pentapolín, but in this case he knows what he is facing. Even when the drovers and their herd have passed over him, sending him rolling head-over-heels on the ground, he continues to abuse them: 'a gran priesa, tropezando aquí y cayendo allí, comenzó a correr tras la vacada, diciendo a voces: — ¡Deteneos y esperad, canalla malandrina, que un solo caballero os espera!' (1208) ('Don Quixote started running after the herd of bulls, stumbling here and falling there, and crying: "Stop, stay, you scurvy knaves: it is but one solitary knight awaiting you!"').[105] The punishment for his arrogance is the supremely humiliating one of being completely ignored: 'Pero no por eso se detuvieron los apresurados corredores, ni hicieron más caso de sus amenazas que de las nubes de antaño' (1208)[106] ('But this didn't make the hasty travellers stop, and they paid no more attention to his threats than to last year's clouds').[107] A sense of weary melancholy — of a world (that of Don Quixote's fantasies) passing away — is transmitted through Cervantes's allusion to the 'nubes de ataño', the mention of Don Quixote sitting down on the ground ('más enojado que vengado' ('more enraged than avenged')) as he waits for Sancho to fetch their animals, and the laconic description (with its artfully deployed reference to the 'false and pretend' Arcadia) of their departure from the scene: 'Llegaron, volvieron a subir amo y mozo, y sin volver a despedirse de la Arcadia fingida o contrahecha y con más vergüenza que gusto, siguieron su camino' (1208) ('They came; master and servant remounted; and without turning back to say goodbye to the make-believe Arcadia, and feeling more shame than satisfaction, they continued on their way').[108]

Don Quixote's most physically and symbolically significant fall — it is described as a dangerous one ('peligrosa caída') (II. 64, 1267) — occurs, of course, when he is defeated on the beach of Barcelona by the Knight of the White Moon (Sansón Carrasco). In effect, although he is not aware of it, it marks the definitive end of his career as a knight errant, and it is simultaneously amusing, sad, and appropriate that, when he continues to insist on Dulcinea's peerless beauty and asks to be killed, his voice, emerging from within the confines of his completely closed up helmet, should be said to sound 'como si hablara dentro de una tumba' (1267)[109] ('as from inside a grave').[110] His reaction to the defeat is eloquently expressed in his conversation with Sancho as they depart the city:

> Al salir de Barcelona, volvió don Quijote a mirar el sitio donde había caído y dijo:
> — ¡Aquí fue Troya! ¡Aquí mi desdicha, y no mi cobardía, se llevó mis alcanzadas glorias, aquí usó la fortuna conmigo de sus vueltas y revueltas, aquí se escurecieron mis hazañas, aquí finalmente cayó mi ventura para jamás levantarse! (II. 66, 1275)
>
> (As they left Barcelona, Don Quixote turned back to gaze at the place where he had fallen, and said:
> 'Here once stood Troy! Here my bad luck, and not my cowardice, deprived me of the glory I had won; here did I feel the fickleness of fortune; here the lustre of my exploits was obscured: here, in short, my joy came crashing to the ground, never again to rise!')[111]

The emphasis on his fall ('el sitio donde había caído'; '¡Aquí fue Troya!'; 'aquí finalmente cayó mi ventura'), and Don Quixote's references to Fortune ('mi desdicha'; 'la fortuna'; 'mi ventura') preface a discussion of Fortune itself.[112] In response to Sancho's amusingly and characteristically earthy dismissal of her as 'una mujer borracha y antojadiza, y sobre todo ciega' (1275) ('a flighty woman who drinks too much, and, what's more, she's blind'),[113] Don Quixote (not always so orthodox on this point)[114] insists on the Christian view that 'no hay fortuna en el mundo' ('there's no such thing as fortune'): 'las cosas que en él suceden, buenas o malas que sean, [no] vienen acaso, sino por particular providencia de los cielos' (1276)[115] ('whatever happens in this world, good and bad, does not occur by chance, but by special providence of heaven').[116] This implies, he claims, that each person, having the duty and the freedom to react appropriately to unforeseen external events, is the 'artífice de su ventura' ('architect of his own fortune') and he concludes that he has made a bad job of this: 'Yo lo he sido de la mía, pero no con la prudencia necesaria, y, así, me han salido al gallarín mis presunciones' (1276) ('And I have been the architect of mine, but not with the necessary prudence, and so my presumption has led to disaster').[117] As with his reaction to the images of the saints, it seems for a moment that his unusually humble references to his own lack of prudence and his 'presunciones' might indicate that he now recognizes the folly of his whole undertaking. But, once again, this is not so; his very next words reveal that what he laments is not some overarching intellectual or moral failing, but merely a tactical miscalculation:[118]

> pues debiera pensar que al poderoso grandor del caballo del de la Blanca Luna no podía resistir la flaqueza de Rocinante. Atrevíme en fin, hice lo que pude, derribáronme, y, aunque perdí la honra, no perdí, ni puedo perder, la virtud de cumplir mi palabra. Cuando era caballero andante, atrevido y valiente, con mis obras y con mis manos acreditaba mis hechos; y agora, cuando soy escudero pedestre, acreditaré mis palabras cumpliendo la que di de mi promesa. Camina, pues, amigo Sancho, y vamos a tener en nuestra tierra el año del noviciado, con cuyo encerramiento cobraremos virtud nueva para volver al nunca de mí olvidado ejercicio de las armas. (II. 66, 1276)

> (because I should have realized that my feeble Rocinante couldn't stand up to the mighty bulk of the horse of the Knight of the White Moon. But I took him on, I did what I could, I was overthrown and although I lost my honour I did not lose, nor can I lose, the virtue of having kept my word. When I was a knight errant, brave and bold, I used to verify my own deeds with my arm and my actions, and now that I am a common squire, I shall verify my own words by keeping the promise that I made. Forward, then, Sancho my friend, and we shall spend our year of mortification in our own land, and in our exclusion we shall gain new strength to return to the profession of arms, which I shall never forget.)[119]

His belief and his pride in his knightly prowess and honour remain very much intact, and he fully intends to resume his chivalric career once the year of enforced retirement is over.

Don Quixote's final and, in a symbolic sense, most humiliating, fall comes in Chapter 68, when he is trampled by a herd of pigs, in the same place (as previously noted) in which he was earlier trampled by the bulls.[120] The similarity between these episodes and the coincidence of place is clearly designed to invite comparison, and, perhaps more importantly, contrast.[121] On this occasion, Don Quixote had not been looking for adventure (or trouble) as indeed he is not allowed to do, but simply sitting chatting peacefully and companionably with Sancho about the nature of sleep and Sancho's unusually eloquent observations on the subject. He only rises and reaches for his sword when he hears 'un sordo estruendo y un áspero ruido, que por todos aquellos valles se estendía' (II. 78, 1290) ('a dull rumble and then a strident cacophony spreading throughout the surrounding valleys')[122] which makes him anticipate some terrible danger and feel the urgent need to defend himself. The deafening noise ('el gruñir y el bufar') (1290) ('the grunting and the snorting')[123] comes from a herd of more than six hundred pigs being driven to market. Before he has time to see what they are, or to get out of their way, 'sin tener respeto a la autoridad de don Quijote, ni a la de Sancho' ('showing no respect for Don Quixote's authority, or for Sancho's') the 'estendida y gruñidora piara' ('the far-spread grunting herd') has passed over them. It is all over in seconds, leaving the two men and their mounts lying flattened on the ground: 'El tropel, el gruñir, la presteza con que llegaron los animales inmundos, puso en confusión y por el suelo a la albarda, a las armas, al rucio, a Rocinante, a Sancho y a don Quijote' (1290) ('This grunting, stampeding herd of of unclean animals appearing from nowhere threw the packsaddle, the armour, the dun, Rocinante, Sancho and Don Quixote into confusion and on to the ground').[124] The word order here is significant. Instead of running in descending hierarchical sequence from greatest to least — from human beings (Don Quixote and Sancho), to animals (Rocinante and the *rucio*), to objects ('las armas' and 'la albarda') — the systematic reversal of that ordering serves to underline the completeness of Don Quixote's humiliation, and the turning upside down and overthrow of his whole world by the action of animals considered to be 'immundo[s] y sucio[s]'.[125] On this occasion, however, he shows no signs of anger, does not get to his feet and makes no attempt to seek to restore his honour. In fact, further amplifying the motif of reversal, it is Sancho who asks to take up his master's sword and (deploying a mangled version of his chivalresque language) informs him that he wants to kill 'media docena de aquellos señores y descomedidos puercos' (1290–91) ('half a dozen of those great unmannerly swine'),[126] and it is Don Quixote who urges him to desist, accepting abjectly that this humiliation is but his due as a defeated knight: 'que esta afrenta es pena de mi pecado, y justo castigo del cielo es que a un caballero andante vencido le coman adivas y le piquen avispas y le hollen puercos' (1290) ('this affront is a chastisement for my sin, and it is heaven's just punishment of a vanquished knight errant for jackals to eat him, wasps to sting him and pigs to trample him').[127] His reaction to this event is, therefore, very different to that of his previous trampling by the bulls: he is much more chastened, and shows much greater humility, but still the same strength of delusion. Even though he speaks of 'mi pecado' and the 'justo castigo del cielo', it seems that he does not intend these terms in their conventional religious sense: his 'sin' is to have been defeated in combat, since in the books of chivalry defeat is often figured allegorically as a sign of, and punishment for, sin. The extreme nature, and bizarre combination, of what he considers the proper agents — 'adivas', 'avispas', 'puercos' — of this divine punishment, also speak of a still very disturbed mind. In all three of these epsiodes, then, we see a pattern emerge — a curious combination of movement and stasis — whereby a progressively humbled and self-doubting Don Quixote seems momentarily to come to the verge of self-knowledge and sanity but, in every case, ends up showing himself to be as deluded as ever.

Fortune and Providence

Through these references to punishment for sin and presumption, Cervantes depicts a world in which characters and narrator believe in a world ruled by Providence, in which pride comes before a fall and in which heaven uses such falls to purify and restore the soul.[128] As Roque Guinart puts it, when trying to draw Don Quixote out of his deep melancholy:

> Valeroso caballero, no os despechéis ni tengáis a siniestra fortuna esta en que os halláis, que podía ser que en estos tropiezos vuestra torcida suerte se enderezase:

que el cielo, por estraños y nunca vistos rodeos, de los hombres no imaginados, suele levantar los caídos y enriquecer los pobres. (II. 60, 1223).

('Valiant knight, do not take umbrage or consider the present setback as some piece of ill luck, because it could well happen that this stumble straightens the crooked path of your fortune; for heaven, in strange, mysterious, roundabout ways, inconceivable to man, raises the fallen and makes the poor wealthy.')[129]

But is this a view of the world that informs the novel as a work of art, and which it vindicates? The culture and time in which it was written, the evidence of Cervantes's biography, and of his other works, might suggest that this is not at all improbable. However, Eduardo Urbina's cautionary words about the widespread tendency to extrapolate Cervantes's views about Fortune from what his characters say about it (notably, 'Cada uno es hijo de sus obras' (I. 4, 70) ('every man is the child of his own deeds')[130], and 'Cada hombre es artífice de su fortuna' (II. 66, 1276) ('every man is the architect of his own fortune')[131]) are equally relevant to discussions of Providence:

> Arriesgado resulta siempre al enfrentarse a un texto irónico-burlesco como el *Quijote* intentar buscar claves consistentes para su interpretación, aunque se trate de una tan omnipresente y fiable como la Fortuna. Pero particularmente fallido en este caso es el extrapolar citas ignorando el contexto paródico de la narración y su desarrollo narrativo. [...] Caso diferente es lo ocurrido en obras como *Numancia*, *Persiles* y *La fuerza de la sangre* en donde género e intención son bien manifestos y no interfieren igualmente la ironía y la parodia.[132]

> (It is always risky, when dealing with an ironic-burlesque text like the *Quixote*, to try to find consistent keys to its interpretation, even if it is one as omnipresent and reliable as Fortune. But, in this case, it is particularly wide of the mark to extrapolate quotations while disregarding the parodic context of the narration and its narrative development. [...] It is a different matter in the case of works like *Numancia*, *Persiles*, and *La fuerza de la sangre* where genre and intention are quite clear and where irony and parody do not interfere in the same way.)

It is only through the internal evidence of the text itself that the question can properly be approached. We have observed that falls (and, if we think of them more broadly as descents, we may include the Cave of Montesinos episode among them) are a consistent feature of Don Quixote's progress throughout Part Two, are often (literally) humiliating, and associated with his ever-deepening melancholy and sense of disillusionment. As events occurring within the fiction, most of them are accidents, but accidents caused ultimately, if not immediately, by Don Quixote's fantasy that he is a knight errant, a fantasy rooted in his pride: thus, for example, he falls off Rocinante as he rides forward to meet the Duke and Duchess because, in his preoccupation with making a good impression ('Don Quijote se gallardeó en la silla, púsose bien en los estribos, acomodóse la visera, arremetió a Rocinante y con gentil denuedo fue a besar las manos a la duquesa'(II. 30, 958) ('Don Quixote sat himself upright and stately in his saddle, made his feet firm in the stirrups, adjusted his visor, spurred Rocinante forward and rode with graceful demeanour to kiss the Duchess's hands')[133]), he fails to notice that Sancho has not yet arrived to help him dismount. Even in the cases where it appears that his fall occurs purely as the result of the more or less malicious interference of others, as in the episodes of 'Las Cortes de la Muerte' (II. 11) and his first entry into Barcelona (II. 61), their interference is provoked (if not justified) by the extravagant strangeness of his words and physical appearance, and, in the second case, by his fame as a bizarre literary character. The only exception is his trampling by the pigs (II. 68), when he is a purely accidental victim, and which happens when he is no longer acting as a knight. We can also point to two other related overarching patterns: first, towards the end of Part Two, Don Quixote's physical or geographical trajectory moves in a consistently downwards direction; he descends to the banks of the river Ebro — twice plunging to the bottom — before travelling on to Barcelona and suffering defeat there at the lowest possible point on land — where it meets the sea;[134] and, second, the deeper he descends into melancholy, and the more he is humiliated, the more his pride (which does not disappear) is softened.

Acknowledging that these patterns exist does not, however, necessarily mean accepting that Providence plays a role in Don Quixote's physical and emotional journey. Urbino, for example, who traces the *altibajos* of the knight's career in detail and believes that, as a motif, they constitute 'un centro de significación clave de cara a la interpretación del *Quijote*' (a key locus of meaning with regard to the interpretation of the *Quixote*), and, further, that they correspond to a moral pattern whereby the 'caídas físicas, humillaciones y reveses' (physical falls, humiliations and setbacks) which are a 'consecuencia de la locura del hidalgo y sus "altas caballerías"' (a consequence of hidalgo's madness and his 'high chivalric deeds') and also 'permiten una segunda trayectoria de ascenso en la que don Quijote, aún si dejar de ser "hijo de sus obras" llega a ser imprevistamente "vencedor de sí mismo"' (allow a second ascending trajectory through which, without ceasing to be 'the child of his deeds', Don Quixote comes, unexpectedly, to be a 'victor over himself'), contends nonetheless that

> en contraste con el devenir de Amadís de Gaula, para quien los cambios de Fortuna tienen un sentido providencial, en el *Quijote* los altibajos marcan certeramente la dirección y sentido de las aventuras del nuevo caballero a través de una serie de inversiones burlescas que niegan precisamente lo sobrenatural-maravilloso como agente de la ficción.[135]
>
> (in contrast with the progess of Amadís de Gaula, for whom shifts of Fortune have a providential sense, the ups and downs in the *Quixote* accurately plot the direction and meaning of the adventures of the new knight through a series of burlesque inversions that precisely negate the 'supernatural-marvellous' as an agent in the fiction.)

Urbina's view that, in the *Quixote*, Cervantes undermined not only the literary conventions of the romances of chivalry but also the view of the world that underpinned them is one shared by a significant number of scholars.[135] However, the fact that Providence is not explicitly and authoritatively said to order particular events, and the absence, or even the parody, in Don *Quixote*, of acts of miraculous supernatural intervention, may have more to do with Cervantes's objections (as a writer concerned with verisimilitude) to the exaggerated and trivializing way in which they are presented in the romances than with any deeper doubts about the existence and agency of Providence itself. As John J. Allen has put it, 'the distinction between novel and romance based upon the presence or absence of Providence in the fictional world would seem to be an oversimplification'. He argues, further, that Cervantes's 'providential arrangement of events [...] is the mildest conceivable use of the Christian supernatural — a domain on the frontiers of the verisimilar explicitly sanctioned by the literary theorists of the day', and, in general terms, that

> in *Don Quixote* Cervantes has steered a middle course between the world of *Amadís* and *La Diana* — a world controlled from without — and that of *Lazarillo* and *Guzmán de Alfarache* — a world out of control. It is a world in which man is autonomous, but not abandoned.[137]

In response to Urbina's particular point about Don Quixote's reversals leading to his becoming 'vencedor de sí mismo', it may be objected that, although his demeanour and attitude do change as result of repeated humiliations and disappointments, his recovery of sanity is not something that he chooses or achieves for himself; rather, at least as he believes, it is 'el poderoso Dios [...] que tanto bien me ha hecho' (II. 74) ('Almighty God, who has done me such good').[138] It is at this point that we come back to the questions of the apparent abruptness of his recovery-conversion, and how it affects and is affected by our reading of what has gone before in Part Two. Williamson, who acknowledges that this mysterious event is presented as a miracle, sees it as a purely functional (and opportunistic?) last-minute reversion to romance convention, as something

> which supervenes at the very end as a kind of *deus ex machina*. It is this sudden and arbitrary cure that permits Cervantes to rid the novel of the power of the Devil and bring his parody of the *libros de caballerías* to a close with a moving death-bed scene that reinserts the Quixote within the ideological framework of Catholic Spain.[139]

The cure is certainly sudden, but because the fact of its happening and the manner in which it happens represent the confluence, and the culmination and fulfilment, of the motifs and thematic patterns that we have been considering, it does not seem to be arbitrary. It happens when Don Quixote has descended into a deep, six-hour-long sleep, and the scene of his recovery and death is closely bounded by multiple references to descending movement: as they return home for the last time, he and Sancho '*bajaron* de la cuesta y se fueron a su pueblo' (II. 73, 1322)[140] ('they went down the hill towards their village');[141] Chapter 74, which is announced as being about 'cómo don Quijote *cayó* malo y del testamento que hizo y su muerte', opens with a reminder of how 'las cosas humanas [...] yendo siempre en *declinación* de sus principios hasta llegar a su último fin' (1328) ('what is human is not eternal, but is in continuous decline from its beginning to its conclusion'),[142] and closes with a valedictory reference to 'las fingidas y disparatadas historias de los libros de caballerías, que [...] *van ya tropezando y han de caer* del todo sin duda alguna' (II. 74, 1337; emphases added) ('those false, absurd histories in books of chivalry, which [...] are even now tottering, and without any doubt, will soon tumble to the ground').[143] As many commentators have observed, this descent into unconsciousness also specifically recalls and fulfils the potential for recovery hinted at in Don Quixote's dream in the Cave of Montesinos.[144] Similarly, Quixote's conversion, which he attributes to divine intervention, represents the culmination and resolution of his series of confrontations with the rival demands of chivalry and sanctity, and, in particular, the fulfilment of the potential latent in his encounter with the image of St Paul.[145] In that episode, as in the scene of Don Quixote's recovery, we find the theme of chivalry versus sanctity converging, not just with the motif of rising and falling, but also with that of omens. Don Quixote had initially interpreted his encounter with the sacred images as a 'buen agüero' and then corrected this to 'felicísimo acontecimiento' (II. 58, 1198). He did not see any connection between himself and the image of St Paul falling from his horse, and in terms of contemporary religious orthodoxy he was right to make this correction. However, the way in which Cervantes has articulated this scene — the fact that this image of a saint, who was not a 'caballero' and who elaborated the metaphor of spiritual warfare (on which Don Quixote based his speech on the subject in Chapter 8), is the last of the four inspected by him and the one that appears to impact him most — suggests that readers are invited to see a connection. The image of St Paul's conversion is not an omen pointing to a particular pre-ordained future, but one that reflects important aspects of Don Quixote's 'present': his temperament,[146] his persistent 'kicking against the pricks' of reality,[147] the pride that motivates this, and the potential concealed in the painful and humiliating but salutary consequences that flow from it. In retrospect, of course, when this potential is realized, the image does assume a prophetic aspect, as it appears to prefigure Don Quixote's being knocked off his horse on the beach of Barcelona — the reason why he returns home (even if, in intention only for a year) — and the suddenness of his conversion with the recovery of sight that it brings: 'tengo juicio ya libre y claro, sin las sombras caliginosas de la ignorancia' (II. 74, 1330) ('My mind [...] is now clear and free without those gloomy shadows of ignorance').[148] In a recent article on Don Quixote's encounter on the outskirts of his village (II. 73) with the hunted hare and the cage of crickets, and recalling that the motif of a hunted hare taking refuge under a horse is also found in the *Galatea* (Book I), Terence O'Reilly notes that St Anselm is said to have had a similar experience, and cites the allegorical interpretation of it attributed to him: 'the hare is an image of a dying man, pursued by evil spirits.' He observes, further, that 'it is not difficult [...] to see in the hare's anguish a symbol of his [Don Quixote's] history [his preoccupation with malevolent enchanters] and his plight', and a pointer towards his impending death, in which 'he finds [...] a safe refuge, like Anselm's hare'. Thus, O'Reilly argues, although the hare and the cage of crickets do not have the meaning as 'agüeros' (related to Dulcinea) that Quixote ascribes to them, neither are they devoid of meaning, as Sancho concludes, but rather constitute an 'enigma' and 'imply that in the events of everyday life there does exist a providential order', one whose 'presence, however, is veiled'; also, because they 'communicate before they are understood', readers not acquainted with the hagiographical tradition can 'apprehend the images as significant'.[149]

Conclusion

In conclusion, it is the cumulative interaction of the themes and motifs studied here, particularly as they converge in the 'enigma' of the image of St Paul's conversion, that suggests that Don Quixote's career has been guided by the hand of Providence, or that at least permits such an interpretation. Unlike the authors of the romances of chivalry, Cervantes does not identify Providence as an agent or 'character' in the narrative, and does not pretend to know how it works, or attempt to reproduce its precise mechanics. In keeping with the spirit of Don Quixote's remark that 'El discreto y cristiano no ha de andar en puntillos con lo que quiere hacer el cielo', he appears to wish to respect its invisibility and its mystery, and confines himself to pointing towards it as an 'off-stage' presence. This is why it is appropriate and symptomatic that Don Quixote's psychological trajectory throughout Part Two, while it has a discernible overarching shape to it, is also, within the parameters of that shape, erratic, unpredictable, and arrhythmical, that his recovery should be both slow and sudden, and that the reader is not made privy to what happened in the six-hour sleep from which Don Quixote emerged as Alonso Quijano.

Notes to Chapter 9

1. Jorge Luis Borges, 'Análisis del último capítulo del *Quijote*', *Revista de la Universidad de Buenos Aires* (5ª época), 1 (1956), 29–36 (p. 36). All translations of passages from texts other than *Don Quixote* are mine, unless otherwise indicated.
2. Jorge Guillén, 'Vida y muerte de Alonso Quijano', *Romanisches Forschungen*, 64 (1952), 102–13 (p. 109).
3. Steven Hutchinson, 'Del anticlímax y sus virtudes en el *Quijote* de 1615 (la muerte parentética)', in *El 'Quijote' de 1615. Dobleces, inversiones, paradojas, desbordamientos e imposibles*, ed. by Antonio Cortijo Ocaña, Gustavo Illades Aguiar, and Francisco Ramírez Santacruz (Santa Barbara, CAL: University of California, Publications of eHumanista, 2016), pp. 120–31 (pp. 121, 127, 124).
4. 'Aunque haya algún que otro autor para quien este final no pasa de ser una chapuza rápida; o bien algo innecesario o forzado, ya que no hay nada en la dinámica fundamental del texto que "exija" la muerte del caballero, la postura general es muy otra' (Although there is the odd writer for whom this ending is nothing more than a hurried blunder; or something unnecessary and forced, since there is nothing in the text that 'requires' the death of the knight, the general critical position is quite different); Jaime Fernández, 'Visión de la crítica en el siglo XX sobre la muerte de don Quijote', *Edad de Oro*, 25 (2006), 141–55 (p. 142).
5. Borges, 'Análisis', p. 31.
6. Edwin Williamson, *The Half-way House of Fiction: 'Don Quixote' and Arthurian Romance* (Oxford: Oxford University Press, 1984), p. 123.
7. Anthony Close, *A Companion to 'Don Quixote'* (Woodbridge, UK; Rochester, NY: Tamesis, 2008), pp. 120, 121, 123. For Williamson, Don Quixote's recovery, however psychologically implausible, performs another aesthetically necessary function: that of resolving 'the punishing contradiction between pathos and parody', allowing 'the reader at last [...] to release those reserves of sympathy for the grieving knight which had been repressed so long as his obsession with chivalric romance held sway over his imagination' (*The Half-way House*, pp. 199–200).
8. See, for example, Jordi Aladro, 'La muerte de Alonso Quijano, un adiós literario', *Anales Cervantinos*, 37 (2005), 179–90; Jordi Aladro, 'La muerte de Alonso Quijano, La última imitación de Don Quijote', in *Actas del XI coloquio internacional de la Asociación de Cervantistas (Seúl, 17–20 de noviembre de 2004)*, ed. by Chul Park (Seoul: Universidad Hankuk de Estudios Extranjeros, 2005), pp. 429–39; Margit Frenk, 'Don Quijote ¿muere cuerdo?', in *Cuatro ensayos sobre el 'Quijote'*

(Mexico, D.F.: Fondo de Cultura Económica, 2013), pp. 49–58; Hutchinson, 'Del anticlímax y sus virtudes'; and Gustavo Illades, 'Locura y religión quijotescas o la doble ejemplaridad del libro (*Quijote* I y II)', in *El 'Quijote' de 1615. Dobleces, inversiones, paradojas, desbordamientos e imposibles*, ed. by Antonio Cortijo Ocaña, Gustavo Illades Aguiar, and Francisco Ramírez Santacruz (Santa Barbara, CAL: University of California, Publications of *eHumanista*, 2016), pp. 132–44.

9. As Rachel Schmidt puts it, 'Don Quijote's life only has meaning through an interpretation of his death, and so all readers must double back to reinterpret his life upon finishing the novel' ('The Performance and Hermeneutics of Death in the Last Chapter of *Don Quijote*', *Cervantes: Bulletin of the Cervantes Society of America*, 20.2 (2000), 101–26 (p.102)); and, in similar vein, Ruth Fine: 'En la hora de su muerte, don Quijote se convierte voluntaria y cristianamente, de loco, en Alonso Quijano, el Bueno, una conversión que podría estar proyectándose retrospectivamente al resto de su pasada existencia, redimiéndola o, por el contrario, ofreciendo un guiño irónico a su misma autenticidad y validez' (As his death approaches, Don Quixote changes willingly and in a Christian spirit from being mad to being Don Alonso, the Good, a conversion that, projected backwards over the rest of his former existence, could be seen to redeem it, or, on the other hand, to cast an ironic glance upon its very authenticity and validity) ('En torno a la narración paradójica o las paradojas de la conversión en el *Quijote* de 1615: los casos del morisco Ricote y de Alonso Quijano, el Bueno', in *El 'Quijote' de 1615. Dobleces, inversiones, paradojas, desbordamientos e imposibles*, ed. by Antonio Cortijo Ocaña, Gustavo Illades Aguiar, and Francisco Ramírez Santacruz (Santa Barbara, CAL: University of California, Publications of *eHumanista*, 2016), pp. 50–61 (p. 58)).

10. Miguel de Cervantes Saavedra, *The Ingenious Hidalgo Don Quixote de la Mancha*, trans. by John Rutherford (London: Penguin, 2000), p. 975. All translations from *Don Quixote* given in inverted commas, or in indented quotations, are from this edition. Otherwise, they are mine.

11. p. 975.

12. As noted by Borges: 'Aquí Cervantes renuncia instintivamente a toda sorpresa. Cervantes anuncia que don Quijote, su amigo y nuestro amigo, va a morir. Este anuncio tranquilo da por sentada la muerte del héroe y hace que la aceptemos' (Here, Cervantes instinctively renounces all sense of surprise. Cervantes announces that Don Quixote, his friend and our friend, is going to die) ('Análisis', p. 29).

13. p. 975.

14. p. 975.

15. p. 976.

16. As Trevor Dadson observes elsewhere in this volume, 'we get absorbed in the novel, all notion of time is suspended when we are reading a good novel, and when we get to the end, we feel something like a loss or bereavement, as if someone had died and left a void behind them' (p. 21). Borges (see note 5 above) also touches on this point but finds another layer to the pathos of the ending by invoking the sense of finality that is likely also to have been felt by the author: 'Cervantes, al escribir estas líneas, pudo pensar que también él estaba cerca de la muerte y que más le hubiera valido escribir libros de devoción y no de arbitraria ficción. Don Quijote se despide de sus fantásticas lecturas y viene a ser una proyección de Cervantes que se despide de su novela, también fantástica' (As he wrote these lines, Cervantes could have been reflecting that he too was close to death, and that it would have been better for him to write works of devotion instead of abitrary fiction) ('Análisis', p. 31). This view is echoed by Hutchinson, 'Del anticlímax', pp. 126–27.

17. Williamson, for example, speaks of his 'new inwardness' (*The Half-way House*, p. 173).

18. As many commentators have observed, Don Quixote, as a mythical or archetypal literary figure, has long survived the death of Alonso Quijano; in answering the related question of 'how [...] this doubly executed demise, in which the protagonist announces the death of his persona and the narrator recounts the death of the protagonist, leave[s] the story so open' by arguing that 'in the re-creation of the protagonist that the reader must then perform through the act of interpretation, Cervantes has achieved Don Quijote's desire: the survival of his name and his fame after death', Rachel Schmidt adds a new layer of depth and direction to the notion of Don Quixote's 'immortality' ('The Performance and Hermeneutics of Death', pp. 102, 123).

19. Williamson, for example, speaks of Don Quixote's recovery taking 'an inevitably abrupt and miraculous form' (*The Half-way House*, pp. 213–14).
20. p. 976.
21. p. 976.
22. pp. 976, 977.
23. p. 976.
24. p. 977.
25. p. 487.
26. p. 493.
27. p. 978.
28. For Henry W. Sullivan, this chapter 'is remarkable for its new manifesto', in that it heralds the shift whereby 'the chivalric project of Part I now becomes a salvific project in Part II' (*Grotesque Purgatory: A Study of Cervantes's 'Don Quixote', Part II* (University Park, Pennsylvania: Pennsylvania State University Press, 1996), p. 54).
29. p. 536.
30. In other words, the deadly sins. In the note *ad loc* in the second volume of the Rico et al. edition, the omission of avarice is explained by the claim that its presence would be redundant 'porque el que la practica es radicalmente indigno de ser caballero' (because anyone practising it is fundamentally unworthy to be a knight).
31. p. 527.
32. p. 533.
33. p. 537. 'Quid est facilius dicere: Dimittuntur tibi peccata tua: an dicere: Surge, et ambula?' (Matthew 9, 5) ('Whether is easier, to say, Thy sins are forgiven thee: or to say, Arise, and walk?'). In echoing these words, and testing his master in this way, Sancho, ironically, and comically, takes on the role of the scribes to whom they were uttered as a reproof.
34. p. 537.
35. p. 537.
36. p. 538.
37. Ironically, of course, Sancho will later be condemned to secure the disenchantment of Dulcinea by giving himself considerably more than two dozen lashes.
38. p. 538.
39. There are clear parallels between this conversation and that between Don Quixote and Vivaldo in I. 13, 151–54: conflating the activities of real soldiers and fictional knights errant, Don Quixote contends that the latter are 'ministros de Dios en la tierra y brazos por quien se ejecuta en ella su justicia' (151–52) ('ministers of God on earth, the arms through which his justice is executed here'; p. 97) and agrees with Vivaldo's disingenuously proffered opinion that 'aun la [profesión] de los frailes cartujos no es tan estrecha' (151) ('not even being a Carthusian monk is as strict'; p. 97). In this case, however, Don Quixote makes no reference to knights engaging in any kind of spiritual warfare. On this point, see Antonio Regalado, 'La religión de don Quijote y la fe de Alonso Quijano', in *Cervantes y las religiones: Actas del Coloquio Internacional de la Asociación de Cervantistas (Universidad Hebrea de Jerusalén, Israel, 19–21 de diciembre de 2005)*, ed. by Ruth Fine and Santiago López Navia, Biblioteca Áurea Hispánica, 51 (Madrid: Iberoamericana, 2008), pp. 199–222 (pp. 199–202).
40. 'Señor — respondió Sancho — , no soy yo religioso para que desde la mitad de mi sueño me levante y me discipline' (II. 68, 1289) ('"Sir", replied Sancho, "I'm not some monk to get up in the middle of the night and start scourging myself"'; p. 944).
41. The interchange also exemplifies Cervantes's all-pervasive thematic interest in how truth and truths are so often distorted or completely travestied by being misappropriated or misapplied amidst the emotional and motivational complexities and cross-currents of human interactions.
42. p. 584.
43. I. 4.
44. p. 27.
45. p. 536.
46. For example, Gil Pérez de Biedma (within the text itself), as noted by Anthony Lappin elsewhere in this volume (pp. 167–69).

47. Williamson argues that 'Cervantes has pre-empted the possibility of moral judgement on Don Quixote by making him not bad but mad', and that, 'since [he] is still as mad as ever when he arrives home, there is no moral to be drawn from the history of his adventures' (*The Half-way House*, pp. 211, 123). Of course, Cervantes, typically, presents Don Quixote's pride (and madness) under shifting lights: often (perhaps predominantly), as a comically exaggerated version of a universal human failing; sometimes as silly vanity; very occasionally, and then only obliquely, as something uglier and darker, as when the mention of Andrés being left for dead by his master is closely followed by: 'Y desta manera deshizo el agravio el valeroso don Quijote; el cual, contentísimo de lo sucedido, pareciéndole que había dado felicísimo y alto principio a sus caballerías, con gran satisfacción de sí mismo iba caminando hacia su aldea' (I. 4, 72) ('This was how the valiant Don Quixote redressed that wrong; and delighted with what had happened, and considering that he had made a most happy and glorious beginning to his knight-errantry, he rode towards his village full of satisfaction'; p. 45).
48. As noted, for example, in the note *ad loc.* in the second volume of the Rico et al. edition: 'El parlamento y en general la función del caballero cristiano se dejan explicar a partir de la idea paulina (Efesios, VI, 10–18) de las armas del cristiano, recogida y glosada desde antiguo' (The speech and the function of the knight in general may be explained by reference to the Pauline idea (Ephesians 6. 10–18), taken up and glossed from antiquity, of the arms of the Christian).
49. For example, Ramon Llull, in his *Llibre de l'Ordre de Cavalleria* (*c.* 1274–76).
50. Echoing St Paul, Bernard writes: 'This is, I say, a new kind of knighthood and one unknown to the ages gone by. It ceaselessly wages a twofold war both against flesh and blood and against a spiritual army of evil in the heavens'. He is scathing about the vanity inherent in the secular cult of chivalry: 'What then, O knights, is this monstrous error and what this unbearable urge which bids you fight with such pomp and labor, and all to no purpose except death and sin? You cover your horses with silk, and plume your armor with I know not what sort of rags; you paint your shields and your saddles; you adorn your bits and spurs with gold and silver and precious stones, and then in all this glory you rush to your ruin with fearful wrath and fearless folly. Are these the trappings of a warrior or are they not rather the trinkets of a woman?'; St Bernard of Clairvaux, *In Praise of the New Knighthood*, trans. by Conrad Greenia OSCO, in *The Works of Bernard of Clairvaux*, Vol. 7 (*Treatises III*) (Kalamazoo, MI: Cistercian Publications, 1977), pp. 115–67 (pp. 129, 132).
51. Regalado, 'La religión de don Quijote', p. 204.
52. Views on this character are notoriously divergent: for a listing by category ('positive', 'negative', and 'moderate'), see Augustin Redondo, 'Nuevas consideraciones sobre el personaje del Caballero del Verde Gabán (*D.Q.*, II, 16–18)', in *Actas del II Congreso Internacional de la Asociación de Cervantistas*, ed. by G. Grilli (Naples: Società Editrice Intercontinentale Gallo, 1995), pp. 513–33 (p. 513, n. 1). The division of opinion persists, in modulated form, in two relatively recently published articles: for Emilio Martínez Mata ('El caballero del verde gabán', *Monteagudo*, 20 (2015), 73–103 (pp. 95, 96)), Don Diego's life, which exemplifies all the positive qualities of 'el epicureísmo cristiano de raíz erasmista' (Erasmian inspired Christian Epicureanism), is 'sensata y productiva' (prudent and productive); for Isabel M. Roger ('Don Quijote y Roque Guinart frente al estilo de vida de los poderosos', *Anales Cervantinos*, 48 (2016), 83–201 (pp. 188, 191)), who acknowledges that he is (although not in an entirely admirable sense) 'el personaje más próximo a los ideales del Renacimiento' (the character who most approximates to the ideals of the Renaissance), his 'actitud vital [...] muestra la ociosidad que desmorona económicamente a un país que pretendía mantener un imperio' (attitude towards life [...] reveals the idleness that was causing a country seeking to maintain an empire to crumble economically).
53. p. 538.
54. However, it is not insignificant that the 'maravilloso silencio' ('marvellous silence') of his house is such that 'semejaba un monasterio de cartujos' (II. 18, 846) ('[it] made it seem like a Carthusian monastery'; p. 604). According to Martínez Mata ('El caballero del verde gabán', p. 93), his appreciation of this silence may signify 'un anticipo o parte del proceso de preparación a la renuncia definitiva que don Quijote terminará por llevar a cabo' (an anticipation or part of the preparatory process for the definitive renunciation [of chivalry] that Don Quixote will end up making).

55. The exception is Cardenio (as noted by Close, *A Companion to 'Don Quixote'*, p. 190).
56. p. 584.
57. p. 584.
58. p. 584.
59. p. 584.
60. pp. 584, 585.
61. p. 598.
62. p. 586.
63. p. 586.
64. Martínez Mata ('El caballero del verde gabán', p. 75) notes that Don Quixote's encounter with Don Diego comes immediately after his victory over Sansón Carrasco (in the guise of the Caballero de los Espejos), and that at the start of Chapter 16 the narrator places particular emphasis on the 'satisfacción que rebosa don Quijote por su reciente victoria: "Con la alegría, contento y ufanidad que se ha dicho seguía don Quijote su jornada"' (smugness over his recent victory with which Don Quixote brims: With the joy, contentment and self-satisfaction aforementioned Don Quixote continued on his way).
65. p. 586.
66. p. 586.
67. p. 597.
68. As noted by, for example, Close, *A Companion to 'Don Quixote'*, pp. 192–93.
69. p. 590.
70. p. 593.
71. As noted by María Caterina Ruta: 'En esta imagen la posición del caballero y del caballo se ha invertido con respecto a las precedentes: el santo está debajo del caballo totalmente dominado por la luz que lo rodea y la voz que le habla. La caída del caballo, en cuanto pérdida del gobierno sobre la fuerza ciega del instinto y de la pasión, tendría que simbolizar la caída en el pecado. En el caso de Saulo, en cambio, el hombre se separa del animal para someterse él mismo a otra clase de dominio que, por medio de la conversión, le llevará hacia la salvación spiritual' (In this image the positions of horseman and horse have been inverted with respect to the previous ones: the saint is beneath his horse, totally dominated by the light that surrounds him and the voice that speaks to him. In as much as it signifies loss of control over the blind force of instinct and passion, it would have to symbolize the fall into sin. In the case of Saul, on the other hand, the man separates himself from the animal in order to submit himself to another kind of dominion which, by means of conversion, will lead him towards spiritual salvation) ('Aspectos iconológicos del *Quijote*', *Nueva Revista de Filología Hispánica*, 38 (1990), 875–86 (p. 882)).
72. p. 874.
73. p. 875.
74. In her 'Lectura Comentada' of this chapter in the second volume of the Rico et al edition (pp. 210–15 (p. 213)), Margherita Morreale notes that Don Quixote may be echoing Pedro de Rivadeneira's comment on St Martin in his *Flos sanctorum* of 1599 — 'más parecía monje que soldado' (he was more like a monk than a soldier).
75. p. 875.
76. p. 875.
77. 'doctor gentium in fide et veritate' (1 Timothy 2.7) ('a teacher of the Gentiles in faith and verity').
78. p. 875.
79. 'evangelium quod evangelizatum est a me [...] non est secundum hominem [...] sed per revelationem Iesu Christi' (Galatians 1. 11–12) ('the gospel which was preached of me is not after man [...] but by the revelation of Jesus Christ').
80. p. 875.
81. p. 875.
82. p. 876.
83. p. 876.
84. The note *ad loc.* in the second volume of the Rico et al. edition posits an echo, in Don Quixote's

words, of 1 Timothy 6.16: 'Qui solus habet inmortalitatem lucem habitans inaccessibilem quem vidit nullus hominum sed nec videre potest' ('Who only hath immortality, dwelling in the light which no man can approach unto; whom no man hath seen, nor can see'). This emphasis on seeing seems to be anticipated in the words with which one of the *labradores* invites Don Quixote to view the images: 'porque vea vuestra merced esta verdad, espere vuestra merced y verla ha por vista de ojos' (1196) (so that you may see the truth of this, let you wait and you will see it with your own eyes).

85. p. 875.
86. p. 876.
87. p. 873.
88. p. 874.
89. p. 875.
90. p. 536.
91. p. 875.
92. Ruta is inclined to link Don Quixote's change in tone to a waning of belief in his mission: 'Este "podría ser" se aleja del tono perentorio que Don Quijote usaba consigo mismo y con los demás cuando la fe en su ideal era muy sólida' (This 'it could be' marks a distance from the peremptory tone that Don Quixote used for himself and to others when his faith in his ideal was very solid) (Ruta, 'Aspectos iconológicos', p. 884). For Close, the doubt is not so much about his mission as about his ability to fulfil it; although he allows that 'the hero's pious admission of self-doubt with his melancholy over Dulcinea's enchantment raises this theme, momentarily, to a new and more serious level', he believes that 'in talking about mental improvement [...] he is probably referring to a cure for grief rather than insanity' (*A Companion to 'Don Quixote'*, pp. 108–09).
93. For Ruta, the episode 'sirve para fijar un momento fundamental del universo semántico de la novela, un momento [...] que puede proporcionar una de las claves de lectura del texto cervantino' (serves to fix a fundamental moment within the semantic world of the novel, a moment [...] that may furnish one of the keys for the reading of Cervantes's text) ('Aspectos iconológicos', p. 885). For Félix Martínez-Bonati, it marks the moment when Don Quixote's 'search for adventures and fame, position and wealth, is transformed into an indefinite, open, disoriented quest that invites thoughts of the abysmal lack of sense the world is taking on' (*'Don Quijote' and the Poetics of the Novel* (Ithaca: Cornell University Press, 1992), p. 105). For Rachel Schmidt, it signals a more positive shift in Don Quixote's attitude: 'al ver el cuadro de la conversión de San Pablo, don Quijote se tiende hacia una nueva especie de caballería' (on seeing the picture of St Paul's conversion, Don Quixote reaches towards a new form of chivalry) ('Leyendo otros que sean luz del alma: el *Quijote* y la literatura del *ars moriendi*', in *Cervantes y el 'Quijote': Actas del Coloquio Internacional*, ed. by Emilio Martínez Mata (Madrid: Editorial Arco, 2007), pp. 113–24 (p. 122)). Ruth Fine concurs: 'podría estimarse que la aventura del capítulo II, 58 proporciona indicios anticipatorios que ayudan a entender los últimos tramos del camino de don Quijote como una conversión cristiana' (it may be considered that the adventure in II. 58 furnishes advance signs that allow the last stages of Don Quixote's journey to be understood as a Christian conversion). ('En torno a la narración paradójica', p. 58).
94. p. 876.
95. p. 876.
96. Sancho shares his master's misfortune in quite a number of these instances: in the River Ebro; (partially) on meeting the Duke and Duchess; with the bulls; on Clavileño; on entering Barcelona; with the pigs; and, of course, experiences his own 'great' fall, into a hole in the ground, on the ducal estate (II. 55). For a study of this motif, see Eduardo Urbina, '"En alas de deseo": el motivo de los altibajos en *Don Quijote*', *Indiana Journal of Hispanic Literatures*, 2.2 (1994), 87–104.
97. p. 584.
98. p. 882.
99. Don Quixote announces his intention to do this as a gesture of thanks to his hosts, and as a proof that he is incapable of ingratitude, in an 'after-dinner speech' whose opening words could not be more ironic: 'Entre los pecados mayores que los hombres cometen, aunque algunos dicen

que es la soberbia, yo digo que es el desagradecimiento' (1205) ('Although some people say the worst sin men commit is pride, I say that it is ingratitude'; p. 880).
100. p. 881
101. The narrator slyly attributes the appearance of the animals and their drovers to 'la suerte, que sus cosas iba encaminando de mejor en mejor' (1207) ('fortune, which was making his affairs progress from good to even better'; p. 882).
102. p. 882.
103. p. 881.
104. His confrontation with the caged lions (II. 17) and his ravings in the episode of the 'Enchanted Boat' (II. 29) are comparable in this sense.
105. p. 883.
106. The expression, 'las nubes de antaño', recurs (with intensified wistfulness, due to context) in Sancho's words to Don Quixote about the inoperancy of the hare and the cage of crickets as 'omens' in the penultimate chapter of Part Two: 'He aquí, señor, rompidos y desbaratados estos agüeros, que no tienen que ver más con nuestros sucesos, según que yo imagino, aunque tonto, que con las nubes de antaño' (II. 73, 1323) ('"Here you are, sir — your omens foiled and come to nought, and I might be a fool but to my mind they haven't got any more to do with our affairs than last year's clouds"'; p. 972). The cognate adage (appropriately, the last to appear in the novel), 'En los nidos de antaño, no hay pájaros hogaño', is cited in the final chapter by Don Quixote as he attempts to persuade his family and friends that he has recovered his sanity: ' — Señores — dijo don Quijote — , vámonos poco a poco, pues ya en los nidos de antaño no hay pájaros hogaño. Yo fui loco y ya soy cuerdo; fui don Quijote de la Mancha y soy agora, como he dicho, Alonso Quijano el Bueno' (II. 74, 1333) ('"Not so fast, gentlemen," said Don Quixote: "you won't find this year's birds in last year's nests. I was mad, and now I am sane: I was Don Quixote de la Mancha and now, as I said, I am Alonso Quixano the Good"'; p. 979).
107. p. 883.
108. p. 883.
109. According to Carlos Alvar, 'la playa barcelonesa se convierte en un espacio simbólico, pues en ella es derrotado y en cierta medida puede decirse que acaba el caballero don Quijote a orillas del mar, como si se tratara de un anuncio del viaje al Más Allá de los textos artúricos' (the Barcelona beach becomes a symbolic space because he is defeated on it and so, to a certain extent, one can say that Don Quixote, the knight, comes to an end on the shore of the sea, seeming, as in Arthurian literature, to presage a journey to the Beyond) ('Del rey Arturo a Don Quijote: Paisaje y horizonte de expectativas en la tercera salida', *Boletín de la Real Academia Española*, 85 (2005), 7–27 (p. 22).
110. p. 928.
111. p. 934.
112. Citing the *Diccionario enciclopédico de la lengua castellana*, ed. by Elias Zerolo and others, 4th ed., 2 vols (Paris, n. d.), s.v. *fortuna*, Eric Ziolkowski notes that 'the Castilian terms *fortuna*, *destino*, *suerte*, and *ventura*, which throughout the *Quijote*'s narrative, refer to "la causa incógnita que se cree presidir el éxito de las cosas" (the unknown cause that is believed to preside over the outcome of things), with their subtle distinctions being summed up as follows: "La *ventura* hace, la *fortuna* quiere ó exige, la *suerte* decide, el *destino* ordena"' (luck does, fortune wishes or demands, fate decides, destiny ordains) ('Don Quixote's Windmill and Fortune's Wheel', *Modern Language Review*, 86 (1991), 885–97 (p.887)).
113. p. 935.
114. As, for example, when he hears the cacophony of animal noises on entering El Toboso ('todo lo cual tuvo el enamorado caballero a mal agüero' (II. 9, 758) ('all of which was taken by the enamoured hidalgo as a bad omen'; p. 539)), and, on the outskirts of his village, in response to the boys' conversation about the cricket cage, and the appearance of the hunted hare ('¡Malum signum! ¡Malum signum! Liebre huye, galgos la siguen: ¡Dulcinea no parece!' (II. 73, 1323) ('*Malum signum! Malum signum!* Hare flees, greyhounds chase: Dulcinea appears not!'; p. 971)).
115. Cervantes restates this oft insisted upon view in *Persiles* IV.14: 'aquella que comúnmente es llamada Fortuna, que no es otra cosa sino un firme disponer del cielo' (what is called Fortune

is nothing else than a firm decree of heaven) (*Los Trabajos de Persiles y Sigismunda*, ed. by Juan Bautista Avalle-Arce (Madrid: Castalia, 1969), p. 474). For a useful summary of the early history of 'Fortune', see Ziolkowski, 'Don Quixote's Windmill', pp. 885–90.
116. p. 935.
117. p. 935.
118. As noted by A. G. Lo Ré, in 'The Three Deaths of Don Quixote: Comments in Favor of the Romantic Critical Approach', *Cervantes: Bulletin of the Cervantes Society of America*, 9.2 (Fall 1989), 21–41 (pp. 30–31).
119. p. 935.
120. 'En estas pláticas iban siguiendo su camino, cuando llegaron al mesmo sitio y lugar donde fueron atropellados de los toros' (II. 67, 1283) ('They were plodding along, chatting away like this, when they came to the place where they'd been trampled by the bulls'; p. 940) Not altogether unsurprisingly, Don Quixote makes no mention of this; for him, 'Este es el prado donde topamos a las bizarras pastoras y gallardos pastores que en él querían renovar e imitar a la pastoral Arcadia (1283) ('This is the meadow where we came across those charming shepherdesses and gallant shepherds who were reviving and imitating the pastoral Arcadia'; p. 940), and it is this memory that leads him to suggest that he and Sancho take to being shepherds during their year of forced retirement from knight errantry. Borges refers to it as 'esta obscena aventura' (this obscene adventure) ('La conducta novelística de Cervantes', in Jorge Luis Borges, *El idioma de los argentinos* (Buenos Aires: Gleizer, 1928; Buenos Aires: Seix-Barral, 1994), pp. 139–46 (p. 146)); Williamson contends that, post-Don Quixote's defeat at Barcelona, 'the novel settles into unmotivated episodic action characterized by the use of recycled ideas and scenes of gratuitous cruelty to the madman', a process of which his being 'needlessly trampled' by pigs following 'the horrible trampling of the old gentleman by a herd of bulls' is symptomatic (*The Half-way House of Fiction*, pp. 190, 192).
121. Having argued (convincingly) that, before being substituted by the trampling by bulls, this episode formed part of an earlier redaction of Chapter 48, and 'contrariamente a cuantos la consideran una inútil reiteración de algo "ya dicho"' (in contrast to those who consider it a pointless reiteration of something 'already said'), Carlos Romero Muñoz writes ('"Animales inmundos y soeces" (*Quijote*, II, 58–59 y 66)', *Rassegna Iberistica*, 63 (1998), 3–24 (p. 6)): 'no dudo en afirmar que nuestro autor acierta al conservar unas paginas con toda probabilidad escritas para un contexto muy distinto. En efecto, la aventura de los toros y la de los puercos son cosas "parecidas", pero, al mismo tiempo, "diferentes" (I have no hesitation in stating that our author was right to keep some pages that, in all probability, were written for a very different context. Indeed, the adventure of the bulls and that of the pigs are 'similar' things but, at the same time, 'different'). He sees the difference as residing in the contrast between Don Quixote's daytime departure from the ducal palace and his forced return to it by night.
122. p. 945.
123. p. 945.
124. p. 946.
125. Sebastián de Covarrubias Horozco, *Tesoro de la lengua castellana o española* [1611], ed. by Ignacio Arellano and Rafael Zafra (Madrid: Iberoamericana, 2006), *s.v. puerco*: 'Del puerco no tenemos ningún provecho en toda su vida, sino mucho gasto, y ruido, y solo da buen día aquel en que le matamos' (We get no good out of the pig in the whole of its life, but rather much expense and noise, and the only good day it gives is the day on which we kill it); *Diccionario de autoridades*, 6 vols (Madrid: Real Academia Española, 1726–39), V, *s.v. puerco*: 'Animal doméstico, immundo y sucio, que se ceba y engorda para que sirva de mantenimiento. [...] Es el más súcio y indocíl de los animales [...]' (Foul and filthy domestic animal that is fattened and fed so that it may serve as sustenance. [...] It is the dirtiest and most intractable of the animals).
126. p. 946.
127. p. 946.
128. Sancho, for example, sees his fall into the pit on the Duke's estate in these terms: '¡Desdichado de mí, y en qué han parado mis locuras y fantasías' (II. 55, 1177) ('What a poor unlucky devil I am, and look what all my follies and my fancies have come to!'; p. 859).

129. p. 895.
130. p. 43.
131. p. 935.
132. Eduardo Urbina, 'El juego de la fortuna en el *Quijote* de 1605', in *Actas de XII Congreso de la Asociación Internacional de Hispanistas 21–26 de agosto de 1995, Birmingham,* 7 vols (Birmingham: Department of Hispanic Studies, University of Birmingham, 1998), III (Estudios áureos II) (ed. by Jules Whicker), pp. 254–62 (p. 262, n.12).
133. p. 690.
134. Famously, of course, it is only in response to what Don Jerónimo tells him, in Chapter 59, about Avellaneda's poorly written account of his 'Don Quixote''s participation in a tourney in Zaragoza, that the real Don Quixote changes his mind about going there and heads for Barcelona instead. Cervantes, clearly, did not originally plan for Don Quixote's physical journey to correspond so closely to the decline in his fortunes and his self-belief, but his choice to make the beach the scene of Don Quixote's defeat suggests that in this respect, as in others, he consciously turned the apocryphal Part Two to his advantage.
135. Eduardo Urbino, ' "En alas de deseo": el motivo de los altibajos en *Don Quijote*', *Indiana Journal of Hispanic Literatures*, 2.2 (1994), 87–104 (pp. 88, 98, 87).
136. Edwin Williamson, for instance, writes: 'His [Cervantes's] parody is aimed increasingly at two of its [romance's] most basic premises: that there is a direct intercourse between the material and the spiritual worlds, and that the destiny of the hero is guided by Providence' (*The Half-way House*, pp. 110–11); see also his article, 'The Devil in *Don Quixote*', *Bulletin of Spanish Studies*, 92.8–10 (2015), 147–66 (esp. pp. 148–49).
137. John J. Allen, 'The Providential World of Cervantes' Fiction', *Thought: Fordham University Quarterly*, 55.2 (1980), 184–95 (pp. 187, 193–94)'; elsewhere, arguing on the basis of the intercalated stories in Part One, he states: 'Pero la rectificación de Cervantes no nos lleva del *deus ex machina* a un mundo desprovisto de Dios, y una de las razones fundamentales por la inclusión en el *Quijote* de los cuentos intercalados es precisamente la reiterada confirmación de la operación de la Providencia divina en el mundo donde viven don Quijote y Sancho' (But Cervantes's rectification does not take us from the *deus ex machina* to a world devoid of God, and one of the fundamental reasons for the inclusion of the interpolated stories in the *Quixote* is precisely the repeated confirmation of the operation of Providence in the world in which Don Quixote and Sancho live) ('La Providencia divina en el *Quijote*', in *Cervantes, su obra y su mundo* (*Actas del I Congreso sobre Cervantes*), ed. by M. Criado de Val (Madrid: EDI-6, 1981), pp. 525–29 (p. 528)).
138. p. 976.
139. Williamson, 'The Devil in *Don Quixote*', p. 166.
140. As noted by Urbina (' "En alas del deseo" ', p. 94).
141. p. 970.
142. p. 975.
143. p. 982.
144. Peter Dunn, for example, observes that Don Quixote's true awakening will only come at the end, when he gets to 'soñar el sueño de la muerte' (dream the dream of death) and awakens 'purgado ya de sueños' (now purged of his dreams) ('La Cueva de Montesinos por fuera y por dentro: Estructura épica, fisonomía', *MLN*, 88.2 Hispanic Issue (March, 1973), 190–202 (p. 202)). See also, Edward Riley, '*Don Quijote*' (London: Allen & Unwin, 1986), p.142: 'It seems right therefore to read the Cave experience in the way most critics have done, as a significant pointer towards Don Quixote's eventual rejection of chivalric fiction and his recovery of sanity'; and Henry W. Sullivan, *Grotesque Purgatory*, p. 113: 'Cervantes is using the Montesinos episode as a kind of forge or crucible in which Don Quixote is recast so that he may finally be reinstated as Don Alonso, his true and final identity.'
145. A point well made by Rachel Schmidt (' "Leyendo otros" ', p. 122), who also notes the particular relevance to the dying, emphasized in the *artes moriendi*, of St Paul's concept of spiritual warfare: 'Esta aventura [...], nos proporciona la pista con que entender los últimos pasos del camino de don Quijote. La imagen del buen cristiano como caballero se remonta a la descripción paulina

del armamento del Cristiano y a la imagen bíblica de una guerra santa entre Dios y el diablo, pero se resucita precisamente en los libros de bien morir. [...] De hecho, el mismo Concilio de Trento, en sesión 14 sobre el sacramento de la extrema unción, enfatiza la necesidad de aparejar al cristiano con las armas necesarias para protegerse del mal en el momento de fallecer. Dicho consejo Joan de Salazar lo comparte con la clerecía en su *Arte de ayudar y disponer a bien morirá todo género de personas* (1608) así: "instituyó Jesucristo Señor nuestro el sacramento de la extrema unción, para ayudar y fortificar al enfermo, en tan grave y estrecho peligro; ungiendo con óleo santo al caballero y soldado cristiano, para que pelee valerosamente en aquel último y postrero combate"' (This adventure [...] gives us the clue to understanding the final steps of Don Quixote's journey. The image of the good Christian as a soldier goes back to St Paul's description of the armour of the Christian and to the biblical image of a holy war between God and the Devil, but it is revived precisely in the books about dying well. [...] Indeed, the Council of Trent itself, in Session 14 on the sacrament of Extreme Unction, emphasizes the need to equip the Christian with the arms necessary to protect himself from evil at the moment of death. This same advice is shared with the clergy by Joan de Salazar in his 'Art of preparing and helping all kinds of people to die well' (1608) as follows: 'Our Lord Jesus Christ instituted the sacrament of extreme unction to assist and strengthen the sick man in such grave and extreme danger; through anointing the Christian knight and soldier with holy oil, so that he can fight valiantly in that last and final combat').

146. Juan Huarte de San Juan, cites St Paul as a prime example of those who are 'melancólicos por adustión' (melancholic by reason of heat): 'veamos lo que hizo Dios cuando quiso fabricar un hombre en el vientre de su madre [...], haciéndole de grande entendimiento y mucha imaginativa, forzosamente (guardando el orden natural) le sacó colérico y adusto. Y que esto sea verdad, déjase entender fácilmente considerando el grande fuego y furor con que perseguía la Iglesia' (let us observe what God did when he wished to put together a [certain] man in his mother's womb [...], in making him of great understanding and imaginative power, he had perforce (observing the natural order) to create him choleric and dry. And that this is true may easily be understood by considering the great fire and fury with which he persecuted the Church) (*Examen de ingenios para las ciencias* [1575], ed. by Guillermo Serés (Madrid: Cátedra, 1989), p. 464).

147. 'Omnesque nos cum decidissemus in terram, audivi vocem loquentem mihi hebraica lingua : "Saule, Saule, quid me persequeris?" durum est tibi contra stimulum calcitrare' (Acts 26, 14) ('And when we were all fallen to the earth, I heard a voice speaking unto me, and saying in the Hebrew tongue, Saul, Saul, why persecutest thou me? it is hard for thee to kick against the pricks').

148. p. 976.

149. Terence O'Reilly, 'The Death of Don Quixote and the Birth of Modernity: The Omens in *Don Quixote*, Part II, Chapter 73', *Bulletin of Spanish Studies*, 94:8 (2017), 1269–85 (pp. 1282, 1285).

CHAPTER 10

Don Quixote, II. 71–74: The Sense of an Ending

Jeremy Lawrance

The last four chapters of *Don Quixote*, Part Two describe the return to his village of the defeated hero, and then his death.¹ Such a melancholy finale is hardly the stock-in-trade of romance, nor what the burlesque conclusion to Part One leads us to expect. Both endings play upon the epic motif of the νόστος or homecoming, the age-old theme of Homer's *Odyssey* and chivalric romance. The second presents several echoes of the first, but the outcome is quite different and the parallels have exactly the effect of pointing up the contrast: the errant knight's unheroic retreat to La Mancha (first escorted in cage and cart, second on his dilapidated nag all alone with Sancho), a none-too-glorious reception by the villagers and Sancho's down-to-earth reunion with his wife, the Niece and Housekeeper's remonstrations, with diverse jeremiads on the dangers of romance and its damnable fictions; and our hero's dazed retreat to his 'old bed' to escape all this — by falling asleep.

The first Part's treatment (I. 52, 644–46) seems expressly designed to emphasize the parodic aspect of the contrast between Quixote's fate and those of Odysseus and the knights of romance. If the Greek hero, too, returns as a beggar and is recognized at first only by his swineherd, nurse, son, and faithful dog, it is all part of a disguise leading to his despatch of the suitors to the dark abode of Hades, reunion with his wife (not a burlesque retainer's return to his), and the triumphant resumption of his throne (*Odyssey*, XIII–XXIV). A similar pattern obtains in the romances; their fictions all turn on a single elementary plot line, the infant prince separated at birth from house and home who, after wandering the ends of the earth in search of adventure, finds out his true identity through some anagnorisis (a birthmark, token, duel) and returns to inherit his rightful kingdom.² As Cervantes makes the Curate observe, such fables do not normally envisage a scenario in which their protagonists 'mueren en sus camas, y hacen testamento antes de su muerte' (I. 6, 91) ('die in their beds, and make their wills before dying').³ True, the cyclical nature of Spanish romances meant the heroes had eventually to shuffle off the mortal coil to make way for their heirs; but Amadís, for example, does not do so till the end of the fifth Book of his interminable series, the one about his son Esplandián, by which time he has long since recovered his kingdom. Even then he does not die, but is summoned by Urganda la Desconocida to the Ínsula Firme with all the cycle's other heroes: emperor Esplandián, kings Galaor, Florestán, Agrajes, and Grasandor, Count Gandalín, Oriana and all the wives, even Amadís's dwarf and the fictional author, Greek sage Elisabat. There they are seated on thrones, restored to youth with a magic potion, then cast up in the air by a spell — enchanted fortress and all — and down a mighty cavern to join King Arthur underground, whence they will in some future age be resurrected to rescue Christendom and reign once more in Gran Bretaña. Montalvo ends with a cheery promise of more of the same in his next instalment on their sons.[4]

We may think this infantile fantasy already sufficiently ridiculous compared to Homer; but no doubt it was supposed to be gravely affecting. At all events Cervantes's scorn was well merited, and his ending to Part One builds up the mocking contrast between romance and real life, carefully maintaining the decorum of comedy throughout; to which end his last lines make clear, in direct parody of the chivalric potboilers' obligatory promise of a sequel, that despite the narrator's failure to discover any 'authentic papers' on the matter, he has it on good authority — i.e. Manchegan hearsay — that Quixote's collapse was nothing serious; he recovered, not indeed his wits, but his health and ventured forth again upon his mad exploits. So the book concludes 'con esperanza de la tercera salida de don Quijote. *Forse altro canterà con miglior plectro*' (I. 52, 653) ('in hopes of Don Quixote's third sally: *Forse altro canterà con miglior plectro*'). However, there is an intervening postscript: a series of inept verses by the 'academicians' of La Argamasilla, written in Gothic script on mouldering parchments dug up in 'a leaden box' on a local building site according to its elderly medic owner, which includes epitaphs by Monicongo, Paniaguado, Cachidiablo, and Tiquitoc for the graves of Quixote, Dulcinea, and Sancho, replete with allusions to Amadís and hints of thrones and caverns. So, contradicting the 'hope' of more adventures and with a heavy-lidded glance towards any *altro* eyeing his plectrum in the delusion it might prove 'better', the postscript seems to hint that the hero is neither dead nor alive, but the story is over (I. 52, 646–53).

On the face of it, then, the subtle deflation by this mention of tombs at the end of Part One is just one component of a rich comedy of literary parody, not an intervention intended to make us ponder on mortality. When Paniaguado warbles *in laudem Dulcineae del Toboso*,

¡Oh dura estrella!,
que esta manchega dama y este invito
andante caballero, en tiernos años
ella dejó, muriendo, de ser bella,
y él, aunque queda en mármores escrito,
no pudo huir de amor, iras, y engaños, (I. 52, 650)

(O hard star!
That this Manchegan dame and worthy knight,
In tender years, when people strongest are,
She lost by death the glimpse of beauty bright,
And he, although in marble richly done,
Yet love's wrath and deceits he could not shun,)[5]

it is hard to ignore the jokes of inept versification and crass pedantry (adjectives all preposed, the sorry mix-up for rhyme's sake of Latinism 'invito' < *invictus* 'undefeated'/*invitus* 'unwilling') or the vacuous triviality of his imprecation against Fate's hard constellation (cutting short her charms, his delusions). Of course, we may ponder on mortality and *engaños* if we wish; but the 'fidedigno autor' ('trustworthy author') asks only that we repay the 'inmenso trabajo' ('vast toil') of his antiquarian endeavours by granting them 'el mesmo crédito que suelen dar los discretos a los libros de caballerías' (647) ('the same credit that people of sense give to the books of chivalry') — that is, none at all. The tone and ethos of the chapter is resolutely comic.

The ending to Part Two is, by contrast, far more complex and ambivalent, teetering on the tightrope between *burlas* and *veras*. It too is full of humour; indeed, parody is if anything increased, for to mockery of the romances it adds satire of the false pretender Avellaneda's spurious Part Two. Yet it terminates with the pathetic scene of Quixote's deathbed conversion, repentance, and renunciation of his chivalric *persona* — and then, in deliberate counterpoint to Part One, with the author's Muslim *alter ego* Cide Hamete hanging up his pen and admonishing readers to fulfil their Christian [*sic*!] duty by preventing the presumptuous Tordesillesque impostor from ever again attempting to raise his hero's tired bones from the grave (II. 74, 1336–37).

This did not accord with the decorum of comedy, which in Cervantes's day was regarded as having the force of law, infringements as felonies. 'In comedy', thundered Cicero, 'anything tragic is unseemly' (*De optimo genere oratorum*, I. I). Renaissance theorists discussed this disjunction between tragedy and comedy at length, and in particular the impermissibility of the latter's mentioning death. The authority most consulted by Cervantes was Alonso López Pinciano, who observed that even in 'very fine and pure comedies' he sometimes found 'fears, laments, and even deaths'. His interlocutor Fadrique explains (emphasis added):

> All those are to make you laugh, not cry; and if you don't laugh at them, you deserve to be laughed at yourself. [...] Yes, some theatregoers are so thin-skinned as to cry at comedies, but [...] this must be *because the action was more tragic and sad than was suitable for comedy* [...] and the poet, failing to observe the rules of pure comedy, slid into tragedy [...]. Tragedy's deaths arouse pity, but when they occur in comedy they are there to amuse and entertain, since the characters who die are persons the world can well do without like a quarrelsome old woman, an old miser, a pimp, or a procuress.[6]

The example López Pinciano had in mind was the report of the death of Chrysis in Roman playwright Terence's *Andria* I. 105, a subject of controversy from the time of Donatus; Fadrique's last three lines are directly imitated from the latter's commentary, though the substitution of Donatus's *meretrix*, *senex*, and surplus wife by 'una vieja zizañadora, un viejo avaro, un rufián, o una alcahueta' was meant to make us think of a modern instance, Fernando de Rojas's *Tragicomedia de Calisto y Melibea* — a work whose hybrid title advertised the notorious fact that Celestina's and the other protagonists' violent murders and suicides are not merely mentioned, but vividly enacted.[7] Cervantes implies that his work, too, is not by any strict generic definition a comedy; rather, as he makes his *amigo* declare in the Prologue to Part One,

> todo él es una invectiva contra los libros de caballerías, de quien nunca se acordó Aristóteles, ni dijo nada San Basilio, ni alcanzó Cicerón, ni caen debajo de la cuenta de sus fabulosos disparates las puntualidades de la verdad, [...] ni tiene para qué predicar a ninguno, mezclando lo humano con lo divino. (I. Prólogo, 18)

> (it is all an attack upon the books of chivalry, of which Aristotle never dreamt, nor St Basil said a word, nor Cicero had any knowledge; the niceties of truth do not come within the range of its fanciful vagaries, [...] nor does it have any need to preach to anybody, mixing up things human and divine.)

Nonetheless, Friend concludes the same speech by stating that the book's aim is to ensure that 'el melancólico se mueva a risa, el risueño la acreciente' (19) ('the melancholy be moved to laughter, and the merry made merrier still'); and cathartic laughter was agreed to be a defining characteristic of comedy.

Does this mean, then, that Cervantes intended us to enjoy the death of Don Quixote in Part Two as a comic matter of 'amusing entertainment', the overdue taking-off of an old dotard belonging to the class of 'persons the world can well do without'? No; it has been the almost universal consensus of readers and critics that this is not the effect, or affect, of the ending. Despite its humorous aspects, its parodic subtext and satire of Avellaneda, it seems hard to argue that the climactic scene of Don Quixote's death (though technically it is not 'Quixote' who dies) is comic in the low sense envisaged by López Pinciano, for it describes, step by step (marked A1–7 in the quotations below) and in overtly religious language, a 'good' death, that is, the orthodox Catholic ritual of an edifying Christian demise as laid down by immemorial tradition and the *Arts of Dying Well*:[8]

> — Yo me siento, sobrina, a punto de muerte [A1]: querría hacerla de tal modo, que diese a entender que no había sido mi vida tan mala que dejase renombre de loco; que, puesto que lo he sido, no querría confirmar esta verdad en mi muerte [A2]. Llámame, amiga, a mis buenos amigos, al cura, al bachiller Sansón Carrasco y a maese Nicolás el barbero, que quiero confesarme y hacer mi testamento.
> Pero de este trabajo se escusó la sobrina con la entrada de los tres. Apenas los vio don Quijote, cuando dijo:
> — Dadme albricias, buenos señores, de que ya yo no soy don Quijote de la Mancha, sino Alonso Quijano, a quien mis costumbres me dieron renombre de 'bueno'. [...] Los [cuentos] de hasta aquí [...], que han sido verdaderos en mi daño, los ha de volver mi muerte, con ayuda del cielo, en mi provecho [A3]. Yo, señores, siento que me voy muriendo a toda priesa: déjense burlas aparte y tráiganme un confesor que me confiese [A4] y un escribano que haga mi testamento [A5], que en tales trances como éste no se ha de burlar el hombre con el alma; y así, suplico que en tanto que el señor cura me confiesa vayan por el escribano. (II. 74, 1330–31)

('Niece, I feel myself at the point of death [A1]; and I would fain meet it in such a way as to show that my life has not been so ill that I should leave behind me the name of a madman; for though I have been one, I would not wish to confirm the fact at my death [A2]. Call in to me, my dear, my good friends the curate, the bachelor Samson Carrasco, and Master Nicholas the barber, for I wish to confess and make my will.'

But his niece was saved the trouble by the entrance of the three. The instant Don Quixote saw them he said:

'Congratulate me on my news, good sirs, for I am no longer Don Quixote of La Mancha but Alonso Quixano, whose way of life won me the name of Good. [...] All that nonsense before, [...] the only true part of which was the harm it did me, my death will, with heaven's help, turn to my good [A3]. I feel, sirs, that I am rapidly dying; put aside jesting and bring me a confessor to confess me [A4] and a notary to make my will [A5], for in extremities like this man must not trifle with his soul; and so, while the curate is confessing me, I beg you go get the notary.')

Apart from this it lays stress on the bonds of human affection and grief felt by the bystanders (B), and inserts authorial apostrophes describing their grief as well merited (C):[9]

Acabose la confesión [A4] y salió el cura diciendo:

— Verdaderamente se muere y verdaderamente está cuerdo Alonso Quijano el Bueno; bien podemos entrar para que haga su testamento.

Estas nuevas dieron un terrible empujón a los ojos preñados de ama, sobrina y de Sancho Panza, su buen escudero, de tal manera, que los hizo reventar las lágrimas de los ojos y mil profundos suspiros del pecho [B]; porque verdaderamente, como alguna vez se ha dicho, en tanto que don Quijote fue Alonso Quijano el Bueno a secas, y en tanto que fue don Quijote de la Mancha, fue siempre de apacible condición y de agradable trato, y por esto no sólo era bien querido de los de su casa, sino de todos cuantos le conocían [C].

Entró el escribano con los demás, y después de haber hecho la cabeza del testamento y ordenado su alma don Quijote, con todas aquellas circunstancias cristianas que se requieren, llegando a las mandas, dijo [...] [A5] (II. 74, 1331–32)[10]

(The confession over [A4], the curate came out saying, "Alonso Quixano the Good is indeed dying, and is indeed in his right mind; we may now go in to him while he makes his will."

This news gave a tremendous impulse to the brimming eyes of the housekeeper, niece, and Sancho Panza his good squire, making the tears burst from their eyes and a thousand deep sighs from their hearts [B]; for in truth, as has been said more than once, whether Don Quixote was plain Alonso Quixano the Good or whether he was Don Quixote of La Mancha, he was always of a gentle disposition and kindly in all his ways, and hence he was beloved not only by those of his own house, but by all who knew him [C].

The notary came in with the rest, and as soon as the preamble of the will had been set out and Don Quixote had commended his soul to God with all the Christian formalities that are required, coming to the bequests, he said [...] [A5])

All three strands, or rather all four, come together in the climax:

> En fin, llegó el último de don Quijote, después de recebidos todos los sacramentos [A6] y después de haber abominado con muchas y eficaces razones de los libros de caballerías. Hallose el escribano presente, y dijo que nunca había leído en ningún libro de caballerías que algún caballero andante hubiese muerto en su lecho tan sosegadamente y tan cristiano como don Quijote [C?]; el cual, entre compasiones y lágrimas de los que allí se hallaron [B], dio su espíritu [A7], quiero decir que se murió. (II. 74, 1334–35)¹¹
>
> (At last Don Quixote's last end came, after he had received all the sacraments [A6] and had in full and forcible terms expressed his abomination of the books of chivalry. The notary was there at the time, and he said that in no book of chivalry had he ever read of any knight errant having died in his bed so calmly and so like a Christian as Don Quixote [C]; who, amid the sorrow and tears of all there present [B], yielded up his spirit [A7]; that is to say, died.)

The ironic parenthesis of the scrivener's dim-witted failure to grasp the drift of Alonso Quijano's 'full and forcible abomination' of the romances of chivalry, insisting still on regarding him as a *caballero andante* and calling him — as does the narrator — by his insane chivalresque name, inadvertently reminding us of the Curate's judgment that the untoward verisimilitude of Tirant lo Blanc's 'dying in his bed and making a will' was a *necedad* ('idiocy') for which its author should have been condemned to the galleys for life (I. 6, 91; see p. 237, above), are heavy winks reminding us of the burlesque nature of Quixote's adventure and the novel that tells it. Yet the design to arouse pathos is unmistakeable. 'Put aside jesting [...], man must not trifle with his soul'; the manner of the description evokes, in terms of Aristotle's classification of comic *vs.* tragic mimesis, not the alienation of looking down on a character inferior to us so much as sympathy for a fellow man.¹²

In this sense the ending of Part Two confronts us, seemingly on purpose, with what has been a battleground of Cervantine critique in modern times: namely, the Romantic reading of the novel not as a funny book, but as a tragic one.¹³ Perhaps the best known, certainly the most concise and striking formulation in English is Byron's:

> I should be very willing to redress
> Men's wrongs, and rather check than punish crimes,
> Had not Cervantes, in that too true tale
> Of Quixote, shown how all such efforts fail.
>
> IX
>
> Of all tales 'tis the saddest — and more sad,
> Because it makes us smile: his hero's right,
> And still pursues the right; — to curb the bad,
> His only object, and 'gainst odds to fight,
> His guerdon: 'tis his virtue makes him mad!
> But his adventures form a sorry sight; —
> A sorrier still is the great moral taught
> By that real Epic unto all who have thought.¹⁴

'Of all tales 'tis the saddest': the words are often quoted out of context, but to do so traduces the point of what Byron was saying, which is encapsulated in the phrase 'too *true* tale': that is, a '*real* Epic' and its great but sorry 'moral' for thinking readers, that to pursue the right against the odds and fight the bad — 'all such efforts fail'. For Byron, in other words, what dies at the end of *Don Quixote* is not so much Alonso Quijano as Quixote's fantasy of utopia; and what makes this sad is that it happens to be the truth, 'reality' — the ineluctable fate of idealistic dreams. Only in this light can it make sense to say, 'more sad, *because* it makes us smile'. What kills the quixotic hope is, precisely, mockery.[15]

Such readings bear in a specific way upon the question posed above as to whether, in accord with renaissance theories of genre, Cervantes portrayed his hero's death in order to make fun of it. The Romantic answer is now regarded with scepticism, but before dismissing it we should be clear about the nuanced amplitude of Byron's judgment; he grants the burlesque elements in the portrayal but argues, in effect, that they serve to make it not more comic but instead more tragic, by highlighting the true reason and deepening the true pathos of Quixote's defeat. We should be clear, if for no other reason, because it seems hard to deny what Harold Bloom calls 'Cervantes's darkening vision' in *Don Quixote*, Part Two.[16] The protagonists' long stay at the Duke and Duchess's castle (28 chapters of 240 pages, over a third of the book), with all the courtly farces invented 'hacerles burlas que llevasen vislumbres y apariencias de aventuras' (II. 34, 996) ('to practise some jokes upon them that should have the look and appearance of adventures'), has often perturbed readers, for it cruelly epitomizes the role of mockery in our hero's downfall. 'Enchained hopelessly in the grovelling fetters of externality', protested Lamb, must be the mind to which 'the image of the high-souled, high-intelligenced Quixote — the errant Star of Knighthood, made more tender by eclipse — has never presented itself':

> Illustrious Romancer! were the 'fine frenzies', which possessed the brain of thy own Quixote, a fit subject, as in this Second Part, to be exposed to the jeers of Duennas and Serving Men? to be monstered, and shown up at the heartless banquets of great men? [...] Why, Goneril would have blushed to practise upon the abdicated king at this rate, and the she-wolf Regan not have endured to play the pranks upon his fled wits, which thou hast made thy Quixote suffer in Duchesses' halls, and at the hands of that unworthy nobleman.[17]

The painful pranks culminate in the charade of a pathetic attempt to scale the heights of heaven on Clavileño, a risible wooden simulacrum of a flying horse, which explodes, aptly symbolizing the manner of Don Quixote's defeat (II. 40–41, 1037–55). It begins with authorial praise of Cide Hamete for not omitting the smallest (discreditable) minim or atom of the truth 'para gusto y general pasatiempo de los vivientes' (1037) ('for the delight and amusement of every living being') — sure enough, the ducal guffaws last 'no sólo aquel tiempo, sino el de toda su vida' (1055) ('not only for the moment, but for all their lives') — but ends with Quixote's nagging doubts about the reality of his entire 'adventure' (1054–55). And later, at the start of his final return to the village, he encounters the noble pranksters again (II. 70), where it emerges that they were also implicated in his crowning defeat at the hands of the Knight of the White Moon on the beach at Barcelona (II. 64–65), for it was they who put Sansón Carrasco on Don Quixote's trail when he consulted them after the failure of his first attempt to bring his friend home, as the Knight of the Mirrors (II. 13–15). Finally, after Sansón returns to recount the success of his second attempt, they cannot resist trapping the dejected hero on his way back to La Mancha for one last sarcastic trick (II. 70, 1302–03). The 'author' sums up the role of these highborn mischief-makers with a damning final comment:

> Y dice más Cide Hamete: que tiene para sí ser tan locos los burladores como los burlados y que no estaban los duques dos dedos de parecer tontos, pues tanto ahínco ponían en burlarse de dos tontos. (II. 70, 1303)
>
> (And Cide Hamete says, moreover, that for his part he considers the concocters of the joke as crazy as the victims of it, and that the Duke and Duchess were not two fingers' breadth removed from looking like fools themselves, when they took such pains to make game of a pair of fools.)

This surely marks a place where Byron's and Lamb's readings find some support in Cervantes's text; but in truth the worm of Don Quixote's disillusionment runs right through the story from the moment of Dulcinea's enchantment, where it is the lady's 'olor de ajos crudos' ('smell of raw garlic') that is most perturbing, for it seems to him a sign of 'spite' on the part of the traitorous enchanters apt to defeat even his most reverent faith in the surpassing romance of chivalry (II. 10, 773). Nabokov perceived the same 'snake of doubt, the coiled consciousness that his quest is a delusion,' in another emblematic chapter where, undressing alone by the light of two dim tapers in his chamber at the Duke's palace and put out by Sancho's absence while governing his *ínsula* ('he felt his loneliness'), Quixote catches sight of a hole in his threadbare green socks and falls into dejection — only to be assailed by another trick, Altisidora's pantomime of lovelorn courting at his window (II. 44, 1074–81). '[C]erró de golpe la ventana' ('He shut the window with a bang') the chapter concludes, 'y, despechado y pesaroso como si le hubiera acontecido alguna gran desgracia, se acostó en su lecho' (1081) ('and out of temper and out of sorts as if some great misfortune had befallen him, stretched himself on his bed') — much as he is to do again at the end in II. 74, though in a still more melancholy state of mind and to different effect.[18]

The narrator prefaces the scene in II. 44 by assuring his 'amiable reader', 'si con ello no rieres, por lo menos desplegarás los labios con risa de jimia' (II. 44, 1072) ('if you do not laugh at it, at any rate you will pucker your lips in an apish grin'). The commentators offer no idea as to what Cervantes meant by *risa de jimia*, though for defining the affect of this part of the novel, and hence of its ending, it seems one of the most important of his thousands of self-reflexive remarks.[19] So far as I know, the only editor to proffer anything is Clemencín:

> *Con risa de jimia*: What connexion is there between wonder [*admiración*] and 'apish laughter'? For the rest, Cervantes well observed [in the conclusion of the same sentence] that 'Don Quixote's adventures must be honoured either with wonder or with laughter'; and to put it more accurately, often with the two together, because *the sublime kind of ridicule* arouses both at the same time.[20]

Though this contributes nothing on the meaning — why a *she*-ape, for example? — it shows some critical acumen. Cervantes's expression was a coinage of his own, so we can only speculate as to what it was supposed to imply; but one thing is certain, 'ape' was never a flattering term. The standard image was of the animal's grotesque mimicry of humankind, on a par with performing elephants, dancing dogs, or cuckoos planting their eggs in other people's nests; and above all, its risible unawareness of its own incongruous ugliness and stupidity. In short, the *jimia* was looked upon as a *scurra* or clown.[21] For Redondo, that role immediately invokes 'the universe of buffoonery (*truhanería*)'; *risa de jimia* was therefore 'festive, but degrading', reducing Don Quixote to nothing more than a court fool.[22] However, *de jimia* implies not so much 'laughter *at* an ape' as 'ape-laughter'; in other words, it is the 'amiable reader' whom Cervantes's phrase casts as pithecoid, not Quixote. The phrase thus appears to cast as much doubt on the humanity or reason of the person who grimaces in simian ridicule as it does upon that of the target of the grimace. What makes it still more perplexing are the immediately following words, 'porque los sucesos de don Quijote o se han de celebrar con admiración o con risa' (1072) ('because Don Quixote's adventures must be honoured either with wonder or with laughter'), which, as Clemencín observed, appear to establish a disjunction between *risa* and *admiración*, which are elsewhere presented as joint effects of any well-constructed work, as for example in Don Quixote's own words to the Curate on marrying *enseñanza* with *deleite* in I. 47, 600: 'Hanse de casar las fábulas mentirosas con el entendimiento de los que las leyeren [...], de modo que anden a un mismo paso la admiración y la alegría juntas' ('Plots in fiction should be wedded to the understanding of the reader, [...] so that wonder and delight may *together* keep pace one with the other'; emphasis added) . Here, in contrast, *risa de jimia* is apparently an alternative to *admiración*.[23]

The cruel insensitivity and heartlessness of early-modern laughter, so prominent not only in the episodes under consideration but in the treatment of Quixote and Sancho throughout Part Two, has attracted much attention in Cervantine criticism, from Nietzsche onwards, and has often been adduced to support historicist 'hard' readings of the novel against the 'soft' Romantic one.[24] Yet, illuminating as such correctives are, need one point out that they cannot play any determining role in critique? Whether or not Cervantes and/or his contemporaries were cruel and heartless, our concern is with the book, *Don Quixote*; and there is no reason why it should not have transcended its own period in this respect as it does in all others. When a text proffers such ironic and ambivalent passages as the one on the seeming madness of the Duke and Duchess's jokes at the expense of two madmen, or on the reader's possibly ape-like grin (at the jests, or at the madmen), we can hardly avoid reflecting on how they contribute to the affect of what we are reading. In this respect, Cécile Hue's illuminating discussions of the Golden Age imagery and symbolism of monkeys and apes offer suggestive nuances and avenues for thought.[25] Again, what are we to make of Quixote's inability to believe the Duke capable of malice, even after discovering that the mock duellist Tosilos is his lackey: '——No vos acuitéis, señoras ——dijo don Quijote——, que ni ésta es malicia ni es bellaquería; y si la es, no ha sido la causa el duque, sino los malos encantadores que me persiguen' (II. 56, 1188) ('"Do not distress yourselves, ladies," said Don Quixote, "for this is no trickery or roguery; or *if it is*, it is not the Duke who is at the bottom of it, but those wicked enchanters who persecute me"'; emphasis added)? His innocence and vanity are comic, to be sure; but is he mad or bad? Perhaps, indeed, the subconscious mental obliquity of refusing to think evil of his host was in the last analysis more generous than stupid; for, though doubtless unconscious of the fact, the Duke was really, as Nabokov observed (n. 18, above), nothing better than a persecuting enchanter himself, and of the meanest kind. 'Nonetheless', remarked Alexander Parker, 'it is trickery, not enchantment'; in one of the first attacks on the Romantic reading, he argued that the novel tells the story not of a noble idealist defeated by an uncomprehending world, but of Don Quixote's Christian conversion from the arrogant egoism of his 'fantastical megalomania', in spite of the lies of those like the 'shameless' Duke who ought to know better but persist in leading him on. His deathbed recovery is no 'defeat', but the 'logical culmination' of this moral journey: 'In his fight with lies [...] he has finally, through suffering and humiliation, recognized the supreme truth'.[26]

All these ironic ambiguities invite us to return to the texture of Part Two's last four chapters with an open mind. In the light of López Pinciano's strictures on death in comedy on one hand, and the Romantic hypothesis of the novel's tragic sense on the other, we may devote attention not to some doomed attempt to divine Cervantes's intention, 'hard' or 'soft', but to the ending's artistry and semantic richness, and how it arouses such a variety of responses.[27]

Once back on the road after the last encounter with the Duke and Duchess, Chapter II. 71 'De lo que a don Quijote le sucedió con su escudero Sancho yendo a su aldea' ('Of What Passed between Don Quixote and his Squire Sancho on the Way to their Village') begins with the matter of Sancho's self-flagellation for the purpose of disenchanting Dulcinea. The treatment is purely comic, starting with the unromantic business of fixing a price per lash and continuing with Sancho's ploy, on discovering after six or eight of the stipulated 3,300 strokes 'ser pesada la burla' (that 'the jest' is 'tiresome'), of whipping trees rather than himself (II. 71, 1310–14). In keeping with the liberating sense of the heroes' having escaped at last from the tortuous machinations of the ducal palace and returned to their proper nature and business, the festive tone is worthy of Part One; the dialogue sparkles with the vivid mixture of friendship and artless self-interest we know of old (Sancho haggling over the price while guilefully asserting that 'el amor de mis hijos y de mi mujer me hace me muestre interesado" (1311) ('the love of my wife and children forces me to seem mercenary'); Quixote concerned that his squire should not tire, or worse, kill himself before completing the task), embellished with otiose proverbs and chivalric pedantry. Nevertheless, the psychology is finely balanced; it is clear that, despite themselves, there is comradeship between the two. After the 'flogging' Quixote covers Sancho with his jacket so he may sleep; and at the end of the chapter when he once more admonishes his squire to desist from larding his talk with proverbs (using two or three himself to say so), Sancho replies that he will do his best (without a single one).

Next day they proceed to a country inn, but Quixote recognizes it as such, not a castle, for 'después que le vencieron con más juicio en todas las cosas discurría, como agora se dirá' (II. 71, 1314) ('ever since he had been vanquished he talked more rationally about everything, as will be shown presently'). If this is a pointer to the coming dénouement, what follows 'presently' seems a presentiment of imminent *desengaño*, disabusal; a scene so paradoxical and inconsequential that it cannot be read otherwise than as symbolic. In the dingy chamber where they are lodged Quixote spots two paintings 'de malísima mano' ('by some very poor hand'), one of the abduction of Homer's Helen by Paris, the other of Virgil's Dido abandoned by Aeneas (1314–15). The incompetent botcher contrived to make Helen look a strumpet ('se reía a socapa' ('she was laughing slyly')), and Dido a crybaby dropping 'lágrimas del tamaño de nueces' ('tears the size of walnuts')). Quixote 'notes' this fact, but his only audible comment is comically by-the-way: far from talking 'more rationally', he blurts out that the ladies were most unfortunate because, had he been there, he could have prevented it all — the fall of Troy and Rome's destruction of Carthage included — by killing Paris (1315). We catch our breath, for while this rewinds his maddest delusions of knight errantry, there is something disturbing about the directness of its allusion to killing; formerly he idealized his dream as a romantic matter of challenges, duels, and vanquished rivals, but this seems to adumbrate an untoward admission of the deadly reality. Sure enough, as Edward Riley points out, it is the last time we ever hear him imagine himself as a chivalric champion of romance.[28] Nonetheless Sancho is prompted by the boast to remark that soon there will be no inn or barber's shop 'donde no ande pintada la historia de nuestras hazañas' ('where the story of our doings won't be painted up') ('ours' is rich!). Even so, he too notices the frightful quality of the daubs in question, provoking a riposte in which Quixote compares the painter to that Orbaneja of Úbeda whose draughtsmanship was so poor that he had to label the subjects of his canvases (1315). All this is designed to lead up to a swipe at the equally incompetent 'painter' of the *Segundo tomo del ingenioso hidalgo don Quixote de la Mancha* published under the name of Alonso Fernández de Avellaneda (licenced 4 July 1614), news of which is thought to have reached Cervantes just before writing II. 59 (1213–18), no more than six months before finishing his book (passed by the censor 27 February 1615).

Biting allusions to Avellaneda's contemptible botch come thick and fast in these final pages, beginning in the previous chapter with Altisidora's account of the devils playing tennis with it in hell (to which Quixote responds that he could not care less 'que ando como cuerpo fantástico por las tinieblas del abismo [...] porque no soy aquel de quien esa historia trata' (II. 70, 1306) ('that I am wandering in a fantastic shape in the darkness of the pit, [...] for *I am not the one* that history treats of'; emphasis added), and escalating in the next, as we see in a moment. The satire is witty and unrelenting, and has led some to see literary polemic as the sole structural motive for our ending, which shows Quixote 'finalmente muerto y sepultado' ('finally dead and buried') — terminally dead this second time — 'porque ninguno se atreva a levantarle nuevos testimonios' (II. Prólogo, 677) 'so that no one may dare to raise any further witness against him'. That, however, is to miss the full point. As the scene of the bad paintings is expressly and exquisitely designed to show,

Cervantes's criticism was not just spleen at 'Avellaneda' having stolen a march on him, but the charge that the impostor's book embodied — as it does — an abject, almost cretinous misrepresentation of the nature of his novel. It was, to be precise, the work of a sneering ape, the sort to paint Dido with walnut-sized tears or Helen with a whorish grin (Avellaneda's Quixote indeed takes up with a fifty-year-old whore); in other words, a buffoon incapable of portraying the truth of the book's heroes or grasping its complex, ironic style of burlesque.[29] By pointing this out, what does the author achieve? Naturally, he implicitly draws attention to the complexity, irony, and truth of what we are reading.

In this last respect there is another striking facet of the scene. The jest about Orbaneja, as no reader can be unaware, is a direct repetition of the same anecdote in II. 3, 711. There, however, Quixote tells it to complain that 'el autor de mi historia' ('the author of *my* history'; emphasis added) the Moorish dog Cide Hamete, 'no ha sido sabio [...] sino algún ignorante hablador, que a tiento y sin algún discurso se puso a escribirla, salga lo que saliere' ('was no sage, but some ignorant chatterer who in a haphazard and heedless way set about writing it, turn out as it might'). That this means Cervantes himself is of course deliberate irony; we may rest assured that Sansón Carrasco's preceding list of 'faults' (*tachas*) in Part One such as intercalated novels were ones of which he was particularly proud, and Sansón is made to respond to the Don's outburst with a lighthearted yet incontestable correction underlining the work's success ('los niños la manosean, los mozos la leen, los hombres la entienden y los viejos la celebran; y, finalmente, [...] la tal historia es del más gustoso y menos perjudicial entretenimiento que hasta agora se haya visto' (711–12) ('children turn its leaves, young people read it, grown men understand it, and old folk praise it; and in a word, [...] the said history is the most delightful and least injurious entertainment that has ever been seen')). The contrast between this first occurrence of the joke and its second in II. 71, virtually identical but now applied to a real 'prattling ignoramus', is no less ironical; but the context of disillusion — Quixote's and Cervantes's — lends the humour a more profound, intentionally ambivalent affect. Hence the reference to Avellaneda goes beyond mere literary satire; metaphorically, it paints the Knight of the Sorry Countenance's growing melancholy in alternate brush-strokes of comedy and pathos. As if to underline this, the narrative brusquely abandons the scene and returns to the story's main burlesque thread as it gathers towards its end: the urgency of Dulcinea's disenchantment ('Pero dejando esto aparte, dime si piensas, Sancho, darte otra tanda esta noche' (II. 71, 1316) ('But leaving this aside, tell me, Sancho, do you have a mind to give yourself another round tonight?')).

The next chapter, II. 72 'De cómo don Quijote y Sancho llegaron a su aldea' ('Of How Don Quixote and Sancho Reached their Village'), returns to the theme in the same manner. It recounts Quixote's weird encounter with a character from Avellaneda's work, Don Álvaro Tarfe; but the treatment again firmly subordinates literary satire to the novel's burlesque and introspective narrative purposes. One is to present the comic spectacle of Quixote's insisting on obtaining a sworn affidavit from Don Álvaro affirming that they have never met before. The other, to show that, whereas Sancho has wholly interiorized his master's old convictions about his chivalric quest ('el famoso, el valiente y el discreto, el enamorado, el desfacedor de agravios, el tutor de pupilos y huérfanos, el amparo de las viudas, el matador de las doncellas' (1318–19) ('the famous, the valiant and the wise, the lover, the undoer of wrongs, the guardian of minors and orphans, the protector of widows, the killer of damsels'), as he proudly introduces Don Quixote, in his eagerness to mimic the language of romance — *desfacedor* — somewhat unfelicitously alluding, with *matador de doncellas*, to the episode of Altisidora's fake demise two chapters earlier), Quixote himself has ceased from speaking in these vainglorious terms. He points out that he has never set foot in Zaragoza, but does not avoid alluding to the matter of his defeat, the 'sucesos [...] no [...] de mucho gusto' ('adventures [...] of great regret') that occurred instead in Barcelona (1319–20). The most striking feature of the scene is its lack of bile or boastfulness; Quixote and Tarfe meet on terms of utmost courtesy, dine together, and exchange pleasantries 'en las cuales mostró el gran manchego su discreción, de modo que desengañó a don Álvaro Tarfe del error en que estaba' (1321) ('in the course of which the great Manchegan displayed his discretion, so that he disabused Don Alvaro Tarfe of the error he was under'). More to the point, he does not demand that the character from the apocryphal version admit that he or it is false, or that Quixote himself is true, only that 'yo no soy el don Quijote impreso en la segunda parte' (1320) ('I am not the Don Quixote in print in the Second Part') — a remark that, while acute from a literary critical and theoretical point of view, shows the Knight's gradual subconscious relinquishment of his make-believe identity. The effect is to leave Don Álvaro wondering whether it is not he who is 'encantado, pues tocaba con la mano dos tan contrarios don Quijotes' (1321) ('enchanted, now that he had been brought face to face with two such opposite Don Quixotes'); but they part the best of friends.

It is clear, then, that in these closing chapters the apocryphal *Don Quijote*, far from being dragged in for petty motives of spite, plays a role parallel to that of Part One in the rest of Part Two. To read the Prólogo or Cide Hamete's concluding words as implying that Cervantes entertained the slightest, most distant worry that 'Avellaneda' would really set about concocting a fourth continuation of the story if he did not kill off its hero is one of the more charming naivetés of Cervantine criticism, its credulity matched only by the innocence of supposing that, had 'Avellaneda' been contemplating such a plan, he would have cared tuppence whether Cervantes killed Don Quixote or not, after he had already done so in Part One; which incidentally should mean that all the many people in Part Two who have read Part One ought to be aware that the 'Quixote' they meet is in fact dead — but this did not deter Cervantes himself from writing Part Two.[30] In other words, the references to *Segundo tomo del ingenioso hidalgo don Quijote de la Mancha* demand to be read with the exactly same critical attention to their narratological function as those to Part One: a function fundamentally humorous, but with both profoundly fantastic epistemological implications (how can one 'meet' a character from a book?) and profoundly verisimilar psychological ones. Two details in II. 72 confirm this careful aesthetic purpose: the seemingly offhand mention by Don Álvaro of the discordant ending of Avellaneda's barren squib, 'osaré yo jurar que le dejo metido en la Casa del Nuncio, en Toledo, para que le curen' (1319) ('I dare swear I left him

[Quixote] shut up in the Casa del Nuncio [madhouse] at Toledo, to be cured'); and the recurrent topic of Dulcinea's disenchantment, the only remnant of Quixote's mad utopian dream, which he is fooled into believing has been completed ('aquella noche [...] acabó Sancho su tarea, de que quedó don Quijote contento sobremodo, y esperaba el día por ver si en el camino topaba ya desencantada a Dulcinea su señora' (1321) ('that night [...] Sancho finished off his task, at which Don Quixote was beyond measure joyful, and looked forward to the day, to see if along the road he should meet his now disenchanted lady Dulcinea'). Both alike foreshadow, *per antithesim*, the imminent dénouement.

With that, the heroes crest the hill and catch sight of the village. Chapter II. 73 'De los agüeros que tuvo don Quijote al entrar de su aldea, con otros sucesos que adornan y acreditan esta grande historia' ('Of the Omens Don Quixote Had as He Entered his Village, and Other Incidents that Embellish and Confirm this Great History') tells of the hero's homecoming, as described in my first paragraph. We need not rehearse again the burlesque echoes of the ending to Part One but attend only to the matter highlighted in the title: the 'omens' that greet the pair as they trot in past the allotments.[31] The simple event takes up a quarter of the chapter. Two boys are arguing and one shouts, 'no la has de ver en todos los días de tu vida' (II. 73, 1322) ('you shall never see her again as long as you live!'); immediately afterwards, a hare being chased by a pack of hounds hides under Sancho's ass. Quixote instantly interprets both as signs he will never in all his days see Dulcinea free of her persecutors. Of course the omen *is* an omen, but not in the sense he says. No one will ever 'see' Dulcinea, because she does not exist; subconsciously Quixote realizes it, and that to 'disenchant' her means to accept the fact. The hare comes to rest under Sancho's beast, not his, because Sancho must be aware, at a level not so subconscious, that he is responsible for his master's delusion that she is enchanted, and hence exists; and so feels guilty that he has done nothing to disenchant her — that is, disenchant him — not so much by failing to flog himself as by not confessing the trick. He hastens to prove that what the boys were discussing was a cage of crickets (apt symbol! Dulcinea caged, two caged madmen), buys it, picks up the hare, and presents both to Quixote with the words:

> — He aquí, señor, rompidos y desbaratados estos agüeros, que no tienen que ver más con nuestros sucesos, según que yo imagino, aunque tonto, que con las nubes de antaño. Y, si no me acuerdo mal, he oído decir al cura de nuestro pueblo que no es de personas cristianas ni discretas mirar en estas niñerías, y aun vuesa merced mismo me lo dijo los días pasados [*cf.* II. 58, 1199], dándome a entender que eran tontos todos aquellos cristianos que miraban en agüeros. (II. 73, 1323–24)

('Here, sir, are your omens, broken and undone; they have no more to do with our affairs, to my way of thinking, stupid though I am, than with the clouds of yesteryear. And if I remember rightly I have heard the curate of our village say that it does not become Christians or sensible people to give heed to these silly things; and even you yourself said the same to me the other day, telling me that all Christians who minded omens were stupid.'

And so — the crowning moment passes in only twelve of the novel's 194,043 words — Quixote quietly hands the hare (Dulcinea) back to the huntsmen: 'Llegaron los cazadores, pidieron su liebre, y diósela don Quijote; pasaron adelante', (1324) ('The sportsmen came up and asked for their hare, and Don Quixote gave her to them; they went on').

So the two proceed into the village, and within minutes Quixote is telling Sansón and the Curate his plan 'dar vado a sus amorosos pensamientos, ejercitándose en el pastoral y virtuoso ejercicio' (1325) ('to give free rein to his thoughts of love by following the virtuous pastoral calling'), declaring in a fine pastiche of bucolic language that his love will still be 'la sin par Dulcinea del Toboso, gloria de estas riberas, adorno de estos prados, sustento de la hermosura, nata de los donaires' (1326) ('the peerless Dulcinea del Toboso, the glory of these brooksides, the ornament of these meadows, the mainstay of beauty, the cream of all the graces') (is *nata*, 'cream', a little *too* shepherd-like? He might have chosen *flor*, 'flower' — more pastoral, less rustic), and even chuckling at the idea of Teresa Panza being called Teresaina. Yet nothing can be the same after the scene we have just witnessed. Whatever Quixote says, in his heart of hearts he knows the dream is over; he wastes no more time scrutinizing the face of every woman they meet to see if she is Dulcinea.

The same extraordinary blend of festive comedy and melancholy disillusion runs through the final chapter, 'De cómo don Quijote cayó malo y del testamento que hizo y su muerte' ('Of How Don Quixote Fell Sick, and the Will He Made, and his Death'). I have pointed out above how, alongside the underlying features of parody of the romances and satire of Avellaneda, the account of Alonso Quijano's death draws on the *Arts of Dying Well* to present it as a devout and serious one, and how the efforts of all his family and friends to comfort and support him reinforce the pathos. As such, Quijano's passing is not tragic; he dies peacefully and well. By the same token it is not comic in López Pinciano's sense, but even so, commentators have not been slow to point out elements of ambivalent irony. The account of his last will and testament skips the requisite dispositions for the salvation of his soul, masses, charitable bequests, etc., to describe the *mandas* ('y después de haber hecho la cabeza del testamento y ordenado su alma don Quijote, con todas aquellas circunstancias cristianas que se requieren, llegando a las mandas' (II. 74, 1332) ('as soon as the preamble of the will had been set out and Don Quixote had commended his soul to God with all the Christian formalities that are required, coming to the bequests')). These show an obsession with denouncing the romances of chivalry that seems only a little less unhealthy than his previous desire to live them out ('creyeron sin duda que alguna nueva locura le había tomado' (1331) ('they thought without doubt some new craze had taken possession of him')), for example in his determination to disinherit his niece should she propose marrying any man who knows 'qué cosas sean libros de caballerías' (1334) ('what books of chivalry are'), or begging pardon of the pseudonymous Avellaneda for having been an unwitting cause of his 'absurdities' (*disparates*, 1334). Perhaps most striking, after all this he falls into a terminal coma for three days:

> Alborotáronse todos y acudieron a su remedio [...], pero, con todo, comía la sobrina, brindaba el ama y se regocijaba Sancho Panza; que esto ´ del heredar algo borra ´ o templa en el heredero ´ la memoria de la pena ´ que es razón que deje el muerto. (II. 74, 1334)

> (All were in a flutter and made haste to take care of him [...]; but still the niece ate, the housekeeper quaffed, and Sancho Panza was cheered; for the thought of an inheritance somewhat blots out or assuages the heir's memory of the grief the dead man ought to leave.)

The joke was proverbial; Hartzenbusch spotted that the words after *que esto* are four rhymed ballad verses (marked ´ in the Spanish), 'produced by chance, or quoted on purpose', which likewise lend it a trite, traditional feel.[32] Such irony is not existential, then, not the scene of bondage and absurdity offered by characters 'inferior in power or intelligence to ourselves' at Frye's bottom level of mimesis (n. 12, above), but the relaxed, sardonic kind proper to middling low mimetic realism. In this sense it runs parallel to the self-reflexive humour of the satiric 'new' epitaphs (replacing those at the end of Part One) of Sansón and Cide Hamete, the gentle leg-pull of the Curate's second affidavit certifying — against his express wishes — the dead man's 'genuine' identity ('llamado comúnmente "don Quijote de la Mancha"' ('commonly called Don Quixote of La Mancha')) in order 'quitar la ocasión de que algún otro autor [...] le resucitase falsamente' (1335) ('to remove the possibility of any other author [...] bringing him to life again *falsely*'; emphasis added), and indeed the constant insistence of all the characters and narrators on calling him Don Quixote (twenty-six times) despite his best efforts to re-form himself as plain (?) Alonso Quijano el Bueno.[33] In the passage already quoted above (at n. 10) the author says: 'en tanto que don Quijote fue Alonso Quijano el Bueno a secas, y en tanto que fue don Quijote de la Mancha, fue siempre de apacible condición' (II. 74, 1332) ('whether Don Quixote was plain Alonso Quixano the Good or Don Quixote of La Mancha, he was always of a gentle disposition') — we almost miss the point, so light is the touch. Isn't this, in reality, precisely the wrong way round?

To define the ethos of Part Two's ending as low mimetic realism excludes the idea that it aims at the derisive comedy of existential 'irony' in Frye's sense, or equally that it is in any sense high tragedy. Yet this does not mean that low mimesis cannot be humorous and serious. The peculiarity of Cervantes's style is its deliberate ambiguity of affect, which is kaleidoscopic in the technical sense that its colours 'may be constantly altered *by rotation of the instrument*', exhibiting 'a constantly changing [...] *succession of shifting phases*' (*OED*). The multiple readings of past centuries tend to play up one phase or another, hard or soft, but I argue that the ambivalence is insoluble; those that come down on one side tend only to focus on one rotation of the instrument. All illuminate aspects of the novel, but perhaps the most suggestive overall are the reactions of creative writers, which stretch from Byron and Lamb to Nabokov, Guillén, and Borges as we have seen; these tend to spring not from theoretical, historicist, or methodological viewpoints, but from a spontaneous practical interest in the novel's technique of 'shifting' — only recall

Borges's suggestion that, if a modern poet were to achieve the 'almost' impossible task of rewriting *Don Quixote* word for word but without copying the original, the resulting 'palimpsest' would be an entirely new, more 'subtle' novel.[34]

In relation to the ending, two strands help round off these remarks. The first is Thomas Mann's perception that, coiled within the 'witty depths and trick mirrors of art and illusion' of Part Two's games (with its various authors, with Part One, with Avellaneda) — 'a romantic puzzle, an ironic trick' in which the heroes 'live on the fame of their fame, [...] step out of the sphere of reality [...] and to a joyous welcome from the readers, wander in person as heightened realities' in a narrative 'naïve' yet 'singularly arbitrary and sovereign in its contradictions' — there lies a yet stranger story of which 'the author himself was not so aware in the beginning':

> His respect for the creature of his own comic invention steadily grows during the narrative, — this process is perhaps the most fascinating thing in the whole novel; indeed, it is a novel in itself, and it keeps step with his growing respect for the work, which was conceived modestly as a crude satirical joke without any notion of the symbolic and human stature to which the figure of the hero was destined to grow. This change of viewpoint permits and causes a wide-ranging identification of the author with his hero.[35]

Mann finds Quijano's death, with its humdrum bourgeois concerns and humour, 'prosaic' (*matt*) and unsentimental, yet inevitable; to die in battle would violate the comedy, to live on once sane be demeaning, to die mad 'neither Christian nor pedagogical'. But all this, plus the fact that although we should feel pleased on Quijano's behalf we feel sorry at Quixote's demise, shows how far the novel has transcended its burlesque premise, while the author's 'jealousy' of Avellaneda only proves his new, proud bond with his 'stepson' ('Para mí sola nació don Quijote, y yo para él' (II. 74, 1336) ('For me alone [Cide Hamete's pen] was Don Quixote born, and I for him')). In fact, the transcendence is so extreme that it effectually 'kills off' the possibility of any 'comforting' (*befriedigend*) ending.[36]

Many critics have spun variations on this theme of the novel's gradual, almost imperceptible 'shifting' or 'rotation' of the point of view so as to secure our — still doubtful and incredulous — identification with the hero, including speculations that the final scene reflected Cervantes's presentiment of his own death a year later. The latter idea has little to do with literary critique, but Borges, who shared it, draws the relevant lessons: the sense of the ending depends on the 'emotional charge' of the preceding chapters, but also on what he calls the 'magic effect' of this chapter's various literary 'tricks' (*astucias*).[37] Prominent among these are two authorial 'eclipses' or 'gaps of silence'. First, Cervantes makes Quijano's conversion to sanity take place through the mysterious medium of a six-hour sleep:

> Rogó don Quijote que le dejasen solo, porque quería dormir un poco. Hiciéronlo así y durmió de un tirón, como dicen, más de seis horas; tanto, que pensaron el ama y la sobrina que se había de quedar en el sueño. Despertó al cabo del tiempo dicho y, dando una gran voz, dijo:
> — ¡Bendito sea el poderoso Dios, que tanto bien me ha hecho! En fin, sus misericordias no tienen límite, ni las abrevian ni impiden los pecados de los hombres. (II. 74, 1329)

> (Don Quixote begged them to leave him alone, as he had a wish to sleep a little. They did so, and he slept at one stretch, as the saying is, more than six hours, so that the housekeeper and niece thought he was going to sleep for ever. At the end of that time he woke up, and in a loud voice exclaimed, 'Blessed be Almighty God, who has shown me such goodness. In short, his mercies are boundless, and the sins of men can neither limit them nor keep them back!')

We are not told by what obscure process the sleep, or dream (*sueño*), effected this cure; as Borges nicely puts it, 'to make it *more believable*, he insinuates the possibility of a miracle' (p. 16). Somewhat the same is true of the second of the 'unknowns or feigned scruples', the author's failure to tell us anything about the hero's confession; all we learn is, 'Hizo salir la gente el cura, y quedose solo con él y confesole' (II. 74, 1331) ('The curate turned them all out and, left alone with him, confessed him'). For Borges, this delicate 'gap' too lends 'more credibility to the other facts' (p. 19). In short, Cervantes's narrative strategies simultaneously create verisimilitude *and* magic, effects calculated to achieve the identification (*Solidarisierung*) of which Mann spoke.

When Don Quixote lies making his will, he begins the bequests by stipulating that any moneys in Sancho's possession should be his and adds that, *if* he could, more than an *ínsula* he would leave him a kingdom 'because the simplicity of his character and the fidelity of his conduct deserve it':

> Y, volviéndose a Sancho, le dijo:
> — Perdóname, amigo, de la ocasión que te he dado de parecer loco como yo, haciéndote caer en el error en que yo he caído de que hubo y hay caballeros andantes en el mundo. (II. 74, 1332–33)
>
> (And turning to Sancho, he said: 'Forgive me, friend, that I led you to seem as mad as myself, making you fall into the same error I myself have fallen into, that there were and are knights errant in the world.')

Sancho bursts into tears, and exclaims for the final time:

> — ¡Ay! [...] No se muera vuestra merced, señor mío, sino tome mi consejo y viva muchos años, porque la mayor locura que puede hacer un hombre en esta vida es *dejarse morir* sin más ni más, sin que nadie le mate ni otras manos le acaben que las de la melancolía. Mire no sea perezoso, sino levántese desa cama, y vámonos al campo vestidos de pastores, como tenemos concertado: quizá tras de alguna mata hallaremos a la señora doña Dulcinea desencantada, que no haya más que ver. Si es que se muere de pesar de verse vencido, écheme a mí la culpa, diciendo que por haber yo cinchado mal a Rocinante le derribaron; cuanto más que vuestra merced habrá visto en sus libros de caballerías ser cosa ordinaria derribarse unos caballeros a otros y el que es vencido hoy ser vencedor mañana. (II. 74, 1333; emphasis added)
>
> ('Ah! [...] Don't die, my lord, but take my advice and live many years; for the craziest thing a man can do in this life is *to let himself die* without rhyme or reason, without anybody killing him, or any hands but melancholy's making an end of him. Come, don't be lazy, but get up from that bed and let us take to the fields in shepherds' dress, as we agreed. Perhaps behind some bush we shall find the lady Doña Dulcinea disenchanted, as fine as fine can be. If it be that

Your Honour is dying of vexation at having been vanquished, lay the blame on me and say you were overthrown because of my having girthed Rocinante badly; besides, Your Honour must have seen in your books of chivalry that it is a common thing for knights to knock one another down, and for the one who is vanquished today to be the winner tomorrow.')

It cannot escape us, in the light of the omens of II. 73, that this is a key moment. For Borges, the fact that Quixote's friends, and Sancho above all, have swapped places with him and now 'carry on living, or pretending to live' his 'illusory world' is part of the magic; Sancho 'cannot grasp that Don Quixote *died during his sleep*, and that now it is useless to invoke enchanters and Dulcineas' (pp. 18, 20). The observation that there are *two* deaths at the end is one of those perceptions that seems perfectly obvious and yet, put in such a way, is illuminating. No less striking, however, is the unvarying humour at the expense of Sancho's simple-mindedness in these, his last words: 'take my advice', don't be 'lazy' and die 'without rhyme or reason' (*sin más ni más*) at the 'hands' of melancholy; we only have to get up to find Dulcinea 'behind some bush'; blame it all on a mix-up with the saddle-girth (no mention of that in II. 64), 'Your Honour must have seen' ... in the romances he cannot read.

That the intended affect inclines more towards a smile than ape-laughter seems overwhelmingly likely, but the speech brings us to the second strand of critique I mentioned above. Sancho attributes Alonso Quijano's decline to melancholy and suggests that his death is voluntary, at least in some passive sense ('dejarse morir'). The idea of suicide has been taken up by a multitude of critics, with earnest discussions as to whether it is Quixote who elects to die for Quijano's salvation, Quijano who makes way to let Quixote's fame live on, and so on.[38] Such arguments find little overt support in the text, which seems to say clearly, not that sanity brings death, but that death brings sanity. Nonetheless, Quijano's reply to Sancho's desperate attempt to comfort him and the last of Part Two's 197 mentions of Dulcinea is memorable:

> — Señores — dijo don Quijote — , vámonos poco a poco, pues ya en los nidos de antaño no hay pájaros hogaño. Yo fui loco y ya soy cuerdo. (II. 74, 1333)

> ('Sirs, not so fast,' said Don Quixote, 'in last year's nests there are no birds this year. I was mad, and now I am sane.')

The language is simple and colloquial, and his use of a proverbial expression provokes a smile, given the history between him and Sancho on the matter (the last time, in II. 71); but 'the birds of yesteryear have flown the nest' evokes disillusion (only months later Cervantes would ruefully apply it to himself in the prologue to his 'unperformed' *Comedias*).[39] Most notable, perhaps, is the elegiac poetic cadence of its *pie quebrado* heptasyllabic metre and rhyme. Borges describes the tone as unfathomable, the 'negligent music' of a master (p. 20). *Melancolía, -cólico* occurs eleven times in Part Two, nine of them in the last section beginning with the Duchess's observation of the hero's loneliness at II. 44, 1072, and all used by or applicable to Quixote; the last three, of his illness in the final chapter, as diagnosed by a doctor. In retrospect the occurrences all seem significant: after the telling one in II. 44, the word crops up twice in II. 58, when Quixote talks about the melancholy caused by omens (1199; cf. II. 73, 1324, which refers back to this), and the girls beg him not to break the nets round their impromptu pastoral lest he 'let in' melancholy (1203); then in II. 60 Roque Guinart finds him 'pensativo, con la más triste y melancólica figura' (II. 60, 1222) ('pensive, with the saddest and most melancholy face') after thinking about 'la convertida en labradora Dulcinea' (1219) ('Dulcinea transformed into a country wench'); and, more ironically, in II. 65 Don Antonio Moreno chides Sansón for the wrong of having brought Quixote to his senses, 'porque con su salud no solamente perdemos sus gracias, sino las de Sancho Panza su escudero, que cualquiera dellas puede volver a alegrar a la misma melancolía' (II. 65, 1270) ('for by his recovery we lose not only his drolleries, but his squire Sancho Panza's too, any one of which is enough to make Melancholia herself merry again').

Paintings, omens, illness, empty nests, death: all are told with unsentimental humour, but the inflexion toward melancholy is palpable. Whether we see the ending of Part Two as comic or sad, the readings to which I have alluded all share the conviction that it marks some kind of peripeteia, or what Frank Kermode, in the book from which I have borrowed my title, defines as 'the equivalent, in narrative, of irony in rhetoric, [...] a disconfirmation followed by a consonance'; a deflection of the generic convention that provides an 'unexpected and instructive' dissonance that is also a resolution. He begins by saying that it is expected of poets 'that they should help us to make sense of our lives'; Cervantes is mentioned only once, when, following in the steps of Ortega y Gasset, Kermode cites him as the first in the long line replacing romance's inherited paradigm of the 'comfortable' but illusory 'unidimensional' narrative order, the stereotypical 'land of fiction' whose remoteness from reality 'we identify as absurd', not with realism but with 'realistic poetry', a new genre that searches how, 'by all manner of dazzling devices and metaphors and stratagems, fiction and reality can be brought together again' — words he applies to Robert Musil, but no less true of *Don Quijote*.[40] Recalling López Pinciano's allusion to tragicomedy, or Byron's description of the novel as a 'real' epic and Sismondi's 'eternal contrast between the spirit of poetry and that of prose', we see that neither concept was so remote from modern critical theory after all. For Cervantes the sense of such an ending by no means excluded humour; nevertheless such recognitions are serious.[41] In his study Northrop Frye points to both comic and tragic forms of low mimesis. For the affect of the latter he suggests a term used several times above:

> In low mimetic tragedy, pity and fear are neither purged nor absorbed into pleasures, but are communicated externally, as sensations. [...] The best word for low mimetic or domestic tragedy is, perhaps, *pathos*, and pathos has a close relation to the sensational reflex of tears. Pathos presents its hero as isolated by a 'weakness' which appeals to our sympathy because it is on our own level of experience.[42]

What the realistic humour and pathos of Cervantes's ending contrives to offer, perhaps, is this special form of catharsis; not the pity and fear Aristotle defined as the end of tragedy, but Kermode's 'sense' of recognizing our own destinies and mortality in those of fictional characters we have been inveigled into regarding with the affection we feel for real persons.[43]

Notes to Chapter 10

1. Miguel de Cervantes, *Don Quijote de la Mancha*, II. 71–74, 1310–37.
2. See Daniel Eisenberg, *Romances of Chivalry in the Spanish Golden Age* (Newark, DE: Juan de la Cuesta, 1982), pp. 55–74.
3. Unless otherwise indicated, all translations are mine; those from *Don Quixote* are, except in one case, adapted from Miguel de Cervantes Saavedra, *The Ingenious Gentleman Don Quixote of La Mancha*, trans. by John Ormsby, 4 vols (London: Smith, Elder & Co., 1885).
4. Garci Rodríguez de Montalvo, *Las sergas de Esplandián* [1496?], in *Libros de caballerías*, ed. by Pascual de Gayangos, Biblioteca de Autores Españoles, 40 (Madrid: Rivadeneyra, 1857), pp. 403–561 (pp. 558–61). The medieval *Amadís* appears to have ended tragically with the hero's death in combat at the hands of unknowing Esplandián, and Oriana's suicide. The kitsch substitute's lack of taste is total and unrelenting; Montalvo ponderously explains, for example, that the heroes' contemptibly vulgar jewel-encrusted chairs showed that though other 'high men might be their equals in dress, they could not match their *seats* [*asentamientos*], which lent them great authority' (henceforth all emphases mine) — even when slumped on them in suspended animation.
5. [Miguel de Cervantes Saavedra], *The History of the Valorous and Wittie Knight-Errant, Don-Quixote of the Mancha: Translated out of the Spanish*, trans. by Thomas Shelton (London: William Stansby for Ed[ward] Blount and W[illiam] Barret, 1612), Pp1^v (modernized).
6. Alonso López Pinciano, 'Epístola nona: De la comedia', in his *Philosophia antigua poetica* (Madrid: Thomas Junti, 1596), pp. 371–417 (pp. 381–82). That Cervantes read this chapter attentively is certain; he even borrowed one of its little jokes, making Sancho say *cananeas* 'Canaanites' for *hacaneas* 'hacks': ' "[V]ienen a caballo sobre tres cananeas remendadas, que no hay más que ver." –Hacaneas querrás decir, Sancho. –Poca diferencia hay –respondió Sancho' (II. 10, 769) (' "They come mounted [the three country trollops he would have Quixote believe are Dulcinea and her ladies] on three piebald *cackneys*, the finest sight ever you saw". "Hackneys, you mean, Sancho". "There is not much difference," said Sancho') ; cf. López Pinciano, pp. 401–02 on laughter from word-play, 'for example [...] saying *cananea* when one means *acanea*'.
7. *Aeli Donati quod fertur Commentum Terenti: Accedunt Eugraphi Commentum et Scholia Bembina*, ed. by Paulus Wessner, 3 vols (Leipzig: Teubner, 1902–08), I, 71 ad *And.* I. i. 78 'he portrays comic deaths in such a way as [...] not to be tragic, making it a whore who is removed, or an old man, or a man's extra wife; a death of this kind is received with moderate sadness, even joy.' See Jeremy Lawrance, 'On the Title *Tragicomedia de Calisto y Melibea*', in *Letters and Society in Fifteenth-Century Spain: Studies Presented to P. E. Russell on his Eightieth Birthday*, ed. by Alan Deyermond and Jeremy Lawrance (Llangrannog: Dolphin, 1993), pp. 79–92.
8. The protocol was public, everyday, and familiar; Philippe Ariès, *Western Attitudes toward Death: From the Middle Ages to the Present*, trans. by Patricia M. Ranum (Baltimore: Johns Hopkins University Press, 1974) calls it 'tamed' (*apprivoisée*), not so much because it took place at home as because its domestication embodied a spontaneous resignation to the collective destiny distinct from our 'savage' (*ensauvagée*) modern interdict upon death: 'mad though he was, Don Quixote made no attempt to flee from death into the daydreams in which he had passed his life. On the contrary, the warning signs of death brought him back to his senses' (p. 5).
9. Ariès also notes this Baroque inflexion towards theatrical emotion (*Western Attitudes*, pp. 55–58 'exalted, dramatized, and [...] already less concerned with [*la mort de soi*, one's] own death than with *la mort de toi*, the death of the other person; [...] the romantic, rhetorical treatment of death'). The rhetorical turn is mirrored in the bystanders' grief at Quixote's death; Cervantes likewise uses it to shape the affect 'romantically', as we see.
10. Unlike a modern will stipulating the disposal of the testator's estate, the pre-modern nuncupative testament concerned the spiritual preparation of his soul to ensure a state of grace in the next life, including charitable bequests, stipulations for exequies and funeral masses, intimate confession of wrongs to be righted, etc.

11. The seven numbered stages of the ceremony of the good death were: A1 recognition that one's 'hour' had come and 'regret de la vie', A2 words of consolation to family, servants, and friends asking pardon for misdeeds, A3 contrition for sins, A4 confession and absolution, A5 dictation of a last will and testament, A6 Extreme Unction, and finally A7 giving up one's soul to God. Nothing is missing, all is performed with fitting dignity.
12. Aristotle, *Poetics*, 1448a1–5, 'the protagonists must necessarily be worthy or cheap, [...] either better, or equal to us, or worse' (ἤτοι βελτίονας ἢ καθ'ἡμᾶς ἢ χείρονας). I follow Northrop Frye, *Anatomy of Criticism: Four Essays* (Princeton: Princeton University Press, 1957), pp. 33–34 in taking this to mean the difference between (*a*) high mimesis, heroes superior to us in kind or degree, i.e. myth/romance (where they are endowed with supernatural powers) or tragedy/epic; (*b*) low mimesis, characters not superior but 'one of us', i.e. realism/comedy; (*c*) irony, characters 'inferior in power or intelligence to ourselves, so that we have the sense of looking down on a scene of [...] absurdity'. The problem is that Cervantes's ending seems to partake of more than one mode. For the same point in relation to Tirant, a likely source, see Jeremy Lawrance, 'Death in *Tirant lo Blanc*', in *'Tirant lo Blanc': New Approaches*, ed. by Arthur Terry (London: Tamesis, 1999), pp. 91–107.
13. For the history behind the controversy, see P. E. Russell, '*Don Quixote* as a Funny Book', *Modern Language Review*, 64 (1969), 312–26; Anthony J. Close, *The Romantic Approach to 'Don Quixote': A Critical History of the Romantic Tradition in 'Quixote' Criticism* (Cambridge: Cambridge University Press, 1978).
14. First published anonymously in *Don Juan: Cantos xii.–xiii.–and xiv* (London: John Hunt, 1823), Canto XIII 8–9, pp. 59–60.
15. Byron probably lifted his famous line from J. C. L. Simonde de Sismondi, *De la littérature du midi de l'Europe*, 4 vols (Paris: Treuttel et Würtz, 1813), III, 337–42, 'quelques personnes ont considéré Don Quichotte comme le livre le plus triste qui ait jamais été écrit' (p. 340). It became a truism of Romantic critique, but this did not mean the Romantics were unaware of the comedy. Sismondi himself talked of 'this book scattered with so much comic salt', 'so amusing [...], laughable', *gaieté, esprit piquant, satire*; the essential point was the work's *blend* of elements, 'the eternal contrast between the spirit of poetry and that of prose' (pp. 332, 338–39).
16. 'Introduction', in *Don Quixote*, trans. by Edith Grossman (New York: HarperCollins, 2003), pp. i–xix (p. x).
17. Charles Lamb, 'Barrenness of the Imaginative Faculty in the Productions of Modern Art', in his *The Last Essays of Elia* (London: Edward Moxon, 1833), pp. 166–86 (pp. 182, 184); he too remarked that to laugh was to read the book 'by halves, mistaking his author's purport, which was — tears'. In Soviet People's Artist Grigory Kozintsev's classic Marxist film adaptation (*Дон Кихот*, Lenfilm 1957; designed to 'rehabilitate' the novel after the death of Stalin, who disliked it) the Duke and Duchess are presented in yet more sinister light as heartless aristocratic villains of the class war — a reading which Cervantes's portrayal does not necessarily exclude.
18. Vladimir Nabokov, *Lectures on Don Quixote*, ed. by Fredson Bowers (New York: Harcourt Brace Jovanovich, 1983), pp. 68–70; the chapter sprouts 'wings', comments Nabokov, to sweep us into the 'dreamworld of permanent and irrational art', by contrast with the 'atrocious' cruelty of those he calls 'the main villainous enchanters in the book', the 'diabolical' Duke and 'tigerish' Duchess (p. 62). But Jorge Guillén, 'Vida y muerte de Alonso Quijano', *Romanische Forschungen*, 64 (1952), 102–13 (p. 103) adds that the impoverished gentleman is 'clearly Alonso Quijano at this moment' (II. 44, 1075–76, 'The *good* gentleman was beyond measure distressed [...], because [the irreparable disaster to his stockings] is one of the greatest signs of poverty an *hidalgo* can show in the course of his long embarrassments'). Thus it directly prefigures our ending.
19. 'We do not know what the laughter denoted by this expression involves', drily observe the editors at II. 74, 1072, n.16. The rest is silence: nothing in John Bowle's pioneering commentary, *Historia del famoso cavallero Don Quixote de la Mancha*, 6 vols (Salisbury/Londres: Edvardo Easton, for B. White & others, 1781), v: *Anotaciones*, 111; the Real Academia's *El ingenioso hidalgo don Quixote de la Mancha: Nueva edición corregida denuevo, con nuevas notas, con nuevas estampas, con nuevo analisis*, ed. by Juan Antonio Pellicer, 5 vols (Madrid: Gabriel de Sancha, 1797–98), v, 46; Luis [Ludwig] Ideler's *Notas al Ingenioso hidalgo Don Quixote de la Mancha*, 2 vols (Berlin: Enrique

Frölich, 1804–05), II, 252; Francisco Rodríguez Marín's *El ingenioso hidalgo don Quijote de la Mancha*, Clásicos Castellanos, 8 vols (Madrid: La Lectura, 1911–13), VII, 128; Rodolfo Schevill & Adolfo Bonilla's *Don Quixote de la Mancha*, 4 vols (Madrid: Gráficas Reunidas, 1935–41), IV, 67; John Jay Allen's edn, 2 vols (Madrid: Cátedra, 1977), II, 351; or Luis Andrés Murillo's, 2 vols (Madrid: Castalia, 1978), II, 368.

20. *El ingenioso hidalgo Don Quijote de la Mancha*, ed. Diego Clemencín, 6 vols (Madrid: E. Aguado, 1833–39), V, 373–74. Clemencín was the first, and long remained the only Spaniard to take the book seriously as a work of art, and he was a Romantic; he adds, '*Don Quijote sintió su soledad* ['felt his loneliness']: This manifestation of the *sensibility and tenderness* of Don Quixote's heart will be rightly appreciated by *sensitive souls*, the only judges of a matter in which those of a different temper find nothing of note. Cervantes made Don Quixote human, emotional, sensitive; observe *the wellspring of the interest that the personality of the Manchegan hidalgo inspires* in readers.'

21. So Bernardino Gómez Miedes, *Commentariorum de sale libri quinque*, enlarg. 2nd edn (Valentiæ: Petrus Huete, 1579), pp. 437–38 (IV. 23), on the comedy of 'nature', not 'wit', also adducing elephants, dogs, cuckoos: 'As for the ape (*Simia*, fem.), its ridiculous imitation of man is well known; Hippocrates said of it, 'a ridiculous mind dressed in a ridiculous body', and it is considered a mimic or clown of man, for there is no gesture, no motion or effort in it that, by its attempt to reproduce the human equivalent, does not provoke man's laughter.' Miedes is cited by Russell, '*Don Quixote* as a Funny Book', p. 321, who observes that ridicule of an ape aping man 'in the post-Darwinian age [...] has, perhaps, turned rather sour'. Real Academia Española's online *Corpus diacrónico del español* (CORDE, <http://corpus.rae.es/cordenet.html> [accessed 23 April 2019]) shows that *jimio* was commoner, in Aesopic tales, etc. (× 186 to 1625), but specifically as an insult feminine was usual (*jimia* × 32), applicable to men and women, e.g. Lupercio Leonardo de Argensola's *Rima* on the old man who dyes his hair 'like a *ximia*' (though cf., for rhyme, *Don Quixote*, I .11, 138 'He ends up adoring a *jimio* [*said by a woman of another woman*] | Thanks to [...] her borrowed braids of hair | And host of made-up beauties') or, still more indicative, medieval testimonia like Juan Fernández de Heredia, *Rams de flors* 'a stupid king sat on a throne is an exalted *ximia*'. The sexist aspect of the usage is noted by Cécile Hue, 'Apelle, saint Luc et le singe: trois figures du peintre dans l'Espagne des XVIe et XVIIe siècles. Fonctions littéraires, théoriques et artistiques' (Thèse de doctorat, Université de la Sorbonne nouvelle-Paris III, 2009, HAL Id : tel-00951404 <https://tel.archives-ouvertes.fr/tel-00951404> [accessed 23 April 2019]), e.g. on pejorative *pintamonas* 'dauber, rotten painter' ('like a monkey behaving inappropriately by copying humans', p. 87; the 'linguistically marked' feminine form 'doubtless stigmatizes the double interest, *condescending and intriguing*, of the human vis-à-vis the animal, [...] certainly a misogynist view', pp. 93–94).

22. Augustin Redondo, 'Fiestas burlescas en el palacio ducal: el episodio de Altisidora', in *Actas del Tercer Congreso Internacional de la Asociación de Cervantistas*, ed. by Antonio Bernat Vistarini (Palma: Universitat de les Illes Balears, 1998), pp. 49–62 (p. 50).

23. This is discussed by Eduardo Urbina, 'El concepto de *admiratio* y lo grotesco en el *Quijote*', *Cervantes: Bulletin of the Cervantes Society of America*, 9.1 (1989), 17–33. Russell, '*Don Quixote* as a Funny Book', p. 324, n. 2 opined, citing Clemencín, that 'the logic of this passage is very unclear and [...] in view of Cervantes' other statements that he regarded wonder as an essential element of the ridiculous we cannot conclude that the particles "o ... o" have here a true disjunctive function rather than [...] a copulative one' (cf. p. 321, on 'failure to understand this close relationship between laughter and the element of wonderment or surprise in Cervantes' day' as the reason why the ducal antics 'baffle' post-romantic critics). E. C. Riley, *Cervantes' Theory of the Novel* (Oxford: Clarendon Press, 1962), pp. 92–93 likewise found the distinction 'not altogether clear'. Curiously, neither considered the possibility that Cervantes was being ironic; it would not be the first time. Urbina argues, reasonably enough, that the problem 'cannot be fixed, reduced to a simple antithesis or assimilated as a figure of ascending approbation' (p. 19).

24. The hard/soft distinction, so named by Oscar Mandel, 'The Function of the Norm in *Don Quixote*', *Modern Philology*, 55.3 (1958), 154–63, is taken as a basis for discussing our passage on *risa de jimia* by Urbina, 'El concepto de *admiratio*', pp. 18–19 and n. 6. On early modern laughter,

Friedrich Nietzsche, *Zur Genealogie der Moral: eine Streitschrift* (Leipzig: Naumann, 1887), p. 53, 2.6, who does not omit to mention apes (I quote, with one or two adaptations, from *On the Genealogy of Morality*, ed. by Keith Ansell-Pearson, trans. by Carol Diethe, Cambridge Texts in the History of Political Thought, rev. 2nd edn (Cambridge: Cambridge University Press, 2007), p. 42–43): 'They could not imagine a princely wedding or folk festival in the grand style without executions, tortures, or some *auto-da-fé*, or likewise any noble household without creatures on whom people could thoughtlessly vent their malice and cruel taunts (remember Don Quixote at the court of the Duchess: today we read the whole of *Don Quixote* with a bitter taste in the mouth, almost as an ordeal [*Tortur*], which would make us very strange and dark to the author and his contemporaries, — they read it with a clear conscience as the most jovial of books, and almost died laughing). To see suffering does one good, to inflict suffering even more so — [...] an ancient, powerful, human, all-too-human principle to which, by the way, even apes might subscribe: for in thinking up bizarre cruelties people say they anticipate and "rehearse" what man will do. Without cruelty, no festivity: that is what the oldest, longest human history teaches.' For more recent work see, for example, *Demócrito áureo: los códigos de la risa en el Siglo de Oro*, ed. by Ignacio Arellano and Victoriano Roncero, Iluminaciones, 26 (Sevilla: Renacimiento, 2006), in particular the editors' essays (pp. 285–359) and Cesáreo Bandera's on *Don Quijote* (pp. 51–74).

25. For instance, on *risa de jimia* 'to denote an amused, *mocking* look'('Apelle, saint Luc et le singe', 192, n. 432, in the excursus on the incompetent painter Orbaneja in *DQ* II. 71; see n. 29 below); on monkeys in art: 'the monkey [*singe*, < SIMIA] implies a prosaic symbolism *coupled with a certain vulgarity*. The animal's gaze [...] is eccentric: *rather than looking inwards or searching for inspiration, it stares out at the material world* and *at us*; the mirror function is *always disturbing*, possibly mocking, [...] a demystified view of the world' (pp. 295–97); and on *singeries* like a satirical portrait of the *valido* Olivares as ape, 'monkeys *love* ugliness and *are* ugly' (pp. 547–48), 'spaces of play in which the monkey-painter and *the monkey-spectator* pirouette, and shot through with humour and derision' (p. 550). The monkey's vulgar, earthbound perspective, allied to its mocking mirror-image as our spectator, further complicate the link between *risa de jimia* and *admiratio*.

26. Alexander A. Parker, 'El concepto de la verdad en el *Quijote*', *Revista de Filología Española*, 32 (1948), 287–305 (pp. 300–01). The approach is problematic, for it entirely ignores the novel's comedy, but remains more plausible in terms of the Baroque ideology of *desengaño* than any solely burlesque reading. See Stephen Boyd, 'Parker and the Anti-Romantic Interpretation of *Don Quijote*', *Bulletin of Spanish Studies*, 85.6 (2008), 3–16.

27. Jaime Fernández, *Bibliografía del 'Quijote' por unidades narrativas y materiales de la novela*, rev. 2nd edn, 2 vols + 1 CD-ROM (Alcalá de Henares: Centro Estudios Cervantinos, 2008) shows that chapters I. 1 and II. 74 have attracted more commentary than all the others; the latter is touched on in *c*. 600 of the 14,000 items. His 'Visión de la crítica en el siglo XX sobre la muerte de don Quijote', *Edad de Oro*, 25 (2006), 141–55, provides an overview of an important part of this output; he too is led to forefront 'the indefinable tone of the whole'.

28. E. C. Riley, *Don Quixote*, Unwin Critical Library (London: Allen & Unwin, 1986), p. 135. A brief *ficción* in Jorge Luis Borges's *El hacedor* imagines this very scenario: Quixote 'discovers [...] that he has killed a man'. How will he react? Not at all, because he hallucinates; pathetically, by waking up to reality; or guiltily, by inventing a reason from within the dream, thereby making it impossible ever to wake up? ('Un problema' [1957], in *Obras completas*, 4 vols (Buenos Aires: Emecé, 1996), II: *1952–1972*, (p. 172).

29. There is no better clue to the absurdity of a one-sided 'hard' reading of Part Two than considering its apocryphal counterpart — an extreme hard reading — and Cervantes's disgust with it; see A. A. Sicroff, 'La segunda muerte de don Quijote como respuesta de Cervantes a Avellaneda', *Nueva Revista de Filología Hispánica*, 24.2 (1975), 267–91. For Orbaneja's simian connotations, see Hue, 'Apelle, saint Luc et le singe', pp. 189–97.

30. Such 'absurdities' are explored by Dian Fox, 'The Apocryphal Part One of *Don Quijote*', *MLN*, 100 (1985), 406–16 (pp. 409–10). The deeper aspects of the role of Part One in Part Two have been extensively studied and are a theme of all serious critique; the parallel with that of Avellaneda's work is well shown by Edward H. Friedman, 'Executing the Will: The End of the Road in *Don Quixote*', *Indiana Journal of Hispanic Literatures*, 5 (1994), 105–25.

31. On this vital episode, see E. C. Riley, 'Symbolism in *Don Quixote*, Part II, Chapter 73', *Journal of Hispanic Philology*, 3 (1979), 161–74.
32. Juan Eugenio Hartzenbusch, *Las 1633 notas puestas a la primera edicion de 'El Ingenioso Hidalgo' reproducida por D. Francisco Lopez Fabra con la foto-tipografía* (Barcelona: Ramirez, 1874), p. 185 n. 1633. Bowle (n. 19 above), V, 165 §569.29 quotes Sebastián de Covarrubias, *Tesoro de la lengua Castellana o Española* (Madrid: Luis Sanchez, 1611), f. 455^v s.v. guesa on the proverb 'El muerto a la güesa y el vivo a la mesa' ('the dead in the earth, the living make mirth'): 'however much the death of the deceased may be regretted, those who have just buried him with sadness and lamentation sit straight down to eat, because both are part of nature'; Rodríguez Marín, VIII, 330 n. 6 adds two more. Rachel Schmidt, 'The Performance and Hermeneutics of Death in the Last Chapter of *Don Quijote*', *Cervantes: Bulletin of the Cervantes Society of America*, 20.2 (Fall 2000), 101–26, comparing the death-bed scene with *artes moriendi*, concludes that Quijano's repentance fails to convince as he still shows desire for fame, not concern for the other world; Jordi Aladro, 'La muerte de Alonso Quijano, un adiós literario', *Anales Cervantinos*, 37 (2005), 179–90 concurs. The readings are refutable ('man must not trifle with his soul', etc.), but the ironies undeniable.
33. Hartzenbusch, *Las 1633 notas*, pp. 184–85 n. 1632 points out that he is called Alonso Quijano el Bueno five times in this chapter, and his niece Antonia Quijana (1st edn, ff. 277^v–280^r); but in I. 1, 39 Quijada, Quesada or 'by probable conjectures' Quejana (f. 1^v; 2nd state 'Quixana'), on 46 Quijada 'y no Quesada' (f. 3^v); in I. 5, 78–79 Quijana twice (f. 16^{r-v}; 2nd state f. 15bis^{r-v} 'Quixada'), in I. 49, 620 Quijada (f. 299^r). He makes the score Quijano 6, Quij/Quesada-Quij/Quejana 6, but it is 5:8. The joke is simply explained: cf. Avellaneda, *Segundo tomo* (Tarragona: Felipe Roberto, 1614), Ch. 1, f. 1^v–2^r '*Madalena*, his niece [...] They no longer call him Don Quixote, but *señor Martín Quijada*, which was his proper name', and thus sixteen times up to the end in the madhouse, Ch. 36, f. 281^r.
34. Jorge Luis Borges, 'Pierre Menard, autor del Quijote' [1939], in *Obras completas*, I: *1923–1949*, pp. 444–50.
35. Thomas Mann, *Meerfahrt mit Don Quijote* [1934] (Frankfurt: Fischer, 2002), entries for 21–22 May, pp. 36–37, 42–43; I quote from the translation by H. T. Lowe-Porter, in *Cervantes: A Collection of Critical Essays*, ed. by Lowry Nelson (Englewood Cliffs: Prentice-Hall, 1969), pp. 49–72 (pp. 55–56).
36. Mann, *Meerfahrt mit Don Quijote*, 28 May, pp. 84–92.
37. Jorge Luis Borges, 'Análisis del último capítulo del Quijote' [1956], in *Textos recobrados: 1956–1986*, 3rd edn (Buenos Aires: Sudamericana, 2011), pp. 13–22. Cervantes, 'while writing these lines, may have thought about his own proximity to death too' (p. 17), but Borges makes clear the novel's ending *had* to be 'the hero's disabusal', and if Quixote was no longer 'a fiction for Cervantes, [...] he isn't for us either'; the bystanders' laments may signify 'Cervantes's sadness', but also trigger ours (pp. 14–15). A. G. Lo Ré, 'The Three Deaths of Don Quixote: Comments in Favor of the Romantic Critical Approach', *Cervantes: Bulletin of the Cervantes Society of America*, 9.2 (Fall 1989), 21–41 reaches similar conclusions by a more detailed route.
38. For such ideas, see, for example, Guillén, 'Vida y muerte de Alonso Quijano'; Aladro, 'La muerte de Alonso Quijano' (nn. 18, 32 above). The panorama is well reviewed by Fernández, 'Visión de la crítica' (n. 27 above).
39. *Ocho comedias y ocho entremeses nuevos, nunca representados* (Madrid: Juan de Villarroel, 1615), 'Prólogo al lector', f. ¶3^v 'thinking the ages when my praises ran abroad were still afoot, I went back to writing a few comedies, but I found no birds in last year's nests [...]. And so, God give you health, and me patience.'
40. Frank Kermode, *The Sense of an Ending: Studies in the Theory of Fiction* [1967], rev. edn (New York: Oxford University Press, 2000), pp. 127–30; and the preceding quotations, pp. 18, 3–4. José Ortega y Gasset's *Meditaciones del Quijote* (Madrid: Residencia de Estudiantes, 1914) is no literary critique of Cervantes's novel, but he offers a profound exposition of this new realist aesthetic (which *Don Quixote*'s polemic against the romances of chivalry made fully conscious, p. 170), notably in 'Poesía y realidad', 'La poesía realista', and 'Tragicomedia' (Meditación primera §§10, 13, 19, pp. 170–73, 179–84, 200–05): 'reality enters poetry to raise adventure to a

higher aesthetic power' (p. 173); 'The theme of realist poetry is the collapse of a certain poetics', and 'reality seems only to acquire an aesthetic interest for some comic intention' (pp. 181, 184); yet 'The novel's overarching line is a tragedy [...], inevitably', so it is by essence tragicomic (p. 201).

41. Martin von Koppenfels, 'Terminar-Abjurar: el último capítulo del *Don Quijote*', *Criticón*, 96 (2006), 69–85 (trans. of 'Don Quijote schwört ab: Versuch über das Schließen', in *Die Endlichkeit der Literatur*, ed. by Eckart Goebel & Martin von Koppenfels (Berlin: Akademie, 2002), pp. 13–25) offers theoretical discussion of exactly what kind of an ending it is; drawing on Benjamin and others, he suggests that, precisely by accepting the 'closure' rejected by the romances, by Part One, and by the apocryphal *Tomo segundo* (see Julio Rodríguez-Luis, 'On Closure and Openendedness in the two *Quijotes*', in *On Cervantes: Essays for L. A. Murillo*, ed. by James A. Parr (Newark: Juan de la Cuesta, 1991), pp. 227–40), it creates its own reflexive form of 'infinity'.
42. Frye, *Anatomy*, p. 38.
43. For this idea of catharsis see Hans Robert Jauss, 'La jouissance esthétique: les expériences fondamentales de la *poiesis*, de l'*aisthesis* et de la *catharsis*', *Poétique*, 10.39 (septembre 1979), 261–74; and Paul Ricoeur, *Soi-même comme un autre* (Paris: Seuil, 1990), pp. 192–93, who expounds the idea of self-identity as formed 'under the constellation of narratives that teach how to articulate retrospection and prospection diegetically', narratives that emplot contingency as meaningful (also pp. 281–90, 381). *Catharsis* in this perspective is 'a poeticization capable [...] of elucidating aporia', a 'transfiguration' not just of the solution, but of the question (see his *Temps et récit*, 3 vols (Paris: Seuil, 1983–85), 1: *L'intrigue et le récit philosophique*, pp. 21–22, and also pp. 82–83).

BIBLIOGRAPHY

Primary Sources

Albornoz, Bartolomé de, *Arte de los contractos* (Valencia: Pedro de Huete, 1573)
Alemán, Mateo, *Guzmán de Alfarache*, ed. by José María Micó, 2 vols (Madrid: Cátedra, 1981)
—— *Guzmán de Alfarache*, ed. by Luis Gómez Canseco, Biblioteca Clásica de la RAE, 42 (Madrid: Real Academia Española, 2012)
Argote de Molina, Gonzalo, *Nobleza del Andaluzia* (Seville: Fernando Díaz, 1588)
Aristotle, *Nichomachean Ethics: With an English translation by H. Rackham*, revised edn, Loeb Classical Library, 73 (Cambridge, MA: Harvard University Press, 1968)
Avellaneda, Alonso Fernández de, *El ingenioso hidalgo don Quijote de la Mancha*, ed. by F. García Salinero (Madrid: Castalia, 1971)
—— *El ingenioso hidalgo Don Quijote de la Mancha*, ed. by Luis Gómez Canseco, (Madrid: Biblioteca Nueva, 2000)
—— *El Quijote apócrifo*, ed. by Alfredo Rodríguez López-Vázquez, Letras Hispánicas, 685 (Madrid: Cátedra, 2011)
—— *Segundo tomo del ingenioso hidalgo don Quixote de la Mancha, que contiene su tercera salida: y es la quinta parte de sus auenturas. Compuesto por el Licenciado Alonso Fernandez de Auellaneda, natural de la Villa de Tordesillas. Al Alcalde, Regidores, y hidalgos, de la noble villa de Argamesilla, patria feliz del hidalgo Cauallero Don Quixote de la Mancha* (Tarragona: Felipe Roberto, 1614)
Azpilcueta, Martín de, *Comentario resolutorio de cambios*, ed. by Alberto Ullastres, José M. Pérez Prendes, and Luciano Pereña (Madrid: Consejo Superior de Investigaciones Científicas, 1965)
B., R. [Nathaniel Crouch], *The History of the Nine Worthies of the World* (London: Nath[aniel] Crouch, 1687)
Libro Primero, del valeroso e invencible principe don Belianis de Grecia; hijo del Emperador don Belanio de Grecia (Medina del Campo: Diego Despinosa, 1564)
[Byron, George Gordon, Lord], *Don Juan: Cantos XII–XIII and XIV* (London: John Hunt, 1823)
Libros de caballerías, ed. by Pascual de Gayangos, Biblioteca de Autores Españoles, 40 (Madrid: Rivadeneyra, 1857)
Cancionero de romances (Anvers, 1550): edición, estudio, bibliografía e índices, ed. by Antonio Rodríguez-Moñino (Madrid: Castalia, 1967)
Cerda, Juan de la, *Libro intitulado vida política de todos los estados de mugeres* (Alcalá de Henares: Juan Gracián, 1599)
Cervantes Saavedra, Miguel de, *El ingenioso hidalgo don Quixote de la Mancha* (Madrid: Juan de la Cuesta, 1605) <http://bdh.bne.es/bnesearch/detalle/bdh0000042946> [accessed 23 April 2019]
—— *The History of the Valorous and Wittie Knight-Errant, Don-Quixote of the Mancha: Translated out of the Spanish*, trans. by Thomas Shelton (London: William Stansby for Ed[ward] Blount and W[illiam] Barret, 1612)

―――― *Historia del famoso cavallero Don Quixote de la Mancha*, ed. Juan Bowle, 6 vols (London: B. White, P. Elmsley and others; Salisbury: Edward Easton, 1781)

―――― *El ingenioso hidalgo don Quixote de la Mancha: nueva edición corregida denuevo, con nuevas notas, con nuevas estampas, con nuevo analisis*, ed. Juan Antonio Pellicer, 5 vols (Madrid: Gabriel de Sancha, for Real Academia Española, 1797–98)

―――― *El ingenioso hidalgo Don Quijote de la Mancha*, ed. by Diego Clemencín, 6 vols (Madrid: E. Aguado, 1833–39; repr. Castilla, 1967)

―――― *The Ingenious Gentleman Don Quixote of La Mancha*, trans. by John Ormsby, 4 vols (London: Smith, Elder & Co., 1885)

―――― *El ingenioso hidalgo don Quijote de la Mancha*, ed. by Francisco Rodríguez Marín, Clásicos Castellanos, 8 vols (Madrid: La Lectura, 1911–13)

―――― *Don Quixote de la Mancha*, ed. by Rodolfo Schevill and Adolfo Bonilla, Obras completas de Miguel de Cervantes Saavedra, 4 vols (Madrid: Gráficas Reunidas, 1935–41)

―――― *Don Quijote de la Mancha*, ed. by John Jay Allen, Letras Hispánicas, 100–01, 2 vols (Madrid: Cátedra, 1977)

―――― *El ingenioso hidalgo don Quijote de la Mancha*, ed. by Luis Andrés Murillo, Clásicos Castalia, 77–78, 2 vols (Madrid: Castalia, 1978)

―――― *Don Quixote*, ed. by Franciso Rico, Unwin Critical Library (London: Allen & Unwin, 1986)

―――― *Don Quijote de la Mancha*, ed. by Francisco Rico (Instituto Cervantes, 1998) <https://cvc.cervantes.es/literatura/clasicos/quijote/default.htm> [accessed 23 April 2019]

―――― *Cervantes: Don Quixote*, trans. by John Rutherford (Harmondsworth: Penguin, 2000)

―――― *Don Quijote de la Mancha*, ed. by Francisco Rico and others, 2 vols (Madrid: Real Academia Española, 2004 and [Barcelona]: Galaxia Gutenberg-Círculo de Lectores, Centro para la Edición de los Clásicos Españoles)

―――― *Don Quixote*, trans. by Edith Grossman (London: Secker & Warburg, 2004; repr. London: Vintage, 2005)

―――― *Don Quijote de la Mancha: Edición del Instituto Cervantes (1605, 1615, 2015)*, ed. by Francisco Rico, Biblioteca Clásica de la Real Academia Española, 47, 2 vols (Madrid: Real Academia Española, 2015)

―――― *Entremeses*, ed. by Eugenio Asensio (Madrid: Castalia, 1970)

―――― *Novelas ejemplares*, ed. by Harry Sieber, 22nd edn, Letras Hispánicas, 105–06, 2 vols (Madrid: Cátedra, 1997)

―――― *The Complete Exemplary Novels*, ed. by Barry Ife and Jonathan Thacker (Oxford: Oxbow Books, 2013)

―――― *Novelas ejemplares*, ed. by Jorge García López (Madrid: Real Academia Española, 2013)

―――― *Obras selectas* (Madrid: EDIMAT, 2000)

―――― *Ocho comedias y ocho entremeses nuevos, nunca representados* (Madrid: Juan de Villarroel, 1615)

―――― *Teatro completo*, ed. by Florencio Sevilla Arroyo (Barcelona: Penguin Random House, 2016)

―――― *The Travels of Persiles and Sigismunda: A Northern History*, anonymous trans., (London: H[umphrey] L[ownes] for M[atthew] L[ownes], 1619), ed. by B. W. Ife and T. L. Darby <http://www.ems.kcl.ac.uk/content/etext/e006.html> [accessed 4 April 2017]

―――― *Los Trabajos de Persiles y Sigismunda*, ed. by Juan Bautista Avalle-Arce (Madrid: Castalia, 1969)

―――― *Los trabajos de Persiles y Sigismunda: Historia septentrional*, ed. by Carlos Romero Muñoz (Madrid: Cátedra, 2004)

CLAIRVAUX, ST BERNARD OF, *In Praise of the New Knighthood*, trans. by Conrad Greenia OSCO, in *The Works of Bernard of Clairvaux*, 7 (*Treatises III*) (Kalamazoo, MI: Cistercian Publications, 1977), pp. 115–67

Contreras, Alonso de, *Vida, nacimiento, padres y crianza del capitán Alonso de Contreras*. ed. by Fernando Reigosa (Madrid: Alianza Editorial, 1967)
Corpus diacrónico del español Corpus (CORDE), Real Academia Española, [n. d.] <http://corpus.rae.es/cordenet.html> [accessed 23 April 2019]
Correas, Gonzalo, *Vocabulario de refranes y frases proverbiales*, ed. by Louis Combet (Bordeaux: Institut d'études ibériques et ibéro-américaines de l'Université de Bordeaux, 1967)
Covarrubias Orozco, Sebastián de, *Tesoro de la lengua castellana o española* (Madrid: Luis Sanchez, 1611)
—— *Tesoro de la lengua castellana o española*, ed. by Ignacio Arellano and Rafael Zafra (Madrid: Iberoamericana, 2006)
Coward, Noël, *Hay Fever*, French's Acting Edition (London: Samuel French, 1927)
Curtius Rufus, Quintus, *De los hechos del magno Alexandre rey de macedonia* (Seville: Juan Cromberger, 1534)
Deza, Lope de, *Gobierno político de agricultura*, ed. by Ángel García Sanz (Madrid: Instituto de Cooperación Iberoamericana, 1991)
Diccionario de autoridades, 6 vols (Madrid: Real Academia Española, 1726–39)
Diccionario enciclopédico de la lengua castellana, ed. by Elias Zerolo and others, 4th edn, 2 vols (Paris, n. d.)
Donatus, Aelius, *Aeli Donati quod fertur Commentum Terenti: Accedunt Eugraphi Commentum et Scholia Bembina*, ed. by Paulus Wessner, 3 vols (Leipzig: Teubner, 1902–08)
Flores de poetas ilustres, in *Poetas líricos de los siglos xvi y xvii*, ed. by Adolfo de Castro, 2 vols (Madrid: Rivadeneyra, 1857)
Fracastoro, Girolamo, *Latin Poetry*, trans. by James Gardner, The I Tatti Renaissance Library, 57 (Cambridge, MA: Harvard University Press, 2013)
Fernández, Gerónimo, *Libro Primero, del valeroso e inuencible principe don Belianis de Grecia* (Medina del Campo: Diego Despinosa, 1564)
García, Francisco, *Tratado utilísimo y muy general de todos los contratos*, ed. by Idoya Zorroza and Horacio Rodríguez Penelas (Pamplona: EUNSA, 2003)
Georgoevitz, Bartholomeus, *De afflictione tam captivorum quam etiam sub turcae tributo viventium* (Antwerp: Copenius, 1514)
Georgii, Franciscus, *De harmonia mundi totus cantica tria* (Venice: Bernardinus de Vitalibus, 1525)
Gomesius Miedes, Bernardinus, *Commentariorum de sale libri quinque*, 2nd edn (Valentiæ: Petrus Huete, 1579)
Góngora y Argote, Luis de, *Romances*, ed. by Antonio Carreira (Barcelona: Quaderns Crema, 1998)
Gracián, Baltasar, *Agudeza y arte de ingenio*, ed. by Evaristo Correa Calderón, Clásicos Castalia, 14–15, 2 vols (Madrid: Castalia, 1987)
Granada, Fray Luis de, *Adiciones al Memorial de la vida Christiana* (Salamanca: Mathias Gast, 1574)
Haedo, Diego de, *Topographia e historia general de Argel, repartida en cinco tratados, do se veran casos estraños, muertes espantosas, y tormentos exquisitos; que conuiene se entiendan en la Christianidad: con mucha doctrina, y elegancia curiosa* (Valladolid: Diego Fernandez de Cordova y Oviedo for Antonio Coello, 1612)
Hartzenbusch, Juan Eugenio, *Las 1633 notas puestas a la primera edicion de 'El Ingenioso Hidalgo' reproducida por D. Francisco Lopez Fabra con la foto-tipografia* (Barcelona: Narciso Ramirez, 1874)
Herrera, Fernando de, *Anotaciones a la poesía de Garcilaso*, ed. by Inoria Pepe and José María Reyes, Letras Hispánicas, 516 (Madrid: Cátedra, 2001)

Horozco, Sebastián de, *Libro de los proverbios glosados*, ed. by Jack Weiner (Kassel: Reichenberger, 1994)

Huarte de San Juan, Juan, *Examen de ingenios para las ciencias* [1575], ed. by Guillermo Serés (Madrid: Cátedra, 1989)

—— *Examen de ingenios para las ciencias* (Baeza: Juan Baptista de Montoya, 1594)

Jurava, Juan de, *Historia de yerbas y plantas con los nombres griegos, latinos y españoles*, ed. by María Jesús Mancho (Salamanca: CILUS, 1999)

El libro del inuencible cauallero Lepolemo hijo del emperador de Alemaña y de los hechos que hizo llamandose el Cauallero de la Cruz (Toledo: Juan Ferrer, 1552)

López, Diego, *Declaración magistral sobre las Emblemas de Andres Alciato* (Nájera: Juan de Mongastón, 1615)

López de Ayala, Pedro, *La cronica del rey do[n] pedro* (Toledo: Remon de Petras, 1526)

López de Ubeda, Francisco, *La Pícara Justina*, ed. by Antonio Rey Hazas, 2 vols (Madrid: Editorial Nacional, 1977)

López Pinciano, Alonso, *Philosophia antigua poetica* (Madrid: Thomas Junti, 1596)

Mariana, Juan de, *La dignidad real y la educación del Rey (De rege et regis institutione)*, ed. by Luis Sánchez Agesta (Madrid: Centro de Estudios Constitucionales, 1981)

Mármol Carvajal, Luis del, *Rebelión y castigo de los moros*, ed. by Cayetano Rosell (Madrid: Ribadeneira, 1852)

Mercado, Tomás de, *Suma de tratos y contratos*, ed. by Nicolás Sánchez Albornoz, 2 vols (Madrid: Instituto de Estudios Fiscales, Ministerio de Hacienda, 1977)

Minsheu, John, *A Dictionarie in Spanish and English* (London: Ed[mund] Bollifant, 1599)

Molina, Juan de, *Descripcion del Reyno de Galizia* (Mondoñedo: Agustín de Paz, 1551)

Molina, Luis de, *La teoría del justo precio*, ed. by Francisco G. Camacho (Madrid: Editora Nacional, 1981)

Molina, Tirso de, *Cigarrales de Toledo*, ed. by Luis Vázquez Fernández, Clásicos Castalia, 216 (Madrid: Castalia, 1996)

Nietzsche, Friedrich, *Zur Genealogie der Moral: eine Streitschrift* (Leipzig: Naumann, 1887)

—— *On the Genealogy of Morality*, ed. by Keith Ansell-Pearson, trans. by Carol Diethe, Cambridge Texts in the History of Political Thought, 2nd edn (Cambridge: Cambridge University Press, 2007)

Novus index librorum prohibitorum et expurgatorum: editus autoritate et jessu D. Antonii Zapata (Seville: Francisco de Lyra, 1632)

Núñez, Francisco, *Libro intitulado del parto humano: Madrid, Universidad Complutense, Facultad de Medicina, MS. 618.4*, transcr. by María Teresa Herrera and María Estela González de Fauve (Madison: Hispanic Seminary of Medieval Studies, 1997)

Oña, Pedro de, 'Tratado y memorial de los inconuenientes y daños que a causado en los Reynos la moneda de Vellon que estos años se labro y doblo en Castilla y del Remedio y reparo de todos ellos', Madrid, Biblioteca Nacional de España, MS 6279, fol. 4^v.

Ortiz, Luis, *Memorial del contado Luis Ortiz a Felipe II*, ed. by José Larraz (Madrid: Instituto de España, 1970)

Pererius, Benedictus, *Centum octoginta tres disputationes selectissimae super libro Apocalypsis beati Ioannis apostoli: quibus adiectae sunt [...] viginti tres disputationes, aduersus eos qui putarunt, Maometem Saracenorum legislatorem fuisse verum illum antichristum* (Venice: Antonius Leonardus, 1607)

Peter of Spain, *Summaries of Logic: Text, Translation, Introduction, and Notes*, ed. and trans. by Brian P. Copenhaver, with Calvin Normore and Terence Parsons (Oxford: Oxford University Press, 2014)

Petrarch (Francesco Petrarca), *Selected Letters: Vol. II*, trans. by Elaine Fantham, The I Tatti Renaissance Library, 77 (Cambridge, MA: Harvard University Press, 2017)

Cronica del muy valiente y esforçado cauallero Platir: hijo del inuencible emperador Primaleón (Valladolid: Nicolas Tierri, 1533)
—— *Platir: Valldolid, Nicolás Tierri, 1533*, ed. María Carmen Marín Pina (Alcalá de Henares: Centro de Estudios Cervantinos, 1997)
PLUTARCH, *La primera y segunda parte de Plutharcho*, trans. by Alfonso de Palencia, 2 vols (Seville: Paulo de Colonia, 1491)
PONS, GASPAR DE, *Untitled Memorial* (Madrid: [n. pub.], 1600), fol. 37^r
QUEVEDO, FRANCISCO DE, *El Buscón*, ed. by Domingo Ynduráin, Letras Hispánicas, 124 (Madrid: Cátedra, 2001)
—— *Obra poética*, ed. by José Manuel Blecua, 4 vols (Madrid: Castalia, 1969–81)
—— *Poesía original completa*, ed. by José Manuel Blecua (Barcelona: Planeta, 2004)
QUINTILIAN, *The Orator's Education*, ed. and trans. by Donald A. Russell, Loeb Classical Library 124–27 and 494, 5 vols (Cambridge, MA: Harvard University Press, 2002)
Recopilación de las leyes de estos reynos, 3 vols (Madrid: Catalina de Barrio y Angulo y Diego Diaz de la Carrera, 1640; repr. Valladolid: Lex Nova, 1982)
Relaciones histórico-geográficas-estadísticas de los pueblos de España: Reino de Toledo, ed. by Carmelo Viñas and Ramón Paz, 3 vols (Madrid: CSIC, 1951–63)
Romancero general, en que se contienen todos los Romances que andan impressos aora nueuamente añadido, y emendado por Pedro Flores (Madrid: Juan de la Cuesta, 1614)
SALINAS, EL CONDE DE, *El conde de Salinas. Obra completa: la poesía desconocida*, ed. by Trevor J. Dadson (Madrid: Anejos de la Real Academia Española, 2016)
SEPÚLVEDA, LORENZO DE, *Cancionero de romances (Sevilla, 1584): Edición, estudio, bibliografía e índices*, ed. by Antonio Rodríguez-Moñino (Madrid: Castalia, 1967)
SHAFFER, PETER, *Amadeus: A Play* (Harmondsworth: Penguin Books, 1984)
SORIANO, JERÓNIMO, *Libro de experimentos médicos, fáciles y verdaderos*, transcr. by María Teresa Herrera and María Estela González de Fauve (Madison: Hispanic Seminary of Medieval Studies, 1997)
SOTO, DOMINGO DE, *De iustitia et iure libri decem / De la justicia y del derecho*, trans. by Marcelino González Ordóñez, 5 vols (Madrid: Instituto de Estudios Políticos, 1967)
VALENCIA, PEDRO DE, 'Discurso de Pedro de Valencia acerca de la moneda de vellón. Zafra, 1605', in *Obras completes IV/I: Escritos sociales I: Escritos económicos*, ed. by Rafael González Cañal (León: Universidad de León, 1994), 111–23
VARGAS LLOSA, MARIO, *Carta de batalla por Tirant lo Blanc* (Barcelona: Seix Barral, 1991)
VEGA, LOPE DE, *El rufián Castrucho* (Madrid: RESAD, 2000)
—— *Obras de Lope de Vega*, ed. by Emilio Cotarelo y Mori, 13 vols (Madrid: Revista de Archivos, Bibliotecas y Museos, 1916–1930)
VILLEGAS, ALONSO DE, *Flos sanctorum: Segunda parte y historia general en que se escrive la vida de la Virgen* (Barcelona: Damian Bages, 1586)
VERGIL, POLYDORE, *On Discovery*, ed. and trans. by Brian P. Copenhaver, The I Tatti Renaissance Library, 6 (Cambridge, MA: Harvard University Press, 2002)
VIRGIL, *Los doze libros de la Eneida de Vergilio, Principe de los Poetas Latinos*, trans. by Gregorio Hernández de Velasco (Toledo: Juan de Ayala, 1555)
—— *Eclogues, Georgics, Aeneid: Books 1–6*, trans. by H. R. Fairclough, rev. by George P. Goold, Loeb Classical Library, 63 (Cambridge, MA: Harvard University Press, 1999)
ZURITA, JERÓNIMO, *Los cinco libros postreros de la primera parte de los Anales de la Corona de Aragón* (Zaragoza: Juan de Lanaja y Quartanet, 1610)

Secondary Sources

ALADRO, JORDI, 'La muerte de Alonso Quijano, un adiós literario', *Anales Cervantinos*, 37 (2005), 179–90
—— 'La muerte de Alonso Quijano, La última imitación de Don Quijote', in *Actas del XI coloquio internacional de la Asociación de Cervantistas (Seúl, 17–20 de noviembre de 2004)*, ed. by Chul Park (Seoul: Universidad Hankuk de Estudios Extranjeros, 2005), pp. 429–39
ALCHALABI, FRÉDÉRIC, 'L'écriture de l'histoire dans la *Crónica sarracina* de Pedro de Corral: le roi et son conseiller sous le regard d'Eleastras, l'historien', *e-Spania* [Online], 12 (2011), <http://dx.doi.org/10.4000/e-spania.20595>
ALLEN, JOHN J., 'The Narrators, the Reader, and Don Quijote', *MLN*, 91 (1976), 201–12
—— 'La Providencia divina en el *Quijote*', in *Cervantes, su obra y su mundo (Actas del I Congreso sobre Cervantes)*, ed. by M. Criado de Val (Madrid: EDI-6, 1981), pp. 525–29
—— 'The Providential World of Cervantes' Fiction', *Thought: Fordham University Quarterly*, 55.2 (1980), 184–89
ALONSO ASENJO, JULIO, '*Quijote* y romances: usos y funciones', in *Historia, reescritura y pervivencia del Romancero: estudios en memoria de Amelia García-Valdecasas*, ed. by Rafael Beltrán (Valencia: Universitat de València, 2000), pp. 25–65
ALVAR, CARLOS, 'Del rey Arturo a Don Quijote: Paisaje y horizonte de expectativas en la tercera salida', *Boletín de la Real Academia Española*, 85 (2005), 7–27
ANDERSON, ELLEN M., and GONZALO PONTÓN, 'La composición del *Quijote*', in *Don Quijote de la Mancha: edición del Instituto Cervantes 1605–2005*, ed. by Francisco Rico and others, 2 vols ([Barcelona]: Galaxia Gutenberg-Círculo de Lectores, Centro para la Edición de los Clásicos Españoles), pp. cxcii–ccxx
ANSON, JOHN, 'The Female Transvestite in Early Monasticism: The Origins and Development of a Motif", *Viator*, 5 (1974), 1–32
ARANDA PÉREZ, FRANCISCO JOSÉ, 'Cide Hamete Benengeli, inventor inventado del Quijote, y otros historiadores arábigos más o menos invencioneros', *eHumanista/Conversos*, 3 (2015), 9–44 <http://www.ehumanista.ucsb.edu/conversos/volumes/3> [accessed 22 February 2018]
ARBESÚ FERNÁNDEZ, DAVID, '*Auctoritas* y experiencia en "El curioso impertinente"', *Cervantes: Bulletin of the Cervantes Society of America*, 25.1 (2005), 23–43
ARBIZU, JOSÉ MARÍA, *Sancho, primer intérprete de don Quijote* (Salamanca: Publicaciones Universidad Pontificia de Salamanca, 2001)
ARELLANO, IGNACIO, and VICTORIA RONCERO (eds), *Demócrito áureo: los códigos de la risa en el Siglo de Oro*, Iluminaciones, 26 (Sevilla: Renacimiento, 2006)
ARIÈS, PHILIPPE, *Western Attitudes toward Death: From the Middle Ages to the Present*, trans. by Patricia M. Ranum (Baltimore: Johns Hopkins University Press, 1974)
—— *Images de l'homme devant la mort*, 2nd edn, 2 vols (Paris: Seuil, 1985)
ARMAS, FREDERICK A. DE, 'The Artful Gamblers: Wagering Danaë in Cervantes' *Don Quixote* I. 33–35', in *Objects of Culture in the Literature of Imperial Spain*, ed. by Mary E. Barnard and Frederick A. de Armas (Toronto: University of Toronto Press, 2013), pp. 54–79
—— 'Don Quijote y Alejandro Magno: vidas paralelas', in *Cervantes, la lectura interminable*, ed. by Roberto González Echevarría (= *Cuadernos hispano-americanos*, 790 (April 2016)), 32–47
ASTRANA MARÍN, LUIS, *La vida turbulenta de Quevedo*, (Madrid: Gran Capitán, 1945)
AVALLE ARCE, JUAN BAUTISTA, *Nuevos deslindes cervantinos* (Barcelona: Ariel, 1975), pp. 17–72
—— 'Don Quijote, Sancho, Dulcinea: Aproximaciones', *Crítica Hispánica*, 11 (1989), 53–67
AZPITARTE, JUAN M., *Pícaros y mercaderes en el 'Guzmán de Alfarache': reformismo burgués y*

mentalidad aristocrática en la España del Siglo de Oro (Granada: Universidad de Granada, 1994)

BAKER, EDWARD, *La biblioteca de don Quijote* (Madrid: Marcial Pons, 1997)

BAÑOS VALLEJO, FERNANDO, 'El transformismo de santa Eugenia: del cuerpo medieval al ingenio barroco', *Bulletin of Hispanic Studies*, 93 (2016), 1–28

BARNÉS VÁZQUEZ, ANTONIO, *'Yo he leído en Virgilio': la tradición clásica en el 'Quijote'*, Biblioteca Cátedra Miguel de Cervantes: Publicaciones Académicas, 12 (Vigo: Editorial Academia del Hispanismo, 2009)

BARNETT, S. J., *Idol Temples and Crafty Priests: The Origins of Enlightenment Anticlericalism* (New York: St Martin's Press, 1999)

BÉCARES, VICENTE, and ALEJANDRO LUIS IGLESIAS, *La librería de Benito Boyer (Medina del Campo 1592)* (Salamanca: Junta de Castilla y León, 1992)

BLANCO AGUINAGA, CARLOS, 'Cervantes y la picaresca: notas sobre dos tipos de realismo', *Nueva Revista de Filología Hispánica*, 11 (1957), 313–42

BLECUA, JOSÉ M., *Sobre poesía de la Edad de Oro: ensayos y notas eruditas*, (Madrid: Gredos, 1970)

BLEIBERG, GERMÁN, MAUREEN IHRIE, and JANET PÉREZ, eds, *Dictionary of the Literature of the Iberian Peninsula*, 2 vols (Westport, Conn: Greenwood, 1993)

BLOOM, HAROLD, 'Introduction', in *Don Quixote*, trans. by Edith Grossman (New York: Ecco/HarperCollins, 2003), pp. i–xix

—— *A Map of Misreading* (Oxford: Oxford University Press, 1980)

—— *The Anxiety of Influence: A Theory of Poetry* (New York: Oxford University Press, 1997)

BOGNOLO, ANNA, 'El "Lepolemo", "Caballero de la Cruz" y el "Leandro el Bel"', *Edad de Oro*, 21 (2002), 271–88

BONDANELLA, PETER, *Umberto Eco and the Open Text: Semiotics, Fiction, Popular Culture* (Cambridge: Cambridge University Press, 1997)

BORGES, JORGE LUIS, 'Análisis del último capítulo del *Quijote*', *Revista de la Universidad de Buenos Aires* (5ª época), 1 (1956), 29–36; repr. in *Textos recobrados*, 3rd edn, 3 vols (Buenos Aires: Sudamericana, 2011), III, 13–22

—— 'La conducta novelística de Cervantes', *El idioma de los argentinos* (Buenos Aires: Gleizer, 1928; Buenos Aires: Seix-Barral, 1994), pp. 139–46

—— 'Pierre Menard, autor del Quijote', in *Obras completas*, 4 vols (Buenos Aires: Emecé, 1996), I: *1923–1949*, 444–50

—— 'Un problema', in *Obras completas*, 4 vols (Buenos Aires: Emecé, 1996), II: *1952–1972*, 172

BOYD, STEPHEN, ed., *A Companion to Cervantes's 'Novelas Ejemplares'*, Serie A: Monografías, 218 (Woodbridge: Tamesis, 2005)

—— 'Parker and the Anti-Romantic Interpretation of *Don Quijote*', *Bulletin of Spanish Studies*, 85.6 (2008), 3–16

BRANCAFORTE, BENITO, *'Guzmán de Alfarache' ¿Conversión o proceso de degradación?* (Madison: Hispanic Seminary of Medieval Studies, 1980)

BROOK, PETER, *The Empty Space* (London: Penguin, 1968)

BROWN, LESLEY, 'What Is the "Mean Relative to Us" in Aristotle's Ethics?', *Phronesis*, 42.1 (1997), 77–93

BURTON, GIDEON O., 'Silva Rhetoricae', <http://rhetoric.byu.edu/> [accessed 26 September 2017]

BURTON, JONATHAN, *Traffic and Turning: Islam and English Drama, 1579–1624* (Newark: University of Delaware Press, 2005)

CABAÑAS AGRELA, JOSÉ MIGUEL, *Breve historia de Cervantes* (Madrid: Nowtilus, 2016)

CARLSON, MARVIN, *Performance: A Critical Introduction*, 2nd edn (New York: Routledge, 2004)

Casalduero, Joaquín, *Sentido y Forma del 'Quijote' (1606–1615)*, 3rd edn (Madrid: Insula, 1975; repr. Colección Biblioteca Cervantina, x, Madrid: Visor Libros, 2006)
Cash, Annette G., 'Formas de tratamiento en "Don Quijote"', in *Tus obras los rincones de la tierra descubren: Actas del VI congreso internacional de la Asociación de Cervantistas*, ed. by Alexia Dotras Bravo (2008), pp. 225–32
Castro, Américo, 'Cervantes y la Inquisición', *Modern Philology*, 27 (1930), 427–33
—— *Cervantes y los casticismos españoles* (Madrid: Alfaguara, 1966)
—— 'La palabra escrita y el *Quijote*', in *Hacia Cervantes* (Madrid: Taurus, 1967), repr. in Américo Castro, *Obra reunida*, ed. by José Miranda, 3 vols (Madrid: Editorial Trotta, 2001–04), I (2002), pp. 341–72.
Cavillac, Michel, *Gueux et marchands dans le 'Guzmán de Alfarache' (1599–1604): Roman picaresque et mentalité bourgeoise dans l'Espagne du Siècle d'Or* (Bordeaux: Études Ibériques, Presses Universitaires de Bordeaux, 1983)
—— *'Guzmán de Alfarache' y la novela moderna* (Madrid: Casa de Velázquez, 2010)
—— *Pícaros y mercaderes en el 'Guzmán de Alfarache'* (Granada: Universidad de Granada, 1994)
Cipriani, Marco, 'Il *De orthographia* di L. Caecilius Minutianus Apuleius: introduzione, edizione, traduzione e commento' (unpublished doctoral thesis, Università degli Studi Roma Tre, 2009)
Clay, Zanna, and Marco Iacobini, 'Mirroring Fictional Others', in *The Aesthetic Mind: Philosophy and Psychology*, ed. by E. Schellekens and P. Goldie (New York: Oxford University Press, 2011), pp. 313–29
Close, Anthony, *Cervantes and the Comic Mind of his Age* (Oxford: Oxford University Press, 2000)
—— *A Companion to 'Don Quixote'*, Serie A: Monografías, 262 (Woodbridge: Tamesis, 2008)
—— 'The Liberation of the Galley Slaves and the ethos of *Don Quijote* Part I', *Cervantes: Bulletin of the Cervantes Society of America*, 27.1 (Spring 2007 [2008]): 7–30
—— *Miguel de Cervantes: 'Don Quixote'*, Landmarks of World Literature (Cambridge: Cambridge University Press, 1990)
—— *The Romantic Approach to 'Don Quixote': A Critical History of the Romantic Tradition in 'Quixote' Criticism* (Cambridge: Cambridge University Press, 1978)
Coleridge, Samuel Taylor, *Biographia Literaria: or, Biographical Sketches of My Literary Life and Opinions* (London: R. Fenner, 1817), <http://www.english.upenn.edu/~mgamer/Etexts/biographia.html> [accessed 23 April 2019]
Comer Kidd, David, and Emanuele Castano, 'Reading Literary Fiction Improves Theory of Mind', *Science*, 342 (2013), 377–80 <http://dx.doi.org/10.1126/science.1239918>
Cotarelo y Mori, Emilio, *Obras de Lope de Vega: obras dramáticas* (Madrid: Tipografía de la Revista de Archivos, Bibliotecas y Museos, 1916)
Croce, Benedetto, *Estetica come scienza dell'espressione e lingüística generale: teoria e storia*, 4th edn (Bari: Laterza, 1912)
Cros, Edmond, *Le protée et le gueux: recherches sur les origines et la nature du récit picaresque dans 'Guzmán de Alfarache'* (Paris: Didier, 1967)
—— *Mateo Alemán: introducción a su vida y a su obra* (Salamanca: Anaya, 1971)
Curtius, Ernst Robert, *European Literature and the Latin Middle Ages*, trans. by Willard R. Trask, rev. edn, intro. by Colin Burrow, Bollingen Series, 36 (Princeton: Princeton University Press, 2013)
Dadson, Trevor J., ed., 'El conde de Salinas y Leonor Pimentel: cuando se juntan el amor y la poesía', in *Spanish Golden Age Poetry in Motion: The Dynamics of Creation and Conversation*, ed. by Jean Andrews and Isabel Torres (Woodbridge: Tamesis, 2014), pp. 185–212

—— 'La difusión de la poesía española impresa en el siglo XVII', *Bulletin Hispanique*, 113.1 (2011), 13–42

—— 'The Dissemination of Poetry in Sixteenth-Century Spain', *Journal of the Institute of Romance Studies*, 8 (2000 [2003]), 47–56

—— 'The Education, Books and Reading Habits of Ana de Mendoza y de la Cerda, Princess of Éboli (1540–1592)', in *Women's Literacy in Early Modern Spain and the New World*, ed. by Anne J. Cruz and Rosilie Hernández-Pecoraro (Aldershot: Ashgate, 2011), pp. 79–102

—— *Historia de la impresión de las 'Rimas' de Lupercio y Bartolomé Leonardo de Argensola* (Zaragoza: Institución 'Fernando el Católico', 2010)

—— 'La librería de Cristóbal López (1606): estudio y análisis de una librería madrileña de principios del siglo XVII', in *El libro antiguo español IV. Coleccionismo y Bibliotecas (Siglos XVI–XVII)*, ed. by Pedro M. Cátedra and María Luisa López-Vidriero (Salamanca: Universidad de Salamanca, Sociedad Española de Historia del Libro, 1998), pp. 167–234

—— 'Los libros de caballerías, *Don Quijote* y sus lectores en el siglo XVII', in *Antes y después del 'Quijote' en el cincuentenario de la Asociación de Hispanistas de Gran Bretaña e Irlanda*, ed. by Robert Archer (Valencia: Biblioteca Valenciana, 2005), pp. 59–78

—— *Libros, lectores y lecturas: estudios sobre bibliotecas particulares españolas del Siglo de Oro* (Madrid: Arco/Libros, 1998)

—— 'Literacy and Education in Early Modern Rural Spain: The Case of Villarrubia de los Ojos', in *The Iberian Book and its Readers: Essays for Ian Michael*, ed. by Nigel Griffin, Clive Griffin, and Eric Southworth, *Bulletin of Spanish Studies*, 81 (2004), 1011–37

—— *Los moriscos de Villarubia de los Ojos (siglos XV–XVIII): Historia de una minoría asimilada, expulsada y reintegrada* (Madrid: Iberoamericana, 2007)

—— 'The Multicultural World of *Don Quijote*', *In Other Words*, 2016 (47), 86–94

—— 'La publicación y diseminación de obras de entretenimiento en la España del siglo XVII', in *Del autor al lector: el comercio y distribución del libro medieval y moderno*, ed. by Manuel José Pedraza Gracia, Yolanda Clemente San Román, and Nicolás Bas Martín (Zaragoza: Prensas de la Universidad de Zaragoza), pp. 69–95

DAVIES, ANN, *Penélope Cruz*, BFI Film Stars (London: Palgrave MacMillan, 2014)

DI PINTO, ELENA, *La tradición escarramanesca en el teatro del Siglo de Oro* (Madrid: Iberoamericana, 2005)

DOMÍNGUEZ ORTIZ, ANTONIO, and BERNARD VINCENT, *Historia de los moriscos: vida y tragedia de una minoría*, Biblioteca de la Revista de Occidente, 36 (Madrid: Revista de Occidente, 1978)

DOODY, MARGARET ANNE, *The True Story of the Novel* (New Brunswick, NJ: Rutgers University Press, 1999)

DOPICO BLACK, GEORGINA, 'Canons Afire: Libraries, Books, and Bodies in *Don Quixote*'s Spain', in *Cervantes' 'Don Quixote': A Casebook*, ed. by Roberto González Echevarría (Oxford: Oxford University Press, 2005), pp. 95–123

DUNN, KEVIN, *Pretexts of Authority: The Rhetoric of Authorship in the Renaissance Preface* (Stanford: Stanford University Press, 1994)

DUNN, PETER N., 'La cueva de Montesinos por fuera y por dentro: estructura épica, fisonomía', *MLN*, 88.2 (1973), 190–202

—— *Spanish Picaresque Fiction: A New Literary History* (Ithaca: Cornell University Press, 1993)

—— 'Two Classical Myths in *Don Quijote*', *Renaissance and Reformation*, 9.1 (1972), 2–10

DURÁN, MANUEL, *La ambigüedad en el 'Quijote'*, Biblioteca de la Facultad de Filosofía y Letras (Xalapa: Universidad Veracruzana, 1960)

ECO, UMBERTO, *Sei passeggiate nei boschi narrativi: Harvard University Norton Lectures 1992–93* (Milan: Bompiani, 1994)

EDGAR, DAVID, *How Plays Work* (London: Nick Hern Books, 2009)
EGIDO, AURORA, 'La cueva de Montesinos y la tradición erasmista de ultratumba', in *Cervantes y las puertas del sueño: estudios sobre 'La Galatea', 'El Quijote', y 'El Persiles'*, Estudios universitarios (Barcelona: PPU, 1994), pp. 137–78 (first publ. as 'Cervantes y las puertas del sueño: sobre la tradición erasmista del ultramundo en el episodio de la cueva de Montesinos', in *Studia in honorem prof. M. de Riquer*, ed. by Carlos Alvar and others, 4 vols (Barcelona: Quaderns Crema, 1988), III. 305–41)
EHLERS, BENJAMIN, *Between Christians and Moriscos: Juan de Ribera and Religious Reform in Valencia, 1568–1614* (Baltimore: Johns Hopkins University Press, 2006)
EISENBERG, DANIEL, 'La biblioteca de Cervantes', in *Studia in honorem prof. M. de Riquer*, 3 vols (Barcelona: Quaderns Crema, 1986–88), II, 271–328
—— 'Did Cervantes Have a Library?', in *Hispanic Studies in Honor of Alan D. Deyermond: A North American Tribute* (Madison: Wisconsin Hispanic Seminary of Medieval Studies, 1986), pp. 93–106
—— *Estudios cervantinos* (Barcelona: Sirmio, 1991)
—— 'The Pseudo-Historicity of the Romances of Chivalry', *Quaderni Ibero-Americani*, 45–46 (1975), 253–59
—— *Romances of Chivalry in the Spanish Golden Age* (Newark, DE: Juan de la Cuesta, [1982])
EISENBERG, DANIEL, and MARÍA CARMEN MARÍN PIÑA, *Bibliografía de los libros de caballerías castellanos* (Zaragoza: Prensas Universitarias de Zaragoza, 2000)
ESCUDERO, JOSÉ ANTONIO, *Estudios sobre La Inquisición* (Madrid: Marcial Pons, 2005)
FAJARDO, SALVADOR J., 'Instructions for Use: The Prologue to *Don Quixote I*', *Journal of Interdisciplinary Literary Studies*, 6.1 (1994), 1–17
FERNÁNDEZ, JAIME, *Bibliografía del Quijote por unidades narrativas y materiales de la novela*, 2nd expanded edn, 2 vols (Alcalá de Henares: Centro de Estudios Cervantinos, 2008)
—— 'Visión de la crítica en el siglo XX sobre la muerte de don Quijote', *Edad de Oro*, 25 (2006), 141–55
FERNÁNDEZ RODRÍGUEZ, NATALIA, '"Suele el disfraz varonil agradar mucho": las santas travestidas de la hagiografía en la comedia nueva', in *Cuatrocientos años del 'Arte nuevo de hacer comedias' de Lope de Vega: actas selectas del XIV Congreso de la Asociación Internacional de Teatro Español y Novohispano de los Siglos de Oro*, ed. by G. Vega García-Luengos and H. Urzáiz Tortajada (Valladolid–Olmedo: Universidad de Valladolid–Ayuntamiento de Olmedo, 2010), pp. 455–66
FINE, RUTH, 'En torno a la narración paradójica o las paradojas de la conversión en el *Quijote* de 1615: los casos del morisco Ricote y de Alonso Quijano, el Bueno', in *El 'Quijote' de 1615. Dobleces, inversiones, paradojas, desbordamientos e imposibles*, ed. by Antonio Cortijo Ocaña, Gustavo Illades Aguiar, and Francisco Ramírez Santacruz (Santa Barbara, CA: University of California, Publications of *eHumanista*, 2016), pp. 50–61
FLORES, RALPH, *The Rhetoric of Doubtful Authority: Deconstructive Readings of Self-Questioning Narratives, St. Augustine to Faulkner* (Ithaca: Cornell University Press, 1984)
FOLGER, ROBERT, *Images in Mind: Lovesickness, Spanish Sentimental Fiction and 'Don Quijote'*, North Carolina Studies in the Romance Languages and Literatures (Chapel Hill: University of North Carolina, 2002)
FOLKENFLIK, ROBERT, '*Tristram Shandy* and Eighteenth-Century Narrative', in *The Cambridge Companion to Laurence Sterne*, ed. by Thomas Keymer (Cambridge: Cambridge University Press, 2009), pp. 49–63
FOUCAULT, MICHEL, 'Qu'est-ce qu'un auteur?', *Bulletin de la Société française de philosophie*, 63:3 (1969), 73–104
FOX, DIAN, 'The Apocryphal Part One of *Don Quijote*', *MLN*, 100 (1985), 406–16

FRENK, MARGIT, 'Don Quijote ¿muere cuerdo?', in *Cuatro ensayos sobre el 'Quijote'* (Mexico, D.F.: Fondo de Cultura Económica, 2013), pp. 49–58

FRESHWATER, HELEN, *Theatre and Audience* (London: Palgrave Macmillan, 2009)

FRIEDMAN, EDWARD H., 'Executing the Will: The End of the Road in *Don Quixote*', *Indiana Journal of Hispanic Literatures*, 5 (1994), 105–25

—— 'Reading Redressed: or, The Media Circuits of *Don Quijote*', *Confluencia*, 9.2 (1994), 38–51

FRYE, NORTHROP, *Anatomy of Criticism: Four Essays* (Princeton: Princeton University Press, 1957)

GAMES, ALISON, *The Web of Empire: English Cosmopolitans in an Age of Empire* (Oxford: Oxford University Press, 2008)

GARCÉS, MARÍA ANTONIA, *Cervantes in Algiers: A Captive's Tale* (Nashville: Vanderbilt University Press, 2002)

GARCÍA GUERRA, ELENA MARÍA, *Las alteraciones monetarias en Europa durante la Edad Moderna*, Cuadernos de Historia, 78 (Madrid: Arco Libros, 2000)

—— *Moneda y arbitrios: consideraciones del siglo XVII* (Madrid: Consejo Superior de Investigaciones Científicas, 2003)

GARCÍA DEL PASO, JOSÉ I., 'El problema del vellón en *El chitón de las tarabillas*', *La Perinola*, 6 (2002), 323–62

GARDAIR, COLOMBINE, 'Performing Places', in *C&C'11: Proceedings of the 8th ACM Conference on Creativity and Cognition* (New York: Association for Computing Machinery, 2011), pp. 51–60

GASTA, CHAD M., 'Cervantes and the Picaresque: A Question of Compatibility', in *The Picaresque Novel in Western Literature: From the Sixteenth Century to the Neopicaresque*, ed. by J. A Garrido Ardila (Cambridge: Cambridge University Press, 2015), pp. 96–112

GAYLORD, MARY MALCOLM, 'Pulling Strings with Master Peter's Puppets', *Cervantes: Bulletin of the Cervantes Society of America*, 18 (1998), 117–47

GENETTE, GÉRARD, *Seuils* (Paris: Éditions du Seuil, 1987)

GERLI, E. MICHAEL, *Refiguring Authority: Reading, Writing, and Rewriting in Cervantes*, Studies in Romance Languages, 39 (Lexington: University Press of Kentucky, 1995)

GINGRAS, GERALD L., 'Relación de cómo Ginés de Pasamonte se desprendió de su cárcel literaria', in *Cervantes y su mundo*, ed. by Kurt Reichenberger and Darío Fernández-Morera, 3 vols (Kassel: Reichenberger, 2004), II, 193–226

GLASER, EDWARD, 'Nuevos datos sobre la crítica de los libros de caballerías en los siglos XVI y XVII', *Anuario de Estudios Medievales*, 3 (1996), 393–410

GOFFMAN, ERVING, *The Presentation of Self in Everyday Life* (Garden City: Doubleday Anchor, 1959)

GONZÁLEZ ECHEVARRÍA, ROBERTO, *Cervantes' 'Don Quixote'*, Open Yale Courses (New Haven: Yale University Press, 2015)

—— *Love and the Law in Cervantes* (New Haven: Yale University Press, 2005)

GREENBLATT, STEPHEN, *Renaissance Self-Fashioning: From More to Shakespeare* (Chicago: University of Chicago Press, 2005)

GREENE, MOLLY, *Catholic Pirates and Greek Merchants: A Maritime History of the Mediterranean* (Princeton: Princeton University Press, 2010)

GUILLÉN, CLAUDIO, 'Luis Sánchez, Ginés de Pasamonte y los inventores del género', in *Homenaje a Rodríguez Moñino: estudios de erudición que le ofrecen sus amigos y discípulos hispanistas norte-americanos* (Madrid: Castalia, 1966), pp. 221–31

—— *Literature as System* (Princeton: Princeton University Press, 1971)

—— 'Luis Sánchez, Ginés de Pasamonte y el descubrimiento del género picaresco', in Claudio Guillén, *El primer siglo de oro: estudios sobre géneros y modelos* (Barcelona: Editorial Crítica, 1988), pp. 197–211

Guillén, Jorge, 'Vida y muerte de Alonso Quijano', *Romanische Forschungen*, 64 (1952), 102–13

Gussow, Mel, *Conversations with Stoppard* (London: Nick Hern Books, 1995)

Gutiérrez Trápaga, Daniel, 'Caracterización, tradición y fuentes caballerescas del personaje de Merlín en el *Quijote*', *Tirant*, 13 (2010), 39–50

Hahn, Juergen, 'Rinconete y Cortadillo in *Don Quijote*: A Cervantine Reconstruction', *MLN* 116.2 (2001), 211–34

Hampton, Timothy, *Writing from History: The Rhetoric of Exemplarity in Renaissance Literature* (Ithaca: Cornell University Press, 1990)

Hart, Thomas R., '¿Cervantes perspectivista?', *Nueva Revista de Filología Hispánica*, 40.1 (1992), 293–303

Hart, Thomas R., and Steven Rendall, 'Rhetoric and Persuasion in Marcela's Address to the Shepherds', *Hispanic Review*, 46.3 (1978), 287–98

Harvey, L. P., *Muslims in Spain, 1500 to 1614* (Chicago: University of Chicago Press, 2005)

Hernández Alonso, César, and Beatriz Sanz Alonso, *Germanía y sociedad en los siglos de oro: la cárcel de Sevilla* (Valladolid: Secretariado de Publicaciones e Intercambio Editorial, Universidad de Valladolid, 1999)

Herrera Puga, Pedro, and Pedro de León, *Grandeza y miseria en Andalucía: testimonio de una encrucijada histórica, 1578–1616* (Granada: Facultad de Teología, 1981)

—— *Sociedad y delincuencia en el siglo de oro: aspectos de la vida sevillana en los siglos XVI y XVII* (Granada: Universidad de Granada, Secretariado de Publicaciones, 1971)

Higuera, Henry, *Eros and Empire: Politics and Christianity in 'Don Quixote'* (Lanham, MA: Rowman & Littlefield, 1995)

Hill, John M. M., *Poesías germanescas* (Bloomington: Indiana University Press, 1945)

Hitchcock, Richard, 'Cervantes, Ricote and the Expulsion of the Moriscos', *Bulletin of Spanish Studies*, 81 (2004), 175–85

Hollan, Douglas., and C. Jaston Throop, 'The Anthropology of Empathy: Introduction', in *The Anthropology of Empathy: Experiencing the Lives of Others in Pacific Societies*, ed. by D. W. Hollan and C. J. Throop (New York: Berghahn Books, 2001), pp. 1–24

Housley, Norman, *Religious Warfare in Europe 1400–1536* (Oxford: Oxford University Press, 2002)

Hue, Cécile, 'Apelle, saint Luc et le singe: trois figures du peintre dans l'Espagne des XVIe et XVIIe siècles: fonctions littéraires, théoriques et artistiques' (doctoral thesis, Université de la Sorbonne nouvelle-Paris III, 2009) <https://tel.archives-ouvertes.fr/tel-00951404> [accessed 23 April 2019]

Hutchinson, Steven, 'Del anticlímax y sus virtudes en el *Quijote* de 1615 (la muerte parentética)', in *El 'Quijote' de 1615. Dobleces, inversiones, paradojas, desbordamientos e imposibles*, ed. by Antonio Cortijo Ocaña, Gustavo Illades Aguiar, and Francisco Ramírez Santacruz (Santa Barbara, CA: University of California, Publications of eHumanista, 2016), pp. 120–31

Ife, B[arry] W., 'Cervantes's Portuguese Lover' in *'A primavera toda para ti': Homenagem a Helder Macedo*, ed. by Margarida Calafate Ribeiro (Lisbon: Presença, 2004), pp. 117–21

—— 'Drama as Novel/Novel as Drama' in *Cervantes–Shakespeare 1616–2016*, ed. by José Manuel González, José María Ferri, and María del Carmen Irles (Kassel: Reichenberger, 2017), pp. 350–68.

—— 'Feliciana's Little Voice', *Bulletin of Hispanic Studies*, 86.1 (December 2009), 867–76

Ihrie, Maureen, 'Classical Skepticism and Narrative Authority in *Don Quijote de la Mancha*', in *Studies on 'Don Quijote' and Other Cervantine Works*, ed. by Donald W. Bleznick (York: Spanish Literature Publications Company, 1984), pp. 31–37

Illades, Gustavo, 'Locura y religión quijotescas o la doble ejemplaridad del libro (*Quijote* I y II)', in *El 'Quijote' de 1615. Dobleces, inversiones, paradojas, desbordamientos e imposibles*, ed. by Antonio Cortijo Ocaña, Gustavo Illades Aguiar, and Francisco Ramírez Santacruz (Santa Barbara, CA: University of California, Publications of *eHumanista*, 2016), pp. 132–44

IZQUIERDO IZQUIERDO, JOSÉ ANTONIO, 'Haya, encina o alcornoque? Ecos de una polémica virgiliana en el *Quijote*', *Minerva: Revista de filología clásica*, 5 (1991), 293–304

JAUSS, HANS ROBERT, 'La jouissance esthétique: les expériences fondamentales de la *poiesis*, de l'*aisthesis* et de la *catharsis*', *Poétique*, 10.39 (1979), 261–74

JOLY, MONIQUE, 'Afición de los extranjeros al vino y al jamón: nota sobre el sentido de una síntesis cervantina', *Nueva Revista de Filología Hispánica* 22.2 (1973), 321–28

JOHNSON, CARROLL B., *Cervantes and the Material World* (Urbana: University of Illinois Press, 2000)

—— *Don Quixote: The Quest for Modern Fiction* (Boston: Twayne, 1990)

KEEN, SUZANNE, 'A Narrative Theory of Empathy', *Narrative*, 14 (2006), 207–36

KERMODE, FRANK, *The Sense of an Ending: Studies in the Theory of Fiction*, rev. edn (New York: Oxford University Press, 2000)

KOPPENFELS, MARTIN VON, 'Terminar-Abjurar: el último capítulo del *Don Quijote*', *Criticón*, 96 (2006), 69–85, repr. from 'Don Quijote schwört ab: Versuch über das Schließen', in *Die Endlichkeit der Literatur*, ed. by Eckart Goebel & Martin von Koppenfels (Berlin: Akademie, 2002) pp. 13–25

LAMARQUE, PETER, and STEIN HAUGOM OLSEN, *Truth, Fiction and Literature: A Philosophical Perspective* (Oxford: Oxford University Press, 1994)

LAMB, CHARLES, 'Barrenness of the Imaginative Faculty in the Productions of Modern Art', in Charles Lamb, *The Last Essays of Elia* (London: Edward Moxon, 1833), pp. 166–86

LANGHOLM, ODD, *The Legacy of Scholasticism in Economic Thought: Antecedents of Choice and Power* (Cambridge: Cambridge University Press, 1998)

LAPPIN, ANTHONY JOHN, 'Introduction' in Lope de Vega, *El Caballero de Olmedo*, ed. by Anthony John Lappin, Hispanic Texts (Manchester: Manchester University Press, 2006)

LARRAZ, JOSÉ, *La época del mercantilismo en Castilla (1500–1700)*, 3rd edn (Madrid: Aguilar, 1963)

LATHROP, THOMAS A., 'The Mysterious Missing Title of Chapter 43, of *Don Quixote*, Part I', in *Cervantes y su mundo*, ed. by A. Robert Lauer and Kurt Reichenberger, 3 vols, (Kassel: Reichenberger, 2005), III. 275–82

LAUSBERG, HEINRICH, *Handbook of Literary Rhetoric: A Foundation for Literary Study*, trans. by Matthew T. Bliss, Annemiek Jansen, and David E. Orton, ed. by David E. Orton and R. Dean Anderson (Leiden, 1998)

LAWRANCE, JEREMY, '"Mal haya el que en señores idolatra" (1609): Poetry of Gardens and Solitude', in *A Poet for All Seasons: Eight Commentaries on Góngora*, ed. by Oliver Noble Wood and Nigel Griffin (New York: Hispanic Seminary of Medieval Studies, 2013), pp. 25–46

—— 'On the title *Tragicomedia de Calisto y Melibea*', in *Letters and Society in Fifteenth-Century Spain: Studies Presented to P. E. Russell on his Eightieth Birthday*, ed. by Alan Deyermond & Jeremy Lawrance (Llangrannog: Dolphin, 1993), pp. 79–92

—— 'Death in *Tirant lo Blanc*', in *'Tirant lo Blanc': New Approaches*, ed. by Arthur Terry, Colección Támesis, A181 (London: Tamesis, 1999), pp. 91–107

LÁZARO CARRETER, FERNANDO, *'Lazarillo de Tormes' en la picaresca* (Barcelona: Ariel, 1972)

LEAHY, CHAD, '"Dineros en Cruzados": The *Morisco* Expulsion, Numismatic Propaganda, and the Materiality of Ricote's Coins', *Hispanic Review* 84.3 (2016), 273–98

LEYS, SIMON, 'The Imitation of Our Lord Don Quixote', *New York Review of Books*, 11 June, 1998

LIU, BENJAMÍN, 'Ricote, Mariana y el patrón oro', in *Cervantes y la economía*, ed. by Miguel-Ángel Galindo Martín (Cuenca: Ediciones de la Universidad de Castilla-La Mancha, 2007), pp. 53–66

López Navío, José, 'Sobre la frase de la duquesa: "las obras de caridad hechas floja y tibiamente" (Don Quijote, 2, 36)', Anales Cervantinos, 9 (1961), 97–112
Lo Ré, A. G., 'The Three Deaths of Don Quixote: Comments in Favor of the Romantic Critical Approach', Cervantes: Bulletin of the Cervantes Society of America, 9.2 (1989), 21–41
Mackey, Mary, 'Rhetoric and Characterization in Don Quijote', Hispanic Review, 42.1 (1974), 51–66
Madariaga, Salvador de, Guía del lector del 'Quijote': ensayo psicológico sobre el 'Quijote', 2nd edn (Buenos Aires: Editorial Sudamericana, 1943)
Maestro, Jesús G., Crítica de los géneros literarios en el Quijote: idea y concepto de género en la investigación literaria (Vigo: Academia del Hispanismo, 2009)
Mañas Núñez, Manuel, 'Sanctius Brocensis, "El Brocense"', Alcántara: Revista del Seminario de Estudios Cacereños, 61–62 (2005), 11–26
Mancing, Howard, Cervantes' 'Don Quixote': A Reference Guide, Greenwood Guides to Multicultural Literature (Westport, CT: Greenwood Press, 2006)
—— 'Cide Hamete Benengeli vs. Miguel de Cervantes: The Metafictional Dialectic of Don Quijote', Cervantes, 1 (1981), 63–81
—— The Chivalric World of 'Don Quijote': Style, Structure, and Narrative Technique (Columbia: University of Missouri Press, 1982)
—— 'Guzmán de Alfarache and After: The Spanish Picaresque Novel in the Seventeenth Century', in The Picaresque Novel in Western Literature: From the Sixteenth Century to the Neopicaresque, ed. by J. A. Garrido Ardila (Cambridge: Cambridge University Press, 2015), pp. 40–59
Mandel, Oscar, 'The Function of the Norm in Don Quixote', Modern Philology, 55.3 (1958), 154–63
Mann, Thomas, Meerfahrt mit Don Quijote (1934): mit einer Übersicht und Photographien von sämtlichen Atlantikreisen Thomas Manns, Fischer Taschenbuch, 50645 (Frankfurt: Fischer, 2002)
Mar, Raymond A., Keith Oatley and Jordan B. Peterson, 'Exploring the Link between Reading Fiction and Empathy: Ruling Out Individual Differences and Examining Outcomes', Communications, 34 (2009), 407–28
Marín, Nicolás, 'La piedra y la mano en el prólogo del Quijote apócrifo', in Homenaje a Guillermo Guastavino: miscelánea de estudios en el año de su jubilación como Director de la Biblioteca Nacional (Madrid: Asociación Nacional de Bibliotecarios, Archiveros y Arqueólogos, 1974), pp. 253–88
Márquez Villanueva, Francisco, 'La interacción Alemán-Cervantes' in Actas del Coloquio Internacional de la Asociación de Cervantistas (Barcelona: Anthropos, 1991), pp. 149–81
—— Personajes y temas del 'Quijote' (Madrid: Taurus, 1975)
Martín Jiménez, Alfonso, Guzmánes y Quijotes: dos casos similares de continuaciones apócrifos (Valladolid: Universidad de Valladolid, Secretario de Publicaciones y Intercambio Editorial, 2010)
Martínez-Bonati, Félix, 'Don Quijote' and the Poetics of the Novel (Ithaca: Cornell University Press, 1992)
Martínez Mata, Emilio, 'El caballero del verde gabán', Monteagudo, 20 (2015), 73–103
—— Cervantes comenta el 'Quijote', intro. by Anthony Close (Madrid: Cátedra, 2008)
Mas, Albert, Les Turcs dans la littérature espagnole du Siècle d'Or: recherches sur l'evolution d'un thème littéraire, 2 vols (Paris: Follope, 1967)
McKenzie, Jon, Perform or Else: From Discipline to Performance (New York: Routledge, 2001)
Micó, José María, 'Prosas y prisas en 1604: el Quijote, el Guzmán y la Pícara Justina', in Hommage à Robert Jammes, ed. by F. Cerdan, 3 vols (Toulouse: Presses Universitaire du Mirail, 1994), III, 827–48

MILLÁN, JOSÉ ANTONIO, 'El Quijote apócrifo de "Alonso Fernández de Avellaneda"', *Revista digital universitaria* 6.5 (2005), 1–8

MILLER, J. HILLIS, 'The Critic as Host', in *Deconstruction and Criticism*, ed. by Harold Bloom and others (London: Routledge, Kegan Paul, 1979), pp. 217–53

MINNIS, ALASTAIR J., *Medieval Theory of Authorship: Scholastic Literary Attitudes in the Later Middle Ages*, 2nd edn (Aldershot: Scolar Press, 1988)

MOLHO, MAURICE, 'Doña Sancha (*Quijote*, II, 60)', in *Homenaje a José Manuel Blecua ofrecido por sus discípulos, colegas y amigos*, ed. by Dámaso Alonso (Madrid: Gredos, 1983), pp. 443–48

—— 'El pícaro de nuevo', *MLN*, 100.2 (1985), 199–222

MONER, MICHEL, 'El problema morisco en los textos cervantinos', in *Las dos grandes minorías étnico-religiosas en la literatura española del Siglo de Oro: los judeoconversos y los moriscos. Actas del 'Grand Séminaire' de Neuchâtel: Neuchâtel 26 a 27 de mayo de 1994*, ed. by Irene Andres-Suárez (Paris: Diffusion les Belles Lettres, 1995), pp. 85–100

MORALES ORTIZ, ALICIA, *Plutarco en España: Traducciones de 'Moralia' en el siglo XVI* (Murcia: Universidad de Murcia, 2000)

MORBY, EDWIN S., 'Some Observations on *tragedia* and *tragicomedia* in Lope', *Hispanic Review* 11.3 (1943), 185–209

MORENO, EMILIO, liner notes to 'Orphénica Lyra', dir. José Miguel Moreno, *Música en el 'Quijote'*, (San Lorenzo de El Escorial: Glossa Music, GCD 920207, 2005)

MORROS MESTRES, BIENVENIDO, 'Cervantes y la revolución cultural del Renacimiento: Acteón y don Quijote', *Anales Cervantinos*, 37 (2005), 167–77

MUNDÓ, A. M., 'La datación de los códices litúrgicos visigóticos toledanos', *Hispania sacra*, 18 (1965), 1–25

MURILLO, LOUIS A., *The Golden Dial: Temporal configuration in 'Don Quijote'* (Oxford: Dolphin, 1975)

NABOKOV, VLADIMIR, *Lectures on 'Don Quixote'*, ed. by Fredson Bowers (San Diego: Harcourt Brace Jovanovich, 1983)

NADEAU, CAROLYN A., '*Moscatel morisco*: The Role of Wine in the Formation of Morisco Identity', *Bulletin of Hispanic Studies*, 90.2 (2013), 153–65

—— *Women of the Prologue: Imitation, Myth, and Magic in 'Don Quixote I'* (London: Associated University Presses, 2002)

NELSON, INGRID, and SHANNON GAYK, 'Introduction: Genre as *form-of-life*', *Exemplaria*, 27 (2015), 3–7

NELSON, LOWRY, ed., *Cervantes: A Collection of Critical Essays* (Englewood Cliffs: Prentice-Hall, 1969)

NELL, VICTOR, *Lost in a Book: The Psychology of Reading for Pleasure* (New Haven: Yale University Press, 1988)

NISHIDA, EMMA, 'Los romances y el lenguaje de germanía en el entremés del *Rufián viudo*: ¿mensajes pícaros de Cervantes hacia Alonso Fernández de Avellaneda?', *Tus obras los rincones de la tierra descubren. Actas VI Congreso Internacional de la Asociación de Cervantistas. Alcalá de Henares, 13 al 16 de diciembre de 2006*, ed. by A. Dotras Bravo and others (Alcalá de Henares: Centro de estudios cervantinos, 2008)

Notas al Ingenioso hidalgo Don Quixote de la Mancha, ed. by Luis [Ludwig] Ideler, 2 vols (Berlin: Enrique Frölich, 1804–05)

OLEZA, JUAN, 'La propuesta teatral del primer Lope de Vega', in *Teatro y prácticas escénicas: II*, ed. by Ana Giordano Gromegna (London: Tamesis, 1986), pp. 251–308

OLID GUERRERO, EDUARDO, *Del teatro a la novela: el ritual del disfraz en las 'Novelas ejemplares' de Cervantes*, Biblioteca de Estudios Cervantinos, 34 (Alcalá de Henares: Universidad de Alcalá Servicio de Publicaciones, 2015)

O'Neill, Sinéad, Joshua Edelman and John Sloboda, *Opera Audiences and Cultural Value: A Study of Audience Experience,* Working Paper, 2 (London: Creativeworks London, 2014) <http://www.creativeworkslondon.org.uk/publications/working-paper-2> [accessed 3 April 2017].

Orduna, Lilia E. F. de, 'Héroes troyanos y griegos en la *Hystoria del magnánimo, valiente e inuencible cauallero don belianís de grecia* (Burgos, 1547)', in *Actas del IX Congreso de la Asociación internacional de hispanistas,* 2 vols (Frankfurt: Vervuert, 1986), I, 559–68

O'Reilly, Terence, 'The Death of Don Quixote and the Birth of Modernity: The Omens in *Don Quixote,* Part II, Chapter 73', *Bulletin of Spanish Studies,* 94.8 (2017), 1269–85

Ortega y Gasset, José, *Meditaciones del Quijote* (Madrid: Residencia de Estudiantes, 1914)

Parker, Alexander A., 'El concepto de la verdad en el *Quijote', Revista de Filología Española,* 32 (1948), 287–305 <http://cvc.cervantes.es/literatura/quijote_antologia/parker.htm> [accessed 23 April 2019]

Parr, James A., *'Don Quixote': A Touchstone for Literary Criticism* (Kassel: Reichenberger, 2005)

Patlagean, Evelyne, 'L'histoire de la femme deguisée en moine et l'évolution de la saintété feminine en Byzance', *Studi medievali,* 3rd series, 17 (1976), 597–623

Pedraza Jiménez, Felipe B., 'De Quevedo a Cervantes: la génesis de la jácara', *Edad de Oro Cantabrigense: Actas del VII Congreso de la Asociación Internacional Siglo De Oro (AISO): (Robinson College, Cambridge, 18–22 Julio, 2005)* (Madrid: Iberoamericana, 2006)

Percas de Ponseti, Helena, *Cervantes y su concepto del arte,* 2 vols, Biblioteca Románica Hispánica, II: Estudios y Ensayos, 217 (Madrid: Gredos, 1975)

—— 'Un misterio dilucidado: Pasamonte fue Avellaneda', *Cervantes: Bulletin of the Cervantes Society of America,* 22.1 (2002), 127–54

Perdices de Blas, Luis, *La economía política de la decadencia de Castilla en el siglo XVII: investigaciones de los arbitristas sobre la naturaleza y causas de la riqueza de las naciones* (Madrid: Editorial Síntesis, 1996)

Pérez de León, Vicente, *Tablas destempladas: los entremeses de Cervantes a examen* (Alcalá de Henares, Madrid: Centro de Estudios Cervantinos, 2005)

Pérez-Villanueva, Sonia, *The Life of Catalina de Erauso, the Lieutenant Nun: An Early-Modern Autobiography* (Madison: Fairleigh Dickinson University Press, 2014)

Perry, Mary Elizabeth, *Crime and Society in Early Modern Seville* (Hanover, NH: University Press of New England, 1980)

Phipps Houck, Helen, 'Substantive Address Used between Don Quijote and Sancho Panza', *Hispanic Review,* 5 (1937), 60–72

Polchow, Shannon L., 'Manipulation of Narrative Discourse: From *Amadís de Gaula* to *Don Quixote', Hispania,* 88 (2005), 72–81

Prendergast, Ryan, *Reading, Writing, and Errant Subjects in Inquisitorial Spain* (Farnham: Ashgate, 2011)

Querol Gavaldá, Miguel, *La música en las obras de Cervantes* (Barcelona: Comtalia, 1948)

Rabone, Richard, 'Fallen Idols? Vice and Virtue in the Iconography of Icarus and Phaethon', in *The Routledge Companion to Iberian Studies,* ed. by Javier Muñoz-Basols, Laura Lonsdale, and Manuel Delgado (London: Routledge, 2017), pp. 249–63

Redondo, Augustin, 'Fiestas burlescas en el palacio ducal: el episodio de Altisidora', in *Actas del Tercer Congreso Internacional de la Asociación de Cervantistas,* ed. by Antonio Bernat Vistarini (Palma: Universitat de les Illes Balears, 1998), pp. 49–62

—— 'Nuevas consideraciones sobre el personaje del Caballero del Verde Gabán (*D.Q.,* II, 16–18)', in *Actas del II Congreso Internacional de la Asociación de Cervantistas,* ed. by G. Grilli (Naples: Società Editrice Intercontinentale Gallo, 1995), pp. 513–33

—— *Otra manera de leer el 'Quijote': historia, tradiciones culturales y literatura,* Nueva Biblioteca de Erudición y Crítica (Madrid: Castalia, 1997)

—— 'La religión de don Quijote y la fe de Alonso Quijano', in *Cervantes y las religiones: Actas del coloquio internacional de la Asociación de Cervantistas (Universidad Hebrea de Jerusalén, Israel, 19–21 de diciembre de 2005)*, ed. by Ruth Fine and Santiago López Navia, Biblioteca Áurea Hispánica, 51 (Madrid: Iberoamericana, 2008), pp. 199–222

REGALADO, ANTONIO, 'La religión de don Quijote y la fe de Alonso Quijano', in *Cervantes y las religiones: Actas del Coloquio Internacional de la Asociación de Cervantistas (Universidad Hebrea de Jerusalén, Israel, 19–21 de diciembre de 2005)*, ed. by Ruth Fine and Santiago López Navia, Biblioteca Áurea Hispánica, 51 (Madrid: Iberoamericana, 2008), pp. 199–222

RICOEUR, PAUL, *Soi-même comme un autre* (Paris: Seuil, 1990)

—— *Temps et récit*, 3 vols (Paris: Seuil, 1983–85)

RICO, FRANCISCO, 'Don Quijote, Cervantes, el justo medio', *Estudios Públicos*, 100 (2005), 63–70

RILEY, EDWARD C., *Cervantes' Theory of the Novel* (Oxford: Clarendon Press, 1962)

—— *'Don Quijote'* (London: Allen & Unwin, 1986)

—— 'Don Quixote and the Imitation of Models', *Bulletin of Hispanic Studies*, 31 (1954), 3–16

—— 'Metamorphosis, Myth, and Dream in the Cave of Montesinos', in *Essays on Narrative Fiction in the Iberian Peninsula in Honour of Frank Pierce*, ed. by R. B. Tate (London: Dolphin, 1982), pp. 105–19

—— *La rara invención: estudios sobre Cervantes y su posteridad literaria* (Barcelona: Editorial Crítica, 2001)

—— 'Symbolism in *Don Quixote*, Part II, Chapter 73', *Journal of Hispanic Philology*, 3 (1979), 161–74

RIQUER, MARTÍN DE, *Para leer a Cervantes*, El Acantilado, 74 (Barcelona: Acantilado, 2003)

RODRÍGUEZ-LUIS, JULIO, 'On Closure and Openendedness in the two *Quijotes*', in *On Cervantes: Essays for L. A. Murillo*, ed. by James A. Parr (Newark: Juan de la Cuesta, 1991), pp. 227–40

ROGER, ISABEL M., 'Don Quijote y Roque Guinart frente al estilo de vida de los poderosos', *Anales Cervantinos*, 48 (2016), 83–201

ROJAS, CRISTOBAL DE, *Teorica y practica de fortificacion, conforme las medidas y defensas destos tiempos, repartida en tres partes* (Madrid: Luis Sanchez, 1589)

ROMERO MUÑOZ, CARLOS, '"Animales inmundos y soeces" (*Quijote*, II, 58–59 y 66)', *Rassegna Iberistica*, 63 (1998), 3–24

—— 'Nueva lectura de *El retablo de Maese Pedro*', *Actas del I Coloquio Internacional de la Asociación de Cervantistas* (Madrid: Anthropos, 1990), pp. 95–130

ROUHI, LEYLA, 'A Handsome Boy Among Those Barbarous Turks: Cervantes's Muslims and the Art and Science of Desire', in *Islamicate Sexualities: Translations Across Temporal Geographies of Desire*, ed. by Kathryn Babayan and Afsaneh Najmabadi (Cambridge, MA: Harvard University Press, 2008), pp. 41–71

RUPP, STEPHEN, 'Soldiers and Satire in *El Licenciado Vidriera*', in *A Companion to Cervantes's Novelas Ejemplares*, ed. by Stephen Boyd (Woodbridge: Tamesis, 2010), pp. 134–47

RUSSELL, PETER E., '*Don Quixote* as a Funny Book', *Modern Language Review*, 64.2 (1969), 312–26

RUTA, MARÍA CATERINA, 'Aspectos iconológicos del *Quijote*', *Nueva Revista de Filología Hispánica*, 38 (1990), 875–86

SAWYER, ROBERT, 'Tilting at Convention: Orson Welles's *Don Quixote* and *Chimes at Midnight*', in *Cervantes — Shakespeare 1616–2016*, ed. by José Manuel González, José María Ferri, and María del Carmen Irles (Kassel: Reichenberger, 2016), pp. 369–85

SCHECHNER, RICHARD, *Performance Theory* (London: Routledge, 2003)

SCHMIDT, RACHEL, 'Leyendo otros que sean luz del alma: el *Quijote* y la literatura del *ars* moriendi', in *Cervantes y el 'Quijote': Actas del Coloquio Internacional*, ed. by Emilio Martínez Mata (Madrid: Editorial Arco, 2007), pp. 113–24

——'The Performance and Hermeneutics of Death in the Last Chapter of *Don Quijote*', *Cervantes: Bulletin of the Cervantes Society of America*, 20.2 (2000), 101–26

SCRUTON, ROGER, *Art and Imagination: A Study in the Philosophy of Mind* (London: Methuen, 1974)

SHEEHAN, MICHAEL M., *The Will in Medieval England* (Toronto: Pontifical Institute of Medieval Studies, 1963)

SICROFF, A. A., 'La segunda muerte de don Quijote como respuesta de Cervantes a Avellaneda', *Nueva Revista de Filología Hispánica*, 24.2 (1975) (*Homenaje a Raimundo Lida*), 267–91

SISMONDI, J. C. L. SIMONDE DE, *De la littérature du midi de l'Europe*, 4 vols (Paris: Treuttel et Würtz, 1813)

SMITH LEWIS, AGNES, 'The Story of the Blessed Mary Who Was Called Marina', *Vox Benedictina*, 2 (1985), 305–17

SMITH, WINIFRED, *The Commedia dell'Arte: A Study in Italian Popular Comedy* (New York: Columbia University Press, 1912)

SNADER, JOE, *Caught between Worlds: British Captivity Narratives in Fact and Fiction* (Lexington: University Press of Kentucky, 2000)

SOBEJANO, GONZALO, 'De la intención y valor del *Guzmán de Alfarache*', *Romanische Forschungen*, 71 (1959), 267–311

SOSA, MARCELA BEATRIZ, '(Más)caras de la sexualidad en el Siglo de Oro español: travestismo y metateatro en géneros breves', *Texturas: estudios interdisciplinares sobre el discurso*, 4 (2004), 105–15

SPITZER, LEO, *Linguistics and Literary History: Essays in Stylistics* (Princeton: Princeton University Press, 1948)

——'Thomas Mann y la muerte de don Quijote', *Revista de Filología Hispánica*, 2 (1940), 46–48

STAGG, GEOFFREY, 'Revision in *Don Quixote* Part I', in *Studies in Honour of I. González Llubera*, ed. by Frank Pierce (Oxford: Dolphin, 1959), pp. 347–66

——'Sobre el plan primitivo del *Quijote*', in *Actas del I Congreso Internacional de Hispanistas*, ed. by Frank Pierce and Cyril A. Jones (Oxford: Dolphin, 1964), pp. 463–71

STYAN, J. L., *The Elements of Drama* (Cambridge: Cambridge University Press, 1960)

SULLIVAN, HENRY W., *Grotesque Purgatory: A Study of Cervantes's 'Don Quixote', Part II* (University Park, Pennsylvania: Pennsylvania State University Press, 1996)

TIGNER, AMY L., 'The Spanish Actress's Art: Improvisations, Transvestism, and Disruption in Tirso's *El vergonzoso en palacio*', *Early Theatre*, 15 (2012), 169–92

TORRES, BÉNÉDICTE, *Cuerpo y gesto en 'El Quijote' de Cervantes* (Alcalá de Henares: Centro de Estudios Cervantinos, 2002)

UNAMUNO, MIGUEL DE, *Vida de Don Quijote y Sancho*, ed. by Alberto Navarro, Letras Hispánicas, 279 (Madrid: [n. pub.], 1905, repr. Cátedra, 1992)

URBINA, EDUARDO, 'El concepto de *admiratio* y lo grotesco en el *Quijote*', *Cervantes: Bulletin of the Cervantes Society of America*, 9.1 (1989), 17–33

——'"En alas de deseo": el motivo de los altibajos en *Don Quijote*', *Indiana Journal of Hispanic Literatures*, 2.2 (1994), 87–104

——'El juego de la fortuna en el *Quijote* de 1605', in *Actas de XII Congreso de la Asociación Internacional de Hispanistas 21–26 de agosto de 1995, Birmingham*, 7 vols (Birmingham: Department of Hispanic Studies, University of Birmingham, 1998), III (Estudios áureos II) (ed. by Jules Whicker), pp. 254–62

——*El sin par Sancho Panza: Parodia y creación* (Barcelona: Anthropos, 1991)

VAN DOREN, MARK, *Don Quixote's Profession* (New York: Columbia University Press, 1958)

VÉLEZ-SAINZ, JULIO, '¿Amputación o ungimiento? Soluciones a la contaminación religiosa en el *Buscón* y el *Quijote* (1615)', *MLN*, 122.2 (2007), 233–50

VIDAL DOVAL, ROSA, '"Nos soli sumus christiani": *Conversos* in the Texts of the Toledo Rebellion of 1449', in *Medieval Hispanic Studies in Memory of Alan Deyermond*, ed. by A. M. Beresford, L. M. Haywood, and J. Weiss (Woodbridge: Tamesis, 2013), pp. 215–36

VIGO, ABELARDO DEL, *Cambistas, mercaderes y banqueros en el Siglo de Oro español* (Madrid: Biblioteca de Autores Cristianos, 1997)

VOSSLER, KARL, *La soledad en la poesía española*, trans. by José Miguel Sacristán, 2nd edn, Biblioteca Filológica Hispana, 49 (Madrid: Visor, 2000)

WAAL, FRANS B. M. DE, *The Age of Empathy: Nature's Lessons for a Kinder Society, With Drawings by the Author* (New York: Harmony, 2009)

WALTON, KENDALL L., *Mimesis as Make-Believe: On the Foundations of the Representational Arts* (Cambridge, MA: Harvard University Press, 1990)

WARDROPPER, BRUCE W., 'Cervantes' Theory of the Drama', *Modern Philology*, 52.4 (1955), 217–21

WASSERMAN, DALE, '*Don Quixote* as Theatre', *Cervantes: Bulletin of the Cervantes Society of America*, 19.1 (1999), 125–30

WHETTER, KEVIN SEAN, *Understanding Genre and Medieval Romance* (Avalon: Ashgate, 2008)

WILLIAMSON, EDWIN, 'La autoridad de Don Quijote y el poder de Sancho: el conflicto político en el fondo del *Quijote*', in *Autoridad y poder en el Siglo de Oro*, ed. by Ignacio Arellano, Christoph Strosetzki, and Edwin Williamson (Madrid: Iberoamericana, 2009), 241–66

—— 'The Devil in *Don Quixote*', *Bulletin of Spanish Studies*, 92.8–10 (2015), 147–66

—— *The Half-way House of Fiction: 'Don Quixote' and Arthurian Romance* (Oxford: Oxford University Press, 1984)

—— 'The Power-Struggle between Don Quixote and Sancho: Four Crises in the Development of the Narrative', *Bulletin of Spanish Studies*, 84 (2007), 837–58

WILLIS, RAYMOND S., JR, *The Phantom Chapters of the 'Quijote'* (New York: Hispanic Institute in the United States, 1953)

WISE, KAREN, *English Touring Opera*, 'Opera in Cinemas' Report, Working Paper 3 (London: Creativeworks London, 2014) <http://www.creativeworkslondon.org.uk/publications/working-paper-3> [accessed 3 April 2017].

WOLF, WERNER, 'Framings of Narrative in Literature and the Pictorial Arts', in *Intermediality and Storytelling*, ed. by Marina Grishakova and Marie-Laure Ryan (Berlin: de Gruyter, 2010), pp. 126–47

WRIGHT, ROGER, 'Humour in the Oral *Romancero*: How Would We Know?', *Bulletin of Hispanic Studies*, 86 (2009), 26–36

ZIOLKOWSKI, ERIC, 'Don Quixote's Windmill and Fortune's Wheel', *Modern Language Review*, 86 (1991), 885–97

ZIPPEL, FRANK, 'Fiction across Media: Towards a Transmedial Concept of Fictionality', in *Storyworlds Across Media: Towards a Media-Conscious Narratology*, ed. by Marie-Laure Ryan and Jan-Noël Thon (Lincoln: University of Nebraska Press, 2014), pp. 103–25

INDEX

Abre los ojos (*Vanilla Sky*) 107
Actaeon 59
Adam and Eve 20
Aeneas 38, 42, 247
Africa 119, 149, 218
Agrajes 238
Albornoz, Bartolomé de 144
Alemán, Mateo 4, 125, 126, 128, 129
 Guzmán de Alfarache 4–5, 119–21, 123–27, 129, 184
Alexander the Great 2, 35, 42, 43, 44, 45, 46, 52, 54, 58, 62 n. 58
Alfonso X (el Sabio) 100
Algiers 163, 166, 168, 169, 172, 182 n. 66, 193
Alifanfarón 219
Allen, John J. 225, 235 n. 137
Altisidora 57, 95, 97, 216, 244, 247, 249
Amadís de Gaula 12, 53, 59, 67, 126, 166, 176 n. 16, 182 n. 70, 257 n. 4
Amadís of Gaul 2, 11, 45, 107, 117 n. 52, 224, 225, 237, 238
 see also *Amadís de Gaula*
Ambrosio 1, 15, 23, 25, 26, 27, 28
Ana Félix 6, 172–73
Anderson, Ellen M. 116 n. 39, 185
Andrés 46, 60 n. 18, 211, 230 n. 47
Angulo el Malo 105
Anselm, St 226
Anselmo 74
Antichrist 162
Antonio (shepherd boy) 1, 4, 15, 22, 102, 103, 116 n. 42
Aquinas, Thomas, St 134
Arabic (language) 3, 6, 14, 32 n. 21, 37, 67, 133, 134, 154, 163, 164, 165, 167, 168, 170, 174, 177 n. 25, 179 n. 35, 180 n. 51
arbitristas 147, 150, 152
Arcadia 20, 24, 219, 220, 234 nn. 120, 128 & 129, 179 n. 35, 180 n. 51
Arcalaus 2, 45
Argensola, Bartolomé Leonardo de 25, 34 n. 67
Argensola, Lupercio Leonardo de 25, 34 n. 67
Ariosto:
 Orlando furioso 11, 31 n. 6
Aristotle 3, 70, 75, 76, 79, 80, 88 n. 36, 89 n. 48, 134, 161, 240, 242, 256, 258 n. 12
Arms and Letters (DQ's speech on) 18, 33 n. 37

Arrian 2, 44
 Anabasis of Alexander 43
Arthur, King 233 n. 109, 238
Arts of Dying Well 240, 251
Asia 42, 43, 45
asientos 147
auctoritas 3, 65, 66–67, 68–74, 76, 77–86, 86 nn. 2–6, 87 nn. 7 & 8
Augsburg 6, 152
 Declaration of 6
Auristela (*Persiles*) 99
Avellaneda, Alonso Fernández de 3, 8, 36, 42, 58, 62 n. 58, 85, 93, 114 nn. 3 & 4, 120, 125, 127, 130 n. 16, 170, 180 n. 47, 193, 205, 235 n. 134, 239, 240, 247–51, 253, 260 n. 30, 261 n. 33
Ávila, Luis de:
 Carlo famoso 17
Azán Agá 169
Azpilcueta, Martín de 142, 143, 145

Babieca 42
baciyelmo 5, 52, 139, 140, 141
baños (of Algiers) 97, 115 n. 23, 169, 193
Barahona de Soto, Luis:
 Las lágrimas de Angélica 17
Barbary 165, 170
barber (*DQ*) 5, 11, 12, 13, 29, 53, 108, 110, 115 n. 19, 139, 140–42, 145, 208, 214, 240, 241, 247
Barcelona (episodes of *DQ* set in) 4, 36, 57, 127, 207, 218, 220, 224, 226, 233 n. 109, 234 n. 120, 235 n. 134, 243, 249
Barnés Vázquez, Antonio 77
Basilio 65, 81
Basil, St 240
Basque, the (Don Sancho de Azpeitia) 67, 68
Belerma 81
Belianís (de Grecia) 161, 162, 164, 175 n. 11
Belmonte, Luis de:
 El afanador el de Utrera 196
Beltenebros 107
Berganza (*El coloquio de los perros*) 125, 138, 150, 151
Bergman, Ted 7
Bernard of Clairvaux, St 213, 230 n. 50
 Liber ad milites Templi: De laude novae militiae 213
Bible 20, 49, 73, 75
 Apocalypse 162

Corinthians II 49
Deuteronomy 49
Ephesians 212, 230 n. 48
Genesis 160
Kings, Book of 73
Blanco Aguinaga, Carlos 125
Blecua, José Manuel 190
Bloom, Harold 120, 121, 122, 127, 243
Borges, Jorge Luis 205, 228 nn. 12 & 16, 234 n. 120, 252, 253, 254, 255, 260 n. 28, 261 n. 37
Boyd, Stephen, 7–8
Boyer, Benito 17, 32 n. 30
Brewer, Brian 5–6
Bucephalus 42
Byron, George Gordon, Lord 8, 242–43, 244, 252, 256, 258 n. 15

Caballero de la Blanca Luna 127, 221
  see also Carrasco, Sansón
caballeros santos, see warrior saints
Cabañas Agrela, José Miguel:
  Breve historia de Cervantes 184–85
Cachidiablo 238
Cairo, Sultan of 164
Calderón de la Barca, Pedro 187
Camila 74
Canavaggio, Jean 113
Canon of Toledo 1, 13, 77, 179–80 n. 44
Cantón Salazar, Juan:
  El valiente Barrionuevo 196
capital flight (problem of in Spain) 147, 148, 149, 151
Captive's Tale 6, 100, 165, 167–68, 173, 174, 179 n. 38
Cardenio 1, 12, 15, 52, 100, 112, 167, 231 n. 55
Carmen, la de Triana 107
Carrasco, Sansón (Samson Carrasco) 76, 111, 123, 170, 218, 220, 231 n. 64, 240–41, 243, 248, 251, 252, 256
  as Knight of the Mirrors 244
  as Knight of the White Moon 220, 221, 243
Carthage 247
Casalduero, Joaquín 188
Castile 2, 55, 58, 127, 144, 152
  kingdom of 56
Castro, Américo 61 n. 45, 125, 126, 146, 155 n. 16
  Cervantes y los casticismos españoles 125
Catalonia 37
Catholic Monarchs 44, 143
Cato 42, 73
Celestina, La, see Rojas, Fernando de
Cervantes, Miguel de:
  captivity of (in Algiers) 119, 168, 170, 193
  and drama 4, 88 n. 20, 93–94, 95, 112–13
  imprisonment of (in Seville) 184
  library of 19, 33 n. 40
  and music 4, 94, 95, 96, 97, 98, 99, 101, 112, 114 n. 12, 115 n. 23

  works:
    El curioso impertinente 15, 86 n. 2, 113
    Don Quijote, see Don Quixote, separate entry
    Entremés del rufián viudo llamado Trampagos 7, 190
    La Galatea 16, 21, 23, 24, 96, 98, 163, 178 n. 32, 226
    Novelas ejemplares:
      El celoso extremeño 98
      El coloquio de los perros 138
      El licenciado Vidriera 187, 195
      La española inglesa 98, 115–16 n. 28
      La fuerza de la sangre 93, 223
      La gitanilla 60 n. 18, 100
      La ilustre fregona 97, 190
      Las dos doncellas 93
      Rinconete y Cortadillo 97, 184, 185, 187
    Obras completas 96
    Ocho comedias y ocho entremeses nuevos, nunca representados 93, 261 n. 39
    Los baños de Argel 97, 115 n. 23
    La casa de los celos 97, 115 n. 23
    Los trabajos de Persiles y Sigismunda 98, 99, 109, 110, 112, 115 n. 28, 193, 223, 233–34 n. 115
    Viaje del Parnaso 128
Charles V, Emperor 147
Chaves, Cristóbal de 7, 186, 187
  Relación de las cosas de la cárcel de Sevilla y su trato 186
Chevalier, Maxime 189
Christ 138, 210, 216, 231 n. 79, 235–36 n. 145
Christianity 6, 165, 168
Church (Catholic) 13, 138, 139, 173, 216, 236 n. 146
Cicero 69, 70, 87 n. 14, 239, 240
  De optimo genere oratorum 239
Cid, El 42
Cide Hamete Benengeli 3, 6, 37, 74, 78, 81, 82, 85, 86, 86–87 n. 6, 104, 133, 138, 164, 165, 166, 167, 168, 170, 173, 174, 239, 243, 248, 249, 252, 253
Circe 73, 88 n. 30
Clavileño 40, 82, 111, 218, 232 n. 96, 243
Clemencín, Diego 8, 35, 37, 55, 60 n. 12, 187, 188, 193, 244, 245, 259 nn. 20 & 23
Close, Anthony 1
  A Companion to 'Don Quixote' 1, 36, 39, 189, 190, 206, 231 n. 55, 232 n. 92
comedias de capa y espada 196
comedias de valiente 7, 196, 199
comedy 5, 8, 36, 102, 126, 129, 135, 140, 238, 239–40, 246, 248, 251, 252, 253, 258 nn. 12 &15, 260 n. 26
Constantinople 163
Contreras, Alonso de:
  Vida, nacimiento, padres y crianza del capitán Alonso de Contreras 195–96
Corbacho, El 187
Correa, Gonzalo:
  Vocabulario de refranes 44

'Cortes de la Muerte', episode of 218, 224
Cortés, Hernán 210
Cotarelo y Mori, Emilio 196
courtly love poetry 2, 29, 30
Covarrubias, Sebastián de:
 Tesoro de la lengua castellana 44, 234 n. 125, 261 n. 32
Covent Garden (London) 109, 118 n. 61
Cros, Edmond 125, 130 n. 23
cross-dressing 172, 195
Cruz, Penélope 107–08
Cubillo, Álvaro:
 Añasco el de Talavera 196
cuentecillos 7, 189
curate, *see* priest
Curioso impertinente, *see* Cervantes, Miguel de, works

Dadson, Trevor 1, 2, 228 n. 16
Davies, Ann 107, 108, 117 n. 55
deadly sins 212, 229 n. 30
decorum 3, 8, 19, 70, 76, 77, 96, 238, 239
desengaño (disillusionment) 16, 27, 125, 127, 247, 260 n. 26
Devil 52, 105, 166, 179 n. 42, 212, 225, 234 n. 128, 235 n. 136, 236 n. 145, 247
Deza, Lope de 149, 151
Dido 8, 42, 247, 248
Donatus 239
Don Gregorio (*DQ*) 172, 173, 181–82 n. 66
Don Juan (*DQ* II. 59) 42
Don Luis (*DQ*) 1, 15, 179 n. 36, 199
Don Quixote:
 as celebrity 110, 111, 112, 170
 death of 1, 3, 7, 48, 82, 125, 205, 206, 207, 208, 225, 226, 227 n. 4, 228 nn. 9 & 18, 237, 239, 240–41, 243, 246, 251, 253, 255, 257 nn. 8 & 9, 261 n. 32
 housekeeper of 208, 237, 241, 252, 254
 as Knight of the Sorry Countenance 248
 library of 11, 16–17, 19, 23, 31 n. 7, 32 n. 31, 110
 as musician 95–96
 names of 31 n. 2, 176 n. 15, 228 n. 18, 241, 261 n. 33
 niece of 31 n. 2, 208, 237, 241, 251, 252, 254, 261 n. 33
 recovery of 5, 7, 206, 207, 208, 209, 225, 226, 227, 227 n. 7, 229 n. 19, 235 n. 144, 246, 256
 and the theatre 95, 103, 105–06, 108, 113, 194
 trampled by bulls 40, 218, 219, 221, 222, 234 n. 121
 trampled by pigs 221–22, 224, 234 n. 120
 as *valiente* 7, 39, 58, 78, 79, 196–99
Don Quixote:
 criminals and criminality in 7, 183, 186–90, 193–95, 197–200
 fiction (mode of) in 3, 4, 5, 7, 66, 93, 98, 159, 163, 164, 169, 174, 186, 187, 196, 199, 235 n. 144
 segundo autor 5, 37, 67, 104, 176 n. 17

Part One 11, 13, 14, 16, 17, 18, 21, 24, 25, 30, 31 n. 2, 32 n. 24, 33 nn. 37 & 39, 42, 43, 61 n. 51, 108, 110, 111, 112, 119, 120, 121, 123, 124, 126, 133, 136, 140, 160, 162, 163, 166, 173, 177 n. 25, 180 n. 47, 183, 209, 235 n. 137, 237, 238, 239, 240, 246, 248, 249, 250, 252, 253, 260 n. 30, 262 n. 41
 intercalated stories in 12, 15, 167, 179 n. 36, 235 n. 137, 248
 prologue 3, 66, 68, 70, 71, 72, 74, 76, 80, 82, 88 n. 33, 93, 114 n. 4, 160, 162, 163, 164, 166, 176 n. 17, 183, 185, 188, 240
Part Two 3, 4, 7, 16, 19, 24, 30, 31 n. 2, 32 n. 24, 36, 75, 81, 82, 105, 110, 111, 112, 113, 123, 124, 126, 127, 130 n. 16, 133, 139, 145, 160, 170, 171, 194, 206, 207, 208, 209, 215, 218, 223, 224, 225, 227, 233 n. 106, 235 n. 134, 237, 239, 240, 242, 245, 246, 249, 252, 253, 255, 256, 260 nn. 29 & 30
 Chapter 28 of: 80
 in contrast to Part One 4, 16, 110, 112, 113, 209, 239, 260 n. 30
 germanía in 7, 188, 189, 190, 193, 195
 Italianisms in 7, 194, 195
 rising and falling (motif of) in 7, 8, 209, 218, 219–26
Don Sancho de Azpeitia, *see* Basque, the
Doña Clara 15, 101, 179 n. 36, 199
Doña Rodríguez 42, 46, 56
Doña Sancha 54–55, 56, 57, 58
Doody, Margaret 127
Dorotea 12, 13, 59, 95, 100, 101
Duke and Duchess 39, 40, 58, 82, 86 n. 6, 216, 217, 218, 223, 232 n. 96, 243, 244, 245, 246, 258 nn. 17 & 18
Dulcinea del Toboso 35, 48, 53, 58, 68, 82, 219, 226, 233 n. 114, 250, 251, 254, 255
 disenchantment of 2, 35, 36, 40, 41, 42, 48, 50, 55, 57, 59, 229 n. 37, 246, 248, 250, 254
 DQ's love for 38–39, 220
 enchantment of 36, 81, 111, 217, 232 n. 92, 244, 256, 257 n. 6
 song in praise of 238
Dunn, Peter N. 89 n. 54, 128, 186, 235 n. 144
duques, *see* Duke and Duchess
Durandarte 3, 84–85

Ebro 218, 224, 232 n. 96
Eco, Umberto 159, 169
Eisenberg, Daniel 19, 130 n. 16
Egypt 163, 165
El guapo Francisco Estevan 196
Eliot, T. S.:
 The Waste Land 106
Elisabat 238
El Toboso 111, 233 n. 114

El valiente Juan de Heredia 197, 198
El valiente Pedro Ponce 196
El valor nunca vencido, hazañas de Juan de Arévalo 196
Enciso, Diego Jiménez de:
    El valiente sevillano, 196
England 11, 94, 106, 118 n. 66
Enrique (of Trastámara) II 2, 55, 56, 63 n. 103
Enríquez Gómez, Antonio:
    El valiente Diego de Camas 196
epic 5, 8, 42, 120, 127, 129, 237, 242, 243, 256, 258 n. 12
    Carolingian 42
Erauso, Catalina de:
    Vida y sucesos de la monja alférez 195
Ercilla, Alonso de:
    La Araucana 16
Esplandián 237, 238, 257 n. 4
ēthos (ethos) 3, 69, 73, 87 n. 16, 88, 167, 182 n. 70, 201 n. 25, 239, 252
Eulalia 15, 22
Europe 127, 152, 160, 169

Fajardo, Salvador J. 71
fame, debate on (episode) 8, 209–13
Fate 43, 239
Feliciana de la Voz (*Persiles*) 99, 100, 101
Ferdinand II of Aragon 44
Fernández, Jaime 205, 227 n. 4, 260 n. 27, 261 n. 38
Fernández, Jerónimo 161
Fernando 12, 15, 199
fiction:
    in *DQ, see* Don Quixote
    nature of 3, 6, 20, 21, 24, 30, 110, 112, 158–60, 163, 170, 173–74, 186, 245, 256
Florestán 238
Fortinbras 160
Fortune 7, 80, 124, 168, 199, 206, 210, 218, 220, 223, 224, 233 nn. 101, 112 & 115
Fracastoro, Girolamo 83, 89 n. 63
Frasso, Antonio de lo:
    Libro de la Fortuna de amor 16
Frye, Northrop 252, 256, 258 n. 12
Fuggers 6, 147

Galaor 11, 238
galeotes, see galley slaves
galley slaves (episode of) 6, 7, 109, 123, 141, 186, 187
Gálvez de Montalvo, Luis:
    El pastor de Fílida 16, 23
Gandalín, Count 238
García, Francisco:
    Tratado utilísimo y muy general de todos los contratos 135
Garcilaso de la Vega 19, 20, 21, 29, 49, 50, 61 n. 26
    Eclogues 49, 50, 61 n. 26
Garzoni, Tomasso 194
George, St 215, 216

Georgievitz, Bartholomeus 169, 179 n. 42, 181 n. 55
Gerli, Michael 187
German pilgrims (*DQ* II. 54) 6, 145, 146, 147, 149, 152, 153, 154, 194
Gil Polo, Gaspar:
    Diana enamorada 16, 23
Ginés de Pasamonte 1, 4, 7, 15, 119, 120, 123, 124, 130 nn. 13 & 16, 186, 187, 194, 195
Gingras, Gerald R. 186
goatherds (episode of) 2, 4, 17, 18, 20, 21, 22, 30, 101, 102, 103, 109
Goffman, Erving 106
Golden Age (DQ's speech on) 4, 18, 19, 20, 21, 22, 24, 26, 30, 34 n. 84, 101, 125
golden mean 3, 75, 80, 88 n. 36
Golden Rule 149
Goliath 73
Gómez Canseco, Luis 128
Góngora, Luis de 177 n. 28
    Soledades 49
González de Bobadilla, Bernardo:
    Ninfas y pastores de Henares 16, 23
González Echevarría, Roberto 36, 180 n. 45
Gordian knot 2, 42, 43, 44, 45, 46, 58, 176 n. 16
Gordium (Phrygia) 43
Gran Bretaña 238
Gran Capitán 160, 162
Granada, Fray Luis de:
    Adiciones al Memorial de la vida Cristiana 54
Grasandor 238
Greenblatt, Stephen 106
Gresham's Law 148
Grisóstomo 1, 2, 4, 11, 15, 22, 23, 24, 25, 26, 28, 29, 30, 95, 102, 103–05, 110, 116 n. 39, 117 n. 46
Guadalupe 99
Guadiana, River 82
Guillén, Jorge 205, 252, 258 n. 18, 261 n. 38
Guinart, Roque 36, 57, 222, 256, 230 n. 52
Guesclin, Bertrand du 55

Hades 237
Haedo, Diego de 169
Hahn, Juergen 186
Hartzenbusch, Juan Eugenio 252, 261 n. 33
Helen of Troy 8, 247, 248
Hernández de Velasco, Gregorio 38, 61 n. 26
Harvey, L. P. 151
Herostratus 209
Herrera Puga, Pedro 185, 200 n. 22
Hesiod 126
Hidalgo, Juan:
    Romances de germanía 190
Hillis Miller, J. 4, 121, 127
Holy Brotherhood 198
Holy League 168
Holy Office, *see* Inquisition

Homer 161, 238
   Iliad 43
   Odyssey 38, 61 n. 26, 237
Horace 19, 73
   Epodes 49
   Odes 20
Horatius 210
Huarte de San Juan, Juan:
   Examen de ingenios para las sciencias 236 n. 146
Hue, Cécile 245, 259 n. 21, 260 n. 29
humanist cousin (*DQ* II) 3, 65, 74, 81, 82–83
Hutchinson, Steven 205, 228 n. 16

Ife, Barry 4
Imperio Argentina 107
Inquisition 49, 160, 165, 170
   inquisitorial flames 11
Ínsula Firme 237
Islam 162, 164, 166, 169, 171, 180 n. 52
Italy 194, 195

jácara(s) 7, 189, 190, 191, 192, 193, 196, 199
James the Great, St 215, 216
Jamón Jamón 107
John of the Cross, St 29
Johnson, Carroll B. 11, 133, 135, 148, 152
Joly, Monique 146, 150, 189
Juan Palomeque 1, 13, 15, 21, 88 n. 20, 140
Julius Caesar 210
Jupiter 37

Kermode, Frank 256

La Argamasilla, academicians of 180 n. 47, 238
La Cava 168, 176 n. 23
La hija de Celestina 188
La Mancha 31 n. 2, 39, 105, 108, 141, 150, 163, 165, 167, 176 n. 15, 180 n. 47, 237, 244
Lamb, Charles 243, 244, 252
La niña de tus ojos 107
Lausberg, Heinrich 68, 86 n. 4
Lawrance, Jeremy 8
La vida del escudero Marcos de Obregón 184, 188
Lazarillo de Tormes 4, 5, 15, 119, 120, 121, 122, 127, 129, 138, 186, 187, 188, 199, 225
Lázaro Carreter, Fernando 120, 121, 125, 130 n. 6
Leahy, Chad 152
León, Fray Luis de 20, 29, 49
León, Pedro de 7
Lepanto, Battle of 119, 195
Lepolemo 164
Lepolemo (Caballero de la Cruz) 163, 164, 165, 166
Lerma, Duke of 105
libros de caballerías, see romances of chivalry
Lisbon 126
Liu, Benjamín 148

Loaysa (*El celoso extremeño*) 98
'loco de Sevilla', tale of 214
López, Cristóbal 17
López de Enciso, Bartolomé:
   Desengaño de celos 16
López Maldonado, Gabriel:
   Cancionero 16
López Pinciano, Alonso 239, 240, 246, 251, 256, 257 n. 6
Los abrazos rotos 107
Lotario 74
Lucifer 59
Luscinda 12, 13, 16

Madariaga, Salvador de 35, 57, 58, 59
Maese Nicolás 11, 240
   see also barber
Maese Pedro 4, 7, 82, 113, 124, 194
Maestro, Jesús G.:
   Crítica de los géneros literarios en el 'Quijote' 187
Magreb 119
Mambrino (helmet of) 5, 6, 29, 42, 96, 115 n. 19, 133, 139, 140, 143, 145, 147, 154
Mancing, Howard 76, 87 n. 6, 176 n. 17
Mann, Thomas 253, 254
Marcela 2, 4, 11, 21–28, 29, 30, 75, 76, 87 n. 16, 95, 102, 103, 104, 105, 110, 116 nn. 39 & 42, 117 n. 46
Marcus Curtius 210
Mariana, Juan de 144, 145, 148, 176 n. 23
   La dignidad real y la educación del Rey 144
   Tratado y discurso sobre la moneda de vellón 144
Marina, St 172
Maritornes 1, 13, 47, 198
Márquez Villanueva, Francisco 153, 173
Marquis of Mantua, ballad of 19, 33 n. 39, 67, 68, 166
Mars 42, 76
Martí, Juan (Mateo Luján de Sayavedra) 120, 121
Martin of Tours, St 215, 216, 231 n. 74
Mary (Virgin) 168
   as Mother of God 173
   as Our Lady 215
McKenzie, Jon:
   Perform or Else 94
Medina del Campo, pragmatic of 143
Mediterranean 152, 168
Mercado, Tomás de 135, 142, 145, 148, 149, 150
Merlin 39, 40, 41, 49, 50, 82, 84
   prophecy of 36, 38–39, 41, 53, 59, 84
metalists 5, 144
Mexía, Pedro 83
Micomicona 59
Middle Ages 6, 150, 159, 165, 213
Middle East 119
Minnis, A. J. 66
Miranda, Don Diego de 1, 8, 16, 17, 33 n. 54, 209, 211, 213, 214, 218
   library of 1, 16, 17

Mirrors, Knight of, *see* Carrasco, Sansón
Molho, Maurice 51, 62 n. 72, 138
Moner, Michel 148
Monicongo 238
Monipodio (*Rinconete y Cortadillo*) 184, 185
Monroy, Cristóbal de:
  El más valiente andaluz, Antón Bravo 196
Montalvo, Garci Rodríguez de 67, 86 n. 5, 238, 257 n. 4
Montemayor, Jorge de 16, 19, 23
  La Diana 16, 23
Montesinos 81, 82
  Cave of 3, 38–39, 68, 74, 81, 110, 111, 176 n. 23, 217, 218, 223, 226, 235 n. 144
Montiel, Battle of 2, 55
Montiel, campo de 108
Moreno, Don Antonio 82, 171, 172, 173, 256
morisco aljamiado (Morisco translator) 5, 14, 32 n. 21, 134, 138
Moriscos 5, 6, 14, 15, 32 n. 21, 133, 138, 139, 145, 146, 148, 150, 151, 152, 153, 154, 158, 165, 166, 170, 171, 173, 174, 180–81 n. 53
  expulsion of 6, 145, 148, 151, 152, 153, 165, 166, 170, 171
Mucius Scaevola 210
Mudarra González 2, 56, 57, 58
Muhammad 162, 166
Murillo, Andrés 127
Musil, Robert 256
Muslims 6, 134, 138, 146, 162, 164, 165, 166, 168, 169, 179 n. 41, 181 n. 63, 239

Nabokov, Vladimir 35, 244, 246, 252, 258 n. 18
Naples 25
Native Americans 149
Nelson, Graham viii
Neo-Stoic virtues 49
Nero 26
Nietzsche, Friedrich 245, 259–60 n. 24
Nine Worthies 43
Nishida, Emma 193, 201 n. 32
Noble Wood, Oliver 2–3
nominalists 5, 144

Oakley, Robert 4–5
Odysseus 237
Olalla, *see* Eulalia
Old Christians 145, 151
omens 7, 8, 218, 226, 233 n. 106, 250, 255, 256
Oña, Pedro de 144, 151, 156 n. 37
Orbaneja of Úbeda 247, 248, 260 n. 25
Oriana 238, 257 n. 4
O'Reilly, Terence 1, 226
Orlando (*Orlando furioso*) 106, 107, 117 n. 52
Ortega y Gasset, José 256, 261 n. 40
Ortiz, Luis 148, 151

Osorio (family) 162
Ovid 20

Padilla, Pedro de:
  Tesoro de varias poesías 16
Palmerín de Inglaterra 11, 43
Paniaguado 238
Panza, Sancho, *see* Sancho Panza
Panza, Teresa 251
Paris (prince of Troy) 161, 247
Parker, Alexander A. 155 n. 16, 246, 260 n. 26
Pasamonte, Jerónimo de 119, 124, 125, 195
  Vida 195
pastoral 34 n. 65, 50, 51, 57, 256
  Arcadia 234 n. 120
  calling 251
  fiction 98
  instruments 115 n. 21
  interlude 17
  novel 21–25, 29, 30, 98, 102
  paradise 127
  romance 2
  setting 105
  topos 37, 49, 58, 60 n. 23
  world 22, 23, 25, 30
Paul, St 8, 212, 215, 216, 218, 226, 227, 230 n. 50, 232 n. 93, 235–36 n. 145, 236 n. 146
Pedraza Jiménez, Felipe
Pedro (goatherd) 22, 26
Pedro I (the Cruel) of Castile 2, 55, 56, 58, 63 n. 103
Penelope 38
Pentapolín 219
Peralta (*Casamiento engañoso y Coloquio de los perros*) 93
Pererius, Benedictus 162
Pérez, Alonso:
  Segunda parte de la Diana 16, 23
Pérez de Andrade, Fernán 55, 63 n. 103
Pérez de Biedma, Gil 168, 229 n. 46
performance 2, 4, 93, 94, 95, 106, 107–08, 110, 112, 113, 114 n. 2, 117 nn. 49, 55 & 58, 228 n. 9
  art movement 94
  audience for 108, 109, 113, 114 n. 2
  DQ as 4, 93, 102, 113, 117 n. 49
  language of 94, 108
  spaces for 108, 109, 113
Periandro (*Persiles*) 110
Perry, Mary Elizabeth 186, 193
  Crime and Society in Early Modern Seville 185
Petrarch 69
Petrarchan lover / beloved 2, 51, 58
Petrarchan poetry 25
Petrus Hispanus:
  Summulae Logicales 68
Philip II 129, 147
Philip III 105, 129, 143, 144, 147

picaresque 4, 7, 119, 120–21, 122, 124, 127, 183, 184–85, 186–89, 192, 193, 195–96, 199–200
Pimentel (family) 162
Pimentel, Leonor 30, 34 n. 83
Platir 162
Plutarch 2, 42, 43, 44
  Life of Alexander 43
Polydore Vergil 83, 84
  De Inventoribus Rerum 82
Pons, Gaspar de 147, 149, 150, 156 n. 53
Pontón Gijón, Gonzalo 116 n. 39, 185
Preciosa (*La gitanilla*) 100
priest (DQ's village) 11, 13, 31 n. 8, 76, 88 n. 39, 108, 110, 140, 163, 208
priests (other) 12, 13, 22, 103, 116 n. 42, 167
Primaleón cycle 162
Propalladia 187
Protestantism 171, 180 n. 52
Protestants 180 n. 52
providence 7, 8, 206, 220, 222, 223, 224–25, 227, 235 n. 137

Quevedo, Francisco de 190, 193
  Vida del Buscón 49, 188
  Historia y vida del Gran Tacaño 187
  Pero Vázquez de Escamilla 196
Quintilian 3, 69
  Institutio Oratoria 69, 86 n. 4
Quintus Curtius 2, 44, 46
  History of Alexander 43
Quijano, Alonso, *see* Quixano, Alonso
Quixano, Alonso 11, 14, 15–16, 17, 19, 21, 23, 24, 25, 29, 31 n. 2, 33 n. 39, 208, 223 n. 106, 205, 206, 207, 208, 227, 233 n. 106, 240, 241, 252, 261 n. 33
  as actor 106–08
  death of 125, 207, 228 nn. 9 & 18, 241–42, 243, 251, 253, 255, 258 n. 18, 261 n. 32

Rabone, Richard 3
Ralegh, Sir Walter 106, 107, 117 n. 52
Redondo, Augustin 195, 230 n. 52, 245
Regalado, Antonio 213, 229 n. 39
Renaissance 8, 106, 175 n. 8, 178 n. 31, 230 n. 52, 239, 243
Ribera, Juan de 151
  see also Valencia, archbishop of
Ricote 6, 31 n. 2, 133, 139, 145–54, 171–72, 173
Riley, E. C. 87 n. 7, 123, 124, 186, 235 n. 144, 247, 259 n. 23, 261 n. 31
Riquer, Martín de 124, 130 n. 16
Robinson Crusoe 5, 129
Rocinante 2, 41, 45, 106, 210, 221, 222, 223, 254–55
Roderick (king of Spain) 168, 176 n. 23
Rodrigo de Lara 2, 56, 58
Rodríguez Marín, Francisco 193, 261 n. 32

Rojas, Fernando de 239
  La Celestina 187, 188, 239
romances de germanía 7, 190, 193, 195
Romances del Marqués de Mantua 17
  see also Marquis of Mantua, ballad of
romances of chivalry 6, 7, 11, 12, 13, 16, 17, 21, 24, 30, 32 n. 29, 66, 161, 209, 224, 227, 239, 242, 251, 255, 261 n. 40
Romans 53, 161
Romantic reading of *DQ* 8, 163, 234 n. 118, 242, 243, 245, 246, 258 nn. 13 & 15, 259 n. 20, 261 n. 37
Romanticism 129
Romantics, German 163
Romero Muñoz, Carlos 194, 195, 234 n. 121
Rubicon 210
Rueda, Lope de:
  Pasos 7, 189
  Registro de representantes 189
Rufo, Juan:
  La Austríada 16
Ruidera, Lake of 82
Russell, Peter 36, 259 nn. 21 & 23

Saavedra (*DQ*) 163
Salamanca, university of 22, 103
Samson 57
Sanazzaro, Jacopo:
  Arcadia 20
Sancho Panza 3, 5, 17, 21, 34 n. 65, 37, 68, 88 n. 39, 112, 123, 169, 194, 213, 215, 216, 219, 220, 223, 235 n. 137, 244, 245, 257 n. 6
  and Aristotle's golden mean 75, 76–80
  and *baciyelmo* 5, 139, 140–41
  and Cave of Montesinos 80–84, 111
  at DQ's deathbed 208, 225, 226, 233 n. 106, 234 nn. 120 & 128, 237, 238, 241, 247, 248–49, 250, 252, 254–55, 256
  and Dulcinea 111
  and fame 170, 209, 210–12, 217
  and femininity 62 n. 72
  goes to Barcelona and galleys 126, 127, 128
  illiterate 14, 15, 20, 70, 76
  and knight errantry 18
  and Merlin's prophecy 39–40
  and penance of lashes 2, 35, 37, 39–42, 45–53, 57, 59, 229 nn. 33, 37 & 40, 246
  and performance 4, 24, 95, 102, 104, 105, 108, 111
  relationship/contrast with DQ 3, 4, 8, 36, 38, 43, 53, 54–59, 63 n. 97, 70, 111, 125, 210, 221–22, 232 n. 96
Ricote episode 6, 133, 139, 145–46, 150–51, 153, 171–72

Scandinavia 99
Schechner, Richard 108, 112, 114

Scipio Africanus 218
Sempere, Jerónimo de:
  La Carolea 17
Seneca:
  Hipolitus 20
Seville (Sevilla) 7, 116 n. 28, 125, 127, 176 n. 21, 184, 185, 186, 187, 189, 192, 195, 208
  Cárcel Real of 7, 184, 185, 186, 187, 188, 189, 193, 195
Shakespeare, William 95, 117 n. 49
Sicily 75
Siete Infantes de Lara 56, 57
Silva y Mendoza, Pedro de, Count of Salinas 30, 34 n. 83
Sismondi, J. C. L. Simonde de 256, 258 n. 15
Smollett, Tobias 93
Sobejano, Gonzalo 120
Soto (*Guzmán de Alfarache*) 128
Soto, Domingo de 142, 145
Starr, Nick 109
Sterne, Laurence 113 n. 1
  Tristram Shandy 93, 113 n. 1
Styan, J. L. 112
styles, hierarchy of 129
suspension of disbelief 21

Tansillo, Luigi [Luis], 175
Tarfe, Don Álvaro 57, 248, 249
Tarquin 26, 34 n. 70
Terence:
  Andria 239
Theocritus:
  Idylls 20
Tiquitoc 238
Tirant lo Blanc 242, 258 n. 12
Toledo 14, 32 n. 21, 49, 133, 134, 137, 138, 154, 184
  Alcaná of 5, 14, 134
  Canon of, *see* Canon of Toledo
  Casa del Nuncio 249–50
  Plaza del Zocodover in 14
Tosilos 245
tragedy 29, 36, 129, 153, 239, 252, 256, 258 n. 12, 261–62 n. 40
tragicomedy 256, 261–62 n. 40
Troy 175 n. 11, 220, 247
Tullia 26, 34 n. 70
Tunis, Battle of 195
Turks 162, 164, 166, 169, 172, 181 n. 54
Twelve Peers of France 43

Úbeda, Francisco de:
  La pícara Justina 5, 126, 128, 187, 188

Uchalí Fartax 169
Unamuno, Miguel de 35

Urbina, Eduardo 223, 224, 225, 232 n. 96, 259 nn. 23 & 24
Urganda la Desconocida 237

Valdivielso, José de 171
Valencia 61, 135, 163
  archbishop of 151, 165
  kingdom of 151
Valencia, Pedro de 144, 145, 147
Vecilla Castellano, Pedro de la:
  El león de España 17
Vega, Bernardo de la:
  El pastor de Iberia 16, 23
Vega, Lope de 16, 93, 113, 114 nn. 4 & 5
  'A mis soledades voy' 49
  El rufián Castrucho 199
  El valiente Céspedes 199
Velasco (family) 162
Velasco, Gregorio Hernández de 38, 61 n. 26
vellón (currency) 143, 144, 145, 147, 148, 151
Vélez de Guevara, Luis:
  El asombro de Turquía y valiente toledano 196
Veracruz 210
Vicky Christina Barcelona 107
Vida del escudero Marcos de Obregón 184, 188
Vida y hechos de Estebanillo González 188
Vinci, Leonardo da 95
Virgil 2, 19, 20, 37, 38, 60 n. 17, 61 n. 26, 73, 88 n. 30, 247
  Aeneid 61 n. 26, 73, 247
  Eclogues 20, 37
Virués, Cristóbal de:
  El Monserrate 16
Vivaldo 15, 25, 26, 104, 229 n. 39
voice, the (in Cervantes) 4, 95, 97, 98, 101, 104, 105, 109, 170, 220, 254
  narrative 3, 67, 72, 104
  plurality of 72, 78, 85, 105, 110, 112
  singing 4, 96, 98, 99, 100, 101, 115–16 n. 28
Volver 107

warrior saints 213, 215
Weslers 147
White Moon, Knight of, *see* Carrasco, Sansón
Williamson, Edward 36, 58, 59, 86 n. 5, 205, 206, 225, 227 n. 7, 228 n. 17, 229 n. 19, 230 n. 47, 234 n. 120, 235 n. 136
Willis, Raymond S. 67, 87 n. 9

Xarton (*Lepolemo*) 163, 164, 165

Zaragoza 36, 85, 119, 235 n. 134, 249
Zárate, Fernando de:
  El valiente Campuzano 196
Zoraida 167, 168, 173, 174, 249

www.ingramcontent.com/pod-product-compliance
Lightning Source LLC
Chambersburg PA
CBHW080541090426
42734CB00016B/3166